THE EDUCATOR'S DESK REFERENCE

The Educator's Desk Reference

(EDR)

A SOURCEBOOK OF EDUCATIONAL INFORMATION AND RESEARCH

Second Edition

Melvyn N. Freed, Ph.D., Robert K. Hess, Ph.D., and Joseph M. Ryan, Ph.D.

AMERICAN COUNCIL ON EDUCATION
PRAEGER
Series on Higher Education

Library of Congress Cataloging-in-Publication Data

Freed, Melvyn N.
  The educator's desk reference : a sourcebook of educational information and research /
  Melvyn N. Freed, Robert K. Hess, and Joseph M. Ryan.—2nd ed.
    p. cm.
  Rev. ed. of: The educator's desk reference (EDR).   c1989.
  Includes bibliographical references and index.
  ISBN 1–57356–359–5 (alk. paper)
    1. Education—United States—Information services—Handbooks, manuals, etc.   2.
  Education—Research—United States—Handbooks, manuals, etc.   3. Education—United
  States—Databases—Handbooks, manuals, etc.   4. Education—Reference
  books—Bibliography.   5. Education—Bibliography.   I. Hess, Robert K.   II. Ryan, Joseph
  M.   III. Freed, Melvyn N. Educator's desk reference (EDR)   IV. Title.
  LB1028.27.U6 F74   2002
  370'.7'2—dc21   2002025344

Formerly ACE/Oryx Press Series on Higher Education

British Library Cataloguing in Publication Data is available.

Library of Congress Catalog Card Number: 2002025344
ISBN: 1–57356–359–5

First published in 2002

Praeger Publishers, 88 Post Road West, Westport, CT 06881
An imprint of Greenwood Publishing Group, Inc.
www.praeger.com

Printed in the United States of America

The paper used in this book complies with the
Permanent Paper Standard issued by the National
Information Standards Organization (Z39.48–1984).

10 9 8 7 6 5 4 3 2 1

Contents

Contents

Contents

SECTION F: ORGANIZATIONS IN EDUCATION
Melvyn N. Freed

Preface

Information is the universal password to knowledge and enlightenment. It is the tool with which new frontiers are discovered and explored. The Internet has propelled the advancement and communication of information, and its potential is yet to be fully understood and maximized. Complementing this new technological phenomenon are the traditional means of discovery and communicating. It is when the old and new are used together that innovation is accelerated and new knowledge is born.

This, the second edition of *The Educator's Desk Reference (EDR)* seeks to facilitate educational research as it identifies both traditional and electronic sources of information. Furthermore, it offers statistical tools and software specifically tailored for behavioral research. As with the first edition, this book has been designed for the professional as a ready-reference handbook both to refresh the reader's technical memory and to provide new developments in research methodology and sources of information.

Distinguishing this second edition are the section on the Internet, the chapter on measurements, and the chapter that addresses techniques for exploratory data analysis. The carryover chapters update information that appeared in the earlier edition. Finally, the section on standardized tests and inventories has been excluded because other significant and traditional texts treat this subject more comprehensively than could be done in this single-volume. The reader is referred to these other titles in several different sections of this second edition.

In the field of education, as in other academic disciplines, information has been highly systematized. The scholar must identify the most direct path to this body of knowledge and be able to access the data accurately and efficiently; the *EDR* is instrumental in this process. It also provides readers with a guide to the information that they may find in specific national and regional education organizations.

An essential component of the research process is the dissemination of the discovery of new knowledge. Hence, the names of book and journal publishers have been presented along with the subject areas in which they publish and their guidelines for authors.

The tools for conducting research are also addressed in this book, including descriptions of the latest software in education and the behavioral sciences. Furthermore, there are guidelines for selecting the proper research design and descriptions of the characteristics, along with uses for various research designs and statistical procedures. Sampling techniques are discussed, and there is a summary of the major concepts and procedures in classical test theory and Item Response Theory. A chapter is dedicated to techniques for exploratory data analysis. Thus, the *EDR* is a concise summary of the means for exploring the field of education and cognate fields.

The *EDR* is not a textbook; instead, it assumes prior professional education. Its purpose is to serve as a ready-reference handbook for the practitioner which synthesizes selected information that is otherwise available only in diverse and sometimes expensive sources. It also provides information that has not been readily available, except to a few. The *EDR* brings to the desktop a compendium of information that will make research easier and more efficient. Because of *EDR*'s breadth of content and the limitation of space, in-depth coverage could not be given to the disparate bibliographic presentations of printed and electronic sources, and not all publishers, software, Web sites, and education organizations could be profiled; however, an effort was made to include those commonly regarded as most important.

This reference book may be used for casual inquiry or for scholarly educational research. Its scope embraces all levels of education, from preschool through graduate school and beyond, and will be of value to teachers, professors, elementary and secondary education administrators, college administrators, librarians, counselors, researchers, and others who are involved in the educational process.

The Educator's Desk Reference is organized by sections with chapters that elaborate on the theme of each section. Where it was deemed helpful to the reader, item entry numbers were used to facilitate cross-referencing between chapters and the identification of individual entries. These numbers follow a coding scheme; namely, the elements include a section's alpha character, the chapter's number, and the item's identification number. For example, A3-1 means Section A, Chapter 3, Item 1. The authors hope the *EDR* will facilitate the discovery process and further educational growth.

DISCLAIMER

The work of the authors was accurate at the time of writing. Due to the ephemeral nature of Web sites on the Internet and the frequent vicissitudes in computer software, changes may have occurred subsequent to the preparation of the manuscript. Also, frequent changes occur in publishing that may affect the section on print publications. The reader is reminded of the time-sensitivity of some of this information.

Acknowledgments

A book of this magnitude necessitated the cooperation and assistance of several persons whose contributions merit recognition. We are grateful to the following individuals at Arizona State University West who provided able assistance in the preparation of Section E: Liz Ramirez for helping with updating the material that appeared in the first edition of this book; Kathy Bliss and Elisha Davidson who were instrumental in the preparation of formulas and figures; and Liz Marini and Rico Rivera who edited the text.

Appreciation is extended to those organizations, associations, book publishers, and journals that took the time to respond to the surveys that were essential to the writing of numerous chapters.

A special word of appreciation is expressed to Susan Slesinger of the Greenwood Publishing Group, whose extraordinary patience under unusual circumstances enabled this publication to come to fruition.

Finally, the authors acknowledge the support, encouragement, and understanding that were given by their respective families over the long period of time that was involved in the writing of this book. Without their loving contributions, this publication would not have been attainable. To all of them, the authors say in unison, "Thank You."

SECTION A

THE EDUCATOR'S PRINTED REFERENCE SOURCES

Melvyn N. Freed

CHAPTER 1

Introduction

The world of print publications maintains its viability despite the emerging prominence of the electronic media. Some printed reference materials are now produced in both hard copy and e-editions. For fruitful and productive research, it is necessary that the researcher explore both of these media. Section A addresses the print domain.

The successful collection of information and productive research depend, in part, on knowing what reference materials are available in an academic discipline. This involves familiarity with the purpose and the unique contribution that each publication makes to the body of knowledge; that is, a competent review of the literature first requires that the researcher know how to find it. To assist the reader in locating information, Section A (1) reviews many of the principal reference publications in and related to education, and (2) directs the reader to the appropriate reference title(s) when searching for the answer to a particular question.

Chapter 2, "Guide to Printed Reference Sources in Education," contains "The Information Locator" which presents questions that are often asked in education and related fields, followed by the reference publications that provide the answers. These questions are based on the major features offered by the reference publications described in Chapter 3; consequently, these two chapters are interrelated.

Chapter 3, "Printed Information Sources by Type," provides an annotated bibliography of reference publications in education. Although not all-inclusive, this bibliography has been designed to be of great value to both the beginning researcher and the experienced professional. For other bibliographical listings, the reader is referred to such publications as Robert Balay's *Guide to Reference Books*, Marda Woodbury's *A Guide to Sources of Educational Information*, the *ARBA Guide to Education*, and specialized bibliographies in the disparate areas of education.

The Information Locator (TIL) in Chapter 2 gives additional details about the titles in Chapter 3. After identifying a needed title in TIL, Chapter 3 provides a full bibliographic citation for that title, along with an accompanying descriptive annotation. To facilitate this cross-referencing, each title has been assigned an item entry number (A3–X). This code means Section A, Chapter 3, followed by the unique item identification number. The titles in Chapter 3 have been listed alphabetically within categories, and they have been numbered consecutively throughout the chapter. For example, A3–1 refers to title 1 in Chapter 3 of Section A. Thus, the reader can move easily between Chapters 2 and 3.

In summary, Section A addresses two needs in the field of education: (1) the need to identify major reference materials available for educational research or for casual inquiry in education, and (2) the need to find answers to questions in education that can be found in the reference works cited herein.

CHAPTER 2

Guide to Printed Reference Sources in Education

INTRODUCTION

The format for this chapter is The Information Locator, which guides the reader to specific reference publications for answers to selected questions. These questions highlight the features of the reference titles cited. The guiding questions should be read carefully to enable the reader to enter The Information Locator at the proper place. Occasionally, there are subtle distinctions between descriptive questions because of the subtle differences between publications.

The questions are arranged in the left column by categories according to the type of information that is being sought. For example, questions seeking information about books are to be found under "Books." Within each category, the questions do not follow a set sequence because their orderliness has been achieved by the categorization. Furthermore, the categories are brief to foster their utilization. The categories for the questions are as follows:

> Agencies, Associations, Foundations, and Organizations
> Biographical Information
> Books
> Certification
> Collective Bargaining
> Definitions
> Educational Resources
> Elementary and Secondary Schools, School Districts, and State Education
>   Officers
> Internet Addresses
> Law and Education
> Periodicals
> Postsecondary Education Institutions
> Potpourri of Educational Information
> Research Findings
> Research Designs, Statistical Procedures, and Measurement
> Software and Hardware
> Statistics on Education
> Tests

In the right-hand column are the titles of reference books that contain the information elicited by the questions in the left-hand column. Also, the item entry number code refers to Chapter 3 for full bibliographic information and a descriptive annotation. In many instances the suggestions for sources of information are not exhaustive; instead, these titles should be viewed as being among the reference publications that contain the information. The Information Locator is a beginning for the researcher.

THE INFORMATION LOCATOR

Agencies, Associations, Foundations, and Organizations

Where Should I Go to Find...	*Try*
a directory of national and international education organizations in the U.S. with addresses, telephone numbers, and descriptive information about each?	*Encyclopedia of Associations* [A3–54]
the identification of higher education-related associations, organizations, and information centers worldwide?	*The International Encyclopedia of Higher Education* [A3–91]
descriptive information on UNESCO, the International Bureau of Education, United Nations University, and international organizations in the academic disciplines?	*The World of Learning* [A3–76]
private organizations as sources of student financial aid for education beyond high school?	*College Blue Book* [A3–48]
graduate and postgraduate financial awards available worldwide for research and study in sundry academic disciplines?	*College Blue Book*, Vol. 5 (U.S. sources, only) [A3–48] *The Grants Register* [A3–57]
a directory of educational and training facilities (residential and nonresidential) that serve the needs of exceptional children?	*Directory for Exceptional Children* [A3–53]
a directory of permanent, nonprofit research centers with their locations and descriptive information?	*Research Centers Directory* [A3–71]

Agencies, Associations, Foundations, and Organizations

Where Should I Go to Find...	*Try*
a directory of statewide higher education agencies, higher education associations, and postsecondary education consortia with their addresses, telephone numbers, and names of chief executive officers?	For some of these organizations, see this book, Section F. *Accredited Institutions of Postsecondary Education* [A3–42] *HEP Higher Education Directory* [A3–58] *Encyclopedia of Associations* (in part) [A3–54]
a directory of educational agencies, organizations, and associations related to elementary and secondary education?	*Patterson's American Education* [A3–64]
a list of foundations and other organizations that offer grants?	*Annual Register of Grant Support* [A3–45] *Foundation Directory* [A3–55] *Foundation Grants Index* [A3–56] *The Grants Register* [A3–57]
the funding interests of individual foundations?	*Annual Register of Grant Support* [A3–45] *Foundation Directory* [A3–55] *Foundation Grants Index* [A3–56] *The Grants Register* [A3–57]
a list of grants awarded by foundations with descriptive titles of the grants?	*Foundation Grants Index* [A3–56]
foundations that offer grants for media-related projects?	*Annual Register of Grant Support* [A3–45] *Educational Media and Technology Yearbook* [A3–142] *Foundation Directory* [A3–55]
a directory of U.S. organizations and associations that service instructional media, computer technology, and related fields?	*Educational Media and Technology Yearbook* [A3–142] *Encyclopedia of Associations* [A3–54]
the names and descriptive information about learned societies, research institutes, libraries, and museums worldwide?	*The World of Learning* [A3–76]

Agencies, Associations, Foundations, and Organizations

Where Should I Go to Find...	*Try*
the names of individual members of national academies throughout the world?	*The World of Learning* [A3–76]

Biographical Information

biographies of prominent American educators?	*Biographical Dictionary of Modern American Educators* [A3–22] *Encyclopedia of American Education* [A3–79]

Books

an index of books in print that discloses the title, author's name, publisher, and price?	*Books in Print* [A3–5]
titles of books in print categorized by subject?	*Subject Guide to Books in Print* [A3–20]
book titles soon to be published in the U.S.?	*Books in Print* [A3–5] *Forthcoming Books* [A3–13]
abstracts of books in sociology and related disciplines?	*Sociological Abstracts* [A3–119]
citations to book reviews in the social sciences?	*Social Sciences Index* [A3–118]
updated information for *Books in Print*?	*Books in Print Supplement* [A3–6]
citations to book reviews in education?	*Education Index* [A3–104]
titles of elementary and high school textbooks in print or forthcoming?	*El-Hi Textbooks and Serials in Print* [A3–12]
titles of books that are written for children?	*Best Books for Children* [A3–2] *Best Books for Young Teen Readers* [A3–3] *Children's Books in Print* [A3–8]

Books

Where Should I Go to Find...	*Try*
titles of reference books for children?	*Reference Books for Children* [A3–18] *Reference Books for Children's Collections* [A3–19]
abstracts of books in psychology and related disciplines?	*Psychological Abstracts* [A3–114]
a comprehensive bibliography for education?	*Bibliographic Guide to Education* [A3–4] *Dictionary Catalog of the Teachers College Library* [A3–10]
an annotated bibliography of reference publications in education?	*American Reference Books Annual* [A3–1] *Guide to Reference Books* [A3–14] *A Guide to Sources of Educational Information* [A3–15]

Certification

certification requirements for teachers, counselors, librarians, administrators, and other public school personnel in each state and U.S. possessions and territories?	*Requirements for Certification* [A3–131]
interstate reciprocal agreements for certification of teachers, administrators, and other professionals in public elementary and secondary schools?	*Requirements for Certification* [A3–131]
the addresses of state officers of certification for public school educators?	*Requirements for Certification* [A3–131]

Collective Bargaining

a bibliography on collective bargaining in higher education?	*Collective Bargaining in Higher Education and the Professions* [A3–9]

Definitions

Where Should I Go to Find . . .	*Try*
a glossary of international terms used in higher education?	*The International Encyclopedia of Higher Education* [A3–91]
acronyms designating higher education organizations around the world?	*The International Encyclopedia of Higher Education* [A3–91]
the controlling terminology and associated definitions used to classify entries in ERIC's *Current Index to Journals in Education* and in *Resources in Education*?	*Thesaurus of ERIC Descriptors* [A3–40]
a taxonomy and definitions of educational terms?	*Thesaurus of ERIC Descriptors* [A3–40]
the controlling terminology and associated definitions used to classify entries in *Psychological Abstracts*?	*Thesaurus of Psychological Index Terms* [A3–41]
the definitions of terms used in special education?	*A Dictionary of Special Education Terms* [A3–37] *Encyclopedia of Special Education* [A3–83] *The Oryx Dictionary of Education* [A3–38] *Special Education Dictionary* [A3–39]
the definitions of terms and phrases used in education?	*American Educators' Encyclopedia* [A3–77] *The Concise Dictionary of Education* [A3–34] *Dictionary of Education* [A3–35] *A Dictionary of Special Education Terms* [A3–37] *Encyclopedia of American Education* [A3–79] *The Oryx Dictionary of Education* [A3–38]
the meaning of an acronym, abbreviation, or initialism used in education?	*Dictionary of Educational Acronyms, Abbreviations, and Initialisms* [A3–36] *The Oryx Dictionary of Education* [A3–38] (Answer continues)

9

Definitions

Where Should I Go to Find . . .	*Try*
the meaning of an acronym, abbreviation, or initialism used in education?	*Special Education Dictionary* [A3–39]
the definitions of legal terms and phrases?	*Black's Law Dictionary* [A3–33]

Educational Resources

a source of free teaching materials for teachers?	*Educator's Grade Guide to Free Teaching Aids* [A3–11]
a list of guidance materials in print?	*El-Hi Textbooks and Serials in Print* [A3–12]
a list of supplementary curriculum materials in print by subject area?	*El-Hi Textbooks and Serials in Print* [A3–12]
the funding interests of individual foundations?	*Annual Register of Grant Support* [A3–45] *Foundation Directory* [A3–55] *The Foundation Grants Index* [A3–56] *The Grants Register* [A3–57]
sources of grants and application information?	*Annual Register of Grant Support* [A3–45] *Foundation Directory* [A3–55] *The Foundation Grants Index* [A3–56] *The Grants Register* [A3–57]
guidelines for writing grant proposals?	*Annual Register of Grant Support* [A3–45]
titles of video programs for educational use?	*The Video Source Book* [A3–21]

Elementary and Secondary Schools, School Districts, and State Education Officers

Where Should I Go to Find . . .	*Try*
a comprehensive directory of public and private elementary schools in the United States?	*Patterson's Elementary Education* [A3–65]
a comprehensive directory of public and private secondary schools in the United States?	*Patterson's American Education* [A3–64]
the names and addresses of school districts, school district superintendents, and principals?	*Patterson's American Education* [A3–64] *Patterson's Elementary Education* [A3–65] *QED State School Guide* (separate volume for each state) [A3–70]
the names and addresses of chief state school officials for elementary, secondary, and higher education?	*Patterson's American Education* [A3–64] *Patterson's Elementary Education* (limited to secondary and higher education) [A3–65]
telephone numbers for state departments of education?	*QED State School Guide* [A3–70]
the names and addresses of superintendents of education in parochial school systems?	*Patterson's American Education* [A3–64] *Patterson's Elementary Education* [A3–65] *QED State School Guide* (separate volume for each state) [A3–70]
the names and contact information for charter schools in the United States?	*Patterson's Elementary Education* [A3–65]
an explanation of the elementary and secondary education systems in the United Kingdom, Canada, France, The Netherlands, and Switzerland?	*Schools Abroad of Interest to Americans* [A3–72]
the names and descriptive information about preK–12 schools in foreign nations that accept American students?	*The ISS Directory of Overseas Schools* [A3–61] *Schools Abroad of Interest to Americans* [A3–72]

Elementary and Secondary Schools, School Districts, and State Education Officers

Where Should I Go to Find . . .   *Try*

certification requirements for teachers,   *Requirements for Certification*
counselors, librarians, administrators,   [A3–131]
and other public school personnel in
each of the states and United States
possessions and territories?

interstate reciprocal agreements for   *Requirements for Certification*
certification of teachers, administrators,   [A3–131]
and other professionals in public
elementary and secondary schools?

high schools abroad that offer the   *The ISS Directory of Overseas Schools*
International Baccalaureate?   [A3–61]

Internet Addresses

Web site addresses for educational   This book, Section B.
associations, organizations, research   *Web Site Source Book* [A3–75]
centers, foundations, and
education-related businesses?

Web site addresses for educational   This book, Section B.
institutions?   *American Universities and Colleges*
                                                [A3–44]
                                                Barron's Profiles of American Colleges
                                                [A3–46]
                                                College Blue Book [A3–48]
                                                The College Board College Handbook
                                                [A3–49]
                                                HEP Higher Education Directory
                                                [A3–58]
                                                International Handbook of Universities
                                                [A3–60]
                                                Peterson's 2 Year Colleges [A3–66]
                                                Peterson's 4 Year Colleges [A3–67]
                                                Web Site Source Book [A3–75]

Law and Education

Where Should I Go to Find . . .	*Try*
an explanation and analysis of court actions affecting education?	*Education Law* [A3–125]
a summary of appellate case law on education?	*Deskbook Encyclopedia of American School Law* [A3–78] *The Yearbook of Education Law* [A3–145]
the text of state and/or federal court cases related to education?	*The Education Law Reporter* [A3–127]
a compilation of major United States Supreme Court decisions on education?	*Encyclopedia of American Education* [A3–79]
the text of federal laws and regulations pertaining to education?	*School Law Register* [A3–132] *United States School Laws and Rules* [A3–133]
the identification and explanation of significant federal legislation on education?	*Encyclopedia of American Education* [A3–79]
state statutes and regulations pertaining to education?	*Education Law* [A3–125] *Education Law: Public and Private* [A3–126]
the legal position of a state on matters of education?	*Education Law: Public and Private* [A3–126]
checklists and model forms for use by educational institutions as guides in matters with legal implications?	*Education Law* [A3–125]

Periodicals

an international bibliography of journals in higher education with contact information?	*Higher Education: A Worldwide Inventory of Centers and Programs* [A3–59]
titles of journal articles with abstracts?	*Current Index to Journals in Education* [A3–102]

Periodicals

Where Should I Go to Find . . .	*Try*
an index, without abstracts, of journal articles in education from 1929 to date?	*Education Index* [A3–104]
a list of periodicals with their addresses?	*Current Index to Journals in Education* [A3–102] *Education Index* [A3–104] *Magazines for Libraries* [A3–17]
an index of British journal articles on education (no abstracts)?	*British Education Index* [A3–99]
a list of periodicals by subject with descriptive information?	*Magazines for Libraries* [A3–17]
the recommended periodicals for a specified type of library?	*Magazines for Libraries* [A3–17]
an index of education articles published in popular (noneducational) periodicals?	*Readers' Guide to Periodical Literature* [A3–115]
an annual bibliography of publications on reading research?	*Annual Summary of Investigations Relating to Reading* [A3–98] For current monthly reviews, see *Current Index to Journals in Education* [A3–102]
a bibliography of journal articles in early childhood education?	*Handbook of Research in Early Childhood Education* [A3–86]
a bibliography of journal articles in special education?	*Encyclopedia of Educational Research* [A3–82] *Handbook of Research on Teaching* [A3–88] *Handbook of Special Education* [A3–89]
abstracted journal articles on educational administration?	*Current Index to Journals in Education* [A3–102] *Educational Administration Abstracts* [A3–105]

Periodicals

Where Should I Go to Find . . .	*Try*
an index of abstracted journal articles on gifted children and those with disabilities?	*Current Index to Journals in Education* [A3–102] *Exceptional Child Education Resources* [A3–106]
an international directory of hard-copy and electronic periodicals, by subject, that provides bibliographic information?	*Ulrich's Periodicals Directory* [A3–74]
the indexing and abstracting services for a selected periodical?	*Ulrich's Periodicals Directory* [A3–74]
an index to, and abstracts of, literature in psychology and related disciplines?	*Current Index to Journals in Education* [A3–102] *Psychological Abstracts* [A3–114]
subject index terms used to search the periodical literature in psychology?	*Thesaurus of ERIC Descriptors* [A3–40] *Thesaurus of Psychological Index Terms* [A3–41]
an index to, and abstracts of, literature in sociology and related disciplines?	*Current Index to Journals in Education* [A3–102] *Sociological Abstracts* [A3–119]
titles of journal articles in the social and behavioral sciences?	*Social Sciences Citation Index* [A3–117] *Social Sciences Index* [A3–118]
journal articles on business education?	*Current Index to Journals in Education* [A3–102] *Education Index* [A3–104] *Social Sciences Citation Index* [A3–117] *Social Sciences Index* [A3–118]
abstracts of journal articles on higher education?	*Current Index to Journals in Education* [A3–102] *Higher Education Abstracts* [A3–109]
manuscript requirements for periodicals in education?	This book, Section C, Chapter 1. *Cabell's Directory of Publishing Opportunities in Education* [A3–47]
an index of articles published in state education journals?	*State Education Journal Index* [A3–121]

Periodicals

Where Should I Go to Find . . .	*Try*
articles pertaining to physical education, health, dance, physical therapy, recreation, sports, and sports medicine?	*Current Index to Journals in Education* [A3–102] *Education Index* [A3–104]
abstracts of journal articles on child growth and development?	*Current Index to Journals in Education* [A3–102] *Child Development Abstracts and Bibliography* [A3–100]
abstracts of journal articles on the sociology of education?	*Current Index to Journals in Education* [A3–102] *Sociological Abstracts* [A3–119] *Sociology of Education Abstracts* [A3–120]
publications in the social and behavioral sciences in which a specific author has been cited?	*Social Sciences Citation Index* [A3–117]
the addresses of authors of journal articles in the social and behavioral sciences?	*Social Sciences Citation Index* [A3–117]
a bibliography of articles on the history of education that are found in periodicals in other academic disciplines?	*An International List of Articles on the History of Education Published in Non-Education Serials* [A3–16]
an annotated bibliography of media-related periodicals?	*Educational Media and Technology Yearbook* [A3–142]

Postsecondary Education Institutions

Where Should I Go to Find . . .	*Try*
a directory of colleges and universities with descriptive information?	*Accredited Institutions of Postsecondary Education* [A3–42] *American Universities and Colleges* [A3–44] *Barron's Profiles of American Colleges* [A3–46] (Answer continues)

Postsecondary Education Institutions

Where Should I Go to Find . . .	*Try*
a directory of colleges and universities with descriptive information?	*College Blue Book* [A3–48] *The College Board College Handbook* [A3–49] *Directory of College and University Administrators* [A3–52] *Peterson's 4 Year Colleges* [A3–67] *Peterson's 2 Year Colleges* [A3–66]
the addresses, telephone numbers, fax numbers, and e-mail addresses of colleges and universities?	*American Universities and Colleges* [A3–44] *The College Board College Handbook* [A3–49] *Directory of College and University Administrators* [A3–52] *HEP Higher Education Directory* (A3–58]
colleges identified by admission selectivity, admission/placement policies, type, special characteristics, and ranges of cost?	*The College Board College Handbook* [A3–49] *Peterson's 4 Year Colleges* [A3–67]
the location of special academic programs in colleges, such as combined bachelor's/graduate programs by field, distance learning, external degrees, study abroad, and others?	*American Universities and Colleges* [A3–44] *The College Board Index of Majors and Graduate Degrees* [A3–50]
comprehensive programs and special services in two-year and four-year colleges designed for students with learning disabilities or attention deficit disorders?	*The K&W Guide to Colleges for Students with Learning Disabilities or Attention Deficit Disorders* [A3–62] *Peterson's Colleges with Programs for Students with Learning Disabilities or Attention Deficit Disorders* [A3–69]
graduate and postgraduate financial awards available worldwide for research and study in sundry academic disciplines?	*College Blue Book*, Vol. 5 (U.S. sources only) [A3–48] *The Grants Register* [A3–57]

Postsecondary Education Institutions

Where Should I Go to Find . . .	*Try*
a worldwide directory of programs, centers, and related agencies dedicated to research and training in higher education?	*Higher Education: A Worldwide Inventory of Centers and Programs* [A3–59]
a list of specialized and professional accrediting agencies with the schools that they have accredited?	*American Universities and Colleges* [A3–44] *Directory of College and University Administrators* [A3–52] *HEP Higher Education Directory* [A3–58]
regional accrediting associations with their addresses?	This book, Section F. *Accredited Institutions of Postsecondary Education* [A3–42] *American Universities and Colleges* [A3–44] *The College Board College Handbook* [A3–49] *Directory of College and University Administrators* [A3–52]
admissions requirements, tuition, fees, and majors offered at individual institutions of higher education?	*American Universities and Colleges* [A3–44] *Barron's Profiles of American Colleges* [A3–46] *College Blue Book* [A3–48] *The College Board College Handbook* [A3–49] Peterson's Annual Guides to Graduate Study [A3–68]
an interpretation of academic costumes and ceremonies?	*American Universities and Colleges* [A3–44]
the first and the most current dates of accreditation for a college or university?	*Accredited Institutions of Postsecondary Education* [A3–42]
the names and telephone numbers of administrators at a college or university?	*Directory of College and University Administrators* [A3–52] *HEP Higher Education Directory* [A3–58]

Postsecondary Education Institutions

Where Should I Go to Find . . .	*Try*
the names of community college, college, and university faculty in the United States with their institutional affiliations and addresses?	*National Faculty Directory* [A3–63]
a directory of community colleges with descriptive information?	*American Community Colleges* [A3–43] *College Blue Book* [A3–48] *Directory of College and University Administrators* [A3–52] *Peterson's 2 Year Colleges* [A3–66]
an index of community colleges by program area?	*American Community Colleges* [A3–43] *The College Board Index of Majors and Graduate Degrees* [A3–50] *Peterson's 2 Year Colleges* [A3–66]
an index of occupational education programs and the schools with programs in each area?	*College Blue Book* [A3–48]
an index of academic majors and the colleges and universities that offer programs in each field?	*Barron's Profiles of American Colleges* [A3–46] *College Blue Book* [A3–48] *The College Board Index of Majors and Graduate Degrees* [A3–50] Peterson's Annual Guides to Graduate Study, Book One [A3–68]
a practical guide to administering the daily academic and nonacademic affairs of colleges and universities?	*Handbook of College and University Administration* [A3–84]
undergraduate courses of study offered in nations worldwide?	*Schools Abroad of Interest to Americans* [A3–72] *Study Abroad* [A3–73]
guidance on how to select and prepare to participate in a collegiate program abroad?	*Study Abroad* [A3–73]
information on graduate programs in specific universities with names of deans and chairpersons?	Peterson's Annual Guides to Graduate Study [A3–68]

Postsecondary Education Institutions

Where Should I Go to Find . . .	*Try*
a directory of British Commonwealth universities with an extensive description of each university?	*Commonwealth Universities Yearbook* [A3–51]
the names of university faculty, by academic area, in British Commonwealth universities?	*Commonwealth Universities Yearbook* [A3–51]
the names of university faculty, by academic area, in universities worldwide?	*The World of Learning* [A3–76]
universities in the British Commonwealth, indexed by subject of study?	*Commonwealth Universities Yearbook* [A3–51]
an international directory of institutions of higher learning at the university level with descriptive information?	*International Handbook of Universities* [A3–60]
the admission requirements and language of instruction at universities worldwide?	*International Handbook of Universities* [A3–60]
the names and addresses of higher education institutes worldwide?	*The World of Learning* [A3–76]

Potpourri of Educational Information

Where Should I Go to Find . . .	*Try*
rules of writing style for academic papers?	*The Chicago Manual of Style* [A3–123] *A Manual for Writers of Term Papers, Theses, and Dissertations* [A3–129] *Publication Manual of the American Psychological Association* [A3–130]
a compilation of articles on international education?	*The International Encyclopedia of Education* [A3–90]
a compilation of articles on higher education worldwide?	*The International Encyclopedia of Higher Education* [A3–91]

Potpourri of Educational Information

Where Should I Go to Find . . .	*Try*
a list of major libraries worldwide and an identification of their major collections?	*The International Encyclopedia of Higher Education* [A3–91]
an index to, and abstracts of, education literature found in sources other than journals?	*Resources in Education* [A3–116]
a subject index of U.S. government publications?	*American Statistics Index* [A3–134] *Cumulative Subject Index to the Monthly Catalog of United States Government Publications* [A3–112] *Federal Government Publications Catalog* [A3–107] *Monthly Catalog of United States Government Publications* [A3–112]
a subject index to newspaper articles?	*New York Times Index* [A3–113]
an index of unpublished education literature, such as speeches, technical reports, research reports, and others?	*Resources in Education* [A3–116]
general reference books on education at all levels with descriptive articles on a broad range of education issues, with bibliographies?	*American Educator's Encyclopedia* [A3–77] *Encyclopedia of American Education* [A3–79] *Encyclopedia of Education* [A3–80]
an annotated bibliography of information materials pertaining to children?	*Childhood Information Resources* [A3–7]
topics of current interest in education from an international perspective?	*World Yearbook of Education* [A3–144]
information on educational media and technology, including grants, information sources, organizations, and more?	*Educational Media and Technology Yearbook* [A3–142]
by state, average teacher salaries?	*Digest of Education Statistics* [A3–136]

Potpourri of Educational Information

Where Should I Go to Find . . .	*Try*
guidelines for documenting a learning disability (LD) or attention deficit/hyperactivity disorder (ADHD) in adolescents and adults?	*The K&W Guide to Colleges for Students with Learning Disabilities or Attention Deficit Disorders* [A3–62]

Research Findings

Where Should I Go to Find . . .	*Try*
a critical synthesis of research findings in education?	*Encyclopedia of Educational Research* [A3–82]
a bibliography of publications on research topics in education?	*Encyclopedia of Educational Research* [A3–82]
a critical summary of research on teaching, including theories and methods of teaching?	*Encyclopedia of Educational Research* [A3–82] *Handbook of Research on Teaching* [A3–88]
a collection of scholarly writings on the history, nature, composition, and influence of the curriculum in elementary and secondary education?	*Handbook of Research on Curriculum* [A3–87]
a compilation of abstracts of master's theses?	*Masters Abstracts International* [A3–110]
the procedure for ordering copies of master's theses?	*Masters Abstracts International* [A3–110]
a list, with no abstracts, of master's theses in education?	*Master's Theses in Education* [A3–111]
an index to, and abstracts of, educational research literature found in sources other than journals?	*Resources in Education* [A3–116]
an index of unpublished research literature?	*Resources in Education* [A3–116]

Research Findings

Where Should I Go to Find . . .	*Try*
published research findings on reading?	*Annual Summary of Investigations Relating to Reading* [A3–98] *Current Index to Journals in Education* [A3–102]
a collection of articles on reading research methodologies and findings?	*Handbook of Reading Research* [A3–85] *Handbook of Research on Teaching* [A3–88]
articles on the theories, practices, and research related to early childhood education?	*Encyclopedia of Educational Research* [A3–82] *Handbook of Research in Early Childhood Education* [A3–86] *Handbook of Research on Teaching* [A3–88]
a compendium of the basic knowledge in special education?	*Handbook of Special Education* [A3–89]
a summary of public attitudes toward U.S. public schools?	*Gallup Polls of Attitudes Toward Education, 1969–88* [A3–128]
graduate research studies in physical education, health, recreation, and dance?	*Dissertation Abstracts International* [A3–103] *Health, Physical Education and Recreation Microform Publications Bulletin* [A3–108]
research studies in business education?	*Current Index to Journals in Education* [A3–102] *Education Index* [A3–104]
a bibliography of publications pertaining to research on teaching?	*Encyclopedia of Educational Research* [A3–82] *Handbook of Research on Teaching* [A3–88]
a compilation of abstracts of doctoral dissertation research?	*Dissertation Abstracts International* [A3–103]

Research Findings

Where Should I Go to Find . . .   *Try*

the procedure for ordering copies of
doctoral dissertations?

Comprehensive Dissertation Index
[A3–101]
Dissertation Abstracts International
[A3–103]

a list of all North American doctoral
dissertations accepted since 1861?

Comprehensive Dissertation Index
[A3–101]

Research Designs, Statistical Procedures, and Measurement

experimental research designs and
related statistical procedures?

*Design and Analysis: A Researcher's
Handbook* [A3–24]
*Experimental Design: Procedures for
the Behavioral Sciences* [A3–25]
Foundations of Behavioral Research
[A3–26]
Measurement, Design, and Analysis
[A3–30]
*Statistical Principles in Experimental
Design* [A3–32]

quasi-experimental research designs
with a discussion of their use and
techniques?

Measurement, Design, and Analysis
[A3–30]
Quasi-Experimentation [A3–31]

articles on the concepts, techniques, and
terms used in educational evaluation?

Encyclopedia of Educational Evaluation
[A3–81]

an integrated approach to measurement,
design, and analysis with an explanation
of the fundamental concepts and
principles?

Measurement, Design, and Analysis
[A3–30]

how to assess student learning using
standardized tests and classroom tests?

Assessment [A3–23]
*Measurement and Assessment in
Teaching* [A3–27]
*Measurement and Evaluation in
Education and Psychology* [A3–28]
*Measurement and Evaluation in
Psychology and Education* [A3–29]

Where Should I Go to Find . . .   *Try*

Research Designs, Statistical Procedures, and Measurement

principles and techniques in measurement and evaluation used in education and psychology?	*Measurement and Evaluation in Education and Psychology* [A3–28] *Measurement and Evaluation in Psychology and Education* [A3–29]
a text on the issues, principles, and techniques for assessing children with special needs?	*Assessment* [A3–23]
a discussion of the legal and ethical considerations involved when assessing children?	*Assessment* [A3–23] *Measurement and Evaluation in Psychology and Education* [A3–29]

Software and Hardware

a comprehensive guide to specific computer software and hardware products with descriptions and prices?	*Data Sources* [A3–124]

Statistics on Education

an index and abstracts of U.S. government statistical publications listed by subject, title, and category?	*American Statistics Index* [A3–97]
national statistical information about American education at all levels?	*American Statistics Index* [A3–97] *The Condition of Education* [A3–135] *Digest of Education Statistics* [A3–136] *Education Statistics of the United States* [A3–137] *Projections of Education Statistics* [A3–140] *The World Almanac and Book of Facts* [A3–143]
sources of statistical information for the U.S. and foreign countries?	*Statistics Sources* [A3–141]
descriptive educational data for the states?	*Education Statistics of the United States* [A3–137] *Fact Book on Higher Education* [A3–138]

Statistics on Education

Where Should I Go to Find . . .	*Try*
national demographic and economic data?	*American Statistics Index* [A3–97] *Fact Book on Higher Education* [A3–138] *Statistics Sources* [A3–141]
descriptive statistical information on the status of women and minorities in higher education?	*Fact Book on Higher Education* [A3–138]
descriptive statistical information on foreign students studying in the U.S.?	*Open Doors: Report on International Educational Exchange* [A3–139]
projections of statistical data on U.S. education?	*Projections of Education Statistics* [A3–140]

Tests

a list of commercially published tests with descriptive information and critical reviews?	*Mental Measurements Yearbook* [A3–92] *The Supplement to the Thirteenth Mental Measurements Yearbook* [A3–93] *Test Critiques* [A3–94]
an index of standardized tests by subject?	*Mental Measurements Yearbook* [A3–92] *The Supplement to the Thirteenth Mental Measurements Yearbook* [A3–93] *Test Critiques* [A3–94]
an index of standardized tests organized by variables/concepts measured?	*Mental Measurements Yearbook* [A3–92] *The Supplement to the Thirteenth Mental Measurements Yearbook* [A3–93] *Tests* [A3–95]

Tests

Where Should I Go to Find . . .	*Try*
a list of test publishers with their addresses?	*Mental Measurements Yearbook* [A3–92] *The Supplement to the Thirteenth Mental Measurements Yearbook* [A3–93] *Test Critiques* [A3–94] *Tests* [A3–95] *Tests in Print V* [A3–122]
a list of standardized tests that are in print with a description of each test?	*Tests* [A3–95] *Tests in Print V* [A3–122]
a descriptive list of unpublished tests that measure children's behavioral traits?	*Tests and Measurements in Child Development: Handbook II* [A3–96]

CHAPTER 3

Printed Information Sources by Type

INTRODUCTION

This chapter contains an annotated bibliography of reference publications that facilitates study, research, and practice in the field of education. Its scope encompasses the full spectrum of education. The publications have been categorized by type as follows:

> Bibliographies
> Biographical Information
> Books on Educational Research, Statistics, and Measurement
> Dictionaries and Thesauri
> Directories
> Encyclopedias and Handbooks
> Indexes and Abstracts
> Miscellaneous
> Statistical Digests and Sources
> Yearbooks

These publications, except for the section titled "Books on Educational Research, Statistics, and Measurement," are considered to be reference tools because of their single-purpose, "look-up" features. "Books on Educational Research, Statistics, and Measurement" was included to complement the research purpose of this book.

As explained in Chapter 1, the titles have been listed alphabetically within category and numbered consecutively throughout this chapter to help the reader move from Chapter 2 to this chapter and find full bibliographic information and annotations. The annotations explain the purpose of the publications as well as some of the special information that is contained in the individual titles.

BIBLIOGRAPHIES

[A3–1]
American Reference Books Annual, 2000. (ARBA) Vol. 31. Bohdan S. Wynar, editor in chief, and Shannon M. Graff, associate editor. Englewood, CO: Libraries Unlimited, 2000.

An annual annotated bibliography and review of reference books published in the U.S. and Canada. Includes education. Additionally, encompasses general reference works, the social sciences, humanities, and science and technology.

[A3–2]

Best Books for Children: Preschool through Grade 6. 6th edition. Edited by John T. Gillespie. New Providence, NJ: R. R. Bowker Co., 1998.

A bibliography of books for children preschool through the sixth grade. Titles are arranged by subject. Includes fiction and nonfiction books. Profiles of publications provide the author's name, title of book, publisher, intended grade level of the reader, a brief description of the theme or purpose, price, and more. Includes an index that classifies all titles by subject and grade level. Also contains author and title indexes.

[A3–3]

Best Books for Young Teen Readers: Grades 7 to 10. Edited by John T. Gillespie. New Providence, NJ: R. R. Bowker Co., 2000.

A subject-organized bibliography of fiction and nonfiction books written for students in grades 7 to 10. A profile of each book includes the author's name, title of the book, publisher, suitable grade level of the reader, a brief statement about the theme or purpose of the book, price, and more. A subject-grade level index categorizes each title according to subject and the intended grade level of the reader. Also contains an author index and one for titles.

[A3–4]

Bibliographic Guide to Education. Boston: G. K. Hall, 1999. Published annually.

A comprehensive bibliography of publications in education that have been cataloged by Teachers College, Columbia University. Also includes selected titles in the field that have been catalogued by The Research Libraries of the New York Public Library. Full bibliographic information is cited for book and nonbook titles (no periodicals) in all areas and on all levels of education. Includes administrative reports from U.S., state, and city departments of education as well as from foreign countries. Lists publications in their native languages. Useful for identifying titles that exist on a subject.

[A3–5]

Books in Print. 53rd edition. Titles section, 4 vols.; Authors section, 4 vols., Subject section [A3–20], 6 vols.; Publishers section, 1 vol.; Supplement [A3–6], 3 vols. New Providence, NJ: R. R. Bowker Co., 2000. Published annually.

A listing of U.S. books in print or soon to be published. Covers nearly all subjects. The books must be available to the trade or general public for purchase. Excludes textbooks, professional medical and law books, pamphlets, subscription-only titles, and other books not available to the general public. Included among the bibliographic information are the author, editor, title, Library of Congress number (infrequently), ISBN number, price, number of pages, publication data, and publisher.

[A3–6]

Books in Print Supplement. 3 vols. New Providence, NJ: R. R. Bowker Co., 2001. Published annually.

Six months after *Books in Print* (BIP) is published, this supplement is issued to update the information in BIP.

[A3–7]

Childhood Information Resources. Marda Woodbury. Arlington, VA: Information Resources Press, 1985.

An annotated bibliography of international materials concerned with American children through age 12. Arranged by type of information format (e.g., books) with an annotation for each title. Indexes by subject, title, and author. The introductory material provides helpful suggestions for the researcher who is studying childhood issues.

[A3–8]

Children's Books in Print. 32nd edition. New Providence, NJ: R. R. Bowker Co., 2001. Published annually.

Lists all books for children that are in print. Whenever possible, indicates the reading or grade level for a title. Entries also include the author, Library of Congress number (not always), ISBN number, publisher, publication date, price, and more.

[A3–9]

Collective Bargaining in Higher Education and the Professions. Lucinda R. Zoe and Beth Hillman Johnson. New York: National Center for the Study of Collective Bargaining in Higher Education and the Professions, Baruch College, 1998. Published annually.

A bibliography of publications that focus on collective bargaining in higher education and the professions. Provides subject and author indexes.

[A3–10]

Dictionary Catalog of the Teachers College Library. 36 vols. Boston: G. K. Hall, 1970. First supplement, 1971, 5 vols.; Second Supplement, 1973, 2 vols.; Third Supplement, 1977, 10 vols. Updated by the *Bibliographic Guide to Education* [A3–4].

A reproduction of the card catalog of Teachers College Library, Columbia University. Contains one of the most extensive collections of literature in education. Books, periodicals, and audiovisual materials are cataloged. The holdings include materials from approximately 200 educational systems throughout the world. When this publication is used in conjunction with the *Bibliographic Guide to Education* [A3–4], it provides a valuable reference tool for a review of the world's literature in education.

[A3–11]

Educator's Grade Guide to Free Teaching Aids. Thomas J. Haider and Kathleen S. Nehmer. Randolph, WI: Educators Progress Service, 1996.

An annotated list of free teaching materials from sundry sources that are available to teachers. Includes books, pamphlets, charts, exhibits, maps, and other teaching aids. Indexed by title, subject, and source.

[A3–12]

El-Hi Textbooks and Serials in Print. New Providence, NJ: R. R. Bowker Co., 2000. Published annually.

Provides bibliographic information for elementary, junior, and senior high school textbooks and supplementary materials in print or forthcoming. Also includes professional books, guidance materials, reference books, and tests. Indexed by author, title, and subject. Prices are reported.

[A3–13]

Forthcoming Books. New Providence, NJ: R. R. Bowker Co. Published bimonthly.

The primary purpose of this title is to supplement *Books in Print* (BIP) [A3–5] by announcing book titles that are to be published in the U.S. during the 12 months to come. Also lists U.S. titles published since the last issue of BIP.

[A3–14]

Guide to Reference Books. 11th edition. Edited by Robert Balay. Chicago: American Library Association, 1996.

A comprehensive annotated bibliography of reference sources in the various subject areas, including education. Reference titles are organized by subject and type of publication. Provides descriptions of the contents along with full bibliographic information. Often explains the evolution of the work, which may include any changes in the title through its history. Coverage is international.

[A3–15]

A Guide to Sources of Educational Information. 2nd edition. Marda Woodbury. Arlington, VA: Information Resources Press, 1982.

An extensive annotated bibliographical list of reference sources in education. These include printed materials and nonprint sources, such as educational organizations, government agencies, and other nonprint sources of information. Organized by type of reference tool and, for selected materials, by subject. Although an older publication, it remains a useful resource.

[A3–16]

An International List of Articles on the History of Education Published in Non-Educational Serials, 1965–74. Joseph M. McCarthy. New York: Garland, 1977.

An international bibliography of articles on the history of education. These articles have not been indexed either in *Education Index* or in *Current Index to Journals in Education.* For the period covered, this publication extends the search for articles to noneducational periodicals. Remains useful for its time parameters.

[A3–17]

Magazines for Libraries. 10th edition. Bill Katz and Linda S. Katz. New Providence, NJ: R. R. Bowker Co., 2000.

An annotated list of about 7,850 periodicals arranged by subject. Includes both print and electronic periodicals. According to the authors, these periodicals were selected as being "the best and most useful for the average primary or secondary school, public, academic, or special library." Descriptions include title, frequency of publication, publisher's address, price, whether refereed, circulation size, targeted audience, description of contents, and more.

[A3–18]

Reference Books for Children. 4th edition. Carolyn S. Peterson and Ann D. Fenton. Metuchen, NJ: Scarecrow Press, 1992.

This bibliography of reference books intended for children contains a description of each title along with the standard bibliographical reference information. The more than 1,000 entries encompass a wide range of topics. Includes guidance on how to evaluate different types of reference sources.

[A3–19]

Reference Books for Children's Collections. 3rd edition. Edited by Dolores Vogliano. New York: Office of Children's Services of the New York Public Library, 1996.

Presents an annotated bibliography of reference books suitable for children. This is a diversified selection of titles, and it is designed for the spectrum of grade levels.

[A3–20]

Subject Guide to Books in Print. 6 vols. New Providence, NJ: R. R. Bowker Co., 2001. Published annually.

A companion to *Books in Print* [A3–5] that lists, by subject, in-print and forthcoming books in the U.S. Excludes fiction, poetry, literature, and drama.

[A3–21]

The Video Sourcebook. 24th edition. 2 vols. Edited by James M. Craddock. Farmington Hills, MI: The Gale Group, 2000. Published annually.

A descriptive list of more than 123,000 video titles. These titles are arranged alphabetically and by subject.

BIOGRAPHICAL INFORMATION

[A3–22]

Biographical Dictionary of Modern American Educators. Frederick Ohles, Shirley M. Ohles, and John G. Ramsay. Westport, CT: Greenwood Press, 1997.

Presents short biographical sketches of prominent American educators. The criteria for inclusion were (1) importance to the field of education, (2) being at least 60 years of age, (3) being retired, or (4) being deceased.

BOOKS ON EDUCATIONAL RESEARCH, STATISTICS, AND MEASUREMENT

[A3–23]

Assessment. 8th edition. John Salvia and James E. Ysseldyke. Boston: Houghton Mifflin Co., 2001.

A major text on assessment that, while applicable to the full spectrum of education, places emphasis on the assessment of children with special needs. Discusses teacher-made tests, standardized achievement tests, and intelligence tests. Covers assessment of sensory acuity, reading, mathematics, oral and written language, perceptual-motor skills, problem behavior, and adaptive behavior. Contains a chapter on the legal and ethical considerations when assessing children, especially those with exceptionalities. A significant publication for the graduate student and practitioner engaged in the assessment of children.

[A3–24]

Design and Analysis: A Researcher's Handbook. 3rd edition. Geoffrey Keppel. Englewood Cliffs, NJ: Prentice-Hall, 1991.

Discusses experimental designs and their associated statistical procedures used in the behavioral, biological, and social sciences. Explains the operational steps involved with the designs, reasons behind the analytical procedures, and the kinds of information that can be obtained from each experimental design. Useful for the researcher who is in the process of planning an experimental research study.

[A3–25]

Experimental Design: Procedures for the Behavioral Sciences. 3rd edition. Roger E. Kirk. Pacific Grove, CA: Brooks/Cole, 1995.

Explains the fundamentals of experimental designs and their related statistical procedures used in education. Includes a description of each design along with a disclosure of the underlying assumptions and the proper operating conditions. Discusses the advantages and disadvantages of the designs. Provides computational examples. A valuable tool for the researcher.

[A3–26]

Foundations of Behavioral Research. 4th edition. Fred N. Kerlinger and Howard B. Lee. Ft. Worth, TX: Harcourt College Publishers, 2000.

A treatment of the scientific approach to conducting behavioral research with emphasis on research designs, statistical procedures, and measurement. Explains the relationship between the research problem, design, and the methodology. Discusses the research problem, hypotheses, definitions of research terminology, types of research, inferential statistics, methods for collecting data, and other essential topics associated with the pursuit of scientific behavioral research. A valuable guide for the researcher.

[A3–27]

Measurement and Assessment in Teaching. 8th edition. Robert L. Linn and Norman E. Gronlund. Upper Saddle River, NJ: Prentice-Hall, 2000.

A recognized graduate-level publication on the role and techniques of measurement and assessment in the teaching process. Its scope includes classroom tests, observational techniques, selection and use of standardized tests, methods for expressing instructional objectives, how to measure complex achievement, use of student portfolios in instruction, assignment of grades for student achievement, and more. Also reviews basic statistics. A comprehensive treatment of educational measurement and how to implement it.

[A3–28]
Measurement and Evaluation in Education and Psychology. 4th edition. William A. Mehrens and Irvin J. Lehmann. Ft. Worth, TX: Holt, Rinehart and Winston, 1991.

Encompassing teacher-made tests; standardized achievement tests; and interest, personality, and attitude inventories, the authors have prepared an important text on measurement and evaluation principles, techniques, and practices. They cover how to build objective and essay tests, norm- and criterion-referenced measurement, observational techniques, and interpretation of test scores.

Standardization instruments include achievement tests, aptitude tests, and inventories for assessing interest, attitudes, and personality. Issues pertaining to assessing exceptionality are discussed. Also considers factors that affect evaluation, such as anxiety, test-wiseness, practice, guessing, and others. A significant text on measurement and evaluation.

[A3–29]
Measurement and Evaluation in Psychology and Education. 6th edition. Robert M. Thorndike. Upper Saddle River, NJ: Prentice-Hall, 1997.

A robust graduate-level and professional text on concepts, principles, and techniques in measurement and evaluation in psychology and education. Discusses current issues in measurement, score interpretation, reliability, validity, guidelines for evaluating a test, use of assessment information, interpretation and use of standardized achievement tests, and how to construct teacher-made tests. Also addresses the characteristics of selected aptitude tests.

Equally important in this book is its consideration of interest measurement, personality assessment, attitudes and rating scales, and the legal and ethical issues involved in the assessment of children. Addresses the impact of computers on test development, scoring, administration, and interpretation of tests. This is a significant publication for the graduate student and the professional.

[A3–30]
Measurement, Design, and Analysis: An Integrated Approach. Elazar J. Pedhazur and Liora Pedhazur Schmelkin. Hillsdale, NJ: Lawrence Erlbaum Associates, 1991.

Presents the principles and concepts of educational measurement along with an explanation of experimental design and analysis. Coverage includes test validity and reliability, as well as basic concepts and principles of research designs, and explains how to construct and implement experimental designs, quasi-experimental designs, and nonexperimental designs. Encompasses sampling strategies and sample size. This versatile book addresses the use of computers and software in data analysis. It also focuses on such statistical procedures as multiple regression analysis, factorial designs, analysis of covariance, exploratory factor analysis, confirmatory factor analysis, and more. This book undertakes an integrated approach to measurement, design, and analysis in behavioral research.

[A3–31]

Quasi-Experimentation: Design and Analysis Issues for Field Settings. Thomas D. Cook and Donald T. Campbell. Boston: Houghton Mifflin Co., 1979.

Presents quasi-experimental designs that are used in the behavioral sciences. A useful book for this type of research design.

[A3–32]

Statistical Principles in Experimental Design. 3rd edition. B. J. Winer, Donald R. Brown, and Kenneth M. Michels. New York: McGraw-Hill, 1991.

An excellent professional source for information on experimental designs and their statistical principles used in behavioral research. Explains single-factor and multifactor experiments, balanced lattice designs, Latin squares, analysis of covariance, and more.

DICTIONARIES AND THESAURI

[A3–33]

Black's Law Dictionary. 7th edition. Henry Campbell Black. Eagan, MN: West Group, 1999.

The long-recognized dictionary of legal terms and phrases. Provides definitions that are often documented by reference to court cases. Includes English and non-English terms and phrases that are used in American and English jurisprudence.

[A3–34]

The Concise Dictionary of Education. Gene R. Hawes and Lynne S. Hawes. New York: Van Nostrand Reinhold Co., 1982.

A dictionary of terms that encompass the full spectrum of education. This specialized dictionary of educational terms spans preschool years through postdoctoral studies and lifelong learning.

[A3–35]

Dictionary of Education. 2nd edition. Edited by Carter V. Good. New York: McGraw-Hill, 1959.

The first edition was the initial comprehensive dictionary of professional and technical terms used in education. The second edition builds on this precedent. Also includes terms meaningful to education from philosophy, psychology, and sociology.

[A3–36]

Dictionary of Educational Acronyms, Abbreviations, and Initialisms. 2nd edition. Edited by James C. Palmer and Anita Y. Colby. Phoenix, AZ: Oryx Press, 1985.

An alphabetical list of more than 4,000 acronyms, abbreviations, and initialisms that are used in education along with the terms that they represent. Also offers a reverse list (i.e.), represented terms appearing first). Includes names of organizations, degrees, tests, processes, equipment, systems, titles, technical terminology, programs, and more.

[A3–37]

A Dictionary of Special Education Terms. Bryon C. Moore, William Abraham, and Clarence R. Laing. Springfield, IL: Charles C Thomas, 1980.

Provides the definitions of terms that are in use in special education. The dictionary's authors state that they focused on the areas of "mental retardation, emotional handicaps, hearing, vision, . . . learning disability, speech, physical handicaps, and giftedness." Includes a pronunciation guide for the terms.

[A3–38]

The Oryx Dictionary of Education. Edited by John W. Collins III and Nancy P. O'Brien. Westport, CT: Oryx Press, 2002.

A dictionary containing approximately 7,000 terms and phrases used in education and related academic disciplines. Includes both traditional terminology and the more recent vocabulary in education. A modern dictionary for the profession.

[A3–39]

Special Education Dictionary. Edited by Susan Gorn. Horsham, PA: LRP Publications, 1997.

Defines terms, phrases, and acronyms used in the field of special education. Entries are for childhood diseases, disabilities, legal terms relating to special education, diagnostic tests, neurological terms, instructional methods, behavior management, early intervention services, and more. Easy to use for concise definitions.

[A3–40]

Thesaurus of ERIC Descriptors. 14th edition. Edited by James E. Houston. Westport, CT: Oryx Press, 2001.

Designed to be the "definitive vocabulary for education." Contains the indexing terminology (descriptors) used to access the *Current Index to Journals in Education* [A3–102] and *Resources in Education* [A3–116]. The hierarchy of descriptors is a valuable tool, especially with its "broader" and "narrower" terms for many of the descriptors. This hierarchy facilitates locating related materials. The *Thesaurus* is the key to accessing the ERIC system.

[A3–41]

Thesaurus of Psychological Index Terms. 8th edition. Edited by Alvin Walker Jr. Washington, DC: American Psychological Association, 1997.

A list of terms and subject headings that are used in *Psychological Abstracts* [A3–114] and in *PsycINFO*, the online database for *Psychological Abstracts*. To facilitate the use of the foregoing, the *Thesaurus* provides such tools as "used for," "broader terms," "narrower terms," and "related terms." Definitions are given for some of the terms in the classification system.

DIRECTORIES

[A3–42]

Accredited Institutions of Postsecondary Education. Edited by Kenneth Von Alt. Washington, DC: American Council on Education. Westport, CT: Oryx Press, 2001. Published annually.

A list, by state, of accredited postsecondary education institutions and an indication of professional programs within those institutions that have been accredited by national or regional accrediting bodies. Includes both degree-granting and non-degree-granting institutions. These bodies have been recognized by the Council for Higher Education Accreditation (CHEA). Also lists candidates for accreditation. Included are the name and address of the institution; type of control, institution, and student body; dates of first and most recent accreditation; the accrediting body; specialized accreditation; and more. Contains an index of accrediting agencies recognized by CHEA.

[A3–43]

American Community Colleges: A Guide. 10th edition. Edited by Robert H. Atwell and David Pierce. Washington, DC: American Council on Education. Phoenix, AZ: Oryx Press, 1995.

A directory, by state, of accredited postsecondary education institutions that offer the associate degree. This publication complements *American Universities and Colleges* [A3–44]. *American Community Colleges* (ACC) provides descriptive information about each institution, including purpose and programs, location, telephone number, accreditation, history, academic calendar, admission requirements, tuition and fees, teaching staff, general degree requirements, special facilities, names of senior administrative officials, and more.

[A3–44]

American Universities and Colleges. 16th edition. 2 vols. Edited by James J. Murray III. Hawthorne, NY: Walter de Gruyter, in collaboration with the American Council on Education, 2001. Published quadrennially.

Published since 1928, a directory of accredited colleges and universities in America that award at least the baccalaureate degree. Each institutional profile includes contact information, institutional characteristics, accreditation, academic calendar, admission requirements, degree requirements, degrees and other formal awards conferred, tuition and other expenses, financial aid, enrollment, institutional finances, description of the library, physical facilities, and more. Also contains a description of the accrediting agency in each professional field along with the names of its member institutions. Presents essays on higher education, including the history and structure of higher education in America. There is an explanation of the academic costume code and a ceremony guide for American colleges and universities.

[A3–45]

Annual Register of Grant Support. 34th edition. New Providence, NJ: R. R. Bowker Co., 2001. Published annually.

A directory of grants available from foundations, community trusts, government agencies, educational and professional associations, unions, special interest organizations, and corporations. Profiles each grant program by offering such information as purpose, types of grants, eligibility requirements, application information, and where to send inquiries. Indexes grant programs by subject, geographical location, and funding organization. Provides guidelines on how to write grant proposals.

[A3–46]

Barron's Profiles of American Colleges. 24th edition. Compiled and edited by the College Division of Barron's Educational Series. Hauppauge, NY: Barron's Educational Series, 2000. Published annually.

Contains brief descriptive information of each college that is cited. The descriptions include enrollment, major offered, admission requirements, median ACT and SAT test scores, student costs, financial aid, and more. Provides an index that groups colleges according to the degree of admissions competitiveness. Includes an index of academic majors that identifies colleges and universities that offer each major.

[A3–47]

Cabell's Directory of Publishing Opportunities in Education. 5th edition. Edited by David W. E. Cabell and Deborah L. English. Beaumont, TX: Cabell Publishing Co., 1998.

For each of more than 400 journals in education, this directory describes the guidelines for submitting a manuscript for publication. Reports on the editorial policy, review process, targeted readers, and other related matters of interest to writers.

[A3–48]

The College Blue Book. 28th edition. 5 vols. New York: Macmillan Reference USA, 2001.

A comprehensive compilation of descriptions of colleges, universities, community colleges, and occupational education schools. Also lists postsecondary education institutions by program area. Offers a directory of private sources of student financial assistance with information on how to apply. A first stop when seeking information about institutions of higher education and related matters.

[A3–49]

The College Board College Handbook, 2001. 38th edition. New York: College Entrance Examination Board, 2000. Published annually.

A well-established guide to postsecondary education institutions in the U.S. Published by the College Board, it serves as a facilitator for college-seeking students. Its pages display institutional profiles of community colleges, four-year institutions, and graduate schools. The profiles are comprehensive yet not exhaustive. A variety of indexes is provided to assist the college-bound student with identifying a suitable college or university. Colleges are listed by type of institution, special characteristics, enrollment size, admission selectivity, admission/placement policies, student life, ROTC availability, and individual NCAA sports that are offered.

Accompanying the 38th edition of this publication is the *College Explorer* CD-ROM, Windows version. It helps students to identify their college of choice and provides direct links to individual college Web sites.

A valuable complement to this directory is *The College Board Index of Majors and Graduate Degrees* [A3–50], which categorizes colleges by academic major.

[A3–50]

The College Board Index of Majors and Graduate Degrees, 2001. 23rd edition. New York: College Entrance Examination Board, 2000. Published annually.

This publication enables the reader to identify colleges and universities that offer specific fields of study and the degree level of each program (associate degree through the doctorate and first professional degree). Organized by major with state subcategories and name of institutions listed under each state. Discloses the institutional location of special academic programs, such as combined bachelor's and graduate programs by major, distance learning, external degrees, independent study, internships, study abroad, teacher certification, weekend colleges, and others.

[A3–51]

Commonwealth Universities Yearbook, 2000. 75th edition. 2 vols. London: Association of Commonwealth Universities, 2000. Published annually.

A directory of the universities in the British Commonwealth. Presents a comprehensive description of each university, including its address and telephone number, names of its faculty (by academic area) and administrators, the university's origin, library collection, degrees and other academic recognitions, admissions, fees, residential facilities, and other related information. A chapter is devoted to each university, and these university chapters are organized by country. Indexes universities by subject area of study.

[A3–52]

Directory of College and University Administrators, 2001. Princeton, NJ: Peterson's, 2001. Published annually.

A directory of institutions of higher education disclosing the names, telephone numbers, and e-mail addresses of the administrators on each campus. Also provides succinct descriptive information for each college or university. Contains the names and contact information for administrative personnel in the offices of higher education systems. Lists the accrediting agencies for institutions of higher education.

[A3–53]

The Directory for Exceptional Children. 13th edition. Boston: Porter Sargent Publishers, 1994.

A list of more than 3,000 educational and training facilities in the U.S. that serve children with special needs. Gives a descriptive profile of each facility that includes the address and telephone number, name of the chief administrative official and the medical director, types of handicaps accepted, curriculum by level, therapy offerings, size of enrollment, staff size, enrollment costs, and other related information. A categorized directory for identifying facilities that serve developmental, emotional, and organic disabilities. Includes public and private facilities and residential and day facilities. Also lists associations, societies, and foundations that address the needs of children with disabilities.

[A3–54]

Encyclopedia of Associations. 37th edition. Vol. 1: *National Organizations of the U.S.* Edited by Patricia T. Ballard. Farmington Hills, MI: The Gale Group, 2001. Published annually.

A directory of national and international organizations headquartered in the U.S. that have voluntary memberships. Includes more than 1,300 educational organizations in addition to those that are commercial, agricultural, scientific, cultural, etc. Organizational profiles include the organization's name, acronym, address, telephone number, Web site address, purpose, name and title of the chief operating officer, founding date, size of membership, computer-based services, official publications, size of operating budget, date and location of annual meeting, and more.

[A3–55]

The Foundation Directory. 23rd edition. David G. Jacobs, associate editor. New York: The Foundation Center, 2001. Published annually.

Foundations are listed by state, and descriptive information for each foundation is given, such as address, telephone number, purpose, types of projects funded, limitations on giving, financial data on the foundation, grant application information, to whom correspondence should be sent, and the names of officers and trustees. Indexes foundations by area of funding interest, geographical location, type of support awarded, and alphabetically. Reports the geographical area of a foundation's activities.

[A3–56]

The Foundation Grants Index, 2001. 29th edition. Edited by Rebecca MacLean. New York: The Foundation Center, 2000. Published annually.

A directory of foundations that award grants of at least $10,000. Discloses a foundation's funding interests and its limitations on giving. Lists the foundation's grant awards for the preceding year. Indexes grants by subject and by the state in which the recipient is located. Also includes a summary directory of foundations with their addresses and the limitations of their grant programs.

[A3–57]

The Grants Register, 2001. 19th edition. Edited by Louise Baynes. New York: St. Martin's Press, 2000.

A worldwide directory of graduate, postgraduate, and professional grants for scholarly studies. Granting organizations include universities, foundations, research centers, and others. Descriptive information includes the grantor's subject area(s) of interest, eligibility requirements, level of study, purpose of the grant, type of financial award, value of the stipend, application procedure, and other relevant information. Persons who are interested in pursuing scholarly studies in the U.S. and abroad will find this directory to be of value in identifying financial awards for supporting their academic pursuits.

[A3–58]

HEP Higher Education Directory. Washington, DC: Higher Education Publications, 2001. Published annually.

A directory of institutions of higher education in America that have some level of accreditation and that offer at least a one-year program of study that leads to a degree. College and university profiles contain such information as name, address, telephone number, enrollment, congressional district, annual undergraduate tuition and fees, academic calendar system, accreditation, highest degree offering, names of key administrators, and other selected institutional characteristics. An index provides the telephone numbers of key administrators. This directory presents the name, address, telephone number, and chief executive officer's name of statewide higher education agencies, higher education associations, and consortia of colleges and universities. There is an index of postsecondary education institutions by specialized and professional accreditation association.

[A3–59]

Higher Education: A Worldwide Inventory of Centers and Programs. Philip G. Altbach and David Engberg. Phoenix, AZ: Oryx Press, 2001.

This is an international directory of higher education programs, centers, and associated agencies. All of these are dedicated to the research and study of higher education and, in some cases, to the preparation of professors and administrators for this field. The list of programs and centers is organized by country. Within the U.S., the entries are categorized by state. Descriptive profiles include the name, address, telephone number, Web site address, organizational focus, titles of courses taught, names of faculty, titles of key books and journals used in the courses taught, and more. A major feature of this directory is its international bibliography of journals in higher education with contact information for each journal.

[A3–60]

International Handbook of Universities. 15th edition. International Association of Universities. New York: Groves Dictionaries, 1998. Published triennially.

A directory of university-level institutions of higher education worldwide. For each university, it presents descriptive information such as location, telephone number, admission requirements, academic calendar, language of instruction, degrees and diplomas conferred, names of administrators, and more. Institutions are alphabetized within each country.

[A3–61]

The ISS Directory of Overseas Schools. Princeton, NJ: International Schools Services, 2000. Published annually.

This is a directory of overseas schools, preK–12, in which English is the language of instruction and where an American or British curriculum is followed. These schools are listed by city within country, and the school profiles include the address, telephone number, name of principal, grade levels offered, enrollment, staff size, nationality composition of the student body, annual tuition, academic calendar, curriculum, and other related information. It lists schools that offer boarding facilities and those that offer the International Baccalaureate Program during the last two years of high school.

[A3–62]

The K&W Guide to Colleges for Students with Learning Disabilities or Attention Deficit Disorders. 5th edition. Marybeth Kravets and Imy F. Wax. New York: Random House, 1999. Published biennially.

Displays descriptive profiles of institutions of higher education that offer programs and services for students with learning disabilities or attention deficit disorders. Includes both a general description of the college and specific information about programs and services for students with LD or ADHD. This publication also offers guidance for the student in the process of selecting a college. For both LD and ADHD, separate guidelines for documentation are provided.

[A3–63]

The National Faculty Directory. 32nd edition. 3 vols. Farmington Hills, MI: The Gale Group, 2001. Published annually.

A list of the teaching faculty at community colleges, four-year colleges, and universities in the U.S. and selected institutions of higher education in Canada. Alphabetized entries include the faculty member's name, department affiliation, institution's name, and institutional address. The primary data source for this directory is the current academic catalog.

[A3–64]

Patterson's American Education. 96th edition. Edited by Wayne Moody. Mount Prospect, IL: Educational Directories, 2000. Published annually.

A directory of secondary and postsecondary schools in the U.S. For secondary education, it lists school districts by state and reports the names and addresses of the superintendents and principals. Also discloses the enrollment of a school district. Includes public and private schools. At the beginning of each state's section, the names of the major state-level officers for secondary and postsecondary education are printed along with their addresses. For postsecondary education, it cites public and private colleges, universities, community colleges, and vocational-technical-trade schools by subject field within a state. Also contains directories of superintendents of education for Roman Catholic, Lutheran, and Seventh-Day Adventist schools. Provides a directory of educational associations, agencies, and organizations.

[A3–65]

Patterson's Elementary Education. 12th edition. Edited by Wayne Moody. Mount Prospect, IL: Educational Directories, 2000. Published annually.

A directory of public and private kindergartens, elementary schools, and middle schools in the U.S. The beginning of each state's section reports the names of the major state officials in the state's department of education along with their address and telephone numbers. Also reports the Web site address of each state department of education.

School districts are listed alphabetically by town. For each school district, it lists the names and addresses of the superintendent and the principals. A brief descriptive profile is provided for individual schools that includes the address, telephone number, enrollment, and grade levels. Also included is a list of charter schools in each state and the schools under the U.S. Bureau of Indian Affairs. This directory contains the names and contact information for superintendents of Catholic, Lutheran and Seventh-Day Adventist schools.

[A3–66]

Peterson's 2 Year Colleges, 2001. 31st edition. Princeton, NJ: Peterson's, 2000. Published annually.

Accredited two-year colleges in the U.S. and U.S. territories are listed with a descriptive profile of each institution. For some, an in-depth narrative description is also provided. An index of majors enables the reader to identify two-year colleges that offer programs in each academic field. Reports admission requirements, tuition and fees, and more. Contains sections that offer guidance on issues involved with selecting a community college, applying for admission, and paying for an education.

[A3–67]

Peterson's 4 Year Colleges, 2001. 31st edition. Princeton, NJ: Peterson's, 2000. Published annually.

This is one of the widely recognized guides to four-year colleges and universities in the U.S. and Canada, with both brief profiles and in-depth narrative descriptions of individual colleges. These provide institutional historical data, an explanation of undergraduate programs, a description of facilities, and information on the faculty, admission requirements, application process, and more. To assist with the selection of a suitable college, institutions of higher education are indexed by academic major, difficulty of being accepted, and ranges of cost. Sections also discuss how to delimit the search to a few colleges, how to pay for a college education, standardized tests required, and how to use the Internet for selecting a college.

Accompanying this directory is a CD-ROM that provides valuable guidance for selecting a college and making application to it. This CD enables direct access to www. CollegeQuest.com.

[A3–68]

Peterson's Annual Guides to Graduate Study. 35th edition. 6 vols. Princeton, NJ: Peterson's, 2001. Published annually. *Note:* At the time of this writing, there was not a current umbrella title for this set of guides; consequently, the publisher's former title has been used.

The individual titles of the six volumes of these guides are as follows:

> *Peterson's Graduate and Professional Programs: An Overview* (Book 1)
> *Peterson's Graduate Programs in the Humanities, Arts, and Social Sciences* (Book 2)
> *Peterson's Graduate Programs in the Biological Sciences* (Book 3)
> *Peterson's Graduate Programs in the Physical Sciences, Mathematics, Agricultural Sciences, the Environment and Natural Resources* (Book 4)
> *Peterson's Graduate Programs in Engineering and Applied Sciences* (Book 5)
> *Peterson's Graduate Programs in Business, Education, Health, Information Studies, Law, and Social Work* (Book 6)

This is a directory of graduate and professional programs in accredited colleges and universities in the U.S. and its territories. It also includes such programs in U.S. accredited postsecondary education institutions in Canada, Mexico, Europe, and Africa. Programs are listed by field; and, for each university, the listing of programs also reports the level of graduate degree offered. Both brief profiles and in-depth descriptions are provided.

[A3–69]

Peterson's Colleges with Programs for Students with Learning Disabilities or Attention Deficit Disorders. 5th edition. Princeton, NJ: Peterson's, 1997.

A directory of accredited two-year and four-year colleges and universities in the U.S., territories of the U.S., and Canada that award associate or bachelor's degrees and that offer comprehensive programs or special services for students with learning disabilities (LD) or attention deficit disorders (ADD). Provides institutional profiles that include general information about the college and specific information on programs and services that are available to students with LD or ADD. Also includes guidance for these students on how to select a college.

[A3–70]

QED State School Guide, 2000–2001. 18th edition. 52 vols. Denver: Quality Education Data, 2000. Published annually.

A set of state directories that list, by county, the public, private, and parochial elementary and secondary schools. For each state, the front section reports an overview of descriptive statistics for education followed by the county listings. Demographic data, contact information, names of key administrators, enrollment statistics, and a variety of program information are provided for the different school districts and schools. A directory of selected telephone numbers is displayed for each state department of education.

[A3–71]

Research Centers Directory. 27th edition. Edited by Donna Wood. Farmington Hills, MI: The Gale Group, 2001. Published annually.

A directory of permanently established research centers, institutes, bureaus, and other similar nonprofit research organizations in education and other fields. Descriptive information in each entry includes the address, telephone number, director's name, sources of support, fields of research, specialized collections and databases, publications, and other related information. Indexes by name of research center, acronym of the center, name of sponsoring institution, research subject field, and special capabilities (equipment, databases, collections, etc.).

[A3–72]

Schools Abroad of Interest to Americans. 9th edition. Boston: Porter Sargent Publishers, 1999.

Brief descriptive information of independent elementary and secondary schools in 125 countries that may be of interest to U.S. students and their families for studying abroad. Reports the language of instruction along with other information. Also contains information on colleges and universities abroad that enroll American students.

[A3–73]

Study Abroad, 2001. 8th edition. Princeton, NJ: Peterson's, 2001. Published annually.

A guide to undergraduate studies in countries worldwide. Reports courses by subject area. Provides guidance for selecting and preparing to enter a program of study abroad. Also reports eligibility requirements for the separate programs, financial aid that is available, procedures for applying, living arrangements, and more.

[A3–74]

Ulrich's Periodicals Directory. 39th edition. New Providence, NJ: R. R. Bowker Co., 2000. Published annually.

An international compilation of serials published in education and other fields. Gives full bibliographic information. Includes serials that are published regularly or irregularly. Reports where a title is indexed and abstracted. Provides a separate subject listing of publications that index and/or abstract periodicals. Contains sections that list serials available online and on CD-ROM. Includes names of providers of online serials and a listing of the serials that each provides. Coverage encompasses both traditional and electronic publications.

[A3–75]

Web Site Source Book. 6th edition. Edited by Pam Gaulin. Detroit: Omnigraphics, 2001. Published annually.

A directory of Web sites for associations, businesses, organizations, institutions, foundations, government agencies, research centers, etc. Organized by subject. Within the field of education are the Web site addresses for colleges and universities, community colleges, vocational and technical schools, early childhood learning centers (i.e., corporate head-quarters), educational research centers, accrediting organizations, U.S. Department of Education, businesses that provide educational materials and services, and many organizations and associations in education. The profiles include, when available, the name, address, telephone number, toll-free telephone number, fax number, E-mail address, and the Web site address.

[A3–76]
The World of Learning, 2000. 50th edition. London: Europa Publications, 1999. Published annually.

A comprehensive international list of learned societies, research institutes, libraries, museums, colleges, and universities arranged alphabetically by and within country. Provides assorted descriptive information about each entry, including location and telephone number. Facilitates the identification of specific entities in each of the foregoing categories in nations worldwide. For universities, provides the names of faculty by academic department, thus aiding in the identification of colleagues throughout the world. As the title suggests, it is a directory for the world's academic community. Also includes information on bodies of the UN and other international organizations.

ENCYCLOPEDIAS AND HANDBOOKS

[A3–77]
American Educators' Encyclopedia. 2nd edition. David E. Kapel, Charles S. Gifford, and Marilyn B. Kapel. Westport, CT: Greenwood Press, 1991.

Contains brief articles on terms and phrases used in education along with entries on prominent educators, educational organizations, and other education-related subjects. Each entry concludes with reference citations.

[A3–78]
Deskbook Encyclopedia of American School Law. Rosemont, MN: Information Research Systems, 2001. Published annually.

Summarizes case law on education. Based on state and federal appellate court decisions. The case law summaries are categorized according to accidents-injuries-death, employment practices, constitutional freedoms, tenure, student rights, and other legal issues.

[A3–79]
Encyclopedia of American Education. 3 vols. Harlow G. Unger. New York: Facts On File, 1996.

A comprehensive encyclopedia of public and private education at all levels. Its scope embraces most areas of education, including pedagogy, administration, school reform, history, educational terminology, biographical profiles of eminent educators, organizations and associations, psychometrics, and more about American education.

Significant federal legislation from 1787 to 1993 pertaining to education is listed, as are the major decisions of the U.S. Supreme Court that addressed issues of education. Displays a chronology of American education from 1607 to 1994.

[A3–80]

The Encyclopedia of Education. 10 vols. Edited by Lee C. Deighton. New York: Macmillan Publishing Co. and The Free Press, 1971.

A compilation of more than 1,000 signed articles that address the broad spectrum of American education at all levels. Although the primary emphasis is on American education, there are articles on international and comparative education. Addresses the history, philosophy, theory, research, and structure of education. Albeit its publication dates back three decades, it remains of value for its historical perspective.

[A3–81]

Encyclopedia of Educational Evaluation. Scarvia B. Anderson, Samuel Ball, Richard T. Murphy, and associates. San Francisco: Jossey-Bass, 1975.

A collection of signed articles that synthesizes the principal concepts and techniques applicable to the evaluation of education and training programs. Both brief and extensive entries are used. Includes definitions of terms encountered in the literature on evaluation. Provides bibliographies for further review of the literature as of 1975. Articles are classified by topical areas for easy access. Subjects addressed include evaluation models, setting program objectives, planning for evaluation, experimental designs, sampling, measurement devices and techniques, statistical concepts and tools, and more. Although published in 1975, much of it remains of value.

[A3–82]

Encyclopedia of Educational Research. 6th edition. 4 vols., Marvin C. Alkin, editor in chief. Published in collaboration with the American Educational Research Association. New York: Macmillan Publishing Co., 1992. Published approximately every 10 years.

Offers a wide range of topics in education with signed articles that summarize recent (as of the publication date) trends and major research findings. This critical synthesis of research is supported by extensive bibliographic references. Intended for graduate students, professionals in education, and thoughtful laypersons. An excellent source for initiating a study of a selected topic in education. First published in 1941.

[A3–83]

Encyclopedia of Special Education. 2nd edition. 3 vols. Edited by Cecil R. Reynolds and Elaine Fletcher-Janzen. New York: John Wiley and Sons, 2000.

A compilation of extended definitions of terms and major concepts used in special education. Contains signed articles that provide scholarly treatment of topics. Presents the names and contributions of the pioneers and eminent professionals in the field of special education.

[A3–84]

Handbook of College and University Administration. 2 vols. Edited by Asa S. Knowles. New York: McGraw-Hill, 1970.

A set of handbooks on the academic and nonacademic administration of two-year colleges and four-year colleges and universities. Volume 1 addresses general (nonacademic) administrative affairs such as legal matters, governing boards, organizational matters, planning, public relations, nonacademic personnel administration, business and financial affairs, and physical plant operations. Volume 2 focuses on academic policies, curriculum planning, research, academic personnel administration, library organization and management, athletics, admissions, student personnel administration, collective bargaining, and other related academic topics. An operational guide for administering the daily affairs of a college or university.

[A3–85]

Handbook of Reading Research. Vol. 3. Edited by Michael L. Kamil, Peter B. Mosenthal, P. David Pearson, and Rebecca Barr. Mahwah, NJ: Lawrence Erlbaum Associates, 2000.

Signed scholarly articles that provide a comprehensive analysis and interpretation of reading research, including methodologies used and research findings. Offers chapters on literacy processes, practices, and policies. Reports on state-of-the-art basic processes and instructional practices. A research-based overview of the field of reading with extensive bibliographies.

[A3–86]

Handbook of Research in Early Childhood Education. Edited by Bernard Spodek. New York: The Free Press, 1982.

Contains articles with research findings on topics in early childhood education. These topics include child development, developmental theories, processes in the classroom, public policy as it relates to early childhood education, and measurement and evaluation methods. Provides lengthy bibliographies.

[A3–87]

Handbook of Research on Curriculum. Edited by Philip W. Jackson. A project of the American Educational Research Association. New York: Macmillan Publishing Co., 1992.

A significant treatment of the curriculum in elementary and secondary education. Encompasses a broad consideration of the subject that includes articles on conceptual and methodological perspectives and issues; curricular history, organization, and policy; cultural determinants of the curriculum; the influence of the curriculum; and more. This is a scholarly publication that is based on professional research.

[A3–88]

Handbook of Research on Teaching. 3rd edition. Edited by Merlin C. Wittrock. New York: Macmillan Publishing Co., 1986.

Presents a critical summary of research findings on teaching along with the theories involved and the methods used to study teaching. The effort has been to present an integrated discussion of research on teaching that discloses the relationships between studies and between the findings and their theoretical foundations. Provides extensive references. This handbook is a project of the American Educational Research Association.

[A3–89]

Handbook of Special Education: Research and Practice. 4 vols. Edited by Margaret C. Wang, Maynard C. Reynolds, and Herbert J. Walberg. Oxford and Elmsford, NY: Pergamon Press, 1987–1991.

A collection of scholarly articles on the fundamental knowledge in special education. Summarizes the research foundation of the field of special education and synthesizes the state of the art and state of practice. This body of work serves as a reference for professionals. The articles address basic concepts, curricula, teaching methods, delivery systems, education of children with different types of disabilities, research efforts in gifted education, and other related topics. Provides extensive bibliographies.

[A3–90]

The International Encyclopedia of Education: Research and Studies. 2nd edition. Edited by Torsten Husen and T. Neville Postlethwaite. New York: Elsevier Science, 1994.

An alphabetized collection of signed scholarly articles which treats a wide range of topics on educational "problems, practices, and institutions" in countries worldwide. This encyclopedia focuses on (1) the state of the art in education, (2) scientifically valid information that is available, and (3) identifying additional research that is needed in the different areas of education. The articles usually run several pages. Provides source bibliographies for further inquiry into international education topics.

[A3–91]

The International Encyclopedia of Higher Education. 10 vols. Edited by Asa S. Knowles. San Francisco: Jossey-Bass, 1977.

Consists of signed articles concerning all major aspects of higher education on the international scene. Presents national systems of higher education; topical essays written by educational leaders from around the world; a discussion of 142 fields of study; citations of hundreds of regional, national, and international education associations, organizations, and societies; centers and institutes of higher education research; major reports on postsecondary education; an international directory of documentation and information centers on higher education; a list of acronyms that designate associations, organizations, and governmental agencies of higher education worldwide; and a glossary that defines English and non-English terms associated with higher education from the nations of the world. There are descriptive essays, instructional entries that explain day-to-day administrative practices of colleges and universities in different nations germane to specific topics, definitive articles that explain a concept or term, and theoretical essays about issues in higher education.

[A3–92]

Mental Measurements Yearbook. 13th edition. Edited by James C. Impara and Barbara S. Plake. Lincoln, NE: Buros Institute of Mental Measurements of the University of Nebraska-Lincoln, 1998. Published approximately every three years.

Published since 1938, the *MMY* has become the principal reference source that lists commercially published tests in the English language. Test entries include a description containing the title; intended examinees; publication date; acronym; special comments; number of part scores; statement on the absence of reliability and/or validity data; statement on the absence of normative data; indication of whether it is a group or individual test; listing of forms, parts, and levels; number of pages; cost; scoring; time to administer; author; publisher; and other related information. Also provides test references and professional critical reviews about the qualities of the tests.

The testing instruments profiled in the *MMY* are arranged alphabetically and numbered consecutively. Indexes include the Index of Titles, Index of Acronyms, Classified Subject Index, Publishers Directory and Index, Index of Names, and a Score Index. The tests are cross-referenced to reviews in earlier editions.

Tests included in this edition were limited to new or revised instruments since the 12th edition; consequently, descriptions and references for older tests may be found in earlier editions of the *MMY* and in the *Tests in Print* [A3–122] series.

[A3–93]

The Supplement to the Thirteenth Mental Measurements Yearbook. Edited by Barbara S. Plake and James C. Impara. Lincoln, NE: Buros Institute of Mental Measurements of the University of Nebraska-Lincoln, 1999.

Supplements the 13th edition of the *MMY* [A3–92] by providing reviews of standardized tests that were either new or revised since the 1998 publication of the *MMY* and before June 15, 1999. The format remains the same as found in the 13th edition of the *MMY*.

[A3–94]

Test Critiques. 10 vols. Edited by Daniel J. Keyser and Richard C. Sweetland. Austin, TX: PRO-ED, 1994.

A presentation of published standardized tests used in psychology, education, and business. Contains a description of each test along with a professional critique. Each instrument's profile includes the "Introduction," which explains the purpose and history of the instrument; a "Practical Applications/Uses" section, which describes the intended settings and appropriate subjects to be tested, and guidelines for administering, scoring, and interpreting; a "Technical Aspects" section, which discusses the psychometric properties of the instrument along with professional comments; and a "Critique" section, which offers a general critique.

[A3–95]

Tests: A Comprehensive Reference for Assessments in Psychology, Education, and Business. 4th edition. Edited by Taddy Maddox. Austin, TX: PRO-ED, 1997.

A guide to standardized assessment instruments. Provides concise descriptions, not evaluations. The profiles include the instrument's title, author, purpose, copyright date, targeted examinees, explanation of the scoring method, cost, and name of the publisher. Describes the format, test items, variables measured, materials used, and the administration of the test. An index categorizes the instruments according to the purposes of the tests, such as intelligence, academic achievement, academic aptitude, development, readiness, personality, and others.

[A3–96]
Tests and Measurements in Child Development: Handbook II. 2 vols. Orval G. Johnson. San Francisco: Jossey-Bass, 1976.

Provides descriptive profiles of unpublished measures of the behavior of children up to age 18. For each test, it reports the title, age of intended examinees, variable being measured, type of measure, description of the measure, validity and reliability, and more related information. The testing instruments are placed in 11 categories. Achievement measures, case history forms, and demographic data-gathering instruments have been excluded.

INDEXES AND ABSTRACTS

[A3–97]
American Statistics Index (ASI). 2 vols. Bethesda, MD: Congressional Information Service. Published in annual editions and monthly supplements.

A master index and abstracts of statistical publications issued by branches and agencies of the federal government. The publisher, CIS, makes available microfiche copies of most publications indexed and abstracted in *ASI*. Materials not included in *ASI* are those that contain highly technical and scientific data, classified information, and other exceptions as noted by the publisher. This publication appears in two volumes: the Index and the Abstract. Indexing is by subjects and names, categories, titles, and agency report numbers. The Abstract section contains a full description of the purpose, content, and format of each publication.

[A3–98]
Annual Summary of Investigations Relating to Reading. Sam Weintraub et al. Newark, DE: International Reading Association. Formerly an annual publication. Last published in 1996.

Provides abstracts of the published reading research literature. The entries include the bibliographic citation followed by an abstract that describes the purpose of the research, subjects studied (age and grade), instruments used, procedures, and principal findings. Facilitates a quick overview of the year's published research on reading. Remains valuable for historical research.

[A3–99]
British Education Index. Edited by Phil Sheffield. London: University of Leeds, 1954–. Published quarterly.

Indexes articles in several hundred English-language education periodicals that are published in the British Isles. Also includes selected international titles. Articles are indexed by subject and author. Available in print, on CD-ROM, and on the Internet (http://www.leeds.ac.uk/bei).

[A3–100]

Child Development Abstracts and Bibliography. Chicago: University of Chicago Press, Society for Research in Child Development. Published three times a year.

Abstracts articles from professional journals concerned with child growth and development. The abstracted articles are categorized by major subject areas, such as health, learning, personality studies, educational processes, and other related broad topics. Also includes reviews of books on the growth and development of children.

[A3–101]

Comprehensive Dissertation Index. Ann Arbor, MI: UMI ProQuest Information and Learning. Published annually.

Endeavors to index every doctoral dissertation accepted by North American universities since 1861. Does not include abstracts. Dissertations are to be found by subject, keyword, and author. Entry information includes subject, keyword, title, author, school, degree date, *Dissertation Abstracts International* [A3–103] citation, UMI dissertation order number, and other information. There are cumulative editions beginning with the 1861–1972 cumulation, and they have been published subsequently with varying intervals. Currently, the cumulations are quinquennial.

[A3–102]

Current Index to Journals in Education (CIJE). Westport, CT: Oryx Press. Published monthly since 1969. Semiannual cumulations.

An indexing and abstracting service for approximately 1,020 education and education-related journals with indexing coordinated by the *Thesaurus of ERIC Descriptors* [A3–40]. Abstracts are brief one-paragraph summaries of the articles indexed. As a component of the ERIC system, *CIJE* functions as ERIC's indexing service for published journal articles. Entries in *CIJE* are by educational journal (EJ) number, subject, and author. The database of *CIJE* is also available online and on CD-ROM.

[A3–103]

Dissertation Abstracts International. Ann Arbor, MI: UMI ProQuest Information and Learning. Published monthly for Sections A and B and quarterly for Section C.

Compiles abstracts of doctoral dissertations accepted by universities in North America and Europe. Section A's abstracts are from the humanities and social sciences (including education), Section B's abstracts are from the sciences and engineering, and Section C's abstracts include all disciplines from European universities, printed in their original languages. Abstracts contain up to 350 words, and each can be found by subject, title keyword, and author. These abstracts are also available online at http://library.dialog.com/bluesheets/html/bl0035.html. The dissertations that are abstracted may be purchased from UMI ProQuest Information Learning.

[A3–104]

Education Index. New York: H. W. Wilson Co. Published monthly except July and August.

Published since 1929, a cumulative and unified subject-author index of 462 English-language professional periodicals in education. Also indexes monographs and yearbooks. Following the subject-author index is a separate listing of citations to book reviews. Subjects span the range of education. Entries are not abstracted. Contains a list of indexed periodicals with addresses, frequency of publication, and subscription prices.

[A3–105]

Educational Administration Abstracts. Edited by Paul McDowell. Thousand Oaks, CA: Corwin Press in cooperation with the University Council for Educational Administration. Published quarterly.

Contains abstracts of more than 120 professional journals, books, and other publications on educational administration. The abstracts are categorized in broad subject areas. Also lists dissertations that have been completed in educational administration at universities affiliated with the University Council for Educational Administration.

[A3–106]

Exceptional Child Education Resources. Arlington, VA: Council for Exceptional Children. Published quarterly.

Indexes and abstracts journal articles concerning children with disabilities and those who are gifted. Articles are indexed by subject, author, and title. The abstracts are brief. Some of the documents can be purchased from the ERIC Document Reproduction Service. The database is available on CD-ROM and on the Internet at http://www.silverplatter.com/usa/schbysch.htm.

[A3–107]

Federal Government Publications Catalog. Williamsport, PA: Brodart Co., 1976–. Updated monthly.

A microform catalog of the U.S. Government Printing Office's publications arranged by subject, author, and title.

[A3–108]

Health, Physical Education and Recreation Microform Publications Bulletin. Eugene, OR: University of Oregon, 1949–.

Indexes master's and doctoral research papers in the areas of health, physical education, and recreation that are available on microfiche. Contains indexes by subject and author.

[A3–109]

Higher Education Abstracts. Claremont, CA: Claremont Graduate School, 1984–. Published quarterly.

Contains abstracts of scholarly journal articles, conference papers, and research reports on sundry topics in higher education. The abstracts are organized according to such broad categories as students, faculty, administration, community colleges, finance, instructional programs, and others. Prior to 1984, this publication was published under the title of *College Student Personnel Abstracts*.

[A3–110]

Masters Abstracts International. Ann Arbor, MI: UMI ProQuest Information and Learning. Published quarterly.

A collection of 150-word abstracts of master's theses and Educational Specialist materials in the humanities, social sciences, engineering, and the sciences that have been accepted for degrees by accredited American colleges and universities. Entries can be found by subject and author. Theses may be ordered from UMI ProQuest Information and Learning.

[A3–111]

Master's Theses in Education. Morehead, IA: Master's Theses Directory. Published annually.

A list of master's theses written on topics in education and accepted by colleges and universities. No abstracts. Identifies the title, author, and institution that accepted the thesis.

[A3–112]

Monthly Catalog of United States Government Publications. Washington, DC: U.S. Government Printing Office, 1895–.

A monthly index of publications issued by the federal government. Offers a bibliographic description of the documents. Indexes them by title, author, subject, and series/report number. The *Cumulative Subject Index to the Monthly Catalog of United States Government Publications* is the composite index to the *Monthly Catalog* for the period 1900–1971.

[A3–113]

New York Times Index: A Book of Record. New York: New York Times, 1913–. Published semimonthly. Cumulated annually.

A subject index of articles that appeared in the *New York Times*. Offers brief summaries of the articles along with bibliographic reference to the full article. Accesses news media coverage of current events, including news related to education. The *Information Bank Thesaurus*, formerly the *New York Times Thesaurus of Descriptors*, is a supplement that facilitates locating information.

[A3–114]

Psychological Abstracts. Edited by Linda Beebe. Washington, DC: American Psychological Association. Published monthly.

Abstracts and indexes journal articles, books, technical reports, and other literature in the field of psychology and related disciplines. Classifies abstracts according to 22 major categories. The database is available online via PsycINFO.

[A3–115]

Readers' Guide to Periodical Literature. New York: H. W. Wilson Co. Published monthly and cumulated annually.

A subject-author index of periodicals that are of interest to the general public vis-à-vis professional journals. Useful to the educational researcher when there is an interest in locating articles germane to education that have been published in popular periodicals. Since these publications are not indexed in the *Education Index* [A3–104], the *Readers' Guide to Periodical Literature* serves as a complementary index for articles on education.

[A3–116]

Resources in Education (RIE). Educational Resources Information Center. Washington, DC: U.S. Office of Educational Research and Improvement. Published monthly. Semiannual indexes published by Oryx Press. Annual cumulations.

The monthly catalog of educational literature from sources other than journals that has been cataloged in the ERIC system. Contains indexes and abstracts of documents that report on research, speeches, and technical reports. Many of the documents are unpublished or of limited distribution. Uses the ERIC descriptor system for indexing. (See *Thesaurus of ERIC Descriptors*, A3–40.) Full documents are usually available in microfiche or paper form. *RIE* documents can also be searched using CD-ROM or online.

[A3–117]

Social Sciences Citation Index. Philadelphia: Institute for Scientific Information, 1973–. Published three times per year with annual and quinquennial cumulations.

Indexes articles in scholarly journals in the social, behavioral, and related sciences. These articles appear in journals from throughout the world. There are four major sections, namely: (1) the Citation Index, which is arranged by author and provides references to publications in which the author's work has been cited; (2) the Source Index, which is also organized by author and provides full bibliographic information and, whenever possible, the author's address; (3) the Permuterm Subject Index, which is arranged by subject using all possible pairs of significant terms in the title and subtitle of the article to classify it; and the (4) Guide/Lists of Source Publications, which explains how to use the *Social Sciences Citation Index* and also lists the publications that are indexed.

[A3–118]

Social Sciences Index. New York: H. W. Wilson Co. Published quarterly.

A cumulative and unified subject-author index of English-language periodicals in the social sciences. Fields include psychology, psychiatry, social work, and sociology in addition to anthropology, political science, urban studies, and other related disciplines. Entries are not abstracted. Following the subject-author index is a separate list of citations for book reviews. Contains a list of indexed periodicals with their addresses, frequency of publication, and subscription prices.

[A3–119]
Sociological Abstracts. Edited by Jill Blaemers. Bethesda, MD: Cambridge Scientific Abstracts. Published in February, April, June, August, October, and December.

Abstracts and indexes journal articles, books, papers presented at professional meetings, and other professional literature from the field of sociology and related disciplines. Classifies abstracts in 29 categories.

[A3–120]
Sociology of Education Abstracts. Edited by Chris Shilling. Abingdon, Oxfordshire, U.K.: Carfax Publishing, Taylor and Francis Ltd., 1965–. Published quarterly.

Abstracts journal articles and books that address the sociological study of education. Only articles that have been published in peer-reviewed journals are abstracted. There are annual cumulative author and subject indexes.

[A3–121]
State Education Journal Index and Educators' Guide to Periodicals Research Strategies. Edited by L. Stanley Ratliff. Westminster, CO: State Education Journal Index Publications, 1963–. Published semiannually.

An index of articles appearing in state education and association publications. Many of these titles are not indexed in the *Education Index* [A3–104]. Arranged by subject. Also includes guidelines for conducting a review of the periodical literature in education.

[A3–122]
Tests in Print V. 2 vols. Edited by Linda L. Murphy, James C. Impara, and Barbara S. Plake. Lincoln, NE: The Buros Institute of Mental Measurements of the University of Nebraska-Lincoln, 1999. Published quinquennially.

The *Tests in Print* (TIP) series serves as a comprehensive index to all of the *Mental Measurements Yearbooks* [A3–92]. TIP is an alphabetized bibliography of commercially published tests in the English language that are in print and can be purchased. Each entry contains a description of the test and a list of test references. Refers the reader to all of the test reviews of a given test that appeared in all of the *Mental Measurements Yearbooks* to date. The test reviews themselves do not appear in TIP. Indexes tests by title, subject, and the variable being measured.

MISCELLANEOUS

[A3–123]
The Chicago Manual of Style. 14th edition. Chicago: University of Chicago Press, 1993.

A stylebook on how to prepare all types of scholarly manuscripts from expository to technical writing. It discusses formal dissertations, journal articles, books, and other forms of writing. Focuses on the use of computers in all areas of publishing. Attention is given to bibliographies, footnotes, endnotes, punctuation, indexing, tables, and many other components of written communication. A widely recognized guide to the art and skill of writing and publishing.

[A3–124]

Data Sources: The Complete Computer Product Book. 2 vols. Farmington Hills, MI: Gale Group, 2001. Published annually.

A guide to computer hardware and software. Volume 1, titled *Hardware, Communications Software, Systems Software*, is a catalog of such products. Names specific products and provides a brief description of the characteristics, functions, and price. Reports profiles of manufacturers. Volume 2, titled *Applications Software Indexes*, lists software packages by function, including education. Product profiles include the function, feature characteristics, system requirements, and price. Company profiles are provided. These two volumes offer a starting place for identifying computer-related products.

[A3–125]

Education Law. 7 vols. James A. Rapp. Albany, NY: Matthew Bender & Co. A loose-leaf service updated semiannually.

Covers the law as it applies to education. Encompasses adjudications of all levels of courts germane to all levels and areas of education. Contains treatises, not digests, of court actions. Explains and interprets education law. Its analyses are useful to administrators and attorneys.

Provides an annotated bibliography of state statutes, organized by state, that pertain to education. Reports the legal citation and brief description of each statute. Also includes operational checklists that apply to many educational situations. These provide guidance to avoid or minimize legal problems. Presents model forms that can be used in a large number of practical situations, such as different types of contracts, code of student conduct, use of educational facilities by outsiders, and many more. In summary, *Education Law* offers an analysis of education law and provides checklists and model forms.

[A3–126]

Education Law: Public and Private. 2 vols. William D. Valente. St. Paul, MN: West Publishing Co., 1989. Pocket parts are published to remain current.

Summarizes state and federal case law, regulations, and legislation that applies to education. Cites specific cases and state standards concerning selected aspects of education. A source for identifying the legal position of a state on an educational issue.

[A3–127]

The Education Law Reporter. Eagan, MN: West Group, 1982–. Published biweekly.

Publishes the text of education-related cases decided in the U.S. Supreme Court, U.S. Courts of Appeals, U.S. District Courts, and state appellate courts. Identifies the litigants, facts of the case, applicable laws and precedent cases, reasoning of the court, and other essential information about the case.

[A3–128]

Gallup Polls of Attitudes Toward Education, 1969–88: A Topical Summary. Edited by Wilmer Bugher. Bloomington, IN: Phi Delta Kappa, 1990.

Reports the results of the Phi Delta Kappa-Gallup survey of the attitudes of the public toward the public schools in America. These annual polls ascertain the attitudes toward selected topics for the year of the study. This publication provides a summary of the findings of these polls from 1969 to 1988. Although the "topical summaries" are no longer being published, the annual survey results are published by Phi Delta Kappa every September in the *Phi Delta Kappan.*

[A3–129]

A Manual for Writers of Term Papers, Theses, and Dissertations. 6th edition. Kate L. Turabian. Revised by John Grossman and Alice Bennett. Chicago: University of Chicago Press, 1996.

A style manual for writing formal, scholarly papers usually described as term papers, theses, and dissertations. Provides guidelines for such matters as abbreviations, punctuation, underlining, footnotes, bibliographies, tables, illustrations, and other related technical matters concerning academic writing.

[A3–130]

Publication Manual of the American Psychological Association. 5th edition. Washington, DC: American Psychological Association, 2001.

The manual of style for preparing manuscripts in the field of psychology. Also adopted by other disciplines and multidiscipline publishers. Addresses most areas of formal writing, including organizing, grammar, punctuation, spelling, underlining, quotations, footnotes, bibliographies, tables, information on APA journals, and other information on scholarly writing.

[A3–131]

Requirements for Certification of Teachers, Counselors, Librarians, Administrators for Elementary and Secondary Schools. 65th edition. Edited by Elizabeth A. Kaye. Chicago: University of Chicago Press, 2000. Published annually.

Reports the certification requirements for public school teachers, administrators, counselors, librarians, and other school personnel in each of the states and U.S. possessions and territories. Apprises the reader where to obtain further certification information. Also identifies interstate reciprocal agreements for certification of public school personnel.

[A3–132]

School Law Register. Arlington, VA: Capitol Publications. Updated monthly.

A compilation of the texts of federal laws and regulations pertaining to education. Valuable for the person who prefers to read the actual laws and regulations instead of summaries.

[A3–133]

United States School Laws and Rules, 2000. Edited by Michael I. Levin. Eagan, MN: West Group, 2000. Published annually.

The only publication that annually compiles in a single volume the federal statutes and related U.S. government regulations germane to education in America. The information on statutes was derived from the *United States Code* and the regulatory matters from the *Code of Federal Regulations*. In this, the 2000 edition, the statutory coverage includes education, labor, civil rights, and the environment. The coverage of federal agency rules embraces education, civil rights, age discrimination, equal employment, labor, disabilities, and the environment.

To facilitate its use, this publication contains pertinent federal documents that assist with interpreting statutes and regulations related to disciplining students with disabilities, continuation coverage of group health plans, responding to sexual harassment of students, and federal posting and notice requirements. This is a valuable aid for school board members, school administrators, teachers, and others.

STATISTICAL DIGESTS AND SOURCES

[A3–134]

American Statistics Index (ASI). 2 vols. Bethesda, MD: Congressional Information Service. Published in annual editions and monthly supplements.

See A3–97.

[A3–135]

The Condition of Education, 2000. U.S. Department of Education, National Center for Education Statistics. Washington, DC: U.S. Government Printing Office, 2000. Published annually.

A summary of the status of education in America for the year published. Covers preschool through postsecondary education. Targets public and private education. Includes statistical data on the academic performance of students, high school dropouts, school revenues and expenditures, student characteristics, student drug and alcohol abuse, and other topics.

[A3–136]

Digest of Education Statistics. 36th edition. Washington, DC: National Center for Education Statistics, 2000. Published annually.

An abstract of statistical information on American education encompassing prekindergarten through graduate school. The information is nationwide in scope and current as of the date of publication. Among the topics included are student enrollment, graduates, libraries, finances, federal funds for education, and other statistical data.

[A3–137]

Education Statistics of the United States. 2nd edition. Edited by Deirdre A. Gaquin and Katherine A. Debrandt. Lanham, MD: Bernan Press, 2000.

Contains a potpourri of statistical data on all levels of education in the U.S. Derived from the U.S. Bureau of the Census and the National Center for Education Statistics, this publication reports on school and college enrollments, educational attainment, and education statistics for states and counties. Profiles of the individual states include educational attainment, revenues and expenditures for education, state requirements for high school graduation, data on faculty and staff in institutions of higher education, and other statistical data.

[A3–138]

Fact Book on Higher Education. Charles J. Anderson. Phoenix, AZ: Oryx Press in cooperation with the American Council on Education, 1998. Published irregularly.

Offers a wide range of statistical information on higher education. Includes published and unpublished data regarding demographic and economic factors, enrollment, institutions of higher education, faculty and staff, students, and earned degrees. Publishes highlights of each of these categories of data and of the status of women and minorities in higher education. This series began in 1958.

[A3–139]

Open Doors: Report on International Educational Exchange. Edited by Todd M. Davis. New York: Institute of International Education, 1999. Published annually.

A demographic profile of foreign students studying in U.S. institutions of higher education. Includes country of origin, fields of study, sources of financial support, and other descriptive statistical information about international students in the U.S.

[A3–140]

Projections of Education Statistics to 2008. 27th edition. U.S. Department of Education, National Center for Education Statistics. Debra E. Gerald and William J. Hussar. Washington, DC: National Center for Education Statistics, 1998.

Presents national statistical projections for different educational indicators. These include enrollments for K–12 and higher education, high school graduates, earned degrees, student charges, educational expenditures, and other statistical projections.

[A3–141]

Statistics Sources, 2002. 25th edition. 2 vols. Edited by Jacqueline Wasserman O'Brien and Steven R. Wasserman. Farmington Hills, MI: The Gale Group, 2001. Published annually.

A guide to sources of statistical information. This reference book does not contain statistical data; instead, it directs the reader to sources of statistical information in education, social sciences, business, industry, finance, and other topics for the U.S. and foreign nations. Includes government and private sources.

YEARBOOKS

[A3–142]

Educational Media and Technology Yearbook. Edited by Robert M. Branch and Mary Ann Fitzgerald. Englewood, CO: Libraries Unlimited, 2001. Published annually.

Offers a variety of information on instructional technology and educational media. Presents treatises that focus on sundry issues in these fields. Provides a descriptive list of organizations and associations that are involved with educational media in the U.S., Canada, the United Kingdom, and other nations. Also contains a descriptive directory of graduate programs in instructional technology and educational computing. Discloses foundations that provide financial support for media-related projects and includes an annotated bibliography of print and nonprint resources in instructional technology and educational media.

[A3–143]

The World Almanac and Book of Facts. Mahwah, NJ: World Almanac Education Group, 2001. Published annually.

A compilation of facts on many subjects, including education. Offers statistics and other succinct descriptive information on education, such as a list of colleges and universities in America; enrollments in elementary, secondary, and postsecondary education; national summaries of SAT and ACT test scores; and other miscellaneous information about education at all levels in America.

[A3–144]

World Yearbook of Education. London: Kogan Page; Sterling, VA: Stylus Publishing, 2001. Published annually.

Each annual issue of this yearbook is dedicated to a current theme that is of significance to international education. The theme is implemented through a series of signed treatises by authors from different nations. Contains a combined bibliography of items referenced in the individual articles. Provides biographical sketches of the contributing authors. A good source with which to begin a literature review.

[A3–145]

The Yearbook of Education Law, 2000. Edited by Charles J. Russo. Dayton, OH: Education Law Association, 2001. Published annually.

Summarizes and analyzes case law decisions handed down by state appellate and federal courts during the year of coverage. Spans all levels and areas of education. Topics include governance, employees, students, collective bargaining, higher education, finance, torts, and property. Includes a table of cited cases.

SECTION **B**

INTERNET INFORMATION SOURCES FOR THE EDUCATOR

Melvyn N. Freed

CHAPTER 1

Finding Education Information on the Web:
The U.S. Domain

INTRODUCTION

In this section we enter the universe of cyberspace, that electronic realm of information that is both vast and challenging to use. Today's content may be tomorrow's history due to its constant state of change. The Internet excites the imagination and offers a threshold to knowledge and communication with limits yet to be explored. Cardinal to the research process is the act of creativity. Successful exploration of the Internet requires maximization of the creative process.

Educational researchers have customarily resorted to journals, books, and other printed materials for their information. During the latter years of the twentieth century, they began to call upon computerized sources, such as online databases and CD-ROMs. Very quickly the progression was made to the World Wide Web, or the Internet. With the advent of cyberspace came access to new sources of information and with such speed that an information revolution was born. It became feasible to extend the search beyond national boundaries with a simple click of a computer mouse. In a short period of time the educational research community became international. The sharing of information among educators in diverse nations became commonplace. The research quest has experienced a renaissance.

This chapter and those to follow in this section have been designed to facilitate the exploration of knowledge in education via use of the Internet. Chapters 1 and 2 focus on the U.S. domain, and Chapters 3 and 4 on the international domain. As in Section A, The Information Locator has been used to identify sources of information. Simply locate the needed question in the left column and then identify the Web site address (URL) in the right column. The item entry number that follows the address refers to a brief bibliographic citation and annotative description in Chapter 2. The URLs have been presented as they appear on their Web sites.

To facilitate use, the item-locator questions have been categorized as follows:

> Agencies, Centers, and Organizations
> Community Colleges: Innovative Practices
> Curricular Matters
> Directories of Educational Institutions and Services
> Education and the Law
> Elementary and Secondary Education: State Profiles
> Facilities for Education
> Faculty in Higher Education
> Finances of Education
> Higher Education: Potpourri of Information Sources

Institutional Research
Instruments for Surveys and Educational and/or Psychological Measurement
Issues and Trends
Libraries
Rankings of Institutions of Higher Education
Sources of Web Site Addresses
Statistical Data
Student Outcomes
Teacher Education and Certification

The Web site addresses in the answers are not all-inclusive (i.e., they are suggested places to start a search). New ones are being regularly created; therefore, the researcher is encouraged to explore the Internet in pursuit of discovery.

It is important for the reader to understand that Web sites are fluid and ephemeral; consequently, their existence, addresses, and content are subject to change. For this reason, the author of this section asserts that the URLs in this section were operational at the time of writing; however, alterations of Web sites may have occurred subsequently.

THE INFORMATION LOCATOR

Agencies, Centers, and Organizations

Where Should I Go to Find...	*Try*
the home page for ERIC?	http://www.accesseric.org/ [B2–52]
the names and addresses of ERIC clearinghouses and other ERIC components?	http://www.accesseric.org/ sites/address.html [B2–54]
the Web site of the ERIC Clearinghouse on Higher Education?	http://www.eriche.org/main.html [B2–76]
the home page for the National Center for Education Statistics?	http://nces.ed.gov/ [B2–19]
the gateway to Web sites of the Regional Educational Laboratories?	http://www.nwrel.org/national/ [B2–102]
the Web site of the National Center for Public Policy and Higher Education?	http://www.highereducation.org/ [B2–84]
the Web site addresses of research centers for the study of higher education?	http://airweb2.org/links/centers.cfm [B2–6]

Agencies, Centers, and Organizations

Where Should I Go to Find...	*Try*
a directory of online organizations that provide a broad range of information and assistance at all levels in education?	http://www.ed.gov/Programs/ EROD/ [B2–70]
an educational research and information support service that offers customized services to school districts?	http://www.ers.org/ [B2–77]
a directory of state associations of public school administrators, citing contact information?	http://www.ers.org/states.htm [B2–78]
a directory of chief state school officials?	http://www.ccsso.org/addres.html [B2–63] http://www.ers.org/states.htm [B2–78]
whom to ask at the American Council on Education for specialized information in higher education?	http://www.acenet.edu/about/WhotoAsk/home.cfm [B2–56]
the home page for the American Association for Higher Education?	http://www.aahe.org/ [B2–47]
the Web site for TIAA-CREF?	http://www.tiaa-cref.org/ [B2–105]
access to information about specific scholarly societies throughout the world?	http://www.scholarly-societies.org/ [B2–103]
the Web site of *The Chronicle of Higher Education*?	http://www.chronicle.com/ [B2–65]
the Web site of *Education Week*?	http://www.edweek.org/ [B2–74]

Community Colleges: Innovative Practices

resources that promote improvements in community colleges through innovation, experimentation, and institutional change?	http://www.league.org/welcome.htm [B2–91]

Curricular Matters

Where Should I Go to Find . . .	*Try*
the translation of educational research findings into practical resources and services for educators?	http://www.nwrel.org/eval/index.html [B2–101]
the eight National Education Goals and information about each goal?	http://www.negp.gov/page3.htm [B2–99]
NCATE's revised unit standards for accreditation of teacher education programs?	http://www.ncate.org/2000/ 2000stds.pdf [B2–96]
access to lesson plans and other educational materials at all grade levels?	http://thegateway.org/welcome.html [B2–42]
the identification of learning resource materials by grade level, subject, and type of media?	http://www.explorasource.com/ educator/ [B2–79]
evaluations of software?	http://www.epie.org [B2–75A]
special education programs, organizations, and materials?	http://ericec.org/factmini.htm [B2–16] http://www.hood.edu/seri/serihome.htm [B2–85] http://www.awesomelibrary.org/ [B2–61]
a service that evaluates foreign education credentials?	http://www.aacrao.org/fees-frame.htm [B2–44] http://www.ierf.org/ [B2–86]
initiatives to reform undergraduate education in science, mathematics, engineering, and technology education?	http://www.aahe.org/ppic/ inst_change.htm [B2–49]
what is being done in colleges to promote the teaching function as being significant scholarly work along with developing new processes for maximizing teaching effectiveness?	http://www.aahe.org/teaching/ Teaching_Initiative_Home.htm [B2–50]
degrees conferred by colleges and universities?	http://nces.ed.gov/pubsearch/ pubsinfo.asp?pubid=98256 [B2–31]

Curricular Matters

Where Should I Go to Find . . .   *Try*

how to convert collegiate credit hours   Http://www.aacrao.org/r&a-frame-asp.
from one calendar system to another?   html (Click on "Credit Hour Conversion
                                              Methods.") [B2–45]

Directories of Educational Institutions and Services

the names and addresses of ERIC   http://www.accesseric.org/
clearinghouses and other components?   sites/address.html [B2–54]

a directory of organizations within a   http://www.ed.gov/BASISDB/EROD/
designated geographical area that   eric/SF [B2–69]
provides access to the ERIC database
and related resources?

a national directory of elementary and   http://nces.ed.gov/nceskids/
secondary schools with descriptive data   school/default.htm [B2–26]
for each school, including its address   http://www.asd.com/ [B2–60]
and telephone number?   http://nces.ed.gov/ccdweb/
                                             school/School.asp [B2–21]

the addresses and telephone numbers of   http://nces.ed.gov/ccdweb/
public school districts, K–12?   school/district.asp [B2–20]

descriptive information on private   http://nces.ed.gov/pubsearch/
schools K–12 germane to students, staff,   pubsinfo.asp?pubid=1999319 [B2–34]
finances, and other characteristics?

the name, location, and other descriptors   http://nces.ed.gov/surveys/
of a specific private school K–12   pss/locator/locator.html [B2–39]
according to its type or program
emphasis?

a directory of state associations of   http://www.ers.org/states.htm [B2–78]
public school administrators, including
contact information?

a directory of chief state school   http://www.ccsso.org/addres.html
officials?   [B2–63]
                                             http://www.ers.org/states.htm [B2–78]

Directories of Educational Institutions and Services

Where Should I Go to Find . . .	*Try*
a national directory of local professionals who provide services for the special education community?	http://www.iser.com/ [B2–89]
a descriptive profile of a specific college or university?	http://nces.ed.gov/globallocator/ [B2–22]
descriptive information for a specific community college based on personally selected criteria?	http://www.gseis.ucla.edu/ERIC/ findcc.html [B2–81]
the names of colleges and universities with their descriptive profiles according to personally selected criteria, such as regional location, degree offerings, enrollment, etc.?	http://nces.ed.gov/ipeds/cool/ Search.asp [B2–23]
names of the land-grant and sea-grant universities along with the history and legislative acts behind them?	http://www.ifas.ufl.edu/WWW/ LS_GRANT/index.htm [B2–87]
a directory of graduate programs and professional development opportunities that specialize in the community college?	http://www.gseis.ucla.edu/ ERIC/gradprog.html [B2–82]

Education and the Law

assistance with keeping abreast of incipient legislation, new laws, and new regulations that impact higher education?	http://www.cphe.org/ [B2–67]
information on the law and special education?	http://www.ed.sc.edu/spedlaw/ LawPage.htm [B2–72] http://www.edlaw.net/frames.html [B2–70A]
citations to full-text constitutional law, case law, regulations, school codes, and supplementary law materials on education at all levels?	http://www.priweb.com/ internetlawlib/99.htm [B2–102A]

Elementary and Secondary Education: State Profiles

Where Should I Go to Find . . .	*Try*
a descriptive statistical profile of public elementary and secondary education for the United States and each state?	http://nces.ed.gov/pubsearch/ pubsinfo.asp?pubid=2000304 [B2–37]

Facilities for Education

information on planning, designing, constructing, financing, operating, and maintaining K–12 school facilities?	http://www.edfacilities.org/an/ index.html [B2–68]
information on the design, construction, management, operations, and maintenance of college facilities?	http://www.appa.org/ [B2–59] http://airweb2.org/links/facility.cfm [B2–9]

Faculty in Higher Education

innovative developments for modernizing reward systems for the faculty in higher education?	http://www.aahe.org/FFRR/ ffrrnew2.htm [B2–48]
a description of new full-time college faculty and a comparison with senior faculty?	http://nces.ed.gov/pubsearch/ pubsinfo.asp?pubid=98252 [B2–30]
the average salaries and tenure data on full-time instructional faculty in higher education?	http://nces.ed.gov/pubsearch/ pubsinfo.asp?pubid=1999193 [B2–33] http://www.nchems.org/ InfoServices/infoserv.htm [B2–97]

Finances of Education

information on higher education finance?	http://airweb2.org/links/finance.cfm [B2–10] http://www.nchems.org/ InfoServices/infoserv.htm [B2–97] http://nces.ed.gov/ipeds/data.html [B2–24] http://nces.ed.gov/pubsearch/ pubsinfo.asp?pubid=1999193 [B2–33] (Answer continues)

Finances of Education

Where Should I Go to Find . . .	*Try*
information on higher education finance?	http://www.acenet.edu/ resources/fact-sheets/home.html [B2–58] http://www.edstats.net/ scripts/calclist/calc_list.cgi [B2–73]
online programs that facilitate budget analysis for colleges and universities, including calculations of management ratios for individual campuses and benchmarks for interinstitutional comparisons?	http://www.edstats.net/ scripts/calclist/calc_list.cgi [B2–73] http://www.jma-inc.net/ [B2–90]
Internet sites that offer information on grants and funding for special and/or gifted education?	http://ericec.org/fact/grants.htm [B2–15]

Higher Education: Potpourri of Information Sources

sources of information on higher education throughout the world?	http://www.higher-ed.org/ [B2–83]
a scheme for grouping higher education institutions for operating comparisons?	http://www.edmin.com/jma/cohort/ [B2–71]

Institutional Research

access to chat groups on institutional research?	http://airweb.org/ [B2–1]
software and Internet tools for the institutional researcher?	http://www.bates.edu/IR/tools/ tools.html [B2–62]
instruments that can be used to survey student outcomes on individual college campuses?	http://www.nchems.org/Surveys/ surveys.htm [B2–98]
instruments that can be used to assess collegiate alumni regarding their pre- and post-baccalaurate experiences?	http://www.nchems.org/Surveys/ surveys.htm [B2–98]

Institutional Research

Where Should I Go to Find . . .	*Try*
instruments that can be used to analyze the performance of individual college campuses concerning their institutional effectiveness, leadership, culture, and other variables?	http://www.nchems.org/Surveys/surveys.htm [B2–98]
national data describing postsecondary institutions that are accessible by subject, topic, question, or keyword?	http://nces.ed.gov/npec/answers [B2–40]
a data element dictionary for key terms used in higher education survey instruments?	http://nces.ed.gov/npec/answers [B2–40]

Instruments for Surveys and Educational and/or Psychological Measurement

reviews of educational and psychological tests and measures?	http://ericae.net/testcol.htm#trev [B2–13] http://www.ets.org/testcoll/ [B2–78A]
guidelines on how to select a standardized test?	http://ericae.net/seltips.txt [B2–11]
the names and addresses of major test publishers?	http://ericae.net/testcol.htm#Testpub [B2–12]
descriptions and content analyses of core national surveys that are used in higher education?	http://nces.ed.gov/npec/answers [B2–40]
a data element dictionary for key terms used in higher education surveys?	http://nces.ed.gov/npec/answers [B2–40]

Issues and Trends

the latest news on issues and trends in higher education?	http://www.acenet.edu/news/home.html [B2–57] http://www.chronicle.com/ [B2–65]

Libraries

Where Should I Go to Find . . .	*Try*
access to libraries worldwide via the Internet?	http://sunsite.berkeley.edu/Libweb/ [B2–41]
information about a specific public library, including its location and a description of its operational characteristics?	http://nces.ed.gov/surveys/ libraries/liblocator/default. asp [B2–38]
indexes to journals in education?	http://ericir.syr.edu/Eric/ [B2–17] http://www.ship.edu/~library/ instruction/edresearch.htm [B2–104]

Rankings of Institutions of Higher Education

rankings of U.S. colleges and universities?	http://www.library.uiuc.edu/ edx/rankings.htm [B2–92] http://www.usnews.com/usnews/ edu/college/corank.htm [B2–107]
rankings of schools of engineering?	http://www.usnews.com/usnews/ edu/beyond/bceng.htm [B2–106]

Sources of Web Site Addresses

sources of Web site addresses for higher education?	http://www.acenet.edu/About/ programs/Programs&Analysis/ Policy&Analysis/policy-research/home. cfm [B2–55] http://airweb2.org/links/commcoll.cfm [B2–7] http://airweb2.org/links/assoc.cfm [B2–4] http://airweb2.org/links/centers.cfm [B2–6] http://www.mcli.dist.maricopa.edu/cc/ [B2–93] http://www.chronicle.com/free/ resources/index.php3 [B2–66] http://www.academicinfo.net/ studentcolleges.html [B2–51]

Sources of Web Site Addresses

Where Should I Go to Find . . .	*Try*
the Web site address of a U.S. college or university?	http://nces.ed.gov/globallocator [B2–22]
the Web site addresses of research centers for the study of higher education?	http://airweb2.org/links/centers.cfm [B2–6]
Web sites that pertain to community colleges?	http://www.aacc.nche.edu/ [B2–43] http://www.gseis.ucla.edu/ ERIC/eric.html [B2–80] http://airweb2.org/links/commcoll.cfm [B2–7] http://www.mcli.dist.maricopa.edu/cc/ [B2–93]
the gateway to Web sites of the Regional Educational Laboratories?	http://www.nwrel.org/national/ [B2–102]
Internet sites that offer a variety of information resources for the institutional research and educational-research communities?	http://www.irp.panam.edu/ more_html/utpa_erlist.html [B2–88]
Web sites that focus on affirmative action and diversity in higher education?	http://airweb2.org/links/affirm.cfm [B2–3]
Web sites that are concerned with disability issues and the college student?	http://airweb2.org/links/ada.cfm [B2–2]
a directory of Web sites that contain enrollment data for higher education?	http://airweb2.org/links/enroll.cfm [B2–8]
learning outcome assessment resources for higher education?	http://www2.acs.ncsu.edu/UPA/ survey/resource.htm [B2–108]
Web sites that are of service to professional counselors?	http://ericcass.uncg.edu/ CounselorConnection.htm [B2–14]
links to the Web sites of individual state departments of education?	http://www.ccsso.org/seamenu.html [B2–64] http://www.negp.gov/page13.htm [B2–100]

Statistical Data

Where Should I Go to Find . . .	*Try*
the ERIC home page?	http://www.accesseric.org/ [B2–52]
access to the ERIC database?	http://www.accesseric.org/ searchdb/searchdb.html [B2–53] http://ericir.syr.edu/Eric/ [B2–17]
a directory of organizations within a designated geographical area that provide access to the ERIC database and related resources?	http://www.ed.gov/BASISDB/EROD/ eric/SF [B2–69]
the Integrated Postsecondary Education Data System (IPEDS) databases?	http://nces.ed.gov/ipeds/data.html [B2–24] http://www.nchems.org/ InfoServices/infoserv.htm [B2–97]
an online method for accessing the education statistics generated by the National Center for Education Statistics?	http://nces.ed.gov/pubs97/97076.html [B2–27]
a potpourri of statistical information about higher education in America?	http://www.acenet.edu/ resources/fact-sheets/home.html [B2–58] http://nces.ed.gov/npec/answers [B2–40] http://nces.ed.gov/ipeds/data.html [B2–24] http://www.nchems.org/ InfoServices/infoserv.htm [B2–97]
descriptive statistics of college students and/or faculty?	http://nces.ed.gov/ipeds/data.html [B2–24] http://nces.ed.gov/pubsearch/ pubsinfo.asp?pubid=98082xxxxx [B2–29] http://www.acenet.edu/ resources/fact-sheets/home.html [B2–58]

Statistical Data

Where Should I Go to Find . . .	*Try*
statistical data relating earnings to level of educational attainment?	http://govinfo.kerr.orst.edu/ earn-stateis.html [B2–18] http://www.acenet.edu/ resources/fact-sheets/home.html [B2–58]
a directory of Web sites that contain enrollment data for higher education?	http://airweb2.org/links/enroll.cfm [B2–8]
data on degrees conferred by postsecondary education institutions?	http://nces.ed.gov/pubsearch/ pubsinfo.asp?pubid=98256 [B2–31]
research on the characteristics of first-generation college students?	http://nces.ed.gov/pubsearch/ pubsinfo.asp?pubid=98082xxxxx [B2–29]
the average salaries and tenure data on full-time instructional faculty in higher education?	http://nces.ed.gov/pubsearch/ pubsinfo.asp?pubid=1999193 [B2–33] http://www.nchems.org/ InfoServices/infoserv.htm [B2–97]
information for implementing federal reporting requirements by institutions of higher education?	http://www.aacrao.org/r&a-frame-asp.html [B2–45]
a descriptive statistical profile of public elementary and secondary education for the United States and each state?	http://nces.ed.gov/pubsearch/ pubsinfo.asp?pubid=2000304 [B2–37]
data and research-based commentary on high school completion and dropout rates?	http://nces.ed.gov/pubsearch/ pubsinfo.asp?pubid=2000022 [B2–36]
a guide to census data on the Internet?	http://airweb2.org/links/census.cfm [B2–5]

Student Outcomes

how to enhance the quality and use of student outcome data in higher education?	http://nces.ed.gov/pubsearch/ pubsinfo.asp?pubid=97992 [B2–28]

Student Outcomes

Where Should I Go to Find . . .	*Try*
information on the post-baccalaureate experiences of college students?	http://nces.ed.gov/pubsearch/ pubsinfo.asp?pubid=1999155 [B2–32]
learning outcome assessment resources for higher education?	http://www2.acs.ncsu.edu/UPA/ survey/resource.htm [B2–108]
instruments that can be used to survey student outcomes on individual college campuses?	http://www.nchems.org/Surveys/ surveys.htm [B2–98]
instruments that can be used to assess alumni of collegiate institutions germane to their pre- and postbaccalaureate experiences?	http://www.nchems.org/Surveys/ surveys.htm [B2–98]
instruments that can be used to analyze the performance of individual college campuses regarding their institutional effectiveness, leadership, culture, and other variables?	http://www.nchems.org/Surveys/ surveys.htm [B2–98]
data and research-based commentary on high school completion and dropout rates?	http://nces.ed.gov/pubsearch/ pubsinfo.asp?pubid=2000022 [B2–36]
an evaluation and report of mathematics achievement of students in grades 4, 8, and 12 as reported by the National Assessment of Educational Progress?	http://nces.ed.gov/ nationsreportcard/96report/97488.shtml [B2–25]
the report of the National Assessment of Educational Progress on the writing ability of 4th, 8th, and 12th grade students?	http://nces.ed.gov/pubsearch/ pubsinfo.asp?pubid=1999462 [B2–35]

Teacher Education and Certification

NCATE's revised unit standards for accreditation of teacher education programs?	http://www.ncate.org/2000/ 2000stds.pdf [B2–96]

Teacher Education and Certification

Where Should I Go to Find . . .   *Try*

national and state information on the national teacher certification program of the National Board for Professional Teaching Standards?

http://www.nbpts.org/nbpts/ [B2–95]

state policy standards regarding qualifications for teachers to teach?

http://www.edweek.org/ sreports/qc00/templates/ article.cfm?slug=policies.htm [B2–75]

teacher certification requirements for each state, the District of Columbia, and Canadian provinces?

http://www.nasdtec.org/manual.html [B2–94]

CHAPTER 2

Descriptive Profiles of U.S. Web Sites

INTRODUCTION

This chapter presents descriptive profiles of the Web sites that were cited in Chapter 1 of this section. These profiles elaborate on the information presented in the preceding chapter. They have been organized alphabetically according to their address names (URLs). Each address has been presented exactly as it appears on the Internet. Any inconsistencies that may exist between URLs are attributed to the formats presented by the different Web masters of the various sites.

As explained in Chapter 1, to find a Web site's profile, simply use the item entry number provided in that chapter and locate it in Chapter 2. Commencing each profile is the item entry number followed by the address of the Web site. The format of these numbers is as follows. The initial letter designates the section (B) and the associated number (2) refers to this chapter. The numerals that appear to the right of the hyphen identify the specific Web site. Thus, B2–1 refers to the first profile in Chapter 2 of Section B.

Next, the title of the Web site has been given. Following it is the name of the site's sponsor. If the site is that of an organization and the title is the name of the organization, then the separate entry for the sponsor's name has been omitted because the title and sponsor's name are the same.

Succeeding the foregoing preliminaries is a brief explanation of the Web site. This includes the purpose and services offered by it. In some cases, the scope of the Web site is narrow; therefore, the annotation is likewise succinct.

PROFILES OF U.S. WEB SITES

[B2–1]   http://airweb.org/
Association for Institutional Research (AIR)

This Web site gives access to the field of institutional research. Using Internet links, it guides the viewer to a cornucopia of sites. Among these are eight "tracks," each of which focuses on a major area of institutional research and allows viewers to "talk" to others on that topic.

The other launching points on this home page of AIR include *Internet Resources for Institutional Research,* which makes accessible the full spectrum of the field by offering links to bibliographies of institutional research studies that, themselves, are accessible Web sites. Also, access is offered to major databases of other organizations. Finally, this site provides entrée to a host of information about the programs and services of the Association for Institutional Research.

[B2–2] http://airweb2.org/links/ada.cfm
Disability Issues. The Association for Institutional Research (AIR)

This Web site is a direct link to multiple sites that address different facets of the topic "disabilities and the college student." Includes links with organizations that focus on this subject and related programs.

[B2–3] http://airweb2.org/links/affirm.cfm
Affirmative Action/Equity. The Association for Institutional Research (AIR)

Sets forth a list of Web sites that are concerned with a potpourri of issues and topics pertaining to affirmative action. These include reports, Internet sites of organizations, and links to other sites on this subject.

[B2–4] http://airweb2.org/links/assoc.cfm
Associations. The Association for Institutional Research (AIR)

A directory of Web sites sponsored by associations in higher education. Click on a selection and enter that site.

[B2–5] http://airweb2.org/links/census.cfm
Census Data. The Association for Institutional Research (AIR)

This Web site serves as a guide to other Internet locations that present a variety of census data. Included are the home page of the U.S. Bureau of the Census, data from the 1990 decennial census, and links to a host of demographic information.

[B2–6] http://airweb2.org/links/centers.cfm
Research Centers/Institutes. The Association for Institutional Research (AIR)

A directory of Web site addresses owned by research centers that concentrate on the study of higher education. Includes both domestic and foreign sites.

[B2–7] http://airweb2.org/links/commcoll.cfm
Community Colleges. The Association for Institutional Research (AIR)

Presents an array of Web sites that provide information on community colleges. Includes links to organizations and other specialized sites. One of the links is to the Community College Web, which in turn links to more than 1,100 community college Web sites in addition to 187 other resource locations. A treasure trove for finding information on community colleges.

[B2–8] http://airweb2.org/links/enroll.cfm
Enrollment Planning. The Association for Institutional Research (AIR)

Contained herein is a guide to Web sites that have useful information for enrollment planning by institutions of higher education. A wide variety of data and analyses is featured.

[B2–9]   http://airweb2.org/links/facility.cfm
Facilities. The Association for Institutional Research (AIR)

A comprehensive presentation of Web sites that pertain to topics on college facilities. Among these are residence hall construction, computer classroom and laboratory designs, research facilities for science and engineering, facilities inventory and classification, and more.

[B2–10]   http://airweb2.org/links/finance.cfm
Finance. The Association for Institutional Research (AIR)

Introduces the viewer to a pool of Internet sites on higher education finance. Topics include cost studies on instruction, research, and service programs; faculty compensation; economic data; student charges; and more. Provides links to organizations and their Web sites germane to higher education finance.

[B2–11]   http://ericae.net/seltips.txt
Test Evaluation. ERIC Clearinghouse on Assessment and Evaluation

Offers tips on how to evaluate and select an educational or psychological standardized test. Reviews professional standards that are commonly employed to implement the evaluation of an instrument of measurement.

[B2–12]   http://ericae.net/testcol.htm#Testpub
Buros/ERIC Test Publisher Directory-Search. ERIC Clearinghouse on Assessment and Evaluation

The viewer may search for the names and addresses of more than 900 major test publishers.

[B2–13]   http://ericae.net/testcol.htm#trev
Test Review Locator-Search. ERIC Clearinghouse on Assessment and Evaluation

This site enables the viewer to access citations that review standardized tests in education and psychology. These citations appear in *Mental Measurements Yearbooks, Tests in Print,* and *Test Critiques.*

[B2–14]   http://ericcass.uncg.edu/CounselorConnection.html
Counselor Connection: Internet Resources for Professional Counselors. ERIC Clearinghouse for Counseling and Student Services

Offers links to Web sites that address topics and themes that correlate with the needs and interests of professional counselors. These span a large array of selections.

[B2–15]   http://ericec.org/fact/grants.htm

Grants/Funding Information. ERIC Clearinghouse on Disabilities and Gifted Education

Provides information about grants and other funds that are available to programs or individuals engaged in special or gifted education. This information is to be obtained from Web links that are identified.

[B2–16]   http://ericec.org/factmini.htm

Fact Sheets, Minibibs (special and gifted education). ERIC Clearinghouse on Disabilities and Gifted Education

Within this online bibliography can be found titles of printed materials and Internet links to sites on special education and gifted education. The topics referenced include special education statistics, names of state directors of special education, funding sources, names of publishers who issue publications on special and gifted education, and more.

[B2–17]   http://ericir.syr.edu/Eric/

Search ERIC Database. Educational Resources Information Center

ERIC is the premier index to the world of educational literature. Using keyword search terms, the visitor to this Web site is able to search the more than one million abstracts of journal articles and documents on educational research and practice. Instructions are provided on how to process a search of ERIC.

[B2–18]   http://govinfo.kerr.orst.edu/earn-stateis.html

Earnings by Occupation and Education, 1990. U.S. Bureau of the Census

This site is a Federal Government Information Sharing Project and reports for all states, an individual state, the District of Columbia, Metropolitan Statistical Areas, Consolidated Metropolitan Statistical Areas, and Primary Metropolitan Statistical Areas data on earnings by occupation and educational level.

[B2–19]   http://nces.ed.gov/

National Center for Education Statistics (NCES)

Here is the Web entrance to the NCES. From here the viewer may access the vast world of education statistics as collected and reported by NCES. Considerable data are available from this site.

[B2–20] http://nces.ed.gov/ccdweb/school/district.asp

National Public School District Locator. National Center for Education Statistics (NCES)

Allows a quick search for basic descriptive information on individual public school districts, K–12. Includes the district's address and telephone number.

[B2–21] http://nces.ed.gov/ccdweb/school/School.asp

National Public School Locator. National Center for Education Statistics (NCES)

This is a natonal Internet directory of public schools, K–12. The visitor to this Web site may either enter the name of a specific public school along with other information that is requested or conduct a search according to state, grade level, and/or size of enrollment. Identifing information is given for each school. The viewer is also led to a description of the school district.

[B2–22] http://nces.ed.gov/globallocator/

IPEDS College Opportunities On-Line. National Center for Education Statistics (NCES)

Insert the name of a college or university, and a profile of that institution will be displayed. Informs the viewer of the important campus telephone numbers, academic year costs, and other descriptive information. This Web site provides access to more than 9,000 postsecondary institutions.

[B2–23] http://nces.ed.gov/ipeds/cool/Search.asp

IPEDS College Opportunities On-Line: Begin Your College Search by Selecting Criteria.... National Center for Education Statistics (NCES)

The visitor to this Web site may enter criteria that describe a type of college or university and then retrieve a list of institutions that satisfy those criteria. Upon receiving the campus names, the viewer may then gain access to a profile of each college.

[B2–24] http://nces.ed.gov/ipeds/data.html

Integrated Postsecondary Education Data System (IPEDS). National Center for Education Statistics (NCES)

Here are the databases of the IPEDS from 1988–1989 to the present. These include fall enrollments of higher education throughout the nation, data on faculty salaries, institutional characteristics of colleges and universities, higher education financial statistics, student degree-completion information, and data on academic libraries and state higher education profiles. These data are collected annually by the National Center for Education Statistics.

[B2–25]   http://nces.ed.gov/nationsreportcard/96report/97488.shtml
NAEP 1996 Mathematics Report Card for the Nation and the States. National Center for Education Statistics (NCES)

Discloses the mathematical achievement levels of students in grades 4, 8, and 12 in public and private schools. Depending on the degree of participation in the study, results are presented for individual states and for the nation.

[B2–26]   http://nces.ed.gov/nceskids/school/default.htm
Find Your School. National Center for Education Statistics (NCES)

A national directory of elementary and secondary schools that cites the address, telephone number, student enrollment, number of faculty, student–teacher ratio, and the racial stratification of the student body.

[B2–27]   http://nces.ed.gov/pubs97/97076.html
EDsearch: Education Statistics on Disk. National Center for Education Statistics (NCES)

The visitor to this Web site will find software that has been developed to provide access to the education statistics that have been published by NCES. Using the standard ERIC descriptors and the NCES index terms, more than 2,600 tables, charts, and text files can be accessed. An assortment of search methods is available. Search results can be saved under user-defined file names, and tables that have been retrieved can be displayed, printed, or stored on disk. Directions are provided for downloading and installing the software.

[B2–28]   http://nces.ed.gov/pubsearch/pubsinfo.asp?pubid=97992
Enhancing the Quality and Use of Student Outcomes Data. National Center for Education Statistics (NCES)

Reports on the state of the art of collecting, analyzing, and disseminating data on student outcomes and makes recommendations on how to improve the quality and usefulness of these data. The full report may be downloaded.

[B2–29]   http://nces.ed.gov/pubsearch/pubsinfo.asp?pubid=98082xxxxx
First-Generation Students: Undergraduates Whose Parents Never Enrolled in Postsecondary Education. National Center for Education Statistics (NCES)

Examines the postsecondary education experiences of first-generation college students and compares them with their peers whose parents attended college.

[B2–30]   http://nces.ed.gov/pubsearch/pubsinfo.asp?pubid=98252
New Entrants to the Full-Time Faculty of Higher Education Institutions. National Center for Education Statistics (NCES)

The findings of this national study disclose comparisons between junior and senior faculty in colleges and universities.

[B2–31]   http://nces.ed.gov/pubsearch/pubsinfo.asp?pubid=98256
Degrees and Other Awards Conferred by Degree-Granting Institutions: 1995–1996. National Center for Education Statistics (NCES)

Reports degrees and other awards conferred by degree-granting institutions of higher education. Summaries include degrees and awards by field of study, gender, and race/ethnicity.

[B2–32]   http://nces.ed.gov/pubsearch/pubsinfo.asp?pubid=1999155
Life after College. National Center for Education Statistics (NCES)

Reports on the follow-up of college students who graduated with a bachelor's degree and describes their experiences in graduate education and/or employment/unemployment. Based on 1992 to 1993 degree recipients and their experiences as of 1997.

[B2–33]   http://nces.ed.gov/pubsearch/pubsinfo.asp?pubid=1999193
Salaries and Tenure of Full-Time Instructional Faculty on 9–10 Month Contracts, 1997–1998. National Center for Education Statistics (NCES)

Reports on the number, average salaries, and tenure of full-time instructional faculty in higher education.

[B2–34]   http://nces.ed.gov/pubsearch/pubsinfo.asp?pubid=1999319
Private School Universe Survey, 1997–1998. National Center for Education Statistics (NCES)

Presents an array of data on private schools, K–12, in the U.S. based on the *Private School Universe Survey* of NCES. Information includes school population, school level, religious orientation, program emphasis, and more. Also leads to data on finances, staffing, etc. This is a comprehensive overview of private education K–12 that is comparable to the NCES *Common Core of Data Universe,* which is generated for public elementary and secondary schools.

[B2–35]   http://nces.ed.gov/pubsearch/pubsinfo.asp?pubid=1999462
NAEP 1998 Writing: Report Card for the Nation and the States. National Assessment of Educational Progress. National Center for Education Statistics (NCES)

Contains a summary of the results of the national assessment of the writing skills of students in grades 4, 8, and 12 for the nation and participating states. Performance on the NAEP assessment is reported according to the average writing score on a scale of 0–300 and relates to the percentage of students who attain each of three achievement levels; namely, Basic, Proficient, and Advanced. This Web site links to the full report.

[B2–36]   http://nces.ed.gov/pubsearch/pubsinfo.asp?pubid=2000022
Dropout Rates in the United States: 1998. National Center for Education Statistics (NCES)

Based on national data collected by NCES, this report analyzes the completion and dropout rates among high school students. It also studied the relationship between selected student characteristics and the probability of completing high school and of dropping out. Using Internet links, this Web site serves as a gateway to an extensive array of reports on the different aspects of student success and student attrition.

[B2–37]   http://nces.ed.gov/pubsearch/pubsinfo.asp?pubid=2000304
State Profiles of Public Elementary and Secondary Education: 1996–97. National Center for Education Statistics (NCES)

For the academic years 1987–1988 and 1996–1997 and based on the Common Core of Data and the Schools and Staffing Survey of NCES, this Web site provides a comprehensive statistical description of elementary and secondary education in the U.S. Using factors such as demographic characteristics, grade levels, race/ethnicity of students, achievement levels, and high school completion and attrition rates, this report presents descriptive and comparative data for the nation and each state. It also includes staffing levels, student–teacher ratios, revenues and expenditures, salaries, and other descriptors. The states are ranked on selected variables.

[B2–38]   http://nces.ed.gov/surveys/libraries/liblocator/default.asp
Public Library Locator. National Center for Education Statistics (NCES)

A guide to public libraries and public library service outlets. When the viewer inputs the name and location of a library, there will be retrieved descriptive information pertaining to that library's size of collection, financial operations, interlibrary relationships, and services.

[B2–39]   http://nces.ed.gov/surveys/pss/locator/locator.html
Private School Locator. National Center for Education Statistics (NCES)

This Web site enables the user to access one or more private schools, K–12, according to the selection criteria that are used. The search may be by the name of a specific school or according to stated criteria that will result in a list of schools. The selection could be of regular elementary or secondary schools according to grade levels offered, Montessori schools, special education schools, vocational-technical schools, denominational schools, early childhood programs or day care centers, or schools that offer alternative or nontraditional programs. The search may be further refined according to size of enrollment, gender specialization, or by a special educational emphasis.

[B2–40] http://nces.ed.gov/npec/answers

Accessing National Surveys with Electronic Research Sources (ANSWERS). National Postsecondary Education Cooperative (NPEC) and the National Center for Education Statistics (NCES)

This Web site is of value to researchers and policy analysts as they seek national survey data on higher education. It is an inventory of core national survey instruments and their data sets. These data sets are presented for viewer-selected subjects and topical areas. The higher education surveys are summarized by use of a matrix of their data sets and the different subject and topical areas. Visitors to this Web site may also access these data by selecting a probing question or keyword.

Supplementing the foregoing are copies of the survey instruments where the viewer can read the questions that generated the data. All known national surveys of higher education institutional data are contained in this Web site. Finally, it is the purpose of this site to provide a dictionary of survey terminology and to encourage standardization of definitions for use by developers of these instruments.

[B2–41] http://sunsite.berkeley.edu/Libweb/

Library Servers via WWW. The Library, UC Berkeley and Sun Microsystems, Inc.

With this Web site and its links, the user is able to contact academic, public, state, specialized, and other types of libraries in more than 100 nations. The information that is available differs with each library's Web site.

[B2–42] http://thegateway.org/welcome.html

Welcome to the Gateway. U.S. Department of Education

This Web site and its associated links provide educators at all grade levels (prekindergarden through higher education) with access to a plethora of educational materials that are on the Internet. These include lesson plans, activities, and projects. The Gateway to Educational Materials (GEM) project makes available educational materials found in a variety of Web sites sponsored by universities, federal and state governments, not-for-profit organizations, and commercial enterprises. Access to the materials is accomplished by browsing and complying with the instructions provided. Many documents can be downloaded.

[B2–43] http://www.aacc.nche.edu/

American Association of Community Colleges (AACC)

Here is the Web site of the national organization that serves as the voice of the community college sector of higher education. Using this site, the visitor can learn about the programs and services of the AACC. Furthermore, via links, the Web sites of individual community colleges that are members of AACC can be reached. The viewer can also access research that focuses on the community college.

[B2–44]   http://www.aacrao.org/fees-frame.htm
Foreign Education Evaluation Service. American Association of Collegiate Registrars and Admissions Officers (AACRAO)

A service for institutions, organizations, and individuals who seek a professional evaluation of foreign education credentials. Important for those who do not have knowledge of a foreign education system.

[B2–45]   http://www.aacrao.org/r&a-frame-asp.html
Research and Analytical Issues. American Association of Collegiate Registrars and Admissions Officers (AACRAO)

This is a source to consult when needing updated information on the different federal reporting requirements with which postsecondary education institutions must comply. It provides guidelines, helpful suggestions, and analyses.

[B2–46]   http://www.aacrao.org/r&a-frame-asp.html (Scroll to "Standard Definitions, Calculation Methods, Institutional Practices")
Credit-Hour Conversion Methods. American Association of Collegiate Registrars and Admissions Officers (AACRAO)

Explains the procedures for converting collegiate credit hours between semester, quarter, and trimester systems.

[B2–47]   http://www.aahe.org/
American Association for Higher Education (AAHE)

This Web site introduces the AAHE and its different service programs for the higher education community. Using links, the viewer may access other sites that disclose national endeavors that are addressing current issues in higher education. Also presents organizational matters such as AAHE's mission, its history, names of its Board of Directors, and staff names. The viewer may also access the AAHE *Online Publications Catalog*. Contact information for this organization is given.

[B2–48]   http://www.aahe.org/FFRR/ffrrnew2.htm
Faculty Roles and Rewards. American Association for Higher Education (AAHE)

Describes the efforts of AAHE to provide national leadership in the endeavor to enhance career development for faculty in colleges and universities. Explores ways to update the reward structure for faculty. In the process, there is an examination of faculty priorities, compensation, and evaluation.

[B2–49]   http://www.aahe.org/ppic/inst_change.htm
Program for the Promotion of Institutional Change. American Association for Higher Education (AAHE)

Explains some programs at the national level that have concentrated on reforming undergraduate education in science, mathematics, engineering, and technology education. Discusses AAHE's Institutional Change Institute. Provides links to other Web sites on this topic.

[B2–50] http://www.aahe.org/teaching/Teaching_Initiative_Home.htm
Teaching Initiatives. American Association for Higher Education (AAHE)

Introduces the AAHE Teaching Initiatives Program, which is intended to enhance the appreciation for the teaching function on the college campus and to stimulate new ideas on how to maximize teaching effectiveness. Links provide access to further information.

[B2–51] http://www.academicinfo.net/studentcolleges.html
The Student Center: Colleges and Universities. Academic Info.

This is a directory of higher education resources that are on the Internet. It contains links to Web sites that address a variety of topics on higher education, including the international realm.

[B2–52] http://www.accesseric.org/
The Educational Resources Information Center (ERIC)

Here is ERIC's home page on the Internet. It serves as an entrée to the services and programs of the ERIC system. Click on this Web site and the world of educational information becomes readily available.

[B2–53] http://www.accesseric.org/searchdb/searchdb.html
Search ERIC Database. Educational Resources Information Center (ERIC)

This is where the educational researcher can go to conduct inquiries of the ERIC database. Updated monthly, this site provides access to more than 1 million abstracts of documents and journal articles on educational research and practice. The ERIC collection dates from 1966 to the present.

[B2–54] http://www.accesseric.org/sites/address.html
Names and Addresses of ERIC Components. Educational Resources Information Center (ERIC)

A directory of ERIC's clearinghouses, adjunct clearinghouses, and support components. Provides their addresses, telephone numbers, e-mail addresses, and other information.

**[B2–55]   http://www.acenet.edu/About/programs/Programs&Analysis/
Policy&Analysis/policy-research/home.cfm**
Internet Sources for Higher Education Policy and Research Topics. American
Council on Education (ACE)

Here is a guide to other Web sites on higher education. The viewer may access these
sites by selected categories; namely, associations; journals; educational research, policy
centers, and institutes; general information on institutions of higher education; and gov-
ernment-funded educational resources. Offers a comprehensive array of information on
higher education.

[B2–56]   http://www.acenet.edu/about/WhotoAsk/home.cfm
Who to Ask. American Council on Education (ACE)

This Web site gives access to the professional staff at ACE. They can be found either
by name or by a specialization search. Biographical profiles are provided along with telephone numbers of the staff.

[B2–57]   http://www.acenet.edu/news/home.html
ACE News. American Council on Education (ACE)

A source of recent news about higher education around the nation. Includes position
letters of the ACE, federal policy analysis, legal updates, and other issues in the news.

[B2–58]   http://www.acenet.edu/resources/fact-sheets/home.html
ACE Fact Sheets on Higher Education. American Council on Education (ACE)

Reports sundry statistical data on American higher education that encompasses such
topics as average earnings of workers by level of educational attainment; educational attainment by age, sex, and race; postsecondary education enrollments; and a summary of
higher education institutions and the degrees which they have conferred. Additionally, descriptive data are presented on college students, and information can be found on financing higher education.

[B2–59]   http://www.appa.org/
APPA: The Association of Higher Education Facilities Officers

This site is a portal to information on facilities at colleges and universities. It presents
news, references to programs and publications, guides to consultants, and links to other
Internet sources. Major categories at this Web site are General Administration; Maintenance and Operations; Energy and Utilities; and Planning, Design, and Construction.

[B2–60]   http://www.asd.com/
American School Directory. ASD

An Internet guide to the public and private K–12 schools in America. Each of the more than 108,000 schools has its own Web site that is accessed by this guide. Contains the address and telephone number of each school in addition to a variety of other information.

[B2–61]   http://www.awesomelibrary.org/
Awesome Library. Evaluation and Development Institute and Dr. R. Jerry Adams

Offers an extensive assortment of professionally reviewed resources on a broad array of topics in education. Subjects included are special education, mathematics, science, English, social studies, and the arts.

[B2–62]   http://www.bates.edu/IR/tools/tools.html
The Toolbox. Bates College

Introduces the viewer to a large bibliography of Web sites that offer useful software and Internet tools for the person engaged in institutional research and educational research.

[B2–63]   http://www.ccsso.org/addres.html
Chief State School Officer Addresses. The Council of Chief State School Officers (CCSSO)

A directory of the names, addresses, telephone numbers, and fax numbers of the chief state public school officers.

[B2–64]   http://www.ccsso.org/seamenu.html
Links to State Education Agencies. The Council of Chief State School Officers (CCSSO)

Using this Web site, the visitor can access the Web sites of the state agencies or departments of education. Simply click on the profile of the targeted state that appears on the map of the U.S.

[B2–65]   http://www.chronicle.com/
The Chronicle of Higher Education

The weekly newspaper for the higher education community that addresses the interests of college and university faculty and administrators. Includes campus news; developments at the federal and state levels that affect higher education; articles about faculty tenure and salaries; job listings; personnel changes on campuses and in state higher education systems; statistics on enrollment, tutition, salaries, and others; and news items on selected topics. Many of the services offered by this Web site are available only to subscribers of *The Chronicle of Higher Education.*

[B2–66]   http://www.chronicle.com/free/resources/index.php3
Internet Resources. The Chronicle of Higher Education

On this Web site the visitor will learn of other sites that are of interest to persons in higher education. A list of keywords is displayed, and the selection of a keyword enables access to a linked site.

[B2–67]   http://www.cphe.org/
Council on Law in Higher Education (CLHE)

This is the Web site of the Council on Law in Higher Education. It is the mission of the Council to provide information on legal issues and legal developments in higher education. Court decisions, regulations, and legislation in process are addressed. Among the main areas of focus are academic affairs, affirmative action, laws on disabilities, campus security, student privacy, records management, and First Amendment issues. Its scope is flexible as the issues of the day expand. Although not a substitute for professional legal advice, this site is an information facilitator for administrators and attorneys in the higher education community.

[B2–68]   http://www.edfacilities.org/an/index.html
National Clearinghouse for Educational Facilities (NCEF)

Affiliated with the ERIC system, this clearinghouse provides information on the planning, designing, building, financing, operations, and maintenance of school facilities, K–12. This Web site allows the visitor to submit a request to NCEF concerning a facility matter, and NCEF will research the answer. Also, persons may submit news items about facilities (K–12) for national dissemination because such an item will become part of the clearinghouse's database. With the use of links, access is available to other sites germane to school facilities.

[B2–69]   http://www.ed.gov/BASISDB/EROD/eric/SF
Directory of ERIC Resource Collections. Educational Resources Information Center (ERIC)

By designating a state or a country, the visitor to this site can obtain a list of organizations that offer online CD-ROM access to the ERIC database, have large collections of ERIC microfiche, and/or subscribe to major ERIC publications. For each center, descriptive information is reported.

[B2–70]   http://www.ed.gov/Programs/EROD/
Education Resource Organizations Directory. U.S. Department of Education

This is a "mother lode" of information about the full spectrum of education. By using this site, the educational researcher may access more than 2,400 Web sites of organizations that facilitate the research process. Resource organizations may be accessed by name, URL, state, subject, and in other ways.

[B2–70A]   http://www.edlaw.net/frames.html
The EDLAW Center

Serving children with disabilities, the EDLAW Center provides a variety of services that include information on legal developments in the field of disabilities and assists parents, schools, and attorneys in solving problems.

[B2–71]   http://www.edmin.com/jma/cohort/
JMA Cohorts for Institutional Comparison. John Minter Associates

Presents a refinement of the Carnegie categories for classifying institutions of higher education. Offers a useful analytical management tool.

[B2–72]   http://www.ed.sc.edu/spedlaw/LawPage.htm
The Law and Special Education. Mitchell L. Yell, Ph.D.

Reviews the law as it applies to special education. Provides updates concerning legal developments, including court cases, statutory changes, and regulatory developments. Covers both federal and state jurisdictions.

[B2–73]   http://www.edstats.net/scripts/calclist/calc_list.cgi
EDSTATS–Higher Education Statistics. John Minter Associates

Presents free online budget benchmark ratios for public and independent colleges and universities. Includes comparative budget benchmarks for instructional activities, academic libraries, unit-level administrative activity, and units of student affairs.

[B2–74]   http://www.edweek.org/
Education Week

A weekly newspaper that serves the K–12 professional community. It reports on educational issues, policies, and a variety of other matters that are of interest to educators. This site offers links to other education-related Web sites.

[B2–75]   http://www.edweek.org/sreports/qc00/templates/article.cfm? slug=policies.htm
Setting Policies for New Teachers. Education Week

Based on a study of all states, this Web site reports on the outcome of a survey of state policies regarding minimum standards for allowing beginning teachers to teach. It discloses both the official standards and the actual practices. The discrepancy is a "wake-up call" germane to assuring quality teaching.

[B2–75A]   http://www.epie.org
The Educational Products Information Exchange. EPIE

With this Web site, the visitor has access to evaluations of more than 19,000 educational software packages. Simply click on the appropriate link and *The Educational Software Selector (T.E.S.S.)* becomes available. Profiles include the purpose, grade level, description, software publisher, and other information about the package. This evaluation service originated as a printed publication in 1967 and has evolved into being available online and on CD-ROM. [*Note:* At the time of this writing, the EPIE Web site was in a state of change; consequently, the reader may experience some alterations to the foregoing description.]

[B2–76]   http://www.eriche.org/main.html
ERIC Clearinghouse on Higher Education. Educational Resources Information Center (ERIC)

This clearinghouse is a center for information on higher education. Its scope is delimited to higher education at the levels of the baccalaureate degree and higher degrees. (*Note:* For the associate degree level, see B2–80 for the ERIC Clearinghouse for Community Colleges.) As part of the ERIC system, it collects materials on a full range of topics in higher education, including planning and evaluation, curriculum matters, teaching methods, financial affairs, legal issues, graduate and professional education, students, faculty, and governmental issues.

[B2–77]   http://www.ers.org/
Educational Research Service (ERS)

Operating under the sponsorship of seven national associations of school administrators, ERS provides research and information services to subscribing local K–12 school districts. It will search the literature for requested information, provide inter-district comparison profiles based on suggested criteria, and conduct customized research for school districts.

[B2–78]   http://www.ers.org/states.htm
State Associations of School Administrators. Educational Research Service (ERS)

This Web site is dedicated to listing, by state, all of the public school administrator associations. For each association, it displays the chief official's name, address, telephone number, fax number, e-mail address, and, when applicable, the Web site address. Also reported is information on each state's chief public school administrator.

[B2–78A]   http://www.ets.org/testcoll/
ETS Test Collection Database. Educational Testing Service, Inc.

Contains an extensive bibliography of standardized tests with an abstract of each instrument. Also provides references to publications that describe the instrument.

[B2–79]   http://www.explorasource.com/educator/

ExplorAsource: ConnectingR esources, Standards, and Learning Needs. MediaSeek Technologies, Inc.

This site enables the educator (K–12) to search for specific teaching materials that are available from commercial sources. The probe is made by grade level, subject, topic, and type of media that is being sought.

[B2–80]   http://www.gseis.ucla.edu/ERIC/eric.html

ERIC Clearinghouse for Community Colleges

This is the clearinghouse within the ERIC system that collects documents and journal articles pertaining to the community colleges. It is comparable to B2–76 except that its mission is the community college sector of higher education.

[B2–81]   http://www.gseis.ucla.edu/ERIC/findcc.html

Find A Community College. ERIC Clearinghouse for Community Colleges

This Web site allows the visitor to obtain information on one or more community colleges by inputting the name of a community college or keywords, such as a location, program, financial aid, or other designator. The latter approach usually produces multiple findings.

[B2–82]   http://www.gseis.ucla.edu/ERIC/gradprog.html

Graduate Studies in the Field of Community Colleges. Educational Resources Information Center (ERIC)

Identifies programs that concentrate on the study of community colleges. These programs include research-based, degree-granting programs and leadership training programs for community college administrators. There is access to descriptive information for each program.

[B2–83]   http://www.higher-ed.org/

Higher Education Resource Network. James J.F. Forest, Ph.D.

Offers a very comprehensive collection of information on higher education worldwide. Includes publications and resources for research on higher education, news about higher education events that are occurring throughout the world, access to associations and organizations, a directory of campus Web sites, access to higher education research centers, employment opportunities in higher education, and much more.

[B2–84]   http://www.highereducation.org/

The National Center for Public Policy and Higher Education

Here is the home page of this national organization, whose raison d'être is to analyze state and federal policies pertaining to higher education. The visitor can learn about the programs and publications of the center and how to make contact with it.

[B2–85] http://www.hood.edu/seri/serihome.htm
Special Education Resources on the Internet. Hood College

Presents a collection of Internet resources that serve those interested in special and gifted education. Encompasses university programs, national organizations and associations, law resources, and other information for parents and educators. Addresses the topics of mental retardation, learning disabilities, attention deficit disorders, autism, speech disorders, hearing impairment, and more.

[B2–86] http://www.ierf.org/
International Education Research Foundation, Inc. Credentials Evaluation Service

This is the Web site of an organization that evaluates foreign academic credentials. Academic credits earned abroad are evaluated for acceptance by U.S. universities, employers, or the military.

[B2–87] http://www.ifas.ufl.edu/WWW/LS_GRANT/index.htm
Land-Grant and Sea-Grant Acts, History, and Institutions. University of Florida

Summarizes the background of the land-grant and sea-grant legislative acts that have culminated in the designation of selected universities as being land-grant or sea-grant universities. This Web site also lists the names of the individual institutions that have received these designations.

[B2–88] http://www.irp.panam.edu/more_html/utpa_erlist.html
The Higher Education Research Meta-Index

To assist the institutional researcher and the educational research community at-large, this Web site provides an index of Internet sites that will be of interest. These hyperlinked sites are sources of statistical data and other research-related information. Listed are Web sites sponsored by federal and state agencies, colleges and universities, independent research centers, and others.

[B2–89] http://www.iser.com/
Internet Special Education Resources

A national directory of professionals who provide services in the field of special education. Discloses their names and addresses. Also offers guidelines for parents and educators who are seeking these services.

[B2–90]   http://www.jma-inc.net/
Management Ratio Calculators. John Minter Associates

A service that offers customized budget management ratios for individual colleges and universities. Also provides interinstitutional data comparisons.

[B2–91]   http://www.league.org/welcome.htm
League for Innovation in the Community College

Since 1968, this organization has been providing leadership for institutional effectiveness and innovation in community colleges. This Web site discloses the variety of services and projects offered for the enhancement of these institutions.

[B2–92]   http://www.library.uiuc.edu/edx/rankings.htm
College and University Rankings. Education and Social Science Library, University of Illinois at Urbana-Champaign

Presents a bibliography of links to various services that rank colleges and universities. These ranking services focus on U.S. and foreign institutions of higher education.

[B2–93]   http://www.mcli.dist.maricopa.edu/cc/
Community College Web. Maricopa Center for Learning and Instruction. Maricopa Community Colleges

A guide to more than 1,100 Web sites of community colleges in the U.S. , Canada, and other countries. Also provides links to 18 sites that treat a variety of topics on community colleges.

[B2–94]   http://www.nasdtec.org/manual.html
NASDTEC Manual. National Association of State Directors of Teacher Education and Certification

This is the authoritative guide to teacher education and certification. It reports requirements for teacher certification in each of the 50 states, the District of Columbia, Canadian provinces, and selected other locations. Discloses the identity of teacher training institutions and their approved programs.

[B2–95]   http://www.nbpts.org/nbpts/
The National Board for Professional Teaching Standards (NBPTS)

Visit this Web site to learn about the operations and programs of this organization, which is establishing national standards for professional teachers. These standards have been set by subject area and student development level, and they are based on five core propositions. This site provides summaries of the standards and links to other sites that report on state and local actions that have been taken in support of this program.

[B2–96]   http://www.ncate.org/2000/2000/stds.pdf
NCATE 2000 Unit Standards. National Council for Accreditation of Teacher Education (NCATE)

Sets forth the standards that are being enforced by NCATE, as of the fall of 2001, for the accreditation of teacher preparation programs.

[B2–97]   http://www.nchems.org/InfoServices/infoserv.htm
NCHEMS Information Services. National Center for Higher Education Management Services

Facilitates access to national data on higher education by mainly drawing on the data derived from the IPEDS and HEGIS surveys. These data include enrollments, finances, faculty salaries, institutional characteristics, and other elements of these national surveys of higher education.

[B2–98]   http://www.nchems.org/Surveys/surveys.htm
NCHEMS Surveys. National Center for Higher Education Management Services

This Web site introduces the viewer to the survey programs of NCHEMS. These surveys enable administrators in higher education to analyze and better understand the environments of their institutions in terms of students, alumni, governance, and other institutional variables. The visitor to this site is given information on whom to contact for initiating an NCHEM institutional study.

[B2–99]   http://www.negp.gov/page3.htm
Goals. National Education Goals Panel

Lists the Year 2000 National Education Goals with links to a presentation of the objectives of each of the eight goals.

[B2–100]   http://www.negp.gov/page13.htm
The National Education Goals Panel

Using this Web site, the visitor has links to state education agencies, the U.S. Department of Education, National Center for Education Statistics, National Education Association, National PTA, National Governors Association, and the National Conference of State Legislators.

[B2–101]   http://www.nwrel.org/eval/index.html
NWREL's Assessment and Evaluation Services. Northwest Regional Educational Laboratory

The NWREL offers an assessment and evaluation program for the purpose of implementing educational research findings in the classroom (i.e., it serves as a bridge from research to practice). Via this Web site, this regional educational laboratory brings resources and services to the teacher.

[B2–102]   http://www.nwrel.org/national/
National Network: Regional Educational Laboratories. Northwest Regional Educational Laboratory

From this Web site access is available to the separate Internet sites of the 10 regional educational laboratories. Additionally, the viewer is provided with the addresses and telephone numbers of the different laboratories along with the names of the states that each serves.

[B2–102A]   http://www.priweb.com/internetlawlib/99.htm
Internet Law Library: Education and the Law. Pritchard Law Webs

This Web site is an entry point to the full text of state education codes, state statutes, selected case decisions, and other legal documents concerning education at all levels. It also includes some foreign legal materials.

[B2–103]   http://www.scholarly-societies.org/
Scholarly Societies Project. University of Waterloo Library

This is the Internet passage to the world of scholarly societies. It extends access to the Web sites of 1,644 scholarly societies and academies worldwide. Searches may be conducted by the name of a society, subject field, geographical area, language, or year of founding. A variety of information is offered for each society. This data bank goes back to the earliest scholarly societies in Europe.

[B2–104]   http://www.ship.edu/~library/instruction/edresearch.htm
Guide to Finding Articles in Education. Shippensburg University

Cites four online databases that index journals in education. In some cases, the full text of an article can be viewed. The advantages and disadvantages of each database are presented along with helpful suggestions for usage.

[B2–105]   http://www.tiaa-cref.org/
TIAA-CREF Web Center. Teachers Insurance and Annuity Association-College Retirement Equities Fund

Known to most persons employed in higher education, TIAA-CREF provides retirement financial services to the higher education community. This Web site describes the services and programs of these two organizations and permits visitors to interact with this Web site.

[B2–106]   http://www.usnews.com/usnews/edu/beyond/bceng.htm
Engineering Rankings. U.S. News and World Report

Provides information on, and rankings of, U.S. schools of engineering. In addition, the visitor to this Web site may access the Web site of a specific school of engineering.

[B2–107]   http://www.usnews.com/usnews/edu/college/corank.htm
2000 College Rankings. U.S. News and World Report

Ranks colleges and universities by type of institution, region, state, undergraduate programs, graduate programs, and other criteria. The visitor to this Web site may also search for one or more institutions of higher education by name or by a specified group criterion.

[B2–108]   http://www2.acs.ncsu.edu/UPA/survey/resource.htm
Internet Resources for Higher Education Outcomes Assessment. North Carolina State University

Contains a bibliography of Web sites that specialize in learning outcomes assessment on college campuses. These sites often provide links to other Web sites that address this subject.

CHAPTER 3

Finding Education Information on the Web: The International Domain

INTRODUCTION

The reader will now enter the international domain of the Internet. Whereas Chapter 2 concentrates on the U.S. domain, this chapter addresses those Web sites for educators that originate from outside of U.S. The same Information Locator system used in Chapter 2 is implemented in this chapter. Again, simply locate the question in the left column that is being pursued and then identify the URL in the right column. The item entry number that follows the URL is associated with a descriptive profile in Chapter 4 of that Web site. The URLs have been presented as they appear on their Web sites.

In this chapter, the item-locator questions have been organized in sections as follows:

> Africa: Multinational
> Australia and Australasia
> Canada
> China
> Europe: Multinational
> Finland (See Nordic Countries)
> France
> Germany
> India
> Ireland
> Israel
> Japan
> New Zealand (See Australia and Australasia)
> Nordic Countries
> Saudi Arabia
> Sweden (See Nordic Countries)
> Turkey
> United Kingdom
> Worldwide

For inclusion in this book, a Web site has to be available in the English language either as its primary language or as a translation. As with sites in the U.S. domain, these Internet locations are fluid and ephemeral; consequently, their existence, addresses, and content are subject to change. For this reason, the author of this section declares that the URLs in this chapter were operational at the time of writing; however, changes of Web sites may have subsequently occurred.

THE INFORMATION LOCATOR

Africa: Multinational

Where Should I Go to Find . . .	*Try*
information on the African Educational Research Network?	http://www2.ncsu.edu/ncsu/aern/ABOUT.HTML [B4–63]
a central organization for obtaining information on education in Africa?	http://www.bellanet.org/partners/adea/index.html [B4–15]
databases that provide baseline information on education in Africa?	http://www.bellanet.org/partners/adea/en_resources.html [B4–14]
a network for the conduct of educational research in West and Central Africa?	http://www.bellanet.org/partners/adea/Vol10No3/en_3.html [B4–17]
a network for the conduct of educational research in East and Southern Africa?	http://www.bellanet.org/partners/adea/Vol10No3/en_2.html [B4–16]

Australia and Australasia

information on the Australian Council for Educational Research?	http://www.acer.edu.au/ [B4–9]
the latest findings of educational research conducted in Australia?	http://www.acer.edu.au/acer/latest/index.html [B4–10]
what research is being conducted in Australia on ways to improve learning outcomes?	http://www.acer.edu.au/acer/research/index.html [B4–11]
access to the leading professional society for higher education in Australia and its neighboring nations?	http://www.herdsa.org.au/ [B4–28]
a directory of universities in Australia with access to individual campus Web sites?	http://www.avcc.edu.au/avcc/uniwebs.htm [B4–13]
information on the New Zealand Council for Educational Research?	http://www.nzcer.org.nz/ [B4–41]

Canada

an explanation of the higher education system in Canada?	http://homer.aucc.ca/english/dcu/highereducation/overview.html [B4–4]

103

Canada

Where Should I Go to Find . . .	*Try*
a directory of Canadian universities?	http://www.oise.utoronto.ca/~mpress/ universities.html [B4–50] http://homer.aucc.ca/english/dcu/index. html [B4–5]
Web sites of Canadian community colleges that are not affiliated with universities?	http://www.oise.utoronto.ca/~mpress/ colleges.html [B4–43]
members of the faculties of education in Canadian universities, including their contact information?	http://www.oise.utoronto.ca/~mpress/ faculties.html [B4–46]
programs of undergraduate and graduate studies in Canada?	http://homer.aucc.ca/english/dcu/ universities/search.html [B4–6]
access to the education libraries in Canada?	http://www.oise.utoronto.ca/~mpress/ libraries.html [B4–48]
access to the full online text of Canadian journals in education?	http://www.oise.utoronto.ca/~mpress/ journals.html [B4–47]
Internet access to the educational organizations and associations, at all levels, in Canada?	http://www.oise.utoronto.ca/~mpress/ canada.html [B4–42]
Web sites of the public and private school districts in Canada?	http://www.oise.utoronto.ca/~mpress/ edboards.html [B4–45]
the names of, and information on, associations of school boards in Canada?	http://www.oise.utoronto.ca/~mpress/ schoolb.html [B4–49]
Web sites of Canadian private enterprise education?	http://www.oise.utoronto.ca/~mpress/ commercial.html [B4–44]

China

information on the Hong Kong Institute of Educational Research?	http://www.fed.cuhk.edu.hk/~hkier/ [B4–25]
the Chinese equivalent of the American ERIC system?	http://www.fed.cuhk.edu.hk/~hkier/ (Answer continues)

China

Where Should I Go to Find . . .	*Try*
the Chinese equivalent of the American ERIC system?	(Note: Click on "The Chinese Educational Resources Information Centre Project.") [B4–26]

Europe: Multinational

information on the European Educational Research Association?	http://www.eera.ac.uk/ [B4–23]
information on the European Center for Higher Education?	http://www.cepes.ro/ [B4–19]
material on policy and reform in European higher education?	http://www.cepes.ro/ (Note: Click on "Policy and Reform in Higher Education.") [B4–19]
what is being done to foster the internationalization of higher education in Europe?	Http://www.eaie.nl/ [B4–22]
information on models of teacher education in Europe?	http://www.cepes.ro/ (Note: Click on "Status of Teachers and the IT Society.") [B4–19]
the qualifications for gaining access to higher education in a selected European country?	http://access.cepes.ro/cgi-bin/dbOleg. plx [B4–1]

Finland

See "Nordic Countries."

France

information on the system of higher education in France?	http://www.cies.fr/uk/comprendre/ home.htm [B4–21]

Germany

Where Should I Go to Find . . .	*Try*
information on the Max Planck Institute for Human Development, including its four research centers?	http://www.mpib-berlin.mpg.de/Viere. htm [B4–39]

India

a central organization for educational research activities conducted in India?	http://ncert.nic.in/ [B4–7]

Ireland

information on the system of higher education in Ireland, along with libraries and scholarly societies?	http://www.heanet.ie/links/irish/ highered.html [B4–27]

Israel

information on the system of higher education in Israel?	http://www.israelemb.org/highered/ highed.html [B4–35]

Japan

information on the National Institute for Educational Research of Japan?	http://www.nier.go.jp/homepage/ kyoutsuu/indexe.htm [B4–40]

New Zealand

See "Australia and Australasia."

Nordic Countries

a focal point for educational research activity in Finland?	http://www.jyu.fi/ktl/index2.html [B4–36]
information on Nordic higher education and the individual universities in the Nordic countries?	http://www.abo.fi/norden/welcom_e. htm [B4–8]

Nordic Countries

Where Should I Go to Find . . .	*Try*
an explanation of higher education in Sweden?	http://helios.hsv.se/english/higher/index.html [B4–3]
the addresses, telephone numbers, and URLs for colleges and universities in Sweden?	http://www.hsv.se/english/addresses.html [B4–30]

Saudi Arabia

information about higher education in Saudi Arabia and its individual universities?	http://www.mohe.gov.sa/english/enmohe.htm [B4–38]

Sweden

See "Nordic Countries."

Turkey

an outline and history of the educational system in Turkey?	http://www.yok.gov.tr/webeng/edusys.html [B4–62]
information on the higher education system in Turkey?	http://www.yok.gov.tr/indexeng.html [B4–61]

United Kingdom

information on the British Educational Research Association?	http://www.bera.ac.uk/ [B4–18]
a focal point of educational research activity in Scotland?	http://www.scre.ac.uk/Homepage.html [B4–52]
databases of educational research conducted in Scotland?	http://www.scre.ac.uk/gateways/index.html [B4–51]

United Kingdom

Where Should I Go to Find . . .	*Try*
an Internet directory of higher education and research libraries in the United Kingdom with the means to search their catalogs?	http://www.ex.ac.uk/library/uklibs.html [B4–24]
Web sites of universities in the United Kingdom?	http://www.webmaster.bham.ac.uk/ ukuwww.html [B4–60]
descriptive statistics on all levels of education in the United Kingdom?	http://www.statistics.gov.uk [B4–57]
Web sites of colleges in the United Kingdom?	http://www.webmaster.bham.ac.uk/ ukcwww.html [B4–59]
descriptive statistics on higher education in the United Kingdom?	http://www.statistics.gov.uk [B4–57] http://www.srhe.ac.uk/index.htm (Note: Click on "HESA Statistics.") [B4–55] http://www.hesa.ac.uk [B4–29]
descriptive data on applicants to full-time undergraduate programs at institutions of higher education in the United Kingdom?	http://www.ucas.ac.uk/figures/archive/ index.html [B4–58]
an organization that is dedicated to research on all aspects of higher education in the United Kingdom?	http://www.srhe.ac.uk/index.htm [B4–54]
subject-matter focus groups in the United Kingdom that concentrate on professional areas of interest in higher education?	http://www.srhe.ac.uk/index.htm (Note: Click on "SRHE Networks.") [B4–56]

Worldwide

Internet access to libraries worldwide?	http://sunsite.berkeley.edu/Libweb/ (Note: Refer back to B2–41.)
an international bibliography of newsletters and/or journals in education with access either to their table of contents or to articles in full text?	http://www.scre.ac.uk/is/webjournals. html [B4–53] http://www.leeds.ac.uk/bei/journals.htm [B4–37]

Worldwide

Where Should I Go to Find ...	*Try*
descriptions of national education systems worldwide?	http://www.ibe.unesco.org/Inf_Doc/ Nat_reps/wdepfome.htm [B4–34]
an annotated list of databases that access information on educational systems worldwide?	http://www.ibe.unesco.org/Inf_Doc/ Nat_reps/database.htm#databas [B4–31]
hyperlinks to databases that offer information on the cultural, historical, political, and economic context of educational systems worldwide?	http://www.ibe.unesco.org/Inf_Doc/ Nat_reps/introde.htm [B4–32]
worldwide hyperlinks to official national information sources on education?	http://www.ibe.unesco.org/Inf_Doc/ Nat_reps/introde.htm [B4–32]
educational statistics, worldwide, that are maintained in the UNESCO database and elsewhere?	http://www.ibe.unesco.org/Inf_ Doc/ Nat_reps/statist.htm#education [B4–33] http://www.cepes.ro/information_ services/statistics.htm [B4–20]
an international source of university Web sites worldwide?	http://geowww.uibk.ac.at/univ/ [B4–2] http://www.asiadragons.com/education/ home.shtml [B4–12]

CHAPTER 4

Descriptive Profiles of International Web Sites

INTRODUCTION

This chapter provides descriptive profiles of the Web sites that are cited in Chapter 3 of this section. These profiles elaborate on the information presented in the Information Locator of the preceding chapter. They have been organized alphabetically according to their address names (URLs). Each address has been presented exactly as it appears on the Internet. Any inconsistencies that may exist between URLs are attributed to the format presented by the different Web masters of the various sites.

To find a Web site's profile, use the item entry number that is provided in Chapter 3 and locate it in Chapter 4. Starting each profile is the item entry number followed by the address of the Web site. The format of these numbers is as follows. The initial letter designates the section (B), and the associated number (4) refers to this chapter. The numerals that appear to the right of the hyphen identify the specific Web site. Thus, B4–1 refers to the first profile in Chapter 4 of Section B.

Next, the title of the Web site is given. Following it is the name of the site's sponsor. If the site is for an organization and the title is the name of that organization, then the separate entry for the sponsor's name has been omitted because the title and the sponsor's name are the same.

The last segment of each profile is a brief explanation of the Web site. This includes the purpose and services offered by it.

PROFILES OF INTERNATIONAL WEB SITES

[B4–1] http://access.cepes.ro/cgi-bin/dbOleg.plx
Access to Higher Education. UNESCO-CEPES (European Center for Higher Education)

Offers a variety of information on the systems of higher education in selected European countries. Reported for each country are the qualifications for gaining access to higher education, an explanation of the grading system, and a discussion of the examinations and other descriptors of each system of higher education.

[B4–2] http://geowww.uibk.ac.at/univ/
Universities Worldwide. University of Innsbruck

Contains links to 5,396 universities in 152 nations. Simply search by country and then click on the preferred university to gain access to its Web site.

110

[B4–3]   http://helios.hsv.se/english/higher/index.html
Higher Education System in Sweden. The National Agency for Higher Education (Högskoleverket)

Using this Web page, which is a component of the larger Web site of the National Agency for Higher Education in Sweden, the visitor learns how the Swedish system of higher education is organized. Also, by making use of this site and its hyperlinks, there is entry to a broad scope of Swedish higher education.

[B4–4]   http://homer.aucc.ca/english/dcu/highereducation/overview.html
Higher Education in Canada: Overview. Association of Universities and Colleges in Canada and SchoolNet

The visitor to this Web site learns about the mission, history, and organization of higher education in Canada. It discloses the uniqueness and richness of this system. Any person who plans to become involved with a Canadian university will find this Web site to be helpful.

[B4–5]   http://homer.aucc.ca/english/dcu/index.html
The Directory of Canadian Universities. Association of Universities and Colleges of Canada and SchoolNet

This site offers a directory of Canadian universities with links to their institutional profiles. It also provides links to Web sites of associations and organizations affiliated with higher education in Canada.

[B4–6]   http://homer.aucc.ca/english/dcu/universities/search.html
Where to Study What in Canada. Association of Universities and Colleges in Canada and SchoolNet

The visitor to this Web site can discover and access descriptions of undergraduate and graduate programs in Canadian universities. This is a central database of university degree programs in Canada.

[B4–7]   http://ncert.nic.in/
National Council of Educational Research and Training (NCERT). India

The NCERT organization was established for the purpose of advising the different levels of government in India on education. It also provides assistance to schools with its research and development activities and with its information dissemination program. This Web site helps those persons who are interested in the educational research efforts that are taking place in India.

[B4–8] http://www.abo.fi/norden/welcom_e.htm
Higher Education in the Nordic Countries. Nordic Association of University Administrators

The Nordic community of eight nations has developed a network of higher education with a form of cooperation that preserves and respects the unique culture of each of the member countries. These nations encompass Denmark, Sweden, Finland, Norway, Iceland, Greenland, the Faeroe Islands, and the Åland Islands. When visiting this Web site, the viewer can learn about this international community and also access the different institutions of higher education within them.

[B4–9] http://www.acer.edu.au/
Australian Council for Educational Research (ACER)

Dedicated to the enhancement of learning, this independent and not-for-profit organization focuses on educational research and development that produces new knowledge and tools for the improvement of learning. This is the key organization for educational research in Australia and the contiguous South Pacific region. Its research program is divided into the areas of measurement, policy research, international training and development, and the teaching and learning processes. ACER offers contract research services to school districts.

[B4–10] http://www.acer.edu.au/acer/latest/index.html
Latest Findings in Educational Research. Australian Council for Educational Research (ACER)

This Web site discloses the latest findings of the educational research projects that have been conducted by the ACER organization. These projects embrace a variety of topics.

[B4–11] http://www.acer.edu.au/acer/research/index.html
Research into Learning Outcomes. Australian Council for Educational Research (ACER)

Described within this Web site are the efforts of ACER to explore ways and processes for enhancing learning outcomes. This research program addresses five areas that are explained at this Web site. The visitor can also learn about the array of educational research projects that are under contract with ACER.

[B4–12] http://www.asiadragons.com/education/home.shtml
International Education Centers. Asiadragons.Com

This Web site gives access to Web sites of universities throughout the world. When clicking on a geographical region and then on a particular nation within that region, the viewer is presented with a list of colleges and universities. By selecting one of these institutions and then clicking on it, that institution's Web site is revealed.

[B4–13] http://www.avcc.edu.au/avcc/uniwebs.htm
Australian Universities WWW Servers. Australian Vice Chancellors' Committee

A list of universities in Australia with links to their respective Web sites. Each site contains a unique spectrum of descriptive information about that institution.

[B4–14] http://www.bellanet.org/partners/adea/en_resources.html
ADEA Databases. Association for the Development of Education in Africa

Contained within these databases are the most comprehensive statistics on education in sub-Saharan Africa. These databases can be downloaded.

[B4–15] http://www.bellanet.org/partners/adea/index.html
About ADEA. Association for the Development of Education in Africa

ADEA fosters partnerships between ministries of education in Africa and with funding agencies. It serves as a catalyst in promoting educational development in African nations. In the process it functions as a network for the exchange of educational information and the sharing of strategies and innovations.

[B4–16] http://www.bellanet.org/partners/adea/Vol10No3/en_2.html
ERNESA: The Educational Research Network in East and Southern Africa. Association for the Development of Education in Africa

ERNESA is a network of educational research associations in 12 nations located in East and Southern Africa. It endeavors to cultivate educational research skills in its region, promote the conduct of educational research at a high professional level, disseminate research findings among its member nations and outside its region, and seek the improvement of education in East and Southern Africa.

[B4–17] http://www.bellanet.org/partners/adea/Vol10No3/en_3.html
ERNWACA: The Educational Research Network for West and Central Africa. Association for the Development of Education in Africa

The ERNWACA network, consisting of 12 countries in West and Central Africa, is dedicated to encouraging educational research that will aid in the development of education in its member nations. It seeks cooperation between educational researchers and academic administrators, promotes the enhancement of educational research skills, and fosters the dissemination of educational research information.

[B4–18]   http://www.bera.ac.uk/
British Educational Research Association (BERA)

Organized to promote a culture of educational research, BERA works to stimulate discussion and activities in research methodology and engagement in the full spectrum of education. It promotes cooperation with other national and international educational research associations. This organization pursues research into matters of curriculum, teaching techniques and learning outcomes, educational policy issues, comparative education, and more. This is the Internet location for visiting BERA.

[B4–19]   http://www.cepes.ro/
UNESCO-CEPES (European Center for Higher Education)

This is an international research center for promoting cooperation in higher education among member nations in Europe. Sponsored by UNESCO and located in Bucharest, Romania, it undertakes projects that develop and reform higher education. This is a center for the study of higher education and conducts research in this field. This Web site is a source of information on what is taking place in European higher education.

[B4–20]   http://www.cepes.ro/information_services/statistics.htm
Statistical Information on Higher Education in Central and Eastern Europe. UNESCO-CEPES (European Center for Higher Education)

For each country in Central and Eastern Europe, this Web site discloses data on the number of public and private institutions of higher education, student enrollment, and the nation's total population.

[B4–21]   http://www.cies.fr/uk/comprendre/home.htm
The French Higher Education System. Égide

This Web site presents a comprehensive explanation of the French system of higher education. Included is a history of French universities, a disclosure of the types of institutions that make up the higher education community, and links to the Web sites of individual universities and specialized schools.

[B4–22]   http://www.eaie.nl/
European Association for International Education (EAIE)

The mission of EAIE is to stimulate and facilitate the internationalization of education in Europe, with special emphasis on higher education. With headquarters in Amsterdam, it works with educational institutions, governments, and associations to advance the cause of international education. For access to this organization via the Internet, consult this Web site.

[B4–23]   http://www.eera.ac.uk/
European Educational Research Association (EERA)

The EERA was organized to foster European collaboration in educational research and to provide independent advice on matters of educational research. It promotes communication between educational researchers and international governmental organizations and between research associations. EERA functions as an international network for educational researchers in Europe. This Web site is the EERA's communication link with the Internet.

[B4–24]   http://www.ex.ac.uk/library/uklibs.html
UK Higher Education and Research Libraries. University of Exeter

This Web site allows the visitor to access more than 150 higher education and research libraries in the United Kingdom. Although each library's Web site is unique, most permit access to their catalog. This Internet site is valuable for the researcher.

[B4–25]   http://www.fed.cuhk.edu.hk/~hkier/
Hong Kong Institute for Educational Research (HKIER). HKIER and The Chinese University of Hong Kong

HKIER is an independent educational research branch of the Chinese University of Hong Kong that is dedicated to being a central resource for fostering educational research. It conducts strategic research for educational development in China.

[B4–26]   http://www.fed.cuhk.edu.hk/~hkier/ (Note: Click on "The Chinese Educational Resources Information Centre Project")
The Chinese Educational Resources Information Centre Project (Chinese ERIC). HKIER and The Chinese University of Hong Kong

Endeavoring to emulate the U.S. ERIC system, the Chinese counterpart offers abstracts of journal articles in education that have been published in China or in Taiwan. Still in its developmental state, not all articles have been abstracted, albeit full abstracting service is the goal. Eventually, it is planned to include master's theses and doctoral dissertations in its collection. This project will become a central location for published information on Chinese education.

[B4–27]   http://www.heanet.ie/links/irish/highered.html
Irish Higher Education Resources. HEAnet

A visit to this Web site will bring to the visitor an explanation of the educational system in Ireland with special emphasis on higher education. Hyperlinks give access to the Web sites of individual universities in Ireland and to academic libraries, public libraries, the National Library, various archives in Ireland, and special collections. Also available from this Web site are scholarly societies and professional bodies.

[B4–28]   http://www.herdsa.org.au/
Higher Education Research and Development Society of Australasia (HERDSA)

This is the Web site of the leading organization in higher education in Australia and its neighboring countries. "Australasia" refers to Australia, New Zealand, and the South Pacific Islands. The membership of HERDSA is international, as it brings together teachers, administrators, researchers, and others in higher education. It promotes quality teaching in higher education and facilitates the exchange of research information on higher education. This Web site offers access to the profession of higher education in Australasia.

[B4–29]   http://www.hesa.ac.uk
Higher Education Statistics Agency (HESA). UK

This is the Web site of an independent organization that collects data on institutions of higher education in the United Kingdom. Its data embrace students, staff, and finances. This Web site offers a customized data inquiry service. HESA has a cooperative relationship with the Society for Research into Higher Education (UK) [See B4–54].

[B4–30]   http://www.hsv.se/english/addresses.html
Universities and Colleges in Sweden. The National Agency for Higher Education (Högskoleverket)

At this Web site the viewer will find a list of universities and colleges in Sweden with information on each, including access to each institution's Web site.

[B4–31]   http://www.ibe.unesco.org/Inf_Doc/Nat_reps/database.htm#databas
Databases on Education Systems. International Bureau of Education, UNESCO

This Web site is the gateway to information about educational systems throughout the world. It encompasses elementary, secondary, and higher education. Hyperlinks to the world of education are provided.

[B4–32]   http://www.ibe.unesco.org/Inf_Doc/Nat_reps/introde.htm
Web Resources. International Bureau of Education. UNESCO

Here is a comprehensive guide to worldwide research and information on education. Provides links to education sources on the Internet and to the social, cultural, and political context of education in individual nations.

**[B4–33]   http://www.ibe.unesco.org/Inf_Doc/Nat_reps/statist.htm#
education**
Statistics and Indicators. International Bureau of Education, UNESCO

A list of databases on the Internet that contain statistics on education in nations worldwide.

[B4–34]   http://www.ibe.unesco.org/Inf_Doc/Nat_reps/wdepfome.htm
World Data on Education. International Bureau of Education, UNESCO

The visitor to this site has access to concise descriptions of national education systems worldwide, preprimary through higher education. The viewer may select the theme, region, country, and keyword for the search. National profiles are based on reports that have been submitted by individual nations to the International Bureau of Education.

[B4–35]   http://www.israelemb.org/highered/highed.html
Higher Education in Israel. Embassy of Israel

Explains the history of Israel's higher education community and the mission of each institution of higher education. Also provides links to the Web sites of the separate universities.

[B4–36]   http://www.jyu.fi/ktl/index2.html
Institute for Educational Research, University of Jyväskylä, Finland

This is the Web site of the national center for educational research and evaluation at the University of Jyväskylä, in Finland. The scope of its activities encompasses the full spectrum of education. Its mission is national and international assessment and evaluation of education.

[B4–37]   http://www.leeds.ac.uk/bei/journals.htm
Journals Indexed by the *British Education Index*. British Education Index

At this Web site is to be found a bibliography of journals that are indexed by the *British Education Index*. The majority of these journal titles function as hyperlinks to their home pages, where the viewer usually can access the table of contents and, in some instances, the full text of the articles.

[B4–38]   http://www.mohe.gov.sa/english/enmohe.htm
Ministry of Higher Education, Saudi Arabia

The higher education system in Saudi Arabia is explained, and descriptive information on each of the seven universities is presented.

[B4–39]   http://www.mpib-berlin.mpg.de/Viere.htm
Max Planck Institute for Human Development

Located in Berlin and dedicated to the study of human development and educational processes, this multidisciplinary research institute's approach embraces educational science, psychology, and sociology. The institute has four research centers; namely, Adaptive Behavior and Cognition, Sociology and the Study of the Life Course, Educational Research, and Lifespan Psychology. The Center for Educational Research targets research on teaching and learning, large-scale assessment, adolescent cognitive and motivational development, and cultural comparisons.

[B4–40]   http://www.nier.go.jp/homepage/kyoutsuu/indexe.htm
National Institute for Educational Research of Japan

This is the governmental research institute in Japan that conducts basic and applied educational research. It serves as a major collecting and disseminating organization of educational information. The institute provides assistance to educators who are engaged in educational research.

[B4–41]   http://www.nzcer.org.nz/
New Zealand Council for Educational Research

This is an independent organization for the promotion and implementation of educational research in New Zealand. It functions as a service organization for educators and others who are interested in education by its engagement in educational research, dissemination of research-based information, and consulting services. The council's research addresses early childhood education, educational policy, educational measurement, research methodology, and more.

[B4–42]   http://www.oise.utoronto.ca/~mpress/canada.html
Canada-Wide Educational Organizations. Marian Press

This Web site gives access to the educational organizations and associations throughout Canada. They include organizations that focus on literacy, home-based education, special education, educational administration, young children, adult learning, institutional research, colleges and universities, and an extensive array of specialty groups.

[B4–43]   http://www.oise.utoronto.ca/~mpress/colleges.html
Community Colleges (Canada). Marian Press

This is the gateway to access the Web sites of Canadian community colleges that are independent of a university. These Web sites are listed by Canadian province. (Note: To access a community college in Canada that is affiliated with a university, go to B4–50.)

[B4–44]   http://www.oise.utoronto.ca/~mpress/commercial.html
Commercial Education Sites (Canada). Marian Press

Presented here are many Web sites of commercial establishments in Canada that are participants in the educational arena. These include publishers, educational television, consultants, tutoring centers, suppliers of teaching materials, and others.

[B4–45]   http://www.oise.utoronto.ca/~mpress/edboards.html
Boards of Education (Canada). Marian Press

Here is entrée to the school districts of Canada. Organized by Canadian province, there is an alphabetical list of the Web sites of the public and private school districts. Clicking on a selected district produces a potpourri of information on that district.

[B4–46]   http://www.oise.utoronto.ca/~mpress/faculties.html
Faculties of Education (Canada). Marian Press

This Web site facilitates communicating with the faculties in education in Canadian universities. Contains the names and contact information for education faculty at each university.

[B4–47]   http://www.oise.utoronto.ca/~mpress/journals.html
Education Journals (Canada). Marian Press

For access to Canadian journals in education, this Web site offers a bibliography of these publications. When clicking on the title of a journal, the viewer is presented with its contents.

[B4–48]   http://www.oise.utoronto.ca/~mpress/libraries.html
Education Libraries (Canada). Marian Press

Here is entrée to the education libraries in Canada. The Web sites of the libraries are presented here. Albeit each one is different, numerous ones offer access to the catalogs of their collections.

[B4–49]   http://www.oise.utoronto.ca/~mpress/schoolb.html
School Board Organizations (Canada). Marian Press

This is a directory of the public and Catholic school board organizations in Canada. The visitor to this site may access the Web sites of the different organizations. Also available are other professional education associations in Canada.

[B4–50]   http://www.oise.utoronto.ca/~mpress/universities.html
Universities and Colleges (Canada). Marian Press

Organized by Canadian province, the universities and colleges are listed. Click on the name of an institution of higher education and gain access to its Web site.

[B4–51]   http://www.scre.ac.uk/gateways/index.html
Information Gateways. The Scottish Council for Research in Education (SCRE)

SCRE maintains databases of educational research that has been conducted in Scotland. These databases are accessible for research via this Web site.

[B4–52]   http://www.scre.ac.uk/Homepage.html
The Scottish Council for Research in Education (SCRE)

The Scottish Council for Research in Education is a national, independent organization that provides educational research, evaluation, and training services in Scotland. It functions as a clearinghouse for educational research findings from throughout Scotland. SCRE is receptive to receiving inquiries concerning educational research.

[B4–53]   http://www.scre.ac.uk/is/webjournals.html
Education Journals and Newsletters Available on the Internet. The Scottish Council for Research in Education (SCRE)

Utilizing this Web site gives the visitor access to journals and newsletters in education from numerous countries. When clicking on a title, there is provided either the table of contents, the full text of selected articles, or the full text of the entire journal or newsletter.

[B4–54]   http://www.srhe.ac.uk/index.htm
Society for Research into Higher Education (UK)

This organization was established for the purpose of promoting research into higher education, with primary emphasis on the United Kingdom. It addresses the organization and management of institutions of higher education, policy issues, and matters of curriculum, teaching, and methods of learning. This Web site links to the Higher Education Statistics Agency of the United Kingdom (see B4–29) and other European organizations.

[B4–55]   http://www.srhe.ac.uk/index.htm (Note: Click on "HESA Statistics")
SRHE/HESA Liaison to Supply HESA Data. Society for Research into Higher Education (UK)

Working in collaboration with the Higher Education Statistics Agency of the United Kingdom, the Society for Research into Higher Education has subsets of data on higher education in the UK. Its database contains descriptive data on students, staff, and institutional finances. Access to these data is guarded. See this Web site for guidelines for accessing these data.

[B4–56]   http://www.srhe.ac.uk/index.htm (Note: Click on "SRHE Networks.")
SRHE Networks. Society for Research into Higher Education (UK)

Open to international members, SRHE sponsors discussion groups, known as Networks, that allow participants with common interests in a particular area of higher education to convene and pursue the subject matter of their interest. Examples of these topical areas include assessment, curriculum development, information specialists, statistical analyses of higher education, and student development. Educators outside the UK may participate.

[B4–57] http://www.statistics.gov.uk
National Statistics: The Official UK Statistics Site. National Statistics 2000

This Web site provides the official descriptive statistics of the United Kingdom, including all levels of education. To access "education," click on "themes" and then select "education."

[B4–58] http://www.ucas.ac.uk/figures/archive/index.html
Data Archive. Universities and Colleges Admissions Service (UK)

The Universities and Colleges Admissions Service is the central organization in the UK that processes applications for admission to full-time undergraduate programs. In the process, it collects descriptive data on applicants for admission. These statistics often complement those statistics assembled by the Higher Education Statistics Agency (See B4–29). Data tables are arranged by subject of study, age distribution, educational background and qualifications, social class, ethnicity, and other criteria.

[B4–59] http://www.webmaster.bham.ac.uk/ukcwww.html
U.K. Further Education, Higher Education, and University Colleges. JANET Users Group for Administration

This Web site offers a complete list of institutions of higher education in the UK below the university level. There is access to each institution's Web site.

[B4–60] http://www.webmaster.bham.ac.uk/ukuwww.html
U.K. Universities. JANET Users Group for Administration

This Web site offers a complete list of universities in the United Kingdom. By clicking on a university's name, access is gained to its Web site.

[B4–61] http://www.yok.gov.tr/indexeng.html
The Turkish Council of Higher Education

This Web site explains the history, governance, and current status of higher education in Turkey.

[B4–62] http://www.yok.gov.tr/webeng/edusys.html
The Turkish Education System. The Turkish Council of Higher Education

Provides a comprehensive review of the history of education in Turkey from before the Ottomans to the present time. This Web site also explains the educational system of today from preschool through higher education.

[B4–63]   http://www2.ncsu.edu/ncsu/aern/ABOUT.HTML
African Educational Research Network (AERN)

AERN is dedicated to educational development in Africa by building the research capacities of African universities. This organization is providing the leadership for the collaborative effort that is being exerted by numerous international organizations within and outside Africa. This Web site gives Internet access to AERN.

SECTION C

GUIDE TO PROFESSIONAL PUBLISHING

Melvyn N. Freed

CHAPTER 1

Journals in Education and Related Fields

INTRODUCTION

Essential to the research process is the dissemination of new knowledge. As Sir Isaac Newton proclaimed, "If I have seen far it is because I have stood on the shoulders of giants." This sagacious statement recognized that knowledge is evolutionary and cumulative. Information is of little value if it is not publicized.

Today, we have numerous means for disseminating knowledge. The journal is one instrument for communicating with the academic community. Faculty in higher education are, in part, motivated to publish because they function in the "publish or perish" academic culture. Their success in this endeavor is partially determined by their ability to select the right journal and convince the editor of the merit of their manuscript. This chapter is designed to assist would-be authors in their quest to become published.

There are certain guidelines that successful writers follow to enhance their opportunity to succeed in the publishing arena. One of the cardinal rules is to select a journal that is the right fit with the manuscript. Each journal has a purpose; therefore, an author must determine if the manuscript that is to be submitted complies with ("fits") the mission and editorial policy of the publication. Many professional journals have a limited focus and consider only themes that fall within a narrow range. An author should ascertain that scope *ante-factum* and screen the manuscript for appropriateness before submission.

Most journals receive far more submissions than they have space and time to publish. To enhance the competitiveness of one's manuscript, it should offer such a significant contribution to its subject that it merits the publication's space and financial resources. This is another preliminary *ante-factum* responsibility of the writer and requires professional objectivity in evaluating the importance of the manuscript before it is sent to a publisher.

Each journal publishes a limited number of issues annually; consequently, the writer should choose a journal that is published frequently enough to accommodate a reasonable number of articles per year. The larger the number of needed articles, the greater the opportunity to be accepted. With many authors competing for limited publishing space, the frequency of publication can be a critical factor in the "publish or perish" environment.

Each journal has established format guidelines, an acceptable manuscript length, the number of copies to be submitted, evaluative criteria, review procedures, and other publishing policies and rules. The writer should ascertain these matters in advance and consider them while preparing the manuscript. This can improve one's chance of being accepted.

Journals differ regarding the length of time that is taken to process a submission and the period of time between acceptance of a manuscript and publishing it. Also, there are varying policies as to whether a manuscript will be considered by one journal if it is concurrently being reviewed by another periodical. Finally, there are sundry practices concerning complimentary copies of the published article for the author.

To assist those in education who wish to publish in a professional journal, this chapter provides a list of selected journals, categorized by their principal fields of interest and followed by a profile of each journal's guidelines for authors. For some journals these guidelines are only a summary because the complete set of instructions is too lengthy for inclusion; however, information on how to obtain the full guidelines either is provided herein or may be obtained directly from the journal's editor. In some cases, these guidelines may be found in one or more issues of the journal or on the journal's Web site.

In this chapter, the reader should initially check the preferred field category to identify a journal and then turn to that publication's profile and guidelines. For more extensive lists of journals in education that do not include author guidelines, see *The Education Index* and *Current Index to Journals in Education*. For an international bibliography, see this book, Section B, Chapter 4, Web site profiles B4–37 and B4–53.

JOURNALS BY PUBLISHING FIELD

Adult and Continuing Education

> *Adult Learning*
> *Community College Journal*
> *Community College Journal of Research and Practice*
> *The Journal of Continuing Higher Education*

Child and Adolescent Development

> *Childhood Education*
> *Early Childhood Education Journal*
> *Early Childhood Research Quarterly*
> *Journal of Experimental Child Psychology*

Computers (see Educational Technology)

Counseling, Guidance, and School Psychology. (For college level, see Higher Education.)

> *The Clearing House*
> *Journal of Counseling and Development*
> *Journal of Counseling Psychology*
> *Journal of Multicultural Counseling and Development*
> *Measurement and Evaluation in Counseling and Development*
> *Professional School Counseling*
> *School Psychology Review*

Curriculum (Structure, content, and evaluation)

The Clearing House
College Composition and Communication
College Teaching
Community College Journal
Community College Journal of Research and Practice
Early Childhood Education Journal
Early Childhood Research Quarterly
Education and Training in Mental Retardation and Developmental Disabilities
Educational Administration Quarterly
Educational Evaluation and Policy Analysis
The Educational Forum
Educational Leadership
Journal of Adolescent and Adult Literacy
Journal of Chemical Education
Journal of Curriculum and Supervision
Journal of Curriculum Studies
Journal of Education for Business
Journal of Health Education
Journal of Higher Education
Journal of Literacy Research
Journal of Teacher Education
Language Arts
Liberal Education
Mathematics Teacher
Mathematics Teaching in the Middle School
The Reading Teacher
Research in Higher Education
Teaching Children Mathematics

Early Childhood Education

Childhood Education
Early Childhood Education Journal
Early Childhood Research Quarterly

Education General (All levels)

American Journal of Education
Childhood Education
Comparative Education Review
The Educational Forum
Harvard Educational Review
Journal of Law and Education

Journal of Negro Education
Phi Delta Kappan

Educational Administration (Elementary and Secondary Education: finance, community relations, personnel affairs, facilities, and other related matters)

American Journal of Education
American School and University
American School Board Journal
American Secondary Education
The Clearing House
Educational Administration Quarterly
Journal of Education Finance
Journal of Law and Education
NASSP Bulletin
Phi Delta Kappan

Educational Measurement and Testing

Applied Measurement in Education
The Clearing House
Educational and Psychological Measurement
Educational Assessment
Educational Evaluation and Policy Analysis
Journal of Educational Measurement
Measurement and Evaluation in Counseling and Development

Educational Psychology

Journal of Educational Psychology

Educational Research and Statistics (Research as a subject per se and potpourri of research in sundry areas. See also other field categories for research reported in subject journals)

American Educational Research Journal
Educational Assessment
Educational Evaluation and Policy Analysis
Educational Researcher
The Journal of Educational Research
Journal of Educational and Behavioral Statistics
The Journal of Experimental Education
Journal of Research in Childhood Education
Review of Educational Research

Educational Technology

The Clearing House
Computers in the Schools
Educational Technology
Educational Technology Review
Information Technology in Children's Education
International Journal of Education in Technology
Journal of Chemical Education
Journal of Computers in Mathematics and Science Teaching
Journal of Education in Multimedia and Hypermedia
Journal of Instruction Delivery Systems
Journal of Interactive Learning Research
Journal of Technology and Teacher Education
TechTrends, For Leaders in Education and Training

Elementary Education—General

American School Board Journal
Childhood Education

English (All topics. See also Curriculum; Methods of Teaching)

College Composition and Communication
College English
English Education
Language Arts

Finance (See Educational Administration; Higher Education)

Foundations of Education (History, Philosophy, and Sociology of Education)

American Journal of Education
Change: The Magazine of Higher Learning
The Clearing House
Community College Journal
Community College Journal of Research and Practice
Comparative Education Review
The Educational Forum
Harvard Educational Review
Liberal Education
Phi Delta Kappan

Higher Education (Administration, faculty affairs, and college student personnel services)

Academe: Bulletin of the AAUP
American School and University
Change: The Magazine of Higher Learning
College and University
College Planning and Management
College Student Affairs Journal
College Teaching
Community College Journal
Community College Journal of Research and Practice
Comparative Education Review
CUPA-HR Journal
Innovative Higher Education
The Journal of College Admission
Journal of College and University Law
Journal of College Student Development
The Journal of Continuing Higher Education
Journal of Counseling and Development
Journal of Counseling Psychology
Journal of Education Finance
Journal of Higher Education
Journal of Law and Education
Journal of Multicultural Counseling and Development
Measurement and Evaluation in Counseling and Development
NASPA Journal
Phi Delta Kappan
Planning for Higher Education
The Presidency
Research in Higher Education
Thought and Action
Trusteeship

In-Service Training

The Clearing House
English Education
Journal of Teacher Education

Mathematics (See also Curriculum; Methods of Teaching)

Mathematics Teacher
Mathematics Teaching in the Middle School
Teaching Children Mathematics

Methods of Teaching

Annals of Dyslexia
Change: The Magazine of Higher Learning
The Clearing House
College Composition and Communication
College Teaching
Computers in the Schools
Early Childhood Education Journal
Early Childhood Research Quarterly
Educational Leadership
Journal of Adolescent and Adult Literacy
Journal of Chemical Education
Journal of Computers in Mathematics and Science Teaching
Journal of Curriculum and Supervision
Journal of Curriculum Studies
Journal of Education for Business
Journal of Educational Psychology
Journal of Health Education
Journal of Instruction Delivery Systems
Journal of Interactive Learning Research
Journal of Literacy Research
Language Arts
Mathematics Teacher
Mathematics Teaching in the Middle School
The Reading Teacher
Research in Higher Education
Teaching Children Mathematics

Philosophy of Education (See Foundations of Education)

Physical Education, Health, and Recreation

Journal of Health Education
Research Quarterly for Exercise and Sport

Public Policy and School Legislation

American Journal of Education
The Clearing House
Educational Administration Quarterly
Educational Evaluation and Policy Analysis
The Educational Forum
Journal of Curriculum Studies

Journal of Law and Education
Phi Delta Kappan

Reading

Annals of Dyslexia
Childhood Education
Journal of Adolescent and Adult Literacy
Journal of Literacy Research
Reading Research Quarterly
The Reading Teacher

Secondary Education—General

American School Board Journal
American Secondary Education

Sociology of Education (See Foundations of Education)

Special Education (Gifted and Learning Disabled)

American Journal on Mental Retardation
Annals of Dyslexia
Behavioral Disorders
The Clearing House
Education and Training in Mental Retardation and Developmental
*   Disabilities*
Exceptional Children
Gifted Child Quarterly
Journal of Autism and Developmental Disorders
Journal of Learning Disabilities
Journal of Special Education
Journal of Speech, Language, and Hearing Research
Learning Disability Quarterly

Sports (See Physical Education, Health, and Recreation)

Teacher and Counselor Education

The Clearing House
Counselor Education and Supervision
Education and Training in Mental Retardation and Developmental
*   Disabilities*
English Education

Journal of Counseling and Development
Journal of Counseling Psychology
Journal of Curriculum Studies
Journal of Teacher Education
Journal of Technology and Teacher Education
Teaching Children Mathematics

JOURNAL GUIDELINES

Academe: Bulletin of the AAUP

American Association of University Professors
Suite 500
1012 14th Street, NW
Washington, DC 20005
(202) 737-5900
http://www.aaup.org

Publishable Topics: All topics of interest to college and university faculty are considered.
Publication Schedule: Bimonthly
Circulation: 45,000
Concurrent Submission to Other Journals: Permitted
Style Guide: The Chicago Manual of Style (14th edition)
Special Format Guidelines: Footnotes are not permitted.
Recommended Length: 2,000 words
Copies to Be Submitted: One
Electronic Submission: Permitted. Windows format required. Diskettes may be sent to the address cited above. E-mail submissions are allowed.
Review Procedure: Evaluate for appropriateness to readership, strength of topic and argument, style and writing ability, and availability of space in the journal.
Return of Rejections: No
Reason Given for Rejection: Yes
Time from Acceptance to Publication: Varies
Author's Complimentary Copies: Five
Miscellaneous Guidelines: For more detailed guidelines, request a copy of *Academe Editorial Guide.*
Send Manuscripts to: See current issue of the journal.

Adult Learning

American Association for Adult and Continuing Education
4380 Forbes Blvd.
Lanham, MD 20706
(301) 918-1913
Fax: (301) 918-1846

Publishable Topics: The primary purpose of this journal is to bridge the gap between research and practice in the field of adult and continuing education. The types of manuscripts that will be considered are applied research, literature reviews, descriptions of practice, perspectives, critical reviews of resources, descriptions of techniques, and discussions of current issues in the field of adult and continuing education.

Publication Schedule: Four times per year

Circulation: 3,500

Concurrent Submission to Other Journals: Not permitted

Style Guide: Publication Manual of the American Psychological Association (5th edition)

Special Format Guidelines: The name of the author(s) should not be placed on any of the pages of the manuscript. Enclose a separate identification page, which should contain the title of the manuscript, type of manuscript in terms of the types cited under "Publishable Topics," full name(s) of the author(s), position(s) held, affiliation(s), mailing address, telephone numbers of all the contributors, and statement of place and date of previous oral presentations of the manuscript, if any. See the journal's "Guidelines for Contributors" for more detailed instructions.

Recommended Length: Varies by type of article. Research, literature, practice, and perspectives manuscripts should be limited to 10–12 double-spaced pages. All other types of articles should be 4–6 double-spaced pages.

Copies to Be Submitted: Three

Electronic Submission: Not permitted

Review Procedure: Refereed using the blind review system. The evaluative criteria include the contribution of the manuscript to the improvement of practice or the understanding of practice in adult and continuing education, clarity, and the quality of research. The review process takes about three months.

Return of Rejections: Yes

Reason Given for Rejection: Yes

Time from Acceptance to Publication: Depends on the topic and if it relates to the themes that are to be published.

Author's Complimentary Copies: Two

Miscellaneous Guidelines: Submit a signed copy of the journal's "Copyright Release Statement," which is found in the journal's "Guidelines for Contributors."

Send Manuscripts to: See current issue of the journal.

American Educational Research Journal

American Educational Research Association
1230 17th Street, NW
Washington, DC 20036
(202) 223-9485
Fax: (202) 775-1824
http://www.aera.net

Publishable Topics: Features articles on state-of-the-art empirical and theoretical educational research regarding educational processes and outcomes. Interested in a broad range of studies in education.

Publication Schedule: Quarterly

Circulation: 19,000

Concurrent Submission to Other Journals: Not permitted

Style Guide: Publication Manual of the American Psychological Association (5th edition) or *The Chicago Manual of Style* (14th edition)

Special Format Guidelines: The first page should have the complete title of the article but not the name(s) of the author(s). On a separate sheet, type the full title of the article and the name(s) of the author(s). Include the address and telephone number of the first author listed. Use subheads at reasonable intervals. Minimize the use of footnotes; however, when they are used, type them on a separate page and number them consecutively throughout the manuscript. Only words that are to be in italics should be underlined. For more detailed guidelines, see "General Information for Contributors to AERA Journals," published in the journal.

Recommended Length: 20–50 double-spaced typewritten pages and include an abstract of 100–150 words.

Copies to Be Submitted: Five. Also, see next section on electronic submissions.

Electronic Submissions: Permitted. Once a manuscript has been accepted, a 3.5″ computer disk should be sent that contains all revisions. Prefers Wordperfect software; however, the journal can convert from RFT, Microsoft Word, and ASCII. Tables or figures on disk cannot be processed. For more detailed guidelines, see "General Information for Contributors to AERA Journals," published in the journal.

Review Procedure: Refereed using the blind review system. 3–4 months for the review decision.

Return of Rejections: Yes

Reason Given for Rejection: Yes

Time from Acceptance to Publication: At least three months

Author's Complimentary Copies: Five

Send Manuscripts to: See current issue of the journal.

American Journal of Education

University of Chicago Press
5835 S. Kimbark Avenue
Chicago, IL 60637
(773) 702-1555

Publishable Topics: Publishes empirical and theoretical articles on fundamental educational issues of policy and practice. AJE encourages research reports, philosophical arguments and theoretical statements about educational issues, critical syntheses of educational inquiry, and integration of educational policy and practice.

Publication Schedule: Quarterly

Circulation: 2,500

Concurrent Submission to Other Journals: Not permitted

Style Guide: The Chicago Manual of Style (14th edition)

Special Format Guidelines: Manuscripts are to be double-spaced throughout, including quotations, notes, and references. AJE is a reference-style journal, not a footnote-style journal. Footnotes are to be used only for substantive observations. They should be numbered consecutively and placed on a separate page titled "Notes." Only the title should appear on the manuscript with a separate cover page bearing the title of the article and the author's name and affiliation. Type each table on a separate page and refer to each in numerical order in the text. Do not use vertical lines, and place footnotes at the bottom of the table. Indicate footnotes with letters.

Recommended Length: 20–40 double-spaced pages and include an abstract containing a maximum of 100 words.

Copies to Be Submitted: Five

Electronic Submission: Not permitted

Review Procedure: Refereed using the blind review system. The evaluative criteria include the significance of the problem, originality, cogency of the method and argument, and the clarity of the presentation. The average length of time for a review decision is three months.

Return of Rejections: No

Reason Given for Rejection: Yes

Time from Acceptance to Publication: 14 months

Author's Complimentary Copies: 10. The author has the alternative choice of a year's free subscription to AJE.

Send Manuscripts to: See current issue of the journal.

American Journal on Mental Retardation

American Association on Mental Retardation
Suite 846
444 N. Capitol Street, NW
Washington, DC 20001
(800) 424-3688
(202) 387-1968
Fax: (202) 387-2193
http://www.aamr.org/Periodicals/periodicals.html

Publishable Topics: Publishes original scholarly contributions to the knowledge of the causes, treatment, and prevention of mental retardation.

Publication Schedule: Six issues per year

Circulation: 15,000

Concurrent Submission to Other Journals: Not permitted

Style Guide: Publication Manual of the American Psychological Association (5th edition)

Special Format Guidelines: See Web site cited above or "Information for Authors" in the journal.

Recommended Length: Maximum of 20 double-spaced pages

Copies to Be Submitted: Four

Electronic Submission: Not permitted for the original submission; however, after the manuscript has been accepted for publication, the final version should be submitted on a 3.5" IBM-compatible disk prepared in either WordPerfect 8.0, ASCII, or RTF.

Review Procedure: Refereed. Evaluated for scientific merit. The review process takes approximately three months.

Return of Rejections: No

Reason Given for Rejection: Yes
Time from Acceptance to Publication: Less than six months
Author's Complimentary Copies: None
Send Manuscripts to: See current issue of the journal.

American School and University
Intertec Publishing
9800 Metcalf Avenue
Overland Park, KS 66212
(913) 967-1960
Fax: (913) 967-1905
http://www.asumag.com

Publishable Topics: Since the readers are educational administrators in K–12 and higher education, articles should address problems that have been solved in some phase of educational administration, such as purchasing, building and grounds maintenance, facilities design, safety and security, accessibility for the handicapped, heating, ventilating, and air-conditioning (HVAC), and other related topics. Articles concerning computers should be limited to their application to school management.
Publication Schedule: Monthly
Circulation: 63,000
Concurrent Submission to Other Journals: Not permitted
Style Guide: Associated Press Stylebook
Recommended Length: 1,500 words
Copies to Be Submitted: One
Electronic Submission: Permitted. Submissions may be made electronically either by e-mail or faxed. After a manuscript has been accepted, it may be resubmitted on a 3.5" disk using Microsoft Word. (Note: For nonelectronic submissions, see last section of this periodical's profile.)
Review Procedure: Manuscripts are reviewed by editors, not refereed. The review decision can take up to one year.
Return of Rejections: Yes
Reason Given for Rejection: Yes
Time from Acceptance to Publication: Up to one year
Author's Complimentary Copies: Two
Miscellaneous Guidelines: Do not submit theses. If graphics are used, they must be of publishable quality, 8" by 10" maximum, and be of a glossy black and white. If color art is submitted, it should be on 35mm slides.
Send Manuscripts to: See current issue of the periodical.

American School Board Journal
National School Boards Association
1680 Duke Street
Alexandria, VA 22314
(703) 838-6722

Fax: (703) 549-6719

http://www.asbj.com

Publishable Topics: Publishes articles on school governance and administration. Also includes articles on public involvement, school operations, student achievement, case studies, and how-to topics.

Publication Schedule: Monthly

Circulation: 41,000

Concurrent Submission to Other Journals: Not permitted

Style Guide: No particular guide is required; however, writers' guidelines are available at the Web site given above or by fax.

Recommended Length: 1,500–2,500 words

Copies to Be Submitted: One

Electronic Submission: Permitted. May be submitted on a 3.5" disk or by e-mail to editor@electronic-school.com.

Review Procedure: Reviewed by editors, not refereed. Evaluated for appropriateness for readers, originality, and clarity. The review process takes about six weeks.

Return of Rejections: No

Reason Given for Rejection: No

Time from Acceptance to Publication: Eight weeks

Author's Complimentary Copies: Three

Send Manuscripts to: The editor at the address cited above.

American Secondary Education

Ashland University

401 College Avenue

Ashland, OH 44805

(419) 289-5273

Fax: (419) 289-5097

Publishable Topics: Invites articles pertaining to current theories, research, and practice in the field of secondary education and its administration.

Publication Schedule: Quarterly (fall, winter, spring, summer)

Circulation: 550

Concurrent Submission to Other Journals: Not permitted

Style Guide: The Publication Manual of the American Psychological Association (5th edition)

Special Format Guidelines: Original manuscripts must be typed on one side of firm paper and have margins of at least one inch. The entire manuscript (including footnotes, references, and tables) must be double-spaced. When employed, headings and subheadings should be consistent. Indentations or other special arrangements of the text should be clearly indicated.

Recommended Length: 10–30 pages, including a 100-word abstract

Copies to Be Submitted: Three

Electronic Submission: Permitted. After a manuscript has been accepted, a disk is required that is formatted with WordPerfect 6+.

Review Procedure: Blind manuscripts are submitted to two reviewers for evaluation with regard to content, organization, style of writing, mechanics, relevance to secondary education and administration, and currency of the bibliography. The editor reserves the right to make any editorial changes in the manuscript to achieve greater clarity. A decision on the acceptability of the manuscript will be made within 2 to 3 months.

Return of Rejections: Yes, if stamped and self-addressed return envelope is provided.

Reason Given for Rejection: Yes

Time from Acceptance to Publication: Six to nine months

Author's Complimentary Copies: Yes

Miscellaneous Guidelines: Include the author's educational affiliation, academic title, and/or qualifications or experiences related to the manuscript.

Send Manuscripts to: The editor at the address cited above.

Annals of Dyslexia

The International Dyslexia Association
Suite 382
Chester Building
8600 LaSalle Road
Baltimore, MD 21286
(410) 296-0232
Fax: (410) 321-5069
http://www.interdys.org

Publishable Topics: Dyslexia and related learning disabilities (i.e., reading, writing, spelling, handwriting, and others). Although this journal is primarily interested in original research papers, it also publishes significant reviews and documented reports of effective practices.

Publication Schedule: Annually

Circulation: 13,500

Concurrent Submission to Other Journals: Not permitted

Style Guide: The Publication Manual of the American Psychological Association (5th edition)

Special Format Guidelines: See "Guidelines for Contributors" in this journal.

Recommended Length: Not to exceed 35 double-spaced pages in 12-point font, including tables, figures, and reference lists. Also, provide an abstract of the paper with a maximum of 200 words.

Copies to Be Submitted: Five by January 10 for full consideration.

Electronic Submissions: Not permitted. If the manuscript is accepted for publication, a request will then be made for a copy of the computer disk containing the manuscript.

Review Procedure: Manuscripts are reviewed by the editor and at least two other qualified reviewers on the topic. Evaluation is based on the manuscript's value to the journal's readership, the specific contribution within the paradigm of focus, the validity of the methodology and the competence demonstrated in interpreting the results, and the organization and clarity of the writing. The initial review process is normally concluded within three months.

Return of Rejections: Yes

Reason Given for Rejection: Yes

Time from Acceptance to Publication: Because this is an annual publication, the time interval to publication depends on when the manuscript is submitted.

Author's Complimentary Copies: 12 copies of the article, not the journal.

Miscellaneous Guidelines: Do not staple the manuscript. Provide a self-addressed and stamped envelope for journal's acknowledgment of receipt of the manuscript.

Send Manuscripts to: See current issue of the journal.

Applied Measurement in Education

The Oscar and Luella Buros Center for Testing

135 Bancroft Hall

University of Nebraska-Lincoln

Lincoln, NE 68588-0352

(402) 472-6203

Fax: (402) 472-6207

http://www.unl.edu/buros

Publishable Topics: This journal focuses on issues in educational measurement and ways to improve measurement techniques in education. As such, it seeks manuscripts that report on original applied educational and psychological measurement research that enhances the educational process. Additionally, invites articles that report on innovative strategies for solving educational measurement problems. Comparative reviews of tests are also published.

Publication Schedule: Quarterly

Concurrent Submission to Other Journals: Not permitted

Style Guide: The Publication Manual of the American Psychological Association (5th edition)

Special Format Guidelines: See "Instructions for Contributors" in the journal.

Recommended Length: No requirements. Include an abstract of 100–175 words.

Copies to Be Submitted: Four

Electronic Submission: Not permitted

Review Procedure: Refereed. Decision to accept or reject takes four to six weeks.

Return of Rejections: No

Reason Given for Rejection: Yes

Time from Acceptance to Publication: Depends on the production schedule.

Author's Complimentary Copies: One

Send Manuscripts to: See current issue of the journal.

Behavioral Disorders

Council for Children with Behavioral Disorders

1920 Association Drive

Reston, VA 20191
(703) 620-3660

Publishable Topics: Primarily research-oriented articles on the education and therapy of BD and ED children and youth.
Publication Schedule: Quarterly
Circulation: 9,000
Concurrent Submission to Other Journals: Not permitted
Style Guide: Publication Manual of the American Psychological Association (5th edition)
Recommended Length: 15–20 double-spaced pages
Copies to Be Submitted: Five
Electronic Submission: Not permitted
Review Procedure: Refereed. Evaluative criteria include originality, relevance, importance of findings, organization of the manuscript, documentation, style of writing, compliance with APA format, and the adequacy of the research. The review process takes three months.
Return of Rejections: No
Reason Given for Rejection: Yes
Time from Acceptance to Publication: 4 to 12 months
Author's Complimentary Copies: One
Send Manuscripts to: See current issue of the journal.

Change: The Magazine of Higher Learning

Heldref Publications
1319 18th Street, NW
Washington, DC 20036-1802
(202) 296-6267
http://www.heldref.org

Publishable Topics: Articles focus on contemporary issues in higher education. They feature trendsetting institutions and individuals, innovative teaching methods, economics and finance, public policy, professional development, educational philosophy, administrative practices and governance, and the social role of higher education.
Publication Schedule: Bimonthly
Circulation: 18,000
Concurrent Submission to Other Journals: Permitted; however, it is discouraged and decreases the chance of acceptance.
Style Guide: The Chicago Manual of Style (14th edition)
Special Format Guidelines: Do not use footnotes. References should be either worked into the text or cited parenthetically. Include a separate title page that includes a brief biographical sketch for each author that does not exceed five lines. Also, on the title page report contact information for the author(s). For figures and illustrations, provide a legend that is typed on pages that follow the last page of text.
Recommended Length: 1,000–5,000 words
Copies to Be Submitted: Two

Electronic Submission: Permitted. Submit on 3.5" disk, preferably using Microsoft Word. If making an electronic submission, a printout copy is not required.

Review Procedure: Refereed. Evaluative criteria include breadth of appeal/usefulness to administrators in higher education, timeliness, and clarity. No educational research or statistical research unless it is treated in a magazine-article fashion. The review process usually takes three to four months.

Return of Rejections: Yes

Reason Given for Rejection: Yes

Time from Acceptance to Publication: Two to four months

Author's Complimentary Copies: Six

Miscellaneous Guidelines: Change is a magazine, not a journal. Its readers are primarily higher education administrators. Before submitting a manuscript, peruse a copy of the magazine to ascertain its style.

Send Manuscripts to: See current issue of the magazine.

Childhood Education

Association for Childhood Education International
Suite 215
17904 Georgia Avenue
Olney, MD 20832
(301) 570-2111
http://www.acei.org

Publishable Topics: Articles address a broad range of topics on the well-being of children from infancy through early adolescence. Includes articles on innovative practices in the classroom and other settings, significant findings in educational research, accounts of important issues and events that affect children, and other related topics.

Publication Schedule: Six issues per year

Circulation: 12,000

Concurrent Submission to Other Journals: Not permitted

Style Guide: Publication Manual of the American Psychological Association (5th edition)

Special Format Guidelines: Send for "Guidelines for Authors," which includes the Copyright Transfer Agreement that must be signed.

Recommended Length: 5 to 15 double-spaced pages

Copies to Be Submitted: One original plus three copies without the author's name and identifying information.

Electronic Submission: Not permitted

Review Procedure: Refereed. Evaluative criteria include appropriateness for the journal, extent to which the manuscript stimulates thinking about issues related to the well-being of children, degree to which it enhances effective teaching practices, clarity, and adequacy of theoretical base. The review process takes three months.

Return of Rejections: Yes, if a self-addressed and stamped envelope is provided.

Reason Given for Rejection: Sometimes

Time from Acceptance to Publication: One year

Author's Complimentary Copies: Five

Miscellaneous Guidelines: Send only completed manuscripts, not proposals or outlines.

Send Manuscripts to: See current issue of the journal.

The Clearing House

Heldref Publications
1319 18th Street, NW
Washington, DC 20036-1802
(202) 296-6267
Fax: (202) 296-5149
http://www.heldref.org

Publishable Topics: Consideration is given to manuscripts of interest to middle-level and high school teachers and administrators on such topics as curriculum, instructional techniques, teaching with computers, testing and measurement, guidance and counseling, educational trends and philosophy, instructional leadership, school law, community involvement, discipline, gifted and talented programs, education of the handicapped, educational climate, and international programs.

Publication Schedule: Six times per year

Circulation: 3,000

Concurrent Submission to Other Journals: Not permitted. Potential contributors must express in writing that their manuscripts are sole submissions.

Style Guide: The Chicago Manual of Style (14th edition)

Special Format Guidelines: Explanatory notes should be avoided whenever possible by including their content in the text. Essential notes should be identified with consecutive superscripts and listed in a "Notes" section at the end of the text. List references alphabetically at the end of the manuscript. In the text, reference citations should be in parentheses (author, date) or (date).

Recommended Length: Approximately 2,500 words of double-spaced text.

Copies to Be Submitted: Two

Electronic Submission: Not permitted

Review Procedure: Refereed. Review procedure takes three to four months.

Return of Rejections: Yes

Reason Given for Rejection: Yes

Time from Acceptance to Publication: Within six months

Author's Complimentary Copies: Two

Send Manuscripts to: See current issue of the journal.

College and University

American Association of Collegiate Registrars
and Admissions Officers (AACRAO)
Suite 520
One Dupont Circle, NW
Washington, DC 20036
(202) 293-9161
Fax: (202) 872-8857

http://www.aacrao.org

Publishable Topics: Consideration is given to manuscripts that are of interest to higher education administrators. Topics should pertain to admissions, financial aid, records, registration, institutional research, and other closely related functions in colleges and universities.

Publication Schedule: Quarterly

Circulation: 9,500

Concurrent Submission to Other Journals: Not permitted

Style Guide: The Chicago Manual of Style (14th edition)

Special Format Guidelines: Exclude the author's name from any text page. Provide a cover sheet with the manuscript's title and the author's name, address, phone and fax numbers, and e-mail address. For further instructions, see "Instructions to Authors" in a current issue of this journal.

Recommended Length: 4,500 words; however, book reviews and commentaries should not exceed 2,000 words.

Copies to Be Submitted: Two

Electronic Submission: Required. Submit an IBM-compatible disk, preferably in Microsoft Word. Also send a hard copy on 8.5" x 11" white paper.

Review Procedure: Refereed. Evaluative criteria include usefulness of the information, appropriateness of the manuscript to AACRAO's members, validity of the research methodology, and clarity of writing. The review process may take three months.

Return of Rejections: Yes, if requested

Reason Given for Rejection: Not usually

Time from Acceptance to Publication: Six months

Author's Complimentary Copies: Four

Send Manuscripts to: See current issue of the journal.

College Composition and Communication

The National Council of Teachers of English
1111 Kenyon Road
Urbana, IL 61801
(217) 328-3870
http://www.ncte.org/ccc/

Publishable Topics: Invites manuscripts that address the theory, practice, and history of composition and its teaching at all college levels. Articles also focus on the processes of writing and research, the preparation of teachers of writing, and the relationship of literature, language studies, rhetoric, and other fields to composition and its teaching.

Publication Schedule: Quarterly

Circulation: 10,000

Concurrent Submission to Other Journals: Not permitted

Style Guide: MLA Style Manual and Guide to Scholarly Publishing (2nd edition)

Special Format Guidelines: Do not include author's name on the title page or on the first page of the manuscript. On a separate sheet provide name, address, phone number, and e-mail address.

Recommended Length: 4,000–7,000 words; however, shorter or longer articles may be accepted.

Copies to Be Submitted: Three copies and postage for mailing to two outside readers.

Electronic Submission: Permitted. Send by e-mail as an attachment, preferably in RTF.

Review Procedure: Refereed. Review time may require up to 16 weeks.

Return of Rejections: Yes, if a self-addressed and stamped envelope is provided

Reason Given for Rejection: Yes

Time from Acceptance to Publication: Less than a year

Author's Complimentary Copies: Two

Send Manuscripts to: See current issue of the journal.

College English

The National Council of Teachers of English
1111 Kenyon Road
Urbana, IL 61801
(217) 328-3870
http://www.ncte.org/ce/

Publishable Topics: Focuses on the interests of college English teachers in the subjects of literature (including nonfiction), literacy, linguistics, critical theory, rhetoric, reading theory, composition, pedagogy, and professional issues.

Publication Schedule: Bimonthly (September, November, January, March, May, July)

Circulation: 16,000

Concurrent Submission to Other Journals: Not permitted

Style Guide: MLA Style Manual and Guide to Scholarly Publishing (2nd edition)

Special Format Guidelines: Manuscripts should be free of internal references to the author's identity. Place author's name only on the letter of transmittal. Avoid footnotes in the manuscript. Use parenthetical references and a Works Cited list.

Recommended Length: Up to 30 double-spaced pages

Copies to Be Submitted: Two printed copies along with three unaddressed manuscript-size envelopes and adequate unattached postage for mailing to two referees.

Electronic Submission: Not permitted for original submission. After acceptance, a copy of the manuscript on a disk will be required using either WordPerfect or Microsoft Word.

Review Procedure: Refereed using the blind review system. The review process takes up to 16 weeks.

Return of Rejections: No

Reason Given for Rejection: Yes

Author's Complimentary Copies: Two

Send Manuscripts to: See current issue of the journal.

College Planning and Management

Peter Li Education Group
330 Progress Road
Dayton, OH 45449

(937) 847-5900
Fax: (937) 847-5910
http://www.cpmmag.com

Publishable Topics: Articles address the construction, facilities, purchasing, physical maintenance, and technology information needs of college and university administrators. The journal's purpose is to provide solutions to operational and management issues. Prefers manuscripts that are "how-to"-oriented (i.e., those that offer practical solutions).

Publication Schedule: Monthly

Circulation: 30,000

Concurrent Submission to Other Journals: Not permitted

Style Guide: Associated Press Style Book

Special Format Guidelines: Manuscripts are to be typed double-spaced and should report the word count at the top of the first page.

Recommended Length: 1,000–1,500 words

Copies to Be Submitted: One

Electronic Submission: Permitted. Submit on a disk, preferably using Microsoft Word; however, other word-processing software is acceptable.

Review Procedure: This is not a refereed journal. A manuscript is evaluated for its theme, style, and the contribution that it makes to the needs of the journal's readers.

Return of Rejections: No

Reason Given for Rejection: No

Time from Acceptance to Publication: Three months

Author's Complimentary Copies: Two

Send Manuscripts to: See current issue of the journal.

College Student Affairs Journal

Southern Association of College Student Affairs
Robert Bowman, Editor
College of Education
Northwestern State University
Natchitoches, LA 71497
(318) 357-6289
Fax: (318) 357-6275

Publishable Topics: Dedicated to serving the practitioner in college student affairs work. Invites manuscripts that focus on concepts, practices, and research in the field. Research-based submissions are welcome contingent on their value to the practitioner in the field of college student affairs. "How-to" articles, updates on professional issues, briefs on campus programs, perusals of legislative issues, and literature reviews are published.

Publication Schedule: Twice a year

Circulation: 1,500

Concurrent Submission to Other Journals: Not permitted

Style Guide: Publication Manual of the American Psychological Association (5th edition)

Special Format Guidelines: The author's name, position, and institutional affiliation should appear on a separate title page. The manuscript's title should be placed on the first text page without the author's name.

Recommended Length: A maximum of 18 double-spaced pages including an abstract, tables, and references.

Copies to Be Submitted: Four

Electronic Submission: Not permitted

Review Procedure: Refereed. Evaluative criteria include significance of the subject, usefulness to practitioners in the field of college student affairs, quality of methodology or program, and clarity and style of writing. The review process usually takes about eight weeks.

Return of Rejections: Yes

Reason Given for Rejection: Yes

Time from Acceptance to Publication: Six months to a year

Author's Complimentary Copies: One per author

Send Manuscripts to: See current issue of the journal.

College Teaching

Heldref Publications
1319 18th Street, NW
Washington, DC 20036
(202) 296-6267
Fax: (202) 296-5149
http://www.heldref.org

Publishable Topics: Articles address issues related to teaching at the undergraduate and graduate levels in college. Prefers manuscripts that pertain to teaching techniques at the college level, research and reviews of research, new classroom procedures, evaluation of innovative programs, and professional development and evaluation of college teachers.

Publication Schedule: Quarterly

Circulation: 2,200

Concurrent Submission to Other Journals: Not permitted

Style Guide: The Chicago Manual of Style (14th edition)

Special Format Guidelines: Avoid explanatory notes whenever possible by incorporating their content in the text. Identify essential notes with consecutive superscripts and list them in a "Notes" section at the end of the text. List references alphabetically at the end of the manuscript.

Recommended Length: Articles, 1,000–5,000 words; editorials, up to 850 words

Copies to Be Submitted: Two

Electronic Submission: Not permitted

Review Procedure: Refereed. Evaluative criteria include whether the subject comes within the scope of the journal, timeliness, multidisciplinarity, awareness of current developments in the field, adequacy of documentation, and clarity. The review process takes two months.

Return of Rejections: Yes

Reason Given for Rejection: Yes
Time from Acceptance to Publication: Up to one year; however, often sooner
Author's Complimentary Copies: Two
Send Manuscripts to: See current issue of the journal.

Community College Journal

American Association of Community Colleges
Suite 410
One Dupont Circle, NW
Washington, DC 20036
(202) 728-0200
Fax: (202) 223-9390
http://www.aacc.nche.edu

Publishable Topics: Devoted exclusively to the interests of community-based, two-year college education. Articles relate to exemplary programs, practices, and policies. Manuscripts must focus on one or more of the areas within the journal's published editorial calendar. Authors may write for a copy of the calendar and subjects designated for each issue of the journal.
Publication Schedule: Bimonthly
Circulation: 11,000
Concurrent Submission to Other Journals: Permitted
Style Guide: The Chicago Manual of Style (14th edition)
Recommended Length: 1,800–2,000 words. Larger manuscripts will be rejected.
Copies to Be Submitted: One
Electronic Submission: Permitted. Submit PC-formatted disk using MS Word or WordPerfect. May elect to send by e-mail.
Review Procedure: Evaluative criteria include appropriateness of the subject matter, adherence to guidelines, and clarity of writing. The review process may take several months.
Return of Rejections: Yes. Send a self-addressed and stamped envelope.
Reason Given for Rejection: No
Time from Acceptance to Publication: Three months
Author's Complimentary Copies: Three
Miscellaneous Guidelines: Include author's biographical information and photograph. When submitting a manuscript, seriously consider including visuals that will enhance the article and improve the opportunity to be published.
Send Manuscripts to: See current issue of the journal.

Community College Journal of Research and Practice

Taylor and Francis, Inc.
Suite 800
325 Chestnut Street
Philadelphia, PA 19106

(800) 354-1420

Fax: (215) 625-8914

http://www.tandf.co.uk/journals/default.html

Publishable Topics: This journal is international in scope and purpose as it publishes origi-nal research manuscripts that focus on any and all topics pertinent to community col-leges and community college education. Its articles address the interests of community college teachers, administrators, counselors, researchers, and others in the higher education community whose interests are in the community college.

Publication Schedule: 10 issues per year

Circulation: 1,300

Concurrent Submission to Other Journals: Not permitted

Style Guide: Publication Manual of the American Psychological Association (5th edition)

Special Format Guidelines: Manuscripts should end with a section on "Implications for Practice" that explains the meaning and implications of the research findings to practi-tioners in community college education and offers recommendations, based on the re-search results, for change.

Recommended Length: 15–20 double-spaced pages. Include an abstract of no longer than 250 words.

Copies to Be Submitted: Three

Electronic Submission: Permitted. Submissions may be sent via PC disk, attachments to e-mail, or fax.

Review Procedure: Refereed. The evaluative criteria include relevance of the topic, con-sistency of the manuscript with the related literature, validity of the methodology, and clarity of the writing. The review process takes approximately three weeks.

Return of Rejections: No

Reason Given for Rejection: Yes

Time from Acceptance to Publication: Six months

Author's Complimentary Copies: Three

Send Manuscripts to: See current issue of the journal.

Comparative Education Review

Comparative and International Education Society

Graduate School of Education & Information Studies

University of California, Los Angeles

Box 951521

Moore Hall, A-036

Los Angeles, CA 90095

(310) 206-6203

http://www.journals.uchicago.edu/CER/

Publishable Topics: Specializes in international and comparative education. Articles ad-dress the various educational systems in individual countries and the political, social, and economic forces that shape education.

Publication Schedule: Quarterly

Circulation: 2,500+

Concurrent Submission to Other Journals: Not permitted

Style Guide: The Chicago Manual of Style (14th edition)

Special Format Guidelines: The cover page should include the author's name, institutional affiliation, address, telephone and fax numbers, e-mail address, and social security number. The second page should contain the abstract with no more than 150 words. Place the manuscript's title on the third page and do not place the author's name on this page.

Recommended Length: A maximum of 40 pages.

Copies to Be Submitted: Four

Electronic Submission: Not permitted

Review Procedure: Refereed. The evaluative criteria include relevance of the manuscript to comparative or international education, use of an explicit conceptual framework, an adequate review of the related literature, originality in method and analysis, appropriateness of the methodology, the degree of contribution to the field of knowledge, and clarity of the writing. The review process takes approximately three months.

Return of Rejections: Yes, if requested and a self-addressed and stamped envelope has been provided by the author.

Reason Given for Rejection: Yes

Time from Acceptance to Publication: 9 to 12 months

Author's Complimentary Copies: Five

Send Manuscripts to: See current issue of the journal.

Computers in the Schools

Haworth Press, Inc.

10 Alice Street

Binghamton, NY 13904

(800) 429-6784

(717) 459-5933

Fax: (717) 459-5934

http://www.haworthpressinc.com

Publishable Topics: Dedicated to articles that discuss the use of computers in the classroom. This is an interdisciplinary journal of practice, theory, and applied research.

Publication Schedule: Quarterly

Circulation: 2,000

Concurrent Submission to Other Journals: Not permitted

Style Guide: Publication Manual of the American Psychological Association (5th edition)

Special Format Guidelines: See the journal's "Instructions for Authors."

Recommended Length: 10–20 pages

Copies to Be Submitted: Four. Also send a 9" x 11" envelope that is self-addressed and with sufficient postage for the return of the manuscript if it is not accepted. Provide a second self-addressed and stamped envelope for use by the editor to acknowledge receipt of the manuscript.

Electronic Submission: Permitted

Review Procedure: Refereed. The evaluative criteria include the contribution of the manuscript to knowledge in the field and the clarity of the writing. The review process takes approximately six months.

Return of Rejections: Yes

Reason Given for Rejection: Yes

Time from Acceptance to Publication: Six months

Author's Complimentary Copies: Two copies of the journal and 25 copies of the article.

Send Manuscripts to: See current issue of the journal.

Counselor Education and Supervision

American Counseling Association
5999 Stevenson Avenue
Alexandria, VA 22304
(703) 823-9800
http://www.counseling.org

Publishable Topics: Invites articles that are concerned with research, theory, development, or program applications pertinent to counselor education or supervision. The journal addresses matters relevant to the preparation or supervision of counselors in agency and school settings, colleges, and universities or at local, state, and federal levels.

Publication Schedule: Quarterly

Circulation: 3,600

Concurrent Submission to Other Journals: Not permitted

Style Guide: Publication Manual of the American Psychological Association (5th edition)

Special Format Guidelines: See "Guidelines for Authors" in the journal.

Recommended Length: Not to exceed 18 double-spaced pages. Provide an abstract of 50–100 words.

Copies to Be Submitted: Four

Electronic Submission: Not permitted until after the manuscript has been accepted. Then submit the final version on a 3.5" diskette, preferably using WordPerfect or MS Word for Windows. Will accept IBM ASCII or MacIntosh Text file format. Files must be in Times Roman font, point size 12. The disk should have placed on it a label that records the author's name and the hardware and software that were used to produce the disk.

Review Procedure: Refereed using the blind review system. The review process takes two months.

Return of Rejections: No

Reason Given for Rejection: Yes

Time from Acceptance to Publication: Six months

Author's Complimentary Copies: One for each author

Miscellaneous Guidelines: A cover letter that accompanies the manuscript should indicate for which of the following categories of the journal the manuscript is intended: (1) Counselor Preparation, (2) Supervision, (3) Professional Development, (4) Current Issues, (5) Special Sections, (6) Innovative Methods, (7) Book and Media Reviews, or (8) Comments. "Guidelines for Authors" in the journal defines each of these categories.

Send Manuscripts to: See current issue of the journal.

CUPA-HR Journal
College and University Professional Association for Human Resources
Suite 301
1233 20th Street, NW
Washington, DC 20036
(202) 429-0133
Fax: (202) 429-0149
http://www.cupahr.org/callsfor/callfor.htm

Publishable Topics: Features articles that report on nonfaculty human resource management in higher education. Among the topics included are human resource management trends, innovative personnel policies and practices, employment law, compensation, labor relations, human resource management research, and analyses of legislative/governmental developments that pertain to human resource management in higher education.
Publication Schedule: Semiannually
Circulation: 1,200
Concurrent Submission to Other Journals: Not permitted
Style Guide: The Chicago Manual of Style (14th edition)
Special Format Guidelines: Manuscripts should not include footnotes. Enclose a cover letter with the manuscript that provides the author's name, address, telephone number, and e-mail address. Send a one-paragraph biography of the author.
Recommended Length: 1,500–3,500 words
Copies to Be Submitted: Three
Electronic Submission: Permitted. Provide a 3.5" IBM-compatible disk using MS Word. Three hard copies should accompany the disk.
Review Procedure: Refereed using the blind review system. Evaluative criteria include relevance of the manuscript to human resource personnel in higher education, the extent to which statements are supported by facts, and clarity of expression. The review process takes two months.
Return of Rejections: No
Reason Given for Rejection: Yes
Time from Acceptance to Publication: Up to one year
Author's Complimentary Copies: Two
Send Manuscripts to: See current issue of the journal.

Early Childhood Education Journal
Kluwer Academic/Human Sciences Press
233 Spring Street
New York, NY 10013
(212) 620-8000
Fax: (212) 463-0742
http://www.wkap.com

Publishable Topics: Dedicated to reporting exemplary practices in early childhood education. Seeks manuscripts that combine theory, research, and practice. This journal embraces the social, emotional, intellectual, and physical development of children from birth through age eight. Reports descriptions of early childhood education programs and case studies of young children.

Publication Schedule: Quarterly

Concurrent Submission to Other Journals: Not permitted

Style Guide: Publication Manual of the American Psychological Association (5th edition)

Special Format Guidelines: See "Guidelines for Contributors" in a current issue of the journal. Accompanying the manuscript should be a cover page that contains the author's name, address, telephone number, and e-mail address. Do not place any of this information on any other part of the manuscript. In the upper right-hand corner of each page of the manuscript type an abbreviated version of the article's title. Also, provide an abstract not to exceed 150 words. Below the abstract type four or five key words that summarize the content and that can be used for indexing. All pages should be typed double-spaced and only left-justified.

Recommended Length: 6–15 double-spaced pages

Copies to Be Submitted: Three complete copies, including cover sheet, abstract, text, references, and artwork. Also provide a 9" x 12" self-addressed envelope. Paper-clip $3.50 postage to the envelope. Do not use metered envelopes.

Electronic Submission: Not permitted for the initial submission; however, after a manuscript has been accepted and all revisions as required by the editor have been made, the final version of the manuscript should be submitted on a disk that is labeled with the software used, journal's name, and author's last name. A hard copy of the final version must accompany the electronic file on disk.

Review Procedure: Blind peer review. The review process usually takes 12–16 weeks.

Return of Rejections: Yes

Reason Given for Rejection: Yes

Time from Acceptance to Publication: Up to one year

Author's Complimentary Copies: Authors may purchase reprints of their articles.

Send Manuscript to: See current issue of the journal.

Early Childhood Research Quarterly

National Association for the Education of Young Children (Sponsor)
Elsevier Science (Publisher)
655 Avenue of the Americas
P.O. Box 945
New York, NY 10159
(888) 437-4636
http://www.udel.edu/ecrq

Publishable Topics: Significant research and scholarship related to the care and education of children from birth to age eight. Prefers articles that address the application and practice of working with young children. Accepts a wide range of related topics.

Publication Schedule: Quarterly

Circulation: 1,500

Concurrent Submission to Other Journals: Not permitted

Style Guide: Publication Manual of the American Psychological Association (5th edition)

Special Format Guidelines: The first page should contain the title of the manuscript; author's name, affiliation, address, telephone number, and e-mail address; and a short form of the title (less than 55 letters and spaces). The second page should contain a brief abstract (100–150 words for a report of an empirical study; 75–100 words for a review or a theoretical article). Complete author information is available at the Web site cited above and in a recent issue of the journal.

Recommended Length: 10–30 double-spaced pages

Copies to Be Submitted: Four

Electronic Submission: Not permitted

Review Procedure: Refereed using the blind review system

Return of Rejections: Only if requested by the author and a self-addressed and stamped envelope has been provided.

Reason Given for Rejection: Yes

Time from Acceptance to Publication: Six to seven months

Author's Complimentary Copies: One. If more are desired, reprints must be ordered when the page proofs are returned to the publisher.

Send Manuscripts to: See current issue of the journal.

Education and Training in Mental Retardation and Developmental Disabilities

Council for Exceptional Children
1110 N. Glebe Road
Arlington, VA 22201
(800) 224-6830

Publishable Topics: Seeks research and expository manuscripts and critical reviews of the literature pertaining to the education and training of the mentally retarded and those with developmental disabilities. Major emphasis is on identification and assessment, educational programming, training of instructional personnel, habilitation, prevention, community understanding and provisions, and related legislation.

Publication Schedule: Quarterly

Circulation: 9,000

Concurrent Submission to Other Journals: Not permitted

Style Guide: Publication Manual of the American Psychological Association (5th edition)

Special Format Guidelines: The cover page should provide the names and affiliations of all authors and their addresses and telephone numbers. Graphs and figures should be originals or sharp, high-quality photographic prints that are suitable, if necessary, for a 50% reduction in size.

Recommended Length: Typical manuscript is 22 pages.

Copies to Be Submitted: Five

Electronic Submission: Not permitted

Review Procedure: Refereed using the blind review system. The evaluative criteria include the importance of the contribution to the literature, significance of content to the field, practical value, and novelty of techniques.

Return of Rejections: Yes

Reason Given for Rejection: Yes
Time from Acceptance to Publication: Six to eight months
Author's Complimentary Copies: One
Send Manuscripts to: See current issue of the journal.

Educational Administration Quarterly

Corwin Press, Inc.
2455 Teller Road
Newburg Park, CA 91320
(805) 499-9734
Fax: (805) 499-5323
http://www.corwinpress.com/j0043.htm#MS

Publishable Topics: Articles address the various topics within the subject area of educational administration. Among the topics of interest are leadership, organizational theory, accountability and liability, educational governance, school reform, politics of education, personnel issues, collective bargaining, education finance, teacher professionalism, and education law. Articles are expected to be conceptually sound and supported by empirical research.
Publication Schedule: Five issues per year
Circulation: 1,400
Concurrent Submission to Other Journals: Not permitted
Style Guide: Publication Manual of the American Psychological Association (5th edition)
Recommended Length: 20–30 pages. Provide a 50-word abstract.
Copies to Be Submitted: Three
Electronic Submission: Not permitted with the original submission. After the manuscript has been accepted, an IBM-compatible disk containing the final version of the manuscript will be requested.
Review Procedure: Refereed. Evaluative criteria include conceptual or theoretical framework, appropriateness and description of methodology, contribution to the field, and clarity of expression. Review time is approximately three months.
Return of Rejections: Yes
Reason Given for Rejection: Yes
Time from Acceptance to Publication: Three months
Author's Complimentary Copies: Two copies of the journal and 25 tear sheets.
Send Manuscripts to: See current issue of the journal.

Educational and Psychological Measurement

Sage Publications
2455 Teller Road
Thousand Oaks, CA 91320
(805) 499-0721
http://www.acs.tamu.edu/~bbt6147/

Publishable Topics: Statistical theory and studies in educational and psychological measurement. Discussion of the measurement of individual differences, research reports on the development and use of tests and measurements, and other reports that are pertinent to the measurement field, such as suggestions for new types of test items or improved methods for treating test data.

Publication Schedule: Bimonthly

Circulation: 2,500

Concurrent Submission to Other Journals: Not permitted

Style Guide: Publication Manual of the American Psychological Association (5th edition)

Special Format Guidelines: See "Author Guidelines" in the journal.

Recommended Length: No specifications

Copies to Be Submitted: Four

Electronic Submission: Not permitted

Review Procedure: Refereed. Evaluative criteria include significance to the field, clarity of writing, and compliance with editorial guidelines. Review time ranges from three to nine months with the average time being seven months.

Return of Rejections: No

Reason Given for Rejection: Yes

Time from Acceptance to Publication: One year

Author's Complimentary Copies: Two

Send Manuscript to: See current issue of the journal.

Educational Assessment

Lawrence Erlbaum Associates, Inc.
10 Industrial Avenue
Mahwah, NJ 07430
(201) 236-9500
Fax: (201) 236-0072
http://www.erlbaum.com

Publishable Topics: Specializes in publishing original research and scholarship on the educational assessment of individuals, groups, and programs. Its articles embrace a range of issues germane to the theory, empirical research, and practice in the assessment of educational achievement. Also invited are manuscripts that report on testing practices and on national assessment issues.

Publication Schedule: Quarterly

Concurrent Submission to Other Journals: Not permitted

Style Guide: Publication Manual of the American Psychological Association (5th edition)

Recommended Length: No specifications

Copies to Be Submitted: Four

Electronic Submission: Not permitted for the original submission. After a manuscript has been accepted for publication, the author is requested to provide a computer disk containing the manuscript file.

Review Procedure: Refereed using the blind review system. Only the title of the manuscript should appear on the first page. A cover sheet should contain the author's name, affiliation, address, telephone number, fax number, and e-mail address. The review time ranges from four to six weeks.

Return of Rejections: No

Reason Given for Rejection: Yes

Time from Acceptance to Publication: Depends on production schedule.

Author's Complimentary Copies: One

Miscellaneous Guidelines: A cover letter should declare that the ethical standards of the American Psychological Association in the treatment of samples have been followed.

Send Manuscripts to: See current issue of the journal.

Educational Evaluation and Policy Analysis

American Educational Research Association
1230 17th Street, NW
Washington, DC 20036
(202) 223-9485
Fax: (202) 775-1824
http://www.aera.net

Publishable Topics: Emphasizes educational evaluation and educational policy analysis and their relationship. The journal features theoretical and methodological issues along with the practical concerns related to educational evaluation and educational policy formulation.

Publication Schedule: Quarterly

Circulation: 6,000

Concurrent Submission to Other Journals: Not permitted

Style Guide: Publication Manual of the American Psychological Association (5th edition) or *The Chicago Manual of Style* (14th edition)

Special Format Guidelines: Use subheads at reasonable intervals and underline only words to be in italics. Minimize the use of footnotes. When they are used, type them on separate pages and number consecutively throughout the manuscript. The first page should have the title of the article but not the name of the author. On a separate sheet, type the full title of the article and the names of all authors. Send the address, telephone number, and e-mail address of the first author listed.

Recommended Length: 25–35 double-spaced pages for articles, 10–20 pages for research notes. Provide an abstract of 100–150 words.

Copies to Be Submitted: Five

Electronic Submission: Not permitted with original submission. After the manuscript has been accepted for publication, a computer disk will be requested, preferably using WordPerfect.

Review Procedure: Refereed using the blind review system. The review time takes up to three months.

Return of Rejections: Yes

Reason Given for Rejection: Yes

Time from Acceptance to Publication: At least three months

Author's Complimentary Copies: Three

Send Manuscripts to: See current issue of the journal.

The Educational Forum

Kappa Delta Pi, International Honor Society in Education
3707 Woodview Trace
Indianapolis, IN 46268
(317) 871-4900
Fax: (317) 704-2323
http://www.kdp.org

Publishable Topics: Publishes scholarly inquiries that generate new knowledge and insights into education. Also publishes book reviews.
Publication Schedule: Quarterly
Circulation: 6,500
Concurrent Submission to Other Journals: Not permitted
Style Guide: The Chicago Manual of Style (14th edition)
Special Format Guidelines: Only the title page should contain the author's name and institutional address, with the title itself being repeated on the first page of the text. State in the cover letter that the work is not under consideration by any other publication.
Recommended Length: 8–20 double-spaced pages
Copies to Be Submitted: Six
Electronic Submission: Permitted. Use MS Word on a 3.5" disk.
Review Procedure: Refereed using the blind review system. The evaluative criteria include significance of the topic, research information, organization of the discourse, heuristic value, and clarity of expression. The review process takes 12–16 weeks.
Return of Rejections: Yes, if the author provides a self-addressed and stamped envelope.
Reason Given for Rejection: No
Time from Acceptance to Publication: Varies
Author's Complimentary Copies: Two issues of the journal
Send Manuscripts to: See current issue of the journal.

Educational Leadership

Association for Supervision and Curriculum Development
1703 N. Beauregard Street
Alexandria, VA 22311
(800) 933-2723
(703) 578-9600
Fax: (703) 575-5400
http://www.ascd.org

Publishable Topics: Articles are concerned with curriculum, instruction, supervision, and leadership in education. Invites reports of effective programs and practices and interpretations of research. Each issue of the journal focuses on a central theme; consequently, authors should request the current themes that have been adopted and target their manuscripts for one of these themes. If a manuscript is on a special topic that is of great interest but does not comply with one of the themes, it may be accepted for publication.

Publication Schedule: September through May, excluding January

Circulation: 180,000

Concurrent Submission to Other Journals: Not permitted

Style Guide: Publication Manual of the American Psychological Association (5th edition) or *The Chicago Manual of Style* (14th edition)

Special Format Guidelines: Double-space the typing, provide generous margins, and number all pages. On a separate cover sheet, report the author's name, address, telephone number, fax number, and e-mail address. The author's name should not appear elsewhere in the manuscript. Also, report the word count of the manuscript.

Recommended Length: 1,500–2,500 words

Copies to Be Submitted: Two. Do not send photos.

Electronic Submission: Not permitted with original submission. After the manuscript has been accepted for publication, there will be a request for either an IBM-compatible disk or Mac disk. The disk should carry a label indicating the computer platform and the word-processing software that were used along with the author's last name and the file name of the manuscript. Disclose if the disk was formatted as high density. Transmission may also be via e-mail (el@ascd.org).

Review Procedure: The decision to publish an article is made by the editor and the editorial staff. Seeks manuscripts that address the needs and interests of K–12 educators. Prefers informal, conversational style of writing and seldom publishes conventional research reports. Looks for manuscripts that emphasize interpretation and explanation vis-à-vis methodology. In the selection process, consideration is given to a balance of articles germane to topics, perspectives, grade levels, and locations. The review time takes up to eight weeks.

Return of Rejections: Yes, if a self-addressed and stamped 9" x 12" envelope has been provided by the author.

Reason Given for Rejection: No

Time from Acceptance to Publication: 2–24 months

Author's Complimentary Copies: Five

Send Manuscripts to: See current issue of the journal.

Educational Researcher

American Educational Research Association

1230 17th Street, NW

Washington, DC 20036

(202) 223-9485

Fax: (202) 775-1824

http://www.aera.net

Publishable Topics: Scholarly articles of general importance to educational researchers. Features articles on the interpretation, implication, or significance of research and development work in education.

Publication Schedule: Nine issues per year

Circulation: 23,000

Concurrent Submission to Other Journals: Not permitted

Style Guide: Publication Manual of the American Psychological Association (5th edition) or *The Chicago Manual of Style* (14th edition)

Special Format Guidelines: Use subheads at reasonable intervals and underline only words to be in italics. Minimize the use of footnotes. When they are used, type them on a separate page and number consecutively throughout the manuscript. The first page should contain the title of the article but not the name of the author. On a separate sheet, type the full title of the article and the name of the author. Provide the address, telephone number, fax number, and e-mail address of the first author listed.

Recommended Length: Articles, 5,000–7,000 words; abstract, 75–120 words; news and comment pieces, not to exceed 6,000 words.

Copies to Be Submitted: Five

Electronic Submission: Not permitted for original submission. If the manuscript is accepted for publication, an IBM-compatible disk containing the manuscript will be requested.

Review Procedure: Refereed using the blind review system. The review process takes up to three months.

Return of Rejections: Yes

Reason Given for Rejection: Yes

Time from Acceptance to Publication: At least three months

Author's Complimentary Copies: Five

Send Manuscripts to: See current issue of the journal.

Educational Technology

Educational Technology Publications, Inc.
700 Palisade Avenue
Englewood Cliffs, NJ 07632
(201) 871-4007
Fax: (201) 871-4009
http://www.bookstoread.com/etp

Publishable Topics: Covers the full range of technology as it applies to education, including computers in the learning process, all other forms of communication media, instructional design and development, systems approaches to teaching and administration, educational evaluation, Web-based learning, and more. This is a magazine, not a research journal. It publishes articles that discuss, in an informal style, the practical application of scientific knowledge in education.

Publication Schedule: Six issues per year

Circulation: 3,000

Concurrent Submission to Other Journals: Not permitted

Style Guide: Publication Manual of the American Psychological Association (5th edition)

Recommended Length: 2,000–2,500 words typed on double-spaced pages

Copies to Be Submitted: Two

Electronic Submission: Permitted

Review Procedure: Manuscripts are reviewed by the editors and evaluated for their significant contribution to knowledge or to the application of knowledge within the field. The review process takes two weeks.

Return of Rejections: Yes, if a self-addressed and stamped envelope is provided by the author.

Reason Given for Rejection: Sometimes
Time from Acceptance to Publication: Four to six months
Author's Complimentary Copies: Two
Miscellaneous Guidelines: This is a high-level international journal with readers in more than 110 nations. It is intended for a sophisticated audience.
Send Manuscripts to: See current issue of the magazine.

Educational Technology Review

Association for the Advancement of Computing in Education
500 East Main Street
P.O. Box 3728
Norfolk, VA 23514-3728
(757) 623-7588
Fax: (703) 977-8760
http://www.aace.org

Publishable Topics: Dedicated to improving education with the use of information technology. Publishes articles that stimulate ideas and practical solutions that utilize information technology to further education.
Publication Schedule: Semiannually
Circulation: 4,000
Concurrent Submission to Other Journals: Not permitted
Style Guide: Publication Manual of the American Psychological Association (5th edition)
Recommended Length: A maximum of 30 pages
Copies to Be Submitted: Four
Electronic Submission: Permitted. Use Mac or IBM-compatible, high-density disk. Prefer files to be in MS Word; however, ASCII or RTF will be accepted.
Review Procedure: Refereed using the blind review system. The review process takes three to six months.
Return of Rejections: No
Reason Given for Rejection: Yes
Time from Acceptance to Publication: Three to six months
Author's Complimentary Copies: One
Send Manuscripts to: See current issue of the journal.

English Education

The National Council of Teachers of English
1111 Kenyon Road
Urbana, IL 61801
(217) 328-3870
http://www.ncte.org/ee

Publishable Topics: Articles of interest to instructors involved in the preparation of teachers of English and the language arts and in their in-service training.
Publication Schedule: Quarterly

Circulation: 2,700

Concurrent Submission to Other Journals: Not permitted

Style Guide: MLA Style Manual and Guide to Scholarly Publishing and *NCTE Guidelines for Nonsexist Use of Language*

Recommended Length: 20–30 pages, double-spaced

Copies to Be Submitted: Six

Electronic Submission: Not permitted for the original submission. After the manuscript has been accepted for publication, a request will be made for a copy on an IBM-compatible disk using MS Word 2000 or another software that is compatible with it.

Review Procedure: Refereed using the blind review system. Evaluative criteria include significance of the manuscript to teacher preparation and professional development in English language arts. Also, seeks manuscripts that are well organized and evidence clarity of expression. The review time takes approximately three months.

Return of Rejections: Yes, if return postage has been provided.

Reason Given for Rejection: Yes

Time from Acceptance to Publication: Approximately six months

Author's Complimentary Copies: Two

Send Manuscripts to: See current issue of the journal.

Exceptional Children

Council for Exceptional Children
1110 N. Glebe Road
Arlington, VA 22201
(800) 224-6830
(703) 620-3660

Publishable Topics: Features articles on professional issues of concern to special educators and on the education and development of exceptional students. Will consider manuscripts that are data-based position papers, data-based research, research integration papers, and policy analyses. The following kinds of manuscripts are discouraged: (1) accounts from individuals of their experiences growing up with a disability; (2) accounts from parents of their experiences raising a child with a disability; (3) accounts from teachers of their experiences teaching children with disabilities; (4) reports of the correlations between performance on several tests for a specific group of students with disabilities (e.g., performance of students with learning disabilities on the WRAT and the PIAT); and (5) reports of innovative programs and techniques that do not have data on the implications of using these programs or techniques.

Publication Schedule: Quarterly

Circulation: 100,000

Concurrent Submission to Other Journals: Not permitted

Style Guide: Publication Manual of the American Psychological Association (5th edition)

Special Format Requirements: The entire manuscript should be double-spaced, including footnotes, quotations, references, and tables. References should refer only to material cited within the text. List references in alphabetical order on separate pages following the manuscript. Place footnotes on separate pages at the end of the manuscript and number consecutively. The cover sheet should include all authors' names, professional affiliations, addresses, and telephone numbers. Place tables and figures on separate pages at the end of the manuscript.

Recommended Length: 5–15 double-spaced pages. Must send an abstract of 80–120 words.

Copies to Be Submitted: Four

Electronic Submission: Not permitted

Review Procedure: Refereed using the blind review system. Evaluative criteria include implications for the practice of special education, originality, importance of the topic, accuracy and validity, and clarity of expression.

Return of Rejections: Yes, if a self-addressed and stamped envelope has been provided by the author.

Reason Given for Rejection: Yes

Time from Acceptance to Publication: Six months to one year

Author's Complimentary Copies: One

Send Manuscript to: See current issue of the journal.

Gifted Child Quarterly

National Association for Gifted Children
Suite 550
1707 L Street, NW
Washington, DC 20036
(202) 785-4268
http://www.nagc.org

Publishable Topics: Publishes articles on the theory and research related to the psychology and education of gifted and talented children.

Publication Schedule: Quarterly

Circulation: 7,000

Concurrent Submission to Other Journals: Not permitted

Style Guide: Publication Manual of the American Psychological Association (5th edition)

Recommended Length: 12–20 double-spaced pages. Submit an abstract of not more than 125 words.

Copies to Be Submitted: Four

Electronic Submission: Not permitted for the original submission. If manuscript is accepted for publication, a request will be made for submission of the final version on an IBM-compatible disk using MS Word.

Review Procedure: Refereed. Evaluative criteria include considering the avoidance of overly technical writing and excessive tables and figures. Do not submit new practices that have not been tried and evaluated by the author. The review process takes three to six months.

Return of Rejections: No

Reason Given for Rejection: Yes

Time from Acceptance to Publication: 4–12 months

Author's Complimentary Copies: Two

Send Manuscripts to: See current issue of the journal.

Harvard Educational Review
Harvard Education Publishing Group
Gutman Library, Suite 349
6 Appian Way
Cambridge, MA 02138
(617) 495-3432
Fax: (617) 496-3584
http://gseweb.harvard.edu/~hepg/her.html

Publishable Topics: Publishes opinion and research articles for a generalist audience. Manuscripts should be of interest to teachers, policymakers, scholars, and researchers in the field of education broadly defined to include topics in psychology, sociology, political science, history, and related endeavors.

Publication Schedule: Quarterly

Circulation: 10,500

Concurrent Submission to Other Journals: Not preferred

Style Guide: The Chicago Manual of Style (14th edition) should be followed for general questions of style, form, grammar, and punctuation. For technical and research manuscripts, use the *Publication Manual of the American Psychological Association* (5th edition). For legal citations, follow *The Bluebook: A Uniform System of Citation* (17th edition).

Recommended Length: 20–30 pages, double-spaced

Copies to Be Submitted: Three and a one-page abstract

Electronic Submission: Not permitted

Review Procedure: Reviewed anonymously by at least two readers. Evaluative criteria include the quality and scholarly integrity of the work, priorities of the editors, and appropriateness for a generalist audience. The review process takes two to three months.

Return of Rejections: Yes, if requested and the author provides a self-addressed and stamped envelope.

Reason Given for Rejection: No

Time from Acceptance to Publication: Four months

Author's Complimentary Copies: Four

Send Manuscripts to: See current issue of the journal.

Information Technology in Children's Education
Association for the Advancement of Computing in Education
500 East Main Street
P.O. Box 3728
Norfolk, VA 23514-3728
(757) 623-7588
Fax: (703) 977-8760
http://www.aace.org

Publishable Topics: Reports research and the applications of research for using information technology in the education of children in early childhood, preschool, and elementary grades.

Publication Schedule: Annually
Circulation: 1,000
Concurrent Submission to Other Journals: Not permitted
Style Guide: Publication Manual of the American Psychological Association (5th edition)
Recommended Length: Maximum of 30 pages
Copies to Be Submitted: Four
Electronic Submission: Permitted. Use Mac or IBM-compatible, high-density disk. Prefer files to be in MS Word; however, ASCII or RTF will be accepted.
Review Procedure: Refereed. Review process takes six months.
Return of Rejections: No
Reason Given for Rejection: Yes
Time from Acceptance to Publication: Three to six months
Author's Complimentary Copies: One
Send Manuscripts to: See current issue of the journal.

Innovative Higher Education

Kluwer Academic/Human Sciences Press
233 Spring Street
New York, NY 10013
(212) 620-8000
Fax: (212) 463-0742
http://www.isd.uga.edu/ihe/ihe.htm

Publishable Topics: Seeks manuscripts that report on innovative responses to the contemporary challenges confronted in higher education. These may be programs, strategies, or other types of responses.
Publication Schedule: Quarterly
Concurrent Submission to Other Journals: Not permitted
Style Guide: Publication Manual of the American Psychological Association (5th edition)
Special Format Guidelines: The title page of the manuscript should contain the author's name and affiliation. Do not place this information in any other part of the manuscript. On the second page, provide a 20-word caption about the article that will be used in the table of contents. Also, provide an abstract not to exceed 100 words. See instructions for authors in a current issue of the journal or "Tips for Authors" on the Web site cited above.
Recommended Length: 15–20 pages, double-spaced
Copies to Be Submitted: Four
Electronic Submission: Not permitted for the initial submission; however, after a manuscript has been accepted and all revisions as required by the editor have been made, the final version of the manuscript should be submitted on a disk that is labeled with the software used, journal's name, and author's last name. A hard copy of the final version must accompany the electronic file on disk.
Review Procedure: Refereed. Evaluative criteria include innovative ideas expounded, valid research, careful organization, and clarity of writing. The review process takes three months or less.
Return of Rejections: No

Reason Given for Rejection: Yes
Time from Acceptance to Publication: Six months
Author's Complimentary Copies: None
Send Manuscripts to: See current issue of the journal.

International Journal of Education in Technology
Association for the Advancement of Computing in Education
500 East Main Street
P.O. Box 3728
Norfolk, VA 23514-3728
(757) 623-7588
Fax: (703) 977-8760
http://www.aace.org

Publishable Topics: This journal is dedicated to fostering the international exchange of theory, research, development, and practice of telecommunications in education and training. It invites articles that promote the educational process via adoptions of advancements in telecommunications.
Publication Schedule: Quarterly
Circulation: 550
Concurrent Submission to Other Journals: Not permitted
Style Guide: Publication Manual of the American Psychological Association (5th edition)
Recommended Length: 30-page maximum
Copies to Be Submitted: Five
Electronic Submission: Permitted. Use Mac or IBM-compatible, high-density disk. Prefer files to be in MS Word; however, ASCII or RTF will be accepted.
Review Procedure: Refereed. Review process takes three to six months.
Return of Rejections: No
Reason Given for Rejection: Yes
Time from Acceptance to Publication: Three months to one year
Author's Complimentary Copies: One
Send Manuscripts to: See current issue of the journal.

Journal of Adolescent and Adult Literacy
International Reading Association
800 Barksdale Road
P.O. Box 8139
Newark, DE 19714-8139
(302) 731-1600
Fax: (302) 368-2449
http://www.reading.org

Publishable Topics: The journal serves as an open forum for the field of reading education (theory, research, and practice) for learners ages 12 and above, including literacy programs for adults. Articles are written for the practitioner, namely, teachers and reading specialists and college professors of reading education.

Publication Schedule: Eight issues per year

Circulation: 14,000

Concurrent Submission to Other Journals: Not permitted

Style Guide: The Chicago Manual of Style (14th edition) or the *Publication Manual of the American Psychological Association* (5th edition)

Special Format Guidelines: Double-space throughout and do not use footnotes. For citations in text, use the author's last name and date in parentheses. In the reference list, provide the author's last name and first initial. Avoid sex stereotyping. Use article style, not the formal style of a research report. Speak directly to the experienced educator. Writers may send for a copy of "Instructions for Authors."

Recommended Length: 20 double-spaced pages

Copies to Be Submitted: Four

Electronic Submission: Permitted. Submit a 3.5" disk in IBM or Macintosh format, preferably using MS Word. May send as an e-mail attachment.

Review Procedure: Refereed using the blind review system. The evaluative criteria include significance of contribution to the field, usefulness to teachers and researchers, timeliness, cohesiveness of presentation, freshness of approach, clarity, and contribution to the overall content balance of the journal. The review process takes about two months.

Return of Rejections: No

Reason Given for Rejection: Yes

Time from Acceptance to Publication: Varies

Author's Complimentary Copies: Five

Send Manuscripts to: See current issue of the journal.

Journal of Autism and Developmental Disorders

Kluwer Academic/Plenum Publishers

233 Spring Street

New York, NY 10013

(212) 620-8013

Fax: (212) 463-0742

http://www.wkap.com

Publishable Topics: Devoted to all severe psychopathologies in childhood. Features articles on (1) experimental studies on the biochemical, neurological, and genetic aspects of the disorder; (2) the implications of normal development for deviant processes; (3) interaction between disordered behavior of individuals and social or group factors; (4) research and case studies involving the entire spectrum of interventions, including behavioral, biological, educational, and community aspects; and (5) diagnosis and classification of disorders reflecting new knowledge. Papers may be experimental studies, theoretical papers, critical reviews, or case studies.

Publication Schedule: Bimonthly

Circulation: 3,500

Concurrent Submission to Other Journals: Not permitted

Style Guide: Publication Manual of the American Psychological Association (5th edition)

Special Format Guidelines: Tables should be numbered and referred to by number in the manuscript. Type each table on a separate sheet and label it with a descriptive title. Number illustrations consecutively. Prepare drawings in India ink. Include the names of all authors and their academic affiliations. Provide the address of one author who will review the proofs. Include an abstract of 120 words.

Copies to Be Submitted: Four

Electronic Submission: Not permitted for the initial submission; however, after a manuscript has been accepted and all revisions as required by the editor have been made, the final version of the manuscript should be submitted on a disk that is labeled with the software used, journal's name, and author's last name. A hard copy of the final version must accompany the electronic file on disk.

Review Procedure: Refereed. The review process takes a few months.

Return of Rejections: Yes, if a self-addressed and stamped envelope has been provided by the writer.

Reason Given for Rejection: Yes

Time from Acceptance to Publication: Up to one year

Author's Complimentary Copies: None

Send Manuscripts to: See current issue of the journal.

Journal of Chemical Education

American Chemical Society
Division of Chemical Education
1155 16th Street, NW
Washington, DC 20036
(202) 872-4600
Fax: (608) 262-7145
http://jchemed.chem.wisc.edu

Publishable Topics: Publishes articles of interest to chemistry teachers from secondary education through graduate school. Topics include descriptions of innovative courses, reports of instructional research, reviews of recent advances in chemistry, new laboratory experiments, classroom demonstrations, opinion pieces concerning education, and feature columns on specific topics, such as the use of computers in teaching.

Publication Schedule: Monthly

Circulation: 13,000

Concurrent Submission to Other Journals: Not permitted

Style Guide: See Web site for instructions to authors.

Recommended Length: No more than 16 double-spaced pages

Copies to Be Submitted: Four

Electronic Submission: Not permitted for initial submission; however, after having been accepted and after all revisions have been executed, the manuscript should be submitted on a disk using either RTF or MS Word. May use either IBM or Macintosh format.

Review Procedure: Refereed. The evaluative criteria include technical accuracy and usefulness to chemistry teachers. The review process takes two to three months.

Return of Rejections: Yes

Reason Given for Rejection: Yes
Time from Acceptance to Publication: 9 to 12 months
Author's Complimentary Copies: None
Send Manuscripts to: See current issue of the journal.

Journal of College Admission

National Association for College Admission Counseling
1631 Prince Street
Alexandria, VA 22314
(703) 836-2222
(800) 822-6285
Fax: (703) 836-8015
http://www.nacac.com/jrnl_writerguide.html
Publishable Topics: Invites manuscripts that address current issues in counseling for postsecondary education admissions, and financial aid.
Publication Schedule: Quarterly
Circulation: 7,000
Concurrent Submission to Other Journals: Not permitted
Style Guide: The Chicago Manual of Style (14th edition)
Special Format Guidelines: Pages are to be double-spaced and numbered. A separate title page should be submitted that provides for each author the name, title, institutional affiliation, address, telephone number, and a short vita.
Recommended Length: Feature articles should be between 2,500 and 5,000 words. Contributions to the Open Forum are limited to a maximum of 2,500 words.
Copies to Be Submitted: Two
Electronic Submission: Permitted. Submit on a 3.5" Macintosh-formatted disk using MS Word. Must be accompanied by a hard copy of the manuscript.
Review Procedure: Manuscripts are reviewed and selected by the Journal Editorial Board of NACAC. Evaluative criteria include level of interest to the audience, timeliness, quality of research, and quality of the writing. Avoid educational jargon. The review process takes four to six weeks.
Return of Rejections: No
Reason Given for Rejection: No
Time from Acceptance to Publication: Within one year
Author's Complimentary Copies: Three
Send Manuscripts to: Journal Editor at the address cited above.

Journal of College and University Law

National Association of College and University Attorneys
Suite 620
One Dupont Circle, NW
Washington, DC 20036
(202) 833-8390
Fax: (202) 296-8379

http://www.nacua.org

Publishable Topics: This is the professional journal for attorneys who specialize in the law and higher education. Seeks manuscripts that address legal issues involving higher education.

Publication Schedule: Quarterly

Circulation: 3,600

Concurrent Submission to Other Journals: Permitted

Style Guide: The Bluebook: A Uniform System of Citation (17th ed.)

Special Format Guidelines: Double-space the manuscript, including block quotations.

Recommended Length: 20–40 double-spaced pages

Copies to Be Submitted: One

Electronic Submission: Not permitted

Review Procedure: Refereed. Evaluative criteria include relevance of the manuscript to the professional interests of university attorneys, depth of treatment, timeliness, and clarity of writing. The review process takes approximately one month.

Return of Rejections: Yes, if requested

Reason Given for Rejection: Yes

Time from Acceptance to Publication: Approximately six months

Author's Complimentary Copies: Two copies of the journal and 25 reprints of the article.

Send Manuscripts to: See current issue of the journal.

Journal of College Student Development

American College Personnel Association
Suite 300
One Dupont Circle, NW
Washington, DC 20036
(202) 835-2272
Fax: (202) 296-3286
http://www.acpa.nche.edu

Publishable Topics: The focus is research on college student development and professional issues in college student personnel affairs. Most articles are data-based.

Publication Schedule: Six issues per year

Circulation: 10,000

Concurrent Submission to Other Journals: Not permitted

Style Guide: Publication Manual of the American Psychological Association (5th edition)

Special Format Guidelines: In the writing, do not use the term "subjects"; instead, use "respondents," "participants," or "students."

Copies to Be Submitted: Three

Electronic Submission: Not permitted

Review Procedure: Review is conducted by the editor and at least two editorial board members. Evaluative criteria include appropriateness, research value, contribution to the field, and clarity of expression. The review process takes about eight weeks.

Return of Rejections: No

Reason Given for Rejection: Yes

Time from Acceptance to Publication: At least six months
Author's Complimentary Copies: Five
Send Manuscripts to: See current issue of the journal.

Journal of Computers in Mathematics and Science Teaching
Association for the Advancement of Computing in Education
500 East Main Street
P.O. Box 3728
Norfolk, VA 23514-3728
(757) 623-7588
Fax: (703) 977-8760
http://www.aace.org

Publishable Topics: Serves as a scholarly forum for the exchange of information on research, development, and application of computer technology in the teaching of mathematics and science.
Publication Schedule: Quarterly
Circulation: 1,125
Concurrent Submission to Other Journals: Not permitted
Style Guide: Publication Manual of the American Psychological Association (5th edition)
Recommended Length: Maximum of 30 pages
Copies to Be Submitted: Five
Electronic Submission: Permitted. Use Mac or IBM-compatible, high-density disk. Prefer files to be in MS Word; however, ASCII or RTF will be accepted.
Review Procedure: Refereed. Review time takes three to six months.
Return of Rejections: No
Reason Given for Rejection: Yes
Time from Acceptance to Publication: Three months to a year
Author's Complimentary Copies: One
Send Manuscripts to: See current issue of the journal.

The Journal of Continuing Higher Education
Association for Continuing Higher Education
c/o Trident Technical College
P.O. Box 118067, CE-M
Charleston, SC 29423-8067
(843) 574-6658
Fax: (843) 574-6470
http://www.charleston.net/org/ache

Publishable Topics: Dedicated to the exchange of information, based on research, observation, and experience, that is relevant to continuing higher education. More specifically, seeks articles that address the organization and administration of continuing higher education, research within the field, adult and nontraditional students, continuing education student programs and services, and the development and application of new programs in the field.

Publication Schedule: Three issues per year

Circulation: 2,000

Concurrent Submission to Other Journals: Not permitted

Style Guide: Publication Manual of the American Psychological Association (5th edition)

Special Format Guidelines: The author's name should not appear on the manuscript; instead, the name, title, address, and telephone number should be placed on a separate sheet. Double-space all pages.

Recommended Length: Up to 5,000 words

Copies to Be Submitted: Four

Electronic Submission: Not permitted for original submission; however, if the manuscript is accepted for publication, the author will be requested to provide the final version on a 3.5" disk that is prepared in MS Word, WordPerfect, or ASCII.

Review Procedure: The blind review procedure is used. Evaluative criteria include relevance to the readership, significance and timeliness of the topic, thoroughness in addressing the topic, quality of the research, and clarity of writing. The review process usually takes 60 days.

Return of Rejections: No

Reason Given for Rejection: Yes

Time from Acceptance to Publication: Approximately four to eight months

Author's Complimentary Copies: Two

Send Manuscripts to: See current issue of the journal.

Journal of Counseling and Development

American Counseling Association

5999 Stevenson Avenue

Alexandria, VA 22304

(703) 823-9800

Fax: (703) 823-0502

http://www.counseling.org

Publishable Topics: Publishes articles that address the full spectrum of counseling practice and issues related to counselor education and supervision. Manuscripts usually fall within the categories of conceptual pieces, research studies, practices, profiles of distinguished practitioners, or assessment and diagnosis.

Publication Schedule: Quarterly

Circulation: 58,000

Concurrent Submission to Other Journals: Not permitted

Style Guide: Publication Manual of the American Psychological Association (5th edition)

Special Format Guidelines: Tables and figures should be used sparingly. A manuscript should not contain more than three tables or two figures. Figures should be camera-ready art. The journal does not publish footnotes; instead, they should be incorporated into the text. Limit the manuscript's title to 80 characters.

Recommended Length: Maximum of 20 double-spaced pages

Copies to Be Submitted: Four

Electronic Submission: Not permitted for the original submission; however, after acceptance of the manuscript for publication, the author will be requested to submit the final edited version on a 3.5" disk in either ASCII format for IBM-compatible computers or in text file format for Macintosh computers.

Review Procedure: Refereed using the blind review system. The evaluative criteria include adherence to the ACA Ethical Standards, appropriateness of the article to the audience, contribution of new knowledge to the field, and that the manuscript was written by a counselor or other mental health practitioner. The review process takes from two to four months.

Return of Rejections: No

Reason Given for Rejection: Yes

Time from Acceptance to Publication: Varies

Author's Complimentary Copies: One

Send Manuscripts to: See current issue of the journal.

Journal of Counseling Psychology

American Psychological Association
750 First Street, NE
Washington, DC 20002
(202) 336-5500
http://www.apa.org/journals/cou.html

Publishable Topics: Features articles on counseling that are of interest to psychologists and counselors in schools, colleges, counseling agencies, and other settings. The journal gives particular attention to reports of empirical studies about counseling processes and interventions, theoretical articles about counseling, and studies concerned with the evaluation of applications of counseling and counseling programs. It also considers manuscripts on the selection and training of counselors, the development of counseling materials and methods, and the application of counseling to special populations and problem areas.

Publication Schedule: Quarterly

Circulation: 9,100

Concurrent Submission to Other Journals: Not permitted

Style Guide: Publication Manual of the American Psychological Association (5th edition)

Special Format Guidelines: See "Instructions to Authors" in the journal.

Recommended Length: No specification

Copies to Be Submitted: Five

Electronic Submission: Not permitted for the initial submission; however, after acceptance of the manuscript for publication, submission of the final version on a computer disk is required. May use any software; however, MS Word is preferred.

Review Procedure: Refereed. Evaluative criteria include originality, validity, and significance of contribution to psychology and counseling. Review process takes up to 90 days.

Return of Rejections: Yes, if requested

Reason Given for Rejection: Yes

Time from Acceptance to Publication: Approximately five to eight months

Author's Complimentary Copies: None
Send Manuscripts to: See current issue of the journal.

Journal of Curriculum and Supervision
Association for Supervision and Curriculum Development
1703 N. Beauregard Street
Alexandria, VA 22311
(703) 578-9600
http://www.ascd.org/pubs/jcs/jcs.html

Publishable Topics: Publishes articles that focus on curriculum and supervision policies and practices. They may take theoretical, speculative, or practical approaches.
Publication Schedule: Quarterly
Circulation: 3,600
Concurrent Submission to Other Journals: Permitted
Style Guide: See "To Our Contributors" in a current issue of the Journal or visit the Web site cited above. Do not use APA style.
Special Format Guidelines: All pages should be typed double-spaced. The author's name, title, affiliation, address, telephone number, fax number, and e-mail address should be provided on a separate sheet. The first page of the manuscript should contain only the title of the manuscript. Tables should be double-spaced on separate pages, and figures should be drawn on white paper in India ink. High-quality computer graphics are acceptable. Provide an abstract of no more than 200 words that summarizes the manuscript's major contribution.
Recommended Length: No specification
Copies to Be Submitted: Four paper copies of the manuscript and abstract and one computer disk copy.
Electronic Submission: Required. The computer disk should contain a label that identifies the author's name, the word-processing program used, and its version. Also, report the name of the disk file.
Review Procedure: The blind review system is used. Guidelines of the journal state that the "highest priority is given manuscripts dealing with comprehensive, holistic, or interactive views embedded in a thorough treatment of related scholarship and the historical context." A variety of research methods are acceptable, including empirical, historical, and interpretive. The review process takes approximately three months.
Return of Rejections: No
Time from Acceptance to Publication: Up to one year
Author's Complimentary Copies: Five
Send Manuscripts to: See current issue of the journal.

Journal of Curriculum Studies
Taylor and Francis, Inc.
Suite 800
325 Chestnut Street
Philadelphia, PA 19106

(800) 354-1420
Fax: (215) 625-8914
http://www.tandf.co.uk/journals/default.html

Publishable Topics: Invites manuscripts that address issues of theory, policymaking, and practice in all areas of curriculum, teaching, and school assessment (K–12) and in teacher education. This journal has an international focus; consequently, it especially welcomes manuscripts that extend the treatment of curriculum beyond national boundaries.

Publication Schedule: Six issues per year

Concurrent Submission to Other Journals: Not permitted

Style Guide: Uses the British convention in the style of writing. See author's guidelines in the journal or visit the Web site cited above.

Special Format Guidelines: See the journal or the Web site above.

Recommended Length: 8,000–10,000 words

Copies to Be Submitted: Four in addition to a 150-word abstract

Electronic Submission: Not permitted for the initial submission; however, after the manuscript has been accepted for publication, the corrected and final version should be submitted on a 3.5" disk in ASCII text only version and in a word-processed version. Also, two hard copy printouts should accompany the disk. Label the disk with the title of the journal, author's name, file names, hardware used (PC or Mac), and name of the software used.

Review Procedure: Refereed. Seeks manuscripts that are written on a significant topic and that will be of interest to an international professional readership. The review process takes about three to four months.

Return of Rejections: Sometimes

Reason Given for Rejection: Yes

Time from Acceptance to Publication: One year

Author's Complimentary Copies: 50 offprints

Send Manuscripts to: See current issue of the journal.

Journal of Education Finance

Association of School Business Officials International
11401 North Shore Drive
Reston, VA 20109
(703) 478-0405
Fax: (703) 478-0205
http://www.uark.edu/misc/jef/home.html

Publishable Topics: Articles related to fiscal affairs in public schools and higher education. Includes matters of fiscal policy, fiscal legislation, and related topics at the local, state, and national levels.

Publication Schedule: Quarterly

Circulation: 1,200

Concurrent Submission to Other Journals: Not permitted

Style Guide: The Chicago Manual of Style (14th edition)

Special Format Guidelines: Does not accept matrix type.
Recommended Length: 15–30 double-spaced pages
Copies to Be Submitted: Five
Electronic Submission: Not permitted
Review Procedure: Refereed. Evaluative criteria include appropriateness for the journal, timeliness, contribution to the field, substantiation of conclusions, and clarity of writing. The review process takes four to eight weeks.
Return of Rejections: Yes, if requested
Reason Given for Rejection: Only if requested
Time from Acceptance to Publication: Varies
Author's Complimentary Copies: One
Send Manuscripts to: See current issue of the journal.

Journal of Education for Business

Heldref Publications
1319 18th Street, NW
Washington, DC 20036
(202) 296-6267
Fax: (202) 296-5149
http://www.heldref.org

Publishable Topics: Dedicated to articles that report on issues and trends in education for business. Seeks research-based articles that are focused on the teaching of business at the secondary, collegiate, and postgraduate levels in the areas of accounting, finance, management, marketing, information systems, and other related business disciplines. Articles address curriculum development, program evaluation, and instructional processes. Innovative practices and programs are of interest to the readership.
Publication Schedule: Bimonthly
Circulation: 1,400
Concurrent Submission to Other Journals: Not permitted
Style Guide: Publication Manual of the American Psychological Association (5th edition)
Special Format Guidelines: See "Instructions to Contributors" in the journal or on the Web site cited above.
Recommended Length: Not to exceed 2,500 words
Copies to Be Submitted: Two
Electronic Submission: Not permitted for the original submission. If the manuscript is accepted, instructions will be sent requesting the final version to be provided on a computer disk.
Review Procedure: Refereed using the blind peer review system. The review process takes two to three months.
Return of Rejections: Yes
Reason Given for Rejection: Yes
Time from Acceptance to Publication: Two to four months
Author's Complimentary Copies: Two
Send Manuscripts to: See current issue of the journal.

Journal of Educational and Behavioral Statistics
American Educational Research Association
1230 17th Street, NW
Washington, DC 20036
(202) 223-9485
Fax: (202) 775-1824
http://www/aera.net

Publishable Topics: Prefers manuscripts that present new methods of statistical analysis in education or new applications of well-known methods. When presenting a statistical method, explain why, when, and how it should be used.

Publication Schedule: Quarterly

Circulation: 3,500

Concurrent Submission to Other Journals: Not permitted

Style Guide: Publication Manual of the American Psychological Association (5th edition) or *The Chicago Manual of Style* (14th edition)

Special Format Guidelines: Use subheads at reasonable intervals and underline only words that are to be italicized. Minimize the use of footnotes; however, when they are used, type them on a separate page and number consecutively throughout the manuscript. The first page should contain the title of the article but not the name of the author. On a separate sheet type the full title of the article and name of the author. When there are multiple authors, provide the address, telephone number, and e-mail address of the first author listed.

Recommended Length: 20–30 double-spaced pages. Include an abstract of 100–120 words.

Copies to Be Submitted: Five

Electronic Submission: Not permitted for original submission. If the manuscript is accepted for publication, an IBM-compatible disk containing the manuscript will be requested.

Review Procedure: Refereed using the blind review system. Up to three months are required for the review process.

Return of Rejections: Yes

Reason Given for Rejection: Yes

Time from Acceptance to Publication: At least three months

Author's Complimentary Copies: Five

Send Manuscripts to: See current issue of the journal.

Journal of Educational Measurement
National Council on Measurement in Education
1230 17th Street, NW
Washington, DC 20036
(202) 223-9318
Fax: (202) 775-1824
http://www.ncme.org

Publishable Topics: Publishes original measurement research and reports on the application of measurement in education. Seeks articles on the research of measurement processes, techniques, tools, and procedures. Also invites manuscripts on measurement philosophy and practices.

Publication Schedule: Quarterly

Circulation: 3,500

Concurrent Submission to Other Journals: Not permitted

Style Guide: Publication Manual of the American Psychological Association (5th edition)

Special Format Guidelines: Manuscripts are to be double-spaced with subheadings used at reasonable intervals. Underline only those words that are to be italicized. Number pages consecutively. Two of the three copies of the manuscript that are submitted should be prepared for blind review by omitting reference to the author and affiliated institution. The first page of the text should contain the complete title but not cite the author's name. For further guidelines, see "Information for Contributors" in a current issue of the journal.

Recommended Length: None specified

Copies to Be Submitted: Three with an abstract of 100–150 words

Electronic Submission: Not permitted

Review Procedure: Refereed using the blind review system. Evaluative criteria include accuracy of the design, analysis, interpretation of the findings, appropriateness for an audience of educational measurement theorists and practitioners, significance and contribution to the field, and novelty of content. The review process takes approximately two to three months.

Reason Given for Rejection: Yes

Send Manuscripts to: See current issue of the journal.

Journal of Educational Multimedia and Hypermedia

Association for the Advancement of Computing in Education
500 East Main Street
P.O. Box 3728
Norfolk, VA 23514-3728
(757) 623-7588
Fax: (703) 977-8760
http://www.aace.org

Publishable Topics: The purpose of this journal is to advance the theory and practice of teaching and learning with the use of multimedia and hypermedia. Invites manuscripts that present research, development, and applications of multimedia and hypermedia in education.

Publication Schedule: Quarterly

Circulation: 1,300

Concurrent Submission to Other Journals: Not permitted

Style Guide: Publication Manual of the American Psychological Association (5th edition)

Recommended Length: Maximum of 30 double-spaced pages

Copies to Be Submitted: Five

Electronic Submission: Permitted. Use Mac or IBM-compatible, high-density disk. Prefer files to be in MS Word; however, ASCII or RTF will be accepted.

Review Procedure: Refereed. The review process takes three to six months.

Return of Rejections: No

Reason Given for Rejection: Yes

Time from Acceptance to Publication: Three months to a year

Author's Complimentary Copies: One

Send Manuscripts to: See current issue of the journal.

Journal of Educational Psychology

American Psychological Association
750 First Street, NE
Washington, DC 20002
(202) 336-5500
http://www.apa.org/journals/edu.html

Publishable Topics: Features articles reporting original research and theoretical work that address learning and cognition as they relate to instruction. Also invites manuscripts that are concerned with the psychological development, interpersonal relationships, and adjustment of the individual. The scope of the journal encompasses all levels of education and all age groups.

Publication Schedule: Quarterly

Circulation: 4,700

Concurrent Submission to Other Journals: Not permitted

Style Guide: Publication Manual of the American Psychological Association (5th edition)

Special Format Guidelines: See "Instructions to Authors" in the journal.

Recommended Length: No specification

Copies to Be Submitted: Five

Electronic Submission: Not permitted for the initial submission; however, after acceptance of the manuscript for publication, submission of the final version on a computer disk is required. May use any software; however, MS Word is preferred.

Review Procedure: Refereed. Evaluative criteria include originality, validity, and significance of contribution to educational psychology. The review process takes three months.

Return of Rejections: Yes, if requested

Reason Given for Rejection: Yes

Time from Acceptance to Publication: Five to eight months

Author's Complimentary Copies: None

Send Manuscripts to: See current issue of the journal.

The Journal of Educational Research

Heldref Publications
1319 18th Street, NW
Washington, DC 20036
(202) 296-6267

Fax: (202) 296-5149
http://www.heldref.org

Publishable Topics: Publishes articles that describe or synthesize research of direct relevance to educational practice in elementary and secondary education. Emphasizes articles that report on variables that can be manipulated in the educational setting. All types of educational research are considered. Manuscripts that rigorously assess the validity of claims for products, testing materials, and educational practices are welcome.

Publication Schedule: Bimonthly

Circulation: 3,000

Concurrent Submission to Other Journals: Not permitted

Style Guide: Publication Manual of the American Psychological Association (5th edition)

Special Format Guidelines: The journal has available its own style sheet with specific instructions for statistical reporting.

Recommended Length: Maximum of about 35 double-spaced pages; very few short notes are accepted.

Copies to Be Submitted: Two

Electronic Submission: Not permitted

Review Procedure: Refereed using the blind review system. Evaluative criteria include appropriateness for the purposes of the journal, significance of the problem, validity of the research procedure, style of presentation, clarity of expression, and other criteria that are normally applicable to evaluating educational research. The review process usually takes six to eight weeks.

Return of Rejections: Yes

Reason Given for Rejection: Yes

Time from Acceptance to Publication: Five to six months

Author's Complimentary Copies: Two

Send Manuscripts to: See current issue of the journal.

Journal of Experimental Child Psychology

Academic Press
Suite 1900
525 B Street
San Diego, CA 92101
(619) 699-6553
Fax: (619) 699-6700
http://www.academicpress.com/jecp

Publishable Topics: Publishes articles reporting research experiments, theoretical treatises, and methodological notes on the cognitive, social, and physical development of children.

Publication Schedule: Monthly

Concurrent Submission to Other Journals: Not permitted

Style Guide: Publication Manual of the American Psychological Association (5th edition)

Special Format Guidelines: See "Information for Authors" in the journal or on the Web site cited above.

Recommended Length: No specification

Copies to Be Submitted: Five

Electronic Submission: Not permitted

Review Procedure: Refereed. Evaluative criteria include methodological adequacy, ability of findings to be replicated, contribution to the understanding of the developmental process and theory, and clarity of the presentation.

Return of Rejections: No

Reason Given for Rejection: Yes

Time from Acceptance to Publication: 3 to 12 months

Author's Complimentary Copies: None

Send Manuscripts to: See current issue of the journal.

The Journal of Experimental Education

Heldref Publications
1319 18th Street, NW
Washington, DC 20036
(202) 296-6267
Fax: (202) 296-5149
http://www.heldref.org

Publishable Topics: Publishes basic and applied research studies that use the range of quantitative and qualitative methodologies used in the behavioral, cognitive, and social sciences. Articles are placed in one of three categories: (1) learning and instruction, (2) motivation and social processes, and (3) measurement, statistics, and research. Authors should indicate the category for which their manuscript is being submitted.

Publication Schedule: Quarterly

Circulation: 1,400

Concurrent Submission to Other Journals: Not permitted

Style Guide: Publication Manual of the American Psychological Association (5th edition)

Special Format Guidelines: See "Guidelines for Contributors" in the journal. With one copy of the manuscript, submit a cover sheet that contains the author's name, address, affiliation, telephone number, fax number, and e-mail address. Because the blind review system is used, the remaining copies of the manuscript should not include any identifying information.

Recommended Length: 15–30 double-spaced pages

Copies to Be Submitted: Three, including an abstract not to exceed 120 words

Electronic Submission: Not permitted for the original submission; however, if the manuscript is accepted for publication, a request will be made for a final copy on disk that was prepared in either MS Word or WordPerfect. A hard copy should accompany the disk.

Review Procedure: Refereed using the blind review system. Evaluative criteria include appropriateness for the journal's purpose, clarity of presentation, thoroughness of the literature review, validity of the research methodology, accuracy, and other criteria normally used in the evaluation of educational research. The review process takes up to three months.

Return of Rejections: Yes

Reason Given for Rejection: Yes

Time from Acceptance to Publication: Three to six months

Author's Complimentary Copies: Two

Send Manuscripts to: See current issue of the journal.

Journal of Health Education

American Association for Health Education
1900 Association Dr.
Reston, VA 20191
(800) 213-7193
(703) 476-3422
Fax: (703) 476-6638
http://www.aahperd.org

Publishable Topics: Publishes articles of interest to health educators who work in a diversity of environments, namely, schools, colleges, clinics, community and public health agencies, and health care settings in the workplace. Manuscripts may be research-based, theoretical, practical, or historical. They should have broad application and implications for health education and fit into one of the following categories: (1) community development, policy, and awareness strategies, (2) professional and instructional programs, or (3) individual health enhancement and maintenance methods.

Publication Schedule: Six issues per year

Circulation: 10,000

Concurrent Submission to Other Journals: Not permitted

Style Guide: Publication Manual of the American Psychological Association (5th edition)

Special Format Guidelines: Include a title page that contains the title of the manuscript; author's name, address, affiliation, telephone number, fax number, and e-mail address. Provide an abstract, not exceeding 200 words, that also includes five keywords or descriptive terms that summarize the manuscript. These should be selected from the *Thesaurus of ERIC Descriptors* or the thesaurus from the Technical and Information and Editorial Services Branch of the National Center for Chronic Disease Prevention and Health Promotion in Atlanta, Georgia. For more detailed instructions, see "Guidelines for Authors" in the journal.

Recommended Length: Not to exceed 15 double-spaced pages

Copies to Be Submitted: Five

Electronic Submission: Not permitted for the original submission; however, if the manuscript is accepted for publication, a request will be made for the final version to be provided on a computer disk.

Review Procedure: Refereed. Evaluative criteria include appropriateness for the journal's audience, relevance and significance to health education, sufficiency of documentation, and clarity of writing. The review process takes approximately three months.

Return of Rejections: Yes, if requested and a self-addressed and stamped envelope has been provided by the author.

Reason Given for Rejection: Yes
Time from Acceptance to Publication: Up to one year
Author's Complimentary Copies: Two
Send Manuscripts to: See current issue of the journal.

Journal of Higher Education

Ohio State University Press
1070 Carmack Road
Columbus, OH 43210
(614) 292-6930
Fax: (614) 292-2065
http://www.ohiostatepress.org/journals.htm

Publishable Topics: Publishes a broad range of topics on higher education that are of interest to higher education faculty and administrators. Discourages manuscripts that emphasize practices of research methodology, except for innovative methodological approaches.
Publication Schedule: Six issues per year
Circulation: 4,300
Concurrent Submission to Other Journals: Not permitted
Style Guide: Publication Manual of the American Psychological Association (5th edition). Also, the journal's manuscript requirements may be requested.
Special Format Requirements: See "Instructions to Contributors" in the journal
Recommended Length: 25–30 double-spaced pages; include an abstract of no more than 50 words
Copies to Be Submitted: Three
Electronic Submission: Not permitted
Review Procedure: Refereed using the blind review system. On a removable cover page, submit the author's name, professional position, and institutional affiliation. Evaluative criteria include significance of the subject, appropriateness to the journal, originality, logical development, and the writing style. Demonstrate a freshness of vision and vitality in the writing. The review process takes about six months.
Return of Rejections: Yes, if a self-addressed and stamped envelope has been provided by the author
Reason Given for Rejection: Yes
Time from Acceptance to Publication: Up to one year
Author's Complimentary Copies: Two
Send Manuscripts to: See current issue of the journal.

Journal of Instruction Delivery Systems

Learning Technology Institute
50 Culpeper Street
Warrenton, VA 20186
(540) 347-0055
Fax: (540) 349-3169

Publishable Topics: Articles are devoted to matters pertaining to instructional delivery systems in education and training for academia, business, industry, and the military. The orientation is on applications, not the technical aspects of design and development. Manuscripts should address some aspect of contemporary instructional delivery systems.

Publication Schedule: Quarterly

Circulation: 1,200

Concurrent Submission to Other Journals: Not permitted

Style Guide: Publication Manual of the American Psychological Association (5th edition)

Special Format Guidelines: The first page should contain the manuscript's title and the author's name, institutional affiliation, and e-mail address. The second page should provide the title, a 100–150-word abstract, and descriptive terms for indexing purposes. On a separate page at the end of the manuscript should be a statement titled "About the Author."

Recommended Length: 2,000–3,000 words

Copies to Be Submitted: Two hard copies and one disk copy labeled with the author's name, software used, and format

Electronic Submission: Permitted. (See preceding section.) No faxes.

Review Procedure: Refereed. The review process takes two to three months.

Return of Rejections: No

Reason Given for Rejection: Yes

Time from Acceptance to Publication: Usually less than four months

Author's Complimentary Copies: Two plus a one-year complimentary subscription to the journal

Send Manuscripts to: See current issue of the journal.

Journal of Interactive Learning Research

Association for the Advancement of Computing in Education
500 East Main Street
P.O. Box 3728
Norfolk, VA 23514-3728
(757) 623-7588
Fax: (703) 977-8760
http://www.aace.org

Publishable Topics: Seeks articles that address the impact of interactive learning environments on education and training. These consider the operating theory, design, implementation, and effectiveness of this type of environment. Interactive learning environments include collaborative learning, performance support systems, multimedia systems, authoring systems, assessment systems, computer-mediated communications, simulations and games, and others.

Publication Schedule: Quarterly

Circulation: 950

Concurrent Submission to Other Journals: Not permitted

Style Guide: Publication Manual of the American Psychological Association (5th edition)

Recommended Length: Maximum of 30 double-spaced pages

Copies to Be Submitted: Four

Electronic Submission: Permitted. Use Mac or IBM-compatible, high-density disk. Prefer files to be in MS Word; however, ASCII or RTF will be accepted.

Review Procedure: Refereed. The review process takes six months to one year.

Return of Rejections: Yes

Reason Given for Rejection: No

Time from Acceptance to Publication: Three to six months

Author's Complimentary Copies: One

Send Manuscripts to: See current issue of the journal.

Journal of Law and Education

Jefferson Law Book Co.
2100 Huntingdon Avenue
Baltimore, MD 21211
(410) 727-7300
Fax: (410) 783-2448
http://www.law.sc.edu/jlawedhp.htm

Publishable Topics: Publishes articles on all aspects of law that relate to education

Publication Schedule: Quarterly

Circulation: 1,400

Concurrent Submission to Other Journals: Not permitted

Style Guide: The Bluebook: A Uniform System of Citation (17th edition)

Special Format Guidelines: Type on a separate page the complete title and the author's name and address. Also, provide a short title on the second page that can be used as a running head. The journal publishes a page of instructions to authors.

Recommended Length: 25–50 double-spaced pages

Copies to Be Submitted: Two

Electronic Submission: Permitted. Submit a 3.5" high-density computer disk using WordPerfect. A printout must accompany the disk.

Review Procedure: Reviewed by the managing editor and the executive editor. The evaluative criteria include originality, insight, accurate understanding of the legal issues involved, timeliness, and appropriateness for the journal. The review process takes one to six months.

Return of Rejections: Yes, if a self-addressed and stamped envelope has been provided by the writer.

Reason Given for Rejection: No

Time from Acceptance to Publication: Three to six months

Author's Complimentary Copies: 25

Send Manuscripts to: See current issue of the journal.

Journal of Learning Disabilities

PRO-ED, Inc.
8700 Shoal Creek Blvd.
Austin, TX 78757

(512) 451-3246
Fax: (512) 302-9129
http://www.proedinc.com

Publishable Topics: The journal is multidisciplinary and publishes articles related to learning disabilities. It accepts major articles; reviews of tests, materials, treatments, and books; opinion papers; and topical series. A major article may be an extensive review of the literature, a theoretical paper, or a nonempirical position paper. "Reports" are shorter and more limited and usually address such topics as studies of test validation, material evaluation, program effectiveness, and remedial technology.

Publication Schedule: Bimonthly

Circulation: 8,000

Concurrent Submission to Other Journals: Not permitted

Style Guide: Publication Manual of the American Psychological Association (5th edition)

Recommended Length: Major articles, 15–25 double-spaced pages with a 75–100-word abstract. Reports are not to exceed 10 double-spaced pages, and should be accompanied by an abstract of 100–150 words.

Copies to Be Submitted: Four

Electronic Submission: Not permitted

Review Procedure: Refereed. Evaluative criteria include relevance to the purpose of the journal, accuracy in delineating the specific characteristics of the LD population being studied, comparison with other manuscripts dealing with similar content, adherence to the APA guidelines, and clarity of writing.

Return of Rejections: Yes

Reason Given for Rejection: Yes

Time from Acceptance to Publication: Six to nine months

Author's Complimentary Copies: One

Send Manuscripts to: See current issue of the journal.

Journal of Literacy Research
National Reading Conference
Suite 5A
11 East Hubbard Street
Chicago, IL 60611
(312) 431-0013
Fax: (312) 431-8697

Publishable Topics: Intended for reading educators with articles reporting original research and presenting theoretical issues. Eligible topics include reading diagnosis, reading instruction in the classroom and clinic, cognitive processes of reading, and the development of literacy.

Publication Schedule: Quarterly

Circulation: 1,500

Concurrent Submission to Other Journals: Not permitted

Style Guide: Publication Manual of the American Psychological Association (5th edition)

Special Format Guidelines: See "Information for Authors" in the journal.

Recommended Length: No limitation
Copies to Be Submitted: Six
Electronic Submission: Not permitted
Review Procedure: Refereed using the blind review system. The review process takes three months.
Return of Rejections: Yes
Reason Given for Rejection: Yes
Time from Acceptance to Publication: Within nine months
Author's Complimentary Copies: Six copies of the journal and 15 reprints of the article
Send Manuscripts to: See current issue of the journal.

Journal of Multicultural Counseling and Development

Association for Multicultural Counseling and Development
Member: American Counseling Association
5999 Stevenson Avenue
Alexandria, VA 22304
(703) 823-9800
http://www.counseling.org/journals/guidelines/JMCD.html

Publishable Topics: Invites manuscripts pertaining to research, theory, or program applications related to multicultural and ethnic minority interests or experiences in the U. S. in all areas of counseling and human development.
Publication Schedule: Quarterly
Circulation: 2,000
Concurrent Submission to Other Journals: Not permitted
Style Guide: Publication Manual of the American Psychological Association (5th edition)
Special Format Guidelines: On a separate page provide the title of the article and the name of the author followed by a paragraph that repeats the author's name and gives the professional title and institutional affiliation. Include the author's address, telephone number, fax number, and e-mail address. Double-space all pages, including the abstract. Do not use footnotes. The use of tables should be kept to a minimum. Each table should be placed on a separate page following the reference section. Figures should be camera-ready.
Recommended Length: Maximum of 20 double-spaced pages, including the references. Provide an abstract not exceeding 50 words.
Copies to Be Submitted: Three
Electronic Submission: Not permitted for the original submission; however, if the manuscript is accepted for publication, the author will be asked to provide a final version on a 3.5" high-density disk prepared either in ASCII or WordPerfect for IBM-compatible computers or in Text file format for Macintosh computers. Label the disk with the first author's name, the journal title, and the software used to prepare the article.
Review Procedure: Refereed using the blind review system. Evaluative criteria include the significance of the topic, relevance to the journal, and clarity of writing. The review process takes from six to eight weeks.
Return of Rejections: Yes
Reason Given for Rejection: Yes

Time from Acceptance to Publication: Six months to a year
Send Manuscripts to: See current issue of the journal.

Journal of Negro Education

Howard University
P.O. Box 311
Washington, DC 20059
(202) 806-8121
Fax: (202) 806-8434

Publishable Topics: Publishes articles on the education of black people. The scope of the journal includes all levels of education, K–12 and higher education. Seeks manuscripts that explore issues addressing this theme.
Publication Schedule: Quarterly
Circulation: 1,600
Concurrent Submission to Other Journals: Not permitted
Style Guide: Publication Manual of the American Psychological Association (5th edition)
Special Format Guidelines: See "Instructions to Contributors" in a current issue of the journal.
Recommended Length: 25 double-spaced pages
Copies to Be Submitted: Three
Electronic Submission: Not permitted for the original submission; however, if the manuscript is accepted for publication, the author will be asked to provide a final version on a 3.5" high-density disk prepared either in MS Word or WordPerfect. Label the disk with the first author's name, the article's title, and the software used to prepare the article.
Review Procedure: Refereed. The review process takes three to four months.
Return of Rejections: Yes, if a self-addressed and stamped envelope has been provided by the author.
Reason Given for Rejection: Yes
Time from Acceptance to Publication: Within one year
Author's Complimentary Copies: Two
Send Manuscripts to: See current issue of the journal.

Journal of Research in Childhood Education

Association for Childhood Education International
Suite 215
17904 Georgia Avenue
Olney, MD 20832
(800) 423-3563
(301) 570-2111
Fax: (301) 570-2212
http://www.udel.edu/bateman/acei/jrceaguides.htm

Publishable Topics: Features articles that advance the knowledge and theory of the education of children, infancy through early adolescence. Consideration is given to empirical research, theoretical studies, ethnographic and case studies, participant-observation studies, and cross-cultural studies. The journal welcomes studies that address international concerns of childhood education. Occasionally accepts small-scale studies that have been implemented in a variety of settings and that are complex and report findings using meta-analytic techniques.

Publication Schedule: Two issues per year

Circulation: 5,000

Concurrent Submission to Other Journals: Not permitted

Style Guide: Publication Manual of the American Psychological Association (5th edition)

Special Format Guidelines: Place author's name and affiliation on only the title page. The first page of text should carry the title with the remaining pages displaying a running head. Double-space everything. Send an abstract of 100–200 words.

Recommended Length: 10–30 double-spaced pages, including the reference list

Copies to Be Submitted: Three

Electronic Submission: Not permitted

Review Procedure: Blind review system that takes three months

Return of Rejections: Yes

Reason Given for Rejection: Yes

Time from Acceptance to Publication: Six months to one year

Author's Complimentary Copies: Three

Send Manuscript to: See current issue of the journal.

Journal of Special Education

PRO-ED, Inc.
8700 Shoal Creek Boulevard
Austin, TX 78757
(512) 451-3246
Fax: (512) 302-9129
http://www.proedinc.com

Publishable Topics: Welcomes articles of research, theory, opinion, and review that are related to special education. The emphasis is on definitive and carefully documented articles. There is less interest in case studies and general surveys, albeit manuscripts of unusual interest will be considered. Extended book reviews of particular significance are invited.

Publication Schedule: Quarterly

Circulation: 3,500

Concurrent Submission to Other Journals: Not permitted

Style Guide: Publication Manual of the American Psychological Association (5th edition)

Special Format Guidelines: Include an abstract not exceeding 125 words. Recommend an in-text summary of the salient points. When using uncommon technical terms, provide short definitions.

Recommended Length: No specifications

Copies to Be Submitted: Four

Electronic Submission: Not permitted for the initial submission; however, after a manuscript has been accepted, the final version is to be submitted on a computer disk. Instructions will be provided.

Review Procedure: Refereed. Evaluative criteria include contribution to the field, adequacy of references, and clarity of writing. The review process takes approximately two months.

Return of Rejections: Yes

Reason Given for Rejection: Yes

Time from Acceptance to Publication: Six to nine months

Author's Complimentary Copies: One

Miscellaneous Guidelines: Provide a brief professional vita of the author

Send Manuscript to: See current issue of the journal.

Journal of Speech, Language, and Hearing Research
American Speech-Language-Hearing Association
10801 Rockville Pike
Rockville, MD 20852
(301) 897-5700
Fax: (301) 571-0457
http://www.asha.org

Publishable Topics: The journal focuses on studies of the processes and disorders of speech, hearing, and language. Manuscripts may take the form of experimental reports or of theoretical, tutorial, or review papers. Also considered are brief research notes that describe a procedure or instrumentation.

Publication Schedule: Bimonthly

Circulation: 49,000

Concurrent Submission to Other Journals: Not permitted

Style Guide: Publication Manual of the American Psychological Association (5th edition)

Special Format Guidelines: Double-space everything. Figures should be camera-ready.

Recommended Length: Not to exceed 40 double-spaced pages

Copies to Be Submitted: Five

Electronic Submission: Not permitted for the initial submission; however, after the manuscript has been accepted for publication, the final version will be requested on a 3.5" disk that preferably has been prepared in MS Word or WordPerfect. The computer disk should contain a label with the author's name and manuscript number that will have been assigned. Provide one hard copy with the disk.

Review Procedure: Refereed. The review process takes about six months.

Return of Rejections: Yes

Reason Given for Rejection: Yes

Time from Acceptance to Publication: Six to nine months

Author's Complimentary Copies: None

Send Manuscript to: See current issue of the journal.

Journal of Teacher Education
American Association of Colleges for Teacher Education (Owner)
Corwin Press, Inc. (Publisher)

2455 Teller Road
Thousand Oaks, CA 91320
(805) 499-9734
Fax: (805) 499-5323
http://www.corwinpress.com

Publishable Topics: Seeks manuscripts on teacher education that address such topics as teacher education programs, testing, standards, accountability, professional development, case studies, and methodologies.

Publication Schedule: Bimonthly

Circulation: 8,500

Concurrent Submission to Other Journals: Not permitted

Style Guide: Publication Manual of the American Psychological Association (5th edition)

Special Format Guidelines: Double-space the entire manuscript. The cover page should include the author's full name, institutional affiliation, address, telephone number, and e-mail address. Provide an abstract, not to exceed 150 words, on a separate sheet. This, too, should be double-spaced.

Recommended Length: Not to exceed 20 double-spaced pages, including references, tables, and charts.

Copies to Be Submitted: Four

Electronic Submission: Not permitted

Review Procedure: Refereed using the blind review system. The evaluative criteria include significance to the field, suitability for the journal's readers, stimulating quality of presentation, originality, comprehensiveness of the literature review, overall quality of the presentation, and clarity of the writing. The review process takes at least two months.

Return of Rejections: Yes

Reason Given for Rejection: Yes

Time from Acceptance to Publication: Three to nine months

Author's Complimentary Copies: Two copies of the journal and 25 tear sheets of the article

Send Manuscript to: See current issue of the journal.

Journal of Technology and Teacher Education

Association for the Advancement of Computing in Education
500 East Main Street
P.O. Box 3728
Norfolk, VA 23514-3728
(757) 623-7588
Fax: (703) 977-8760
http://www.aace.org

Publishable Topics: Seeks manuscripts that discuss the use of information technology in teacher education. Coverage includes preservice and in-service teacher education and graduate programs in curriculum and instruction, educational administration, educational computing, and instructional technology.

Publication Schedule: Quarterly

Circulation: 950
Concurrent Submission to Other Journals: Not permitted
Style Guide: Publication Manual of the American Psychological Association (5th edition)
Recommended Length: Maximum of 30 double-spaced pages
Copies to Be Submitted: Four
Electronic Submission: Permitted. Use Mac or IBM-compatible, high-density disk. Prefer files to be in MS Word; however, ASCII or RTF is accepted.
Review Procedure: Refereed. The review process takes three to six months.
Return of Rejections: No
Reason Given for Rejection: Yes
Time from Acceptance to Publication: Three months to one year
Author's Complimentary Copies: One
Send Manuscripts to: See current issue of the journal.

Language Arts

National Council of Teachers of English
1111 W. Kenyon Road
Urbana, IL 61801
(217) 328-3870
http://www.ncte.org

Publishable Topics: Publishes original contributions on all aspects of language arts teaching and learning. The contents are of primary interest to teachers of children in the preschool through middle-school years. Welcomes viewpoints not only from education but also from other academic areas that have implications for language arts teaching.
Publication Schedule: Monthly, September through April
Circulation: 18,000
Concurrent Submission to Other Journals: Not permitted
Style Guide: The Chicago Manual of Style (14th edition)
Special Format Guidelines: Double-space the manuscript. Include a cover sheet containing the author's name, position, and address. Identifying information should not appear elsewhere in the manuscript.
Recommended Length: No specifications
Copies to Be Submitted: Three
Electronic Submission: Not permitted
Review Procedure: Refereed. The review process takes up to nine months.
Return of Rejections: Yes, if a self-addressed and stamped envelope has been provided by the writer
Reason Given for Rejection: No
Time from Acceptance to Publication: Approximately three months
Author's Complimentary Copies: Two
Send Manuscripts to: See current issue of the journal.

Learning Disability Quarterly

Council for Learning Disabilities
P.O. Box 40303
Overland Park, KS 66204

(913) 492-8755
Fax: (913) 492-2546
http://www.cldinternational.org

Publishable Topics: The primary purpose of the journal is to publish educational articles with an applied focus in the area of learning disabilities. The main emphasis should be on learning disabilities, not on topics or studies that incidentally use learning-disabled subjects or only indirectly relate to the field of learning disabilities. Invites manuscripts with an educational theme in learning disabilities on such topics as reports of techniques in identification, assessment, remediation, or programming; interpretive reviews of the literature; advancement of theory and discussion of pertinent issues; original applied research; and the description of model programs for preservice and in-service training of professionals and paraprofessionals in learning disabilities.

Publication Schedule: Quarterly

Circulation: 2,500

Concurrent Submission to Other Journals: Not permitted

Style Guide: Publication Manual of the American Psychological Association (5th edition)

Special Format Guidelines: Authors are requested to define operationally the populations used in reported studies and to delineate clearly the parameters of settings. Research articles are to translate major findings into practice and to specify the implications for application to learning disability populations or to learning disability settings. Also, articles that develop a given theory or model are to relate such to practice. Include a cover sheet that gives the names and affiliations of all authors and the address of the principal author. Submit a 100–150-word abstract.

Recommended Length: 20–25 double-spaced pages

Copies to Be Submitted: Four

Electronic Submission: Not permitted for the original submission; however, after the manuscript has been accepted for publication and after corrections have been implemented, the final version is to be submitted on a 3.5" high-density disk that is either Mac or IBM-compatible. Prefers files to be in MS Word or WordPerfect; however, other software may be acceptable. Check first.

Review Procedure: Refereed using the blind review system. The review process takes approximately three months.

Return of Rejections: Yes

Reason Given for Rejection: Yes

Time from Acceptance to Publication: 6 to 12 months

Author's Complimentary Copies: One

Send Manuscript to: See current issue of the journal.

Liberal Education

Association of American Colleges and Universities
1818 R Street, NW
Washington, DC 20009
(202) 387-3760
Fax: (202) 265-9532

http://www.aacu-edu.org

Publishable Topics: This journal's mission is to promote liberal education. As such, it serves as a forum for the discussion of ideas on liberal education in higher education. Among the topics on which its articles have been written are collaborative leadership, building faculty capacities, curriculum and general education, diversity, and global awareness.

Publication Schedule: Quarterly

Circulation: 4,500

Concurrent Submission to Other Journals: Not permitted

Style Guide: The Chicago Manual of Style (14th edition)

Special Format Guidelines: See "Publications" on Web site cited above.

Recommended Length: Depending on the section of the journal, 1,800–3,500 words

Copies to Be Submitted: Two

Electronic Submission: Permitted. Submit on a 3.5" high-density disk prepared in MS Word or WordPerfect 6.1 (or earlier version). One hard copy should accompany the disk.

Review Procedure: Not refereed. The review process takes two months.

Return of Rejections: No

Reason Given for Rejection: No

Time from Acceptance to Publication: Varies

Author's Complimentary Copies: Five

Send Manuscript to: See current issue of the journal.

Mathematics Teacher

National Council of Teachers of Mathematics
1906 Association Drive
Reston, VA 20191
(703) 620-9840
Fax: (703) 476-2970
http://www.nctm.org/mt/writers/guidelines.htm

Publishable Topics: This journal is devoted to the improvement of mathematics instruction in the senior high schools, two-year colleges, and teacher education colleges. Articles on the teaching of standard mathematical content in creative and productive ways are especially welcome.

Publication Schedule: Nine issues per year

Circulation: 50,000

Concurrent Submission to Other Journals: Not permitted, except to affiliates of the National Council of Teachers of Mathematics

Style Guide: The Chicago Manual of Style (14th edition)

Special Format Guidelines: Author identification should be limited to a separate sheet. There should be no author identification in the manuscript. Writers may request a copy of NCTM's "Information and Guidelines for Contributors to the Official NCTM Journals" or visit the Web site cited above for more instructions.

Recommended Length: Not to exceed 10 double-spaced pages

Copies to Be Submitted: Five

Electronic Submission: Not permitted

Review Procedure: Refereed using the blind review system. The evaluative criteria include appropriateness for the audience, accuracy of the content, originality, and clarity. The review process takes three to four months.

Return of Rejections: No

Reason Given for Rejection: Yes

Time from Acceptance to Publication: At least six months

Author's Complimentary Copies: 10

Send Manuscript to: See current issue of the journal.

Mathematics Teaching in the Middle School

National Council of Teachers of Mathematics

1906 Association Drive

Reston, VA 20191

(703) 620-9840

Fax: (703) 476-2970

http://www.nctm.org/mtms/writers/guidelines.htm

Publishable Topics: This journal serves as a medium for the exchange of ideas and a source of techniques for teaching mathematics in grades 5–9. Articles present new developments in instruction, curriculum, learning, and teacher education as they relate to mathematics.

Publication Schedule: Nine issues per year

Circulation: 34,000

Concurrent Submission to Other Journals: Permitted only to journals that are affiliated with the National Council of Teachers of Mathematics

Style Guide: The Chicago Manual of Style (14th edition)

Special Format Guidelines: For detailed instructions, see the Web site cited above or write for a copy of "Information and Guidelines for Contributors to the Official NCTM Journals."

Copies to Be Submitted: Five

Electronic Submission: Not permitted

Review Procedure: Refereed. Evaluative criteria include appropriateness for the journal and its readers, importance and uniqueness of the ideas and theories presented that will advance the field of mathematics education, and clarity of expression.

Return of Rejections: No

Reason Given for Rejection: Yes

Time from Acceptance to Publication: At least six months

Author's Complimentary Copies: 10

Send Manuscripts to: See current issue of the journal.

Measurement and Evaluation in Counseling and Development

Association for Assessment in Counseling

Member: American Counseling Association

5999 Stevenson Avenue
Alexandria, VA 22304
(703) 823-9800
http://www.counseling.org/journals/guidelines/MECD.html

Publishable Topics: Invites manuscripts that are of interest to the measurement specialist, counselor, and personnel worker in schools and colleges, public and private agencies, business, industry, and government. All manuscripts must have clearly described implications for practitioners in measurement and evaluation. Articles may include research, theoretical works, and interpretation of test information.

Publication Schedule: Quarterly

Circulation: 3,200

Concurrent Submission to Other Journals: Not permitted

Style Guide: Publication Manual of the American Psychological Association (5th edition)

Special Format Guidelines: Minimize the use of tables and footnotes. Artwork for figures should be camera-ready. Present detailed descriptions of samples used in the reported research and provide the effect size estimates as well as the statistical significance tests that were used. Authors should assist the reader in interpreting the statistical significance of the results. Identification of the author should appear only on the cover page. Accompanying the manuscript should be an abstract of no longer than 25 words. For further instructions, see the Web site cited above or "Guidelines for Authors" in the journal.

Recommended Length: Feature articles should be between 1,500 and 3,000 words

Copies to Be Submitted: Four

Electronic Submission: Not permitted for the original submission; however, after the manuscript has been accepted for publication, a final version should be provided on a 3.5" high-density disk prepared in either MS Word, WordPerfect, ASCII for IBM-compatible computers, or Text File format for Macintosh computers. The disk's label must contain the author's name along with identification of the hardware and software that were used.

Review Procedure: Refereed using the blind review system. The review process takes three to six months.

Time from Acceptance to Publication: Approximately six months

Author's Complimentary Copies: Five

Send Manuscripts to: See current issue of the journal.

NASPA *Journal*

National Association of Student Personnel Administrators
Suite 418
1875 Connecticut Avenue, NW
Washington, DC 20009
(202) 265-7500
Fax: (202) 797-1157
http://www.naspa.org

Publishable Topics: Seeks manuscripts that have been written for the college student affairs practitioner and/or scholar and that provide thorough and concise treatment of relevant topics. General topics may include issues related to leadership and management of higher education, student learning and development, policy, and governance. Specific topics relate to functional areas in which student affairs professionals work. Research articles should describe the stimulus for the research, clearly state the methodology followed, and offer a full discussion of the findings, implications, and conclusions.

Publication Schedule: Quarterly

Circulation: 10,000

Concurrent Submission to Other Journals: Not permitted

Style Guide: Publication Manual of the American Psychological Association (5th edition)

Special Format Guidelines: Place the author's name, position, and institutional affiliation on a separate title page. Double-space all portions of the manuscript. Avoid sexist terminology. Do not use footnotes; instead, incorporate the information in the text. Use the past tense for the literature review and description of procedures and the present tense for the results and discussion.

Recommended Length: Not to exceed 3,000 words, including references, tables, and figures.

Copies to Be Submitted: Four

Electronic Submission: Not permitted for the original submission; however, if the manuscript is accepted for publication, the final version must be submitted in DOS, not Mac.

Review Procedure: Refereed using the blind review system. The evaluative criteria include appropriateness for the student affairs generalist and the clarity and style of writing. The review process takes approximately two months.

Return of Rejections: No

Reason Given for Rejection: Yes

Time from Acceptance to Publication: Six months

Author's Complimentary Copies: Five

Send Manuscripts to: See current issue of the journal.

NASSP Bulletin

National Association of Secondary School Principals
1904 Association Drive
Reston, VA 20191
(703) 860-0200
Fax: (703) 476-5432
http://www.nassp.org

Publishable Topics: Publishes articles on all aspects of school administration, describing trends, innovations, and practices in secondary schools.

Publication Schedule: Monthly (September through May)

Circulation: 40,000

Concurrent Submission to Other Journals: Not permitted

Style Guide: Publication Manual of the American Psychological Association (5th edition)

Special Format Guidelines: Author's identifying information must be restricted to a separate title page that provides the manuscript's title, the author's name and affiliation, and the date of submission. In a cover letter, provide the author's name, address, telephone and fax numbers, and e-mail address. Double-space the manuscript and provide a brief abstract. For further guidelines, see the Web site cited above.

Recommended Length: 3,000–4,000 words

Copies to Be Submitted: Two

Electronic Submission: Permitted. Submit on a 3.5" high-density disk, preferably prepared in MS Word 7.0 or in RTF. Also provide two printouts with the disk. May submit via e-mail to bulletin@principals.org. An e-mail submission must comply with the same guidelines as a hard copy. Do not fax a manuscript.

Review Procedure: There are three reviews; namely, an editorial review, blind peer review, and an advisory council review. These address the appropriateness for the journal, scholarly content and treatment, and significance to secondary school administrators. The evaluative criteria also include timeliness of the topic, technical suitability, and clarity of the writing. The review process takes approximately eight weeks.

Return of Rejections: Yes, if requested and a self-addressed and stamped envelope has been provided by the author.

Reason Given for Rejection: No

Time from Acceptance to Publication: Approximately eight months

Author's Complimentary Copies: Two

Send Manuscript to: See current issue of the journal.

Phi Delta Kappan

Phi Delta Kappa
P.O. Box 789
Bloomington, IN 47402
(812) 339-1156
Fax: (812) 339-0018
http://www.pdkintl.org/kappan/kappan.htm

Publishable Topics: Seeks manuscripts that are concerned with educational research, service, and leadership. Emphasis is on current issues, trends, controversy, and policy in education. Manuscripts should address real problems confronting the field of education.

Publication Schedule: Monthly (September through June)

Circulation: 120,000

Concurrent Submission to Other Journals: Permitted

Style Guide: The Chicago Manual of Style (14th edition). Do not use APA style for footnotes.

Special Format Guidelines: Manuscripts should be factual, logical, and sharply focused. Avoid being pedantic and do not use a dissertation or textbook style. Do not place the conclusions last; instead, the first paragraph should state the major point of the article. Double-space the manuscript.

Recommended Length: 4–20 double-spaced pages

Copies to Be Submitted: One
Electronic Submission: Not permitted
Review Procedure: Not refereed; reviewed by the editors. The evaluative criteria include educational significance, readability, usefulness to the readers, clarity of writing, and concreteness (use an example for every principle or generalization). The review process takes a maximum of eight weeks.
Return of Rejections: Yes, if a self-addressed and stamped envelope has been provided by the writer.
Reason Given for Rejection: Sometimes
Time from Acceptance to Publication: Varies
Author's Complimentary Copies: Five
Send Manuscripts to: See current issue of the journal.

Planning for Higher Education

Society for College and University Planning
311 Maynard Street
Ann Arbor, MI 48104
(734) 998-7832
Fax: (734) 998-6532
http://www.scup.org

Publishable Topics: Articles highlight academic, administrative, financial, and physical planning for higher education in the institutional, state/provincial, national, or international contexts. More favorable consideration will be given to manuscripts that focus on a particular aspect of planning if the focus is related to the broader planning function or to higher education generally. Manuscripts that include an analysis of information or experience are preferred to the mere reporting or description of research findings or work in progress.
Publication Schedule: Quarterly
Circulation: 4,700
Concurrent Submission to Other Journals: Permitted if the author indicates that the manuscript has been submitted elsewhere and, if selected for *Planning for Higher Education,* agrees to publish only in this journal.
Style Guide: The Chicago Manual of Style (14th edition)
Special Format Guidelines: Place author identification information only on first page. Include the mailing address and telephone number. Double-space the manuscript and number each page. A format for manuscripts may be obtained from the society's office.
Recommended Length: 4,000 words
Copies to Be Submitted: Three hard copies and one electronic copy
Electronic Submission: Prefer electronic submission. Do so either on disk or e-mail attachment using MS Word. Also provide three hard copies.
Review Procedure: Refereed using the blind review system. The evaluative criteria include originality, readability, accuracy, contribution to the field, breadth of appeal, the practical benefit to planning in a variety of settings, and benefit to higher education generally. The review process takes from 8 to 10 weeks.

Return of Rejections: Yes
Reason Given for Rejection: Yes
Time from Acceptance to Publication: Three months
Author's Complimentary Copies: Two
Send Manuscripts to: See current issue of the journal.

The Presidency

American Council on Education
One Dupont Circle, NW
Washington, DC 20036
(202) 939-9380
Fax: (202) 833-4760
http://www.acenet.edu

Publishable Topics: This magazine serves as a forum for college and university presidents on issues of policy and leadership in higher education. Manuscripts must address timely topics and provide information and perspectives that are "must reading" for higher education policymakers.

Publication Schedule: Fall, winter, and spring

Circulation: 8,000

Concurrent Submission to Other Journals: Not permitted

Style Guide: The Chicago Manual of Style (14th edition)

Special Format Guidelines: Favors a clear, lively, nonacademic writing style that is comparable to a popular commentary magazine, such as *The New Yorker* or *Harper's*. Endnotes should not be used; however, if thought necessary, minimize their use. If used, number endnotes consecutively throughout the manuscript and place them on a separate page at the end of the manuscript. Sidebars and fact boxes are encouraged. Tables, graphs, and charts are allowable provided their data are interpreted in narrative form.

Recommended Length: 2,000–2,500 words for feature articles and approximately 800 words for columns

Copies to Be Submitted: Two

Electronic Submission: Not permitted for unsolicited manuscripts

Review Procedure: Not a refereed magazine; however, the input of an editorial advisory board is sought. It evaluates manuscripts based on originality, relevance to the readership, timeliness of topic, insightfulness, logical organization of ideas, and clarity of writing. The review process takes six to eight weeks.

Return of Rejections: Yes, if a self-addressed and stamped envelope has been provided by the writer.

Reason Given for Rejection: Sometimes

Time from Acceptance to Publication: Three to six months

Author's Complimentary Copies: Three

Send Manuscript to: See current issue of the magazine.

Professional School Counseling
American School Counselor Association
Suite 310
801 N. Fairfax Street
Alexandria, VA 22314
(800) 306-4722
(703) 683-2722
Fax: (703) 683-1619
http://www.schoolcounselor.org

Publishable Topics: Considers manuscripts on school counseling research, practices, and issues. Publishes articles on the latest theory, research, materials, techniques, and ideas in the field of school counseling.
Publication Schedule: Five issues per year
Circulation: 15,000
Concurrent Submission to Other Journals: Not permitted
Style Guide: Publication Manual of the American Psychological Association (5th edition)
Special Format Guidelines: Double-space the manuscript and do not use footnotes. A cover page should provide the author's name, telephone number, and affiliation in addition to the manuscript's title and date of submission. Include an abstract of 50–75 words.
Recommended Length: 25 pages
Copies to Be Submitted: Three
Electronic Submission: Not permitted for original submission; however, after the manuscript has been accepted for publication, the final version should be submitted on a 3.5" high-density disk that has been IBM formatted and prepared in MS Word, WordPerfect, or ASCII. Affix a label that identifies the author's name and software used. A hard copy should accompany the disk.
Review Procedure: Anonymously refereed by editorial board members
Reason Given for Rejection: Yes
Time from Acceptance to Publication: Varies
Author's Complimentary Copies: Three
Send Manuscript to: See current issue of the journal.

Reading Research Quarterly
International Reading Association
800 Barksdale Road
P.O. Box 8139
Newark, DE 19714
(302) 731-1600
Fax: (302) 368-2449
http://www.reading.org

Publishable Topics: Features reading research and theories of the reading process. Accepts manuscripts that report experimental or descriptive research within a theoretical context. Topics that will be considered include reading acquisition, reading instruction, typical and atypical reading processes, and historical and sociological perspectives on reading. Manuscripts on spelling and writing will not be accepted unless they are specifically applied to reading.

Publication Schedule: Quarterly

Circulation: 12,000

Concurrent Submission to Other Journals: Not permitted

Style Guide: Publication Manual of the American Psychological Association (5th edition)

Special Format Guidelines: At the top of each page type an identifying word or phrase and the page number. Do not place a name on each page. Type the author's full name and address only on a cover sheet. Double-space everything in the manuscript, including quotations and references. Minimize the use of footnotes. When they are used, they should be typed on a separate page following the references. Avoid sexist language.

Recommended Length: No specifications

Copies to Be Submitted: Five

Electronic Submission: Not permitted

Review Procedure: Refereed using the blind review system. The evaluative criteria include contribution to the field, quality of presentation and scientific validity, appropriateness for the journal, and style of writing. The review process takes about three months.

Return of Rejections: No

Reason Given for Rejection: Yes

Time from Acceptance to Publication: Six months

Author's Complimentary Copies: 10

Send Manuscript to: See current issue of the journal.

The Reading Teacher

International Reading Association

800 Barksdale Road

P.O. Box 8139

Newark, DE 19714

(302) 731-1600

Fax: (302) 368-2449

http://www.reading.org

Publishable Topics: Features articles about the teaching and learning of reading that address theory, research, and practice. This journal is delimited to the preschool and elementary school years (i.e., reading among children up to age 12).

Publication Schedule: Eight issues per year

Circulation: 71,000

Concurrent Submission to Other Journals: Not permitted

Style Guide: Publication Manual of the American Psychological Association (5th edition)

Special Format Guidelines: Write in article style, not the style of a formal research report. Manuscripts that are based on research should have a strong focus on meaningful results rather than on the research methodology. Double-space throughout, including references and quotations. At the top of each page type an identifying word or phrase and the page number. Do not place the author's name on each page. On a cover sheet, type the author's full name, return address, telephone number, and a summary of the manuscript. Avoid the use of sexist language.

Recommended Length: 20 double-spaced pages

Copies to Be Submitted: Four

Electronic Submission: Permitted. Send a 3.5" high-density disk formatted in either DOS or Macintosh. Prepare in either MS Word or WordPerfect. Four hard copies should accompany the disk.

Review Procedure: Refereed using the blind review system. The evaluative criteria include appropriateness for the journal, meaningfulness to practitioners in education, quality of presentation, and writing style. The review process takes about two months.

Return of Rejections: No

Reason Given for Rejection: Yes

Time from Acceptance to Publication: 2 to 12 months

Author's Complimentary Copies: Five

Send Manuscript to: See current issue of the journal.

Research in Higher Education

Association for Institutional Research (Sponsor)
Kluwer Academic/Human Sciences Press (Publisher)
233 Spring Street
New York, NY 10013
(212) 620-8000
Fax: (212) 463-0742
http://www.wkap.com

Publishable Topics: Focuses on the study of the processes and operations of institutions of higher education. RHE is a journal for institutional research and is directed to the interests of institutional researchers, planners, faculty, administrators, and others interested in institutional research. Seeks empirical studies that aid in the understanding of institutions of higher education. Topics that are considered include administration, faculty, curriculum and instruction, student characteristics, recruitment and admissions, student academic achievement, retention, attrition, campus climate, and other topics pertaining to collegiate performance.

Publication Schedule: Six issues per year

Concurrent Submission to Other Journals: Not permitted

Style Guide: See "Information for Authors" in the journal. Also, *Publication Manual of the American Psychological Association* (5th edition).

Special Format Guidelines: Double-space throughout the manuscript. The first page should contain the manuscript's title and the author's name, affiliation, and address. No identification should be placed on other pages. Type the tables on separate pages at the end of the manuscript. Cite references by name and year in the text and list alphabetically in the reference list. Provide an abstract of approximately 150 words. See "Information for Authors" in the journal for more guidelines.

Recommended Length: No specifications

Copies to Be Submitted: Three

Electronic Submission: Not permitted for the initial submission; however, after a manuscript has been accepted and all revisions as required by the editor have been made, the final version of the manuscript should be submitted on a disk that is labeled with the software used, journal's name, and author's last name. A hard copy of the final version must accompany the electronic file on disk.

Review Procedure: Refereed using the blind review system. The evaluative criteria include significance to the field, technical adequacy, appropriateness to the journal, and clarity of writing. The review process takes 30–45 days.

Return of Rejections: Yes

Reason Given for Rejection: Yes

Time from Acceptance to Publication: 9 to 12 months

Author's Complimentary Copies: None

Send Manuscripts to: See current issue of the journal.

Research Quarterly for Exercise and Sport

American Alliance for Health, Physical Education, Recreation, and Dance

1900 Association Drive

Reston, VA 20191

(800) 213-7193

(703) 476-3484

Fax: (703) 476-9527

http://www.aahperd.org/publications-rqes.html

Publishable Topics: Publishes research articles in the art and science of human movement. These articles must contribute to knowledge and to the development of theory. The focus may be on new information, confirmation or denial of previous findings, or the application of new or improved techniques.

Publication Schedule: Four issues plus one supplement annually

Circulation: 7,500

Concurrent Submission to Other Journals: Not permitted

Style Guide: Publication Manual of the American Psychological Association (5th edition)

Special Format Guidelines: See "Guide for Contributors" in the journal or at the Web site cited above.

Recommended Length: 28 double-spaced pages for feature articles, 14 double-spaced pages for research notes. These counts include text, references, tables, and figures.

Copies to Be Submitted: Four

Electronic Submission: Not permitted for the original submission; however, after the manuscript has been accepted for publication, provide the final version of the manuscript on a 3.5" high-density disk that has an IBM-compatible format. Prefer preparation done in MS Word. One hard copy should accompany the disk.

Review Procedure: Blind review. The review process takes two to three months.

Return of Rejections: No

Reason Given for Rejection: Yes

Time from Acceptance to Publication: Four to six months

Author's Complimentary Copies: One

Send Manuscript to: See current issue of the journal.

Review of Educational Research
American Educational Research Association
1230 17th Street, NW
Washington, DC 20036
(202) 223-9485
http://www.aera.net/pubs/pubinfo.htm

Publishable Topics: Contains critical integrative reviews of educational research literature. The journal does not accept original empirical research because it is a journal of reviews. Each review should have conceptualizations, interpretations, and syntheses of scholarly work. RER encourages submissions from other disciplines related to educational issues.

Publication Schedule: Quarterly

Circulation: 18,000

Concurrent Submission to Other Journals: Not permitted

Style Guide: Publication Manual of the American Psychological Association (5th edition) or *The Chicago Manual of Style* (14th edition)

Special Format Guidelines: Use subheads at reasonable intervals and underline only words that are to be in italics. Minimize the use of footnotes; however, when they are used, type them on a separate page and number consecutively throughout the manuscript. The first page should contain the title of the manuscript but not the name of the author. On a separate sheet, type the full title of the manuscript and name of the author. If there are multiple authors, provide the address and telephone number of the first author listed. Send an abstract of 100–150 words.

Recommended Length: 25–50 double-spaced pages

Copies to Be Submitted: Four

Electronic Submission: Not permitted for the original submission; however, after the manuscript has been accepted for publication, provide the final version of the manuscript on a 3.5" high-density disk that preferably has been prepared in MS Word. Also accepts WordPerfect or RTF. One hard copy should accompany the disk.

Review Procedure: Refereed using the blind review system. The review process takes up to three months.

Return of Rejections: Yes

Reason Given for Rejection: Yes

Time from Acceptance to Publication: At least three months

Author's Complimentary Copies: Five

Send Manuscript to: See current issue of the journal.

School Psychology Review
National Association of School Psychologists
Suite 402
4340 East West Highway
Bethesda, MD 20814
(301) 657-0270
Fax: (301) 657-0275

http://www.naspweb.org

Publishable Topics: Invites manuscripts that address the interests of practicing school psychologists. Seeks original research, reviews of theoretical and applied topics, case studies, and descriptions of intervention techniques that are useful to school psychologists.

Publication Schedule: Quarterly

Circulation: 22,000+

Concurrent Submission to Other Journals: Not permitted

Style Guide: Publication Manual of the American Psychological Association (5th edition)

Special Format Guidelines: Double-space the manuscript and submit a 100–150-word abstract

Recommended Length: 30 double-spaced pages

Copies to Be Submitted: Five

Electronic Submission: Not permitted

Review Procedure: Refereed using the blind review system by members of the editorial board and ad hoc reviewers. The evaluative criteria include importance of the topic for school psychologists, contribution to the field, and clarity of writing. The review process takes two to three months.

Return of Rejections: Yes

Reason Given for Rejection: Yes

Time from Acceptance to Publication: 6 to 12 months

Author's Complimentary Copies: One

Send Manuscript to: See current issue of the journal.

Teaching Children Mathematics

National Council of Teachers of Mathematics
1906 Association Drive
Reston, VA 20191
(703) 620-9840
Fax: (703) 476-2970
http://www.nctm.org/tcm/writers/guidelines.htm

Publishable Topics: This journal serves as a medium for the exchange of ideas and a source of techniques for teaching mathematics in grades preK–6. Articles present new developments in instruction, curriculum, learning, and teacher education as they relate to mathematics at the specified grade levels.

Publication Schedule: Nine issues per year

Circulation: 40,000

Concurrent Submission to Other Journals: Permitted only to journals that are affiliated with NCTM.

Style Guide: The Chicago Manual of Style (14th edition)

Special Format Guidelines: For detailed instructions, see the Web site cited or write for "Information and Guidelines for Contributors to the Official NCTM Journals."

Copies to Be Submitted: Five

Electronic Submission: Not permitted

Review Procedure: Refereed. Evaluative criteria include appropriateness for the journal and its readers, importance and uniqueness of ideas presented, clarity of expression, and the offering of ideas and theories that will advance the field of mathematics education.

Return of Rejections: No
Reason Given for Rejection: Yes
Time from Acceptance to Publication: At least six months
Author's Complimentary Copies: 10
Send Manuscript to: See current issue of the journal.

TechTrends, For Leaders in Education and Training
Association for Educational Communications and Technology
Suite 2
1800 North Stonelake Drive
Bloomington, IN 47404
(812) 335-7675
Fax: (812) 335-7678
http://www.aect.org

Publishable Topics: Publishes articles that report on a broad range of topics related to the application of new technological developments in the educational setting.
Publication Schedule: Six issues per year
Circulation: 6,000
Concurrent Submission to Other Journals: Not permitted
Style Guide: Publication Manual of the American Psychological Association (5th edition)
Special Format Guidelines: This publication styles itself as a popular magazine, not an academic journal. Write in a conversational style. Do not use footnotes. Double-space the manuscript. Author identification should be with only one copy of the manuscript. Submit a brief biographical profile of the author and an abstract not exceeding 150 words. Figures, tables, photographs, and other graphics are encouraged.
Recommended Length: 3–16 double-spaced pages
Copies to Be Submitted: Three hard copies and one computer disk
Electronic Submission: Permitted. Accompanying the printouts should be a computer disk preferably prepared in MS Word or as an RTF file. Do not send by fax or e-mail. Illustrations should be sent as separate files on the disk. Save photographs as .eps, .tif, or .jpg files. Line art and graphics should be saved as .eps, .tif, or .gif files.
Review Procedure: Refereed using the blind review system. The evaluative criteria include suitability to the journal, timeliness of the topic, contribution to the field, and cogent writing style to enhance understanding. The review process takes two to four months.
Return of Rejections: Yes, if the writer provides a self-addressed and stamped envelope
Reason Given for Rejection: Yes
Time from Acceptance to Publication: Varies
Author's Complimentary Copies: Two
Send Manuscripts to: See current issue of the magazine.

Thought and Action

National Education Association
1201 16th Street, NW
Washington, DC 20036
(202) 833-4000
Fax: (202) 822-7206
http://www.nea.org/he/taguid.html

Publishable Topics: Welcomes manuscripts that offer theoretical and practical information on issues in higher education. Considers a broad range of topics that are of interest to faculty.
Publication Schedule: Fall and spring
Circulation: 80,000
Concurrent Submission to Other Journals: Not permitted
Style Guide: The Chicago Manual of Style (14th edition)
Special Format Guidelines: Double-space the manuscript. Place the author's name, address, and telephone number on only the title page.
Recommended Length: Maximum of 15 double-spaced pages
Copies to Be Submitted: One hard copy and a computer disk copy
Electronic Submission: Prefers an IBM-PC compatible 3.5" high-density disk prepared in MS Word or WordPerfect; however, accepts Macintosh and other word-processing formats.
Review Procedure: Refereed. Manuscripts are evaluated on the basis of their overall interest to the professoriate. The review process takes approximately six months.
Return of Rejections: Yes, if requested
Reason Given for Rejection: No
Time from Acceptance to Publication: Up to six months
Author's Complimentary Copies: Five
Send Manuscript to: See current issue of the journal.

Trusteeship

Association of Governing Boards of Universities and Colleges
Suite 400
One Dupont Circle, NW
Washington, DC 20036
(202) 296-8400
Fax: (202) 223-7053
http://www.agb.org

Publishable Topics: Designed primarily for lay trustees of all types of colleges and universities, this magazine serves to inform trustees and senior administrators on topics germane to higher education governance and policy-making. Manuscripts are sought that provide practical advice, information, and how-to examples; disclose emerging trends or findings of research on higher education management and policy-making; and discuss ideas and issues of interest to trustees and presidents.

Publication Schedule: Bimonthly

Circulation: 34,000

Concurrent Submission to Other Journals: Not permitted

Style Guide: None. Articles are suitable for a popular-style magazine, not an academic journal.

Special Format Guidelines: Write in a lively and jargon-free style in the active voice. Use many examples to illustrate the theme. Footnotes and references are not published. Double-space the manuscript. Provide the author's name, telephone and fax numbers, and e-mail address.

Recommended Length: 2,000–2,500 words

Copies to Be Submitted: One

Electronic Submission: Permitted. May submit initial manuscript via fax or e-mail. After the manuscript has been accepted for publication, submit it on a PC-compatible disk or as an e-mail attachment in MS Word or text-only format. Macintosh disks cannot be accepted.

Review Procedure: Not refereed. Reviewed by the editorial staff and, occasionally, others. The review process takes about one month.

Return of Rejections: No, unless requested by the writer and a self-addressed stamped envelope has been provided to the editor

Reason Given for Rejection: No

Time from Acceptance to Publication: Up to three months

Author's Complimentary Copies: Three

Send Manuscript to: See current issue of the magazine.

CHAPTER 2

Authors' Guide to Book Publishers

INTRODUCTION

This chapter introduces writers in education and related fields to the world of book publishers. Following the feat of writing a book-length manuscript is the challenge to have it accepted by a publisher. This process involves identifying a company that has a need for the manuscript in terms of its publishing purposes and targeted market. It is a matter of selling (i.e., convincing the publishing house that the manuscript is right for it). Writers should understand that publishers of professional material have specific objectives and that all submissions are evaluated in reference to them. To be accepted, the material's and publisher's purposes must be compatible.

In some fields, such as elementary education, a publisher develops an organized series of textbooks according to a master plan. To execute this plan, the company assembles a team of authors who have been chosen with the assistance of professionals in the field. In this situation, an unsolicited manuscript is rarely accepted because it usually does not fit in with the planned publications; however, there are some exceptions regarding supplementary teaching materials.

Success in having a book published requires producing a manuscript of professional quality and finding the proper publisher. The author's first contact with a publisher should be with a prospectus that explains the purpose of the proposed book, a table of contents that contains a brief description of each chapter, a sample chapter, a list of competing titles already in the market, and a curriculum vita. Most publishers do not want to receive a completed manuscript as part of the initial inquiry of interest.

To help scholarly writers with their search for a publisher, this chapter identifies publishing houses that consider unsolicited manuscripts for publication. First, these publishers are categorized according to the subject areas in which they publish. Professional education subjects that are usually associated with the curriculum found in a college of education are listed first, and the associated publications are either college-level textbooks or professional materials for practitioners in education. The latter may be teachers, professors, counselors, or administrators at any level within the education profession.

The second categorization of publishers is by subject areas outside professional education. Although most of these publications are textbooks at the different levels, they may also be professional materials for teachers and others. In a few cases, supplementary teaching materials are the publishing services of the publishers. The categories are deliberately broad to accommodate the diversified programs of the publishing industry. Furthermore, the reader should recognize that the objectives of publishing companies periodically change due to shifts in market demand, curricular emphases, and corporate situations.

During recent years, the book publishing industry has undergone major adjustments as corporate mergers have caused publishing companies to be absorbed into new corporate structures, and some companies have even become extinct. Some giants of yesterday have either disappeared or become organizational units of other companies. As a consequence, at the time of this writing, the foci and direction of publishing houses remain in flux as they engage in a reassessment of the market, and this impacts their individual publishing missions. Due to this condition, the information contained within the guidelines, which is based on responses from publishers, was valid at one time, but subsequent corporate changes may occur because of the dynamics in the publishing industry.

Following the categorizations of publishing companies are their guidelines for considering manuscripts. It is incumbent upon would-be authors to know and follow these guidelines. Information concerning internal procedures and policies of interest to writers accompanies the guidelines. The reader is advised first to identify the publisher in the subject categorization list and then read the entry on guidelines.

BOOK PUBLISHERS BY PUBLISHING FIELD

Professional Education Subjects

Adult and Continuing Education

> American Council on Education/Praeger
> Lawrence Erlbaum Associates
> Jossey-Bass Inc., A Wiley Company
> Weidner & Sons Publishing
> John Wiley & Sons, Inc., College Division

Agriculture Education

> Interstate Publishers, Inc.
> Weidner & Sons Publishing

Child and Adolescent Development

> American Counseling Association
> American Press
> Lawrence Erlbaum Associates
> Houghton Mifflin Co., College Division
> McGraw-Hill Higher Education
> National Association for the Education of Young Children
> Prentice Hall Direct
> Sage Publications
> Waveland Press
> Weidner & Sons Publishing
> John Wiley & Sons, Inc., College Division

Child Psychology

American Press
Lawrence Erlbaum Associates
McGraw-Hill Higher Education
Prentice Hall Direct
Waveland Press
Weidner & Sons Publishing
John Wiley & Sons, Inc., College Division

Comparative Education

Phi Delta Kappa International
Weidner & Sons Publishing

Counseling and Guidance

American Counseling Association
American Press
McGraw-Hill Higher Education
Prentice Hall Direct
Research Press
Sage Publications
Charles C Thomas, Publisher
J. Weston Walch, Publisher
Waveland Press
Weidner & Sons Publishing
John Wiley & Sons, Inc., College Division

Curriculum

American Council on Education/Praeger
American Press
Lawrence Erlbaum Associates
Houghton Mifflin Co., College Division
McGraw-Hill Higher Education
Phi Delta Kappa International
Prentice Hall Direct
Sage Publications
Scholastic, Inc.
Charles C Thomas, Publisher
Waveland Press
Weidner & Sons Publishing
John Wiley & Sons, Inc., College Division

Early Childhood Education

American Press
Lawrence Erlbaum Associates
Houghton Mifflin Co., College Division
McGraw-Hill Higher Education
National Association for the Education of Young Children
Prentice Hall Direct
Charles C Thomas, Publisher
Waveland Press
Weidner & Sons Publishing

Educational Administration

American Press
Lawrence Erlbaum Associates
McGraw-Hill Higher Education
Phi Delta Kappa International
Prentice Hall Direct
Sage Publications
Charles C Thomas, Publisher
Waveland Press
Weidner & Sons Publishing

Educational Foundations

American Press
Lawrence Erlbaum Associates
Houghton Mifflin Co., College Division
McGraw-Hill Higher Education
Phi Delta Kappa International
Sage Publications
Waveland Press
Weidner & Sons Publishing
John Wiley & Sons, Inc., College Division

Educational Measurement and Testing

American Press
Lawrence Erlbaum Associates
Houghton Mifflin Co., College Division
Jossey-Bass Inc., A Wiley Company
McGraw-Hill Higher Education
Prentice Hall Direct
PRO-ED, Inc.
Sage Publications

Waveland Press
Weidner & Sons Publishing

Educational Psychology

American Press
Lawrence Erlbaum Associates
Houghton Mifflin Co., College Division
McGraw-Hill Higher Education
Prentice Hall Direct
Sage Publications
Waveland Press
Weidner & Sons Publishing

Educational Research and Statistics

American Press
Lawrence Erlbaum Associates
Houghton Mifflin Co., College Division
McGraw-Hill Higher Education
Sage Publications
Charles C Thomas, Publisher
Waveland Press
Weidner & Sons Publishing

Educational Technology

American Press
Educational Technology Publications, Inc.
Lawrence Erlbaum Associates
McGraw-Hill Higher Education
Prentice Hall Direct
Scholastic, Inc.
Waveland Press
Weidner & Sons Publishing
John Wiley & Sons, Inc., College Division

Higher Education

American Council on Education/Praeger
ERIC Clearinghouse on Higher Education
Lawrence Erlbaum Associates
Houghton Mifflin Co., College Division
Jossey-Bass Inc., A Wiley Company
Octameron Press
Charles C Thomas, Publisher

Weidner & Sons Publishing
John Wiley & Sons, Inc., College Division

Methods of Teaching

American Council on Education/Praeger (higher education)
American Press
Educators Publishing Service, Inc.
Lawrence Erlbaum Associates
Houghton Mifflin Co., College Division
International Reading Association
McGraw-Hill Higher Education
The Modern Language Association of America
National Council of Teachers of English
Oryx Press (K–12)
Phil Delta Kappa International
Prentice Hall Direct
Sage Publications
Scholastic, Inc.
Charles C Thomas, Publisher
Waveland Press
Weidner & Sons Publishing

Physical Education, Health, and Recreation

American Press
Human Kinetics Publishers, Inc.
McGraw-Hill Higher Education
Prentice Hall Direct
Charles C Thomas, Publisher
Waveland Press
Weidner & Sons Publishing

School Law

Phi Delta Kappa International
Weidner & Sons Publishing

Special Education

Academic Therapy Publications
American Press
Educators Publishing Service, Inc.
Lawrence Erlbaum Associates
Houghton Mifflin Co., College Division
McGraw-Hill Higher Education

215

Prentice Hall Direct
PRO-ED, Inc.
Research Press
Charles C Thomas, Publisher
J. Weston Walch, Publisher
Waveland Press
Weidner & Sons Publishing

Teacher Education: Conditions, Issues, and Trends

Lawrence Erlbaum Associates
McGraw-Hill Higher Education
Sage Publications
Waveland Press
Weidner & Sons Publishing

Academic Subjects

Agriculture

American Press
Interstate Publishers, Inc.
McGraw-Hill Higher Education
Waveland Press
Weidner & Sons Publishing

Behavioral Sciences

American Counseling Association
American Press
Lawrence Erlbaum Associates
Houghton Mifflin Co., College Division
McGraw-Hill Higher Education
F. E. Peacock Publishers, Inc.
Waveland Press
Weidner & Sons Publishing
John Wiley & Sons, Inc., College Division

Business

American Press
Lawrence Erlbaum Associates
Houghton Mifflin Co., College Division
McGraw-Hill Higher Education
Prentice Hall Direct

Weidner & Sons Publishing
John Wiley & Sons, Inc., College Division

Communications

American Press
Lawrence Erlbaum Associates
Houghton Mifflin Co., College Division
McGraw-Hill Higher Education
Prentice Hall Direct
Waveland Press
Weidner & Sons Publishing

Computer Science

American Press
Lawrence Erlbaum Associates
Houghton Mifflin Co., College Division
McGraw-Hill Higher Education
Prentice Hall Direct
Weidner & Sons Publishing
John Wiley & Sons, Inc., College Division

Engineering

American Press
McGraw-Hill Higher Education
Waveland Press
Weidner & Sons Publishing
John Wiley & Sons, Inc., College Division

English as a Second Language

Lawrence Erlbaum Associates
Houghton Mifflin Co., College Division
The Modern Language Association of America
National Textbook Company
J. Weston Walch, Publisher
Weidner & Sons Publishing

Fine Arts

American Press
McGraw-Hill Higher Education
Prentice Hall Direct
Waveland Press
Weidner & Sons Publishing

Foreign Languages

    See World Languages

Health Sciences/Human Services

    American Press
    McGraw-Hill Higher Education
    Waveland Press
    Weidner & Sons Publishing
    John Wiley & Sons, Inc., College Division

Home Economics

    American Press
    Weidner & Sons Publishing

Horticulture

    Interstate Publishers, Inc.
    McGraw-Hill Higher Education
    Weidner & Sons Publishing

Journalism

    McGraw-Hill Higher Education
    Waveland Press
    Weidner & Sons Publishing

Language Arts (K–Graduate School): Reading, Basic Writing Skills, Composition, Literature, Spelling, Vocabulary

    American Press
    Lawrence Erlbaum Associates
    Educators Publishing Service, Inc.
    Houghton Mifflin Co., College Division
    Houghton Mifflin Co., School Division
    International Reading Association
    McDougal Littell Co., Division of Houghton Mifflin Co.
    McGraw-Hill Higher Education
    The Modern Language Association of America
    National Council of Teachers of English
    National Textbook Company
    Oryx Press
    Prentice Hall Direct
    Scholastic, Inc.

J. Weston Walch, Publisher
Waveland Press
Weidner & Sons Publishing

Library Science

Oryx Press

Mathematics

American Press
Lawrence Erlbaum Associates
Educators Publishing Service, Inc.
Houghton Mifflin Co., College Division
Houghton Mifflin Co., School Division
McDougal Littell Co., Division of Houghton Mifflin Co.
McGraw-Hill Higher Education
Prentice Hall Direct
Scholastic, Inc.
J. Weston Walch, Publisher
Waveland Press
Weidner & Sons Publishing
John Wiley & Sons, Inc., College Division

Philosophy

American Press
McGraw-Hill Higher Education
Waveland Press
Weidner & Sons Publishing

Physical Education, Health, and Recreation (K–12)

Human Kinetics Publishers
Prentice Hall Direct

Sciences (Biological and Physical)

American Press
Houghton Mifflin Co., College Division
Houghton Mifflin Co., School Division
McDougal Littell Co., Division of Houghton Mifflin Co.
McGraw-Hill Higher Education
Oryx Press
Prentice Hall Direct
Scholastic, Inc.

J. Weston Walch, Publisher
Waveland Press
Weidner & Sons Publishing
John Wiley & Sons, Inc., College Division

Social Sciences/Social Studies

American Press
Lawrence Erlbaum Associates
Houghton Mifflin Co., College Division
Houghton Mifflin Co., School Division
McDougal Littell Co., Division of Houghton Mifflin Co.
McGraw-Hill Higher Education
Oryx Press
F. E. Peacock Publishers, Inc.
Prentice Hall Direct
Sage Publications
Scholastic, Inc.
J. Weston Walch, Publisher
Waveland Press
Weidner & Sons Publishing
John Wiley & Sons, Inc., College Division

Statistics

American Press
Lawrence Erlbaum Associates
McGraw-Hill Higher Education
Weidner & Sons Publishing

Thinking Skills: Critical and Creative

Lawrence Erlbaum Associates
Houghton Mifflin Co., College Division
McGraw-Hill Higher Education
Weidner & Sons Publishing

World Languages

American Press
Houghton Mifflin Co., College Division
McDougal Littell Co., Division of Houghton Mifflin Co.
McGraw-Hill Higher Education
The Modern Language Association of America
National Textbook Company
Prentice Hall Direct

Weidner & Sons Publishing
John Wiley & Sons, Inc., College Division

BOOK PUBLISHERS' GUIDELINES

Academic Therapy Publications

20 Commercial Boulevard
Novato, CA 94949
(800) 422-7249
Fax: (415) 883-3720
http://www.atpub.com

Professional Education Subjects: Special Education (learning disabilities only), Testing, Curriculum, and High/Low Readers
Academic Subjects: NA
Education and Academic Titles in Print: 350
Materials for Preliminary Review: Abstract, table of contents, sample chapters
Preliminary Review Response Time: Two weeks
Style Guide: The Chicago Manual of Style (14th edition)
Required Copies of Manuscript: One
Electronic Submission: The final version of an accepted manuscript may be submitted on a 3.5" high-density disk that has been formatted either as IBM-compatible or in Macintosh and prepared in Microsoft Works or Word. If an electronic version is submitted, it should be accompanied with a printout.
Acceptance/Rejection Response Time: One month
Reasons Given for Rejection: Yes
Royalties: Variable rates
Copyright Holder: Varies between author and publisher
Send Inquiries to: Publisher

American Council on Education

Publications Department
One Dupont Circle, NW
Washington, DC 20036
(202) 939-9380
Fax: (202) 833-4760
E-mail: pubs@ace.nche.edu
http://www.acenet.edu

Professional Education Subjects: ACE/Praeger "Series on Higher Education": Topics in higher education, such as Governance, Policy-making, Financing Higher Education, Academic Affairs, Teaching Techniques, Faculty Development, Technology, Adult and Continuing Education, and Assessment and Evaluation
Academic Subjects: NA
Education Titles in Print: 85+

Materials for Preliminary Review: Statement of purpose, table of contents, sample chapter, and résumé.

Preliminary Review Response Time: Two to four weeks

Style Guide: The Chicago Manual of Style (14th edition)

Required Copies of Manuscript: One hard copy and one disk copy

Electronic Submission: Prefers manuscripts prepared with IBM PC operating systems. The software of preference is Microsoft Word for Windows or WordPerfect; however, other software packages are acceptable. Macintosh is permitted. Disks may also be prepared in ASCII or "text only" files. If the writer plans to use a software other than one of the preferred ones, contact the publisher before preparing the manuscript. Use only double-sided, high-density disks and label the disks with the name of the software used.

Acceptance/Rejection Response Time: At least two weeks

Reasons Given for Rejection: Yes

Royalties: 10% on net

Copyright Holder: ACE/Praeger

Send Inquiries to: Vice President of External Affairs

American Counseling Association

5999 Stevenson Avenue

Alexandria, VA 22304

(800) 347-6647

(703) 823-9800

Fax: (703) 823-0252

http://www.counseling.org

Professional Education Subjects: Considers all topics in counseling. Manuscripts must be for either undergraduate or graduate textbooks or materials for professional counselors. Does not accept manuscripts written for the general public or clients.

Academic Subjects: Mental health (undergraduate- and graduate-level textbooks)

Education Titles in Print: 100+

Materials for Preliminary Review: Statement of the purpose of the proposed book, an annotated table of contents with a brief description of each chapter, one or two sample chapters, estimate of the number of pages in the proposed book, timeline for writing, and a description of competing books on the market

Preliminary Review Response Time: Two to four weeks

Style Guide: Publication Manual of the American Psychological Association (5th edition)

Required Copies of Manuscript: One hard copy and one disk copy

Electronic Submission: Prefers that the manuscript be prepared using MS Word 97. Use an IBM-compatible format. Macintosh not acceptable.

Acceptance/Rejection Response Time: One month

Reasons Given for Rejection: Yes

Royalties: 10–15% of net sales

Copyright Holder: American Counseling Association

Send Inquiries to: Director of Publications

American Press
Publishing Division
Suite 1100
28 State Street
Boston, MA 02109
(617) 247-0022
Fax: (617) 247-0022

Professional Education Subjects: Textbooks in undergraduate courses in the following subjects: Child and Adolescent Development, Child Psychology, Counseling and Guidance, Curriculum, Early Childhood Education, Educational Administration, Educational Foundations, Educational Measurement and Testing, Educational Psychology, Educational Research and Statistics, Educational Technology, Methods of Teaching, Physical Education and Health, Special Education

Academic Subjects: Undergraduate textbooks in the following subjects: Agriculture, Behavioral Sciences, Business, Communications, Computer Science, Engineering, Fine Arts, World Languages, Health/Human Sciences, Home Economics, Language Arts, Mathematics, Philosophy, Sciences, Social Sciences/Social Studies, Statistics

Education Titles in Print: 220

Materials for Preliminary Review: Preface (including rationale for the book), table of contents, one chapter from each author (not introductory chapter)

Preliminary Review Response Time: Four weeks

Style Guide: Publication Manual of the American Psychological Association (5th edition)

Required Copies of Manuscript: Prefers one hard copy along with a computer disk

Electronic Submission: Publisher is flexible regarding software used and accepts either IBM-compatible or Macintosh

Acceptance/Rejection Response Time: Four months

Reasons Given for Rejection: Yes

Royalties: 10%–15% depending on the type of book, market, and extent of publisher's assistance

Copyright Holder: Publisher

Miscellaneous Guidelines: Prefer authors who are actively involved in teaching the course for which the book is intended.

Send Inquiries to: Editor of the subject field

Educational Technology Publications, Inc.
700 Palisade Avenue
Englewood Cliffs, NJ 07632
(800) 952-2665
(201) 871-4007
Fax: (201) 871-4009
E-mail: edtecpubs@aol.com
http://www.BooksToRead.com/etp

Professional Education Subjects: All aspects of educational technology. Books published for upper undergraduate or graduate levels.

Academic Subjects: NA

Education Titles in Print: 300

Materials for Preliminary Review: Detailed outline including statement of purpose and description of each chapter.

Preliminary Review Response Time: Two weeks

Style Guide: Publication Manual of the American Psychological Association (5th edition)

Required Copies of Manuscript: Two

Electronic Submission: Prefer Macintosh-compatible disk. Hard copy should accompany the electronic submission.

Acceptance/Rejection Response Time: 30 days

Reasons Given for Rejection: Yes

Royalties: Negotiable

Copyright Holder: Educational Technology Publications, Inc.

Send Inquiries to: Publisher

Educators Publishing Service, Inc.

31 Smith Place
Cambridge, MA 02138
(800) 435-7728
(617) 547-6706
Fax: (617) 547-3805
E-mail: epsbooks@epsbooks.com
http://www.epsbooks.com

Professional Education Subjects: Methods of teaching (K–12) and special education (K–12).

Academic Subjects: Seeks supplementary workbooks for use in K–12 that teach reading, spelling, vocabulary, grammar, comprehension, and math. Although particularly interested in workbook series, will consider any proposal for high-quality material that is useful to teachers and students.

Education Titles in Print: 800+

Materials for Preliminary Review: A statement of the unique features of the proposed publication, an outline, sample chapter, and a résumé. Send a self-addressed and stamped envelope for return of materials if they are not accepted.

Preliminary Review Response Time: Up to three months

Style Guide: The Chicago Manual of Style (14th edition). An in-house style manual is also available to authors.

Required Copies of Manuscript: One hard copy and a disk copy

Electronic Submission: Prefer MS Word or WordPerfect. May format as IBM-compatible or Macintosh.

Acceptance/Rejection Response Time: Up to three months

Reasons Given for Rejection: Usually

Royalties: 8%–15% of net sales

Copyright Holder: Negotiable
Send Inquiries to: Acquisitions Department

ERIC Clearinghouse on Higher Education
Suite 630
One Dupont Circle, NW
Washington, DC 20036
(800) 773-3742
(202) 296-2597
Fax: (202) 452-1844
http://www.eriche.org

Professional Education Subjects: ASHE-ERIC *Higher Education Report Series*
(Jossey-Bass, Publishers): All topics in higher education
Academic Subjects: NA
Education Titles in Print: Approximately 200
Materials for Preliminary Review: Only proposals are considered. Submit an outline disclosing the purpose of each chapter, a writing sample, and a résumé. Will not consider manuscripts for preliminary review. See the Web site cited above for further guidelines.
Preliminary Review Response Time: Two to three days
Style Guide: Publication Manual of the American Psychological Association (5th edition)
Required Copies of Manuscript: One hard copy and one disk
Electronic Submission: Use either MS Word or WordPerfect
Acceptance/Rejection Response Time: Two months
Reasons Given for Rejection: Yes
Compensation: $1,500 honorarium
Copyright Holder: Jossey-Bass, Publishers
Send Inquiries to: Editor

Lawrence Erlbaum Associates, Inc.
10 Industrial Avenue
Mahwah, NJ 07430
(800) 926-6579
(201) 236-9500
Fax: (201) 236-0072
http://www.erlbaum.com

Professional Education Subjects: Higher Education, Adult Education, Child and Adolescent Development, Child Psychology, Curriculum and Instruction, Early Childhood Education, Educational Administration and Leadership, Educational Foundations, Educational Assessment and Measurement, Educational Psychology, Educational Research and Statistics, Educational Technology, Methods of Teaching, Special Education, Teacher Education

Academic Subjects: (College and professional levels) Behavioral Sciences (psychology and social psychology), Business, Communication Sciences and Disorders, Computer Science, English as a Second Language, Language Arts, Mathematics, Social Studies, Thinking Skills

Titles in Print: 500

Materials for Preliminary Review: Detailed prospectus, table of contents, sample chapter, and titles of competitive publications

Preliminary Review Response Time: Three to six weeks

Style Guide: Publication Manual of the American Psychological Association (5th edition)

Required Copies of Manuscript: One disk copy and one hard copy

Electronic Submission: Format in IBM-compatible or Macintosh. Flexible regarding word-processing software; however, prefer either MS Word or WordPerfect.

Acceptance/Rejection Response Time: Four to six weeks

Reasons Given for Rejection: Yes

Royalties: 8%–18% depending on size of market for the book

Copyright Holder: Publisher

Send Inquiries to: Editorial Director

Houghton Mifflin Co.

College Division
222 Berkeley Street
Boston, MA 02116
(617) 351-5000
Fax: (617) 351-1134
http://www.hmco.com/college/AuthorGuide/prospectus.html

Professional Education Subjects: (Undergraduate and graduate levels) Higher Education, Early Childhood Education, Child and Adolescent Development, Foundations of Education, Curriculum and Instruction, Educational Measurement and Testing, Educational Psychology, Educational Research and Statistics, Methods of Teaching, Special Education

Academic Subjects: (Undergraduate and graduate levels) Accounting, Business, Management, Communications, Computer Science, Developmental English, World Languages, Language Arts, English as a Second Language, Economics, Mathematics, Sciences, Social and Political Sciences, Psychology, Thinking Skills

Education Titles in Print: 75

Materials for Preliminary Review: Prospectus with table of contents and a curriculum vita. Explain purpose of proposed book and provide titles of competing books. See Web site cited above for more guidelines.

Preliminary Review Response Time: Three to four weeks

Style Guide: See Web site cited above for Author's Guide.

Required Copies of Manuscript: One hard copy and one disk

Electronic Submission: Prefers MS Word; however, other programs are acceptable

Acceptance/Rejection Response Time: Approximately two months

Reasons Given for Rejection: Yes

Royalties: 10%–15% of net sales

Copyright Holder: Houghton Mifflin Co.
Send Inquiries to: Education Editor for professional education topics. "Editor of (specify academic discipline)" for academic topics.

Houghton Mifflin Co.

School Division
222 Berkeley Street
Boston, MA 02116
(617) 351-5000
http://www.eduplace.com

Professional Education Subjects: NA
Academic Subjects: (Grades K–6) Language Arts (English), Language Arts (Bilingual), Mathematics, Science, Social Studies
Materials for Preliminary Review: Prospectus stating the purpose of the proposed book, outline of chapters, and a curriculum vita.
Preliminary Review Response Time: 8 to 10 weeks
Style Guide: Houghton Mifflin's in-house style guide
Required Copies of Manuscript: One
Electronic Submission: Equipped to receive any standard word-processing software.
Acceptance/Rejection Response Time: 10 weeks
Reasons Given for Rejection: Sometimes
Royalties: Negotiable
Copyright Holder: Houghton Mifflin Co.
Send Inquiries to: Editor in Chief

Human Kinetics Publishers

1607 N. Market Street
Champaign, IL 61820
(800) 747-4457
(217) 351-5076
Fax: (217) 351-2674
http://www.humankinetics.com

Professional Education Subjects: (Undergraduate and graduate levels) Physical Education, Recreation and Leisure, Dance, Health (as related to physical activity), Kinesiology, Exercise Science, Sport Medicine
Academic Subjects: Physical Education (K–12)
Education Titles in Print: 600
Materials for Preliminary Review: Preface of the proposed book, table of contents, a sample chapter, and the author's résumé
Preliminary Review Response Time: Two weeks
Style Guide: The Chicago Manual of Style (14th edition)
Required Copies of Manuscript: Two

Electronic Submission: Flexible regarding selection of software; however, prefers MS Word 6.0 or RTF. When submitting electronically, send two disks and two printouts.

Acceptance/Rejection Response Time: Four to six weeks

Reasons Given for Rejection: Yes

Royalties: 10%–15% of net income

Copyright Holder: Author

Send Inquiries to: For physical education, recreation, and dance, send to the HPERD Acquisitions Editor. For scientific, technical, and medicine, send to STM Acquisitions Editor.

International Reading Association

800 Barksdale Road
P.O. Box 8139
Newark, DE 19714-8139
(800) 336-7323
(302) 731-1600
Fax: (302) 731-1057
http://www.reading.org

Professional Education Subjects: Methods of Teaching Reading, Writing Instruction

Academic Subjects: Reading, Language Arts (English), Children's and Young Adult Literature

Education Titles in Print: 110

Materials for Preliminary Review: Completion of the International Reading Association's proposal form

Preliminary Review Response Time: Six to eight weeks

Style Guide: The Association's in-house style guidebook.

Required Copies of Manuscript: Four hard copies

Electronic Submission: When submitting the final version of the manuscript, it is preferable that it be prepared in MS Word; however, WordPerfect is also acceptable. Formatting may be either IBM-compatible or in Macintosh.

Acceptance/Rejection Response Time: 7 to 10 weeks

Reasons Given for Rejection: Yes

Royalties: 8% of net sales for the first 5,000 copies sold outside of the association's Book Club and 10% of net sales for over 5,000 copies sold outside of the Book Club.

Copyright Holder: International Reading Association

Send Inquiries to: Publications Secretary. Request a proposal form.

Interstate Publishers, Inc.

510 N. Vermilion Street
P.O. Box 50
Danville, IL 61834-0050
(800) 843-4774
(217) 446-0500

Fax: (217) 446-9706
E-mail: info-ipp@IPPINC.com
http://www.interstatepublishers.com

Professional Education Subjects: (college level) Agriculture Teacher Education
Academic Subjects: (middle school through college) Agriscience and Technology, Horticulture, Agrimarketing, Agribusiness, Production Agriculture
Education Titles in Print: Four
Materials for Preliminary Review: A prospectus that explains the purpose of the proposed book, a table of contents with a brief description of each chapter, the intended grade level of the book, and two or three sample chapters
Preliminary Review Response Time: Three to four weeks
Style Guide: The Chicago Manual of Style (14th edition)
Required Copies of Manuscript: One
Electronic Submission: Format should be IBM-compatible. Prefer WordPerfect; however, MS Word is acceptable. If submitting a disk, also send one hard copy.
Acceptance/Rejection Response Time: Normally, seven to nine weeks
Reasons Given for Rejection: Yes
Royalties: 10% of proceeds from sales
Copyright Holder: Interstate Publishers, Inc.
Miscellaneous Guidelines: The publisher is interested in publishing books that will be adopted as class textbooks, not sold as single copies
Send Inquiries to: Vice President—Editorial

Jossey-Bass Inc., A Wiley Company
5th Floor
350 Sansome Street
San Francisco, CA 94104
(415) 433-1740
Fax: (415) 433-0499
http://www.josseybass.com

Professional Education Subjects: The publisher does not publish textbooks; instead, its books are intended for professionals, such as college administrators and professors of higher education; nevertheless, some of its books are used as textbooks for advanced graduate courses. It publishes professional materials in Adult and Continuing Education and in Higher Education. Subjects include Teaching and Learning, College Student Services, Student and Faculty Assessment, Higher Education Management and Administration, Institutional Research, Development and Advancement, College and University Governance and Policy-making, Community College Administration, Literacy, and other topics in higher education.
Academic Subjects: NA
Education Titles in Print: 300
Materials for Preliminary Review: A detailed overview of the proposed book with a statement of need for it, contribution that the material will make, intended audience, com-

peting books, tentative schedule for completion, sample chapters, and a curriculum vita

Preliminary Review Response Time: Three to four weeks

Style Guide: Publisher's in-house style manual

Required Copies of Manuscript: Three hard copies

Electronic Submission: Prefers using either MS Word or WordPerfect; however, other word-processing programs are acceptable. Format in either IBM-PC or Macintosh.

Acceptance/Rejection Response Time: Four to eight weeks

Reasons Given for Rejection: Yes

Royalties: 10% of net sales for the first 3,000 copies sold, 12.5% on the next 2,000 copies, and 15% thereafter

Copyright Holder: John Wiley & Sons, Inc.

Send Inquiries to: Acquisitions Editor

McDougal Littell Co.

A Division of Houghton Mifflin Co.

1560 Sherman Avenue

Evanston, IL 60201

(847) 869-2300

http://www.mcdougallittell.com

Professional Education Subjects: NA

Academic Subjects: This company is the secondary education publishing division of Houghton Mifflin. As such, it publishes books in Language Arts, World Languages, Mathematics, Social Studies, American History, World History, and Science.

Materials for Preliminary Review: Statement of purpose, annotated table of contents, sample chapters

Preliminary Review Response Time: Two to three weeks

Style Guide: Contact Editor in Chief

Required Copies of Manuscript: One

Copyright Holder: The publisher

Send Inquiries to: Editor in Chief

McGraw-Hill Higher Education

A Division of McGraw-Hill Companies

1333 Burr Ridge Parkway

Burr Ridge, IL 60521

(630) 789-4000

Fax: (630) 678-6942

E-mail: first_last@mcgraw-hill.com

http://www.mhhe.com/catalogs/work/candidate.mhtml

Professional Education Subjects: Child and Adolescent Development; Child Psychology; Counseling and Guidance; Curriculum; Early Childhood Education; Educational Administration; Educational Foundations; Educational Measurement and Testing; Educational Psychology; Educational Research and Statistics; Educational Technology; Methods of Teaching; Physical Education, Health, and Recreation; Special Education; Teacher Education: Conditions, Issues, and Trends

Academic Subjects: (college level) Agriculture; Behavioral Sciences; Business; Economics; Marketing; Management; Communications; Computer Science; Engineering; Fine Arts; Health Sciences/Human Services; Horticulture; Journalism; Language Arts; Mathematics; Philosophy; Religion; Physical, Biological, and Geological Sciences; Social Sciences; Statistics; Thinking Skills: Critical and Creative; World Languages

Titles in Print: 10,000+

Materials for Preliminary Review: Statement of purpose of the proposed book, annotated table of contents, sample chapters, description of the intended audience, list of competing publications, and a curriculum vita. For more information, visit the Web site cited above.

Preliminary Review Response Time: One to three months

Style Guide: The Chicago Manual of Style (14th edition)

Required Copies of Manuscript: One

Electronic Submission: Flexible on acceptance of word-processing software; however, prefers MS Word. If submitting a disk, also send one hard copy. For further information, see Web site cited above.

Acceptance/Rejection Response Time: Four to eight weeks

Reasons Given for Rejection: Yes

Royalties: Rates vary

Copyright Holder: McGraw-Hill

Send Inquiries to: This varies by academic discipline. See Web site cited above for further information.

The Modern Language Association of America

3rd Floor
26 Broadway
New York, NY 10004-1789
(646) 576-5000
Fax: (646) 458-0030
E-mail: bookpub@mla.org
http://www.mla.org

Professional Education Subjects: Methods of teaching languages and literature (no textbooks, only professional publications)

Academic Subjects: Publishes literary-linguistic research. The MLA invites works that present information and opinions or that challenge established views within the profession. Academic subjects include English as a Second Language, World Languages, and Literature. The MLA does not publish monographs.

Education and Academic Titles in Print: 180

Materials for Preliminary Review: Detailed outline (not the manuscript) and a curriculum vita

Preliminary Review Response Time: Two months

Style Guide: MLA Style Manual
Required Copies of Manuscript: One
Electronic Submission: Any word-processing software language is acceptable. If submitting a disk, also send a hard copy.
Acceptance/Rejection Response Time: Three to four months
Reasons Given for Rejection: Usually
Royalties: Rates vary
Copyright Holder: The MLA
Send Inquiries to: Director of Book Publications

National Association for the Education of Young Children
1509 16th Street, NW
Washington, DC 20036
(800) 424- 2460
(202) 232-8777
Fax: (202) 328-2460
E-mail: editorial@naeyc.org
http://www.naeyc.org

Professional Education Subjects: Publishes professional books for adults on child development and early childhood education. Focuses on children from birth through eight years of age. Does not consider children's books, curriculum guides, or research reports.
Academic Subjects: NA
Education Titles in Print: 120
Materials for Preliminary Review: Submit a detailed outline of the proposed book that describes the purpose of the book, how each chapter will be developed, and the intended audience. Indicate the approximate length of the manuscript and any other pertinent information, such as the qualifications of the author to write the book. Any recommendations for practice should be based on substantial research and a theoretical framework.
Preliminary Review Response Time: Four to six weeks
Style Guide: The Chicago Manual of Style (14th edition)
Required Copies of Manuscript: Four
Electronic Submission: Prefer MS Word. If submitting a computer disk, also send one hard copy of the manuscript.
Acceptance/Rejection Response Time: Three months
Reasons Given for Rejection: Yes
Royalties: None
Copyright Holder: National Association for the Education of Young Children
Send Inquiries to: Publications Editor

National Council of Teachers of English
Books Division
1111 W. Kenyon Road

Urbana, IL 61801
(800) 369-6283
(217) 328-3870
Fax: (217) 328-0977
http://www.ncte.org

Professional Education Subjects: Publishes only professional books for teachers, not text-books. These in-service books focus on the teaching of English and language arts.

Academic Subjects: Language Arts (professional literature for teachers; no textbooks)

Education and Academic Titles in Print: 240

Materials for Preliminary Review: Send a formal proposal (not a completed manuscript) that describes the purpose of the proposed book, objectives and reasons for writing it, titles of competitive books in the market, size of the targeted market, and a definition of the anticipated readership. Also, provide an annotated table of contents that includes chapter titles and a brief description of each chapter. Indicate the estimated length (double-spaced) of the manuscript that is to be written and how long it will take to write it. Two or three sample chapters should be provided. Finally, submit a short résumé of the author(s).

Preliminary Review Response Time: Six weeks

Style Guide: The Chicago Manual of Style (14th edition)

Required Copies of Manuscript: One

Electronic Submission: Prefer MS Word. Label each disk with the author's name, book title, and the name of the word-processing program and its version. Indicate whether used IBM PC-compatible or Macintosh format. Create a separate disk file for each chapter and provide a printed directory showing each filename. Submit one disk and one printout.

Acceptance/Rejection Response Time: Two to four months

Reasons Given for Rejection: Yes

Royalties: 8% of net sales of the first 5,000 copies sold and 10% of net sales in excess of 5,000 copies sold

Copyright Holder: Publisher

Miscellaneous Guidelines: The following are available upon request from the Senior Editor: *NCTE Submission Guidelines, Publishing a Book with NCTE,* and *NCTE Manuscript Preparation Guidelines.*

Send Inquiries to: Senior Editor

National Textbook Company

NTC/Contemporary Publishing Group
4255 West Touhy Avenue
Lincolnwood, IL 60712-1975
(800) 323-4900
(847) 679-5500
Fax: (847) 679-1549
http://www.ntc-cb.com

Professional Education Subjects: NA
Academic Subjects: English as a Second Language (adult education), World Languages (K–college), Language Arts (junior high school–undergraduate college)
Academic Titles in Print: 2,500
Materials for Preliminary Review: Overview that includes a statement of purpose, titles of competing books, and identification of the market to be targeted; annotated table of contents; sample chapter; and a curriculum vita
Preliminary Review Response Time: Four to six weeks
Style Guide: The Chicago Manual of Style (14th edition)
Required Copies of Manuscript: One
Electronic Submission: Accepts Macintosh or PC format. Must submit manuscript on a disk, sending one copy of the disk and one printout. Save as RTF, MS Word, WordPerfect. Label each disk with name and version of the software used, contents of the disk, and name of author.
Acceptance/Rejection Response Time: Four to six weeks
Reasons Given for Rejection: Usually
Royalties: Negotiable
Copyright Holder: Publisher
Send Inquiries to: Editor of the subject

Octameron Press

P.O. Box 2748
Alexandria, VA 22301
(703) 836-5480

Professional Education Subjects: Higher Education (college selection, admission, and financial aid directed toward high school and college students)
Academic Subjects: NA
Education Titles in Print: 14
Materials for Preliminary Review: Annotated table of contents, sample chapter, vita
Preliminary Review Response Time: One week
Style Guide: No specific one required
Required Copies of Manuscript: One
Acceptance/Rejection Response Time: One month
Reasons Given for Rejection: When requested
Royalties: 7.5% of list price; no advance
Copyright Holder: Author
Send Inquiries to: Editorial Director

The Oryx Press

An Imprint of Greenwood Publishing Group
88 Post Road West
P.O. Box 5007
Westport, CT 06881-5007
(203) 226-3571

Fax: (203) 222-1502
http://www.greenwood.com

Professional Education Subjects: Methods of Teaching (K–12). For higher education subjects, see profile of American Council on Education, "Series on Higher Education."

Academic Subjects: High school and undergraduate levels: Language Arts, Media Arts, Music, Sciences, Social Sciences. Graduate level: Library Science.

Education Titles in Print: 250

Materials for Preliminary Review: Statement of purpose and the intended audience, annotated table of contents, the introduction or a sample chapter, curriculum vita

Preliminary Review Response Time: Two weeks

Style Guide: The Chicago Manual of Style (14th edition)

Required Copies of Manuscript: One copy on disk and one hard copy

Electronic Submission: Prefers manuscripts prepared with IBM PC operating systems. The software of preference is Microsoft Word for Windows or WordPerfect; however, other software packages are acceptable. Macintosh is permitted. Disks may also be prepared in ASCII or "text only" files. If the writer plans to use a software other than one of the preferred ones, contact the publisher before preparing the manuscript. Use only double-sided, high-density disks and label the disks with the name of the software used.

Acceptance/Rejection Response Time: Six weeks

Reasons Given for Rejection: Yes

Royalties: 10% of net sales

Copyright Holder: Publisher

Miscellaneous Guidelines: Full guidelines for authors may be found at the Web site cited.

Send Inquiries to: Acquisitions Department

F. E. Peacock Publishers, Inc.

115 W. Orchard
Itasca, IL 60143
(630) 775-9000
Fax: (630) 775-9003
E-mail: fepeacock@aol.com
http://www.fepeacock.com

Professional Education Subjects: NA

Academic Subjects: (College level) Behavioral Sciences and Social Sciences

Academic Titles in Print: 80

Materials for Preliminary Review: Proposal containing a statement of purpose, annotated table of contents, intended audience, and titles of competing books on the market. Submit three sample chapters.

Preliminary Review Response Time: Varies

Style Guide: Publication Manual of the American Psychological Association (5th edition)

Required Copies of Manuscript: Two

Electronic Submission: Not required; however, if a computer disk is sent, it should be formatted as being IBM-PC-compatible and preferably prepared in MS Word. Submit one disk and a hard copy.
Acceptance/Rejection Response Time: Usually up to six months
Reasons Given for Rejection: Yes
Copyright Holder: F. E. Peacock Publishers, Inc.
Send Inquiries to: The Publisher

Pearson Higher Education Division
One Lake Street
Upper Saddle River, NJ 07458
(201) 236-7000

Contact for further information.

Phi Delta Kappa International
408 North Union
P.O. Box 789
Bloomington, IN 47402-0789
(800) 766-1156
(812) 339-1156
Fax: (812) 339-0018
E-mail: headquarters@pdkintl.org
http://www.pdkintl.org

Professional Education Subjects: Educational Administration, Curriculum, Methods of Teaching, Educational Policy, Educational Philosophy, Educational History, School Law, Comparative Education
Academic Subjects: NA
Education Titles in Print: 220
Materials for Preliminary Review: A statement of purpose, annotated table of contents, and a sample chapter
Preliminary Review Response Time: Three to four weeks
Style Guide: The Chicago Manual of Style (14th edition)
Required Copies of Manuscript: One
Electronic Submission: Prefers hard copy for electronic scanning
Acceptance/Rejection Response Time: Three months
Reasons Given for Rejection: Sometimes
Royalties: No royalties; however, an honorarium of $500–$5,000 is paid upon publication. The amount depends on the manuscript.
Copyright Holder: Usually the author
Send Inquiries to: Editor of Special Publications

Prentice Hall Direct

Pearson Education
240 Frisch Court
Paramus, NJ 07652
(201) 909-6440
Fax: (201) 909-6361
http://www.phedu.com

Professional Education Subjects: Publishes only professional books (not textbooks) and practical resources for in-service teachers, specialists, and administrators who serve preK–12. Considers all content areas and positions.

Academic Subjects: Publishes supplementary materials for teaching and learning. Addresses all subjects and grade levels preK–12.

Education Titles in Print: 400

Materials for Preliminary Review: Preface that explains the purpose and the intended reader, outline of contents, and a sample chapter (other than the first)

Preliminary Review Response Time: Two to four weeks

Style Guide: None specified; however, request copy of the Prentice-Hall *Author's Guide*.

Required Copies of Manuscript: Two; however, if submitting manuscript on a computer disk, send one disk copy and one hard copy.

Electronic Submission: Optional. If used, format in either PC or Macintosh. Prefer MS Word or WordPerfect.

Reasons Given for Rejection: Yes

Royalties: 10% net of trade sales (bookstores), 5% direct mail sales

Copyright Holder: Usually the publishing company

Send Inquiries to: Either the Elementary Education Editor or the Secondary Education Editor

Prentice Hall, School

Pearson Education
One Lake Street
Upper Saddle River, NJ 07458
(201) 236-7000

Contact for further information.

PRO-ED, Inc.

8700 Shoal Creek Boulevard
Austin, TX 78757
(800) 897-3202
(512) 451-3246
Fax: (800) 397-7633
E-mail: books@proedinc.com
http://www.proedinc.com

Professional Education Subjects: Professional books in special education, remedial education, and educational assessment and measurement

Academic Subjects: NA

Education Titles in Print: 310

Materials for Preliminary Review: Prospectus that explains the purpose of the proposed book and the intended audience, annotated table of contents, one or two sample chapters, and a curriculum vita

Preliminary Review Response Time: One to two weeks

Style Guide: The publisher's guide for authors

Required Copies of Manuscript: One

Electronic Submission: Accepts any word-processing software. Send one disk copy and one hard copy.

Acceptance/Rejection Response Time: One to two months

Reasons Given for Rejection: Usually

Royalties: Rates vary

Copyright Holder: Publisher

Send Inquiries to: Editor, Books and Materials Division

Research Press Co.

2612 North Mattis Avenue
Champaign, IL 61822
(800) 519-2707
(217) 352-3273
Fax: (217) 352-1221
E-mail: rp@researchpress.com
http://www.researchpress.com

Professional Education Subjects: Counseling and Guidance, Special Education

Academic Subjects: NA

Education Titles in Print: 100

Materials for Preliminary Review: Prospectus, annotated table of contents, sample chapter, research documentation, vita

Preliminary Review Response Time: Two to four weeks

Style Guide: Publication Manual of the American Psychological Association (5th edition)

Required Copies of Manuscript: Two hard copies along with a computer disk

Electronic Submission: Must be PC-formatted and prefers use of MS Word; however, other word-processing software is acceptable

Acceptance/Rejection Response Time: Four to eight weeks

Reasons Given for Rejection: Yes

Royalties: Rates usually start at 10% of net sales and escalate to 15%

Copyright Holder: Author

Send Inquiries to: Managing Editor

Sage Publications, Inc.

2455 Teller Road

Thousand Oaks, CA 91320
(805) 499-0721
Fax: (805) 499-0871
E-mail: info@sagepub.com
http://www.sagepub.com

Professional Education Subjects: Child and Adolescent Development, Counseling and Guidance, Curriculum, Educational Administration, Educational Foundations, Educational Measurement and Testing, Educational Psychology, Educational Research and Statistics, Methods of Teaching, Teacher Education: Conditions, Issues, and Trends

Academic Subjects: (college level) Social Sciences

Materials for Preliminary Review: Prospectus, annotated table of contents, pertinent reviews from professionals in the field

Preliminary Review Response Time: Two to four weeks

Style Guide: Publication Manual of the American Psychological Association (5th edition)

Required Copies of Manuscript: One

Electronic Submission: Prefers receiving hard copy only

Acceptance/Rejection Response Time: Four to eight weeks

Reasons Given for Rejection: Yes

Royalties: Rates vary

Copyright Holder: Publisher

Send Inquiries to: Acquisitions Editor

Scholastic, Inc.

Professional Books Division
555 Broadway
New York, NY 10012
(212) 343-6511
Fax: (212) 343-6804
http://www.scholastic.com

Professional Education Subjects: Professional books and resources for teachers in grades preK–8 in matters of curriculum, methods of teaching, and educational technology. Publishes activity books and other materials that facilitate the classroom teacher.

Academic Subjects: Resource books for teachers in preK–8 in all subjects, such as Language Arts, Reading, Mathematics, Social Studies, Science, Writing, and Classroom Management

Education Titles in Print: 600

Materials for Preliminary Review: Proposal that includes the purpose of the book, intended audience, annotated table of contents, and sample chapters, lessons, or activities

Preliminary Review Response Time: Two months

Style Guide: None specified. An in-house guide for authors is provided after an author is under contract with the publisher.

Required Copies of Manuscript: One disk copy and one hard copy

Electronic Submission: Requires submission on a computer disk. Flexible regarding the word-processing software that is used.
Acceptance/Rejection Response Time: Two months
Reasons Given for Rejection: Sometimes
Royalties: Rates are negotiable
Copyright Holder: Author
Send Inquiries to: Editorial Assistant

Charles C Thomas, Publisher

2600 South First Street
Springfield, IL 62704
(800) 258-8980
(217) 789-8980
Fax: (217) 789-9130
E-mail: books@ccthomas.com
http://www.ccthomas.com

Professional Education Subjects: Curriculum; Counseling and Guidance; Methods of Teaching; Early Childhood Education; Educational Administration; Educational Research and Statistics; Higher Education; Physical Education, Health, and Recreation; Special Education
Academic Subjects: NA
Education Titles in Print: 141
Materials for Preliminary Review: Prospectus with scope of the work, purpose, and plan. Provide an annotated table of contents, anticipated size of the publication, and the titles of any competing books on the market. Explain what graphics will be included. Send a curriculum vita.
Preliminary Review Response Time: Two weeks
Style Guide: Publication Manual of the American Psychological Association (5th edition)
Required Copies of the Manuscript: One disk and one hard copy
Electronic Submission: Use either MS Word, Works, or WordPerfect
Acceptance/Rejection Response Time: Two weeks
Reasons Given for Rejection: Yes
Royalties: The publisher's royalties are paid from first sales, once a year at the end of January, and according to the following schedule: (1) 10% on sales receipts of bound copies sold from 1 to 3,000 copies, (2) 12.5% on sales receipts of bound copies sold from 3,001 to 10,000 copies, and (3) 15% on sales receipts of bound copies sold from 10,001 copies and thereafter
Copyright Holder: Publisher
Send Inquiries to: Editor

J. Weston Walch, Publisher

321 Valley Street
P.O. Box 658
Portland, ME 04104-0658

(207) 772-2846
http://www.walch.com

Professional Education Subjects: Counseling and Guidance, Special Education
Academic Subjects: (Grades 7–adult) Language Arts, English as a Second Language, Mathematics, Science, Social Studies, School to Career
Education and Academic Titles in Print: 500
Materials for Preliminary Review: Proposal letter that explains the purpose and targeted audience along with an annotated table of contents, at least one sample chapter, and a marketability study
Preliminary Review Response Time: One month
Style Guide: Words into Type
Required Copies of Manuscript: One
Electronic Submission: Contact publisher for specifications
Acceptance/Rejection Response Time: Three months
Reasons Given for Rejection: No
Royalties: 8%–10% of sales or a flat fee
Copyright Holder: The publisher. Upon discontinuation, a request may be made to the publisher that the rights to the book be transferred to the author.
Send Inquiries to: Editor in Chief

Waveland Press

P.O. Box 400
Prospect Heights, IL 60070
(847) 634-0081
Fax: (847) 634-9501
E-mail: info@waveland.com
http://www.waveland.com

Professional Education Subjects: Child and Adolescent Development; Child Psychology; Counseling and Guidance; Curriculum; Early Childhood Education; Educational Administration; Educational Foundations; Educational Measurement and Testing; Educational Psychology; Educational Research and Statistics; Educational Technology; Methods of Teaching; Physical Education, Health, and Recreation; Special Education; Teacher Education: Conditions, Issues, and Trends
Academic Subjects: College textbooks in Agriculture; Anthropology; Archaeology; Behavioral Sciences; Biological Sciences; Chemistry; Chemical Engineering; Civil Engineering; Communications; Criminology; Economics; Electronics, Electrical Engineering; Environmental Studies; Government, Political Science; Health, Nutrition; History; Journalism; Language Arts, Linguistics; Literature, Literary Criticism, Essays; Mathematics; Mechanical Engineering; Music, Dance; Outdoor Recreation; Philosophy; Psychology, Psychiatry; Radio, Television; Social Sciences, Sociology; Women's Studies
Education Titles in Print: 549
Materials for Preliminary Review: Prospectus with outline of book
Preliminary Review Response Time: Three to six weeks

Style Guide: No specific guide is required

Required Copies of Manuscript: One

Electronic Submission: If submitting manuscript on a computer disk, use either MS Word or WordPerfect. Must be PC-compatible. Send one disk copy and one hard copy.

Acceptance/Rejection Response Time: Two months

Reasons Given for Rejection: Yes

Royalties: Rates are negotiable

Copyright Holder: Publisher

Send Inquiries to: Publisher

Weidner & Sons Publishing

P.O. Box 2178

Riverton, NJ 08077

(856) 486-1755

Fax: (856) 486-7583

E-mail: weidner@waterw.com

http://www.weidnerpublishing.com

Professional Education Subjects: Adult and Continuing Education; Agriculture Education; Child and Adolescent Development; Child Psychology; Comparative Education; Counseling and Guidance; Curriculum; Early Childhood Education; Educational Administration; Educational Foundations; Educational Measurement and Testing; Educational Psychology; Educational Research and Statistics; Educational Technology; Higher Education; Methods of Teaching; Physical Education, Health, and Recreation; School Law; Special Education; Teacher Education: Conditions, Issues, and Trends

Academic Subjects: (college level) Agriculture, Behavioral Sciences, Business, Communications, Computer Science, Engineering, English as a Second Language, Fine Arts, Health Sciences/Human Services, Home Economics, Horticulture, Journalism, Language Arts, Mathematics, Philosophy, Sciences, Social Sciences, Statistics, Thinking Skills (Critical and Creative), World Languages

Education and Academic Titles in Print: 100+

Materials for Preliminary Review: Statement of purpose, intended readers, outline, sample chapter, and credentials (not résumé) to establish authority in the subject. Also, if intended as a college textbook, mention the author's teaching position and number of students in the author's classes who would use the book. Send self-addressed and stamped envelope for return communication. Provide author's e-mail address.

Preliminary Review Response Time: Six to eight weeks

Style Guide: The Chicago Manual of Style (14th edition)

Required Copies of Manuscript: One computer disk copy and three hard copies. Send self-addressed and stamped envelope if necessary to return manuscript. Provide author's e-mail address.

Electronic Submission: Prefer MS Word; however, will accept WordPerfect or other standard word-processing programs. Must be PC-formatted.

Acceptance/Rejection Response Time: Six to eight weeks

Reasons Given for Rejection: Yes

Royalties: 2%–5% for unpublished authors; 5%–10% for published authors

Copyright Holder: Negotiable
Send Inquiries to: Editor

John Wiley & Sons, Inc.

College Division
605 Third Avenue
New York, NY 10158
(800) 225-5945
(212) 850-6000
Fax: (212) 850-6088
E-mail: info@wiley.com
http://www.wiley.com/authors/guidelines/

Professional Education Subjects: Adult and Continuing Education, Child and Adolescent Development, Child Psychology, Counseling and Guidance, Curriculum, Educational Foundations, Educational Technology, Higher Education

Academic Subjects: (college level) Behavioral Sciences, Business, Computer Science, Engineering, Health Sciences, Mathematics, Sciences, Social Sciences, World Languages

Education and Academic Titles in Print: 12,000

Materials for Preliminary Review: A proposal that states the purpose of the proposed book, annotated table of contents, targeted audience, demand for the book, name(s) of competing titles on the market, and author's assessment of competing titles. Submit a sample chapter and qualifications to write the book.

Preliminary Review Response Time: Four to six weeks

Style Guide: None specified

Required Copies of Manuscript: One disk copy and one hard copy

Electronic Submission: Prefers preparation using MS Word; however, accepts most major word-processing programs. Format either as PC or Macintosh. See Web site cited above for further guidelines.

Acceptance/Rejection Response Time: Approximately four months

Reasons Given for Rejection: Yes

Royalties: Negotiable

Copyright Holder: Publisher

Miscellaneous Guidelines: See the Web site cited above.

Send Inquiries to: Acquisitions editor for the subject

SECTION D

COMPUTER SOFTWARE FOR EDUCATIONAL RESEARCH AND MEASUREMENT

Robert K. Hess

CHAPTER 1

Nonstatistical Packages for Computers

INTRODUCTION

When one explores the history of computers, it is quite evident that computers were developed initially to perform large and tedious calculations. Their evolution into the systems now represented by the new supercomputer generation has not suppressed this early purpose. Computers are still the fastest and most accurate methods available for calculating large sets of data. Today, packages for mainframe computers, microcomputers, and minicomputers are available to all educational researchers. The choice of packages is limited mostly by the quality of the computer system and the expertise of the user. In the last decade the speed and the memory capacity of the desktop computer have changed dramatically. For today's modern researchers desktop systems are available that approach speeds that were once thought impossible even for the large mainframe computers. Furthermore, the memory capacity both in RAM (Random Access Memory) and in storage is literally phenomenal. A well-designed research desktop computer is capable of having over 1 gigabyte of RAM and upward of 100 gigabytes of storage capacity.

Some of the best programs for descriptive data analysis are spreadsheets, database managers, and multiprogram integrated packages. These are all, to some extent, effective for input, storage, and organization of data. While these programs are not designed for intense and in-depth analyses, the selective use of such programs can increase the efficiency of the user.

The descriptions of packages in this chapter include current suggested prices of the manufacturers. These prices are subject to change. Often the price for a piece of software may vary dramatically from the suggested list of the producer to the actual price on the street. Furthermore, discount houses, which buy in quantity, often have prices on the software far below the suggested list price; therefore, the price listed for each software piece is a rounded value designed to provide an estimate for the user rather than a firm value.

A decade ago there were a dozen or more major word-processing programs, spreadsheets, and database programs. Today that number is extremely limited. While there are a few nonmajor word-processing programs available, most have been designed for a very particular purpose and function. The number of all purpose word processing programs is probably less than six today; for spreadsheets, databases, and presentation packages the number is even smaller.

In this chapter, the truly integrated packages are presented first; next is a discussion of the office suites and the independent software pieces that make up those suites; and, finally, analysis of the few remaining stand-alone programs is presented. Prior to the analysis of the software, the chapter describes the types of nonstatistical software often utilized by educational researchers.

Integrated Packages

A decade ago, there were very few integrated packages (word processor, spreadsheet, database, and presentation packages), and every software program seemed to stand alone, with every company claiming compatibility among its programs. Compatibility was often a question of user skill rather than the actual seamless movement between programs. Today, the integrated packages are truly integrated. An integrated package of today usually has some type of built-in task manager from which users must select the type of task that they wish to perform (e.g., create a written document, utilize a spreadsheet, or build a database).

Calling the various office suites integrated packages is somewhat of a misnomer. Most of the office suites really are stand-alone programs that have been integrated as part of a package. Each of the modules of the suites is basically a stand-alone unit. For example, each of the spreadsheets in the suites offered by Corel, Lotus, and Microsoft functions quite perfectly outside its suite environment (the same may be said for the word processors, databases, and slide show developers). On the other hand, the two really integrated packages still available today—Apple Works and Microsoft Works—are indeed integrated packages. The subprograms within each (spreadsheet, database, and word processor) do not operate externally to the overall package.

Spreadsheets

The fundamental purpose of an electronic spreadsheet is the collection, analysis, and reporting of numerical information. In other words, spreadsheets are designed to handle the type of information typically used by educational researchers, namely, numbers. Spreadsheets range from the style designed for the home budget user to the corporate-level financial planner—that is, from a very limited need to a very complex one. This discussion focuses upon programs at the mid-level or advanced application level.

A spreadsheet is an electronic worksheet that utilizes a series of cells to store numerical information and/or contain the formulas used to analyze data. The information is stored in a table format of rows and columns. Typically, the data coded by researchers are categorized into rows (data values or observations) and columns (data labels or data types). This format is perhaps the major strength of a spreadsheet, especially for educational researchers. The spreadsheet permits the calculations of counts, sums, averages, standard deviations, and variances for the data sets.

In addition to the descriptive calculations permitted by spreadsheets, all of the more advanced programs enable the user to create graphic representations of the data values. The types of graphs available differ from program to program, but most possess bar graphs, line graphs, and pie graphs as well as a variety of line graphs and histograms (and all of the major programs now produce 3-D graphics as well). Thus, a relatively advanced spreadsheet program calculates descriptive statistics and produces visual images of the data. A limitation of spreadsheets is in their primary purpose: they are designed for financial analysis (nonstatistical analysis). All of the big three (Lotus 1-2-3, Microsoft Excel, and Corel Quattro Pro) also permit some in-depth statistical analysis (including inferential analysis).

Database Managers

The management of data is one of the aspects of research that often get lost in the haste of research. Researchers are ready to compile information into a computer program and analyze the results, but before an analysis can take place, the data must be organized in some manner. The practice of organizing the data can be tedious and time-consuming, yet effective organization not only increases the speed of analysis but may lead to the discovery of unanticipated contingencies within the data.

Database managers have been a dominant force in the use of microcomputers since their inception. Database managers allow a researcher to develop a format to describe the data and input the data into that structure. A well-developed database permits the user to sort, categorize, subset, and review the information contained in it.

The type and quality of a database selected by a researcher should reflect several aspects: (1) the expertise of the user; (2) the amount of information—data; (3) the degree of manipulation (i.e., sorting, categorizing, etc.) required; and (4) the ability of the database program to obtain data from external programs. A second level of concern associated with the selected database manager is the monetary resources available to the researcher. Huge, enterprise-level database programs can cost upward of tens of thousands of dollars, far beyond the fiscal level of most researchers. For modern educators the typical database program needed functions directly on their desktop computer.

The type of database selected depends, largely, upon the nature of the data sets and the degree of manipulation required by the user. For example, provided the data set is not exceptionally large and requires only minimal sorting, a spreadsheet with sorting features such as possessed by Lotus, Excel, or Quattro Pro would be adequate. In fact, these three spreadsheets have evolved so much over the last decade that multiply layered sorts are quite possible for them. Furthermore, one of the strengths of early databases was their ability to perform two critical functions: search and search/replace. Both of these functions are now available on almost every full-function spreadsheet. What is not available in most spreadsheets is the creation of a nice data entry form for direct entry of data from the keyboard. This is where databases still are the best option for users. In addition, while relational tables can be built on most full-function spreadsheets, this is not their purpose. Every major database program is a relational database, meaning that relations between critical (key) elements shared among two or more tables may be specified. Thus, a table may be created containing student information, including a field identifying "Teacher-Name." Similarly, a table may be created for all teachers that would include the field "Teacher-Name"; thus, these two tables would be linked to each other by this key field (related).

Slide Show Developers

No type of program captured the interest and fancy of the business and scientific world faster than presentation programs over the last decade. A decade ago, very few presentation programs were available on the market. Those that were available were very fundamental and lacking in sophistication. Today, very few businesses would even consider operating without a sales force equipped with a top-of-the-line slide show presentation development program. These programs allow the user to present computer-based slide shows to large groups and to develop handouts of these presentations, and they permit the user to integrate graphics, sound, animation, and more into a complete visual and auditory presentation.

For educational researchers, this means that the results of their work may be organized beyond the historic research paper or article and put into a form that is very palatable for a large audience presentation or presentation via the World Wide Web. A good presentation package permits a wide use of backgrounds, font styles, importation and/or development of graphics, importation of graphs and charts, predetermined template styles to facilitate presentation development, linkage to other programs such as word processors, spreadsheets, and databases. Most of the higher-end programs available today even permit the presentations to be saved in HTML format for publication to the Web (another strategy now being utilized by more and more educational researchers).

Word Processors

A good word processor should permit easy entry of material, provide multiple types of formatting and multiple types of organization, permit both portrait and landscape printing and, in today's WYSIWYG (*what you see is what you get*) world, it should provide a print simulation view as well as a keyboard-related view. It should have a fast spell-checking program as well as a thesaurus. It should provide a choice between seen or not-seen formatting markers. One should be able to cut and paste pictures, graphics, and tables from a variety of different programs (e.g., presentations, statistical packages, spreadsheets, and databases). One should be able to import documents produced by other word-processing programs, as well as exporting to the same programs.

For the educational researcher, a word processor's value lies more in the ability to generate reports and integration of information created by various statistical packages (or databases or spreadsheets). The strength of the word processor, then, is how well it integrates information from a variety of sources into a single document suitable for presentation or publication. The trick is to make the word processor work for the researcher, not make the researcher do the work for the word processor. The more that the word processor provides the ready interface to the types of activities needed for report writing and documentation production, the more the researcher can concentrate on the work, not on the production of the report. Word processors historically have had a nearly religious following. For many people, whatever word processor they first started working with is the one that they intend to keep. Changing word processors can be very difficult, particularly having to learn new commands and new operations that seemed so simple with the previous program.

INTEGRATED SOFTWARE PACKAGES

Name: **602Office**
Company: Software602, Inc.
Address: Suite 3125, One Independent Drive, Jacksonville, FL 32205
URL: www.software602.com
Price: Free

System: Windows (32-bit)
RAM Requirement: 16 MB
Hard Drive Requirement: 14 MB
Comments: 602Office is one of a trio of interesting anomalies in the integrated office suites genre. 602Office is freeware; this means that for the individual user there is no charge for the software. The suite itself includes a Microsoft Word-compatible word processor (602Text), Excel-compatible spreadsheet (602Tab), a photo enhancement program (602Photo), and a photo album storage program (602Album). Even though 602Office resembles an office suite, the various components cannot be purchased separately, and therefore it is classified as an integrated package.

Name: **602Tab**
Comments: 602Tab is a very close rival to the "big three" spreadsheets (e.g., Excel, Corel Quattro Pro, and Lotus 1-2-3). The fact that it reads and writes in Excel format is a plus feature. In fact, 602Tab has the look and feel of Excel. All the general operations that one would expect in a spreadsheet are present in 602Tab.

For the researcher, 602Tab has an enormous array of statistical functions. In total, there are 80 different statistical functions ranging from the expected descriptive all the way through some very unexpected inferential statistics (e.g., Fisher's Exact Test, chi-square tests, calculation of confidence intervals, z-tests).

602Tab produces 35 different types of graphics/charts; while this number does not rival that of Excel, it is nonetheless quite acceptable. Graphics/charts that are produced by 602Tab are easily exported to 602Text for inclusion in a document.

Name: **602Text**
Comments: 602Text is very similar to Microsoft Word 2000 and XP documents. Importation and transportation between the two systems are very smooth. 602Text is capable of nearly every type of formatting action that Microsoft Word is capable of performing.

602Text is capable of importing spreadsheet tables and graphics, performing mail merges, and saving files in .PDF and HTML format. It has a built-in spell checker, grammar checker, and a full dictionary to look up the meaning of an unknown word. 602Text does nearly everything that most regular users of Microsoft Word will ever need.

602Text opens just about any file created by Microsoft Word from version 6.0 forward. Similarly, it saves files in a form that any version of Microsoft Word 6.0 forward can read. In addition, 602Text saves a file into HTML format, as well as saving files as Web style sheets. 602Text imports any graphics created by 602Tab or Excel.

The major difference between the two word processors is in the use of document templates (.DOT files). Microsoft Word's use of document templates permits the user to create (or make use of predeveloped) style guides designed to meet certain format constraints (such as a specially designed template for a publication manual). 602Text does not utilize templates in the same fashion that Microsoft Word utilizes them. 602Text does make use of style sheets (part of the function of Microsoft Word's document templates), but these style sheets are stored with the individual document rather than independently of the document.

Name: **AppleWorks 6.2**
Company: Apple Computer, Inc.
Address: Retail
URL: www.apple.com/appleworks
Price: $79.00
System: Apple Mac OS 8.1 or later (PowerPC)
RAM Requirement: 24 MB
Hard Drive Requirement: 50 MB
Comments: A completely integrated program, AppleWorks possesses a word processor, a spreadsheet, a database, a presentation program, a drawing program, and a painting program. Each of these programs is activated in two stages: first, the apparent program—AppleWorks—is activated; and second, the user then selects one of the six internal programs.

The AppleWorks spreadsheet is a fundamental spreadsheet. It handles most descriptive statistics (mean, standard deviation, variance, minimum, maximum, etc.). While there are not any built-in inferential statistical functions, a clever programmer could readily produce t-tests, F-tests (ANOVA), and even multiple regression analyses. The spreadsheet produces very simple charts/graphs: vertical and horizontal bar graphs, line graphs, pie charts, and scatterplots. The charts/graphs may be imported for inclusion in a document in the word processor; likewise, so may the spreadsheet itself be imported to a word-processor document.

The AppleWorks database is also a very fundamental, flat field table. Very good for maintaining information, it does not have the ability to be linked to other information in separate tables; it functions like an electronic card file. Tables generated by the database may be used for mail merging with the word processor.

The presentations component of AppleWorks is very fundamental. It produces slide shows, but these lack the considerable flair that one has come to typically expect in a slide show presentation.

The AppleWorks word processor is more like a glorified electronic typewriter. It does have the capacity to change fonts and to do some fundamental formatting, but actions beyond this basic level are not possible. On the other hand, it is an ideal word processor if one is simply looking to write simple memos, letters, or uncomplicated short reports.

Name: **EasyOffice Suite, version 3.34**
Company: E-Press Corporation
Address: 70 East Beaver Creek Road, Industrial Unit 203, Richmond Hill, Ontario L4B 3B2 Canada
URL: www.e-press.com
Price: Free
System: Windows (32-bit)
RAM Requirement: 16 MB
Hard Drive Requirement: 28 MB
Comments: EasyOffice is one of a trio of interesting anomalies in the integrated office suites genre. EasyOffice is freeware; this means that for the individual user there is no charge for the software. The suite itself includes a Microsoft Word-compatible word processor (EasyWord), an Excel-compatible spreadsheet (EasySpreadsheet), and a slide show

presentation program (EasyPresentation) as well as a contact manager, a bookkeeping program, a calculator program, a voice reproduction program, and a scaled-down version of the word-processing program.

Name: **EasyWord**

Comments: EasyWord is surprisingly compatible with Microsoft Word 2000 and XP documents. Importation and transportation between the two systems are very smooth. EasyWord is capable of nearly every type of formatting action that Microsoft Word is capable of performing.

EasyWord is capable of importing spreadsheet tables and graphics, performing mail merges, and saving files in .PDF and HTML format. It has a built-in spell checker, grammar checker, and a full dictionary to look up the meaning of an unknown word. In short, EasyWord does nearly everything that most regular users of a word processor will ever need.

The major difference between the two word processors is in the use of document templates (.DOT files). Microsoft Word's use of document templates permits the user to create (or make use of predeveloped) style guides designed to meet certain format constraints (such as a specially designed template for a publication manual). These templates (.DOT files) then stand alone to be used with any document. EasyWord does not utilize templates in the same fashion that Microsoft Word utilizes them. EasyWord uses templates as design layouts and saves these separately. EasyWord does make use of style sheets (part of the function of Microsoft Word's document templates), but these style sheets are stored with the individual document rather than independently of the document.

Name: **EasySpreadsheet**

Comments: EasySpreadsheet is a very close rival to the "big three" spreadsheets (Excel, Corel Quattro Pro, and Lotus 1-2-3). The fact that it reads and writes in Excel format is a plus feature. In fact, if one modifies the menu to employ only the advanced buttons and removes the annoying column and row totals that are automatic upon initial start-up, the spreadsheet closely resembles Excel's. All the general operations of a good spreadsheet are present in EasySpreadsheet.

For the data analyst, there is some significant difference between EasySpreadsheet and the other top three programs. First, there are a limited number of descriptive statistics available, and these are available only through an antiquated system of hand-keying row and column values in a function statement. Second, there are no inferential statistics available (although, utilizing the built-in functions one could develop t-tests, F-tests, z-tests, as well as create templates to handle ANOVA and multiple regression analyses).

Graphics/charts that are produced by EasySpreadsheet are easily exported to EasyWord for inclusion in a document. While the quality of the graphics/charts is good, the quantity and depth of the available types are restricted, although two- and three-dimensional charts are offered in about 11 different forms.

Name: **Microsoft Works 6.0**
Company: Microsoft Corp.
Address: Retail

URL: www.Microsoft.com
Price: $54.95
System: Windows (32-bit)
RAM Requirement: 60 MB
Hard Drive Requirement: 165 MB
Comments: Microsoft Works 6.0 masquerades as an integrated package through a Task Manager interface, but, in reality, each of the packages does stand alone. Included with the Works 6.0 package are a word processor, spreadsheet, database, calendar manager, Microsoft Money, Internet Explorer 5.5, and Outlook Express.

The re-done spreadsheet in Works rivals what Microsoft Excel was just a short time ago. While it does not possess functions for inferential statistics, all of the primary functions for descriptive statistics are present. An innovative user could readily develop appropriate inferential analyses using the existing built-in functions and a little programming. The graphic/chart capacity of the spreadsheet has increased considerably in the last several versions. Graphs/charts can be easily imported into a document being written by Works' word processor. Spreadsheets as well may be copied into a word processor document. Spreadsheets may be saved in native form, in Excel form, or in Lotus 1-2-3 (.wks) form. Similarly, data may be imported from the same forms.

The database management program is really a program designed for home use. It is a flat-field, single-table model designed along the lines of the typical note card. Nonetheless, it can be very useful for gathering information that might be transported to other programs for later use. A database can be used as a mail-merge table for the word processor.

The Microsoft Works 6.0 word processor is a fully functional, albeit somewhat restrained, cousin to Microsoft Word. It maintains much of the premise of Word but without all the flare. It is very capable of producing a good, sound, and fundamental document, but it would be very difficult to work with if one had to embed multiple tables and multiple spreadsheets, and/or if the document were very long. The word processor in Works was designed for home use, not designed to write long reports. The word processor will import a variety of different types of files ranging from Microsoft Word documents (although Word files of 2000 and above must be brought in as RTF type), WordPerfect files, and Macintosh Word files.

Name: **Microsoft Works 2002 Suite**
Company: Microsoft Corp.
Address: Retail
URL: www.Microsoft.com/
Price: $109.00
System: Windows (32-bit)
RAM Requirement: 64 MB
Hard Drive Requirement: 1045 MB
Comments: Microsoft Works 2002 Suite is no longer the small kid on the block. In fact, a complete installation requires more than 1 GB of hard drive space. The suite includes the same Microsoft Word program included with the Office XP suite. In addition to a spreadsheet and database that have historically been part of the Works package, Works 2002 now includes Money 2002, Encarta 2002, Picture It! Photo 2002, and Streets and Trips 2002—as well as a complete upgrade of Internet Explorer 5.5.

Name: **StarOffice Version 5.2**
Company: Sun Microsystems
Address: Available at retailers
URL: www.sun.com/dot-com/staroffice.html
Price: Free download (a CD may be purchased from retailers for $39.95)
System: Windows, Linux, OS/2, and Solaris SPARC/Intel
RAM Requirement: 16 MB
Hard Drive Requirement: 32 MB
Comments: StarOffice includes a word processor (Writer), a spreadsheet (Calc), a slide show creator (Impress), a graphics program (Draw), a calendar program (Schedule), an e-mail program, (Mail), a program designed to allow you to read existing databases (Base), an Internet newsreader (Discussion), and a program for creating complex mathematical formulas (Math). The suite itself is one of the most comprehensive available on the market. It covers almost every need that better researchers would have except for statistical package, and part of that is covered through the Math program.

Name: **Calc**
Comments: Calc is a full-function, Excel reading spreadsheet. While it does not visually duplicate Excel, it does duplicate nearly everything that Excel is capable of doing. The spreadsheet is easy to maneuver through; it offers every statistical function (descriptive and inferential) that Excel provides. Spreadsheets and graphics created by Calc are easily imported into a word processor. The graphics/charts created by Calc also rival those created by Excel in quality and quantity.

Name: **Writer**
Comments: While Writer does not mimic in the precise look and feel of Microsoft Word, it does mimic most of the operations and functions of Word. It imports a wide range of documentation from other word processors, in fact, more than Word itself without the special add-ins. Writer readily imports graphics produced by Calc (or Excel or any other Windows-based spreadsheet). Writer imports tables as well from the spreadsheet. Writer handles mail merges and duplicates most of the other text-related tools of Microsoft Word. Writer employs style sheets, and these may be modified readily by the user. Writer imports the styles created in Microsoft Word and links these directly to a particular document. Microsoft Word documents can be successfully imported to Writer. While the compatibility is not 100%, it is nearly so.

Name: **Impress**
Comments: Impress is the only slide show presentation program that completely imports files created in Microsoft PowerPoint without the apparent loss of any other features created with PowerPoint. While the general layout of Impress resembles the PowerPoint layout, it lacks the frames for viewing slide buttons, user notes, etc. For the most part, Impress does indeed impress. It is user-friendly, capable of the same quality of general presentation that one finds with all the major slide presentation programs.

STAND-ALONE SOFTWARE: OFFICE SUITES

Name: **Corel WordPerfect Office 2002**
Company: Corel Software, Inc.
Address: Retail
URL: www.Corel.com
Price: $399 (Standard); $499 (Professional)
System: Windows (32-bit); Macintosh (PowerPC)
RAM Requirement: 16 MB (Minimum); 32 MB (Recommended)
Hard Drive Requirement: 165 MB

Name: **Quattro Pro 10**
Comments: Quattro Pro rivals Microsoft Excel in many ways. Its capacity for building related spreadsheets is exceptional, and its graphics package is very similar. Forty-four different file charts are standard within Quattro Pro (in addition using a build-in "Wizard"). It is possible to modify the charts in a wide variety of ways. The charts are easily imported into WordPerfect 10 as well as Presentations 10 for a slide presentation.

Quattro Pro's built-in statistics are extremely user-friendly since they are directly accessible through pull-down menu. Furthermore, 20 extended statistical functions are available, including ANOVA, 2-way ANOVA, t-test, z-test, F-test, advanced regression, and so on. In addition, a function exists for calculating ranks and percentiles of data set.

Spreadsheets may be readily imported into any other member of the WordPerfect office suite. In particular, a spreadsheet (or portion of a spreadsheet) may be linked to a WordPerfect document so that any changes made in the spreadsheet would be automatically changed in the document as well. Any graph produced by Quattro Pro is also easily ported into a WordPerfect document either as a stand-alone or as a linked action (again, any changes made in the spreadsheet graphic would then be reflected in the word graphic).

Name: **Paradox 10 (available only in Professional package)**
Comments: Paradox is itself a paradox. Paradox is a holdover from the days when a database was a true industrial-sized engine, along the lines of a FoxPro or a dBase. Paradox itself is designed to answer large-scale questions to provide large-scale means to find solutions to database management. Paradox provides full-blown access to multiple-level tables in a true classic relational database structure. Not really a suitable program for nonprogrammers, it is highly usable for those comfortable with using code to create their database structures.

Data from Paradox is not readily imported into other parts of the Corel Office system. Although data can be imported, it is neither an easy task nor one readily accomplished in a drag-and-drop fashion.

Name: **Presentations 10**
Comments: Presentations is Corel's slide show maker. It includes support for MP3 audio and employs animated gets. It allows you to share your presentations on the Internet without too much difficulty. Furthermore, your slide show may be published rather easily as

HTML in a single set. Cross-platform sharing of slide shows developed under Presentations is a little difficult, although not impossible.

Name: **WordPerfect 10**
Comments: WordPerfect is still WordPerfect. It is a nice upgrade from the previous version of the program (WordPerfect 9). WordPerfect functions essentially as it always has, an ideal piece of software for long documents. Editing long documents has always been a real strength of WordPerfect and continues to be a valuable feature. Classical features such as Reveal Codes are still available, as well as the special F-Key functions often employed by regular users.

Moving documents between WordPerfect and Microsoft Word is very easy, although some other features of Word do not directly transfer, and vice versa. Transfer of documents to other word processors (e.g., Microsoft Works or Lotus WordPro) is not as readily accomplished.

Name: **Lotus SmartSuite Millennium Edition 9.6**
Company: Lotus Development Corp.
Address: Retail
URL: www.lotus.com
Price: $389
System: Windows (32-bit)
RAM Requirement: 16 MB
Hard Drive Requirement: 96 MB

Name: **Lotus 1-2-3**
Comments: Lotus 1-2-3 is the original spreadsheet program that changed the desktop world. It still has all of features that made it at one time the number one spreadsheet in world. It has added the ability to publish worksheets to a Web site and to pull a table down from a Web site.

Lotus 1-2-3 still offers the full statistical functions as it did previously, with the addition of a few more inferential operations (advanced regression, F-test, t-test, z-test, chi-square, etc.). The difficulty with Lotus 1-2-3 has always been that it uses @ operations, which require the user to create formula (albeit through a drag-and-drop type of operation).

Spreadsheet tables may be readily copied into the word processor of Lotus SmartSuite (WordPro). Tables may be imported as complete or as linked (meaning that changes in the table within Lotus 1-2-3 are reflected on changes in the linked document table).

Name: **Approach**
Comments: Approach is Lotus' relational database. Creating a simple, straightforward database is easily accomplished with Lotus Approach. Tables can be copied to WordPro for inclusion in reports. Approach is not as sophisticated as other database programs included with office suites, but it is probably the easiest to work with for a nonprogrammer. Approach offers a "Wizard-like" mock-up to build surveys. This mock-up also provides the guide to create summary statistics. This is a nice addition for researchers trying to cre-

ate a form for a survey being completed by outside parties (or even one that might be created for use on desktop). The created database may be saved to HTML format, but the linking and subsequent application must be created directly by the user.

Name: **Freelance Graphics**
Comments: Freelance has not changed much over the years, although it has added a function to convert presentations into Web-ready pages. The Freelance transfers from a slide show presentation to a Web-ready presentation and is one of the easiest available.

The strength of Freelance has never really been its slide presentation format (although this is a relatively simple activity). The strength of Freelance is that it is a much more manageable graphics design program than some of the other slide presentation programs in the office suite genre. The weakness of Freelance is that it is limited in the quality of its built-in templates and provided graphic images.

Name: **WordPro**
Comments: As word processors run, WordPro offers the least number of bells and whistles of the big three suites. The good news is that most of these bells and whistles are not effects that most run-of-the-mill users need. WordPro does what we expect a fully powered word processor to do, create documents. WordPro easily imports and exports documents produced by Microsoft Word and Corel WordPerfect. Mail merge is a simple function, and tables may be utilized that have been developed by Lotus 1-2-3. Graphics produced by Lotus 1-2-3 or Freelance Graphics may also be imported into a document.
One of the real strengths of WordPro is the flexibility that users have in creating their own version of menus. Menu tabs may be created and modified as the user sees appropriate. A very interesting feature that seems to be unique to WordPro is the ability to use Smart Masters to create a menu system that imitates either Microsoft Word or Corel WordPerfect menus.

Name: **Microsoft Office XP**
Company: Microsoft Corp.
Address: Retail
URL: www.Microsoft.com/office
Price: $460 (Standard); $590 (Professional)
System: Windows (32-bit)
RAM Requirement: 32 MB
Hard Drive Requirement: 260 MB

Name: **Microsoft Office X**
Company: Microsoft Corp.
Address: Retail
URL: www.Microsoft.com/office
Price: $499
System: Macintosh (PowerPC with OS 10.1)
RAM Requirement: 128 MB
Hard Drive Requirement: 196 MB

Comments: Office X is the newly released version of Microsoft Office for the Macintosh PowerPC.

Name: **Excel XP**

Comments: Excel, in its most recent reincarnation, is probably one of the most complex spreadsheet programs ever thought of, let alone created. It offers more functions and operations than most educational researchers would ever have the time to explore. Its ability to provide quick data summary is exceptional. Data may be quickly summarized by built-in functions (mean, standard deviation, variance, etc.). Furthermore, Excel has an add-in data analysis package that allows for 18 different inferential activities, plus an advanced descriptive option. These inferential analyses include ANOVA, t-test, correlations, regression, etc. In addition, it is also possible to rank order and produce a percentile ranking of data from within Excel. Add to this a total of 72 different stock graph types plus 20 customizable operations for these graphs.

Spreadsheets may be readily imported into any other member of the Microsoft office suite. In particular, a spreadsheet (or portion of a spreadsheet) may be linked to a Microsoft Word document so that any changes made in the spreadsheet would be automatically changed in the document as well. Any graph produced by Excel is also easily ported into a Word document either as a stand-alone or as a linked action (again, any changes made in the spreadsheet graphic would then be reflected in the word graphic).

Excel is one of the most common imported types of files accepted by almost all of the major statistical packages. Furthermore, almost all of these packages export to an Excel file as well.

Name: **Access XP**

Comments: Access has developed into a full-fledged, powerful, yet flexible, database program. When Access was first introduced, it seemed as if it was almost a second thought on the part of Microsoft since it was pushing FoxPro as the database of choice for power users. While FoxPro is still available today, it is primarily seen as a server-based system for use in corporate structures rather than a desktop individualized program. Although Access has the capacity to be utilized in a networked environment, it is very effective as a personal database manager. Access has a relatively intuitive data interface and a relatively moderate learning curve. Microsoft has provided several different predeveloped database prototypes to serve as models for database development. The advantage of using a database is that a researcher may develop a template to use for data input, which may then be ported over to Excel or a statistical package for analysis purposes. Otherwise, Access provides good summary statistics as part of the general package.

Name: **PowerPoint XP**

Comments: As presentation programs go, PowerPoint may be considered the standard by which all others seem to be measured. Its learning curve is not steep, and all of the models that it provides as learning assistance as well as the various wizards provided by Microsoft serve as exceptional guides in the development of presentations. Materials from other parts of the Office package may be imported quickly into PowerPoint without any difficulty whatsoever. PowerPoint has recently added a Wizard to quickly convert presentations into HTML-ready slides for use in a Web site.

Name: **Microsoft Word XP**
Comments: Word XP has become the benchmark by which all word-processing programs are now gauged. Word provides more options than most users will ever need. Its ease of operation on a surface level is exceptional, but its real strength comes when a user is able to develop and make use of document templates, graphic importation and modification, importation of spreadsheets and database results, and the like.
Word's facility to manage through mail-merge document compilation is also outstanding. Word can import and export a wide range of different document types, but most of these must be added from the installation disk since they are not considered part of a regular install.

Stand-Alone Software: Database Managers

Name: **Crystal Reports 8** (Standard)
Company: Seagate Technologies Inc.
Address: Retail
URL: www.Seagate.com
Price: $250
System: Windows (32-bit)
RAM Requirement: 32 MB
Hard Drive Requirement: 30 MB
Comments: Seagate has entered the database market with a very user-friendly program. Crystal Reports uses a drop-down menuing system to build relational tables, input forms, and reports forms. Utilizing the same menuing structure, it is also relatively easy for the user to build search queries and application macros. A bit of good database programming knowledge is necessary to really make this program work.

Name: **FileMaker Pro 5.5**
Company: FileMaker
Address: Retail
URL: www.FileMaker.com
Price: $250
System: Windows (32-bit); Macintosh (Mac OS 8.1)
RAM Requirement: 32 MB (Windows); 128 MB (Macintosh)
Hard Drive Requirement: Not Available
Comments: FileMaker pro has long been a favorite of individual researchers, small businesses, and educational institutions. FileMaker Pro is a pull-down menu, graphic user interface system that is relatively user-friendly with a moderate learning curve. FileMaker builds relational tables; a wide variety of input forms and reports, summary tables, and statistics are readily developed, and these may be linked to word-processing or spreadsheet programs (and vice versa). While to really tap the subtle features of FileMaker, one should

be a good database programmer, a relative neophyte can make use of the features offered by this program.

Name: **Microsoft Visual FoxPro 7.0**
Company: Microsoft
Address: Retail
URL: www.Microsoft.com
Price: $575
System: Windows (32-bit); Windows 2000, Windows NT
RAM Requirement: 64 MB (minimum)
Hard Drive Requirement: 115 MB
Comments: FoxPro is probably the most complex database engine available at the retail level today for stand-alone desktop computers. While it is still possible for this program to be utilized by an individual user, this generally is not the case. FoxPro will do just about anything that one needs done in a large database system (the key is a large database system). FoxPro is not for the untutored in database programming. Its learning curve is relatively steep, and just to make some of the simplest functions work takes quite a bit of finesse. FoxPro's best use is in a networked environment (hence, the Windows NT and Windows 2000 systems). Nevertheless, FoxPro really does everything that one ever wanted done in a database. However, for the individual user to utilize FoxPro requires considerable database programming skill.

TEXT EDITORS

While word processors are very effective to enter reports and other written work, they are very ineffective to enter data. Although each of the word processors reviewed previously has the capacity to enter raw text and to save this text in a form that may be utilized by a statistical package, it is very inconvenient and sometimes nearly impossible. Furthermore, most statistical packages accept data entered by one or more of the big three spreadsheet programs; but this can be very inconvenient.

The most effective way to enter raw data to be used by a statistical piece of software is through a text editor. Moreover, since most statistical packages make use of some type of command-driven actions, a text editor permits the user to create these commands later to be submitted for batch runs by the statistical package.

Interestingly enough, while there are several very good commercial editors available, the vast majority of editors are available through what is known as "shareware." Shareware is software produced by private persons or small, independent companies that is made available to users of one or more outlets on the Internet. With shareware, users are offered the opportunity to utilize a piece of software for a restricted period of time (often 35 or 45 days), after which the user is expected either to make a payment (usually considerably far below what the price would be if the product were commercially developed) to the developer or to delete the software from the computer. In the following reviews, if a piece of is software is designated as shareware, then a download site is identified where a link to the software may be found. Following this link, the software may be downloaded for evaluating it for potential use. Shareware software has a habit of "disappearing," meaning that the author or developer is no longer supporting it.

Table D.1.1 presents a breakdown of the desired functions sought in text editors. This table is replicated (in an abbreviated form) for each of the text editors reviewed. The list of functions summarized in Table D.1.1 is not meant to be exhaustive; instead; it is only illustrative of a minimum level expected in a particular category of text editors.

Table D.1.1
Critical Functions in Text Editors

Classification ☑ = Full functions ✓ = Limited functions ☐ = Unknown

Large files	**Multiple files**
at least one megabyte	two or more simultaneously
Find functions	**Search & replace**
locate by name	replace text in entire document
locate by number	**Print options**
Undo and redo	print with line numbers
correct mistakes	print two pages on one page
Line blocks	**Column blocks**
Line numbering	**Macro applications**
Import options	create and save for multiple operations
import beyond ASCII file	**Export options**
	export beyone ASCII file

Name: **Boxer 9.0**
Company: Boxer Software
Address: P.O. Box 14545, Scottsdale, AZ 85267-4545
URL: www.boxersoftware.com
Price: $59.00
System: Windows (32-bit) (versions also available for DOS and OS/2)

Functions:	☑	Large files	☑	Multiple files
	☑	Find functions	☑	Search & replace
	☑	Undo and redo	☑	Print options
	☑	Line blocks	☑	Column blocks
	☑	Line numbering	☑	Macro applications
	☑	Import option	☑	Export options

Comments: Boxer is an editor that has been around for a long time. It has developed into a truly speedy and highly functional text editor. Capable of handling large files (maximum file size 16 MB), it is also able to handle multiple windows on multiple files simultaneously.

Name: **Code Edit 2.0**
Company: Shareware
Address: Shareware
URL: www.CNet.com/shareware
Price: Free
System: Windows (16-bit & 32-bit)
Functions:
- ☑ Large files
- ☑ Find functions
- ☑ Undo and redo
- ☑ Line blocks
- Line numbering
- ✓ Import option
- ☑ Multiple files
- ☑ Search & replace
- ✓ Print options
- Column blocks
- ✓ Macro applications
- ✓ Export options

Comments: Code Edit is very small (less than 300K in size), yet it is a very efficient text editor. It is quite capable of loading multiple files up to 80. It was able to handle a 5 MB file without much of a problem. Code Edit does not handle column blocks.

Name: **ConText**
Company: Shareware
Address: Shareware
URL: www.CNet.com/shareware
Price: Free
System: Windows (32-bit)
Functions:
- ☑ Large files
- ☑ Find functions
- ☑ Undo and redo
- ☑ Line blocks
- ✓ Line numbering
- ✓ Import option
- ☑ Multiple files
- ☑ Search & replace
- ✓ Print options
- Column blocks
- Macro applications
- ✓ Export options

Comments: ConText is a very capable text editor. ConText has an unlimited number of files that may be opened simultaneously, and the size of the files is limited only by the available memory in a system.

Name: **Edit Pad (Lite or Pro)**
Company: RegSoft.com Inc.
Address: PMB 201, Suite 220, 10820 Abbotts Bridge Road, Duluth, GA 30097
URL: www.editpadlite.com
Price: Lite is freeware; Edit Pad Pro $29.95
System: Windows (32-bit)
Functions:
- ☑ Large files
- ☑ Find functions
- ☑ Undo and redo
- ☑ Line blocks
- ☑ Line numbering
- ☑ Import option
- ☑ Multiple files
- ☑ Search & replace
- ☑ Print options
- ☑ Column blocks
- ☑ Macro applications
- ☑ Export options

Comments: Edit Pad Pro is a full-function, text-editing program. It is capable of loading extremely large files and handling multiple files simultaneously. The user interface is friendly and easy to operate. Edit Pad Lite is freeware but should be able to handle most of the operations necessary for data entry. The one limitation to Edit Pad Lite is that it does not do column blocking. Nonetheless, at the price for Edit Pad Pro, obtaining all the full functions is very reasonable.

Name: **GWD Text Editor**
Company: GWD Soft
Address: Shareware
URL: www.gwdsoft.com
Price: $29.95 (without CD); $35.95 (with CD)
System: Windows (32-bit)
Functions:

☑	Large files	☑	Multiple files
☑	Find functions	☑	Search & replace
☑	Undo and redo	☑	Print options
☑	Line blocks	☑	Column blocks
☑	Line numbering	☑	Macro applications
☑	Import option	☑	Export options

Comments: GWD Text Editor is a comprehensive, full-function text editor. Not only does it edit and read ASCII files, but it also edits and reads Macintosh files. GWD Text Editor comes fully operational and ready to edit even the largest of files (it handled a 250 MB file without a problem).

Name: **Prolix 3.0**
Company: Kobayashi Software
Address: Shareware
URL: www.CNet.com/shareware
Price: Free
System: Windows (32-bit)
Functions:

☑	Large files	☑	Multiple files
☑	Find functions	☑	Search & replace
☑	Undo and redo	✓	Print options
☑	Line blocks		Column blocks
	Line numbering	☑	Macro applications
✓	Import option	✓	Export options

Comments: Prolix handles files up to 16 MB in size. It offers multiple windows, permitting multiple files to be loaded. It is somewhat limited in its ability to handle large data files. The cut-and-paste between files is rather straightforward.

Name: **Programmers File Editor—PFE**
Company: Shareware
Address: Shareware
URL: www.CNet.com/shareware
Price: Free

System: Windows (32-bit)

Functions:

☑	Large files	☑	Multiple files
☑	Find functions	☑	Search & replace
☑	Undo and redo	☑	Print options
☑	Line blocks	☑	Column blocks
☑	Line numbering	☑	Macro applications
☑	Import option	☑	Export option

Comments: PFE is a flexible, user-friendly, and fully functional editing program. It permits multiple files and is able to handle file sizes in excess of 200 MB in size. A recordable macrofeature makes this a very useful program for repetitive operations. This program, developed by Alan Phillips of the United Kingdom, is given away as freeware. There may not be a more comprehensive program available for under $50.

Name: **TextEd 2.0**

Company: Green House Multimedia

Address: Shareware

URL: www.CNet.com/shareware

Price: Free

System: Windows (32-bit)

Functions:

☑	Large files	☑	Multiple files
☑	Find functions	☑	Search & replace
☑	Undo and redo	✓	Print options
☑	Line blocks		Column blocks
	Line numbering	✓	Macro applications
✓	Import option	✓	Export options

Comments: TextEd is a small, user-friendly text editor. While somewhat limited in its data manipulation functions, TextEd does serve as a general text ASCII file editor.

Name: **TextPad 4.5**

Company: Helios Software Solution

Address: Shareware

URL: www.CNet.com/shareware

Price: $23

System: Windows (32-bit)

Functions:

☑	Large files	☑	Multiple files
☑	Find functions	☑	Search & replace
☑	Undo and redo	☑	Print options
☑	Line blocks	☑	Column blocks
☑	Line numbering	✓	Macro applications
✓	Import option	✓	Export options

Comments: TextPad is another multiple-file text editor. It is comprehensive with a very straightforward and user-friendly interface. Handles large files without any apparent difficulty. Fully compatible with Windows XP operating system.

Name: **Ultra-Editor 9.0**
Company: IDM Computer Solutions, Inc.
Address: 5575 Lesourdsville West Chester Road, Liberty Township, OH, 45011
URL: www.cnet.com/shareware
Price: $35.00
System: Windows
Functions:
- ☑ Large files
- ☑ Find functions
- ☑ Undo and redo
- ☑ Line blocks
- ☑ Line numbering
- ✓ Import option

- ☑ Multiple files
- ☑ Search & replace
- ☑ Print options
- ☑ Column blocks
- ☑ Macro applications
- ✓ Export options

Comments: Ultra-Editor is a full-function, multiwindowed text editor. It is capable of handling files in excess of 200 MB. It offers the user the opportunity to make personal modifications on program operations. Sold strictly as shareware, Ultra-Editor provides a lot of bang for the buck.

Name: **VEDIT 6.0**
Company: Greenview Data, Inc.
Address: P.O. Box 1586, Ann Arbor, MI 48106-1586
URL: www.vedit.com
Price: $99
System: Windows (32-bit)
Functions:
- ☑ Large files
- ☑ Find functions
- ☑ Undo and redo
- ☑ Line blocks
- ☑ Line numbering
- ☑ Import option

- ☑ Multiple files
- ☑ Search & replace
- ☑ Print options
- ☑ Column blocks
- ☑ Macro applications
- ☑ Export options

Comments: VEDIT has been in business for more than 20 years. Over the years VEDIT has developed into perhaps the fastest editing program available today. Reasonably priced, considering all the features that it presents. It handles multiple files as well as data files in excess of 2 GB. Its speed of operations (especially with large files) is phenomenal. VEDIT has a full library of the user-developed macros that may be used to speed operations.

Name: **Winedit Propack 2001a**
Company: Winedit Software Co.
Address: P.O. Box 1435, Hilo, MI, 96721
URL: www.winedit.com
Price: $129
System: Windows
Functions:
- ☑ Large files
- ☑ Find functions
- ☑ Undo and redo
- ☑ Line blocks

- ☑ Multiple files
- ☑ Search & replace
- ☑ Print options
- ☑ Column blocks

   ☑ Line numbering   ☑ Macro applications
   ✓ Import option   ✓ Export options

Comments: Winedit is one the most comprehensive text-editing packages available. To be precise, it probably has more features than most statistics-oriented researchers are going to ever need. It is really a programmer's editing package. It opens multiple files with file size essentially unlimited (limited primarily to the amount of RAM available). It prints with a variety of different options selected by the user. The user can modify the coding structures so that different types of lines of code appear, both on the screen and in print, in different colors.

Name: **Zeus for Windows 3.70**
Company: Xidicone
Address: P.O. Box 697, Lanecove NSW 1595, Australia
URL: Shareware—www.CNet.com/shareware
Price: $95
System: Windows (32-bit)
Functions:
   ☑ Large files   ☑ Multiple files
   ☑ Find functions   ☑ Search & replace
   ☑ Undo and redo   ☑ Print options
   ☑ Line blocks   ☑ Column blocks
   ☑ Line numbering   ☑ Macro applications
   ✓ Import option   ✓ Export options

Comments: Zeus is a shareware program. It handles files of 5 MB in size without any difficulty. It offers multiple windowing with a very comfortable user interface.

CHAPTER 2

Statistical Packages for Computers

INTRODUCTION

The range of available computer statistical packages runs from the simple, menu-driven to the complex, statistical model-driven. Most menu-driven packages are designed for ease of use and application. In the last decade even some of the more complex model-driven packages have moved into a menu-driven environment as the operating systems for computers have become more dependent upon icon-based applications (Windows and Macintosh OSs). In the final consideration, any package chosen must be dictated more by the sophistication of the user than by the limits of the machine.

The type and quality of the available packages are vast. One may choose from single-task packages (e.g., to do only regression) or fully integrated systems (i.e., performing most, if not all, descriptive and inferential analyses). The integrated packages are also divided into complete systems (buy the packaging and you get all the available analyses) or package sets where you may purchase various combinations of programs to perform only specific analyses. Again, the package chosen is mandated by the type of task, the size of the data, and the skill of the user.

Most of the packages reviewed for this work operate in a GUI (graphic user interface) environment (e.g., Microsoft Windows or Macintosh). Most of these packages are also pull-down, menu-operated. This means that most of the operations for these packages are accomplished by pointing the cursor at the desired category of operation and then selecting a subaction from this category (and possible subselections from this subcategory). In the previous edition of this work over 90% of the software reviewed was command line-driven, rather than menu-driven. Today it is almost impossible to find a program that is strictly command line-driven (unless that program operates only in a DOS or UNIX environment). While almost all the programs operate as menu-driven environments, many do offer the experienced user the opportunity to use command line features (often described as "Syntax" or "Command" actions). The advantage of a command line feature is the ability of the user to "tweak" the desired process to reflect more a personal preference of analyses. The strength of many of the available statistical packages is their appearance as "nontechnical" software. This means that the user may effectively operate the software without necessarily possessing technical skills in statistics. This strength is also a weakness since it does not permit the experienced user the opportunity to "tweak" a particular function to obtain a desired outcome.

Getting data in and out of statistical packages, spreadsheets, and database programs has often been tedious and sometimes nearly impossible. Generally, the user is forced to input data using the built-in editor of a program or using an external editor such as those reviewed in an earlier chapter. The problem raised by many cross-program users has been how to move data from one program to another. This dilemma is generally solved by transferring data to a third program, for example, by saving a data file created by Systat into an

Excel spreadsheet and then reading the Excel spreadsheet into SAS. While this solves the problem, it is nevertheless a wearisome job at times. Two programs available make this task far less complex.

Name: **DBMS/Copy**
Company: Conceptual Software, Inc.
Address: Suite 510, 9660 Hillcroft, Houston, TX 77096
URL: www.conceptual.com
Price: $295
System: Windows (32-bit); UNIX
Functions: DBMS/Copy transfers data between more than 80 different statistical packages, spreadsheet programs, and database programs. The transfer between the programs is easily done with a user-friendly, pull-down menu system. DBMS/Copy handles files as large as the user has memory for storage (users report transferring data in excess of 200 MB). An additional set of features includes the ability to view the data and to select subsets of variables and subsets of records for transfer. DBMS/Copy further has the ability to select variables based on "if-then-else" statements as well as provide the user with a library of over 100 different built-in mathematical functions to create new variables as part of the transfer.
Comments: For more than 10 years, DBMS/Copy has been an essential tool for anyone utilizing different programs to analyze data. Its speed and quality of transfer make it a useful program for any data analyst.

Name: **Stat/Transfer 6.0**
Company: Stata Corporation
Address: 4905 Lakeway Drive, College Station, TX 77845
URL: www.Stata.com
Price: $249
System: Windows (32-bit)
Functions: Stat/Transfer transfers data between 27 different statistical programs, spreadsheets, and databases. Data may be transferred between all three of the big spreadsheets (Excel, Lotus 1-2-3, and Quattro Pro) as well as the major databases (Access, FoxPro, and Paradox). Stat/Transfer also produces HTML tables from any one of the supported programs.
Comments: Stat/Transfer is an easy-to-use data transfer program. StataCorp is not the producer of the software (Circle Systems of Seattle is the originator), but StataCorp acts as the selling agent.

Table D.2.1 presents a breakdown of the desired functions sought in statistical packages. This table is replicated (in an abbreviated form) for each of the statistical packages reviewed. The list of functions summarized in Table D.2.1 is not meant to be exhaustive; instead, it is only illustrative of a minimum level expected in a particular category of statistical analysis.

Table D.2.1.
Critical Functions in Statistical Programs

Classification   ☑= Full functions ✓= Limited functions ☒=Indirectly Available

Descriptive Statistics
  mean & standard deviation
  standard error of mean
  variance
  simple correlations

Advanced Descriptive
  median
  confidence intervals
  quartiles
  percentiles
  advanced correlations

ANOVA/ANCOVA
  one-way & factorial
  between and repeated
  multiple comparisons (a priori &
    post hoc)

Hypothesis Tests
  goodness of fit
  single sample tests
  independent and dependent t-tests

Regression
  simple and multiple
  linear and nonlinear
  stepwise
  multiple correlations
  residual analysis
  confidence intervals
  tests of homogeneity
  polynomial regression

Multivariate
  factor analysis
  rotation options
  logistic regression
  discriminate analysis
  canonical analysis

Distributions (Cross tabs)
  frequency tables
  cross tabulation
  1,2,3 level tables

Nonparametric
  chi-square
  sign test
  Mann-Whitney
  Friedman ANOVA
  Wilcoxon signed-rank

Statistical Graphs
  histogram
  bar charts
  line plots
  scatterplots
  boxplots and whisker plots

Advanced Graphing
  axis control
  XYZ scatterplots
  3D plots
  distribution plotting
  regression residuals
  factor plotting

Test Analyses
  item scoring
  biserial correlation
  Alpha coefficients
  standardized scores

Time Series
  ARIMA modeling
  difference modeling
  seasonal modeling
  smoothing models

Classification   ☑= Full functions ✓= Limited functions ☒=Indirectly Available

Test Analyses (continued)	**Time Series** (continued)
standard error of measure	forecast values
	graphics

Import	**Export**
ASCII	ASCII
Excel	Excel
Lotus	Lotus
Access	Access
dBase	dBase
Paradox	Paradox
Quattro Pro	Quattro Pro
other statistical programs	other statistical programs

COMPREHENSIVE PACKAGES

Name: **ASP: A Statistical Package, Version 3**
Company: DMC Software, Inc.
Address: 6169 Pebbleshire Drive, Grand Blanc, MN
URL: www.dmcsoftware.com
Price: $125 (educational); $199.95 (corporate)
System: Windows (95); DOS (Version 2 only)
Functions:

☑	Descriptive Statistics	☑	Advanced Descriptive
☑	ANOVA/ANCOVA	☑	Hypothesis Tests
☑	Regression	✓	Multivariate
✓	Distributions (Cross tabs)	☑	Nonparametric
☑	Statistical Graphs	☑	Advanced Graphing
✓	Test Analyses	☑	Time Series
✓	Import	✓	Export

Comments: ASP is a surprisingly complete, yet compact, statistical package. It provides a wide majority of the traditional descriptive and inferential functions. Furthermore, it provides quite a large proportion of the more advanced features traditionally found in the more expensive statistical packages. Its one major limitation is in its import and export of data; ASP accepts only ASCII files.

Name: **BMDP New System 2.0**
Company: Statistical Solutions
Address: Stonehill Corporate Center, Suite 104, 999 Broadway, Saugus, MA 01906
URL: www.statsol.ie/bmdp/bmdp.htm
Price: $395 (standard); $1,095 (professional)
System: Windows (32-bit)
Functions:

☑	Descriptive Statistics	☑	Advanced Descriptive
☑	ANOVA/ANCOVA	☑	Hypothesis Tests
☑	Regression	☑	Multivariate

271

☑ Distributions (Cross tabs)	☑ Nonparametric
☑ Statistical Graphs	☑ Advanced Graphing
☑ Test Analyses	☑ Time Series
☑ Import	☑ Export

Comments: BMDP was one of the original big three statistical packages developed for mainframe computing systems. Several years ago the American producer of BMDP was bought out by SPSS, and BMDP ceased to exist as a product in this country. In Europe, on the other hand, Statistical Solutions (an Irish company) retained the rights to market BMDP in Europe and to develop a new product to be called BMDP New System. Statistical Solutions opened an office in Boston in 1996 and began developing a Windows-based version of BMDP.

BMDP New System 2.0 is the most recent version of the software. BMDP New System is a full-function statistical package based upon all of the original libraries for BMDP. BMDP's strongest points were its ability to handle factorial analysis of variance, factor analysis, and regression analysis. Not only have these libraries been maintained, they have been enhanced. BMDP covers all the expected (and then some) descriptive and inferential statistics. Its graphing capacities have been increased over the years but still fall behind some of the high-resolution graphics available in other systems.

At this time, BMDP (standard) does not employ a graphic user interface. It is still command line-driven and therefore probably not useful to someone who has not worked in a code-based environment.

Name: **Data Desk (6.1)**
   Data Desk Plus (6.1)—includes ActivStats
Company: Data Description, Inc.
Address: Suite 9, 840 Hanshaw Road, Ithaca, NY 14850
URL: www.dataDesk.com
Price: Data Desk (6.1) $650 (commercial), $390 (academic)
Data Desk Plus (6.1) $795 (commercial), $477 (academic)
Data Desk/XL—Excel add-on—$50
System: Windows '95 and above (including 2000); Macintosh

Functions:			
☑ Descriptive Statistics	☑ Advanced Descriptive
☑ ANOVA/ANCOVA	☑ Hypothesis Tests
☑ Regression	☑ Multivariate
☑ Distributions (Cross tabs)	☑ Nonparametric
☑ Statistical Graphs	☑ Advanced Graphing
Test Analyses	Time Series
✓ Import	✓ Export

Comments: Performs all classical descriptive data analyses as well as most common inferential analyses (comparative, correlation, ANOVA, MANOVA, etc.). Provides quick interactive analyses of data in numerous graphical formats. The number of cases is limited simply to the amount of memory available on one's disk.

Data Desk is perhaps the most comprehensive statistical package available for Exploratory analysis. Because of its speed, Data Desk permits the user to examine alternative views of data in a manner not readily available in other programs. The addition of ActivStats provides a direct interactive link to demonstrations, simulations, and practice exercises, as well as self-training guides in the applications of statistical procedures and graphic exploratory techniques.

Name: **dbStat**
Company: None
Address: Soo-Nyung Kim, Department of Obstetrics and Gynecology, Konkuk University Medical Center Minjoong Hospital, 1 Hwayang-dong, Kwangjin-gu, Seoul 143-914, Korea
URL: www.dbstat.com
Price: $25
System: Windows
Functions:

☑ Descriptive Statistics	Advanced Descriptive
☑ ANOVA/ANCOVA	☑ Hypothesis Tests
✓ Regression	✓ Multivariate
☑ Distributions (Cross tabs)	✓ Nonparametric
✓ Statistical Graphs	Advanced Graphing
Test Analyses	Time Series
✓ Import	✓ Export

Comments: An easy-to-use statistical program providing three levels of information: (1) a database function for data entry and manipulation. Data may be imported through a variety of formats (Excel, Lotus 1-2-3, FoxPro, etc.); (2) statistical functions including descriptive, comparative, nonparametric, regression, and several multivariate procedures; (3) the Graphic Wizard, permitting a quick visual representation of data in a format very similar to that typically found in a spreadsheet program. Imports Excel 5 spreadsheets.

An interesting program that permits quick data analysis for most of the common descriptive and inferential statistical procedures. A privately developed piece of software available through Internet download at a very reasonable price.

Name: **EcStatic**
Company: Someware in Vermont, Inc.
Address: 18 Summer Street, Montpelier, VT 05602
URL: www.somewareinvt..com
Price: $89.95 (discounts available for 10 or more copies)
System: Windows 16-bit
Functions:

☑ Descriptive Statistics	Advanced Descriptive
✓ ANOVA/ANCOVA	✓ Hypothesis Tests
✓ Regression	✓ Multivariate
☑ Distributions (Cross tabs)	✓ Nonparametric
✓ Statistical Graphs	Advanced Graphing
Test Analyses	Time Series
Import	Export

Comments: EcStatic handles most traditional descriptive and inferential statistics, including nonparametric and cross tabs. Produces scatterplots, histograms, and frequency distributions. Has a built-in editor for direct data entry. No data import capacity at this time.

A relatively inexpensive statistical package that functions within the Windows environment but produces results similar to DOS output. Major limitations at this time are its lack of import ability and proprietary file formatting.

Name: **ESBStats**
Company: ESB Consultancy
Address: P.O. Box 2259, Boulder, WA 6449, Australia
URL: www.esbconsult.com.au/
Price: $99 – Standard Edition; $59—Light Edition
System: Windows (32-bit)
Functions:
- ☑ Descriptive Statistics
- ☑ ANOVA/ANCOVA
- ☑ Regression
- ✓ Distributions (Cross tabs)
- ✓ Statistical Graphs
-    Test Analyses
- ✓ Import
- ☑ Advanced Descriptive
- ☑ Hypothesis Tests
- ✓ Multivariate
- ✓ Nonparametric
- ✓ Advanced Graphing
- ✓ Time Series
- ✓ Export

Comments: ESBStats is an interesting package. It provides most of the standard descriptive and inferential statistics as well as some of the more sophisticated multivariate statistics. Its price is very reasonable, and it is available through download from its Web site.

Name: **GB-Stat 7.0**
Company: Dynamic Microsystems, Inc.
Address: 13003 Buccaneer Road, Silver Spring, MD 20904
URL: www.gbstat.com
Price: $699.95 (Windows); $699.95 (Power Mac)
   Substantial discounts often available, contact Dynamic Microsystems, Inc.
System: Windows (16-bit & 32-bit); Macintosh (Power Mac)
Functions:
- ☑ Descriptive Statistics
- ☑ ANOVA/ANCOVA
- ☑ Regression
- ☑ Distributions (Cross tabs)
- ☑ Statistical Graphs
- ☑ Test Analyses
- ✓ Import
- ☑ Advanced Descriptive
- ☑ Hypothesis Tests
- ☑ Multivariate
- ☑ Nonparametric
- ☑ Advanced Graphing
- ☑ Time Series
- ✓ Export

Comments: GB Stat is a very comprehensive statistical package. It provides the user with a multiple set of tools at the fundamental level as well as at the advanced level. Its graphics have greatly improved over the last several years so that it now rivals many of the other PC-only packages. Its strength is in its user interface. GB-Stat employs a very easy-to-navigate, pull-down menu system. Its primary limitation is that it has a restricted import and export facility.

Name: **Instat**
Company: Graph Pad Software
Address: 5755 Oberlin Drive, #110, San Diego, CA 92121

URL: www.graphpad.com
Price: $99.99 (online); $139 (disk by mail)
System: Windows (16-bit or 32-bit); Macintosh (PowerPC)
Functions:
☑ Descriptive Statistics	Advanced Descriptive
✓ ANOVA/ANCOVA	☑ Hypothesis Tests
✓ Regression	Multivariate
☑ Distributions (Cross tabs)	✓ Nonparametric
✓ Statistical Graphs	Advanced Graphing
Test Analyses	Time Series
✓ Import	✓ Export

Comments: InStat is a user-friendly statistical package. It is designed primarily to provide fundamental descriptive and inferential analyses as well as very clear guidance and suggestions for appropriate use of a given procedure. InStat offers very few bells and whistles but does provide sound statistical results. The results from any analysis are presented in clear and straightforward language with key terms and definitions provided to help the user understand the results. Graphing is left to a minimum since the publishers also publish a program called "Prism," a high-end biostatistical graphing program designed to provide very clear and high-quality graphs. InStat has an extremely limited import and export capacity.

Name: **JMP**
Company: SAS Institute, Inc
Address: SAS Campus Drive, Carey, NC 27513
URL: www.JMPdiscovery.com
Price: $895 (corporate); $395 (academic) [single user]
System: Windows (32-bit); Macintosh OS 8.1/9.0
Functions:
☑ Descriptive Statistics	☑ Advanced Descriptive
☑ ANOVA/ANCOVA	☑ Hypothesis Tests
☑ Regression	☑ Multivariate
☑ Distributions (Cross tabs)	☑ Nonparametric
☑ Statistical Graphs	☑ Advanced Graphing
✓ Test Analyses	✓ Time Series
✓ Import	✓ Export

Comments: JMP is an interactive, pull-down menu-operated, comprehensive statistical package. It provides a nearly complete series of univariate as well as multivariate descriptive and inferential statistics. Advanced ANOVA (and ANCOVA) as well as very sophisticated multiple regression analyses are readily available. Presentation quality graphics are easily created and modified as needed.

Name: **Minitab, Release 13**
Company: Minitab, Inc.
Address: 3081 Enterprise Drive, State College, PA 16801
URL: www.Minitab.com
Price: $1,195 (corporate); academic users should contact Minitab for special pricing.
System: Windows (32-bit, 2000, XT, NT 4)

Functions:
- ☑ Descriptive Statistics
- ☑ ANOVA/ANCOVA
- ☑ Regression
- ☑ Distributions (Cross tabs)
- ☑ Statistical Graphs
- Test Analyses
- ☑ Import

- ☑ Advanced Descriptive
- ☑ Hypothesis Tests
- ☑ Multivariate
- ☑ Nonparametric
- ☑ Advanced Graphing
- ☑ Time Series
- ☑ Export

Comments: Minitab is one of the three remaining mainframe systems that have been ported successfully to a desktop environment. Minitab has a long and successful history as a top-of-the-line, comprehensive statistical package. It offers all traditional descriptive and inferential techniques as well as numerous advanced applications, especially in inferential statistics. Release 13 offers 33 new or enhanced applications over the previous releases. Minitab continues to offer strong support to users with exceptional documentation available not only from Minitab but from third-party sources as well.

A Minitab-based version of ActivStats is available through the Addison Wesley publishing company. This CD-based software is literally an interactive training program (statistics class, if you will). The current cost of this software is listed as $295.

Name: **NCSS 2001**
Company: NCSS
Address: 329 North 1000 East, Kaysville, UT 84037
URL: www.NCSs.com
Price: $299.99 (CD only); $399.99 (with user's guide)
System: Windows (32-bit)
Functions:
- ☑ Descriptive Statistics
- ☑ ANOVA/ANCOVA
- ☑ Regression
- ☑ Distributions (Cross tabs)
- ☑ Statistical Graphs
- ☑ Test Analyses
- ☑ Import

- ☑ Advanced Descriptive
- ☑ Hypothesis Tests
- ☑ Multivariate
- ☑ Nonparametric
- ☑ Advanced Graphing
- ☑ Time Series
- ☑ Export

Comments: NCSS has been around since 1981. Originally called "Number Cruncher Statistical System" because of its facility for easy numeric analysis, NCSS 2001 continues this heritage. The program is easy to navigate and offers all the major statistical functions (descriptive and inferential). NCSS 2001 is reasonably priced and, considering all that it offers, is a good bargain. One feature that NCSS does offer that many of its higher-priced competitive programs should consider is a built-in word processor. This feature makes it very easy for the user to generate and create reports directly within the statistical package.

Name: **SAS 8.2**
Company: SAS Institute, Inc
Address: SAS Campus Drive, Carey, NC 27513
URL: www.SAS.com
Price: Annual License Only – contact SAS for current pricing
System: Windows (32-bit)—and numerous other systems.

Functions: ☑ Descriptive Statistics   ☑ Advanced Descriptive
             ☑ ANOVA/ANCOVA   ☑ Hypothesis Tests
             ☑ Regression   ☑ Multivariate
             ☑ Distributions (Cross tabs)   ☑ Nonparametric
             ☑ Statistical Graphs   ☑ Advanced Graphing
             ☑ Test Analyses   ☑ Time Series
             ☑ Import   ☑ Export

Comments: SAS is the other remaining granddaddy of all statistical packages. Originally published in the 1970s as a mainframe system under the name "Statistical Analysis System," SAS has grown beyond the confines of merely a statistical package. Today it is probably better seen as a total information management system. SAS may be used to handle all information management that a corporation (or, as in many cases, government) may need.

The basic needs of most educational researchers may be filled with two modules: (1) SAS/Base and (2) SAS/Stat. Together, these two packages provide several hundred statistical procedures (descriptive and inferential). A simple listing of these procedures would cover an entire book (and, in fact, does). There is literally very little that any social science researcher cannot find in these two modules.

Add to the Base and Stat modules the SAS/Graph module, and the researcher would have an entire package capable of producing some of the most in-depth statistics and high-resolution graphics available. There are over 19 additional modules; interested users should contact SAS directly for more information.

A major complaint by users of the SAS system has been the fact that, historically, SAS has been a command-driven operation. The newest release of SAS (8.2) is still command-driven, but users may choose to purchase another module, SAS/Assist, which provides a user-friendly, pull-down menuing procedure for accessing SAS operations. This system is very easy to operate and produces syntax that may later be employed in command batch operations.

Name: **Simstat for Windows Version 1.3 and Version 2.0**
Company: PROVALIS RESEARCH
Address: 2414 Bennett Street, Montreal, QC, Canada, H1V 3S4
URL: www.simstat.com
Price: $149
System: Version 1.3 (Windows 16-bit) Version 2.0 (Windows 32-bit)
Functions: ☑ Descriptive Statistics   ☑ Advanced Descriptive
             ☑ ANOVA/ANCOVA   ☑ Hypothesis Tests
             ☑ Regression   Multivariate
             ☑ Distributions (Cross tabs)   ☑ Nonparametric
             ☑ Statistical Graphs   ✓ Advanced Graphing
               Test Analyses   ☑ Time Series
             ✓ Import   ✓ Export

Comments: Simstat provides quite a bit of statistical information at the descriptive and inferential level. A reasonably priced, menu-driven package that combines ease of use with some fairly sophisticated data analysis. Simstat is available directly through the Internet.

Simstat has an add-on package called Easy Factor Analysis (Version 3) for an additional $35 that is a comprehensive factor analysis program. Easy Factor Analysis integrates completely into the Simstat environment (or may be used as a stand-alone). Simstat also offers and item analysis package (StatItem, Version 1.0b) as an add-on program for $35.

Name: **SPSS 10.1**
Company: SPSS Inc.
Address: 11th floor, 233 S. Wacker Drive, Chicago, IL 60606
URL: www.SPSS.com
Price: SPSS Base $599 (other modules available range in price from $199 to $799)
System: Windows (32-bit); Macintosh (PowerPC OS 8 and above)

Functions:	☑	Descriptive Statistics	☑	Advanced Descriptive
	☑	ANOVA/ANCOVA	☑	Hypothesis Tests
	☑	Regression	☑	Multivariate
	☑	Distributions (Cross tabs)	☑	Nonparametric
	☑	Statistical Graphs	☑	Advanced Graphing
	☑	Test Analyses	☑	Time Series
	☑	Import	☑	Export

Comments: SPSS is one of the remaining granddaddies of statistical packages. Originally developed as a mainframe system under the name "Statistical Package for the Social Sciences," SPSS has been under constant development and improvement since the 1970s. Today it is one of the leading statistical systems in the world.

The basic SPSS package (SPSS Base) meets (and probably exceeds) the needs of 90% of all users. SPSS Base has over 100 descriptive and inferential applications that provide an extraordinary amount of information for the user. In addition to built-in graphics, provides an excellent visual representation of data.

SPSS is menu-driven but employs a syntax command line system as well. All menu-driven commands are recorded in a syntax journal and may then be employed for use in repetitive tasks. Alternatively, the user may simply choose to employ the syntax structure for all his or her work. Files may be saved as ASCII, Excel, Lotus, or Systat formats. Files may be imported from the same set of sources. Output and graphics may be imported directly into word processor documents and slide show presentations.

There are numerous additional modules available from SPSS, including SmartViewer, Advance Models, Tables, Conjoint, Regression Models, and Report Writer. Interested parties should contact SPSS Inc. directly for more information on these modules.

Name: **Stata 7**
Company: Stata Corporation
Address: 4905 Lakeway Drive, College Station, TX 77845
URL: www.Stata.com
Price: $499
System: Windows (32-bit); Macintosh (PowerPC)

Functions:	☑	Descriptive Statistics	☑	Advanced Descriptive
	☑	ANOVA/ANCOVA	☑	Hypothesis Tests
	☑	Regression	☑	Multivariate
	☑	Distributions (Cross tabs)	☑	Nonparametric

☑ Statistical Graphs   Advanced Graphing
☑ Test Analyses   ☑ Time Series
☑ Import   ☑ Export

Comments: Stata is a full powered, PC-based statistical package. It carries all of the descriptive and inferential statistical procedures that one would look for in a comprehensive package. The graphics component of Stata is good, but not up to the level of several other packages and their high-resolution graphics. Stata uses a pull-down menuing system that is relatively easy to navigate. As an added bonus, Stata offers several interesting direct Internet capabilities not offered in similar statistical packages.

Name: **Statgraphics Plus 5**
Company: Manugistics, Inc.
Address: 2115 East Jefferson Street, Rockville, MD 20852
URL: www.statgraphics.com
Price: $749 (standard); $1649 (professional)
System: Windows (32 bit)
Functions:

☑ Descriptive Statistics	☑ Advanced Descriptive
☑ ANOVA/ANCOVA	☑ Hypothesis Tests
☑ Regression	☑ Multivariate
☑ Distributions (Cross tabs)	☑ Nonparametric
☑ Statistical Graphs	☑ Advanced Graphing
☑ Test Analyses	☑ Time Series
☑ Import	☑ Export

Comments: In its professional package, Statgraphics is indeed a statistical monster, rivaling some of the older, more established packages. Statgraphics in its standard version leaves a bit to be desired in general statistical functions. While the standard version performs most of the needed descriptive and inferential statistics, the user must move to the professional package in order to access advanced regression activities, multivariate activities (including factor analysis and canonical analysis), and time-series analysis.

Statgraphics includes two very interesting components only partially available in other packages. The first component is called StatAdviser. This component is designed to help users understand the meaning of their results and guides users to a better understanding and interpretation of the results. The second component is called StatWizard. The purpose of StatWizard is to help the user select the best possible statistical technique to answer a particular question under scrutiny. StatWizard also helps users design new experiments as well as guides them through sampling strategies for the proposed study.

Statgraphics really shines in its production of graphic representation of data and relationships among variables. The high-resolution graphics produced by Statgraphics are very good. They are easily ported to word processors or presentation packages.

Name: **Statistica 6**
Company: StatSoft, Inc.
Address: 2300 East 14th Street, Tulsa, OK 74104
URL: www.statsoft.com
Price: STATISTICA Base-$795

Multivariate Exploratory Techniques (add-on product) $395
Advanced Linear/Non-Linear Models (add-on product) $395
STATISTICA for Macintosh $695

System: Windows (32-bit); Macintosh OS 8.1 and above

Functions:

☑	Descriptive Statistics	☑	Advanced Descriptive
☑	ANOVA/ANCOVA	☑	Hypothesis Tests
☑	Regression	☑	Multivariate
☑	Distributions (Cross tabs)	☑	Nonparametric
☑	Statistical Graphs	☑	Advanced Graphing
☑	Test Analyses	☑	Time Series
✓	Import	✓	Export

Comments: A total comprehensive statistical package. Features both basic as well as advanced statistical operations plus exceptional, ready-for-presentation, graphic output (screen as well as printer). Statistica is a comprehensive, integrated package with complete descriptive and inferential statistical tests (including parametric and nonparametric, multivariate, regression and multiple regression). Statistica is a modular system program; in order to meet all the requirements detailed in the table, a user must purchase the base package, the multivariate add-on, and the advanced linear add-on. This requirement raises the total cost of the program to nearly $1,600.

An exceptional user interface employing a pull-down menu system. Extremely easy to maneuver and make user-directed adjustments to standard statistical actions presented by the program menu.

Name: **StatsDirect**
Company: CamCode
Address: One Westbury Barnes, West End, Ashwell, HERTS SG7 5PJ, UK
URL: www.Statsdirect.com
Price: $145 (academic); $265 (corporate)
System: Windows (32-bit)

Functions:

☑	Descriptive Statistics	✓	Advanced Descriptive
☑	ANOVA/ANCOVA	☑	Hypothesis Tests
☑	Regression		Multivariate
☑	Distributions (Cross tabs)	☑	Nonparametric
✓	Statistical Graphs		Advanced Graphing
	Test Analyses	☑	Time Series
✓	Import	✓	Export

Comments: StatsDirect is a relatively low-priced statistical package that performs most descriptive and inferential analyses. It is available for Internet purchase or by mail. It does not offer any multivariate analyses, and its graphics are rather limited.

Name: **StatView**
Company: SAS Institute, Inc
Address: StatView Sales, SAS Campus Drive, Carey, NC 27513
URL: www.StatView.com
Price: $650 (corporate); $350 (academic)

System: Windows (32-bit); Macintosh (OS 9.0.4)

Functions:
- ☑ Descriptive Statistics
- ☑ ANOVA/ANCOVA
- ☑ Regression
- ☑ Distributions (Cross tabs)
- ☑ Statistical Graphs
- ✓ Test Analyses
- ✓ Import
- ☑ Advanced Descriptive
- ☑ Hypothesis Tests
- ☑ Multivariate
- ☑ Nonparametric
- ☑ Advanced Graphing
- ✓ Time Series
- ✓ Export

Comments: StatView is a complete statistical package available for all Windows environments and most Macintosh environments (including PowerPC).

Name: **Systat 10.2**

Company: Systat Software Inc.

Address: 501 Suite F, Point Richmond Tech Center, Canal Boulevard, Richmond, CA 94804

URL: www.systat.com

Price: $799 (academic); $1,299 (corporate)

System: Windows (32-bit)

Functions:
- ☑ Descriptive Statistics
- ☑ ANOVA/ANCOVA
- ☑ Regression
- ☑ Distributions (Cross tabs)
- ☑ Statistical Graphs
- ☑ Test Analyses
- ☑ Import
- ☑ Advanced Descriptive
- ☑ Hypothesis Tests
- ☑ Multivariate
- ☑ Nonparametric
- ☑ Advanced Graphing
- ☑ Time Series
- ☑ Export

Comments: Systat is one of the truly complete statistical packages on the market today. It has been around for nearly 20 years. It was recently acquired from SPSS, and has continued to improve the quality of the product since this acquisition. Systat requires 32 MB of RAM and 30 MB of hard drive space.

There are no additional modules needed to produce some of the most complex descriptive and inferential statistics imaginable. Systat graphics are simply extraordinary. Over 100 different types of graphs and plots may be produced.

While Systat is a pull-down, menu-operated program, users may create command files to automate repetitive tasks. Alternatively, users may choose to simply employ command line operations for all their statistical activities. Systat's capacity for user "tweaking" to produce nonstandard analyses is exceptional.

SPECIAL APPLICATION PACKAGES

Name: **Amos: Analysis of Moment Structures**

Company: Smallwaters Corp.

Address: 1507 E. 53rd St. # 452, Chicago, IL 60615

URL: www.smallwaters.com

Price: $395 (academic); $495 (all others)

System: Windows (32-bit)

Functions: ☑ Descriptive Statistics   Advanced Descriptive
         ANOVA/ANCOVA   Hypothesis Tests
         ✓ Regression   ✓ Multivariate
         Distributions (Cross tabs)   Nonparametric
         ✓ Statistical Graphs   ✓ Advanced Graphing
         Test Analyses   Time Series
         ✓ Import   ✓ Export

Comments: Amos is a Structural Equation Modeling (SEM) program that employs a graphic interface for creating SEM actions. It employs a combination of strategies, including regression analysis, factor analysis, and ANOVA as well as SEM into a complete package. It handles missing data quite readily. It produces graphic representations of the data relationships as well as permits users to make adjustments in the graphic to produce new results in their analysis.

Structural Equation Modeling (SEM) is a very complex statistical technique. When utilized properly, it can help you understand a multitude of multivariate relationships in your data. Amos is a very flexible program in the hands of a skilled user. It is not a program appropriate for individuals not trained in SEM.

Name: **Comprehensive Meta-Analysis**
Company: Biostat
Address: 14 North Dean Street, Englewood, NJ 07631
URL: www.meta-analysis.com
Price: $795 (academic); $995 (commercial)
System: Windows
Functions: ☑ Descriptive Statistics   Advanced Descriptive
         ANOVA/ANCO   Hypothesis Tests
         Regression   Multivariate
         Distributions (Cross tabs)   ☑ Nonparametric
         ☑ Statistical Graphs   Advanced Graphing
         Test Analyses   Time Series
         ✓ Import   ✓ Export

Comments: A program specifically designed for research synthesis (meta- analysis). Provides output focusing on effect size with odds ratios, mean differences, correlations, etc. The summary is also displayed with a visual model that can be modified as part of an ongoing analysis. Studies are stored in a database format, high-resolution graphics are easily created, and exporting data to PowerPoint or MS Word is easily completed. A must-have program for anyone working in meta-analytic research on a large scale.

Name: **EQS 6.0**
Company: Multivariate Software, Inc.
Address: Suite 306, 15720 Ventura Boulevard, Encino, CA 91436
URL: www.mvsoft.com
Price: $595 (Windows); $595 (Power Mac)
System: Windows (32-bit); Macintosh (Power Mac)
Functions: ☑ Descriptive Statistics   Advanced Descriptive
         ANOVA/ANCOVA   Hypothesis Tests

      ✓ Regression   ✓ Multivariate
         Distributions (Cross tabs)   Nonparametric
       ✓ Statistical Graphs   ✓ Advanced Graphing
         Test Analyses   Time Series
       ✓ Import   ✓ Export

Comments: Full-fledged, state-of-the-art structural equation modeling, including confirmatory factor analysis, path analysis, direct modeling, diagram building, and improved user interface. Output may be saved in HTML format.

    Structural equation packages do not get much better than EQS. The improved user-interface's ability to graphically manipulate models makes this a very viable program. *Warning:* This program is not particularly friendly to anyone unfamiliar with structural equation modeling.

Name: **EViews 4**
Company: Quantitative Micro Software
Address: Suite 336, 4521 Campus Drive, Irvine, CA 92612
URL: www.eviews.com
Price: $895 (full); $575 (EViews 4 Basics)
System: Windows (32-bit)
Functions: ☑ Descriptive Statistics   Advanced Descriptive
               ANOVA/ANCOVA   Hypothesis Tests
             ☑ Regression   ✓ Multivariate
             ☑ Distributions (Cross tabs)   Nonparametric
             ☑ Statistical Graphs   ✓ Advanced Graphing
               Test Analyses   ☑ Time Series
             ✓ Import   ✓ Export

Comments: Primarily designed for econometric analyses, EViews would be very useful for descriptive, correlation, and regression-based studies in education. EViews permits import of Lotus and Excel spreadsheet files. Data management is a very strong feature of this program. Really designed more for its econometric analysis, but many educational institutions are examining data in this area.

Name: **Lisrel 8.51**
Company: Scientific Software International, Inc.
Address: Suite 100, 7383 North Lincoln Avenue, Lincolnwood, IL 60712
URL: www.ssicentral.com
Price: $575 (Windows 32-bit); $475 (Macintosh—beta version)
System: Windows (32-bit); Macintosh (Power Mac)
Functions: ☑ Descriptive Statistics   Advanced Descriptive
               ANOVA/ANCOVA   Hypothesis Tests
             ✓ Regression   ✓ Multivariate
               Distributions (Cross tabs)   Nonparametric
             ✓ Statistical Graphs   ✓ Advanced Graphing
               Test Analyses   Time Series
             ✓ Import   ✓ Export

Comments: Lisrel is considered the oldest statistical package for Structural Equation Modeling (SEM). Lisrel 8.5 employs a graphic interface for creating SEM actions and a combination of strategies including regression analysis, factor analysis, and ANOVA as well as SEM into a complete package. Lisrel handles missing data quite readily. It produces graphic representations of the data relationships as well as permits users to make adjustments in the graphic to produce new results in their analysis.

SEM is a very complex statistical technique. When utilized properly, it can help you understand a multitude of multivariate relationships in your data. Lisrel is a very flexible program in the hands of a skilled user. It is not a program appropriate for individuals not trained in SEM.

SSI offers numerous training programs and materials to assist in the development of competent Lisrel users. In addition, numerous third-party books are available as well as a professional journal dedicated to SEM.

Name: **HLM: Hierarchical Linear Modeling, Version 5**
Company: Scientific Software International, Inc.
Address: Suite 100, 7383 North Lincoln Avenue, Lincolnwood, IL 60712
URL: www.ssicentral.com
Price: $430
System: Windows (32-bit, 2000)

Functions:			
✓	Descriptive Statistics	✓	Advanced Descriptive
	ANOVA/ANCOVA	✓	Hypothesis Tests
	Regression	✓	Multivariate
	Distributions (Cross tabs)		Nonparametric
	Statistical Graphs		Advanced Graphing
	Test Analyses		Time Series
☑	Import	☑	Export

Comments: HLM is a program specifically designed to deal with multilevel nested variables often found in policy and similar studies in education. It is a very sophisticated program designed to provide analytic strategies for two- and three-level models.

Name: **Pass 2000**
Company: NCSS
Address: 329 North 1000 East, Kaysville, UT 84037
URL: www.ncs.com
Price: $199.99 (CD only); $249.95 (with user's guide)
System: Windows (32-bit)
Functions: Power analysis and sample size
Comments: Pass 2000 is designed to provide users with a quick and simple means to calculate sample size and the statistical power necessary for a particular statistical test. Pass 2000 provides power and sample analysis for nearly 100 different statistical tests.

Name: **SigmaPlot**
Company: Statistical Solutions

Address: Stonehill Corporate Center, Suite 104, 999 Broadway, Saugus, MA 01906
URL: www.statsol.ie/
Price: $445
System: Windows (32-bit)

Functions:

	Descriptive Statistics		Advanced Descriptive
	ANOVA/ANCOVA		Hypothesis Tests
	Regression		Multivariate
	Distributions (Cross tabs)		Nonparametric
☑	Statistical Graphs	☑	Advanced Graphing
	Test Analyses		Time Series
☑	Import	✓	Export

Comments: SigmaPlot is one extraordinary graphing program. While the actual number of possible graphs produced by SigmaPlot is indeed finite, it may often appear as if the number is limitless. SigmaPlot's speed at producing graphs is exceptional, and it is able to make changes and adjustments on the fly in order for the user to examine the data in greater profile. Porting the graphics to presentation packages is trouble-free and effortless.

Name: **Xlstat Version 5.0 (Windows); Version 4.4 (Macintosh)**
Company: AddinSoft
Address: 6 rue de Clignancourt, 75018 Paris, France
URL: www.xlstat.com
Price: $195 (downloaded from Internet); $225 (CD-ROM)
System: All Windows 32 bit; Macintosh OS 8

Functions:

☑	Descriptive Statistics	☑	Advanced Descriptive
☑	ANOVA/ANCOVA	☑	Hypothesis Tests
☑	Regression	☑	Multivariate
☑	Distributions (Cross tabs)	☑	Nonparametric
☑	Statistical Graphs	☑	Advanced Graphing
☑	Test Analyses		Time Series
✓	Import	✓	Export

Comments: Xlstat is not truly a statistical package. It is actually an "add-in" package for Microsoft Excel. While Excel does contain some very good fundamental statistical functions (see earlier chapter on spreadsheets), Xlstat takes what Microsoft has offered and extends this into a nearly complete and comprehensive statistical program. In addition to some very sophisticated descriptive and inferential techniques, Xlstat also performs some very interesting analyses for survey-type data (which are not readily available on most comprehensive packages). Xlstat is easily obtained by downloading from the Web site—a 30-day grace period is offered to allow users a trial run.

CHAPTER 3

Software for Educational Measurement

INTRODUCTION

Historically, the analysis of educational measurement instruments has been done either by hand or by specially designed measurement software. The problem for the general user has always been that the software tended to be available only on mainframe systems, or, if it was available for desktop, it took a computer programmer to run the software. In the last decade a number of measurement packages became available for the desktop computer that do not require a Ph.D. in programming to use them properly.

For the traditional classroom-level assessment, most spreadsheets can be utilized with appropriate "if-then" statements to analyze the results of a multiple-choice test. Furthermore, if the spreadsheet has a correlation function, then point biserial correlations are readily calculated. Utilizing the graphing features of the spreadsheet, a user may then produce bar charts and line graphs profiling the results of the examinees as well as items from the test. While the use of a spreadsheet may take a little preprogramming, the results are generally quite satisfactory for most classroom needs.

When the level of assessment extends beyond the classroom and moves into the realm known as "large-scale assessment," then a more specialized package is needed to perform the analyses. This need is further expanded when the results of the measurement activity require a measurement model beyond what is known as "classical." Such typical "modern" models include the various Item Response Theory models: one-parameter (typically known as the Rasch model), two-parameter, and three-parameter. The extent of calculations necessary to provide item-level and student-level scores for these models is generally beyond the skills of most users (and doing such calculations by hand would be extremely time-consuming).

The following computer software packages for educational measurement provide a variety of models and strategies for analyzing test items and producing student results. Part of the process of analyzing any measurement instruments is ensuring that the components of the instrument meet the expectations of the particular model (this strategy is typically referred to as a "fit" analysis). In many cases, the software listed in this section is actually produced by an individual or a small group of individuals. This type of software is often marketed by a reseller rather than by the actual developer of the package. In many cases, the retailer/reseller of the particular package may indeed be an organization or a professional special interest group. Many of the packages in this section are available through a download from the Internet and a direct payment via the Internet to the retailer. An Internet address is provided for every software piece described in this section.

Table D.3.1 presents a breakdown of the desired functions sought in educational measurement packages. This table is replicated (in an abbreviated form) for each of the measurement packages reviewed. The list of functions summarized in Table D.3.1 is not meant to be exhaustive; instead, it is only illustrative of a minimum level expected in a particular category of educational measurement.

Table D.3.1
Critical Functions in Educational Measurement Programs

Classification   ☑= Full functions   ✓= Limited functions   ☒=Indirectly Available

Item Scoring
pre-scored items (0/1)
actual student response scored

Advanced Item Scoring
dichotomous
polytomous

Item Level Statistics
mean
standard deviation and variance
point bisereal correlations

Test Level Statistics
mean
standard deviation and variance
standard error of estimating (SEM)
percentile ranks

Reliability
Cronbach's Alpha and/or
KR-20
split-half

Missing Items
omitted
not scored

Item Option Analyses
percent correct for each option
point bisereal for each option

Multiple Forms (or Subsets of Items)

For IRT: Choice of Models
one-, two- or three-parameter model

For IRT: Choice of Estimations

Graphics (text)
item plots
test plots

Advanced Graphics
high-resolution plots
item plots
total test plots

Equating (Items and/or People)
vertical
horizontal

For IRT: Tests of Fit
item level
test level

INDIVIDUAL SOFTWARE PACKAGES

Name: **Bilog 3**
Company: Scientific Software International
Address: Suite 100, 7383 N. Lincoln Avenue, Lincolnwood, IL 60712-1704
URL: www.ssicentral.com
Price: $400 (Windows); $375 (PowerPC)
System: Windows (32-bit); Macintosh (PowerPC)
Functions: ☑ Item Scoring   ☑ Advanced Item Scoring
               ☑ Item Level Statistics   ☑ Test Level Statistics
               ☑ Reliability   ☑ Missing Items

☑ Item Options Analysis ☑ Multiple Forms
☑ Choice of Models ☑ Choice of Estimations
☑ Graphics ☑ Advanced Graphics
☑ Equating ☑ Tests of Fit

Comments: Bilog is an exceptional program for analyzing various measurement instruments. It is capable of implementing one-, two-, or three-parameter models on the same set of data. Graphics produced by Bilog are very good and easily moved into word processor documents or presentation slides.

Name: **Bilog MG**
Company: Scientific Software International
Address: Suite 100, 7383 N. Lincoln Avenue, Lincolnwood, IL 60712-1704
URL: www.ssicentral.com
Price: $385
System: DOS
Functions:
☑ Item Scoring ☑ Advanced Item Scoring
☑ Item Level Statistics ☑ Test Level Statistics
☑ Reliability ☑ Missing Items
☑ Item Options Analysis ☑ Multiple Forms
☑ Choice of Models ☑ Choice of Estimations
☑ Graphics ☑ Advanced Graphics
☑ Equating ☑ Tests of Fit

Comments: Bilog-MG is designed to provide a variety of information on multiparameter IRT assessment instruments. Bilog MG is also capable of producing DIF level information and allows the user to examine a variety of equating models as well. The primary drawback is that currently Bilog MG is available only for DOS systems.

Name: **ConQuest**
Company: Assessment Systems Corporation
Address: Suite 200, 2233 University Avenue, St. Paul, MN 55114
URL: www.assess.com
Price: $675
System: Windows platform
Format: Windows 3.1x and above; NT 3.51
Functions:
☑ Item Scoring ☑ Advanced Item Scoring
☑ Item Level Statistics ☑ Test Level Statistics
☑ Reliability ☑ Missing Items
☑ Item Options Analysis) ☑ Multiple Forms
Choice of Models Choice of Estimations
Graphics Advanced Graphics
☑ Equating ☑ Tests of Fit

Comments: Fits item response and latent regression models, permits examination of a variety of performance assessments, traditional assessments, and rating scales. ConQuest provides an integrated analysis of item response and regression. The analyses are based on the Rasch (1-parameter IRT) model.

A relatively easy-to-use program but one that does require some sophisticated under-standing of IRT models, in particular, the Rasch model.

Name: **DIMTEST** and **Poly-DIMTEST**
Company: Assessment Systems Corporation
Address: 2233 University Avenue, Suite 200, St. Paul, MN 55114
URL: www.assess.com
Price: $150 (Academic); $80 (student); $300 (all others) each. Both may be purchased for $200 (academic); $120 (student); $400 (all others).
System:
Functions:

Item Scoring	Advanced Item Scoring
Item Level Statistics	Test Level Statistics
Reliability	Missing Items
Item Options Analysis	Multiple Forms
Choice of Models	Choice of Estimations
Graphics	Advanced Graphics
Equating	Tests of Fit

Comments: DIMTEST is designed to establish the dimensionality of traits in a dichoto-mously scored educational or psychological instrument. DIMTEST may be used in either a confirmatory or an exploratory mode. It functions in a nonparametric perspective and therefore does not require IRT modeling or estimation of item functions.

Poly-DIMTEST is designed to provide the same results as DIMTEST but for polytomous data.

A very easy-to-use DOS-based program designed to assess whether a given instru-ment is unidimensional. Poly-DIMTEST is very useful with polytomous data such as Likert-type scales or partial-credit, open-ended items.

Name: **Facets**
Company: Winsteps
Address: P.O. Box 811322, Chicago, IL 60681-1322
URL: www.winsteps.com
Price: $495 (Educational)
System: Windows (32-bit)
Functions:

☑ Item Scoring	☑ Advanced Item Scoring
☑ Item Level Statistics	☑ Test Level Statistics
☑ Reliability	☑ Missing Items
☑ Item Options Analysis	☑ Multiple Forms
Choice of Models	Choice of Estimations
Graphics	Advanced Graphics
☑ Equating	☑ Tests of Fit

Comments: Facets is the most general of the Rasch models produced out of the Winsteps organization. Facets has been designed primarily to analyze rating scales and partial-credit models where judges are used to evaluate performance of examinees. Facets is fully capa-ble of handling a multitude of models, including dichotomously scored items. The amount of information produced by Facets is exceptional on the individual examinee level and the item level, as well as other factors such as raters.

Name: **MicroFACT**

Company: Assessment Systems Corporation

Address: Suite 200, 2233 University Avenue, St. Paul, MN 55114

URL: www.assess.com

Price: $299 (academic); $325 (others)

System: DOS only

Functions:	
Item Scoring	Advanced Item Scoring
Item Level Statistics	Test Level Statistics
Reliability	Missing Items
Item Options Analysis	Multiple Forms
Choice of Models	Choice of Estimations
Graphics	Advanced Graphics
Equating	Tests of Fit

Comments: A factor analysis program designed to assess the number of factors in an examination. Designed to determine the number of underlying dimensions in a test. MicroFACT works with dichotomous or polytomous data. It employs tetrachoric correlations in determining the number of factors in a test. It allows several different rotation options in determining the number of factors in a test.

A simple-to-use program that helps to verify whether the test you're employing is unidimensional. A significant drawback is the fact that this program is available only in DOS.

Name: **Multilog**

Company: Scientific Software International

Address: Suite 100, 7383 N. Lincoln Avenue, Lincolnwood, IL 60712-1704

URL: www.ssicentral.com

Price: $270

System: DOS

Functions:	
☑ Item Scoring	☑ Advanced Item Scoring
☑ Item Level Statistics	☑ Test Level Statistics
☑ Reliability	☑ Missing Items
☑ Item Options Analysis	☑ Multiple Forms
☑ Choice of Models	☑ Choice of Estimations
✓ Graphics	Advanced Graphics
☑ Equating	☑ Tests of Fit

Comments: Multilog is the most generic of the three-parameter models produced by Scientific Software International. Multilog handles a variety of partial-credit and rating scale models in addition to the binary 1-, 2-, or 3-parameter IRT models. At this time Multilog is available only for DOS.

Name: **Parscale**

Company: Scientific Software International

Address: Suite 100, 7383 N. Lincoln Avenue, Lincolnwood, IL 60712-1704
URL: www.ssicentral.com
Price: $385
System: DOS
Functions: ☑ Item Scoring   ☑ Advanced Item Scoring
            ☑ Item Level Statistics   ☑ Test Level Statistics
            ☑ Reliability   ☑ Missing Items
            ☑ Item Options Analysis   ☑ Multiple Forms
            ☑ Choice of Models   ☑ Choice of Estimations
            ✓ Graphics   Advanced Graphics
            ☑ Equating   ☑ Tests of Fit

Comments: Parscale is probably the most used software package by those in the testing industry, producing large-scale assessments employing 2- and 3-parameter IRT models. Parscale handles rating scales and makes adjustments for the influence of raters upon examinees' scores. Parscale also handles binary scored items and a mix of binary and rating scale items on the same set of examinees.

Name: **Quest**
Company: Assessment Systems Corporation
Address: Suite 200, 2233 University Avenue, St. Paul, MN 55114
URL: www.assess.com
Price: $460 (Professional); $230 (Student)
System: DOS, Windows, Macintosh (PowerPC)
Functions: ☑ Item Scoring   ☑ Advanced Item Scoring
            ☑ Item Level Statistics   ☑ Test Level Statistics
            ☑ Reliability   ☑ Missing Items
            ☑ Item Options Analysis   ☑ Multiple Forms
              Choice of Models   Choice of Estimations
            ☑ Graphics   Advanced Graphics
            ☑ Equating   ☑ Tests of Fit

Comments: Quest offers a full range of test and questionnaire analyses based upon Rasch measurement theory. Quest analyzes both dichotomous and polytomous data. Analyses may be produced for multiple-choice, Likert-type items, restricted response open-ended items, and partial credit items. Provides a full analysis of item calibrations and estimations for both IRT and classical models. Quest can be run in a batch or interactive mode. Results may be viewed immediately on-screen.

   A very flexible and easy-to-use program based upon the Rasch (1-parameter) IRT model. Perhaps the most flexible and user-friendly piece of software currently available for this type of analysis.

Name: **RASCAL**
Company: Assessment Systems Corporation
Address: Suite 200, 2233 University Avenue, Suite 200, St. Paul, MN 55114
URL: www.assess.com
Price: $299

System: 386 processor Windows 3.1 or Windows 95
Format: Windows or DOS
Functions:

☑ Item Scoring	☑ Advanced Item Scoring
☑ Item Level Statistics	☑ Test Level Statistics
☑ Reliability	☑ Missing Items
☑ Item Options Analysis	☑ Multiple Forms
☑ Choice of Models	☑ Choice of Estimations
☑ Graphics	Advanced Graphics
☑ Equating	☑ Tests of Fit

Comments: Rascal provides a Rasch-based analysis of test data. Rascal is capable of calibrating up to 30,000 examinees with as many as 250 items for the DOS version, while the Windows versions may handle up to 750 items and no limit on examinee count. Rascal generates full sets of item statistics and person-level statistics. Person and item scores may also be outputted to extraneous files for later reporting. The data entry is based upon ASCII format. Data may be answered either through the built-in editor, an external text entry program, or a typical optical scanner that produces an external ASCII file.

Rascal is another of the easy-to-use programs. Setup is very simple and employs a very straightforward ASCII-based data file for its analysis. Output from Rascal is very easy to understand and interpret providing one has a sound understanding of Rasch IRT modeling.

Name: **RUMM 2010**
Company: RUMM Laboratory Pty Ltd
Address: 14 Dodonaea Court, Duncraig 6023, Western Australia
URL: www.faroc.com.au/~rummlab/main.html
Price: $500
System: Windows (32-bit)
Functions:

☑ Item Scoring	☑ Advanced Item Scoring
☑ Item Level Statistics	☑ Test Level Statistics
☑ Reliability	☑ Missing Items
☑ Item Options Analysis	☑ Multiple Forms
☑ Choice of Models	☑ Choice of Estimations
☑ Graphics	☑ Advanced Graphics
☑ Equating	☑ Tests of Fit

Comments: Visually, RUMM may be the most appealing of all the Rasch model programs. Its interface is very easy to operate, the amount of information that it provides is extraordinary, and graphics produced by it are very good. RUMM handles dichotomous as well as polytomous data (and handles these data simultaneously if desired).

Name: **TestFact**
Company: Scientific Software International
Address: Suite 100, 7383 N. Lincoln Avenue, Lincolnwood, IL 60712-1704
URL: www.ssicentral.com
Price: $385
System: DOS

Functions: ✓ Item Scoring   ✓ Advanced Item Scoring
            ☒ Item Level Statistics   ☒ Test Level Statistics
            ✓ Reliability   ✓ Missing Items
            Item Options Analysis   ☑ Multiple Forms
            Choice of Models   Choice of Estimations
            Graphics   Advanced Graphics
            Equating   ✓ Tests of Fit

Comments: TestFact is a program designed to produce factor analysis for binary scoring test items. TestFact is a comprehensive program designed to help the user establish the number of dimensions present in a measurement instrument.

Name: **TESTINFO**
Company: Assessment Systems Corporation
Address: Suite 200, 2233 University Avenue, St. Paul, MN 55114
URL: www.assess.com
Price: $49 (DOS); $75 (Windows—16-bit/32-bit)
System: DOS 3.3, Windows 3.1 or Windows '95 and above
Functions: Item Scoring   Advanced Item Scoring
            ✓ Item Level Statistics   ✓ Test Level Statistics
            ☒ Reliability   Missing Items
            Item Options Analysis   Multiple Forms
            Choice of Models   Choice of Estimations
            Graphics   Advanced Graphics
            Equating   Tests of Fit

Comments: TESTINFO provides a very quick means to analyze dichotomously scored IRT tests for the impact of shortening the original test for use in adaptive testing situations. TESTINFO provides test- and item-level information on KR-20, expected and average test information, as well as test-level information for 4 lengths of tests (full, ¼, ½, ¾). A very useful program if one's purpose is to design test length and to determine the level of test information that one could obtain through shortening a test. Most useful with one- or two-parameter IRT models.

Name: **Winsteps 3.31**
Company: Winsteps
Address: P.O. Box 811322, Chicago, IL 60681-1322
URL: www.winsteps.com
Price: $495 (educational)
System: Windows (32-bit)
Functions: ☑ Item Scoring   ☑ Advanced Item Scoring
            ☑ Item Level Statistics   ☑ Test Level Statistics
            ☑ Reliability   ☑ Missing Items
            ☑ Item Options Analysis   ☑ Multiple Forms
            Choice of Models   Choice of Estimations
            ☑ Graphics   Advanced Graphics
            ☑ Equating   ☑ Tests of Fit

Comments: Winsteps is the latest version of the Rasch model software for dichotomous and polytomous measurement instruments. Fully functional within a Windows environment, Winsteps provides a full range of item- and person-level information. With a huge user base, Winsteps is constantly being revised and updated with feedback from various users.

Name: **XCALIBRE**
Company: Assessment Systems Corporations
Address: Suite 200, 2233 University Avenue, St. Paul, MN 55114
URL: www.assess.com
Price: $399
System: Windows
Functions:

☑ Item Scoring	☑ Advanced Item Scoring
☑ Item Level Statistics	☑ Test Level Statistics
☑ Reliability	☑ Missing Items
☑ Item Options Analysis	☑ Multiple Forms
☑ Choice of Models	Choice of Estimations
☑ Graphics	Advanced Graphics
☑ Equating	☑ Tests of Fit

Comments: XCALIBRE employs a maximum-likelihood estimation model for obtaining IRT calibrations. XCALIBRE provides item and person estimations for both 2- and 3-parameter IRT models. Because XCALIBRE employs a maximum likelihood estimation strategy, fewer examinees and items are required than with other similar programs. XCALIBRE permits the use of anchor items to link across forms. XCALIBRE is one of a group of software produced by Assessment Systems that employs an ASCII-based data entry model. Data may be entered either by the internal editor, an external text editor, or from an optical scan engine that produces an external ASCII file. The program itself is very simple to operate and obtain reasonable output. Its very simple interface hides the complexity of the information generated by the program.

RESEARCH PURPOSES, PROCESSES, AND PROCEDURES IN EDUCATION

Joseph M. Ryan

CHAPTER 1

Introduction

PURPOSE

A vast array of research procedures can be used to gather useful information about important educational questions. Becoming facile with the wide variety of useful educational research procedures and remaining so, however, are difficult, time-consuming, and perhaps impossible tasks. The purpose of Section E is to summarize the most commonly used educational research procedures and compile this material into a concise reference compendium. This section is designed to help educators as they plan, conduct, and review educational research. Educators can use these chapters to refresh their understanding of research procedures, to clarify vaguely remembered details of various methodologies, to verify the appropriateness of using a procedure in a particular situation, and to review limitations or assumptions that need to be considered.

INTENDED AUDIENCES

The information in Section E is intended primarily for readers who have some familiarity with basic research procedures. Those with more extensive preparation in research methodology will also find the section useful because it provides a single, concise collection of a large quantity of detailed information. The more typical procedure for locating this information often involves reviewing various textbooks in research design, statistics, measurement, and sampling. Students who are novices in their study of educational research will also find these chapters helpful. Students can use the section as a simplified supplement to the traditional comprehensive and detailed textbook treatment of the various topics.

SECTION OVERVIEW

To help the reader use this section, a brief overview of its eight chapters is provided.

CHAPTER 1: SECTION INTRODUCTION AND OVERVIEW

This introductory chapter describes the purpose, content, and delimitations of this section, the content and organization of the different chapters, and some suggestions for how the information might be most effectively used.

CHAPTER 2: LINKING RESEARCH QUESTIONS TO RESEARCH DESIGNS AND STATISTICAL PROCEDURES

This chapter is designed to function as a "directory" of educational research questions or research problems. A classification system for categorizing research questions is developed and explained. An educator wanting to investigate a research problem uses information in Chapter 2 to classify the research question. Based on this classification, the researcher is directed to a specific portion of Chapter 3, where the appropriate research design for addressing the question is described, and, in addition, the researcher is directed to specific portions of Chapter 4, where the appropriate statistical procedure is described. Thus, Chapter 2 facilitates the investigation of a research problem by identifying the appropriate design and statistical tool.

CHAPTER 3: A SUMMARY OF RESEARCH DESIGNS

This chapter begins with a brief review of major concepts of research design. The review is followed by a detailed description of 22 common research designs and their variations. Each description includes (1) a visual representation of the design, (2) discussion of situations in which the design is commonly used, and (3) commentary on the strengths and weaknesses of the design. The descriptions conclude with references to specific statistical procedures in Chapter 4 that can be used to analyze data related to the design. This chapter does not function as a textbook; instead, it is a summary for those who have already been trained and need only a refresher or for current graduate students who can benefit from supplementary material.

CHAPTER 4: A SUMMARY OF STATISTICAL PROCEDURES

This chapter contains a description of 97 commonly used statistical procedures. These procedures are presented in the following nine categories:
1. Descriptive Statistics
2. Measures of Relationships
3. Regression Analysis
4. Comparisons: One Sample
5. Comparisons: Two Samples (Parametric)
6. Comparisons: Two Samples (Nonparametric)
7. Comparisons: Two or More Samples (Nonparametric)
8. Comparisons: Two or More Samples, Analysis of Variance (ANOVA)
9. Multiple Comparison Procedures

The information for each statistical procedure includes (1) a description, (2) common applications, (3) the type of data to which it is applied, and (4) limitations of the procedure, including assumptions of the procedure. Like Chapter 3, this chapter is meant as a review for trained professionals or as supplementary material for graduate students, not as a textbook.

CHAPTER 5: A SUMMARY OF SAMPLING TECHNIQUES

This chapter discusses basic sampling concepts and sampling techniques. The information about each concept or technique includes (1) a description, (2) common applications, and (3) strengths and weaknesses.

CHAPTER 6: A SUMMARY OF MEASUREMENT CONCEPTS, APPROACHES, AND PROCEDURES

This chapter begins by offering educators a description of the major concepts, terms, and approaches used in educational measurement. This is followed by an explanation of different types of score interpretation and different scales used to report test results. The critical issues of reliability and validity are covered in the next section, followed by a conceptual description of test-equating and standard-setting procedures.

CHAPTER 7: A SUMMARY OF GRAPICAL PROCEDURES FOR EXAMINING, SUMMARIZING, AND REPORTING DATA

This chapter provides examples of the most commonly used forms of charts and graphs that educators can use to examine, report, and summarize data. The graphical displays in this chapter can be produced by software available in most office applications. The use of such graphics is designed as an aid both to interpreting data and to disseminating the results of various types of data analysis.

CHAPTER 8: A RESEARCH PROCESS CHECKLIST

The Research Process Checklist is a general guide for conducting educational research. The checklist is a series of statements and questions that call attention to major decisions and issues that must be addressed in the research process. The checklist is organized under the headings of five major steps in the research process:

1. Defining the research question and the nature of the research
2. Defining variables, subjects, and the research design
3. Verifying the objectivity, reliability, and validity of observation instruments and procedures
4. Analyzing data
5. Interpreting research results

CHAPTER "ENTRY" CODES

Each research design in Chapter 3, statistical procedure in Chapter 4, sampling concept and technique in Chapter 5, etc., is listed as an "entry" in its respective chapter. Each entry has a unique code for ready reference. An example of a typical entry code is "**E4–17**." Each entry code contains three pieces of information: the letter "E" indicates Section

E; the number "3," "4," or "5" indicates which chapter (3, 4, or 5, respectively); and the one- or two-digit number after the hyphen is the item identification number. For example, the entry code "**E4–17**" refers to Section E, Chapter 4, entry 17.

DELIMITATIONS

Although qualitative/ethnographic research methods and multivariate statistical procedures are useful and appropriate for educators in many research settings, the major focus of Section E is on traditional, hypothesis-testing research methods that use univariate statistical procedures. When space limitations demanded the selection of some procedures over others, the procedures summarized here were chosen for their widespread applicability in educational research situations and their appropriateness to the background of many educators.

USING SECTION E

A considerable amount of information is contained in the eight chapters of this section, each of which begins with an "Introduction." Regardless of a reader's interests, the usefulness of the information would be increased by reading the Introduction before reading any of the chapters in complete detail.

CHAPTER 2

Linking Research Questions to Research Designs and Statistical Procedures

INTRODUCTION

Research questions in education are very numerous and are spread across widely diverse areas of interest. Most of them can be classified, however, in one of three general categories. The research questions are concerned with (1) description, (2) relationships, and (3) differences. Questions of description generally ask about some characteristic of a group of subjects such as their average performance or the variability in their performance. Questions about relationships are generally concerned with whether two different characteristics of some group of subjects are systematically related (correlated) to each other. Questions about differences generally focus on whether two or more groups are different on some characteristic of interest.

The purpose of this chapter is to provide a link between (1) research questions that fall into these three broad categories, (2) the research designs in Chapter 3, and (3) statistical tools in Chapter 4. Following is a step-by-step explanation of how to use this chapter. Three parts follow this, one for each of the three categories of research questions. At the beginning of each part, the nature of the research question is identified (entries in Chapter 3, "A Summary of Research Designs"), and the appropriate statistical procedure(s) is identified (entries in Chapter 4, "A Summary of Statistical Procedures").

HOW TO USE THIS CHAPTER

The following is an eight-step procedure for using this chapter to identify research questions and link them to research designs (Chapter 3) and statistical procedures (Chapter 4). The eight steps are:

Step 1. Read the Introductions to Chapters 3 and 4 to become familiar with the format and organization of the entries.

Step 2. Explicitly state the research question.

Step 3. Classify the research question into one of the three question categories: (1) description, (2) relationships, or (3) differences. The classification of research questions can be facilitated by examining the definitions at the beginning of the sections on description, relationships, and differences.

Step 4. Turn to the part (Part 1, 2, or 3) in this chapter that corresponds to the category identified in Step 3.

Step 5. Read the description of the research question for the section. Notice that subsections are identified and described.

Step 6. Locate the appropriate subsection as required.

Step 7. In the appropriate part (Step 5) or subsection (Step 6), the design(s) that should be used for the research question is identified by reference to an entry number in Chapter 3. Turn to the entry in Chapter 3 to read about the design.

Step 8. In the appropriate part (Step 5) or subsection (Step 6), the statistical procedure(s) that should be used for the research question is identified by reference to an entry number in Chapter 4. Turn to the entry in Chapter 4 to read about the procedure.

The following example uses the eight-step procedure.

Step 1. Read the Introductions to Chapters 3 and 4.

Step 2. Explicitly state the research question, for example, "Is there a significant difference in the achievement of three groups of sixth grade students who study using calculators (group 1), computers (group 2), and no electronic devices (group 3) on a test of arithmetic computation?"

Step 3. Classify the research question into one of three question categories: (1) description, (2) relationships, or (3) differences. The research question stated in Step 2, belongs in category 3, research questions about differences.

Step 4. Go to Section 3 of this chapter.

Step 5. Read the description of the research question for Part 3. Note that subsection 3-A of Part 3 refers to research questions about difference among multiple groups, observed once.

Step 6. Locate the appropriate subsection as required. Since the research question concerns three groups measured once, the appropriate subsection is 3-A of Part 3.

Step 7. Identify the appropriate research design in Chapter 3. The appropriate research design for research questions in subsection 3-A of Section 3 is described in **E3–7**, Multiple Groups, One Observation. Turn to **E3–7** to study this design.

Step 8. Identify the appropriate statistical procedures in Chapter 4. The appropriate statistical procedures for research questions in subsection 3-A of Section 3 are **E4–71**, One-Way Analysis of Variance (ANOVA), and **E4–87**, Randomized Block Designs. Turn to **E4–71** and **E4–87** to study these procedures.

A SYNOPSIS OF "LINKING RESEARCH QUESTIONS TO RESEARCH DESIGNS AND STATISTICAL PROCEDURES"

The final section of this chapter contains a synopsis of the information needed to link research questions to research designs and statistical procedures.

PART 1: RESEARCH QUESTIONS DEALING WITH DESCRIPTION

Research dealing with description is the most basic type of research activity. The accurate and comprehensive description of a sample of subjects with respect to some characteristic of interest is critical in the early stages of research on any topic. Careful description is always important, even in areas that have been thoroughly researched and in areas where experimental research designs are used to test specific hypotheses. Description provides a background and context within which to understand other research findings.

Research questions that deal with description generally pertain to one sample of subjects and one characteristic of that sample. A typical research question of this type might be, "What are the characteristics of basic skills performance at Woodlawn Junior High School?" In answering this question, the researcher might divide the sample into three groups (seventh, eighth, and ninth graders) and then obtain reading and mathematics basic skills test scores. Even with three groups and two variables, the description would be provided for one group and one variable at a time, for instance, the reading scores of seventh graders. In this example, the one-group, one-variable approach could be applied eight times to provide a complete description. These would include the three classes on reading, the three classes on mathematics, all students on reading, and all students on mathematics.

Design
      E3–1: One Group, One Observation
Statistical Procedures
      E4–1 to **E4–4:** Central Tendency
      E4–5 to **E4–10:** Variability or Dispersion
      E4–11 to **E4–13:** Distribution Shapes

PART 2: RESEARCH QUESTIONS DEALING WITH RELATIONSHIPS

Questions about relationships between and among characteristics or variables can be categorized into three subsections: (1) relationships between two variables, (2) relationships among sets of three or more variables, and (3) relationships involving the prediction of one variable from one or more variables.

Subsection 1: Relationships between Two Variables

Relationships between two variables are called correlations and can be examined (1) when one group is observed once and measured on several variables or (2) when one group is observed twice, and variables from the two observations are correlated.

Designs
      E3–1: One Group, One Observation (Multiple Variables)
      E3–2: One Group, Two Observations
Statistical Procedures
      E4–14 to **E4–29:** Correlation coefficients and other measures of relationship
          selected based on the nature of the variables involved.

Subsection 2: Relationships among Sets of Three or More Variables

Relationships among groups of variables are generally studied when one sample of subjects is observed on one occasion and measured on several variables. The research question is concerned with whether three or more variables are so highly related to each other that they are all basically measuring one single characteristic of a sample.

Design
> **E3–1:** One Group, One Observation (Multiple Measurements)

Statistical Procedure
> **E4–30:** Factor Analysis

Subsection 3: Relationships Involving the Prediction of One Variable from One or More Variables

Research questions about relationships involving predictions ask whether and how well some characteristic of a sample of subjects can be predicted from some other characteristic(s) of the subjects. The prediction of one variable from one or more other variables is performed (1) when one group is observed once and measured on multiple variables, or (2) when one group is observed more than once, and prediction is made over time, for example, from a pretest to a posttest.

Designs
> **E3–1:** One Group, One Observation (Multiple Measurements)
> **E3–2:** One Group, Two Observations

Statistical Procedures
> **E4–31** to **E4–39:** Regression Analysis

PART 3: RESEARCH QUESTIONS DEALING WITH DIFFERENCES

A wide variety of research questions deals with differences. For this reason, these research questions are organized into seven major subsections, which are further subdivided.

The seven major subsections address differences related to:

1. One Group
2. Two Groups
3. Multiple Groups
4. Groups in Factorial Arrangements
5. One or More Groups Measured on Two or More Occasions
6. Groups in Nested or Hierarchical Arrangements
7. Group Differences Involving a Control Variable

These subsections are not mutually exclusive, and the reader is urged to refer to all subsections that might be relevant. For example, a researcher who wishes to know if four groups of students differ on a posttest might examine subsections 3 and 4. In most cases, the subsection information overlaps and directs the researcher to the same design entries in Chapter 3 and statistical entries in Chapter 4.

Subsection 1: Differences Related to One Group

A. *One Group, One Observation*

Research questions about one group of subjects generally ask whether some statistical characteristic of the sample, such as the group's average performance (i.e., sample mean), differs from some particular value of interest, such as a population average (i.e., population mean). The sample statistical characteristic of interest might be the mean, variance, proportion, correlation, or the overall sample distribution.

Design
> **E3–1:** One Group, One Observation

Statistical Procedures
> **E4–40** to **E4–47:** Comparisons for One Group, including the mean, variance, proportion, correlation coefficient, and overall distribution.

B. One Group, Two Observations

This situation is common in pretest-posttest designs with one group. The research question asks, Is there a significant difference in some sample characteristic when it is measured during two different observations, normally on two different occasions? Statistical tests used in this situation must be designed for dependent or correlated samples.

Design
> **E3–2:** One Group, Two Observations

Statistical Procedures
> **E4–50, 52, 54, 56:** Parametric tests for means, variances, proportions, and correlations, using dependent or correlated samples.
> **E4–61, 63, 64, 65:** Nonparametric tests for dependent or correlated samples.

C. One Group, Multiple Observations

This situation is concerned with research questions about differences in some sample characteristic when it is measured during several different observations, usually on different occasions. Such questions are common in longitudinal research in which one group is followed across many occasions and hypotheses about changes in the characteristics of the group over time are tested.

Design
> **E3–3:** One Group, Multiple Observations over Time

Statistical Procedures
> **E4–79:** One Group, Repeated Measures Analysis of Variance
> **E4–90:** Time-Series Analysis

Subsection 2: Differences Related to Two Groups

A. *Two Groups, One Observation*

This situation is very common in educational research and is generally encountered when a researcher wants to know if two groups differ with respect to some statistical characteristic of a variable. The performance of two groups on some variable can be compared in terms of means, variability in performance, some proportion, correlation, or the overall distribution of performance.

Design
        E3–4: Two Groups, One Observation
Statistical Procedures
        E4–48 to **E4–56:** Comparisons for Two Groups, including the means,
            variances, proportions, correlation coefficients, and overall distributions.
        E4–57 to **E4–65:** Nonparametric tests for two groups.

B. *Two Groups, Two Observations*

Research questions about differences between two groups observed twice generally involve a pretest and a posttest administered to the two groups. Often the two groups are an experimental group and a control group.

Designs
        E3–5: Two Groups, Two Observations
Statistical Procedures
        E4–49: Comparing Two Sample Means Independent Samples
        E4–71: One-Way Analysis of Variances on Gain Scores
        E4–80: Two-Way Split-Plot Analysis of Variance
        E4–89: Analysis of Covariance

C. *Two Groups, Multiple Observations*

Research questions that ask about differences between two groups observed on multiple occasions are common in longitudinal research. Such research questions are also appropriate in experimental research when an experimental group and a control group are compared before, during, immediately after, and sometimes considerably after the application of the experimental treatment.

Design
        E3–6: Two Groups, Multiple Observations
Statistical Procedures
        E4–80: Split-Plot Design
        E4–90: Time-Series Analysis

Subsection 3: Differences Related to Multiple Groups

Research questions about three or more groups generally ask about differences among group means. Either naturally occurring groups or experimentally created groups might be compared. An example using naturally occurring groups might involve comparing students from rural, suburban, and urban settings. An example using experimentally created groups might involve comparing students in two treatment groups and a control group.

A. *Multiple Groups, One Observation*

Research questions about difference among multiple groups observed once are often concerned with group differences on a posttest after some experimental treatment has been applied. Comparisons among naturally occurring groups are also common.

Design
> **E3– 7:** Multiple Groups, One Observation

Statistical Procedures
> **E4–71:** One-Way Analysis of Variance
> **E4–87:** Randomized Block Design

B. *Multiple Groups, Two Observations*

Research questions about differences among multiple groups (three or more) observed twice are generally asked when the first observation refers to a pretest and the second observation refers to a posttest. The groups often include experimental groups and a control group, observed before and again after some experimental treatment has been applied.

Design
> **E3– 8:** Multiple Groups, Two Observations

Statistical Procedures
> **E4–80:** Two-Way, Split-Plot Analysis of Variance
> **E4–89:** Analysis of Covariance

Subsection 4: Differences Related to Groups in Factorial Arrangements

Factorial arrangements of groups refer to situations in which groups are viewed as differing along a common dimension or common factor. For example, a group of males and a group of females differ on the common dimension or factor "gender." Gender is a two-level factor because there are two groups. Three groups of students, each taught by a different instructional method, can be represented on one factor, "method of instruction." Method of instruction, in this example, has three levels. Groups can be organized or arranged on two, three, or more factors simultaneously. A two-factor arrangement or design, for example, might include "gender" and "method of instruction" together. In such a case, each of the three instructional treatment groups would have males and females, the two levels of the "gender" factor. The critical attribute of factorial arrangements is that all levels of each factor are represented in all levels of all other factors. For the example males and females, both levels of "gender" appear in all three instructional groups.

Designs

      E3–10: One-Way Factorial Analysis of Variance

      E3–11: Two-Way Factorial Analysis of Variance

      E3–12: Three-Way Factorial Analysis of Variance

Statistical Procedures

      E4–71 to **E4–78:** One-, Two-, and Three-Way Analysis of Variances

Subsection 5: Differences Related to One or More Groups Measured on Two or More Occasions (Repeated Measures/Split-Plot Arrangements)

A "repeated measures" arrangement or design refers to a situation in which a sample of subjects is measured on the same variable on two or more occasions. For example, subjects are measured repeatedly. This situation is very common in longitudinal research. Research questions related to repeated measures arrangements are concerned with changes or growth in the performance of subjects over time.

A "split-plot" arrangement or design refers to a situation in which subjects in two or more groups are measured on the same variable on two or more occasions. Research questions related to split-plot arrangements are concerned with (1) differences between the groups regardless of when they are measured, (2) differences between the measurements on different occasions regardless of the groups measured, and (3) differences between the occasions in the differences between the groups.

Designs

      E3–13 to **E3–16:** Repeated Measures and Two-, Three-, and Four-Way
          Split-Plot Designs

Statistical Procedures

      E4–79 to **E4–83:** Repeated Measures and Two-, Three-, and Four-Way
          Split-Plot Analyses

Subsection 6: Differences Related to Groups in Nested or Hierarchical Arrangements

In nested or hierarchical arrangements, groups of subjects at one level—for example, classrooms—are organized within groups at a second level—for example schools. A research question in this situation might ask about differences in the performance of students in five classrooms in schools 1, 2, and 3. "Classrooms" and "schools" constitute two factors in this situation. This is not a factorial arrangement because only some (5 out of 15) of the groups in the classroom factor appear under each group of the school factor.

Designs

      E3–17 and **E3–19:** Two- and Three-Factor Hierarchical Designs

Statistical Procedures

      E4–84 to **E4–86:** Two- and Three-Factor Hierarchical Analysis of Variance

Subsection 7: Group Differences Involving a Control Variable

Many research questions about differences between groups are asked in a research situation in which a control variable(s) is used to minimize the effect of an extraneous variable(s) that might obscure the group comparisons. For example, a research question might ask, Are there differences in the performance of three groups of students studying under different methods of instruction when controlling for initial differences among the students? Control variables can be incorporated into the research design as independent variables, matching variables, or blocking variables. Control variables can be incorporated into statistical analyses as covariates.

Designs

       E3–20: Randomized Block Designs

       E3–21: Latin Square Designs

       E3–22: Analysis of Covariance Designs

Statistical Procedures

       E4–87: Randomized Block Analyses

       E4–88: Latin Square Analyses

       E4–89: Analysis of Covariance

Table E.2.1 contains a synopsis of the information needed to link research questions to research designs and statistical procedures without narrative explanations. It is designed to facilitate the use of the information in this chapter and in Chapters 3 and 4.

Table E.2.1
Research Processes in Education

Chapter 2 *Research Questions Dealing With:*	**Chapter 3** *Research Designs*	**Chapter 4** *Statistical Procedures*
Part 1. Description	E3–1	**E4–1 to E4–13**
Part 2. Relationships		
S_1 Two Variables	**E3–1, E3–2**	**E4–14 to E4–29**
S_2 Three or More Variables	**E3–1**	**E4–30**
S_3 Prediction	**E3–1, E3–2**	**E4–31 to E4–39**
Part 3. Differences		
S_1 One Group		
A. One Observation	**E3–1**	**E4–40 to E4–47**
B. Two Observations	**E3–2**	**E4–50, 52, 54, 56, 61, 63, 64, 65**
C. Multiple Observations	**E3–3**	**E4–79, E4–90**

Chapter 2 *Research Questions Dealing With:*	Chapter 3 *Research Designs*	Chapter 4 *Statistical Procedures*
S_2 Two Groups		
A. One Observation	**E3–4**	**E4–48** to **E4–56**; **E4–57** to **E4–65**
B. Two Observations	**E3–5**	**E4–49, 71, 80, 89**
C. Multiple Observations	**E3–6**	**E4–80, E4–90**
S_3 Multiple Groups		
A. One Observation	**E3–7**	**E4–71, E4–87**
B. Two Observations	**E3–8**	**E4–80, 89**
S_4 Factorial Arrangements	**E3–10** to **E3–12**	**E4–71** to **E4–78**
S_5 One or More Groups Two or More Occasions	**E3–13** to **E3–16**	**E4–79** to **E4–83**
S_6 Nested or Hierarchical Arrangements	**E3–17** to **E3–19**	**E4–84** to **E4–86**
S_7 Involving Control Variables	**E3–20** to **E3–22**	**E4–87** to **E4–89**

CHAPTER 3
A Summary of Research Designs

PURPOSE OF RESEARCH DESIGNS

The purpose of a research design is to isolate and study the influence of an independent variable on some dependent measure. The research design is constructed to increase the validity of the claim that variation in the dependent measure can be attributed exclusively to variation in the independent variable. The influence of all other extraneous variables on the dependent measure must, accordingly, be eliminated, held constant, or controlled in some other fashion. Research designs are used to achieve the desired control over extraneous variables that could confound the independent–dependent variable relationship. The efficiency of designs varies according to the degree to which they control the influence of extraneous variables.

EXTERNAL AND INTERNAL VALIDITY

For a variety of reasons, the control of extraneous variables is difficult to achieve in many educational research settings. The general difficulty is that educational researchers rarely have control over all the factors that need to be manipulated in order to create a true experimental situation. It is often impossible for a researcher to randomly select subjects from a population or randomly assign subjects to experimental treatment conditions. The lack of both random selection and random assignment of subjects constitutes the major roadblock to conducting true experimental research in education. The lack of random selection greatly limits external validity, while the lack of random assignment greatly limits internal validity of research studies.

External validity refers to the extent to which the results of a study can be generalized to a larger population. The major tool for increasing external validity is random selection from the population of the sample being used in the study. Random sampling (**E5–5**) increases the probability that the sample is truly representative of the population with respect to the relevant variables so that the research results for the sample can be generalized to the population.

Internal validity refers to the extent to which variation in the dependent measure can be attributed exclusively to the independent variable. A major tool for increasing internal validity is random assignment, generally called randomization, which controls the influence of extraneous variables by causing them to be equally present in all treatment conditions. In this way the influence of the extraneous variables on the dependent measure is constant across all treatment conditions. Thus, any difference between treatment groups must be due to treatment conditions since the influence of the extraneous variables is a constant.

There are many specific threats to external validity and internal validity. These are examined in great detail in the classic *Experimental and Quasi-Experimental Designs for*

Research, by D. T. Campbell and J. C. Stanley (1966). The interested reader is strongly urged to study this informative work.

DESCRIPTIVE AND EXPERIMENTAL RESEARCH

In studying research designs, it is useful to imagine that designs run along a continuum from purely descriptive at one end to purely experimental on the other. Descriptive studies simply present the characteristics of the sample being studied. There is no attempt to show causal relationships among variables even if two variables are highly correlated. The description of a sample may be generalizable to a population if the sample was randomly selected. Experimental studies, however, are designed to study a causal relationship between independent and dependent variables, in which variation in the dependent variable may be attributed to variation in the independent variable. Experimental studies provide generalizable results when conducted using random samples.

As mentioned before, it is useful to think of descriptive and experimental research designs as varying in degree along a continuum from purely descriptive to purely experimental, rather than as being mutually exclusive dichotomous categories. Between the two ends of the descriptive-experimental continuum is a wide variety of designs referred to as "quasi-experimental" or "pseudoexperimental" designs. Exactly where a research design is located on the continuum depends on how well the design controls for the various threats to internal and external validity. The intricacies of these issues, while beyond the scope of this book, are discussed in detail by Campbell and Stanley (1966), Cook and Campbell (1979), and Maxwell and Delaney (1990).

RESEARCH DESIGNS AND ANALYSES

Research designs are often discussed from two slightly different perspectives. When examined from a strictly design point of view, research designs are often discussed in terms of arrangements of subjects or groups of subjects, the application of independent variable treatment conditions, the measurement of control variables, and dependent variable outcome measures. Using this approach, a study might be described as an experimental group-control design or one-group, pretest-posttest design. When examined from a strictly statistical point of view, however, research designs are often discussed in terms of the statistical procedures used to analyze data obtained in a study. For example, a study that has two independent variables, namely, gender and treatment, and is designed so that all levels of each variable appear along with all levels of the other independent variable, might be described simply as a two-way factorial analysis of variance, gender by treatment. Both the "design" and the "statistical" approaches are used in this chapter.

THE DESIGN PERSPECTIVE

From the design perspective, research designs are organized in the following general categories because they involve

1. One Group, One Observation

2. One Group, Two Observations (Pretest-Posttest)
3. One Group, Multiple Observations over Time
4. Two Groups, One Observation (Posttest)
5. Two Groups, Two Observations (Pretest-Posttest)
6. Two Groups, Multiple Observations over Time
7. Multiple Groups, One Observation (Posttest)
8. Multiple Groups, Two Observations (Pretest-Posttest)
9. Multiple Groups, One and Two Observations over Time

A number of abbreviation and graphic formats are used in presenting these designs. (These are the symbols used by Campbell and Stanley, with modifications in some cases.) The letter "O" indicates that an observation or measurement has been made on some group. An "X" indicates that some experimental treatment condition has been applied to a group. A "C" indicates a control group and generally appears opposite an "X." The control group does not receive the experimental treatment. The sequence of events for a single group is represented on one horizontal line. The temporal order in which events occurred is reflected in the sequence, from left to right, on each line. Events that occurred for different groups are shown on different horizontal lines. Events that occurred at the same time, but for different groups, are on different horizontal lines but appear one over the other. Parallel rows separated by a dashed line indicate comparison groups of subjects who were not randomly assigned to groups. For one-sample designs, the distinction between randomly selected and nonrandomly selected samples is made explicit. In all other cases, the reader must understand that the designs could be presented twice, once for randomly and once for nonrandomly selected samples.

Designs are described in terms of the number of groups involved and the number of observations made of each group. In the context of research designs, an "observation" refers to a single period of observation. Within this single observational period, however, multiple measurements might be made. Thus, a two-observation design includes two periods of observation, within each of which multiple measurements might be made.

The concept of matching is used in two different ways when describing research designs. First, matching used with random assignment involves grouping subjects together into "blocks," so that all the subjects in a "block" are as similar to each other as possible, with respect to the matching variable. Subjects are then randomly assigned from these blocks to different groups so that each group has a subject or subjects from each block. These procedures constitute randomized block designs (**E3–20**). Second, matching is also used in a less rigorous and less useful way in designs that employ a "matched" comparison group. In these designs, the subjects receiving the experimental treatment condition are compared to some nonrandomly selected and nonrandomly assigned group. This comparison group is used because it "matches" the treatment group with respect to variables that might influence the dependent measure. This so-called matching is thought to "control" these confounding variables because the two groups are equated on these measures. This type of matching is vastly overrated as a mechanism for improving research designs.

THE STATISTICAL PERSPECTIVE

From the statistical analysis perspective, research designs are organized into the following general categories, listed by entry number:

Factorial Analysis of Variance Designs

   10.   One-way ANOVA
   11.   Two-Way ANOVA
   12.   Three-Way ANOVA

Repeated Measures/ Split-Plot Analysis of Variance (ANOVA) designs

   13.   One-way Repeated Measures Designs
   14.   Two-way Split-Plot Designs
   15.   Three-way Split-Plot Designs (A and B)
   16.   Four-way Split-Plot Design

Nested or Hierarchical Designs

   17.   Two Nested Factors
   18.   Three Nested Factors
   19.   Cross and Nested Designs
   20.   Randomized Block Designs
   21.   Latin Square Designs
   22.   Analysis of Covariance Designs

RESEARCH DESIGN PROFILES

E3–1
Category: One Group, One Observation

Designs:			
A. Nonrandom Selection:			O
B. Random Selection:			O
C. Nonrandom Selection:		X	O
D. Random Selection:		X	O

Description: The single-group, one-observation designs involve a single measurement or set of measurements for one sample. The sample may be a nonrandom convenience sample (A and C) or a true random sample (B and D). The observations may be preceded by an experimental treatment (C and D).

Applications: Single-group, one-observation studies are commonly used in the earliest stages of research in an area for obtaining basic descriptive information. Such designs are generally employed when the researcher has no control over the research setting but would like to begin collecting baseline information. Often the subjects in a one-group, one-observation design are a convenience sample. One-group, one-observation designs are often used for correlational studies when multiple measurements are made during the observational period.

Comments: This is the weakest of all designs. Nonrandom single observation studies are strictly descriptive in nature and should always be viewed as exploratory. Very useful information can be obtained from such designs, but caution should be exercised in making strong claims from such studies. Findings from single-group, one-observation designs can be very helpful in generating hypotheses to be explored in subsequent research and for identifying possible extraneous variables that should be controlled in future research.

Analysis: One-sample designs are analyzed using a variety of procedures depending on the purpose of the research. Purely descriptive statistics are routinely calculated, using **E4–1** to **E4–13**. Inferences related to one sample, generally comparing a sample statistic to some value of interest, like a population parameter, are tested with **E4–40** to **E4–47.** When several different variables are measured for one sample, the relationships or correlations between pairs of variables are examined with **E4–14** to **E4–30**. Regression analysis might also be conducted with multiple measurements taken on one sample using **E4–31** to **E4–39**.

E3–2

Category: One Group, Two Observations (Pretest-Posttest Design)

Designs: A. Nonrandom Selection: O_1 O_2
            B. Random Selection: O_1 O_2
            C. Nonrandom Selection: O_1 X O_2
            D. Random Selection: O_1 X O_2

Description: The pretest-posttest design involves two observations of the same sample of subjects. The samples may be random (B and C) or nonrandom (A and D). In some cases, no specific experimental manipulation occurs between the two observations (A and B). In many cases, an observation or set of observations is made prior to some experimental treatment condition and then again following the application of the treatment.

Applications: The pretest-posttest designs are commonly used in education to examine changes over time (A and B) and the effects due to some treatment (C and D). The treatments of interest are often curriculum programs or instructional strategies. Such approaches are very common in evaluation designs that are devised to demonstrate the impact of new programs.

Comments: The pretest-posttest design, frequently used in educational research, is a weak design. Substantiating the claim that the experimental treatment X actually accounts for observed posttest-pretest differences can be problematic. In many cases, plausible alternative explanations can be advanced to explain posttest-pretest differences. These alternative explanations are often as likely as the explanation that the experimental treatment caused the difference. In most cases, findings based on pretest-posttest designs should be considered descriptive and exploratory unless rigorous experimental controls have been employed. However, such designs can be useful in generating or refining hypotheses for more rigorous future study and for identifying extraneous variables that need to be controlled in subsequent research.

Analysis: Pretest-posttest designs are analyzed using procedures for dependent or correlated samples. Dependent sample tests for means, variances, proportions, and correlations are described, respectively, in **E4–50, E4–52, E4–54,** and **E4–56.** Nonparametric tests for dependent samples are found in **E4–63** to **E4–65.** A one-way repeated measure analysis, **E4–79,** might be applied to test pretest-posttest differences.

E3–3

Category: One Group, Multiple Observations over Time

Designs: A. Nonrandom Selection: $\quad O_1 \quad\quad O_2 \quad\quad O_i ....O_L$

B. Random Selection: $\quad\quad O_1 \quad\quad O_2 \quad\quad O_i ....O_L$

C. Nonrandom Selection: $\quad O_1 \quad\quad O_2 \quad\quad O_i .. X .. O_L$

D. Random Selection: $\quad\quad O_1 \quad\quad O_2 \quad\quad O_i .. X ..O_L$

Description: The one-group, multiple-observation designs involve repeated measurements of the same subjects. Samples can be random (B and D) or nonrandom (A and C). The repeated observation may occur over time without intervening experimental treatment condition (A and B) or with an experimental treatment condition within the series of measurements (C and D). These designs are called Time-Series Designs when many observations are used.

Applications: Designs involving repeated measurements of a single sample are commonly used in longitudinal research, especially in longitudinal developmental research. Designs with multiple observations and an intervening experimental treatment are quasi-experimental designs generally referred to as Interrupted Time-Series Designs. Such designs are applicable when periodic baseline measurements have been made prior to some treatment condition, and measurements continue to be made after the treatment has been implemented. These designs can be used to assess the impact of social policy changes or changes in regulations, such as changes in the highway speed limit. These types of changes can be considered an experimental treatment, and data associated with these changes, for example, rate of highway accidents by month or year from before and after the change, are regarded as the periodic measures.

Comments: Repeated measures and time-series designs are more powerful than the simple pretest-posttest designs. These multiple-observation designs allow for a careful analysis of systematic trends before, during, and after the introduction of the experimental treatment condition. The impact of certain threats to internal validity can be examined using these designs, and thus their influence can be ruled out in some cases. It is important to remember, however, that these are quasi-experimental designs.

Analysis: One-group, multiple-observation designs are analyzed using one-way repeated measures analysis of variance (**E4–79**) or time-series analysis procedures (**E4–90**).

E3–4

Category: Two Groups, One Observation

Designs: A. Randomized $\qquad\qquad\qquad\quad$ X $\qquad$ O

Randomized $\qquad\qquad\qquad\quad$ C $\qquad$ O

B. Matched $\qquad\qquad\qquad\qquad\;$ X $\qquad$ O

Matched $\qquad\qquad\qquad\qquad\;$ C $\qquad$ O

C.	Matched and Randomized	X	O
	Matched and Randomized	C	O
D.	Treatment	X	O
	Convenience	O	C

Description: The two-group, one-observation designs involve a single measurement or set of measurements on two groups. The single observation or measurement is generally a posttest as depicted in designs A, B, C, and D. The two groups are referred to as the experimental group, which receives treatment X, and the control group, C, which does not receive the treatment. The classification of groups as experimental and control groups can be based on (A) randomization, (B) matching on what are thought to be salient background variables, (C) sequential matching and randomization together, and (D) convenience or mere availability.

Applications: The two-group, one-observation designs are very commonly used to assess the effects of some treatment condition, X, by comparing two groups of subjects in a situation where one group receives the treatment and one group does not. All other things being equal, the difference between the two groups after the treatment reflects the impact of the treatment. These designs are often used to examine the impact of different instructional strategies, curriculum materials, or training methods.

Design C, involving both matching and randomization, is a type of randomized block design (**E3–20**). The variable (or variables) on which the subjects are matched is a blocking variable the influence of which is controlled by matching. Subjects are matched to be as similar as possible on the blocking variable and are formed into blocks.

With a two-group design, the blocks contain two subjects who are as similar as possible on the blocking variable. The two subjects in each block are then randomly assigned to one of the two groups, experimental or control. The subjects from each block are treated as if they were the same subject measured twice, once under each condition. Thus, statistical comparisons appropriate for dependent samples are used with design C.

Comments: The two-group, one-observation design with randomization, as in designs A and C above, is a true experimental design despite the absence of a pretest. The random assignment of subjects to groups is used to create comparability between groups and equivalent distributions of confounding variables within the two groups. The randomization equalizes the influence of potential extraneous variables so that groups differ on the independent variable, but all other characteristics of the groups are equivalent.

An approximation to randomization involves matching (design B) two groups based on demographic variables or some other variables that might influence the dependent measure. The matching is thought to minimize the differences between the groups prior to the application of the experimental treatment. The validity of the inference that posttreatment differences are due to the independent variable is improved by documenting pretreatment similarities through matching. Despite some apparent advantages, matching is not an adequate substitute for randomization and cannot be used to support independent-dependent variable causal inferences.

317

The use of a convenience sample (design D) as a comparison group or pseudocontrol group, is common in educational research. Often, such designs include the suggestion that the treatment group and comparison group were similar prior to the treatment and thus are "matched" samples. These designs are very weak and are most usefully thought of as single-group, one-observation designs. Information about the control group can be used to describe the general context within which the treatment group is studied. This information cannot be used to strengthen independent-dependent variable causal inferences.

Analysis: Two-group, posttest-only designs are generally used to test differences between groups after some treatment has been applied. Parametric procedures for comparing means, variances, proportions, and correlations for two groups are described in **E4–48** to **E4–56**. Nonparametric tests for two groups are described in **E4–57** to **E4–65**. The difference between two groups might be examined using a one-way analysis of variance (**E4–71**) or a randomized block design (**E4–87**).

E3–5

Category: Two Groups, Two Observations
(Pretest-Posttest Designs)

Designs:
A.	Randomized	O_1	X	O_2	
	Randomized	O_1	C	O_2	
B.	Matched	O_1	X	O_2	
	Matched	O_1	C	O_2	
C.	Matched and Random	O_1	C	O_2	
	Matched and Random	O_1	C	O_2	
D.	Treatment	O_1	X	O_2	
	Convenience	O_1	C	O_2	
E.	Randomized		X	O_2	Treatment Group
	Randomized		O_1	C	Control Group

Description: Designs involving two groups and two observations generally include a pretest and posttest for an experimental group and a control group. Subjects can be assigned to experimental or control groups at random, based on matching or on convenience sampling. The pretest and posttest are frequently the same test or alternate forms of the same test used to assess subjects' knowledge before and after the treatment.

Design C involves matching and randomization. In a two-group design, subjects most similar to each other on the matching variable(s) are paired together into blocks. From each block each subject is randomly assigned to either the experimental group or the control group. In this randomized block design, subjects from the same block are treated as the same subject measured twice. Statistical procedures for dependent samples are applied.

Campbell and Stanley refer to design E above as a "separate-sample pretest-posttest" design. In this design, a randomly assigned experimental group is measured after the treatment has been administered, and a randomly assigned control group is measured before the treatment. The posttest for the treatment group is compared to the pretest for the control group. The effect of the treatment on the control group is not assessed.

Application: The pretest-posttest experimental group-control group design is very commonly used to test the impact of an experimental treatment. In educational research, the experimental treatment of interest is often an instructional strategy, a set of curriculum materials, or some teacher training procedure.

Comments: The value of the design for testing hypotheses about treatment effects and for making independent-dependent variable causal inferences depends directly on how the groups are assigned. Designs in which subjects are randomly assigned to treatment and control groups (designs A and C) are true experiments and allow for independent-dependent variable causal inferences. Randomization, however, is not practical in many educational settings.

Matching designs (design B) can be informative but are clearly limited by the nature of the matching variables and the care with which matching is performed. Even under the best of conditions, matching designs should be considered more descriptive than experimental. Matching designs are very common when a teacher or group of teachers is implementing some new program (e.g., teaching strategy or curriculum), and a "matched" group of teachers who do not use the new program is identified.

Design C is a randomized block design, which is very powerful. The test statistic for such designs basically eliminates between-subject variation in the estimate of random error that is used as the denominator in hypothesis testing.

Design D represents a pretest-posttest design with an experimental group and a comparison group that is used simply because it is conveniently available. Often, such designs include the suggestion that the treatment group and comparison group were similar prior to the treatment and thus are "matched" samples. Such comparison groups provide little, if any, useful information. Indeed, the use of a convenience sample can easily be misleading since it gives the design the appearance of an experiment without providing the controls over confounding variables that true experimental designs provide. Moreover, the convenience sample itself may actually introduce additional confounding variables.

Analysis: Two-group, pretest-posttest designs are used to assess the impact of some experimental treatment applied to one group compared to a second group that does not receive the treatment. Data from these designs can be analyzed using a variety of procedures. Gain scores, defined as the difference between posttest and pretest, can be examined using a t-test, **E4–49**, or **E4–50** (for matched samples in design C above). A one-way analysis of variance, **E4–71**, might also be used to examine the gain scores. Gain scores are not very reliable, however. Many researchers would examine these designs using analysis of covariance, **E4–89**, or a split-plot design, **E4–80**.

E3–6

Category: Two Groups, Multiple Observations over Time

Designs: A. Randomized $\quad O_1 \quad O_2 \quad O_3 \quad X \quad O_4 \quad O_5 \quad O_6$
Randomized $\quad O_1 \quad O_2 \quad O_3 \quad X \quad O_4 \quad O_5 \quad O_6$

B.	Matched	O_1	O_2	O_3	X	O_4 O_5 O_6
	Matched	O_1	O_2	O_3	X	O_4 O_5 O_6
C.	Treatment	O_1	O_2	O_3	X	O_4 O_5 O_6
	Convenience	O_1	O_2	O_3	X	O_4 O_5 O_6

Description: The two-group, multiple-observation designs involve a treatment group that receives some experimental treatment condition and a control group that does not receive the treatment. Observations of both groups are made at different times before (O_1 O_2 O_3) and after (O_4 O_5 O_6) the treatment is applied. As with the preceding two-group, two-observation designs, the samples may be randomly assigned, matched, or convenience samples.

Applications: Two-group, multiple-observation designs are commonly used to assess the impact of some experimental treatment condition applied to one group but not to the other. Designs of this sort are very useful in determining long-term treatment effects in contrast to pretest-posttest designs, which assess the impact of an experimental treatment only once, immediately following the application of the treatment. In addition, the multiple observations preceding the treatment are useful in detecting emerging pretreatment trends or shifts.

Comments: The two-group, multiple-observation designs are also called Time-Series Designs if there are a large number of observations. In general, these designs are very useful when the experimental treatment can be randomly assigned to one of the two groups.

Analysis: Two-group, multiple-observation designs are analyzed using a split-plot analysis, **E4–80**, or time-series analysis procedures, **E4–90**.

E3–7

Category: Multiple Groups, One Observation (Posttest)

Designs:	A. Randomized	X	O
	Randomized:	X	O
	Randomized:	C	O
	B. Matched	X	O
	Matched	X	O
	Matched	C	O
	C. Matched and Randomized	X	O
	Matched and Randomized	X	O
	Matched and Randomized	C	O
	D. Nonrandomized	X	O
	Nonrandomized	X	O
	Nonrandomized	C	O

Description: The multiple-group, one-observation designs generally involve a posttest administered to three or more groups. The specific designs illustrated above show two experimental groups and one control group (group 3). There can be any number of groups in varying combinations of experimental and control groups. Subjects can be randomly assigned to groups (as in A and C). Groups can be matched on some confounding variable the influence of which the researcher wishes to control (designs B and C). Design C is a randomized block design (see entries **E3–20** and **E4–87**). Design D involves the comparison of convenience samples or nonequivalent groups.

Applications: Multiple-group, one-observation (posttest) designs are extremely common in educational research. Such designs are commonly used to compare different experimental treatments to each other and to a control group. Often, the different experimental groups represent subjects who are receiving different variations of the same experimental treatment. Multiple control groups are also frequently incorporated into such designs.

Comments: The value of multiple-group, one-observation (posttest) designs depends directly on how subjects are assigned to groups. Design A involves randomization and is a true experimental design. Design C is a randomized block design (**E3–20** and **E4–87**). Such designs are not always practical since they require considerable control over the experimental setting. The randomized block design is a powerful experimental design that should be considered whenever possible. Multiple-group designs often involve "matching" based on the fact that groups are similar with respect to background variables or other measures. Comparing these matched groups is not equivalent to the experimental control of extraneous variables achieved through randomization. Studies using this type of matching or convenience samples may be informative; however, they should be interpreted with great caution. Often it is useful to consider such studies as descriptive studies even if they are analyzed using inferential statistical procedures.

Analysis: Multiple-group, posttest-only designs are generally examined using one-way analysis of variance procedures (**E4–71**) or a randomized block analysis (**E4–87**).

E3–8

Category: Multiple Groups, Two Observations
(Pretest-Posttest Designs)

Designs:	A.	Randomized	O_1	X	O_2
		Randomized	O_1	X	O_2
		Randomized	O_1	C	O_2
Designs:	B.	Matched	O_1	X	O_2
		Matched	O_1	X	O_2
		Matched	O_1	C	O_2
Designs:	C.	Matched and Random	O_1	X	O_2
		Matched and Random	O_1	X	O_2
		Matched and Random	O_1	C	O_2
Designs:	D.	Nonrandomized	O_1	X	O_2
		Nonrandomized	O_1	X	O_2
		Nonrandomized	O_1	C	O_2

Description: Multiple-group, two-observation designs are generally pretest-posttest designs with three or more groups. The designs shown have two experimental groups (groups 1 and 2) and one control group (group 3). There can be any number of groups in varying combinations of experimental and control groups. Subjects can be assigned to experimental or control groups in different ways. In designs A and C, subjects are randomly assigned to groups. In design B, groups are matched on a variable the influence of which the researcher wishes to control. Design C is a randomized block design, the details of which are described elsewhere (**E3–20**, **E4–87**), and D involves the comparison of convenience samples or nonequivalent groups.

Applications: Multiple-group, two-observation (pretest-posttest) designs are often used to test the impact of experimental treatments. In educational research, the experimental treatments of interest are often instructional strategies, curriculum materials, or teacher training procedures.

These designs can be used in many different ways. An analysis of students' gains can be performed by testing hypotheses about the differences between posttest and pretest performance. Pretest and posttest scores can be used in a repeated measures and split-plot analyses (**E3–13** to **E3–16**). Finally, the pretest can be used as a control variable in an analysis of covariance procedure (**E3–22**).

Multiple-group, two-observation (pretest-posttest) designs are used to compare different experimental treatments to each other and to a control group. Multiple control groups are occasionally incorporated into such designs.

Comments: The value of the multiple-group, pretest-posttest designs is directly related to how subjects are assigned to the groups. Randomization, as always, is the key. Designs A and C, which include randomization, are more useful and are true experimental designs. These designs can support independent-dependent variable causal inferences. Design B involves comparisons among groups that are "matched," based on the fact that they are similar with respect to some relevant variables that the researcher thinks should be controlled. Such matching is not very useful in controlling the effects of extraneous variables unless it is accompanied by random assignment, as in design C. Design D involves the comparison of convenience samples or nonequivalent groups. Such designs are very weak and should be considered descriptive in nature even if they are analyzed using inferential techniques.

Analysis: Multiple-group, two-observation (pretest-posttests) designs can be analyzed in several ways. Gain scores can be examined using a one-way analysis of variance, but the lack of reliability typical of gain scores makes this approach undesirable. Analysis of covariance, **E4–89**, is commonly used for these designs. A split-plot analysis, **E4–80**, with one between-subjects factor and one within-subjects factor would also be appropriate.

E3–9

Category: Multiple Groups, One and Two Observations

Design: Solomon Four-Group Design

Randomized	O_1	X	O_2 Group 1
Randomized	O_1	C	O_2 Group 2
Randomized		X	O_2 Group 3
Randomized		C	O_2 Group 4

Description: The Solomon Four-Group Design involves four randomly assigned groups. This is a true experimental design since all subjects are randomly assigned to groups.

There are two experimental groups (groups 1 and 3), one of which takes a pretest and posttest (group 1) and the other of which takes the posttest only (group 3). There are two control groups (groups 2 and 4), one of which takes a pretest and posttest (group 2) and the other of which takes the posttest only (group 4).

Applications: The Solomon Four-Group Design is used to examine the effects of experimental treatment conditions, X, while controlling for a variety of extraneous variables. The design requires considerable control over the experimental situation.

Comments: The Solomon Four-Group Design is useful and powerful in detecting the effects of experimental treatment conditions. A comparison of the posttest for groups 1 and 2 examines treatment effects in the presence of a pretest. A comparison of groups 3 and 4 examines the treatment effects without the influence of a pretest. The effects of the experimental treatment are tested when groups 1 and 3 are compared to groups 2 and 4. The effects of the pretest are examined with a comparison of the posttests of groups 1 and 2 to the posttests of groups 3 and 4.

This is an informative and useful design that requires a large number of subjects as well as considerable control over the experimental situation.

Analysis: The Solomon Four-Group Design is generally analyzed using a one-way analysis of variance, **E4–71**, with four groups, using the posttest as the dependent measure. Scheffé contrasts, **E4–94**, are used to compare groups 1 and 2 against groups 3 and 4. This examines the effect of the pretest. The contrast of groups 1 and 3 against 2 and 4 examines the treatment effect.

E3–10

Category: Factorial Analysis of Variance (ANOVA) Designs
Design: One-Way Analysis of Variance
Description: The one-way analysis of variance design contains a single independent variable, Factor A. The independent variable can have two or more levels forming different groups. The groups are compared when the analysis of variance is performed (**E4–71**).

The basic arrangement for a one-way analysis of variance:

Factor A, A Levels
1 2 3 . . A

Applications: This one-way design with accompanying analysis has many applications in educational research and evaluation. The one-way analysis of variance is appropriate anywhere two or more groups are being compared on some measure. The procedure is commonly used with multiple-group, posttest-only designs.

Comments: The one-way analysis of variance is one of the most commonly used research designs. For details, see **E4–71**.

Analysis: One-Way Analysis of Variance, **E4–71**.

E3–11

Category: Factorial Analysis of Variance (ANOVA) Designs

Design: Two-Way Analysis of Variance

Description: The two-way analysis of variance contains two independent variables, or factors, on the basis of which subjects are classified. Each factor can have two or more levels. If Factor A has A levels, and Factor B has B levels, then subjects are classified into A × B individual cells.

The basic arrangement for a two-way analysis of variance is shown below. Factor A is shown with A levels and Factor B is shown with 3 levels.

Factor A, A Levels
1 2 3 . . A

Factor B 1
2
3

Applications: Two-way analysis of variance designs with accompanying analyses are used whenever there are two independent variables, and all levels of each variable appear under all levels of the other variable. Such designs are very common when subjects in different treatment groups, represented by the levels of Factor A, can be classified on some second variable, represented by Factor B. For example, a two-way analysis of variance, treatment × gender, might have 3 levels of treatment and 2 levels of gender. Such a design would be a 3 × 2 two-way analysis of variance. Two-way analysis of variance is commonly used in aptitude-treatment research in which aptitude levels are represented by Factor A and treatment groups by Factor B.

Comments: Two-way analysis of variance designs are used to test hypotheses about the two independent variables and their interaction. The levels of the factors can be fixed, random, or mixed. For details, see **E4–72**, **E4–73**, and **E4–74**, respectively.

Analysis: Two-Way Analysis of Variance
Fixed Effects Model, **E4–72**
Random Effects Model, **E4–73**
Mixed Effects Model, **E4–74**

E3–12

Category: Factorial Analysis of Variance (ANOVA) Designs

Design: Three-Way Analysis of Variance

Description: The three-way analysis of variance contains three independent variables or factors on the basis of which subjects are classified. Each factor can have two or more levels. If Factor A has A levels, Factor B has B levels, and Factor C has C levels, then subjects are classified into A × B × C individual cells.

The basic arrangements for a three-way analysis of variance is shown below. Factor A is shown with A levels, Factor B is shown with 3 levels, and Factor C is shown with 3 levels.

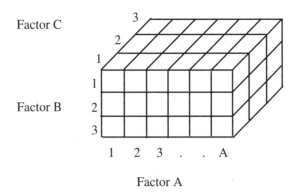

Factor C

Factor B

Factor A

Applications: Three-way analysis of variance designs with accompanying analyses are used whenever there are three independent variables and all levels of each variable appear under all levels of the other variable. Such designs are used when subjects can be classified on three different variables simultaneously. For example, a three-way ANOVA, treatment × gender × SES (socioeconomic status), might have 3 levels of treatment, 2 levels of gender, and 3 levels of SES. Such a design would be a 3 × 2 × 3 three-way ANOVA.

Comments: Three-way analysis of variance designs are used to test hypotheses about three independent variables, their two-way interactions, and their three-way interaction. The levels of the factors can be fixed, random, or mixed. For details, see **E4–75** to **E4–78**, respectively.

Analysis: Three-Way Analysis of Variance
  Fixed Effects Model, **E4–75**
  Mixed Effects Model
    One Fixed, Two Random Factors, **E4–76**
    Two Fixed, One Random Factor, **E4–77**
  Random Effects Model, **E4–78**

E3–13
Category: Repeated Measures and Split-Plot Analysis of Variance (ANOVA) Designs
Design: One-Way Repeated Measures Design
Description: One-way repeated measures designs involve the repeated measurement of the same group of subjects over several occasions. From a design perspective, there is one factor, occasions, with A levels (see **E4–79**). From an analysis perspective, these designs are treated as a two-way mixed model (see **E4–74**). The two factors are subjects (the random factor) and occasions (the fixed factor).

The basic arrangement for a one-way repeated measures analysis of variance is illustrated with Factor A, occasions, consisting of 4 levels.

Factor A, Occasions–(4 Levels)

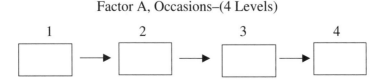

Applications: Repeated measures designs are used anywhere a group of subjects is measured on more than one occasion. Such designs are common in developmental and longitudinal research.

Comments: Repeated measures designs are statistically very powerful. They are the extension of the dependent sample t-test (**E4–50**). For details, see entry **E4–79**.

Analysis: One-Way Repeated Measures Analysis of Variance, **E4–79**.

E3–14

Category: Repeated Measures and Split-Plot Analysis of Variance (ANOVA) Designs

Design: Two-Way Split-Plot Design, One Between-Subjects Factor, One Within-Subjects Factor

Description: The two-way, split-plot design with one within-subjects and one between-subjects factor involves repeated measurements (Factor B) for subjects arranged into different groups (Factor A). The repeated measurements across occasions is the within-subjects factor (B), and the classification of subjects into different groups is the between-subjects factor (A).

The basic arrangement for this design is illustrated with 4 levels of Factor B (Occasions) and 2 levels of Factor A (Groups)

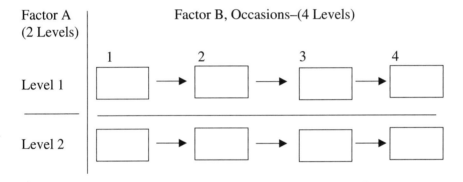

Applications: This design is used when groups of subjects defined on some independent variable (Factor A) are measured on more than two occasions (Factor B). By way of illustration, a very common application might have three levels of Factor B, namely, measurements taken before, during, and after an experimental intervention, and two levels of Factor A, a treatment group and a control group.

Longitudinal research on groups that develop at different rates with respect to the dependent variable would employ this design.

Comments: The one-between, one-within, two-factor, split-plot design is an informative, useful, and powerful design. For details, see entry **E4–80**.

Analysis: Two-Way Split-Plot Analysis of Variance
One Between-Subjects Factor
One Within-Subjects Factor, and **E4–80**.

E3–15A

Category: Repeated Measures and Split-Plot Analysis of Variance (ANOVA) Designs

Designs: Three-Way Split-Plot Design, One Between-Subjects Factor, Two Within-Subjects Factors

Description: This design is used when subjects in different groups (between-subjects, Factor A) are measured two or more times (within-subjects, Factor B) on two or more occasions (within-subjects, Factor C). Such situations arise when subjects in different groups (Factor A) attempt a task several times under different conditions (Factor B), before, during, and after some experimental intervention (Factor C).

The basic arrangements for this design are illustrated below. Factor A, between-subjects, has 2 levels; Factor B, within subjects, has 3 levels; and Factor C, within subjects, has 4 levels.

Applications: A three-way, split-plot design with one between-subjects factor and two within-subjects factors is used when subjects in different groups are measured repeatedly (e.g., trials) on different occasions.

Comments: For details, see entry **E4–81**.

Analysis: Three-Way, Split-Plot Analysis of Variance, One Between-Subjects Factor, Two Within-Subjects Factors, **E4–81**.

E3–15B

Category: Repeated Measures and Split-Plot Analysis of Variance (ANOVA) Designs

Designs: Three-Way, Split-Plot Design, Two Between-Subjects Factors, One Within-Subjects Factor

Description: This design is used when subjects in different groups (between-subjects, Factor A) are at the same time assigned to different levels of a second between-groups factor (Factor B), and all subjects in the A × B between-groups design are measured two or more times (within-subjects, Factor C). Such situations arise when subjects in a two-way factorial ANOVA are measured on repeated occasions. The basic arrangements for this design are illustrated. Factor A, between subjects, has 2 levels; Factor B, between subjects, has 3 levels; and Factor C, within subjects, has 3 levels.

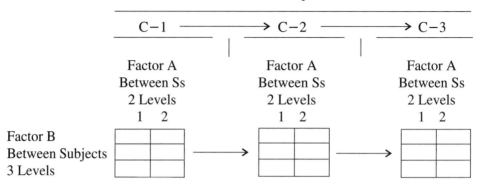

Factor C, Within Subjects, 3 Levels

Applications: A three-way, split-plot design with two between-subjects factors and one within-subjects factor is used when subjects in a two-way factorial ANOVA design are measured on different occasions. Such applications occur when subjects in a two-way design (e.g., gender × treatment), are measured before, during, and after some experimental treatment is applied.

Comments: For details, see entry **E4–82**.

Analysis: Three-Way, Split-Plot Analysis of Variance, Two Between-Subjects Factors, One Within-Subjects Factor, **E4–82**.

E3–16

Category: Repeated Measures and Split-Plot Analysis of Variance (ANOVA) Designs

Design: Four-Way, Split-Plot Design, Two Between-Subjects Factors, Two Within-Subjects Factors

Description: This four-way, split-plot design involves two between-subjects factors and two within-subjects factors. The between-subjects factors have the form of a two-way factorial analysis of variance. The two within-subjects factors indicate that subjects, in the two-way factorial design, are measured two or more times on two or more occasions.

Applications: By way of illustration, this four-way design would be used in an experiment in which gender is crossed with treatment in the form of a two-way factorial ANOVA. Both gender and treatment are between-subjects factors. All subjects are measured over repeated trials of some tasks, and the measurements over trials occur before, during, and after the application of the experimental treatment conditions. Trials and occasions are within-subjects factors.

Comments: For details, see **E4–83**.

Analysis: Four-Way, Split-Plot Analysis of Variance, Two Between-Subjects Factors, Two Within Subjects Factors, **E4–83**.

E3–17

Category: Nested (Hierarchical) Analysis of Variance (ANOVA) Designs

Designs: Two-Factor Nested Design, Factor B Nested in Factor A

Description: Two-factor nested designs involve two independent variables. Only some of the levels of one variable appear under the levels of the other variable. For example, if Factor A has 2 levels, and Factor B nested in Factor A has 10 levels, then levels 1, 2, 3, 4, and 5 of Factor B might appear under level 1 of Factor A. Levels 6, 7, 8, 9, and 10 of Factor B might appear under level 2 of Factor A. This differs from a two-way factorial design with factors A and B. In a factorial design, all the levels of Factor B would appear under all the levels of Factor A.

The general arrangement of a two-factor nested design is illustrated below for Factor A with 2 levels and Factor B with 10 levels.

Factor A

Level 1	Level 2
Factor B	Factor B
Level 1	Level 6
Level 2	Level 7
Level 3	Level 8
Level 4	Level 9
Level 5	Level 10

Applications: Two-factor nested designs are used when only some of the levels of one factor appear under the levels of the other factor. This situation commonly occurs when experimental treatments are administered to different sets of subjects. The example illustrated above could be such a situation.

The illustration applies if Factor A represents levels of treatment, with level 1 being an experimental treatment and level 2 being a control. The 10 levels of factor B are classrooms, with classrooms 1 through 5 receiving the treatment and classrooms 6 through 10 acting as the control. Two-factor nested designs are common in educational research when new instructional methods or curriculum materials are assigned to experimental classes, and other classes serve as controls.

Comments: Two-factor nested designs, with classrooms nested within treatment conditions, are common in education. These designs are frequently analyzed incorrectly as a one-way analysis of variance, with treatment conditions as the one independent variable. For details, see **E4–84**.

Analysis: Two-Factor Nested Analysis of Variance, Factor B Nested in Factor A, **E4–84**.

E3–18

Category: Nested (Hierarchical) Analysis of Variance (ANOVA) Designs

Design: Three-Factor Nested Design, Factor C Nested in Factor B, Factor B Nested in Factor A

Description: Three-factor nested designs involve a double nesting. One factor is nested within a second, and the second is nested in the third. The basic arrangement for such a design is shown below. Factor A has 2 levels, Factor B has 4 levels, and Factor C has 12 levels.

Factor C, levels 1, 2, and 3, are nested under level 1 of Factor B. Factor C, levels 4, 5, and 6, are nested under level 2 of Factor B. Factor C, levels 7, 8, and 9, are nested under Factor B, level 3. Factor C, levels 10, 11, and 12, are nested under Factor B, level 4. Factor B, levels 1 and 2, are nested under Factor A, level 1. Factor B, levels 3 and 4, are nested under Factor A, level 2.

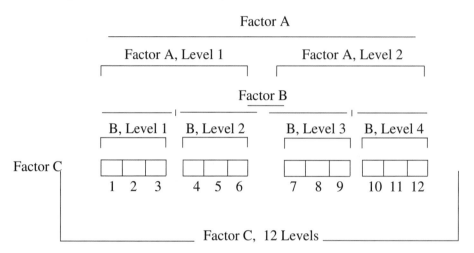

Applications: The illustration above will be used to describe an application of this design in educational research. In this sample application, Factor A is treatment, with 2 levels (a new experimental curriculum and the current curriculum). Factor B is schools, with 4 levels. Two schools, levels 1 and 2 of factor B, are assigned to use the new curriculum, and two schools, levels 3 and 4 of Factor B, are assigned the current curriculum. There are 12 different teachers in the study. Teachers are Factor C. Three different teachers are nested under each of the 4 levels of factor B.

Comments: For details, see **E4–85**.

Analysis: Three-Factor Nested Analysis of Variance, Factor C Nested in Factor B, Factor B Nested in Factor A, **E4–85**.

E3–19

Category: Nested (Hierarchical) Analysis of Variance (ANOVA) Designs

Design: Three Factor Design, Two Factors Nested, One Factor Crossed

Description: The Three-Factor Design with two factors nested and one factor crossed is a combination of a two-factor nested design and a factorial design. In this design, one factor is crossed with the second, and the second is nested under the third. The basic arrangement for this type of design is illustrated below. In this illustration, Factor C, with 2 levels, is crossed with Factor B, with 6 levels. These factors are crossed because all levels of Factor C appear under all levels of Factor B. Factor B is nested in Factor A, with 2 levels. These factors are nested since only some of the levels of Factor B appear under some of the levels of Factor A. Levels 1, 2, and 3 of Factor B are nested under level 1 of Factor A. Levels 4, 5, and 6 of Factor B are nested under level 2 of Factor A.

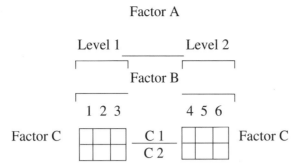

Applications: This illustration will be used to describe an application of this design in educational research. Factor A is treatment, with 2 levels (a new experimental curriculum and the current curriculum). Factor B represents teachers, each of whom teaches a group of students using one of the two curriculum approaches. Teachers 1, 2, and 3 use the new curriculum, while teachers 4, 5, and 6 use the current curriculum. Factor C is students' gender, which is crossed with "teacher," since the teachers all have female and male students in their classes. This design allows the researcher to examine differences in the impact of the treatments, gender differences, and the interaction of gender and treatment.

Comments: For details, see **E4–86**.

Analysis: Three-Factor Analysis of Variance, Two Factors Nested, One Factor Crossed, **E4–86**.

E3–20

Category: Randomized Block Designs

Designs: Randomized Block Designs in General

Description: Randomized Block Designs represent a large class of research designs in which an independent variable is used as a blocking variable to control the influence of a possible extraneous variable and to increase the statistical power of the analysis. A blocking variable can be added to almost any type of analysis of variance design. A blocking variable is selected based on the researcher's belief that it is related, or possibly highly related, to the dependent measure. A general procedure for a simple randomized block design begins by ordering the subjects on the blocking variable. Subjects who are adjacent to each other in this ordering are then grouped into blocks. In some cases, the number of subjects in each block is equal to the number of treatment conditions. In other cases, the number of subjects in each block is a multiple of the number of treatments. Subjects are then randomly assigned from each block to each treatment group. As a result of this procedure, each group has an equal number of subjects from each block, and each group has subjects from all blocks. In this way, the effects of the blocking variable are spread evenly across all treatment groups. Thus, differences between groups cannot be due to the blocking variable.

It is imperative that the blocking variable be incorporated as an independent variable (factor) in the statistical analysis of a randomized block design. Variation on the dependent measure attributable to the blocking variable is removed from the estimate of random error in the analysis. This increases the statistical power of the analysis since the estimate of random error (reduced) is the denominator in testing hypotheses about treatment effects. The use of a randomized block design without incorporating the blocking variable into the statistical analysis inflates the estimate of random error because it increases within-cell variance. This reduces the power of the statistical analysis.

Applications: Randomized block designs can be incorporated into virtually any type of analysis of variance design by adding the blocking factor to the design and analysis. Randomized block designs are used when the researcher wants to control for the effects of a confounding variable and increase the statistical power of the analysis.

Comments: For a description of additional applications and details, see entry **E4–86**.

Analysis: Randomized Block Designs, **E4–86**.

E3–21

Category: Latin Square Designs

Design: Latin Square Designs in General

Description: Latin square designs represent a large class of analysis of variance procedures used to control for potential sources of extraneous variation. Latin square designs incorporate factors as independent variables that otherwise might confound the analysis of the effects due to some experimental treatment. The effects due to the order in which treatment conditions are presented and to the effects due to the practice that students receive under different treatment conditions are often controlled using Latin square designs. These designs are analyzed as fixed-effects, factorial ANOVA models with no interactions among the independent variables.

Applications: Latin square designs are commonly used to control variation due to order, sequence, practice effects, and other possible confounding effects in experimental studies.

Comments: For details, see **E4–87**.

Analysis: Latin Square Designs, **E4–87**.

E3–22

Category: Analysis of Covariance (ANCOVA)

Design: Analysis of Covariance Designs in General

Description: Analysis of covariance represents a large class of designs that are structurally identical to analysis of variance designs but include an additional variable. The additional variable is a continuous independent variable. This continuous, independent variable is called a covariate. The covariate is systematically related to the dependent measure. The variation in the dependent measure that can be attributed to the covariate is estimated and thus removed from the estimate of random error. This reduces the size of the estimate of random error, which is used as the denominator in testing various hypotheses. The statistical power of the design is thereby increased.

Applications: Analysis of covariance is used in a wide range of educational research situations. It is commonly used in pretest-posttest design with the pretest as a covariate. Scores on alternate forms of the dependent measure can be used as covariates. Analysis of covariance is sometimes used to adjust for sampling bias or sampling error. This application can be misleading.

Comments: For details, see **E4–88**.

Analysis: Analysis of Covariance, **E4–88**.

REFERENCES AND RESOURCES

Campbell, D. T., and Stanley, J. C. (1966). *Experimental and Quasi-Experimental Designs for Research.* Chicago: Rand McNally.

Cook, T. D., and Campbell, D. T. (1979). *Quasi-Experimentation: Design and Analysis Issues for Field Settings.* Boston: Houghton Mifflin.

Dean, A., and Voss, D. (1999). *Design and Analysis of Experiments.* New York: Springer-Verlag.

Keppel, G. (1982). *Designs and Analysis: A Researcher's Handbook.* 2nd ed. Englewood Cliffs, NJ: Prentice-Hall.

Kirk, R. E. (1982). *Experimental Designs: Procedures for the Behavioral Sciences.* 2nd ed. Belmont, CA: Brooks/Cole.

Leedy, P. D. (1985). *Practical Research: Planning and Design.* 3rd ed. New York: Macmillan.

Lunneborg, C. E. (1994). *Modeling Experimental and Observational Data.* Belmont, CA: Duxbury Press.

Maxwell, S. E., and Delaney, H. D. (1990). *Designing Experiments and Analyzing Data: A Model Comparison Perspective.* Pacific Grove, CA: Brooks Cole.

Spector, P. E. (1981). *Research Designs.* Sage University Paper series on Quantitative Applications in the Social Sciences, 07-023. Beverly Hills, CA, and London: Sage, 1981.

Winer, B. J., Brown, D. R., and Michels, K. M. (1991). *Statistical Principles in Experimental Design.* New York: McGraw-Hill.

CHAPTER 4

A Summary of Statistical Procedures

INTRODUCTION, PURPOSE, AND OVERVIEW

The purpose of this chapter is to provide the reader a concise summary of the statistical procedures commonly used in educational research. The chapter is designed for both reference and review use. Some readers, with a need to use or properly understand a specific statistical procedure, will find that this chapter contains all the information needed to proceed in many research situations. Other readers, more interested in refreshing their familiarity with various statistical procedures, will find this a convenient source of information on a wide range of statistical topics.

In this chapter, a balance is struck between breadth and depth of content coverage. A broad range of statistical procedures is covered at a depth that is designed to be useful and informative. This chapter is not designed as a textbook in statistics but as a resource for educators with some basic background in statistics. Information about each statistical procedure is presented as a separate "entry," consistent with the format used throughout the book. Each entry contains eight sections:

1. Category—basic classification for the procedure
2. Statistic or Statistical Procedure—the name of the procedure
3. Description—basic information about the procedure
4. Application(s)—research situations in which the procedure is used and how it is used
5. Data—the nature of the data to which the procedure is applied
6. Limitations—assumptions and weaknesses of the procedure
7. Comments—additional information about the procedure
8. Formula—the statistical expression for the procedure

COMPUTER APPLICATIONS

The effective use of this chapter assumes that a researcher has access to a reasonably powerful computer. This assumption has influenced the way that certain procedures are described. For example, in presenting a formula for many procedures, there was often a choice between an expression that reflected the statistical concept of the procedure and an expression that would be used if the procedure were being applied by hand. The expression of the basic statistical concept is presented for two reasons. First, for most procedures, it is adequate for actual applications. Second, in most research situations, actual calculations are performed with a computer or a powerful calculator with basic statistical functions.

The description of many procedures, especially different analysis of variance procedures, assumes that the researcher will use one of the available computer packages for actual applications. Many appropriate packages are reviewed in Section D. Thus, the formula sections of the analysis of variance procedures emphasize showing what term goes in the numerator and what term goes in the denominator to test hypotheses about different factors. The actual computations are left to the computer.

CONTENT OVERVIEW

Ninety-seven statistical procedures, organized into nine general categories, are described in this chapter. A complete listing of the procedures is presented here to serve as a chapter overview and directory.

These nine general categories of statistical procedures are assigned entry numbers and appear in the text with a listing of the statistical procedures for each category. These category listings serve as subdirectories to facilitate cross-referencing and using the book's index.

(E4–1) DESCRIPTIVE STATISTICS

Central Tendency

(E4–2) Mean
(E4–3) Median
(E4–4) Mode

Variability or Dispersion

(E4–5) Range
(E4–6) Mean Deviation
(E4–7) Variance
(E4–8) Standard Deviation

Disarray (Nonparametric)

(E4–9) Sum of D-square
(E4–10) S

Distribution Shapes

(E4–11) Frequency Distributions—Raw and Proportional Frequencies and Cumulative Frequencies
(E4–12) Skewness
(E4–13) Kurtosis

(E4–14) MEASURES OF RELATIONSHIPS

(E4–15) Covariance
(E4–16) Pearson Product-Moment Correlation
(E4–17) Spearman's Rank Order Correlation—Rho
(E4–18) Kendall's Tau
(E4–19) Point Biserial Correlation

(E4–20) Biserial Correlation
(E4–21) Phi-Coefficient
(E4–22) Tetrachoric Correlation
(E4–23) Contingency Coefficient
(E4–24) Kendall's Coefficient of Concordance
(E4–25) Intraclass Correlation
(E4–26) Part Correlation
(E4–27) Partial Correlation
(E4–28) Multiple Correlation
(E4–29) Eta-Squared
(E4–30) Factor Analysis

(E4–31) REGRESSION ANALYSIS

(E4–32) Simple Linear Regression
(E4–33) Regression Coefficient
(E4–34) Y-Intercept
(E4–35) Standard Error of Estimate
(E4–36) Multiple Regression
(E4–37) R-Squared
(E4–38) Curvilinear Regression
(E4–39) Stepwise Regression

(E4–40) COMPARISONS: ONE SAMPLE

(E4–41) Sample Mean Compared to Some Value
(E4–42) Sample Variance Compared to Some Value
(E4–43) Sample Proportion Compared to Some Value
(E4–44) Sample Correlation Compared to 0
(E4–45) Sample Correlation Compared to Some Value
(E4–46) Chi-square Test for Goodness of Fit
(E4–47) Kolomogorov-Smirnov One Sample Test

(E4–48) COMPARISONS: TWO SAMPLES (PARAMETRIC)

(E4–49) Comparing Two Sample Means, Independent Samples
(E4–50) Comparing Two Sample Means, Dependent or Correlated Samples
(E4–51) Comparing Two Sample Variances, Independent Samples
(E4–52) Comparing Two Sample Variances, Dependent or Correlated Samples
(E4–53) Comparing Two Sample Proportions, Independent Samples
(E4–54) Comparing Two Sample Proportions, Dependent or Correlated Samples
(E4–55) Comparing Two Sample Correlations, Independent Samples

(E4–56) Comparing Two Sample Correlations, Dependent or Correlated Samples

(E4–57) COMPARISONS: TWO SAMPLES (NONPARAMETRIC)

(E4–58) Median Test—Sign Test for Independent Samples
(E4–59) Wilcoxon Rank Sum Test—Rank Test for Independent Samples
(E4–60) Mann-Whitney U-Test, Signed Rank Test for Independent Samples
(E4–61) Chi-Square Test of Independence
(E4–62) Kolomogorov-Smirnov Two Sample Test Comparing Distributions
(E4–63) McNemar's Test for Significance of Change—Dependent or Correlated Samples
(E4–64) Sign Test for Dependent Samples
(E4–65) Wilcoxon Matched-Pairs Signed-Rank—Test for Dependent Samples

(E4–66) COMPARISONS: TWO OR MORE SAMPLES (NONPARAMETRIC)

(E4–67) Sign Test for K-Independent Samples
(E4–68) Kruskal-Wallace Rank Test for K-Independent Samples
(E4–69) Friedman Two-Way Analysis of Variance by Ranks for Dependent or Correlated Samples

(E4–70) COMPARISONS: TWO OR MORE SAMPLES—ANALYSIS OF VARIANCE (ANOVA)

Factorial Analysis of Variance

(E4–71) One-Way Analysis of Variance
(E4–72) Two-Way Analysis of Variance—Fixed Effects Model
(E4–73) Two-Way Analysis of Variance—Random Effects Model
(E4–74) Two-Way Analysis of Variance—Mixed Effects Model
(E4–75) Three-Way Analysis of Variance—Fixed Effects Model
(E4–76) Three-Way Analysis of Variance—Mixed Model, One Factor Fixed, Two Factors Random
(E4–77) Three-Way Analysis of Variance—Mixed Model, Two Factors Fixed, One Factor Random
(E4–78) Three-Way Analysis—Random Model

Repeated Measures Analysis of Variance/Split-Plot Analyses

(E4–79) One-Way Repeated Measures—Subjects by Occasions
(E4–80) Two-Way Split-Plot, One Between-Subjects Factor and One within-Subjects Factor
(E4–81) Three-Way Split-Plot, One Between-Subjects Factor and Two Within-Subjects Factors

(E4–82) Three-Way Split-Plot, Two Between-Subjects Factors and One Within-Subjects Factor

(E4–83) Four-Way Split-Plot, Two Between-Subjects Factors and Two Within-Subjects Factors

Nested/Hierarchical Analysis of Variance

(E4–84) Two Factor Design, B Nested in A

(E4–85) Three Factor Designs, C Nested in B, B Nested in A

(E4–86) Three Factor Designs, B Nested in A, C Crossed with B Nested in A

General Analysis of Variance Designs

(E4–87) Randomized Block Designs

(E4–88) Latin Square Designs

Related Designs

(E4–89) Analysis of Covariance

(E4–90) Time-Series Analysis

(E4–91) MULTIPLE COMPARISON PROCEDURES

A Priori Planned Comparisons

(E4–92) Orthogonal Contrasts

(E4–93) Orthogonal Polynomial Contrasts

Post Hoc Comparisons

(E4–94) Scheffé Contrasts

(E4–95) Tukey's Honestly Significant Difference

(E4–96) Newman-Keuls Test

(E4–97) Duncan Multiple Range Test

PROFILES OF STATISTICAL PROCEDURES

E4–1
DESCRIPTIVE STATISTICS
Central Tendency
      (E4–2) Mean
      (E4–3) Median
      (E4–4) Mode
Variability or Dispersion
      (E4–5) Range
      (E4–6) Mean Deviation
      (E4–7) Variance

(E4–8) Standard Deviation

Disarray (Nonparametric)

    (E4– 9) Sum of D-square

    (E4–10) S

Distribution Shapes

    (E4–11) Frequency Distributions—Raw and Proportional Frequencies and Cumulative Frequencies

    (E4–12) Skewness

    (E4–13) Kurtosis

E4–2

Category: Descriptive, Measure of Central Tendency

Statistic: Mean or Arithmetic Mean

Description: The arithmetic average value of a variable in a sample or population.

Application: Used when the performance of a group is to be represented by a single value.

Data: Used with data that are interval- or ratio-level and normally or otherwise symmetrically distributed around the mean.

Limitations: Not an appropriate measure of central tendency if the data are skewed (**E4–12**). Sensitive to extreme cases.

Comments: Generally, the statistic referred to when the term "average" is used.

Formula:

$$\overline{X} = \frac{\sum_{i=1}^{n} X_i}{n}$$

E4–3

Category: Descriptive, Measure of Central Tendency

Statistic: Median

Description: The value of a variable such that half the values in the distribution are above it and half the values in the distribution are below it. The value of a variable obtained by the subject in the 50th percentile.

Application: Used when the performance of a group is to be represented by a single value and the data are not normally or symmetrically distributed.

Data: Used when data are ordinal-, interval-, or ratio-level. Used with raw distributions or frequency distributions.

Limitations: Can be difficult to calculate. The median does not reflect performance on the extreme ends of the distribution.

Comments: The median is not sensitive to the influence of extreme cases on either end of the distribution. Commonly used measure of central tendency when data are known to be skewed.

Formula:

$$\text{Median} = L + \frac{(n/2) - F}{f_m} \times I$$

where

L = exact lower limit of interval containing median

n = number of cases

F = sum of all frequencies below L

I = width of the class intervals

f_m = frequency of interval containing the median

E4–4

Category: Descriptive, Measure of Central Tendency

Statistic: Mode

Description: The most frequently occurring value of a variable in a distribution.

Application: The mode is used as a rough estimate of central tendency. Used to identify "typical" performance.

Data: Used with data that are nominal, ordinal, interval, or ratio.

Limitations: With small samples, the mode is very unstable.

Comments: Distributions can be unimodal or bimodal or have no mode if all values of the variable occur equally often. The only measure of central tendency appropriate for nominal data.

Formula: Often determined by inspection without calculation.

E4–5

Category: Descriptive, Variability or Dispersion

Statistic: Range

Description: The difference between the highest and lowest values of a variable.

Application: Used as a rough estimate of variability with small samples.

Data: Used with ordinal-, interval-, or ratio-level data.

Limitations: The range is sensitive to extreme values in the distribution, generally unstable, and influenced by sample size.

Comments: Useful as a rough, first estimate of variability; more useful with small samples than with large samples.

Formula:

Range = (Largest Value − Smallest Value) + 1

E4–6

Category: Descriptive, Variability or Dispersion

Statistic: Mean Deviation

Description: The average of the absolute values of the deviations from the mean.

Application: An estimate of the average deviation around the mean.

Data: Can be used with data that are interval- or ratio-level.

Limitations: Not easily manipulated algebraically; affected by extreme scores.

Comments: Used frequently when teaching the concept of variability but rarely used in statistical practice.

Formula:

$$\text{Mean Deviation} = \frac{\sum_{i=i}^{n} |X_i - \overline{X}|}{n}$$

E4 –7

Category: Descriptive, Variability or Dispersion

Statistic: Variance

Description: The average of the squared deviations from the mean.

Applications: Used as a common index of variability in a wide range of situations, it is the basic element in a general set of procedures known as analysis of variance (ANOVA) **(E4–70)**.

Data: Used with interval or ratio data.

Limitation: Not in the metric or scale of the original data since all deviations from the mean have been squared. Sensitive to extreme values.

Comments: Dividing the sum of squared deviations by n yields a biased estimate of the population variance (systematically smaller than the true population variance); dividing the sum of squared deviations by $(n-1)$ yields an unbiased estimate of the population variance.

Formula:

$$S^2 = \frac{\sum_{i=1}^{n}(X_i - \overline{X})^2}{n-1}$$

E4 –8

Category: Descriptive, Variability or Dispersion

Statistic: Standard Deviation

Description: The square root of the variance.

Application: Used as a standard index of variability.

Data: Used with interval- or ratio-level data.

Limitations: Sensitive to extreme cases but otherwise broadly useful in describing the typical level of dispersion.

Comments: One of the most common measures of variability; preserves the original scale by taking the square root of the sum of squared deviations. Provides a standard unit or scale for interpreting departures from the mean.

Formula:

$$S = \sqrt{S^2} = \sqrt{\frac{\sum_{i=1}^{n}(X_i - \overline{X})^2}{n-1}}$$

E4–9

Category: Descriptive, Measure of Disarray

Statistic: Sum of D-squared

Description: The sum of the squared differences in the rankings of subjects on two variables.

Application: Used as an index of differences in rank orderings; roughly analogous to the variance for interval or ratio data.

Data: Used when both variables are ordinal-level.

Limitations: Is difficult to interpret.

Comments: Has a minimum value of 0; a maximum of $(N(N^2-1))/3$; a random value of $(N(N^2-1))/6$.

Formula:

$$\sum d^2 = \sum_{i=1}^{n} (\text{Rank}_i \text{ (variable 1)} - \text{Rank}_i \text{ (variable 2)})^2$$

E4–10

Category: Descriptive, Measure of Disarray

Statistic: S

Description: The sum of the weights +1 and -1 assigned for each of $(N(N-1))/2$ ordered pairs for rankings on some variable, assigning +1 for a pair in natural order and -1 for a pair in reverse order.

Application: Used as an index of disarray in rank orderings; roughly analogous to the variance for interval- or ratio-level data.

Data: Ordinal

Limitations: Difficult to interpret

Comments: Has a minimum value of $-(N(N-1))/2$; a maximum value of $+(N(N-1))/2$; and a random value of 0.

Formula:

$$S = \sum_{i=1}^{(N(N-1))/2} \text{Weight}_i, \text{ (for all pairs of values on variable Y)}$$

weight $= +1$, if the pair of values is in natural order
weight $= -1$, if the pair of values is in reverse order

E4–11

Category: Descriptive, Shapes of Distributions

Statistic: Raw and Proportional Frequencies and Cumulative Frequencies

Description: A basic descriptive device for displaying the distribution of some variable in table form. The table lists the frequency with which each value of the variable occurs in terms of raw and proportional frequency and also commonly lists the raw and proportional cumulative frequency. Values of the variable are often grouped into class intervals.

Application: The frequency distribution is the most basic form of descriptive information. The mode and median generally can be read directly or easily estimated from the frequency table. The basic shape of the distribution also can be seen or approximated from the frequency table.

Data: The categories or class intervals used for the frequency distribution are discrete and may represent single values or intervals containing a range of values for the variable in question.

Limitations: With certain samples, the choice of class intervals can influence the general "picture" presented by the frequency distribution. Other descriptive measures should be used along with the examination of the frequency distribution.

Comments: The researcher interested in getting a basic description of a set of data should always examine the frequency distribution along with corresponding visual representations, such as the histogram, frequency polygon, and cumulative frequency polygon. The frequency distribution provides a general picture of the distribution's skew (**E4–12**) and kurtosis (**E4–13**).

Formula: The following table shows a standard presentation of a frequency distribution for 200 subjects on a variable that ranges from 1 to 70, grouped into class intervals of size 5.

Table E.4.1
SAMPLE FREQUENCY DISTRIBUTION

Class Interval	Raw Frequency	Raw Proportional Frequency	Proportional Cumulative Frequency	Cumulative Frequency
66 – 70	11	.055	200	1.000
61 – 65	16	.080	189	.945
56 – 60	19	.095	173	.865
51 – 55	29	.145	154	.770
46 – 50	26	.130	125	.625
41 – 45	27	.135	99	.495
36 – 40	22	.110	72	.360
31 – 35	18	.090	50	.250
26 – 30	11	.055	32	.160
21 – 25	9	.045	21	.105
16 – 20	7	.035	12	.060
11 – 15	4	.020	5	.025
6 – 10	1	.005	1	.005
1 – 5	0	.000	0	.000

E4–12

Category: Descriptive, Shape of Distribution

Statistic: Skewness

Description: An index of a distribution's asymmetry about the mean. The skewness is reflected in the average value of the cubed deviations from the mean, also known as the third moment about the mean. This index of skewness is generally standardized to be independent of the variable's scale.

Application: Commonly used to indicate whether or not the distribution of some variable is normal. In a normal distribution, the skew is 0.

Data: Used when the data are interval or ratio.

Limitations: Can be an artifact of the scale being used, especially if the scale has a limited range.

Comments: Very important in the application of inferential procedures that assume that the dependent variable is normally distributed.

Formula:

$$\text{Skewness} = g_1 = \frac{m_3}{m_2 \sqrt{m_2}}$$

where

$$m_3 = \frac{\sum_{i=1}^{n}(X_i - \overline{X})^3}{n}$$

$$m_2 = \frac{\sum_{i=1}^{n}(X_i - \overline{X})^2}{n}$$

E4–13

Category: Descriptive, Shape of Distribution

Statistic: Kurtosis

Description: An index of nonnormality in a distribution. Kurtosis indicates whether the distribution is nonnormally flat or peaked. The kurtosis is the average of the deviations from the mean raised to the fourth power and standardized.

Application: Used as an indication of normality in a distribution.

Data: Used with interval or ratio data.

Limitations: Can be an artifact of the scale being used, especially if the scale has a limited range.

Comments: A useful descriptive statistic, especially in the application of inferential procedures that assume that the dependent variable is normally distributed.

Formula:

$$\text{Kurtosis} = g_2 = \frac{m_4}{m_2^2} - 3$$

where

$$m_4 = \frac{\sum\limits_{i=1}^{n}(X_i - \overline{X})^4}{n} \quad \text{and} \quad m_2 = \frac{\sum\limits_{i=1}^{n}(X_i - \overline{X})^2}{n}$$

E4–14
MEASURES OF RELATIONSHIPS
    (E4–15) Covariance
    (E4–16) Pearson Product-Moment Correlation
    (E4–17) Spearman's Rank Order Correlation, Rho
    (E4–18) Kendall's Tau
    (E4–19) Point Biserial Correlation
    (E4–20) Biserial Correlation
    (E4–21) Phi-Coefficient
    (E4–22) Tetrachoric Correlation
    (E4–23) Contingency Coefficient
    (E4–24) Kendall's Coefficient of Concordance
    (E4–25) Intraclass Correlation
    (E4–26) Part Correlation
    (E4–27) Partial Correlation
    (E4–28) Multiple Correlation
    (E4–29) Eta-Squared
    (E4–30) Factor Analysis

E4–15
Category: Measures of Relationship
Statistic: Covariance
Description: A statistic that reflects the degree to which two variables are related. The covariance is the average product of deviation scores for two variables.
Application: Used as a general index of relationship between two variables and in the calculation of many other statistics.
Data: Interval or ratio.
Limitations: The covariance is calculated and reported in the unstandardized scale of the original variables. Hence, comparisons among the covariances for different pairs of variables are difficult.
Comments: Not a commonly reported statistic. The covariance is standardized by dividing by the product of the standard deviations of the two variables involved. The standardized covariance is the Pearson product-moment correlation coefficient.
    The covariance **(E4–15)**, the statistical measure of the relationship between two variables, is often confused with the analysis of covariance **(E4–89)**, a statistical procedure for testing hypotheses about differences between group means.
Formula:

$$S_{xy} = \frac{\sum\limits_{i=1}^{n}(X_i - \overline{X})(Y_i - \overline{Y})}{n-1}$$

E4–16

Category: Measures of Relationship

Statistic: Pearson Product-Moment Correlation Coefficient

Description: The average product of the deviation scores for two variables, divided by the product of their standard deviations. This is the same as the average product of the standardized (Z) scores for two variables.

Application: An informative and very commonly used measure of the relationship between two variables. Perhaps the best-known measure of relationship. Generally, the statistic referred to when the phrase "the correlation" is used.

Data: Interval or ratio.

Limitations: Reflects only linear relationships. Assumes both variables are normally distributed.

Comments: Generally described as ranging from -1 to $+1$. Can approximate these minimum and maximum values only when the assumption is true that both variables are normally distributed.

Formula:

$$r_{xy} = \frac{\sum_{i=1}^{n}(X_i - \overline{X})(Y_i - \overline{Y})}{(n-1)S_x S_y}$$

E4–17

Category: Measures of Relationship

Statistic: Spearman's Rank Order Correlation, Rho

Description: A special case of the Pearson product-moment correlation in which both variables are rankings on an ordinal scale.

Application: Commonly used as a measure of relationship when subjects are ranked on two variables.

Data: Both variables ordinal rankings.

Limitations: Some loss of information because ordinal-level data, as opposed to interval or ratio data, are used.

Comments: Equivalent to the Pearson product-moment correlation except that the data are ranks. Tied ranks are assigned the average rank for the rank order position in which they fall.

Formula:

$$\rho = 1 - \frac{6\sum_{i=1}^{n}d_i^2}{n(n^2 - 1)}$$

where $\sum d_i^2$ is the sum of the squared differences in rank (**E4–9**)

E4–18

Category: Measures of Relationship

Statistic: Kendall's Tau

Description: A measure of relationship for two variables ranked on ordinal-level scales; tau is the measure of disarray, S, divided by the maximum value that S can take (**E4–10**).

Application: An alternative to Spearman's Rho.

Data: Both variables ordinal.

Limitations: Some information is lost because ordinal scales are used.

Comments: Tau is an ordering statistic and does not have the same meaning as product-moment correlations. Tied ranks are assigned the average rank order position into which they fall.

Formula:

$$\tau = \frac{S}{\left\{ n(n-1) \right\}/2}$$

where S, a measure of disarray, is defined as in **E4–10**, n = number of Ss

E4–19

Category: Measures of Relationship

Statistic: Point Biserial Correlation

Description: A special case of the Pearson product-moment correlation in which one variable is measured on an interval or ratio scale and the other variable is nominal and dichotomous with no underlying continuous normal distribution.

Application: Used to examine relationships between discrete dichotomous variables and continuous variables.

Data: One variable interval or ratio, the other variable nominal, discrete dichotomous.

Limitations: The direction of the correlation (+ or −) is arbitrary depending on how the values of the dichotomous variable are assigned.

Comments: Commonly used in measurement applications to correlate scored item responses (0 or 1) with total test score as an index of item discrimination.

Formula:

$$r_{pb} = \frac{\overline{X}_{\cdot 1} - \overline{X}_{\cdot 0}}{S_x} \sqrt{\frac{n_1 \, n_0}{n(n-1)}}$$

where

$\overline{X}_{\cdot 1}$ = mean score on X of Ss scoring 1 on variable Y

$\overline{X}_{\cdot 0}$ = mean score on X of Ss scoring 0 on variable Y

S_x = standard deviation of X for all Ss

n_1 = number of Ss scoring 1 on Y

n_0 = number of Ss scoring 0 on Y

n = total number of Ss

.

E4–20

Category: Measures of Relationship

Statistic: Biserial Correlation

Description: A special case of the Pearson product-moment correlation in which one variable is measured on a continuous interval or ratio scale, and the other variable is nominal and dichotomous. The dichotomous variable has an underlying continuous normal distribution, unlike the somewhat similar point biserial **(E4–19)**.

Application: Used as a measure of relationship between a continuous variable and a dichotomous variable, when the dichotomous variable has an underlying continuous normal distribution. For example, students' SAT scores, a continuous variable, can be dichotomized into "above average" and "below average." The biserial correlation could be used to correlate SAT scores, in this dichotomous form, with students' grade point average.

Data: One variable is interval or ratio, and the other variable is dichotomous with an underlying continuous normal distribution.

Limitations: Information is lost by representing a continuous normal variable as a dichotomous variable.

Comments: The biserial correlation is informative and useful when data from a dichotomous variable, with an underlying normal distribution, are readily available or are easy and inexpensive to collect.

Formula:

$$r_{bis} = \left(\frac{\overline{X}_{\cdot 1} - \overline{X}_{\cdot 0}}{S_x} \right) \bullet \frac{n_1 \; n_0}{Un\sqrt{n_2 - n}}$$

where

$\overline{X}_{\cdot 1}$ = mean score on X of Ss scoring 1 on variable Y

$\overline{X}_{\cdot 0}$ = mean score on X of Ss scoring 0 on variable Y

S_x = standard deviation of X for all Ss

n_1 = number of Ss scoring 1 on Y

n_0 = number of Ss scoring 0 on Y

n = total number of Ss

U = ordinate of the Z distribution, unit normal distribution, at the point above which is located $(n_1/n) \times 100$ percent of the area under the curve

E4–21

Category: Measures of Relationship

Statistic: Phi-Coefficient

Description: A measure of relationship between two variables used when both variables are discrete dichotomous variables. A special case of the Pearson product-moment correlation. The Phi-coefficient is calculated from a 2×2 contingency table with the following form:

Variable 2

	0	1	
1	A	B	A+B
0	C	D	C+D
	A+C	B+D	N=A+B+C+D

Variable 1 (label for rows)

Application: Used to measure the relationship between two nominal dichotomous variables.
Data: Both variables are measured on discrete dichotomous scales.
Limitations: Ranges between +1 and −1 only when the proportional marginals all equal .5. That is,

$$\frac{A + B}{N} = \frac{C + D}{N} = \frac{A + C}{N} = \frac{B + D}{N} = .5$$

Comments: The direction of the correlation, either + or −, is arbitrary and must be interpreted carefully inspecting the arrangement of the contingency table. The phi-coefficient can be converted into a 1-degree of freedom chi-square by multiplying the squared phi-coefficient by N.
Formula:

$$\phi = \frac{BC - AD}{\sqrt{(A + C)(B + D)(C + D)(A + B)}}$$

E4–22
Category: Measures of Relationship
Statistic: Tetrachoric Correlation Coefficient
Description: A measure of relationship between two variables used when both variables are dichotomous but have an underlying continuous normal distribution.
Application: Used as a measure of relationship between two variables that are thought to have continuous and normal distributions but are measured on dichotomous scales. This is a commonly used statistic in studying the relationship between two test items. In such a situation, the data are configured as follows:

Item 2

	0	1	
1	A	B	A+B
0	C	D	C+D
	A+C	B+D	N=A+B+C+D

Item 1 (label for rows)

Data: Both variables have underlying continuous normal distributions but are operationalized on dichotomous scales.

Limitations: Information is lost when continuous normal variables are dichotomized.

Comments: The tetrachoric correlation coefficient was often used to facilitate computation of inter-item correlations before the widespread availability of computing devices. It is used when continuous data are difficult or expensive to collect on the variables of interest.

Formula:

$$r_{tet} = cosine \frac{180°}{1 + \sqrt{BC/AD}}$$

where A, B, C, and D are defined as in the application section above. Many statistics books have tables for the value of the tetrachoric correlation as a function of BC/AD.

E4–23

Category: Measures of Relationship

Statistic: Contingency Coefficient, C

Description: A measure of relationship when both variables are measured on scales that are discrete and nominal but not dichotomous.

Application: Used as an index of correlation for nominal variables that have two or more categories.

Data: Both variables are discrete and nominal and have two or more categories.

Limitations: Does not range between -1 and $+1$. The direction of the correlation coefficient is arbitrary and must be determined from the contingency table. Contingency coefficients are comparable only for tables with the same numbers of rows and columns.

Comments: The maximum value of C is estimated by the square root of $((k-1)/k))$ where k is the number of categories in the variable with the fewest categories.

Formula:

$$C = \sqrt{\frac{\chi^2}{N + \chi^2}}$$

where χ^2 is the chi-square for the contingency table for the two discrete variables

E4–24

Category: Measures of Relationship

Statistic: Kendall's Coefficient of Concordance W

Description: A measure of relationship or agreement among multiple rankings of a set of subjects on some criterion. Generally involves three or more rankings.

Application: Used as an index of similarity for multiple rankings of the same elements. Commonly used as an index of agreement among raters who are ranking several subjects or objects.

Data: Elements are arranged on an ordinal scale.

Limitations: Not directly comparable to correlation coefficients.

Comments: W = 0 when maximum disagreement among raters occurs, and W = 1 when maximum agreement occurs.

Formula:

$$W = \frac{12S}{m^2(n^3 - n)}$$

where

$$S = \sum_{j=1}^{n}\left(R_j - \frac{R_j}{n}\right)^2$$

R_j = sum of the ranks assigned to the jth person
m = number of judges
n = number of Ss being ranked

E4 –25

Category: Measures of Relationship

Statistic: Intraclass Correlation

Description: The correlation between two interval- or ratio-level variables for subjects in different groups. The intraclass correlation is generally viewed from an analysis of variance perspective (**E4–71**). It is the correlation between two variables for subjects within groups, for all groups of subjects.

Application: Often used in studies of twins. Used for correlating variables within classrooms with different teachers and with nested designs (**E3–17**).

Data: Used with interval or ratio scales.

Limitations: Can be difficult to interpret and explain. Computationally more complex than typical correlation coefficients.

Comments: Generally conceptualized and calculated within an analysis of variance framework or component analysis framework. The intraclass correlation is basically the within-group correlation removing between-group variation.

Formula:

$$r_I = \frac{MSB - MSW}{MSB + (n-1)MSW}$$

where

MSB = mean square between groups
MSW = mean square within groups
n = number of Ss in groups

E4–26

Category: Measures of Relationship

Statistic: Part Correlation

Description: The correlation between two variables when the effect of some third variable has been removed from one of the two variables being correlated. This differs from the partial correlation (**E4–27**), which is the correlation between two variables with the effect of some third variable removed from both variables being correlated.

Application: Used to examine the influence of some variable on the correlation between two other variables and to examine correlations removing the influence of a confounding variable.

Data: Used with interval or ratio scales.

Limitations: May result in a correlation based on a statistically created condition that does not have practical meaning.

Comments: Usually conceptualized in the context of regression analysis as the correlation between two variables, where one is the residual from the regression in which the control variable is the independent variable.

Formula:

$$r_{x(y \bullet z)} = \frac{r_{xy} - r_{xz} r_{yz}}{\sqrt{1 - r_{yz}^2}}$$

E4–27

Category: Measures of Relationship

Statistic: Partial Correlation

Description: The correlation between two variables removing from both the influence of a third variable. This differs from the part correlation (**E4–26**), which is the correlation between two variables when the effect of some third variable has been removed from one of the two variables being correlated.

Application: Used to examine the influence of some variable on the correlation between two other variables and to examine correlations removing the influence of a confounding variable.

Data: Used with interval or ratio scales.

Limitations: May result in a correlation based on a statistically created condition that does not have any practical or real-life meaning.

Comments: Usually conceptualized in the context of regression analysis as the correlation between two variables, both of which are residuals from separate regressions in which the control variable is the independent variable.

Formula:

$$r_{(xy) \bullet z} = \frac{r_{xy} - r_{xz} r_{yz}}{\sqrt{\left(1 - r_{xz}^2\right)\left(1 - r_{yz}^2\right)}}$$

E4–28

Category: Measures of Relationship

Statistic: Multiple Correlation, R

Description: The Pearson product-moment correlation between a criterion variable and its predicted value from a regression equation.

Application: Used as an index of how well the criterion variable is predicted.

Data: Used with interval or ratio scales.

Limitations: The multiple correlation is limited by the extent to which the variables in the regression equation meet the assumptions for regression analysis.

Comments: The multiple correlation is particularly useful when it is squared. R-squared is the ratio of the variance in the predicted values over the total variance. (See R-squared, **E4–37**.)

Formula:

$$R = r_{y \cdot \hat{y}} \quad \text{or}$$

$$R = \frac{\text{Sum of Squares Regression}}{\text{Sum of Squares Total}} = \frac{\text{SS Reg}}{\text{SS Tot}}$$

E4–29

Category: Measures of Relationship

Statistic: Eta-squared (Correlation Ratio)

Description: An index of relationship that does not assume a linear relationship. Eta-squared varies between 0 and 1 and reflects relationships that may be curvilinear. Eta-squared is also known as the correlation ratio. Eta-squared is comparable to R-squared (**E4–37**), not simply to the correlation between two variables.

Application: Used when an examination of a scatterplot, previous research, or theoretical considerations suggest a nonlinear relationship.

Data: The Y variable is interval or ratio. The X variable can be any level, but eta-squared is more interpretable if X is at least ordinal.

Limitations: Is not symmetric like other correlations; for example, eta-squared (x,y) may not equal eta-squared (y,x).

Comments: Very useful in describing many situations in which linear correlations indicate no relationship. It is essential to examine the scatterplot when interpreting eta-squared.

Formula:

$$\eta^2_{yx} = 1 - \frac{\text{Sum of Squares Within}}{\text{Sum of Squares Total}}$$

where Ss are grouped on X values

E4–30

Category: Measures of Relationship

Statistical Procedure: Factor Analysis

Description: A large category of analytic procedures used to identify relationships among subsets of variables. In general, factor analysis is used to identify underlying traits or constructs called "factors" to which observed measures are related. Observed measures that are highly correlated to each other tend to be related to the same underlying factor. The correlations of the observed measures to the underlying factors are called factor loadings. The factors form a simplified structure within which the original measures can be plotted using a variety of procedures.

Applications: Factor analysis is used in a wide range of applications. In general, factor analysis is used to reduce the data from a large set of measures to a smaller set of factors that retain all the basic information from the measures but do not reflect redundancies found in the original measures. Factor analysis can be used as an exploratory procedure to provide initial identification of factors and to identify commonalities among a set of measures. Factor analysis can also be used as a confirmatory procedure to verify theoretically or empirically derived constructs.

Data: Factor analysis is applied to the intercorrelations of the observed measures.

Limitations: The details of factor analysis are difficult to explain and computationally complex. The results of factor analysis procedures must be interpreted with special care and expertise. Technical expertise alone is not sufficient for providing appropriate interpretation of factor analyses.

Comments: The technical details of factor analysis are beyond the scope of this publication. The researcher interested in more details should examine Mulaik (1972), Kim and Mueller (1978), Cureton and D'Agostino (1993), and Rencher (1995).

As suggested earlier, exceptional care should be used in interpreting the results of factor analyses. Expertise with the variables, the constructs they measure, and the conceptual context within which the measures are made is necessary.

E4–31
REGRESSION ANALYSIS

- **(E4–32)** Simple Linear Regression
- **(E4–33)** Regression Coefficient
- **(E4–34)** Y-Intercept
- **(E4–35)** Standard Error of Estimate
- **(E4–36)** Multiple Regression
- **(E4–37)** R-squared
- **(E4–38)** Curvilinear Regression
- **(E4–39)** Stepwise Regression

E4–32
Category: Regression Analysis

Statistic: Simple Linear Regression

Description: A procedure for predicting some variable Y from variable X by using a linear weighting of X added to a constant. The weighting is the regression coefficient, and the constant is the intercept.

Application: Commonly used to make predictions; to identify the proportion of one variable accounted for by knowledge of another; to estimate residual values on Y having removed the effects of X.

Data: Used with interval or ratio scales.

Limitations: Addresses only linear relationships. Uses only one predictor; therefore, it is not sensitive to more complex relationships. Assumes Y and X are normally distributed.

Comments: Despite some limitations, a very useful procedure for understanding the strength of the relationship.

Formula:

$$\hat{Y} = b_1 X + b_0$$

where

$\hat{Y}$ = the predicted value of Y

b_1 = the regression coefficient (**E4–33**)

X = the independent variable

b_0 = the Y-intercept (**E4–34**)

E4–33

Category: Regression Analysis

Statistic: Regression Coefficient

Description: The regression coefficient is the amount of change in the dependent variable Y that occurs when the independent variable X changes by 1 scale unit. In simple linear regression, the regression coefficient is the slope of the "best-fitting" line defined by the criterion of least squared error.

Application: The regression coefficient is the rate of change in Y as a function of X and is central to all regression analyses.

Data: Regression analysis assumes that both the Y and X variables are interval or ratio. The regression coefficient, a multiplier of X, is ratio in nature (e.g., a regression coefficient of 4 is twice the size of a regression coefficient of 2).

Limitations: Regression coefficients from different analyses cannot be compared directly because they are scale specific.

Comments: The regression coefficient is the product of the ratio of the standard deviations of Y to X multiplied by the correlation between Y and X. When the standard deviations are equal, the regression coefficient and correlation coefficient are equal. The magnitude of the regression coefficient is directly proportional to the correlation coefficient.

Formula:

b_{yx} = the regression coefficient for predicting Y

$$b_{yx} = \frac{\sum_{i=1}^{n}(X_i - \overline{X})(Y_i - \overline{Y})}{\sum(X_i - \overline{X})^2}$$

also,

$$b_{yx} = \frac{S_y}{S_x} \bullet r_{xy}$$

E4–34

Category: Regression Analysis

Statistic: Y-Intercept

Description: In a regression analysis, the Y-intercept is the value of predicted dependent variable, Y, when the independent predictor variable, X, is zero. Geometrically, the intercept is the place on the Y-axis that is crossed by the regression line.

Application: The Y-intercept is an integral part of any regression analysis since it defines the location or origin (X = 0) needed as the starting point for predicting Y.

Data: The Y-intercept is calculated and reported on the same scale as the Y variable.

Limitations: The Y-intercept is not very useful without the regression coefficient.

Formula:

$$b_0 = \overline{Y} - b_{yx} \overline{X}$$

E4–35

Category: Regression Analysis

Statistic: Standard Error of Estimate (SE)

Description: The standard error of estimate is the standard deviation of the residual difference between the observed and predicted values of the dependent variable in a regression analysis. This standard deviation of the residuals is the mean square due to error in the analysis of variance for the regression.

Application: The standard error of estimate is used to place confidence intervals of some desired range around predicted scores. For example, a predicted value plus and minus 1.96 × (SE) yields a 95% confidence interval.

Data: The standard error of estimate is reported in the scale of the predicted variable.

Limitations: Common practice generally involves reporting a single standard error for all possible predicted values. This practice ignores the fact that predicted values in the center of a distribution are known with more precision than values at the tails of a distribution.

Comments: The standard error of the estimate is very helpful in making decisions based on predicted values of some variable. Confidence intervals of any desired range can be established to control the likelihood of making false positive or false negative decisions based on the predicted values.

Formula:

$$S_e = \sqrt{\frac{\sum_{i=1}^{n}\left(e_i - \overline{e}\right)^2}{n-1}} = \sqrt{\frac{\sum_{i=1}^{n} e_i^2}{n-1}}$$

or

$$S_e = S_y \sqrt{1 - r_{xy}^2}$$

where e_i is the residual for person i.

E4–36

Category: Regression Analysis

Statistic: Multiple Regression

Description: A procedure for predicting some dependent variable Y from a set of n independent variables, $\{X_1 X_2 X_3 \ldots X_n\}$, by using a weight on each X_i and a constant. The weights are regression coefficients, and the constant is the intercept. Multiple regression is sometimes used to test theoretical constructs about relationships among variables.

Application: A powerful technique commonly used (1) to make predictions from several independent variables, (2) to identify the proportion of variance in one variable accounted for by knowledge of a set of other variables, and (3) to control the influence of confounding variables. Multiple regression is sometimes used to test theoretical constructs about relationships among variables.

Data: The dependent and independent variables are interval or ratio.

Limitations: The dependent and independent variables involved are assumed to be normally distributed.

Multiple regression lends itself to "blind" empiricism in which some measures that happen to be available are used as independent variables to predict a dependent measure without any conceptual framework to suggest a rationale for such prediction. Multiple regression used in this fashion should be considered exploratory and descriptive.

Comments: The independent variables in a multiple regression analysis can be included in the regression equation (1) one at a time in a series of steps **(E4–39)**, (2) grouped into subsets of variables and included in a series of steps, or (3) all together at one time. Polynomial terms as well as the linear term for the independent variables can be used to perform curvilinear regression.

Formula: Multiple regression equations are of the form:

$$\hat{Y} = b_1 X_1 + b_2 X_2 + \ldots + b_i X_i + \ldots + b_n X_n + b_0, \text{ where}$$

$\hat{Y}$ = the predicted dependent variable

$b_1 b_2 \ldots b_i \ldots b_n$ = the regression coefficients for the respective independent variables

$X_1 X_2 \ldots X_i \ldots X_n$ = the independent variables

b_0 = the Y-intercept

E4–37

Category: Regression Analysis

Statistic: R-squared (R^2)

Description: R-squared is a statistic used in regression analysis that provides an index of how well the independent variable(s) is predicting the dependent measure. R-square is the proportion of the variation in the dependent measure that is accounted for by the prediction made from the independent variable(s). In regression analysis, R-squared is the sum of squares due to regression divided by the sum of squares total. R-squared is equal to the square of the correlation or multiple correlation between the dependent and independent variable(s).

Application: R-squared is a commonly used index of how well the dependent measure is predicted by the independent measure(s). Changes in R-squared are studied to determine if a variable added to a regression equation actually improves the predictive power of the regression equation.

Limitations: R-squared is a useful descriptive index that must not be interpreted as suggesting a causal explanation between the dependent and independent variable(s), even though R-squared is described as the proportion of variation in the dependent variable accounted for by the independent variables.

Comments: R-squared is a very useful index of the power of a regression equation and of each independent variable's contribution to the equation in terms of increased R-squared.

Formula: R-squared can be calculated in two ways:

1. $$R^2 = r^2_{xy}$$

2. $$R^2 = \frac{\text{Sum of Squares Regression}}{\text{Total Sum of Squares}}$$

E4–38

Category: Regression Analysis

Statistic: Curvilinear Regression

Description: A particular type of multiple regression in which the independent variables include the linear and polynomial representations of the predictor variables. The dependent variable Y is predicted from a set of n independent variables, $\{X_1 X_2 X_i ... X_n\}$, where these can be the original independent variables and the independent variables squared, cubed, raised to the fourth power, etc. Other nonlinear transformations of the independent variables may be employed, for example, logs and trigonometric functions.

Application: This is a special application of multiple regression when the relationship between the dependent and independent variables is not linear. Curvilinear regression is commonly used when the relationship between the dependent variable and independent variable(s) is one of "diminishing returns." In such situations, increases in Y are associated with increases in X, up to a certain value of X. After the particular value of X has been reached, further increases in X are associated with a decrease in the values of Y. For example, agricultural yields, in terms of bushels per acre, have a simple curvilinear relationship with rainfall.

Curvilinear regression is sometimes used to test theoretical constructs about relationships among variables.

Data: The dependent and independent variables are interval or ratio.

Limitations: The variables involved are assumed to be normally distributed in their linear form.

Comments: Curvilinear regression is helpful in exploring a wide range of dependent-independent variable relationships in which the values of the dependent variable, Y, increase or decrease as the values of the independent variable, X, increase up to a point on the X scale; after that point has been reached, the direction of the relationship reverses.

Formula: Curvilinear regression equations are of the form:

$$\hat{Y} = b_1 X_1 + b_2 X_1^2 + b_3 X_1^3 + \dots + b_3 X_j^k + b_n X_n^L + b_0,$$

where

$\hat{Y}$ = the predicted dependent variable

$b_1 b_2 b_3 \dots b_i \dots b_n$ = the regression coefficients for the respective independent variables

$X_1 \ X_1^2 \ X_1^3 \dots X_j^k \dots X_n^L$ = the independent variables in linear and various polynomial forms

b_0 = the Y-intercept

E4–39

Category: Regression Analysis

Statistic: Stepwise Multiple Regression

Description: A procedure in multiple regression in which the independent variables are entered into the regression equation one at a time to build a regression equation in steps. As each independent variable is added to the equation, the new equation is evaluated by comparing it to the equation in the previous step in terms of how well the two equations account for variation in the dependent variable.

Application: A powerful technique commonly used to make predictions from several independent variables in a way that examines the power of the different independent variables to predict the dependent measure. Stepwise regression is often used to study theoretical constructs about relationships among variables. Independent variables that provide redundant information about the dependent measure are easily detected and eliminated by using stepwise regression.

Data: The dependent and independent variables are interval or ratio.

Limitations: The variables involved are assumed to be normally distributed.

Comments: A variety of criteria may be used for building equations in a stepwise regression analysis. The common stepwise procedure involves starting with the independent variable that has the highest correlation with the dependent measure and then building up the equation one independent variable at a time. The independent variable added at each step is the one that has the highest correlation with the residuals in the previous step.

Formula: Stepwise multiple regression equations are of the form:

$$\hat{Y} = b_1 X_1 + b_2 X_2 + \dots + b_i X_i + \dots + b_n X_n + b_0,$$

where

$\hat{Y}$ = the predicted variable

$b_1 \ b_2 \dots b_i \dots b_n$ = the regression coefficients for the respective independent variables

$X_1 X_2 \dots X_i \dots X_n$ = the independent variables

b_0 = the Y-intercept

E4–40

COMPARISONS: ONE SAMPLE

      (E4–41) Sample Mean Compared to Some Value

      (E4–42) Sample Variance Compared to Some Value

      (E4–43) Sample Proportion Compared to Some Value

      (E4–44) Sample Correlation Compared to 0

      (E4–45) Sample Correlation Compared to Some Value

      (E4–46) Chi-Square Test for Goodness of Fit

      (E4–47) Kolmogorov-Smirnov One-Sample Test

E4–41

Category: Comparison: One Sample

Statistic: Sample Mean Compared to Some Value, t-test and z-test

Description: A t-statistic or z-statistic is used to determine whether a sample mean differs from some hypothesized value by an amount that exceeds a specified significance level.

Application: Commonly used to test whether some sample mean differs significantly from the population mean on some variable.

Data: Used with interval or ratio scales.

Limitations: Assumes that the sample has been randomly selected and that the dependent variable is normally distributed.

Comments: The t-statistic is used if the population variance must be estimated from the sample variance. The z-statistic is used if the population variance is known.

Formula:

$$t = \frac{\overline{X} - \mu}{s / \sqrt{n}}, \quad (n-1) \text{ df.}$$

$$z = \frac{\overline{X} - \mu}{\sigma_{\overline{x}}}, \quad \sigma_{\overline{x}} = \sigma / \sqrt{n}$$

E4–42

Category: Comparisons: One Sample

Statistic: Sample Variance Compared to Some Value, Chi-Square Test

Description: A chi-square statistic used to test whether a sample variance differs from some hypothesized value by an amount that exceeds some specified levels of significance.

Application: Used to determine whether a sample variance differs significantly from some expected or hypothesized value.

Data: Interval or ratio.

Limitations: Like all chi-square tests, this test is sensitive to sample size.

Comments: Helpful in educational settings to determine whether students are more or less homogeneous than some value of interest.

Formula:

$$\chi^2 = \frac{(n-1)S^2}{a}, \quad (n-1)\ df$$

where
S^2 = variance
a = hypothesized value

E4–43

Category: Comparisons: One Sample

Statistic: Sample Proportion Compared to Some Value, z-statistic

Description: A z-statistic used to determine whether a sample proportion differs from some hypothesized value by an amount that exceeds a specified level of significance.

Application: Often used to check if a sample differs significantly from the population on some demographic characteristic.

Data: Used with interval or ratio scales.

Limitations: Sensitive to sample size. This test may be overly powerful with very large samples.

Comments: Helpful in determining if the proportional representation of some group in a sample is equivalent to that group's proportional representation in the population.

Formula:

$$z = \frac{p - P}{\sqrt{\dfrac{P(1-P)}{n}}}$$

where
p = sample proportion
P = hypothesized value

E4–44

Category: Comparisons: One Sample

Statistic: Sample Correlation Compared to 0, t-statistic

Description: A t-statistic used to determine whether a sample correlation differs from 0 by an amount that exceeds a specified significance level.

Application: This test is used to answer the basic question involved in determining whether a correlation is statistically significant.

Data: Pearson correlation coefficient

Limitations: Direct calculation is rarely needed since critical values for correlations are found in tables in most statistics books.

Comments: It is important to note that testing the correlation coefficient against 0 is not always the relevant question.

Formula:

$$t = r \sqrt{\frac{(n-2)}{1-r^2}}, \quad (n-2) \text{ degrees of freedom}$$

E4–45

Category: Comparisons: One Sample

Statistic: Sample Correlation Compared to Some Value, z-statistic

Description: A z-statistic used to determine whether a sample correlation coefficient differs from some hypothesized value by an amount that exceeds a specified significance level. The test statistic is applied to the correlation coefficients after they have been transformed using Fisher's z-transformation.

Application: Often used to test whether a sample correlation differs significantly (1) from the correlation in the population or (2) from some value suggested by a review of the literature.

Data: Applies to Pearson product-moment correlation coefficient.

Limitations: This procedure is sensitive to sample size.

Comments: Based on Fisher's z-transformation. Fisher's z-transformation is:
z = 1/2{log (1+r)} − 1/2{log (1−r)}

Formula:

$$z = \frac{Z_r - Z_\rho}{\sqrt{\dfrac{1}{n-3}}}$$

where

z = the z-statistic, unit normal deviate

Z_r = the Fisher z-transformation of r

Z_ρ = the Fisher z-transformation of ρ, the hypothesized value

E4–46

Category: Comparisons: One Sample

Statistic: Chi-Square Test for Goodness of Fit

Description: A procedure used with one sample to describe whether the observed frequencies on some variable with C categories are statistically equivalent to the frequencies expected based on theoretical or empirical criteria.

Application: Often used to determine if the frequency distribution for a sample across levels of some variable of interest is statistically equivalent to known population values.

Data: Categories are discrete and defined on a nominal, ordinal, interval, or ratio variable.

Limitations: Like all chi-square tests, the goodness of fit application of the chi-square is sensitive to sample size. With small samples, the test is not very powerful, but with large samples the test can be overly powerful.

Comments: The chi-square goodness of fit test is very useful in describing the extent to which the frequency distribution of some sample on a nominal variable resembles population values.

Formula:

$$\chi^2 = \sum_{i=1}^{c} \frac{(O_i - E_i)^2}{E_i}$$

where
O = observed frequency
E = expected frequency
For C-categories, there are $(C-1)$ degrees of freedom.

E4–47

Category: Comparisons: One Sample

Statistic: Kolmogorov-Smirnov One-Sample Test Comparing Distributions

Description: The Kolmogorov-Smirnov one-sample test is used to determine whether the distribution of some variable for a given sample is statistically equivalent to some particular distribution of interest. Often the criterion distribution is a theoretical distribution such as the normal distribution. The statistical test is based on the largest difference between the proportional cumulative frequencies for the observed and criterion distributions evaluated across all points on the distributions. The sampling distribution of the maximum difference in proportional cumulative frequencies is known, and critical values at various significance levels can be found in nonparametric tables.

Application: The Kolmogorov-Smirnov one-sample test is a goodness of fit test (**E4–46**) used when a researcher wants to test the hypothesis that the distribution of some variable for a sample of interest follows some particular theoretical distribution. This test is often used to test whether a variable is distributed normally.

Data: Groups are classified on a discrete variable and measured on a continuous variable that may be ordinal but is typically interval or ratio.

Limitations: The Kolmogorov-Smirnov test is not a statistically powerful test.

Comments: The Kolmogorov-Smirnov test requires few assumptions, but at the same time it is not a statistically powerful test.

Formula:

$$D = \text{Maximum} \left| F_c(X) - F_s(X) \right|,$$

where
$F_c(X)$ = cumulative frequency distribution for the criterion group at each value of X
$F_s(X)$ = cumulative frequency distribution for the sample at each value of X

E4–48
COMPARISONS: TWO SAMPLES (PARAMETRIC)
> **(E4–49)** Comparing Two Sample Means, Independent Samples
> **(E4–50)** Comparing Two Sample Means, Dependent or Correlated Samples
> **(E4–51)** Comparing Two Sample Variances, Independent Samples
> **(E4–52)** Comparing Two Sample Variances, Dependent or Correlated Samples
> **(E4–53)** Comparing Two Sample Proportions, Independent Samples
> **(E4–54)** Comparing Two Sample Proportions, Dependent or Correlated Samples
> **(E4–55)** Comparing Two Sample Correlations, Independent Samples
> **(E4–56)** Comparing Two Sample Correlations, Dependent or Correlated Samples

E4–49
Category: Comparisons: Two Samples (Parametric)
Statistic: Comparison of Two Independent Sample Means, t-Test
Description: A t-statistic to determine if two sample means are significantly different from each other. More generally, a test of whether the difference between two means differs significantly from some value.
Application: Commonly used to determine if two sample means represent samples from the same population, that is, if the difference between the two sample means is not different from 0.
Data: Dependent variable is interval or ratio.
Limitations: Assumes that the variables are distributed normally in the population and that the variances for the two populations are equal.
Comments: Fairly robust with respect to the assumptions. Does not require equal sample sizes, but the sample sizes cannot be widely different because of the effect on the assumptions.
Formula:

For equal sample sizes:

$$t = \frac{\overline{X}_1 - \overline{X}_2}{\sqrt{\dfrac{S_1^2 + S_2^2}{n}}}$$

(2n−2) or
2(n−1) degrees of freedom

For unequal sample sizes:

$$t = \frac{\overline{X}_1 - \overline{X}_2}{\sqrt{\dfrac{(n_1 - 1)\,S_1^2 + (n_2 - 1)\,S_2^2 \left[\dfrac{1}{n_1} + \dfrac{1}{n_2}\right]}{n_1 + n_2 - 2}}}$$

with $n_1 + n_2 - 2$ degrees of freedom

E4–50
Category: Comparisons: Two Samples (Parametric)
Statistic: Comparison of Two Sample Means, Dependent or Correlated Samples, t-test
Description: A t-statistic used to determine if the means of two dependent or correlated samples are significantly different from each other. More generally, a test of whether the difference between the means of two dependent or correlated samples differs significantly from some value.
Application: Commonly used to determine if the means from two correlated samples are drawn from the same population. A standard procedure in one-group, pretest-posttest designs and in matching designs.
Data: Dependent variable is interval or ratio.
Limitations: Assumes that the variables are normally distributed in the population. Assumes that the variances of the two populations are equal (homogeneity of variance).
Comments: A more powerful statistical test than the independent sample t-test **(E4–49)** because it removes between-subject variance from the estimates of error variance.
Formula:

$$t = \frac{\overline{d}}{S_d / \sqrt{n}}, \quad (n-1) \text{ df}$$

$$\overline{d} = \frac{\sum_{i=1}^{n} (X_{1i} - X_{2i})}{n}$$

and

$$S_d = \sqrt{\frac{\sum_{i=1}^{n} (d_i - \overline{d})^2}{n-1}}$$

E4–51
Category: Comparisons: Two Samples (Parametric)
Statistic: Comparison of Two Independent Sample Variances, F-statistic
Description: An F-statistic used to determine if the variances from two independent samples are equivalent.
Application: Commonly used to test the assumption of homogeneity of variance.
Data: Variances from interval or ratio scales.
Limitations: Assumes normal distributions in the populations.
Comments: Can be used to test the effect of some independent variable on the variance of a dependent variable measured on an experimental group and a control group.
Formula:

$$F = \frac{S_1^2}{S_2^2}$$

with $(n_1 - 1)$ and $(n_2 - 1)$ degrees of freedom

E4–52

Category: Comparisons: Two Samples (Parametric)

Statistic: Comparison of Two Sample Variances—Dependent or Correlated Samples, t-statistic

Description: A t-statistic used to determine if the variances from two dependent or correlated samples are equivalent.

Application: Used to test whether the variance on a pretest is equivalent to the variance on the posttest.

Data: Variances from interval or ratio data and the correlation between the matched scores.

Limitations: The comparison of variances for two samples is confounded by any differences in the scale of the two variables.

Comments: Can be used to test the effect of some independent variable on the variance of the dependent measure in a pretest-posttest design.

Formula:

$$t = \frac{S_1^2 - S_2^2}{\sqrt{\dfrac{4S_1^2 S_2^2}{n-1}(1 - r_{12}^2)}}$$

with $(n-2)$ degrees of freedom

E4–53

Category: Comparisons: Two Samples (Parametric)

Statistic: Comparison of Two Independent Sample Proportions, z-statistic

Description: A z-statistic used to compare proportions from two independent samples.

Application: Used to determine if two samples are drawn from populations with similar proportions with respect to some variable. Commonly used to determine if two samples were proportionally equivalent with respect to some demographic variable.

Data: Used with proportions.

Limitations: The sample size (n) must be large enough so that two quantities (1) (n × proportion) and (2) [n × (1-proportion)] are greater than 5 for both groups.

Comments: If the requirements for sample size are not met, a chi-square test for independence **(E4–61)** must be used.

Formula:

$$Z = \frac{(p_1 - p_2)}{\sqrt{p(1-p)\left(\dfrac{1}{n_1} + \dfrac{1}{n_2}\right)}}$$

$$\text{where } p = \frac{(f_1 + f_2)}{(n_1 + n_2)}$$

366

$$f_1 = \text{frequency in sample 1}$$
$$f_2 = \text{frequency in sample 2}$$

E4–54

Category: Comparisons: Two Samples (Parametric)

Statistic: Comparison of Two Sample Proportions—Dependent or Correlated Samples, z-statistic

Description: A z-statistic used to compare proportions from two dependent or correlated samples. Calculated from a 2 × 2 contingency table with the form:

Posttest

		−	+	
Pretest	+	A	B	A+B
	−	C	D	C+D
		A+C	B+D	N=A+B+C+D

Application: Used to compare proportions before and after some treatment in a pretest-posttest design. In the contingency table shown, for example, subjects indicate whether they are positive (+) or negative (−) about some stimulus before (pretest) and after (posttest) some intervention program. Often used to compare preferences of one group to two stimuli.

Data: Proportions or frequencies in a 2 × 2 contingency table.

Limitations: In the 2 × 2 contingency table, the sum of the frequencies in the cells of both diagonals must be greater than 10. If the frequency limitation is not met, a chi-square test may be used.

Comments: When used in a pretest-posttest design, this test is the same as McNemar's test for change with dependent samples (**E4–63**).

Formula:

$$z = \frac{A - D}{\sqrt{A + D}}$$

A and D as shown in the description

E4–55

Category: Comparisons: Two Samples (Parametric)

Statistic: Comparison of Two Independent Sample Correlations, z-statistic

Description: A z-statistic used to determine if correlation coefficients from two independent samples are significantly different.

Application: Used to test whether the relationship between two variables is statistically equivalent for two different samples.

Data: Applies to Pearson correlation coefficients.

Limitations: The test can be overly powerful with large samples.

Comments: Based on the Fisher's z-transformation of correlation coefficients. Fisher's z-transformation is:

$$Z = \tfrac{1}{2}\{\log(1+r)\} - \tfrac{1}{2}\{\log(1-r)\}$$

Formula:

$$z = \frac{Z_{r1} - Z_{r2}}{\sqrt{\dfrac{1}{n_1 - 3} + \dfrac{1}{n_2 - 3}}}$$

where
Z_{r1} = Fisher Z transformation of r_1
Z_{r2} = Fisher Z transformation of r_2

E4–56

Category: Comparisons: Two Samples (Parametric)

Statistic: Comparison of Two Samples Correlation Coefficients, Correlated or Dependent Samples, t-statistic

Description: A t-statistic used to determine if correlations between pairs of variables from two dependent samples are significantly different.

Application: Often used to determine if pairs of correlations for different variables for the same sample are statistically equivalent.

Data: Used with Pearson product-moment correlation coefficients.

Limitations: Sensitive to sample size.

Comments: Commonly used in the case of three variables, X, Y, Z, to determine if the correlations of each of two variables with the third are equivalent, for example, if r_{xy} is equal to r_{xz}.

Formula:

$$t = \frac{(r_{xy} - r_{xz})\sqrt{(n-3)(1 - r_{yz})}}{\sqrt{2(1 - r_{xy}^2 - r_{xz}^2 - r_{yz}^2 + 2r_{xy}r_{xz}r_{yz})}}$$

with (n –3) degrees of freedom

E4–57

COMPARISONS: TWO SAMPLES (NONPARAMETRIC)
- **(E4–58)** Median Test, Sign Test for Independent Samples
- **(E4–59)** Wilcoxon Rank Sum Test, Rank Test for Independent Samples
- **(E4–60)** Mann-Whitney U-Test, Signed Rank Test for Independent Samples
- **(E4–61)** Chi-Square Test of Independence
- **(E4–62)** Kolmogorov-Smirnov Two-Sample Test Comparing Distributions
- **(E4–63)** McNemar's Test for Significance of Change, Dependent or Correlated Samples
- **(E4–64)** Sign Test for Dependent Samples
- **(E4–65)** Wilcoxon Matched Pairs Signed-Rank Test for Dependent Samples

E4–58

Category: Comparisons: Two Samples (Nonparametric)

Statistic: Median Test, Sign Test for Two Independent Samples, Chi-Square Statistic

Description: A test that compares the median for two independent samples of sizes n_1 and n_2, respectively. The median for the two samples combined is calculated, and then the number of subjects above and below the combined median is then determined within each of the two separate samples. A 2×2 chi-square table composed of samples $(1, 2)$ by position relative to the combined median (above, below) is constructed to test the hypothesis that there is no significant difference between the medians of the population from which the samples are drawn. The 2×2 table is:

Position Relative to Combined Groups Median

		Below	Above	
Sample 1	1	A	B	A+B
Sample 2	2	C	D	C+D
		A+C	B+D	N=A+B+C+D

Application: Used to test differences between the central tendency of two samples when the assumptions required for an independent sample t-test (**E4–49**) are not met. Used when the dependent variable is ordinal.

Data: Dependent variable is at least ordinal but could be interval or ratio. The independent variable on the basis of which groups are defined is discrete.

Limitations: The sign test is not as statistically powerful as the parametric t-test.

Comments: A useful test when assumptions needed for the t-test have not been met. With small samples, Yates' correction for continuity may be required. Yates' correction for continuity increases by .5 observed frequencies that are less than expected and decreased by .5 observed frequencies that are greater than expected.

Formula:

$$\chi^2 = \frac{N(AD - BC)^2}{(A+B)\,(C+D)\,(B+D)\,(A+C)}$$

with 1 degree of freedom

E4–59

Category: Comparisons: Two Samples (Nonparametric)

Statistic: Wilcoxon Rank Sum Test—Rank Test for Independent Samples

Description: The Wilcoxon rank sum test is a nonparametric equivalent to the independent sample t-test (**E4–49**). It is very close to being as statistically powerful as the t-test for normal and rectangular distributions. For samples of size n_1 and n_2, all $N = n_1 + n_2$ observations are combined and rank-ordered from 1 to N. The test statistic is R_1, which is the sum of the ranks for the smaller of the two samples, or either sample, if they are the same size. The exact distribution of R_1 is known, and for situations in which both samples are less than 25, the appropriate critical value for R_1 can be found in tables.

There is a normal approximation for R_1 when n_1 and n_2 are greater than, or equal to 10. The expression for the z-statistic used in this approximation is shown in the formula section.

Application: The Wilcoxon rank sum test is used when distributional assumptions needed for the appropriate application of the independent sample t-test have not been met. This Wilcoxon test is used if the dependent variable is ordinal because the t-test assumes that the dependent measure is interval or ratio.

Data: The dependent variable is at least ordinal. The independent variable, on the basis of which groups are classified, is discrete.

Limitations: The Wilcoxon rank sum test is slightly less powerful than the independent sample t-test in some cases.

Comments: The Wilcoxon rank sum test is a useful and powerful alternative to the independent sample t-test.

Formula:

$$Z = \frac{\left| R_1 - \overline{R}_1 \right| - 1}{\sqrt{\dfrac{n_1 n_2 (n_1 + n_2 + 1)}{12}}}$$

where

$$\overline{R}_1 = \frac{n_1 (n_1 + n_2 + 1)}{2}$$

R_1 = sum of the ranks for the smaller of the two groups when ranked in the combined distribution

E4–60

Category: Comparisons: Two Samples (Nonparametric)

Statistic: Mann-Whitney U-Test, Signed Rank Test for Independent Samples

Description: A nonparametric procedure used to test differences between two independent samples. The Mann–Whitney U-test is a nonparametric alternative to the independent sample t-test (**E4–49**) and is also statistically equivalent to the Wilcoxon rank sum test (**E4–59**). The test statistics U_1 and U_2 are calculated for samples 1 and 2, respectively. The calculations for U_1 and U_2 are shown in the formula section. The smaller of these two test statistics is tested against tabled values for the U-statistic. The null hypothesis is rejected if the observed U-statistic is *less than the critical value.*

Application: The Mann-Whitney U-test is used when distributional assumptions needed for the appropriate application of the independent sample t-test have not been met. In addition, the Mann-Whitney U-test is used if the dependent variable is ordinal because the t-test assumes that the dependent measure is interval or ratio.

Data: The dependent variable is at least ordinal. The independent variable, on the basis of which groups are classified, is discrete.

Limitations: Like all nonparametric tests, the Mann-Whitney U-test is less powerful than corresponding parametric tests.

Comments: The Mann-Whitney U-test is a useful and powerful alternative to the independent sample t-test. The Mann-Whitney U-test yields results identical to those obtained by using the Wilcoxon rank sum test.

Formula:

$$U_1 = n_1 n_2 + \frac{n_1(n_1 + 1)}{2} - R_1$$

$$U_2 = n_1 n_2 + \frac{n_2(n_2 + 1)}{2} - R_2$$

where R_1 and R_2 are the sum of the ranks for samples 1 and 2, respectively, in the combined $(n_1 + n_2)$ distribution

E4–61

Category: Comparisons: Two Samples (Nonparametric)

Statistic: Chi-Square Test of Independence

Description: A nonparametric test used to compare two groups on a nominal variable with two or more categories. If the nominal variable has only two categories, a phi-coefficient (**E4–21**) can be used, or a test for the difference between proportions for two independent samples (**E4–53**) can be performed. Neither test is appropriate when the nominal variable has three or more categories. The chi-square test for independence for two groups on a nominal variable involves a standard chi-square calculation. It tests the hypothesis that the proportion of subjects in the two groups is equivalent across the categories of the nominal variable.

Application: The chi-square test for independence is used to test the hypothesis that two or more groups are statistically equivalent with respect to some nominal variable that has two or more categories.

Data: Groups are defined on some discrete variable and measured on a nominal variable with two or more categories.

Limitations: The chi-square test for independence is not a statistically powerful test of group differences.

Comments: This is a useful test when subjects in two groups are measured on a nominal level variable.

Formula:

For two variables with C categories and K categories

$$\chi^2 = \sum_{j=1}^{k} \sum_{i=1}^{c} \left(\frac{(O_{ij} - E_{ij})^2}{E_{ij}} \right)$$

with $(C-1)(K-1)$ degrees of freedom

E4–62

Category: Comparisons: Two Samples (Nonparametric)

Statistic: Kolmogorov-Smirnov Two-Sample Test Comparing Distributions

Description: The Kolmogorov-Smirnov two-sample test is used to determine whether two independent samples were drawn from the same population or from populations with the same distribution. The test is based on the largest difference between the proportional cumulative frequencies for the two distributions evaluated across all points on the distribution. The sampling distribution of the maximum difference in proportional cumulative frequencies and critical values at various significance levels can be found in nonparametric tables.

Application: This test is used when a researcher wants to test the hypothesis that two samples are equivalent with respect to their overall distributions.

Data: Groups are classified on a discrete variable and measured on a continuous variable that is typically interval or ratio.

Limitations: The Kolmogorov-Smirnov test is not a statistically powerful test.

Comments: This test is flexible in that it requires few assumptions, but, again, it is not a statistically powerful test.

Formula:

$$D = \text{Maximum} \left| F_1(X) - F_2(X) \right|$$

where
$F_1(X)$ = cumulative frequency distribution for group 1
at the corresponding value of X
$F_2(X)$ = cumulative frequency distribution for group 2
at the corresponding value of X

E4–63

Category: Comparisons: Two Samples (Nonparametric)

Statistic: McNemar's Test for Significance of Change, Dependent or Correlated Samples, or Correlated Chi-Square

Description: A nonparametric test used when two correlated samples are categorized on a dichotomous nominal variable. The test statistic is a chi-square. The McNemar test is often used in pretest-posttest designs in which one group of subjects is classified into two levels of a dichotomous nominal variable before and after some treatment. Such designs yield a 2 × 2 contingency table (pre, post X category 1, category 2). Only the two cells representing pretest-posttest change in classification are of interest. Such a table would be:

Posttest

		1	2	
	2	A	B	A+B
Pretest	1	C	D	C+D
		A+C	B+D	N=A+B+C+D

Application: The McNemar test is often used in pretest-posttest designs in which one group of subjects is classified into the two levels of a dichotomous nominal variable before and after some treatment. For example, the McNemar test would be used in situations in which a group of subjects declared themselves "for" or "against" some stimulus (e.g., an issue, political position, or candidate) on two different occasions. If "for" is defined as Category 1, and "against" is defined as Category 2, the design fits the 2×2 contingency table shown above.

Data: Subjects are categorized on a nominal dichotomous variable.

Limitations: McNemar's test is not as statistically powerful as a parametric test like the dependent sample t-test (**E4–50**).

Comments: This is a useful and informative test when a dependent measure at the ordinal, interval, or ratio level is not available.

Formula:

$$\chi^2 = \frac{(A + D)^2}{A + D}, \quad 1 \text{ degree of freedom}$$

A and D as shown in the description

E4–64

Category: Comparisons: Two Samples (Nonparametric)

Statistic: Sign Test for Dependent Samples

Description: This test is used to compare two correlated or dependent samples with N paired observations. The sign of the difference between subjects in each pair of observations is determined and tested against the null hypothesis that there should be an equal number of pairs with (+) plus and (−) minus signs. Pairs with a difference of zero are discarded. The exact probability of getting n pairs with a (+) plus sign and n pairs with a (−) minus sign out of N total pairs is calculated from the binomial expansion of the form $(.5 + .5)^N$, where N is the number of paired observations less the number of pairs with zero differences. With small Ns, a chi-square approximation to the binomial may be used, with each sign having an expected value of (N/2). Yates' correction should be applied in such cases. A computationally convenient formula is shown in the formula section.

Application: The sign test for dependent samples is used to test the difference between two correlated samples. Often, this would be used for the same sample measured twice in a pretest-posttest design. This test is analogous to the dependent sample t-test (**E4–50**) but does not require distributional assumptions. It is used when the dependent variable is ordinal.

Data: The dependent variable is at least ordinal. The independent variable, on the basis of which groups are defined, is discrete.

Limitations: The sign test for correlated samples is not as statistically powerful as the parametric dependent sample t-test.

Comments: The sign test for correlated samples is useful when the dependent variable is ordinal and when assumptions needed for the dependent sample t-test are not met. The sign test for dependent samples is not statistically very powerful compared with the dependent sample t-test (**E4–50**).

Formula:

$$Z = \frac{|D| - 1}{\sqrt{n}}$$

where D = difference in the number of plus and number of minus signs

E4–65
Category: Comparisons: Two Samples (Nonparametric)
Statistic: Wilcoxon Matched-Pairs, Signed-Rank Test for Dependent Samples
Description: A nonparametric test used with matched pairs commonly encountered in pre-test-posttest designs. This test is analogous to the dependent sample t-test **(E4–50)**. For small samples, n less than, or equal to, 25, the test statistic called "T" is used (this is not Student's t). T is determined by (1) calculating the difference between the matched scores for each subject or pair of subjects; (2) ranking the absolute value of the differences; (3) giving the average of the ranks occupied for tied rankings; (4) assigning the appropriate sign, (+) plus or (−) minus, depending on the direction of the difference; and (5) summing the ranks of the less frequently occurring signed values, (+) or (−). T is the sum of the ranks with the less frequent sign. Critical values for T at various significance levels are found in nonparametric tables. With samples greater than 25, the sampling distribution of T has an approximation to the normal distribution. This approximation is given in the formula section.
Application: The Wilcoxon matched-pairs, signed-rank test is used for correlated samples in much the same way that the dependent sample t-test is used. Such applications include pretest-posttest designs and designs in which pairs of subjects are matched on some variable the influence of which the researcher wants to control.
Data: The dependent variable is converted to ordinal differences. Groups are defined on a discrete independent variable.
Limitations: The Wilcoxon matched-pairs, signed-rank test is not as powerful as its parametric counterpart, the dependent sample t-test.
Comments: In many situations, this test is a useful alternative to the dependent sample t-test, although it is somewhat less powerful than the parametric test. The lack of distributional assumptions makes the Wilcoxon test broadly applicable in situations where the assumptions of the dependent sample t-test are questionable.
Formula:

$$Z = \frac{T - \frac{(n)(n+1)}{4}}{\sqrt{\frac{n(n+1)(2n+1)}{24}}}$$

where T is defined in the description

E4–66
COMPARISONS: TWO OR MORE SAMPLES (NONPARAMETRIC)
  (E4–67) Sign Test for K-Independent Samples
  (E4–68) Kruskal–Wallis Rank Test for K-Independent Samples
  (E4–69) Friedman Two-Way Analysis of Variance by Ranks for Dependent or
    Correlated Samples

E4–67
Category: Comparisons: Two or More Samples (Nonparametric)
Statistic: Sign Test for K-Independent Samples Chi-Square
Description: An extension of the median test **(E4–58)** used to compare two or more independent samples.

  The median for all samples combined is calculated, and then the number of subjects above and below the combined median is determined within each of the separate samples. The (K × 2) chi-square table composed of samples (K) by position relative to the combined median (above, below) is constructed to test the hypothesis that there is no significant difference between the medians of the populations from which the samples are drawn. The chi-square is tested with K−1 degrees of freedom.

  The K × 2 table is of the form:

Position Relative to Combined Median

Below   Above
   1   2

Sample 1
Sample 2
Sample 3
  .
Sample K

Application: Used to test differences between two or more samples when the assumptions required for an independent sample t-test **(E4–49)** or analysis of variance **(E4–71)** are not met. Used when the dependent variable is ordinal.
Data: Dependent variable is at least ordinal but could be interval or ratio. The independent variable, on the basis of which groups are defined, is discrete.
Limitations: The sign test is not as statistically powerful as the parametric t-test or analysis of variance.
Comments: A useful test when assumptions needed for the t-test or analysis of variance have not been met. With small samples, Yates' correction for continuity may be required.

Formula:

$$\chi^2 = \sum_{k=1}^{k} \sum_{i=1}^{2} \frac{(O_{ki} - E_{ki})^2}{E_{ki}}$$

where $(K-1)$ degrees of freedom

E4–68

Category: Comparison: Two or More Samples (Nonparametric)

Statistic: Kruskal–Wallis Rank Test for K-Independent Samples

Description: The Kruskal–Wallis rank test for K-independent samples is a nonparametric equivalent to the one-way analysis of variance **(E4–71)** and is an extension of the Wilcoxon rank sum test **(E4–59)**. The Kruskal–Wallis is calculated by combining all the observations from all groups and then rank-ordering them from 1 to N. The sum of the ranks for each of K groups is then determined and used in calculating the test statistic "H," shown in the formula section. For K=3 and n's less than, or equal to, 5, the exact distribution of H is known. In other cases, H approximates a chi-square distribution with $K-1$ degrees of freedom.

Application: The Kruskal–Wallis rank test is used when distributional assumptions needed for the appropriate application of an analysis of variance procedure have not been met. It is commonly applied when the dependent variable is ordinal.

Data: The dependent variable is at least ordinal. The independent variable, on the basis of which groups are classified, is discrete.

Limitations: The Kruskal–Wallis rank test for independent samples is somewhat less powerful than a one-way analysis of variance, but the difference in statistical power, in most cases, is slight.

Comments: The Kruskal–Wallis rank test is a useful and powerful alternative to the one-way analysis of variance when the assumptions required for the analysis of variance have not been met.

Formula:

$$H = \frac{12}{n(n+1)} \sum_{i=1}^{k} \left(\frac{R_i^2}{n_i} \right) - 3(n+1)$$

where R_i = sum of the ranks for i groups on the combined distribution

E4–69

Category: Comparison: Two or More Samples (Nonparametric)

Statistic: Friedman Two-Way Analysis of Variance by Ranks, Dependent or Correlated Samples

Description: The Friedman two-way analysis of variance by ranks is a rank test for correlated samples. The Friedman test is commonly used when some samples of N subjects is measured on K different occasions. The Friedman test is performed by arranging the data into N rows with one row for each person and K columns with one column for each occasion. The K entries in each row are then rank-ordered from 1 to K and assigned rank order values 1 through K. A test statistic "S" is then calculated as shown in the formula section. For small values of K and N, the exact distribution of S is known. In general, the Friedman test statistic is a chi-square statistic derived from S as shown in the formula section. This statistic approximates a chi-square with $K-1$ degrees of freedom.

Application: The Friedman two-way analysis of variance by ranks is used to test hypotheses about differences among correlated samples when the assumptions needed to perform a repeated measures analysis of variance (**E4–79**) have not been met.

Data: The dependent variable is at least ordinal, while the independent variables are discrete.

Limitations: The Friedman test is not as statistically powerful as the parametric repeated measures analysis of variance, but the Friedman test is a useful approach when the assumptions of the parametric procedure have not been met.

Comments: The Friedman test is the nonparametric equivalent to the two-way, mixed model analysis of variance with subjects being the random factor and occasions being the fixed factor (**E4–74**).

Formula:

$$S = \sum_{i=1}^{k} \left(R_i - \overline{R}^2 \right)$$

where

R_i = sum of the ranks for group i

$\overline{R}$ = mean of the R_i's

$\chi^2 = \dfrac{12S}{nK(K-1)}$ with $(K-1)$ degrees of freedom

E4–70
COMPARISON: TWO OR MORE SAMPLES—ANALYSIS OF VARIANCE (ANOVA)

Factorial Analysis of Variance

(**E4–71**) One-Way Analysis of Variance
(**E4–72**) Two-Way Analysis of Variance, Fixed Effects Model
(**E4–73**) Two-Way Analysis of Variance, Random Effects Model
(**E4–74**) Two-Way Analysis of Variance, Mixed Effects Model
(**E4–75**) Three-Way Analysis of Variance, Fixed Effects Model
(**E4–76**) Three-Way Analysis of Variance, Mixed Model, One Factor Fixed, Two Factors Random
(**E4–77**) Three-Way Analysis of Variance, Mixed Model, Two Factors Fixed, One Factor Random
(**E4–78**) Three-Way Analysis of Variance, Random Model

Repeated Measures Analysis of Variance/Split-Plot Analyses

(E4–79) One-Way Repeated Measures, Subjects by Occasions
(E4–80) Two-Way Split-Plot, One Between-Subjects Factor and One
Within-Subjects Factor
(E4–81) Three-Way Split-Plot, One Between-Subjects Factor and Two
Within-Subjects Factors
(E4–82) Three-Way Split-Plot, Two Between-Subjects Factors and One
Within-Subjects Factor
(E4–83) Four-Way Split-Plot, Two Between-Subjects Factors and Two
Within-Subjects Factors

Nested/Hierarchical Analysis of Variance

(E4–84) Two-Factor Design, B Nested in A
(E4–85) Three-Factor Designs, C Nested in B, B Nested in A
(E4–86) Three-Factor Designs, B Nested in A, C Crossed with B Nested in A

General Analysis of Variance Designs

(E4–87) Randomized Block Designs
(E4–88) Latin Square Designs

Related Designs

(E4–89) Analysis of Covariance
(E4–90) Time-Series Analysis

E4–71

Category: Analysis of Variance (ANOVA)

Statistical Procedure: One-Way Analysis of Variance

Description: A procedure for examining the variance in some dependent variable in terms of the portion of variance that can be attributed to certain factors. In one-way analysis of variance, total variance is partitioned into (1) variation due to different levels of the independent variable, called between-group variance, and (2) variation within the levels of the independent variable, called within-group or random variance. The basic arrangement for a one-way analysis of variance is:

Factor A, A Levels

1   2   3   .   .   A

Application: Commonly used to test hypotheses about different groups. The groups may be naturally occurring or represent different levels of some treatment variable.

Data: The dependent variable is interval or ratio. The independent variable is discrete and may be nominal, ordinal, or, in some cases, interval.

Limitations: Assumes homogeneity of variance within group, normal distributions in the populations, and independence among observations (e.g., the subjects are not correlated).

Comments: Robust with respect to the assumption of homogeneity of variance. Often used with a priori or post hoc contrasts.

Formula: One-Way ANOVA

Source of Variation	Degrees of Freedom	Mean Squares	F-Ratio
Between Groups	A–1	MSB	MSB/MSW
Within Groups	N–A	MSW	
Total	N–1		

E4–72

Category: Analysis of Variance (ANOVA)

Statistical Procedure: Two-Way Analysis of Variance, Fixed Effects Model

Description: A procedure for examining the variance in some dependent measure in terms of the portion of variance that can be attributed to certain factors. In the two-way analysis of variance, total variation is partitioned into variation due to independent variables (1) A (with A levels), (2) B (with B levels), (3) the interaction of the independent variables (A*B), and (4) within-cell or random variation. In the fixed effects model, all possible levels of the independent variables are represented in the design and analysis.

The basic arrangements for a two-way analysis of variance are shown in (**E4–73**). Factor A is shown with A levels and Factor B is shown with 3 levels.

Application: Two-way ANOVA is the standard procedure for designs with two independent variables. All levels of the independent variables are represented in the design. One of the independent variables may be a blocking variable used to reduce within-cell variance as it occurs in the context of a one-way design (**E4–71**).

Data: The dependent variable is interval or ratio. The independent variable is discrete and may be nominal, ordinal, or, in some cases, interval.

Limitations: Assumes homogeneity of variance within groups, normal distributions in the populations, and independence among observations (e.g., the subjects are not correlated).

Comments: Robust with respect to the assumption of homogeneity or variance. Often used with a priori or post hoc contrasts. One of the independent variables may be a blocking variable designed to increase statistical power by reducing within-cell variance, the MSW or error term for hypothesis testing. Main effects cannot be interpreted directly if there is a significant interaction term.

Formula: Two-Way Analysis of Variance, Fixed Effects Model

Source of Variation	Degrees of Freedom	Mean Squares	F-Ratio
Between A	A–1	MSA	MSA/MSW
Between B	B–1	MSB	MSB/MSW
Interaction of A*B	(A–1)(B–1)	MSAB	MSAB/MSW
Within	N–(AXB)	MSW	
Total	N–1		

E4–73

Category: Analysis of Variance (ANOVA)

Statistical Procedure: Two-Way Analysis of Variance, Random Effects Model

Description: A procedure for examining the variance in some dependent measure in terms of the portion of variance that can be attributed to certain factors. In the two-way analysis of variance, total variation is partitioned into variation due to independent variables (1) A (with A levels), (2) B (with B levels), (3) the interaction of the independent variables (A*B), and (4) within-cell or random variation. In the random effects model, the levels of both independent variables are sampled from larger sets of possible levels.

Factor A, A Levels

Application: A procedure used with designs that have two independent variables, when levels of the independent variables are sampled. One of the independent variables may be a blocking variable that is used to reduce within-cell variance as it occurs in the context of a one-way design.

Data: The dependent variable is interval or ratio. The independent variables have discrete levels and may be nominal, ordinal, or, in some cases, interval.

Limitations: Assumes homogeneity of variance within groups, normal distributions in the populations, and independence among observations (e.g., the subjects are not correlated).

Comments: Robust with respect to the assumption of homogeneity or variance. Often used with a priori or post hoc contrasts (**E4–91**). One of the independent variables may be a blocking variable designed to increase statistical power by reducing error variance for hypothesis testing. Main effects cannot be interpreted directly if there is a significant interaction term.

Formula: Two-Way Analysis of Variance, Random Effects Model

Source of Variation	Degrees of Freedom	Mean Squares	F-Ratio
Between A	A–1	MSA	MSA/MSAB
Between B	B–1	MSB	MSB/MSAB
Interaction of A*B	(A –1)(B –1)	MSAB	MSAB/MSW
Within	N –(AXB)	MSW	
Total	N–1		

E4–74

Category: Analysis of Variance (ANOVA)

Statistical Procedure: Two-Way Analysis of Variance, Mixed Effects Model

Description: A procedure for examining the variance of some dependent measure in terms of the portion of variance that can be attributed to certain factors. In the two-way mixed effects model analysis of variance, there are a fixed independent variable and a random independent variable. All levels of the fixed variable are reflected in the design. The levels of the random independent variable are sampled from a larger set of levels. Total variation is partitioned into variation due to (1) a fixed independent variable A (with A levels), (2) a random independent variable B (with B levels), (3) the interaction of the independent variables (A*B), and (4) within-cell or random variation.

Application: A common application of the two-way mixed effects model is the repeated measures design **(E4–79),** in which subjects are measured on multiple occasions or trials. "Subjects" is the random factor, while "occasions," or "trials," is the fixed factor. (There is no within-cell variance in the mixed model repeated measures analysis.) The two-way mixed effects model is also used in randomized block designs when levels of the blocking variable are randomly selected and used to reduce error variance as it occurs in the context of a one-way design.

Data: The dependent variable is interval or ratio. The independent variable is discrete and may be nominal, ordinal, or, in some cases, interval.

Limitations: Assumes homogeneity of variance within groups, normal distributions in the populations, and independence among observations (e.g., the subjects are not correlated).

Comments: Robust with respect to the assumption of homogeneity of variance. Often used with a priori or post hoc contrasts. One of the independent variables may be a blocking variable that is designed to increase statistical power. (See randomized block designs, **(E4–87.)** The repeated measures analysis is the multiple-group equivalent to the two-group dependent t-test (**E4–50**). Main effects cannot be interpreted directly in the presence of a significant interaction effect.

Formula: Two-Way Analysis of Variance, Mixed Effects Model

Source of Variation	Degrees of Freedom	Mean Squares	F-Ratio
Between A	A–1	MSA	MSA/MSAB
Between B	B–1	MSB	MSB/MSW
Interaction of A*B	(A–1)(B–1)	MSAB	MSAB/MSW
Within	N–(AXB)	MSW	
Total	N–1		

E4–75

Category: Analysis of Variance (ANOVA)

Statistical Procedure: Three-Way Analysis of Variance, Fixed Effects Model

Description: A procedure for examining the variance in some dependent measure in terms of the portion of variance that can be attributed to certain factors. In the three-way ANOVA, the total variation is partitioned into variation due to independent variables (1) A (with A levels), (2) B (with B levels), and (3) C (with C levels); the two-way interactions (4) A*B, (5) A*C, and (6) B*C; the (7) A*B*C three-way interaction; and (8) the within-group variance. In the fixed effects model, all levels of each independent variable are fixed and represented in the design and analysis.

The basic arrangement for a three-way analysis of variance is shown. Factor A is shown with A levels, Factor B is shown with 3 levels, and Factor C is shown with 3 levels.

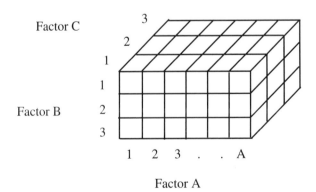

Factor A

Application: The appropriate procedure when the design involves three independent variables and all levels of each variable are represented in the design. One of the independent variables may be a blocking variable used to reduce within-cell variance as the error term in a two-way analysis of variance without the blocking variable. (See randomized block designs **E4–87**.)

Data: The dependent variable is interval or ratio. The independent variables are discrete and may be nominal, ordinal, or, in some cases, interval.

Limitations: Assumes homogeneity of variance within groups (cells), normal distributions in the populations, and independence among observations (e.g., the subjects are not correlated).

Comments: Robust with respect to the assumption of homogeneity of variance. Often used with a priori or post hoc contrasts. One of the independent variables may be a blocking variable designed to increase statistical power by reducing error variance for hypothesis testing. Main effects cannot be interpreted directly in the presence of a significant interaction effect.

Formula: Three-Way Analysis of Variance, Fixed Effects Model

Source of Variation	Degrees of Freedom	Mean Squares	F-Ratio
Between A	A–1	MSA	MSA/MSW
Between B	B–1	MSB	MSB/MSW
Between C	C–1	MSC	MSC/MSW
Interaction of A*B	(A–1)(B–1)	MSAB	MSAB/MSW
Interaction of A*C	(A–1)(C–1)	MSAC	MSAC/MSW
Interaction of B*C	(B–1)(C–1)	MSBC	MSBC/MSW
Interaction of A*B*C	(A–1)(B–1)(C–1)	MSABC	MSABC/MSW
Within	N – (AXBXC)	MSW	
Total	N–1		

E4–76

Category: Analysis of Variance (ANOVA)

Statistical Procedure: Three-Way Analysis of Variance
Mixed Effects Model
One Fixed Independent Variable
Two Random Independent Variables

Description: A procedure for examining the variance in some dependent measure in terms of the portion of variance that can be attributed to certain factors. In the three-way analysis of variance, the total variation is partitioned into variation due to independent variables (1) A (with A levels), (2) B (with B levels), and (3) C (with C levels); the

two-way interactions (4) A*B, (5) A*C, and (6) B*C; the (7) A*B*C three-way interaction; and (8) the within-group variance. In the mixed effects model, all levels of one
independent variable (A) are fixed and represented in the design, and the levels of two
of the independent variables (B and C) are sampled from a larger set of possible levels.

Application: The appropriate procedure when the design involves three independent variables with one variable being fixed and the other two being random. One of the independent variables may be a blocking variable used to reduce within-cell variance (used
as the error term) in a two-way analysis of variance without the blocking variable.

Data: The dependent variable is interval or ratio. The independent variables are discrete
and may be nominal, ordinal, or, in some cases, interval.

Limitations: Assumes homogeneity of variance within groups (cells), normal distributions
in the populations, and independence among observations (e.g., the subjects are not
correlated.)

Comments: Robust with respect to the assumption of homogeneity of variance. Often used
with a priori or post hoc contrasts. One of the independent variables may be a blocking
variable designed to increase statistical power by reducing error variance for hypothesis testing. Main effects cannot be interpreted directly in the presence of a significant
interaction effect.

Formula: Three-Way Analysis of Variance, Mixed Effects Model, One Factor Fixed (A),
Two Factors Random (B,C)

Source of Variation	Degrees of Freedom	Mean Squares	F-Ratio
Between A	A–1	MSA	$\dfrac{MSA}{MSAB + MSAC - MSABC}$
Between B	B–1	MSB	MSB/MSBC
Between C	C–1	MSC	MSC/MSBC
Interaction of A*B	(A–1)(B–1)	MSAB	MSAB/MSABC
Interaction of A*C	(A–1)(C–1)	MSAC	MSAC/MSABC
Interaction of B*C	(B–1)(C–1)	MSBC	MSBC/MSW
Interaction of A*B*C	(A–1)(B–1)(C–1)	MSABC	MSABC/MSW
Within	N – (AXBXC)		
Total	N–1		

E4–77

Category: Analysis of Variance (ANOVA)

Statistical Procedure: Three-Way Analysis of Variance, Mixed Effects Model, Two Fixed Independent Variables, One Random Independent Variable

Description: A procedure for examining the variance in some dependent measure in terms of the portion of variance that can be attributed to certain factors. In the three-way ANOVA, the total variation is partitioned into variation due to independent variables (1) A (with A levels), (2) B (with B levels), and (3) C (with C levels); the two-way interactions (4) A*B, (5) A*C, and (6) B*C; the (7) A*B*C three-way interaction; and (8) the within-group variance. In this mixed effects model, all levels of two independent variables (A and B) are fixed and represented in the design, and the levels of one of the independent variables (C) are sampled from a larger set of possible levels.

Application: The appropriate procedure when the design involves three independent variables with the levels of two variables being fixed and the levels of the other variable being sampled in the design. One of the independent variables may be a blocking variable used to reduce within-cell variance (used as the error term) in a two-way analysis of variance without the blocking variable.

Data: The dependent variable is interval or ratio. The independent variables are discrete and may be nominal, ordinal, or, in some cases, interval.

Limitations: Assumes homogeneity of variance within groups (cells), normal distributions in the populations, and independence among observations (e.g., the subjects are not correlated).

Comments: Robust with respect to the assumption of homogeneity of variance. Often used with a priori or post hoc contrasts **(E4–91)**. One of the independent variables may be a blocking variable designed to increase statistical power by reducing error variance for hypothesis testing. Main effects cannot be interpreted directly in the presence of a significant interaction effect.

Formula: Three-Way Analysis of Variance, Mixed Model, Two Factors Fixed (A, B), One Factor Random (C)

Source of Variation	Degrees of Freedom	Mean Squares	F-Ratio
Between A	A–1	MSA	MSA/MSAC
Between B	B–1	MSB	MSB/MSBC
Between C	C–1	MSC	MSC/MSW
Interaction of A*B	(A–1)(B–1)	MSAB	MSAB/MSABC
Interaction of A*C	(A–1)(C–1)	MSAC	MSAC/MSW
Interaction of B*C	(B–1)(C–1)	MSBC	MSBC/MSW

Source of Variation	Degrees of Freedom	Mean Squares	F-Ratio
Interaction of A*B*C	(A–1)(B–1)(C–1)	MSABC	MSABC/MSW
Within	N – (AXBXC)	MSW	
Total	N–1		

E4–78

Category: Analysis of Variance (ANOVA)

Statistical Procedure: Three-Way Analysis of Variance, Random Effects Model

Description: A procedure for examining the variance in some dependent measure in terms of the portion of variance that can be attributed to certain factors. In the three-way ANOVA, the total variation is partitioned into variation due to independent variables (1) A (with A levels), (2) B (with B levels), and (3) C (with C levels); the two-way interactions (4) A*B, (5) A*C, and (6) B*C; the (7) A*B*C three-way interaction, and (8) the within-group variance. In the random effects model, all levels of each independent are sampled from a larger set of possible levels.

Application: The appropriate procedure when the design involves three independent variables when the levels of each variable are sampled from a larger set of levels. One of the independent variables may be a blocking variable used to reduce within-cell variance (used as the error term) in a two-way analysis of variance without the blocking variable.

Data: The dependent variable is interval or ratio. The independent variables are discrete and may be nominal, ordinal, or, in some cases, interval.

Limitations: Assumes homogeneity of variance within groups (cells), normal distributions in the populations, and independence among observations (e.g., the subjects are not correlated).

Comments: Robust with respect to the assumption of homogeneity of variance. Often used with a priori or post hoc contrasts (**E4–91**). One of the independent variables may be a blocking variable designed to increase statistical power by reducing error variance for hypothesis testing. Main effects cannot be interpreted directly in the presence of a significant interaction effect.

Formula: Three-Way Analysis of Variance, Random Effects Model

Source of Variation	Degrees of Freedom	Mean Squares	F-Ratio
Between A	A–1	MSA	$\dfrac{MSA}{MSAB + MSAC - MSABC}$
Between B	B–1	MSB	$\dfrac{MSB}{MSAB + MSBC - MSABC}$

Source of Variation	Degrees of Freedom	Mean Squares	F-Ratio
Between C	C–1	MSC	$\dfrac{MSC}{MSAC + MSBC - MSABC}$
Interaction of A*B	(A–1)(B–1)	MSAB	MSAB/MSABC
Interaction of A*C	(A–1)(C–1)	MSAC	MSAC/MSABC
Interaction of B*C	(B–1)(C–1)	MSBC	MSBC/MSABC
Interaction of A*B*C	(A–1)(B–1)(C–1)	MSABC	MSABC/MSW
Within	N– (AXBXC)	MSW	
Total	N–1		

E4–79

Category: Analysis of Variance (ANOVA)

Statistical Procedure: Repeated Measures Analysis of Variance, Subjects by Occasions

Descriptions: An analysis of variance procedure used to test hypotheses about one group of subjects measured on two or more occasions. The procedure examines the total variance in some dependent measure in terms of variance attributable to be-tween-subjects variance (variation between different subjects) and within-subject variance (variation for the same subject across occasions). The procedure is described as a one-way repeated measures analysis. Nonetheless, it is equivalent to the two-way mixed model analysis of variance (**E4–74**) when subjects are viewed as a random vari-able and occasions as a fixed variable.

The basic arrangement for a one-way repeated measures analysis of variance is il-lustrated with Factor A, Occasions, consisting of 4 levels, and n subjects (not shown) measured on each occasion.

Factor A, Occasions (4 Levels)

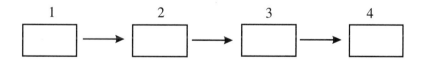

Application: The appropriate analysis when subjects are measured on multiple occasions. Commonly used in longitudinal designs. Appropriate analysis for randomized block designs when A subjects in each block are randomly assigned to one of A levels of the fixed independent variable (see **E4–87**).

Data: Dependent variable is interval or ratio. Independent variables are discrete, nominal, ordinal, and, sometimes, interval.

Limitations: Assumes homogeneity of variance within groups, homogeneity of covariance between groups and normal distributions in the populations and that the scale on which the dependent variable is measured is equivalent across occasions.

Comments: A powerful technique in which subjects act as their own controls. Analogous to the dependent sample t-test **(E4–50)** but appropriate for two or more occasions. Orthogonal polynomial contrasts are often used to test trends across occasions.

Formula: One-Way Repeated Measures Analysis of Variance for n Subjects on O Occasions

Source of Variation	Degrees of Freedom	Mean Squares	F-Ratio
Between Subjects	n–1	MSSUB	
Within Subjects			
Occasions	O–1	MSO	$\dfrac{MSO}{MSsub \bullet Occ}$
Sub*Occ	(n–1)(O–1)	MSsub*Occ	
Total	(n × O)–1		

E4–80

Category: Analysis of Variance (ANOVA)

Statistical Procedure: Two-Way Split-Plot Analysis of Variance
  One Between-Subjects Factor
  One Within-Subjects Factor (Repeated Measures on Within-
    Subjects Factors)

Description: An analysis of variance procedure that examines the variance in some dependent measure in terms of the portion of variance attributable to a between-subjects Factor A (with A levels) and a within-subjects Factor B (with B levels). Subjects within the levels of Factor A are measured repeatedly across the levels of Factor B. Factor A may be different treatment conditions, experimental and control, and Factor B might be measures taken before, during, immediately after, and long after the experimental treatment. Factors A and B are generally considered fixed factors, and n subjects are randomly assigned to the levels of Factor A.

  The basic arrangement for this design is illustrated below with 4 levels of Factor B (Occasions) and 2 levels of Factor A (Groups).

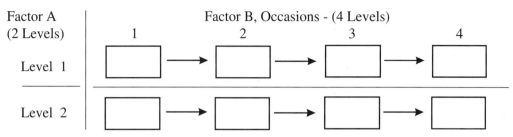

Factor A
(2 Levels)

Factor B, Occasions - (4 Levels)

Level 1

Level 2

Application: The appropriate analysis when subjects in different groups or categories are measured across multiple occasions. For example, Factor A could be a classification variable such as gender, and Factor B might be successive treatment conditions. Commonly used in longitudinal designs when subjects in different groups are measured across time on several occasions. The appropriate analysis with a randomized block design when subjects are grouped into blocks and measured across successive treatment conditions.

Data: Dependent variable is interval or ratio. Independent variables are discrete, nominal, ordinal, and, sometimes, interval.

Limitations: Assumes homogeneity of variance within groups, homogeneity of covariance between groups, and normal distributions in the populations and that the scale on which the dependent variable is measured is equivalent across occasions.

Comments: A powerful technique in which variation between subjects is removed as a source of variation in error terms that are used to test the hypothesis of interest. Orthogonal polynomial contrasts are often used to test trends across occasions.

Formula: Two-Way Split-Plot Analysis of Variance
Factor A, Between-Subjects, has A levels.
There are n subjects (Ss) in each level of A.
Factor B, Within-Subjects, has B levels.

Source of Variation	Degrees of Freedom	Mean Squares	F-Ratio
Between Subjects			
A	A–1	MSA	$\dfrac{MSA}{MS \bullet (Ss\,in\,A)}$
Ss in A	A (n–1)	MS(Ss in A)	
Within Subjects			
B	B–1	MSB	$\dfrac{MSB}{MSB \bullet (Ss\,in\,A)}$
A*B	(A–1)(B–1)	MSAB	$\dfrac{MSAB}{MSB \bullet (Ss\,in\,A)}$
B*(Ss in A)	(B–1)[A (n–1)]	MSB*(Ss in A)	
Total	(A × B × n)–1		

E4–81

Category: Analysis of Variance (ANOVA)

Statistical Procedure: Three-Way Split-Plot Analysis of Variance
   One Between-Subjects Factor
   Two Within-Subjects Factors (Repeated Measures on Within-
      Subjects Factors)

Description: An ANOVA procedure that examines the variance in some dependent measure in terms of the portion of variance attributable to a between-subjects Factor A
   (with A levels) and a within-subjects Factor B (with B levels) and Factor C (with C
   levels). Subjects within the levels of Factor A are measured repeatedly across the levels of Factor B and across the levels of Factor C. Factor A (between-subjects) may be
   different treatment conditions. Factor B (within-subjects) might be repeated trials on
   some task. The trials of Factor B are attempted on two or more occasions, and these
   occasions represent Factor C. Factor A could be a classification variable such as gender. Factor B might be a set of trials on an experimental task, and Factor C might be
   successive treatment conditions under which the trials of Factor B are attempted. Factors A, B, and C are generally considered fixed factors, and n subjects are randomly assigned to the levels of Factor A.

   The basic arrangement for this design is illustrated. Factor A, between-subjects,
   has 2 levels; Factor B, within-subjects, has 3 levels; and Factor C, within-subjects, has
   4 levels.

Application: The appropriate analysis when subjects in different groups or categories
   (Factor A) are measured repeatedly (Factor C) across multiple occasions (Factor B).
   Commonly used in longitudinal designs when subjects in different groups are measured under different conditions across time on several occasions. This analysis could
   be used with a randomized block design (**E4–87**) when subjects are grouped into
   blocks and measured repeatedly across successive treatment conditions.

Data: Dependent variable is interval or ratio. Independent variables are discrete, nominal,
   ordinal, and, sometimes, interval.

Limitations: Assumes homogeneity of variance within groups, homogeneity of covariance
   between groups, and normal distributions in the populations and that the scale on
   which the dependent variable is measured is equivalent across occasions.

Comments: A powerful technique in which variation between subjects is removed as a source of variation in error terms that are used to test the hypothesis of interest. Orthogonal polynomial contrasts are often used to test trends across occasions.

Formula: Three-Way Split-Plot Analysis of Variance

Factor A, Between-Subjects, has A levels.

There are n subjects (Ss) in each level of A.

Factor B, Within-Subjects, has B levels.

Factor C, Within-Subjects, has C levels.

Factors A, B, and C are fixed.

Source of Variation	Degrees of Freedom	Mean Squares	F-Ratio
Between Subjects			
A	A–1	MSA	$\dfrac{\text{MSA}}{\text{MS} \bullet (\text{Ss in A})}$
Ss in A	A(n–1)	MS(Ss in A)	
Within Subjects			
B	B–1	MSB	$\dfrac{\text{MSB}}{\text{MSB} \bullet (\text{Ss in A})}$
A* B	(A–1)(B–1)	MSAB	$\dfrac{\text{MSAB}}{\text{MSB} \bullet (\text{Ss in A})}$
B*(Ss in A)	(B–1)[A (n–1)]	MSB*(Ss in A)	
C	C–1	MSC	$\dfrac{\text{MSC}}{\text{MSC} \bullet (\text{Ss in A})}$
C*A	(C–1)(A–1)	MSAC	$\dfrac{\text{MSAC}}{\text{MSC} \bullet (\text{Ss in A})}$
C*(Ss in A)	(C–1)[A (n–1)]	MSC*(Ss in A)	
C*B	(C–1)(B–1)	MSCB	$\dfrac{\text{MSBC}}{\text{MSCB} \bullet (\text{Ss in A})}$
C*B*A	(C–1)(B–1)(A–1)	MSABC	$\dfrac{\text{MSABC}}{\text{MSCB} \bullet (\text{Ss in A})}$
C*B*(Ss in A)	(C–1)(B–1)[A(n–1)]	MSCB*(Ss in A)	
Total	(A × B × C X n)–1		

E4–82

Category: Analysis of Variance (ANOVA)

Statistical Procedure: Three-Way Split-Plot Analysis of Variance

Two Between-Subjects Factor

One Within-Subject Factor (Repeated Measures on Within-Subjects Factors)

Description: An analysis of variance procedure that examines the variance in some dependent measure in terms of the portion of variance attributable to between-subjects Factor A (with A levels) and Factor B (with B levels) and within subjects Factor C (with C levels). Subjects within the levels of Factor B are within the levels of Factor A and are measured repeatedly across the levels of Factor C. Factor A (between-subjects) might be a classification variable such as gender, Factor B (between-subjects) might be a set of treatment conditions, and Factor C (within-subjects) might be successive measurements of the subjects before, during, and after the treatments are applied. Factors A, B, and C are generally considered fixed factors, and n subjects in the different levels of Factor A are randomly assigned to the levels of Factor B.

The basic arrangement for this design is illustrated. Factor A, between-subjects, has 2 levels; Factor B, between-subjects, has 3 levels; and Factor C, within-subjects, has 3 levels.

Factor C, Within Subjects, 3 Levels

Application: The appropriate analysis when subjects in different groups or categories (Factor A) are assigned to different levels of a second Factor B and measured repeatedly across multiple occasions (Factor C). Commonly used in longitudinal designs where subjects in different groups are assigned to different treatment conditions and measured on several occasions.

Data: Dependent variable is interval or ratio. Independent variables are discrete, nominal, ordinal, and, sometimes, interval.

Limitations: Assumes homogeneity of variance within groups, homogeneity of covariance between groups, and normal distributions in the populations and that the scale on which the dependent variable is measured is equivalent across occasions.

Comments: A powerful technique in which variation between subjects is removed as a source of variation in error terms that are used to test the hypotheses of interest. Orthogonal polynomial contrasts are often used to test trends across occasions.

Formula: Three-Way Split-Plot Analysis of Variance
Factor A, Between-Subjects, has A levels.
Factor B, Between-Subjects, has B levels.
There are n subjects (Ss) in each AB level.
Factor C, Within-Subjects, has C levels.
Factors A, B, and C are fixed.

Source of Variation	Degrees of Freedom	Mean Squares	F-Ratio
Between Subjects			
A	A–1	MSA	$\dfrac{MSA}{MS \bullet (Ss\ in\ AB)}$
B	B–1	MSB	$\dfrac{MSB}{MS \bullet (Ss\ in\ AB)}$
AB	(A–1)(B –1)	MSAB	$\dfrac{MSAB}{MS \bullet (Ss\ in\ AB)}$
Ss in AB	AB(n–1)	MS(Ss in A)	
Within Subjects			
C	C–1	MSC	$\dfrac{MSC}{MSC \bullet (Ss\ in\ AB)}$
C*A	(C–1)(A–1)	MSCA	$\dfrac{MSAC}{MSC \bullet (Ss\ in\ AB)}$
C*B	(C–1)(B–1)	MSCB	$\dfrac{MSBC}{MSC \bullet (Ss\ in\ AB)}$
C*AB	(C–1)(A–1)(B–1)	MSCAB	$\dfrac{MSCAB}{MSC \bullet (Ss\ in\ AB)}$
C*(Ss in AB)	(C–1)[AB(n–1)]	MSC*(Ss in AB)	
Total	$(A \times B \times C \times n)–1$		

E4–83

Category: Analysis of Variance (ANOVA)
Statistical Procedure: Four-Way Split-Plot Analysis of Variance
Two Between-Subjects Factors
Two Within-Subjects Factors (Repeated Measures on Within-Subjects Factors)

Description: An ANOVA procedure that examines the variance in some dependent measure in terms of the portion of variance attributable to a between-subjects Factor A (with A levels), Factor B (with B levels), and within-subjects Factor C (with C levels), and Factor D (with D levels). Subjects within the levels of Factor A are randomly assigned to the levels of Factor B and measured repeatedly across the levels of Factor C on multiple occasions, which are the levels of Factor D. Factor A (between-subjects) might be a classification variable such as gender, Factor B (between-subjects) might be a set of treatment conditions, and Factor C (within-subjects) might be repeated trials on some task attempted before and after (Factor D) the treatments are applied. Factors A, B, C, and D are generally considered fixed factors, and n subjects in the different levels of Factor A are randomly assigned to the levels of Factor B.

Application: The appropriate analysis when subjects in different groups or categories (Factor A) are assigned to different levels of a second Factor B and measured repeatedly (Factor C) on multiple occasions (Factor D). This procedure is used in longitudinal designs when subjects in different groups are assigned to different treatment conditions and are measured several times on several occasions.

Data: Dependent variable is interval or ratio. Independent variables are discrete, nominal, ordinal, and, sometimes, interval.

Limitations: Assumes homogeneity of variance within groups, homogeneity of covariance between groups, and normal distributions in the populations and that the scale on which the dependent variable is measured is equivalent across occasions.

Comments: A powerful technique in which variation between subjects is removed as a source of variation in error terms that are used to test the hypotheses of interest. Orthogonal polynomial (**E4–93**) contrasts are often used to test trends across occasions.

Formula: Four-Way Split-Plot Analysis of Variance
        Factor A, Between-Subjects, has A levels.
        Factor B, Between-Subjects, has B levels.
        There are n subjects (Ss) in each AB level.
        Factor C, Within-Subjects, has C levels.
        Factor D, Within-Subjects, has D levels.
        Factors A, B, and C are fixed.

Source of Variation	Degrees of Freedom	Mean Squares	F-Ratio
Between Subjects			
A	A–1	MSA	$\dfrac{MSA}{MS \bullet (Ss\ in\ A)}$
B	B–1	MSB	$\dfrac{MSB}{MS \bullet (Ss\ in\ A)}$
AB	(A–1)(B–1)	MSAB	$\dfrac{MSAB}{MS \bullet (Ss\ in\ A)}$
Ss in AB	AB(n–1)	MS(Ss in A)	

Source of Variation	Degrees of Freedom	Mean Squares	F-Ratio
Within Subjects			
C	C–1	MSC	$\dfrac{MSC}{MSC \bullet (Ss\ in\ A)}$
C*A	(C–1)(A-1)	MSCA	$\dfrac{MSCA}{MSC \bullet (Ss\ in\ A)}$
C*B	(C–1)(B–1)	MSCB	$\dfrac{MSCB}{MSC \bullet (Ss\ in\ A)}$
C*AB	(C–1)(A–1)(B–1)	MSCAB	$\dfrac{MSCAB}{MSC \bullet (Ss\ in\ AB)}$
C* (Ss in AB)	(C–1)[AB(n–1)]	MSC*(Ss in AB)	
D	D–1	MSD	$\dfrac{MSD}{MSD \bullet (Ss\ in\ AB)}$
D*A	(D–1)(A–1)	MSDA	$\dfrac{MSDA}{MSD \bullet (Ss\ in\ AB)}$
D*B	(D–1)(B–1)	MSDB	$\dfrac{MSDB}{MSD \bullet (Ss\ in\ AB)}$
D*AB	(D–1)(B–1)(A–1)	MSDAB	$\dfrac{MSDAB}{MSD \bullet (Ss\ in\ AB)}$
D* (Ss in AB)	(D–1)[AB(n–1)]	MSD*(Ss in AB)	
CD	(C–1)(D–1)	MSCD	$\dfrac{MSCD}{MSCD \bullet (Ss\ in\ AB)}$
CD*A	(C–1)(D–1)(A–1)	MSCDA	$\dfrac{MSCDA}{MSCD \bullet (Ss\ in\ AB)}$
CD*B	(C–1)(D–1)(B–1)	MSCDB	$\dfrac{MSCDB}{MSCD \bullet (Ss\ in\ AB)}$
CD*AB	(C–1)(D–1)(A-1)(B–1)	MSCDAB	$\dfrac{MSCDAB}{MSCD \bullet (Ss\ in\ AB)}$
CD* (Ss in AB)	(C–1)(D–1)[AB(n–)]	MSCD*(Ss in AB)	
Total	(ABCDn)–1		

E4–84

Category: Analysis of Variance (ANOVA)

Statistical Procedure: Two-Factor Nested (Hierarchical) Design

One-Factor Nested in Another Factor

Description: An analysis of variance procedure that examines the variance in some dependent measure that can be attributed to different levels of some Factor B (with B levels), which are nested within the levels of Factor A (with A levels). Not all levels of Factor B appear across all levels of Factor A. Rather, a subset of levels of Factor B appears under the different levels of Factor A.

For example, Factor B might be teachers and Factor A might be two different methods of instruction. If half of the teachers use one method of instruction and half use the other, then teachers are nested under treatment.

The general arrangement of a two-factor nested design is illustrated for Factor A with 2 levels and Factor B with 10 levels.

<table>
<tr><td colspan="2" align="center">Factor A</td></tr>
<tr><td align="center">Level 1</td><td align="center">Level 2</td></tr>
<tr><td align="center">Factor B</td><td align="center">Factor B</td></tr>
<tr><td>Level 1</td><td>Level 6</td></tr>
<tr><td>Level 2</td><td>Level 7</td></tr>
<tr><td>Level 3</td><td>Level 8</td></tr>
<tr><td>Level 4</td><td>Level 9</td></tr>
<tr><td>Level 5</td><td>Level 10</td></tr>
</table>

Application: The appropriate analysis in two-factor designs when only some of the levels of one Factor (B) appear under each of the levels of the other Factor (A). Applicable when teachers or classrooms (Factor B) are assigned to use one of a set of different teaching methods (Factor A). Teachers/classrooms are nested under treatment in such designs. The appropriate procedure when intact groups such as classrooms are assigned to levels of some treatment.

Data: Dependent variable is interval or ratio. Independent variables are discrete, nominal, ordinal, and, sometimes, interval.

Limitations: Assumes homogeneity of variance within the nested cells and normal distributions in the populations. The subjects in the nested cells are not independent, but the levels of the nested factor are independent. Assumes no interaction between factors.

Comments: The appropriate, but often ignored, analysis when different teachers use different instructional methods in studies designed to assess differences in instructional methods. Often analyzed with a one-way analysis of variance (**E4–71**) with teaching method as the only independent variable. Such analyses violate the assumption of subject independence since sets of subjects within treatment conditions are related by reason of being in the same classroom with the same teacher. Furthermore, the one-way analysis of variance incorporates the variation between teacher within teaching method into the within-cell variance used to test hypotheses about treatment effects.

Formula: Two-Factor Nested Analysis of Variance (ANOVA)

Factor A with A levels.

Factor B with B levels nested in each level of A.

Factor B is random.

There are n subjects in each level of B nested in A.

Source of Variation	Degrees of Freedom	Mean Squares	F-Ratio
A	A–1	MSA	$\dfrac{\text{MSA}^{a}}{\text{MSB(in A)}}$
B (in A)	A(B–1)	MSB(in A)	$\dfrac{\text{MSB(in A)}}{\text{MSE}}$
Error Within cell	AB(n–1)	MSE	
Total	(ABn)–1		

[a] If Factor B is fixed, $F = \dfrac{\text{MSA}}{\text{MSE}}$

E4–85

Category: Analysis of Variance (ANOVA)

Statistical Procedure: Nested (Hierarchical) Design

Three Factors, Two Levels of Nesting

Factor C Nested in Factor B

Factor B Nested in Factor A

Description: An ANOVA procedure that examines the variance in some dependent measure that can be attributed to different levels of some Factor C (with C levels), which are nested within the levels of Factor B (with B levels). The levels of Factor B are themselves nested within the levels of Factor A (with A levels). Not all levels of Factor C appear across all levels of Factor B, and not all levels of Factor B appear across all levels of Factor A. Rather, a subset of levels of Factor C appears under the different levels of Factor B, and a subset of the levels of Factor B appears under the different levels of Factor A. For example, teachers might be Factor C nested in different schools (Factor B), using different instructional methods (Factor A). The basic arrangement for such a design is illustrated on page 398. Factor A has 2 levels, Factor B has 4 levels, and Factor C has 12 levels. Factor C, levels 1, 2, and 3, are nested under level 1 of Factor B. Factor C, levels 4, 5, and 6, are nested under level 2 of Factor B. Factor C, levels 7, 8, and 9, are nested under Factor B level 3. Factor C, levels 10, 11, and 12, are nested under Factor B, level 4. Factor B, levels 1 and 2, are nested under Factor A, level 1. Factor B, levels 3 and 4, are nested under Factor A, level 2.

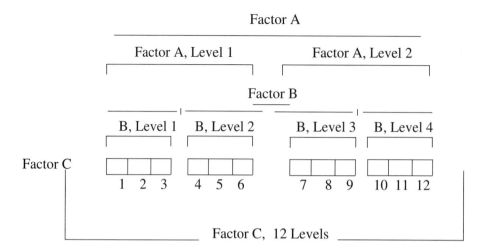

Application: The appropriate analysis in three-factor designs when only some of the levels of one Factor (C) appear under each of the levels of the other Factor (B), which itself is nested under a third Factor (A). Applicable when teachers/classrooms (Factor C) within different schools (Factor B) are assigned to use one of a set of different teaching methods (Factor A). Teachers/classrooms are nested under schools and under treatment in such designs. The appropriate procedure when intact groups such as classrooms are assigned to levels of some treatment factor.

Data: Dependent variable is interval or ratio. Independent variables are discrete, nominal, ordinal, and, sometimes, interval.

Limitations: Assumes homogeneity of variance within the nested cells and normal distributions in the populations. The subjects in the nested cells are not independent, but the levels of the nested factor are independent. Assumes no interaction between factors.

Comments: The appropriate, but often ignored, analysis when different teachers in different schools use different instructional methods in studies designed to assess differences in instructional methods. Schools and methods are not independent. Often analyzed (inappropriately) with a one-way analysis of variance (teaching method). Such analyses violate the assumption of subject independence since sets of subjects within treatment conditions are related by reason of being in the same classroom with the same teacher.

Formula: Three-Factor Nested Analysis of Variance

Factor A with A levels.

Factor B with B levels nested in each level of A.

Factor C with C levels nested in each level of B.

Factors B and C are random.

There are n subjects in each level of C nested in B nested in A.

Source of Variation	Degrees of Freedom	Mean Squares	F-Ratio
A	A–1	MSA	$\dfrac{\text{MSA}^{\text{a}}}{\text{MSB(in A)}}$
B (in A)	A(B–1)	MSB(in A)	$\dfrac{\text{MSB(in A)}}{\text{MSC(in A in B)}}$
C (in B in A)	AB(C–1)	MSC(in B in A)	$\dfrac{\text{MSC(in B in A)}}{\text{MSE}}$
Error within cell	ABC(n–1)	MSE	
Total	(ABCn)–1		

[a]If all factors are fixed, the MSE is the denominator in all the F-ratios.

E4–86

Category: Analysis of Variance (ANOVA)

Statistical Procedure: Three-Factor Design

One Factor Nested in Another

Third Factor Crossed with the Nested Factors

Description: An analysis of variance procedure that examines the variance in some dependent measure in terms of the portion of variance that can be attributed to (1) Factor B (with B levels), which is nested in (2) Factor A (with A levels) and (3) Factor C (with C levels), which is crossed with Factor B nested in A. Appropriate in nested designs that have a third factor crossing all levels of the nested factors.

The basic arrangement for this type of design is shown below. In this illustration, Factor C, with 2 levels, is crossed with Factor B, with 6 levels. These factors are crossed because all levels of Factor C appear under all levels of Factor B. Factor B is nested in Factor A, with 2 levels. These factors are nested since only some of the levels of Factor B appear under some of the levels of Factor A. Levels 1, 2, and 3 of Factor B are nested under level 1 of Factor A. Levels 4, 5, and 6 of Factor B are nested under level 2 of Factor A.

Factor A

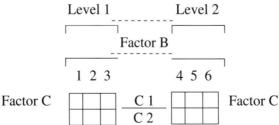

Application: Used when some classification or categorical Factor C crosses the levels of some nested Factor B within the levels of some third Factor A. For example, the analysis would be used in a design in which teachers (Factor B) were nested within experimental teaching method (Factor A) and students' gender (Factor C) was crossed with teachers nested within method.

Data: Dependent variable is interval or ratio. Independent variables are discrete, nominal, ordinal, and, sometimes, interval.

Limitations: Assumes homogeneity of variance within groups, normal distributions in the populations, and no interactions between the nested factors (e.g., Factor B and Factor A).

Comments: An appropriate analysis when teaching methods (Factor A) are assigned to schools and taught by different teachers (Factor B). Factor C might be gender of students or some aptitude measure employed to assess aptitude-treatment interaction (C × A) effects.

Formula: Crossed and Nested Analysis of Variance
        Factor A with A levels.
        Factor B with B levels nested in each level of Factor A.
        Factor C with C levels crossed with B in Factor A.
        Factors A and C are fixed; Factor B is random.
        There are n subjects in each level of C crossed with B in A.

Source of Variation	Degrees of Freedom	Mean Squares	F-Ratio
A	A–1	MSA	$\dfrac{\text{MSA}^{a}}{\text{MSB(in A)}}$
B (in A)	A(B–1)	MSB(in A)	$\dfrac{\text{MSB(in A)}}{\text{MSE}}$
C	(C–1)	MSC	$\dfrac{\text{MSC}^{a}}{\text{MSC} \bullet [\text{B(inA)}]}$
C*A	(C–1)(A–1)	MSCA	$\dfrac{\text{MSCA}^{a}}{\text{MSC} \bullet [\text{B(in A)}]}$
C*[B(in A)]	(C–1)[A(B–1)]	MSC*B(in A)	$\dfrac{\text{MSC} \bullet [\text{B(in A)}]}{\text{MSE}}$
Error within cell	ABC(n–1)	MSE	
Total	(ABCn)–1		

[a]If all factors are fixed, the MSE is the denominator in all the F-ratios.

E4–87

Category: Analysis of Variance (ANOVA)

Statistical Procedure: Randomized Block Designs

Description: A large class of research designs and analysis of variance procedures in which a blocking variable is used in the design and analysis to reduce error variance. The blocking variable is an independent variable added to the design and analysis. Hypotheses about the blocking factor are not usually of any particular interest. There are always statistically significant differences in the levels of the blocking factor or the blocking factor is of no value in reducing error variance. The analysis with a blocking factor, in contrast to the same analysis without the blocking factor, partitions the error term into a new source of systematic variation, namely, variation due to the blocking factor.

Application: Randomized block designs can be used with virtually any analysis of variance model. The levels of the blocking factor may contain one subject in each cell, in which case a repeated measures design is appropriate with replications on the blocking variable. Such a design would be treated as a two-way mixed model **(E4–74)**, with treatments fixed and subjects (the blocking factor) random. In all applications, the researcher must determine whether the levels of the blocking factor are fixed or random and whether each cell will contain one or more subjects.

Data: Dependent variable is interval or ratio. Independent variables are discrete, nominal, ordinal, and, sometimes, interval.

Limitations: Assumes homogeneity of variance within groups, normal distributions in the populations, and other assumptions depending on the specific nature of the design.

Comments: Randomized block designs with appropriate analyses are a class of very powerful, error-reducing procedures. Occasionally, a factor can be both a blocking variable and a variable of interest, as in the case of aptitude-treatment interaction research. Levels of the aptitude factor reduce within-group variance and thus increase the power to detect treatment effects and, at the same time, enable the researcher to check for aptitude-treatment interactions.

Care must be exercised in using randomized block designs. If the blocking variable does not account for a significant proportion of variation, the analysis becomes less powerful in detecting effects on the other factors because degrees of freedom for error are reduced when the blocking factor is partitioned out of the error term. In addition, it is essential that all blocking factors in the design be incorporated into the analysis because, otherwise, within-cell error is maximized, and degrees of freedom for error are reduced.

Formula: Randomized block designs can be incorporated into virtually all of the previously described ANOVA procedures **(E4–71** to **E4–83),** with the blocking factor simply becoming one of the factors in the design and analysis.

E4–88

Category: Analysis of Variance (ANOVA)

Statistical Procedure: Latin Square Designs

Description: A large class of research designs and analysis of variance procedures in which two sources of potential extraneous variation can be controlled by including factors in the design analysis that represent them. Very often used to control for effects due to the order in which treatments are presented. Also used to control for practice effects that are related to the order of the treatments.

Latin squares is described by using a 3 × 3 model to assess the effects of three treatments, A, B, and C. The design is constructed by first selecting a Latin square of the appropriate size from a table of Latin square designs. In the 3 × 3 case with treatments A, B, and C, one such design would have the form:

	Columns		
	1	2	3
Row 1	A	B	C
Row 2	B	C	A
Row 3	C	A	B

Each treatment appears once in each row and column. This is referred to as the standard form. The three rows are then randomly repositioned, and the three columns are randomly repositioned. Each treatment still appears only once in each row and column.

Application: Latin square designs are commonly used to control variation due to order, sequence, practice effects, and other possible confounding effects in experimental research. In this example of a 3 × 3 Latin square design, suppose A, B, and C were experimental treatments and n subjects were assigned to each of the 9 cells in the design. The row and column effects would partition out from the error term variation due to order (A,B,C;B,C,D;C,D,A) and ordinal position (first, second, third).

Latin square designs are commonly used to simplify higher-order factorial designs by using the Latin square as an incomplete factorial design. With a 3 × 3 × 3 design, for example, two of the factors could be used as row and column control variables in the Latin square that could be used to study the third factor.

Data: Dependent variable is interval or ratio. Independent variables are discrete, nominal, ordinal, and, sometimes, interval.

Limitations: Assumes homogeneity of variance within groups and normal distributions in the populations, and, with repeated measures designs, the assumption of homogeneity of covariance is made.

Comments: Latin square designs are useful and powerful in controlling sources of confounding variance in experimental research. The application of Latin square designs requires considerable control in conducting an experiment, and thus, such designs often cannot be used in applied educational research where rigorous control is not possible.

Formula: For L × L Latin Square Design

With Rows (R), Columns (C), and Treatments (T), each with L levels, and n subjects in each cell.

Source of Variation	Degrees of Freedom	Mean Squares	F-Ratio*
Rows	L–1	MSR	MSR/MSW
Columns	L–1	MSC	MSC/MSW

Source of Variation	Degrees of Freedom	Mean Squares	F-Ratio*
Treatment	L–1	MSTrt	MSTrt /MSW
Residual	(L–1)(L–2)	MSRes	MSRes/MSW
Within	L × L × (n–1)	MSW	
Total	(L × L × n)–1		

*In Latin squares with repeated measures such that n = 1, the denominator for all F-ratios is MSRes.

E4–89

Category: Analysis of Variance (ANOVA)
Related Designs
Analysis of Covariance (ANCOVA)

Statistical Procedure: Analysis of Covariance

Description: A large class of designs and associated analyses in which a continuous, independent variable known as a covariate is introduced into an analysis of variance design to increase the statistical power of the analysis. The covariate is sometimes called a concomitant variable, and more than one covariate can be used. The covariate is systematically related to the dependent variable and is used to reduce the estimate of random or error variance in the dependent measure. The reduction of error variance is accomplished by regressing the dependent variable onto the covariate and extracting the sum of squares due to regression from the sum of squares due to error. Covariates can be used in virtually all analysis of variance designs.

Applications: Analysis of covariance is commonly used in pretest-posttest designs with the pretest as the covariate. Alternative forms of tests can be used as covariate and dependent measures. Aptitude measures are often used as covariates in analyses that have achievement measures as dependent variables.

Analysis of covariance is sometimes used to correct for sampling bias or error. This application of analysis of covariance can be misleading.

Data: The dependent variable is interval or ratio. Independent variables are discrete and may be nominal, ordinal, or, sometimes, interval. The covariate is continuous and is interval or ratio.

Limitations: All assumptions of the corresponding analysis of variance procedure apply to the analysis of covariance. In addition, analysis of covariance assumes that the relationships between the covariates and the dependent measure are statistically equivalent within all groups or cells in the design. With a one-way analysis of covariance, this assumption means that the regression lines of the dependent variable that has been regressed onto the covariate within each group are all parallel. In general, this assumption is referred to as parallelism of regression. Violations of the assumption seriously jeopardize the validity of inferences drawn from the analysis.

Comments: The value of analysis of covariance is directly related to the strength of the relationship between the dependent variable and the covariate. The stronger the relationship, the greater the gain in power and precision. Using a covariate that is weakly related to the dependent variable can be counterproductive and actually reduce power and precision. This is because the covariate reduces the error degrees of freedom without reducing the sum of squares due to error.

Using analysis of covariance to correct for bias or errors in sampling or for the actual difference between groups can be problematic. Such applications create statistical conditions that may have no real-life counterpart. For example, consider an experiment in which a remedial education treatment group is compared to a control group of children in regular classes, using a one-way analysis of covariance with a pretest as covariate and posttest as the dependent measure. The analysis of covariance leads to inferences about group differences on the posttest under the statistical condition that the two groups were equivalent at the beginning of the study. Such inferences are valid and generalize to other situations only if the same conditions exist—that is, only if the groups are equivalent at the beginning of the instruction. In real school settings, however, students referred for remedial instruction and students in regular classes are not equivalent prior to instruction. Thus, the conditional inference from the analysis of covariance could be misleading since it does not apply to the context of greatest interest.

Formula: The analysis of covariance is quite similar to the analysis of variance into which the covariate is introduced. The analysis of covariance has an additional source of variation due to the covariate(s). This source of variation has one degree of freedom for each covariate, and the degrees of freedom extracted from the error degrees of freedom.

The number of Covariates = 1.

Factor A, Between Groups, has A levels.

There are n subjects in each group.

Source of Variation	Degrees of Freedom	Mean Squares	F-Ratio
Covariate	I	MSCOV	MSCOV/MSW
Between Groups	A–1	MSB	MSB/MSW
Within Groups	N–(A–I)–1	MSW	
Total	N–1		

E4–90

Category: Analysis of Variance (ANOVA)

     Related Designs

     Time-Series Analysis

Statistical Procedure: Time-Series Analysis

     Interrupted Time-Series Analysis

Description: Time-series analysis and interrupted time-series analysis refer to a large class of procedures and analyses used to examine trends or changes over time. These procedures can be performed using various regression procedures or a specialized set of procedures called auto regressive integrated moving average (ARIMA) models. The ARIMA models are useful in a wide variety of applications. ARIMA models are designed to deal with three sources of "noise" that confound the study of change over time. These are (1) trend—gradual but consistent drifts upward or downward over time, (2) seasonality—cyclic trends repeating at certain times, and (3) random error. ARIMA models have three structural parameters, namely, P, D, and Q. ARIMA models are specified in terms of these parameters as ARIMA (P, D, Q) models. P refers to the autoregressive relationship. D refers to the series being "differenced," for example, subtracting successive values in the series. Q refers to the number of moving average structures in the model. For more information, interested readers should consult Ostrom (1978); Cook and Campbell (1979); McDowall, McCleary, Meidinger, and Hay (1980).

Application: Time-series analysis can be applied to any situation where there are periodic observations or measurements over some period of time. Time-series analysis is used in a wide range of disciplines, including economics, education, history, psychology, and sociology. Interrupted time-series analysis is used to assess the impact of some event or treatment on some dependent measure. In education, for example, these procedures could be used to assess the impact of changes in school policy on dropout rates. Dropout rates for a period of years before and after the policy change would be examined using the appropriate ARIMA. The ARIMA model would be used to determine if there had been a change in the dropout rate associated with the policy change.

Data: A wide range of data can be used with these procedures. Many data points are required for their application.

Limitations: Time-series analysis is not applicable to many educational situations because a large number of observations or measurements must be made over time.

Comments: Time-series procedures are generally applied in quasi-experimental settings where the researcher does not have control over the selection and assignment of subjects. The application of these procedures can, nonetheless, be quite informative.

The number of periodic observations required for the application of these procedures is difficult to specify; 20 observations would constitute a relatively short series of observations. With a small number of observations, repeated measures and split-plot analysis of variance (**E4–79** to **E4–83**) procedures need to be considered if the necessary assumptions are met.

Formula: The references in the description section provide the various formulas for time-series analysis.

E4–91
MULTIPLE COMPARISON PROCEDURES

A Priori Planned Comparisons

(**E4–92**) Orthogonal Contrasts
(**E4–93**) Orthogonal Polynomial Contrasts

Post Hoc Comparisons

(**E4–94**) Scheffé Contrasts
(**E4–95**) Tukey's Honestly Significant Difference

(**E4–96**) Newman-Keuls Test
(**E4–97**) Duncan Multiple Range Test

E4–92

Category: Multiple Comparison Procedures—A Priori, Planned Comparisons
Statistical Procedures: Orthogonal Contrasts
Description: A general procedure for independent tests of particular hypotheses about specific means or combinations of means in the context of analysis of variance when the overall test of the null hypothesis is not of interest. The use of orthogonal contrasts maintains the Type I error rate for the individual comparisons and for the total set of analyses. Orthogonal contrasts test particular hypotheses by partitioning the sum of squares and degrees of freedom for a given factor into separate and independent sources of variation. For Factor A (with A levels), there are A–1 degrees of freedom for orthogonal contrasts. There can be only A–1 orthogonal contrasts. Contrasts are orthogonal if the sum of the cross products of their corresponding coefficients is equal to zero. These contrasts do not require equal cell sizes.
Application: Orthogonal contrasts are used to test particular hypotheses about the difference between specific means or combinations of means. In such cases, the overall F-test for the null hypothesis may be of no particular interest. Studies involving experimental treatment conditions and a control group often use orthogonal contrasts to compare different experimental treatment conditions with the control group.
Data: The same data are used in the orthogonal contrasts as are used in the analysis of variance.
Limitations: All assumptions of the analysis of variance procedures apply. By definition, the orthogonal contrasts are independent of each other, which means that the sum of the cross products of the corresponding coefficients is zero. There can be only as many orthogonal contrasts as there are degrees of freedom for the factor in question.
Comments: Orthogonal contrasts are used when the researcher has specific hypotheses within the overall analysis of variance design. Often used in experimental research in which theoretical considerations lead to specific hypotheses designed to test theoretical claims.
Formula: Orthogonal contrasts are tested with an F-statistic using 1 and the degrees of freedom within from the analysis of variance procedure, for example, the degrees of freedom for contrast = (1, df within).

$$F = \frac{\left(\sum_{J=1}^{A} C_j \overline{X}_j \right)^2}{MSW \left[\sum_{j=1}^{A} (C_j^2 / n_j) \right]}$$

where
C_j = contrast coefficient for Group j
MSW = mean square within from ANOVA

E4–93

Category: Multiple Comparison Procedures—A Priori, Planned Comparisons

Statistical Procedures: Orthogonal Polynomial Contrasts

Description: A special type of orthogonal contrast that tests geometric trends in the differences among means. Orthogonal polynomial contrasts have all the characteristics of general orthogonal contrast. In addition, they specifically test whether differences among group means are linear, quadratic, cubic, quartic, etc.

Data: The same data are used in orthogonal polynomial contrasts as are used in the analysis of variance.

Limitations: All assumptions of the analysis of variance procedure apply. By definition, there are as many orthogonal polynomial contrasts as there are degrees of freedom for the factor in question.

Comments: Orthogonal polynomial contrasts are used when the research has specific hypotheses about the nature of the differences among groups in the overall analysis of variance design. Often used in developmental research with repeated measures designs to examine the nature of growth that occurs across developmental periods.

Formula: Orthogonal polynomial contrasts are tested with an F-statistic with 1 and the degrees of freedom within from the analysis of variance.

Levels	Trend	Coefficients
3	Linear	−1 0 1
3	Quadratic	1 −2 1
4	Linear	−3 −1 1 3
4	Quadratic	1 −1 −1 1
4	Cubic	−1 3 −3 1
5	Linear	−2 −1 0 1 2
5	Quadratic	2 −1 −2 −1 2
5	Cubic	−1 2 0 −2 1
5	Quartic	1 −4 6 −4 1

$$F = \frac{\left(\sum_{j=1}^{A} C_j \overline{X}_j \right)^2}{MSW \left[\sum_{j=1}^{A} (C_j^2 / n_j) \right]}$$

where

C_j = contrast coefficient for Group j

MSW = mean square within from ANOVA

E4–94

Category: Multiple Comparison Procedures, Post Hoc Comparisons

Statistical Procedure: Scheffé Contrasts

Description: A general procedure for comparing two or more means in the context of analysis of variance. Specific hypotheses about pairs of means or other combinations of more than two means can be tested with Scheffé contrasts. The calculation of the Scheffé contrasts is identical to the calculation of orthogonal contrasts **(E4–92)**.

The critical value for testing the significance of Scheffé contrasts is the critical value from the analysis of variance for the factor involving the contrasts, multiplied by the degrees of freedom for that factor. The critical value is thus inflated, making this a conservative test.

Application: Used when a significant overall F-test in an analysis of variance is obtained. Scheffé contrasts are used to determine exactly which means or sets of means are different from each other at a statistically significant level. Often used in experiments with multiple treatment conditions and a control group to test the difference between specific treatments and the difference between all treatments combined and the control group.

Limitations: Scheffé contrasts are not independent (orthogonal). Scheffé contrasts are conservative and result in fewer significant differences than are observed using Tukey **(E4–95)** or Newman-Keuls **(E4–96)**. Because of the conservative nature of Scheffé contrasts, they may not be desirable for pairwise contrasts with equal n's. Scheffé contrasts should be used for complex contrasts or situations with unequal cells.

Comments: The use of Scheffé contrasts maintains the experiment-wise Type I error rate. Scheffé contrasts are very versatile but conservative in testing hypotheses.

Formula:

$$F = \frac{\left(\sum_{j=1}^{A} C_j \overline{X}_j \right)^2}{MSW \left[\sum_{j=1}^{A} (C_j^2 / n_j) \right]}$$

where

C_j = contrast coefficents for group j
MSW = mean square within from ANOVA
n_j = number of Ss in group j

Tested against $(A-1) \times F$,
where F is the critical value from
the ANOVA for Factor A with A Levels

E4–95

Category: Multiple Comparison Procedures—Post Hoc Comparisons
Statistical Procedure: Tukey's Honestly Significant Difference Using the Q-Statistic
Description: A procedure for comparing all pairs of means in the context of analysis of variance to test for significant differences between pairs of means. The Tukey procedure maintains the overall experiment-wise error rate at the predetermined alpha level. The Q-statistic is used to test whether differences between pairs of means are statistically significant. The Q-statistic is the difference between the means divided by the

square root of the ANOVA error mean square after it is divided by the number of subjects in each cell. The Tukey procedure is not as powerful as the Newman-Keuls procedure (E4-96), but the Tukey method maintains the Type I error rate. The degrees of freedom for the critical value of Q is (r, and df-within), where r is the number of means, and df-within is the degrees of freedom within group from the ANOVA.

Application: A standard procedure for examining pairwise differences after a significant overall F-ratio has been found in an analysis of variance. Often tests of all pairwise differences are made when the researcher does not have conceptually based hypotheses that focus attention on specific pairs of means or combinations of means.

Data: Dependent variable is interval or ratio. The independent variable defining groups in nominal, ordinal, or, sometimes, interval.

Limitations: The Tukey method is appropriate only when there are equal cell sizes in all levels of the independent variable in question. The Tukey method is not as statistically powerful as some other methods, notably, Newman-Keuls, but Tukey maintains the Type I error rate at the predetermined level.

Comments: The Tukey method is somewhat conservative, but pairwise differences detected using this method would be detected using any other method. Although the procedure requires equal cell sizes for the levels of the independent variable in question, an approximation of the Tukey method can be made for unequal cell sizes by using the harmonic $\hat{n}$ for the cell size. The harmonic $\hat{n}$ is of the form:

$$\hat{n} = \frac{A}{\dfrac{1}{n_1} + \dfrac{1}{n_2} + \ldots + \dfrac{1}{n_A}} \qquad A = \text{Number of groups}$$

Formula:

$$Q = \frac{\overline{X}_i - \overline{X}_j}{\sqrt{MSW / n}}$$

where MSW = mean square within ANOVA

E4–96

Category: Multiple Comparison Procedures—Post Hoc Comparisons

Statistical Procedure: Newman-Keuls Test for Pairwise Differences Using the Q-Statistic

Description: A procedure for comparing all pairs of means in the context of analysis of variance to test for significant differences between pairs of means. The procedure requires that the means be ordered for testing, generally from the lowest to the highest, left to right. Pairwise differences between all means are calculated, and, since the means are ordered, adjacent pairs are closer in value than other pairs. The Q-statistic is used to test whether differences between pairs of means are statistically significant. The Q-statistic, calculated as in the Tukey method, is the difference between the means divided by the square root of the ANOVA error mean square after it has been divided by the number of subjects in each cell. The Newman-Keuls method is more powerful in detecting significant pairwise differences than the Tukey procedure (**E4–95**). The Newman-Keuls method, however, inflates the experiment's Type I error rate. The critical values of Q used in the Newman-Keuls tests are determined sequentially as a function of r and the error degrees of freedom, where r is the number of steps between ordered means tested plus 1, and the error degrees of freedom are the degrees of freedom-within from the ANOVA.

Application: A standard procedure for examining pairwise differences after a significant overall F-ratio has been found in an analysis of variance. Often, tests of all pairwise differences are made when the researcher does not have conceptually based hypotheses that focus attention on specific pairs of means or combinations of means.

Data: Dependent variable is interval or ratio. The independent variable defining groups is nominal, ordinal, or, sometimes, interval.

Limitations: The Newman-Keuls method is appropriate only when there are equal cell sizes in all levels of the independent variable in question. The Newman-Keuls method is statistically powerful but inflates the experiment's overall experiment-wise Type I error rate.

Comments: The Newman-Keuls method is statistically powerful and hence detects pairwise differences that might not be detected using other methods. Although the procedure requires equal cell sizes for the levels of the independent variable in question, an approximation to the Newman-Keuls method can be made for unequal cell sizes by using the harmonic $\hat{n}$ for the cell size. The harmonic $\hat{n}$ is of the form:

$$\hat{n} = \frac{A}{\dfrac{1}{n_1} + \dfrac{1}{n_2} + \ldots + \dfrac{1}{n_A}} \qquad A = \text{Number of groups}$$

Formula:

$$Q = \frac{\overline{X}_i - \overline{X}_j}{\sqrt{MSW / n}}$$

where MSW = mean square within from ANOVA

E4–97

Category: Multiple Comparison Procedures—Post Hoc Comparisons

Statistical Procedure: Duncan Multiple Range Test for Pairwise Differences Using the Q-Statistic

Description: A procedure for comparing all pairs of means in the context of analysis of variance to test for significant differences between pairs of means. The procedure requires that the means be ordered for testing, generally from the lowest to the highest, left to right. Pairwise differences between all means are calculated, and, since the means are ordered, adjacent pairs are closer in value than other pairs. The Q-statistic is used to test whether differences between pairs of means are statistically significant. The Q-statistic, calculated as in the Tukey and Newman-Keuls methods, is the difference between two means divided by the square root of the analysis of variance error mean square after it has been divided by the number of subjects in each cell. The Duncan multiple range test detects more significant differences than the Newman-Keuls method (**E4-96**), which, in turn is more powerful than the Tukey procedure (**E4-95**). However, the Duncan method, like the Newman-Keuls method, inflates the experiment's Type I error rate. Like the Newman-Keuls method, the critical values of Q used in the Duncan method are determined sequentially as a function of r and the error degrees of freedom, where r is the number of steps between ordered means tested plus 1, and the error degrees of freedom are the degrees of freedom-within from the analysis of variance. The Duncan method differs substantially from the Newman-Keuls method in that it inflates the significance level for each paired-comparison depending on how many other means fall between the two means being compared. The farther apart two means are in the ordering of means, the more lenient the significance level used to test the difference. The adjustment is of the form $1-(1-\alpha)^{r-1}$, where α is the Type I error rate and r is the number of means between the two ordered means being compared plus 1.

Application: A common procedure for examining pairwise differences after a significant overall F-ratio is found in an analysis of variance. Often, tests of all pairwise differences are made when the researcher does not have conceptually based hypotheses focusing attention on specific pairs of means or combinations of means.

Data: Dependent variable is interval or ratio. The independent variable defining groups is nominal, ordinal, or, sometimes, interval.

Limitations: The Duncan multiple range test is appropriate only when there are equal cell sizes in all levels of the independent variable in question. The Duncan test is statistically powerful but inflates the overall experiment-wise Type I error rate.

Comments: The Duncan test is statistically powerful and, hence, detects pairwise differences that might not be detected using other methods. Although the procedure requires equal cells for the levels of the independent variable in question, an approximation to the Duncan method can be made for unequal cell sizes by using the harmonic $\hat{n}$ for the cell size. The harmonic $\hat{n}$ is of the form:

$$\hat{n} = \frac{A}{\dfrac{1}{n_1} + \dfrac{1}{n_2} + \ldots + \dfrac{1}{n_A}} \qquad A = \text{number of groups}$$

Formula:

$$Q = \frac{\overline{X}_i - \overline{X}_j}{\sqrt{MSW / n}}$$

where MSW = mean square within from ANOVA

REFERENCES AND RESOURCES

Campbell, D. T., and Stanley, J. C. (1966). *Experimental and Quasi-Experimental Designs for Research.* Chicago: Rand McNally.

Cody, R. P., and Smith, J.K. (1887). *Applied Statistics and the SAS Programming Language.* 2nd ed. New York: North Holland.

Cook, T. D., and Campbell, D.T. (1979). *Quasi-Experimentation: Design and Analysis Issues for Field Settings.* Chicago: Rand McNally.

Cureton, E. E., and D'Agostino, R. B. (1993). *Factor Analysis: An Applied Approach.* Hillsdale, NJ: Lawrence Erlbaum Associates.

Glass, G. V., and Stanley, J. C. (1970). *Statistical Methods in Education and Psychology.* Englewood Cliffs, NJ: Prentice-Hall.

Hays, W. L. (1994). *Statistics.* 5th ed. Fort Worth: Harcourt Brace.

Hinkle, D. E., Wiersma, W., and Jurs, S. G. (1998). *Applied Statistics for the Behavioral Sciences,* 5th ed. Boston: Houghton Mifflin.

Kim, J., and Mueller, C. W. (1978). *Introduction to Factor Analysis: What It Is and How to Do It.* Sage University Paper series on Quantitative Application in the Social Sciences, 07-013. Beverly Hills, CA, and London: Sage.

Marascuilo, L. A., and McSweeney, M. (1977). *Nonparametric and Distribution Free Methods for the Social Sciences.* Monterey, CA: Brooks/Cole.

Maxwell, S. E., and Delaney, H. D. (1990). *Designing Experiments and Analyzing Data.* Pacific Grove, CA: Wadsworth.

McDowall, D., McCleary, R., Meidinger, E. E., and Hay, R., Jr. (1980). *Interrupted Time Series Analysis.* Sage University Paper series on Quantitative Application in the Social Sciences, 07-021. Beverly Hills, CA, and London: Sage.

Mulaik, S. A. (1972). *The Foundations of Factor Analysis.* New York: McGraw-Hill.

Ostrom, C. W., Jr. (1978). *Time Series Analysis: Regression Techniques.* Sage University Paper series on Quantitative Application in the Social Sciences, 07-009. Beverly Hills, CA, and London: Sage.

Rencher, A. C. (1995). *Methods of Multivariate Analysis.* New York, NY: John Wiley and Sons.

Seigel, S. (1956). *Nonparametric Statistics for the Behavioral Sciences.* New York: McGraw-Hill.

Winer, B. J., Brown, D. R., and Michels, K. M. (1991). *Statistical Principles in Experimental Design.* 3rd ed. New York: McGraw-Hill.

CHAPTER 5

A Summary of Sampling Techniques

INTRODUCTION

The issues involved in obtaining a useful sample of subjects from some population are many and complex. Choices have to be made in a process that contains numerous steps, each with several options. Educators should consider the following four helpful criteria for assessing sampling designs: (1) goal orientation, (2) measurability, (3) practicality, and (4) economy (Kish 1965). "Goal orientation" refers to the need to consider the overall purpose of the research project in making decisions about sampling issues. "Measurability" means that the sampling design allows for the computation of valid estimates of sampling variability or sampling error. "Practicality," as the term suggests, means that the procedures required by the design can actually be carried out in practice, not just in theory. "Economy" refers to the productive use of the often limited resources available for collecting the data needed to complete the research project. All four of these criteria should be carefully considered by the researcher as decisions are made about a sampling design.

The goal orientation criterion focuses the researcher's attention on the purpose of the research project. Broadly speaking, sampling designs can be used in two different types of research settings, each with a different research purpose or orientation. These differences have significant implications for the sampling procedures.

First, sampling designs are critical in survey research and are generally referred to as survey sampling. In this setting, samples are selected from a population and used to estimate directly characteristics of that population, such as the mean, the sum of a variable, or a proportion of subjects in some category. Survey sampling has two integral components: the selection process and the estimation process. These components are not considered separately but are interactive. Often, the researcher determines which type of estimation is desired, and this dictates the selection process. In other situations, the criteria of practicality and economy dictate the selection process, which, in turn, determines the estimation process.

Second, sampling designs are critical in experimental research. In this application, a sample is selected from a population and then assigned to groups receiving different experimental treatment conditions to test hypotheses about the effects of those various treatments. In this setting, careful sampling procedures are employed to improve the generalizability of the experimental research. The generalizability of an experimental study is also called the study's external validity.

This chapter is concerned primarily with sampling as it relates to the second of these two applications, namely, experimental research and hypothesis testing. Major sampling concepts and procedures used to improve the external validity of experimental studies are reviewed. The technical issues involved in the estimation processes of survey sampling are not examined in detail.

413

SELECTION AND ASSIGNMENT

It is important to differentiate two separate steps in the use of samples in experimental research. These are sample selection and sample assignment. Sample selection refers to a set of procedures used to obtain a sample from a population. Sample assignment refers to a set of procedures used to allocate subjects from the sample to different treatment conditions or groups. The role of sample selection and assignment is illustrated in the following figure:

Sample selection, the process of obtaining a sample from a population, is concerned primarily with generalizability or external validity. Sample assignment procedures, used for allocating subjects from the sample to treatment groups, are concerned primarily with internal validity. The example shows four groups, but any number of groups might be involved.

In this chapter, entries are organized according to three major categories: (1) sampling concepts, (2) sampling procedures, and (3) assignment procedures.

SAMPLING CONCEPTS AND PROCEDURES

Sampling Concepts

> **(E5–1)** Population
> **(E5–2)** Sampling Frame
> **(E5–3)** Sampling Unit
> **(E5–4)** Model Sampling (Nonrandom Sampling)
> **(E5–5)** Probability Sampling (Random Sampling)
> **(E5–6)** Estimators
> **(E5–7)** Sampling without Replacement
> **(E5–8)** Multistage Sampling
> **(E5–9)** Multiple Matrix Sampling

Sampling Procedures

> **(E5–10)** Simple Random Sampling
> **(E5–11)** Stratified Sampling
> **(E5–12)** Homogeneous Sampling
> **(E5–13)** Systematic Sampling
> **(E5–14)** Cluster Sampling

Assignment Procedures

(E5–15) Assigning Subjects to Groups

PROFILES OF SAMPLING CONCEPTS AND PROCEDURES

E5–1

Category: Sampling Concepts

Concept: Population

Description: The aggregation of elements or subjects for which the results of a study are to be generalized. A precise definition of a population would describe it in terms of (1) content, (2) units, (3) extent, and (4) time (Kish 1965, p. 7), for example, (1) all students, (2) in third grade classrooms, (3) in Arizona, (4) in spring 2002. The population of interest is called the target population. For practical reasons, samples cannot always be obtained from the target poulation as defined. In such cases, the definition of the target population is modified to define the accessible or operational population.

Application: Carefully defining the population is a critical and often overlooked step in educational research. The difference between the target population and accessible population should be noted with care. When nonrandom samples are used in educational research, hypothetical populations are sometimes defined to reflect the characteristics of the available sample. The sample is then alleged to represent the theoretical population.

Comments: The external validity of a study is not enhanced by defining a hypothetical population to which research results, based on nonrandom samples, can be generalized. If the researcher wishes to generalize the results of a study, a well-defined population must be identified from which some type of random sample can be drawn.

E5–2

Category: Sampling Concepts

Concept: Sampling Frame

Description: The sampling frame is the actual listing of members of the population from which the sample is drawn. In a sense, the sampling frame is the authoritative operational definition of the accessible population. The ideal sampling frame lists every element of the target population only once and lists no other extraneous elements. In practice, sampling frames rarely have a perfect, one-to-one matching with the target population. In such cases, the target population might be redefined to match the sampling frame. Alternatively, the sampling frame might be edited or augmented with other lists to increase the congruence between the target population and the sampling frame.

Applications: All sampling designs involve the use of a sampling frame at some point. In educational research, the sampling frame might be a list of students, teachers, schools, or school districts. In practice, sampling frames are often used because they are conveniently available, and little care is taken to assess the quality of the sampling frame. For example, a common problem is that lists of students and teachers often do not reflect recent changes. In such cases, the sampling frames do not reflect transfer students, students who drop out, new teachers, teachers on leave, and teachers who retire.

Comments: The careful selection, preparation, or documentation of a sampling frame is a critical step in the sampling process because it is the operational definition of the accessible population.

E5–3

Category: Sampling Concepts

Concept: Sampling Unit

Description: Populations are defined in terms of the elements or units for which the researcher seeks information. The sampling unit refers to these basic elements, which are sampled to represent the accessible population.

Applications: In educational research, the sampling unit can be any one of a number of basic elements. For example, the sample unit might be individual students, classrooms of students, a school district, or an entire state.

Comments: It is important to clearly define the sampling unit because, in most cases, must be the unit used in the statistical analysis, and generalization can be made only to these units. For example, if classrooms are the sampling unit, data must be analyzed at the classroom level, not at the student level.

E5–4

Category: Sampling Concepts

Concept: Model Sampling or Nonrandom Sampling

Description: Model sampling refers to nonrandom sampling procedures that are based on an implicit "model." The model makes general assumptions about the distribution of the relevant variable or variables in the population. The assumption implicit in the use of the model is that the variable or variables of interest are distributed in the population in such a way that the researcher can obtain representative samples without random selection.

Applications: Many types of model sampling or nonrandom sampling are well known. These include:

> VOLUNTEER SAMPLES. Subjects are invited to participate in a study in which they volunteer.
>
> CONVENIENCE SAMPLES. Subjects are chosen because they are readily available.
>
> PAID SAMPLES. Subjects are encouraged to participate in a study with some form of payment.
>
> JUDGMENT SAMPLES. Subjects are selected based on expert judgment of their representativeness.
>
> QUOTA SAMPLES. Subjects are selected to match the population proportion on certain demographic variables.

Comments: Model sampling is based on the general assumption (or hope) that the variable or variables of interest is distributed in the population in a way that yields a representative sample, using the techniques described earlier. This assumption is rarely appropriate. For example, judgment sampling would assume that a school principal could identify "typical classrooms" for use in an experiment. Samples obtained using these procedures cannot be considered representative.

Such samples may be useful for pilot studies and for field testing measuring instruments; however, these sampling procedures do not support the external validity of research studies.

E5–5

Category: Sampling Concepts

Concept: Probability Sampling or Random Sampling

Description: In general, probability sampling, referred to more generally as random sampling, has three defining attributes. First, all sampling units in the population have some probability of being selected that is greater than zero. It is not necessary that these probabilities are equal. Second, the probability that any sampling unit might be selected must be specifiable prior to selection. Third, the potential sampling units that constitute the population and those that are excluded from the population are explicitly identified.

Applications: Four major types of random sampling are generally applicable in educational research. These are simple random sampling (**E5–10**); stratified sampling (**E5–11**); systematic sampling (**E5–13**); and cluster sampling (**E5–14**). The major purpose of these procedures is to obtain a sample that is representative of the population and thus improves external validity.

Comments: It is important to recognize that it is not always possible to draw a random sample in applied educational research. The sampling unit (**E5–3**) of interest, whether it is a student, teacher, classroom, or school, cannot always be selected in a way that meets the three criteria for a random sample. In such cases, the researcher must address the issue of generalizability by seeking to replicate the research in different settings with different samples.

E5–6

Category: Sampling Concepts

Concept: Estimator

Description: An estimator is a formula for calculating sample estimates for population parameters. An estimator is a property of a sample design that includes both the selection procedure and the procedure for estimation. The sample design defines an estimator and can be used to generate the sampling distribution of the estimator. Important properties of estimators include:

BIAS. An estimator is biased if, for all possible samples of a particular size, the average estimate for all the samples is larger or smaller than the population value. An estimator is unbiased if the average estimate for all samples is equal to the population parameter.

ERROR OF ESTIMATION. The difference between the sample estimate and the population parameter. The variance of an unbiased estimator is the average squared error of estimation over all samples of a particular size.

MEAN SQUARE ERROR. The sum of the estimator variance and the square of the estimator bias.

EFFICIENCY. One estimator is said to be more efficient than another if, for a given sample size, it has a smaller mean square error.

CONSISTENCY. An estimator is consistent if its mean square error decreases as the sample size increases.

Applications: The careful study of estimators and their properties is critical in survey sampling because the purpose of survey sampling is estimating population values from sample statistics.

Comments: It is important to emphasize that the properties of estimators are determined by the sample design, which includes both the selection procedure and the estimation procedure.

"Bias," as a property of an estimator, should not be confused with "bias" used in a more general sense. "Bias" is sometimes used to mean that a sample is not representative.

E5–7

Category: Sampling Concepts

Concept: Sampling without Replacement

Description: Sampling without replacement is a characteristic of sampling procedures that means that sampling units are removed from the accessible population after they have been selected for the sample. Sampling units can appear in the sample only once using this procedure. Sampling with replacement describes sampling procedures in which sampling units remain in the accessible population even if they are selected to be in the sample. Sampling units can appear in the sample more than once using this procedure.

Applications: In most educational research settings, sampling is done without replacement. Sampling with replacement might be used in multistage sampling (**E5–8**).

Comments: Sampling without replacement is used in most educational research studies. In selecting a random sample of students from a school, for example, students are removed from the accessible population after they have been selected to be in the sample.

E5–8

Category: Sampling Concepts

Concept: Multistage Sampling

Description: Multistage sampling refers to sampling procedures carried out in stages or steps. Large units are sampled first; then smaller units are sampled from these larger units. The large units, sampled first, are called primary sampling units. The small units, sampled second, are elements or elementary units. The number of stages depends on the sampling situation and a variety of other criteria (e.g., practicality, economy).

Applications: Multistage sampling is often used in educational research. In the study of statewide student achievement, for example, school districts might be sampled first as the primary sampling unit. Schools within the school districts chosen in step 1 would then be selected as the elementary sampling unit. The National Assessment of Educational Progress (NAEP) uses a three-stage sampling process. First, counties or groups of counties are sampled. Second, schools are then sampled from the counties chosen in step 1. Third, students are selected from the schools selected in step 2.

Comments: Multistage sampling can be a practical necessity in many situations.

E5–9

Category: Sampling Concepts

Concept: Multiple Matrix Sampling

Description: Multiple matrix sampling refers to situations in which sampling is used for both subjects and material/conditions to which the subjects are assigned.

Applications: Multiple matrix sampling is used in large-scale assessment programs, such as for the National Assessment of Education Progress (NAEP). In the NAEP studies, a sample of subjects is selected (see **E5–8**, Applications); then the subjects are randomly assigned to different test booklets. The test booklets contain a sample of the test questions from the population of questions of interest. No student answers all the test questions, and no test question is answered by all students. By using careful sampling procedures, however, very informative estimates of how the student population would do on all test questions are obtained.

Comments: Multiple matrix sampling is very useful for field-testing large numbers of items in test development activities.

E5–10

Category: Sampling Procedures

Procedure: Simple Random Sampling

Description: Simple random sampling (SRS) refers to a sampling procedure in which all elements of the population have an equal probability of being selected. This is equivalent to saying that all possible samples that could be drawn from the population have an equal probability of being selected. Simple random sampling is performed without replacement (**E5–7**).

Applications: The application of SRS generally involves the use of a table of random numbers. To use this procedure, the N elements in the population are each assigned an individual listing number. For a sample of size n, n equally probable random numbers are then selected from the table of random numbers. The random sample is composed of the n elements in the population whose listing numbers match the n randomly selected numbers from the table.

Comments: Simple random sampling is useful and practical in many small-scale research settings if the mechanics of the procedure are followed carefully. SRS is not very useful in large-scale research projects.

E5–11

Category: Sampling Procedures

Procedure: Stratified Sampling

Description: Stratified sampling involves both the sampling variable (i.e., the variable of interest) and a classification or stratification variable or variables. The classification variable is used to sort population elements into categories or strata.

Subjects are selected to be included in the sample from the strata, not directly from the population at large. It is quite common to select subjects from each stratum in proportion to the size of the stratum in the population. This procedure for allocating subjects is called proportional stratified random sampling. Optimal allocation, used in survey sampling, is another procedure for allocating subjects. With this procedure, the number of subjects from each stratum is proportional to the product of the stratum size and standard deviation. The basic arrangement for a proportional stratified random sample is illustrated in the following figure:

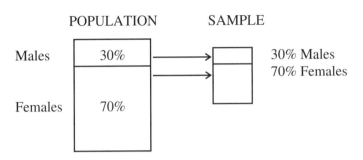

In this example, the stratification variable is gender. In the population, 30% of the people are males, and 70% are females. If a sample of size n is drawn, the number of males will be (.3 × n), and the number of females will be (.7 × n). SRS **(E5–10)**, or any other method, can be used to select the appropriate number of males and females from the population.

Applications: Stratified sampling has many applications in educational research. Classification variables are often selected because they are correlated with the dependent measure and thus are potential extraneous variables. Stratified samples provide a mechanism for controlling the influence of the extraneous variable; in contrast, simple random selection would, at best, randomly distribute the extraneous variable. When stratified sampling is used in experimental research, the stratification variables are sometimes used in the assignment of subjects to groups **(E5–15)** and as independent variables in the statistical analysis.

Comments: Stratification variables have different roles in survey sampling and in experimental research. In survey sampling, stratification variables are used to improve the properties of the estimators of the sampling variable of interest. In experimental research, designed to test hypotheses, stratification variables are used to improve the representativeness of the sample and, also, as variables of interest themselves. The stratification variables may be independent variables for which the researcher has specific hypotheses or potential extraneous variables that the researcher wishes to control.

E5–12

Category: Sampling Procedures

Procedure: Homogeneous Sampling

Description: Homogeneous sampling is a special adaptation of stratified selection in which elements or subjects from only one stratum are selected for the sample. With this procedure, the sample is homogeneous with respect to the stratification variable or variables. This approach is generally not identified as a specific sampling procedure.

Homogeneous sampling is a design procedure used in experimental research to control variation due to the stratification variable. This approach can increase the internal validity of a study. It always decreases a study's external validity.

Applications: Homogeneous sampling is used when the researcher chooses to improve the internal validity of a study at the expense of the study's external validity. Often this choice is made when the researcher recognizes potentially serious confounding variables and stratifies the population on these variables but does not have the resources to sample from all strata created by this stratification.

Comments: Homogeneous sampling is often a practical necessity in many educational research situations. It is critical to recognize, of course, that generalizations cannot be made if homogeneous sampling has been employed. In such cases, the research must be replicated using subjects selected from different strata on the various replications.

E5–13

Category: Sampling Procedures

Procedure: Systematic Sampling

Description: Systematic sampling refers to a set of procedures in which (1) the elements of the population are arranged in an ordered sequence, and (2) the elements are selected at a fixed interval from the ordered sequence. In general, the basis for ordering the elements can be arbitrary as long as each element in the sampling frame can be assigned a unique position in the sequence. In practice, however, the ordering is often systematic and should be examined with care. For example, the elements can be ordered alphabetically, grouped by classrooms, or arranged along an achievement scale from low to high. The nature of the ordering has a major effect on the characteristics of the sample. The sampling interval k is a function of both N, the number of elements in the sampling frame, and also n, the number of elements required for the sample. The sampling interval k is equal to N/n, or the integer that is closest to N/n. A random number r, between 1 and k, is selected from a table of random numbers as the first case. Every k-th element after this first case is then selected as part of the sample.

Applications: Systematic sampling is a very practical and useful procedure in many educational research settings. Lists of schools, teachers, and students are often readily available and can be used as sampling frames (**E5–2**). The procedures for determining the sampling interval, k, and the first case, the r-th element, are straightforward. Selecting every k-th element after the first case basically involves counting. Systematic sampling is especially convenient when elements of the sampling frame are stored electronically. Once r and k are determined, the researcher basically needs a program that counts and stores selected cases.

Comments: Systematic sampling is very useful; however, several problems can arise in its application. The most serious problems arise when subjects are systematically ordered within groups, such as classrooms or schools, and groups are listed sequentially in the sampling frame. For example, consider a situation in which students are ordered within classrooms from low to high on some achievement measure, and the classrooms have approximately the same number of students. In this case, the systematic selection of every k-th student will yield a sample of students who have approximately the same level of achievement. Problems of this sort can occur with other, far less obvious, systematic orderings within groups. If the entire population of elements across the whole sampling frame is ordered from low to high on some achievement measure, then systematic sampling resembles stratified sampling. One subject is selected from each interval where intervals function as achievement strata.

E5–14

Category: Sampling Procedures

Procedure: Cluster Sampling

Description: Cluster sampling refers to a set of procedures in which groups of elements, rather than individual elements, are sampled. These groups, or clusters, are often naturally occurring (e.g., residents of a neighborhood, town, or city). In educational research, the clusters are often classrooms, schools, or school districts. Clusters can be selected using a variety of procedures. Two common procedures for selecting clusters of elements are:

SIMPLE RANDOM SELECTION. All clusters are equally likely to be selected.

PROBABILITY PROPORTIONAL TO SIZE (PPS). The probability that a cluster will be selected is directly proportional to its size. For example, clusters with large numbers of elements are more likely to be selected than clusters with a smaller number of elements.

Applications: Cluster sampling is commonly used in educational research, with classrooms, schools, or school districts serving as the cluster, and is often the only realistic or practical approach. Cluster sampling is often used in a multistage sample design. When the clusters, for example, classrooms, are to be randomly assigned to treatment conditions in experimental research, cluster sampling is required.

Comments: Cluster sampling is often a practical necessity and can be very useful in many educational applications. Special care must be taken in the analysis of data obtained from a cluster sample used in an experiment. If clusters are randomly sampled and then randomly assigned to treatment conditions, the clusters are the unit of analysis for the statistical procedure used for hypothesis testing. For example, if classrooms are sampled and randomly assigned to treatment conditions, it would be incorrect to analyze the performance of individual students to test hypotheses about treatment effects. A nested analysis of variance (**E4–83**), with classrooms nested in treatment, would be the correct approach.

E5–15

Category: Assignment Procedures

Procedure: Assigning Subjects to Groups

Description: In experimental research, subjects in the sample must be assigned to different treatment conditions. The relationship between sample selection and assignment was illustrated earlier and is repeated here:

The assignment of subjects to groups can be performed in ways that are directly analogous to the procedures used to select samples from the population. For example, nonrandom or random assignment can be employed. In some cases, nonrandom assignment is necessary because subjects must consent to being assigned to a treatment condition. In general, nonrandom assignment diminishes internal validity.

The random assignment of subjects from a sample to treatment groups is generally called randomization. Randomization can be performed using a variety of procedures. Simple random assignment is most common. Stratifying the sample on a variable of interest and then randomly assigning from strata to treatment groups can be very useful. In such cases, the stratification variable is generally used in the sample selection process. The stratification variable may be an independent variable of interest or an extraneous variable, the influence of which the researcher wishes to control. In either case, the stratification variable is used as an independent variable in the statistical analysis phase of the research.

Applications: The assignment of subjects from the sample to different treatment groups is a critical step in experimental research. Random assignment of subjects is a major safeguard against threats to internal validity. Characteristics of the subjects that might influence the dependent measure are evenly spread across all treatment groups with random assignment. Procedures that include the stratification of subjects in the sample, followed by random assignment from each stratum to groups, are called randomized block designs **(E4–86)**.

Comments: Random assignment is critical in experimental research if the researcher wishes to make causal inferences. Random assignment does not ensure the validity of such inferences (i.e., the internal validity of the study), but the absence of randomization virtually prohibits causal inferences. Randomization is not practical in many applied educational research settings. In the absence of randomization, other procedures for controlling threats to internal validity should be employed, and attempts at causal inferences should be qualified.

REFERENCES AND RESOURCES

Cochran, W. G. (1977). *Sampling Techniques.* (3rd ed. New York: Wiley.

Jaeger, R. (1984). *Sampling in Education and the Social Sciences.* New York: Longman.

Kish, L. (1965). *Survey Sampling.* New York: John Wiley and Sons.

Lohr, S. L. (1999). *Sampling: Design and Analysis.* Pacific Grove, CA: Duxbury Press.

Stuart, A. (1984). *The Ideas of Sampling.* New York: Oxford University Press.

Sudman, S. (1976). *Applied Sampling.* San Diego: Academic Press.

Thompson, M. E. (1997). *Theory of Sample Surveys.* London: Chapman and Hall.

Thompson, S. K. (1992). *Sampling.* New York: Wiley.

CHAPTER 6

A Summary of Measurement Concepts, Approaches, and Procedures

INTRODUCTION

Educational measurement is the process of assigning numeric values that indicate varying degrees of quality reflected in students' work. Students' work may include responses to multiple-choice questions, answers to short open-ended questions, extended essays, speech, theatrical performances, laboratory experiments, or elaborate projects completed over a period of days or even weeks. Information from different forms of student work is often used to obtain a comprehensive assessment of what students know and are able to do. Students' work can be scored using a number of different procedures. Scoring procedures range from simple dichotomous scoring, with a "0" indicating an incorrect answer and a "1" a correct answer to rating scales with ordered values assigned to students' work such as 1 = novice level, 2 = partially proficient, 3 = proficient, and 4 = advanced. Scoring procedures applied to students' work result in numeric values that are analyzed, evaluated, and standardized using a wide range of measurement procedures.

The purpose of this chapter is to review and describe basic measurement concepts, principles, and procedures. The chapter material is divided into five major sections. Section 1 provides a description of typical applications and uses of tests, commonly used assessment and item formats, approaches to scoring including scoring rubrics, and a description of two important assessment development tools. The final entries of Section 1 deal with classical test theory (CTT) and item response theory (IRT) approaches to measurement. Section 2 deals with norm-referenced and criterion-referenced frameworks for score interpretation as well as a description of nine commonly used score reporting scales. Section 3 deals with procedures for item review including item analysis and differential item functioning. Section 4 addresses the all-important procedures for evaluating test reliability and validity. Test equating and standard setting are covered in Section 5. References useful in reviewing and evaluating specific tests conclude the chapter. An overview of the entries in this chapter is presented below.

(E6–1) Basic Concepts and Approaches

Test Applications and Uses

- **(E6–2)** Selection
- **(E6–3)** Placement
- **(E6–4)** Formative Assessment
- **(E6–5)** Diagnostic Assessment
- **(E6–6)** Summative Assessment

Assessment and Item Formats

(E6–7) Selected Response
Multiple Choice
True-False
Matching
(E6–8) Constructed Response
Short Answer
Extended Response
Performance Assessment
(E6–9) Portfolio Assessment

Approaches to Scoring

(E6–10) Dichotomous Scoring
(E6–11) Ratings and Partial Credit Using Scoring Rubrics
Holistic
Modified Holistic
Analytic
Modified Analytic

Assessment Development Tools

(E6–12) Item Specifications
(E6–13) Test Specifications

Approaches to Measurement

(E6–14) Classical Test Theory (CTT)
(E6–15) Item Response Theory (IRT)

(E6–16) Score Interpretation and Scales

Frames of Reference for Interpretation

(E6–17) Norm-referenced
(E6–18) Criterion-referenced

Types of Scores and Scales

(E6–19) Raw Score
(E6–20) Standardized Score, Z-score
(E6–21) Standardized Score, T-score
(E6–22) Standardized Score, General Form
(E6–23) Grade Equivalent
(E6–24) Percentile Score
(E6–25) Normalized T-score
(E6–26) Normal Curve Equivalent (NCE)

(E6–27) Stanines

(E6–28) Item Analysis and Review

Item Analysis

(E6–29) Item Difficulty
(E6–30) Item Discrimination
(E6–31) Distractor Analysis

Differential Item Functioning (DIF)/Item Bias

(E6–32) Item Sensitivity Review Panels
(E6–33) Delta Measures of Item Difficulty
(E6–34) Chi-Square-Based Approaches
(E6–35) Item Response Theory (IRT) Approaches

(E6–36) Criteria for Evaluating Test Quality

Reliability and Related Concepts and Procedures

(E6–37) Test-Retest Reliability
(E6–38) Alternate Form Reliability, Parallel Form Reliability
(E6–39) Internal Consistency, Split-Half Reliability
(E6–40) Spearman-Brown Prophecy Formula
(E6–41) Internal Consistency, Kuder-Richardson 20 (KR-20)
(E6–42) Internal Consistency, Coefficient Alpha
(E6–43) Inter-rater Agreement or Consistency
(E6–44) Standard Error of Measurement
(E6–45) Classification Reliability
(E6–46) Generalizability

Validity

(E6–47) Content
(E6–48) Criterion-Related, Concurrent
(E6–49) Criterion-Related, Predictive
(E6–50) Construct
(E6–51) Validity Related to Consequence

(E6–52) Test Equating and Standard Setting

(E6–53) Equating
Linear
Equipercentile
Item Response Theory (IRT) Approaches

E6–54) Standard Setting
>> Test- and Item-Focused Approaches
>> Student-Focused Approaches

E6–1 BASIC CONCEPTS AND APPROACHES

Test Applications and Uses

>> **(E6–2)** Selection
>> **(E6–3)** Placement
>> **(E6–4)** Formative Assessment
>> **(E6–5)** Diagnostic Assessment
>> **(E6–6)** Summative Assessment

E6–2

Measurement Category: Test Applications and Uses
Concept/Procedure: Selection
Description: Tests used for selection are designed to identify the most appropriate students for particular educational programs or activities. Sometimes these are relatively low-achieving students who will benefit most from the experiences. At other times, these are relatively high-achieving students who will perform at the highest levels in the programs or activities.

E6–3

Measurement Category: Test Applications and Uses
Concept/Procedure: Placement
Description: Tests used for placement are administered prior to instruction and are used to identify the most appropriate point in an instructional sequence for a student to begin. Placement tests may also be used to identify the most appropriate type of instruction for students.

E6–4

Measurement Category: Test Applications and Uses
Concept/Procedure: Formative Assessment
Description: Formative assessments are employed during instruction to provide feedback used for monitoring students' progress and for reviewing the efficacy of instruction. Formative tests are scored, and students, teachers, and others may receive score reports from the formative tests. Scores from formative tests, however, are not used in grading.

E6–5

Measurement Category: Test Applications and Uses
Concept/Procedure: Diagnostic Assessment

Description: Diagnostic assessments are given during instruction in order to provide a detailed and comprehensive analysis of weaknesses that students seem to have developed. Diagnostic tests are more detailed than formative tests and may be prescribed based on a general deficiency identified through a formative test.

E6–6
Measurement Category: Test Application and Uses
Concept/Procedure: Summative Assessment
Description: Summative tests are given to determine what students know and are able to do after instruction. Summative test results are often used to evaluate the impact of instruction in terms of the extent to which instructional goals have been met. Teacher-made summative tests are used in grading students.

Assessment and Item Formats

(E6–7) Selected Response
Multiple Choice
True-False
Matching
(E6–8) Constructed Response
Short Answer
Extended Response
Performance Assessment
(E6–9) Portfolio Assessment

E6–7
Measurement Category: Assessment and Item Formats
Concept/Procedure: Selected Response
Description: Selected-response assessment and item formats refer to approaches in which a problem or a task is presented to students, and a set of possible correct answers is provided. Students respond by selecting the choice they believe is the correct answer. The selected-response allows for a broad range of content coverage because students can take a large number of such items in a fixed period of time. Selected-response items can be scored objectively by machine, making the scoring process very accurate and efficient. Not all important learning goals, however, can be easily or validly (**E6–43** to **E6–46**) assessed with selected-response items.

The most common forms of selected-response items are multiple-choice, true-false, and matching questions. Readers may wish to consult Haladyna (1994) as an excellent reference on planning, writing, and evaluating selected-response items.

E6–8
Measurement Category: Assessment and Item Formats
Concept/Procedure: Constructed Response
Description: Constructed-response assessment and item formats present students with stimulus materials, tasks to be accomplished, and guidelines within which students must re-

spond to the tasks. Choices of correct answers are not provided. Students must develop or construct a response to the task, often an answer to an open-ended question or an essay in response to a writing prompt. The constructed-response format is commonly used to assess students' writing and their ability to perform scientific investigations and has always been routinely used to assess students in physical education. Constructed-response formats are especially appropriate for assessing complex, integrated processes like writing and problem solving. Students can complete only a small number of constructed response items in a fixed period of time, and thus this format does not provide the opportunity to assess a wide range or broad area of achievement. Individual raters must score students' answers to constructed-response questions. The scoring of constructed responses is time-consuming and costly and also introduces a source of error that could influence validity (**E6–47** to **E6–51**). The most common forms of constructed-response formats include short answer/completion items, open-ended questions, extended response questions, essays, and performance assessments.

E6–9

Measurement Category: Assessment and Item Formats

Concept/Procedure: Portfolio Assessment

Description: Portfolio assessments are not a specific assessment format but refer to collections of students' work. So-called working portfolios are used during the course of instruction and may function as formative (**E6–4**) or diagnostic (**E6–5**) assessments. Assessment portfolios are used at the end of a course or some other period of instruction as a summative assessment (**E6–6**) to evaluate what students know and are able to do. Portfolios may include a wide variety of materials that provide a basis for making inferences about students' knowledge and skills. Portfolios can include samples of students' work done in school or at home, reports from extended projects, classroom and standardized test scores, self-reports, and peer reviews. Portfolios facilitate the assessment of growth or progress over time since portfolio entries are dated as they are placed in the portfolio.

Many teachers use portfolios as an instructional strategy to support students' learning. Portfolios as formal assessment devices, however, require considerable care and effort in planning and developing scoring rubrics (**E6–11**) and in training scorers to apply the rubrics consistently and validly. There has been limited success in using portfolios as summative assessments in large-scale assessment programs.

Approaches to Scoring

> (**E6–10**) Dichotomous Scoring
> (**E6–11**) Ratings and Partial Credit Using Scoring Rubrics
> > Holistic
> > Modified Holistic
> > Analytic
> > Modified Analytic

E6–10

Measurement Category: Approaches to Scoring

Concept/Procedure: Dichotomous Scoring

Description: Selected-response item formats (**E6–7**) present problems or tasks to students and a set of possible correct answers. Students select the option that they believe is the correct answer, and this response is scored as incorrect or correct. Incorrect answer choices are scored a "0" and correct choices are scored a "1." Students' choices are subject to a variety of other analyses (see Item Analysis, **E6–29** to **E6–31**) in addition to being scored dichotomously as wrong or right.

E6–11

Measurement Category: Approaches to Scoring

Concept/Procedure: Ratings and Partial Credit Using Scoring Rubrics

Description: Constructed-response assessments (**E6–8**) present students with stimulus materials, tasks to be accomplished, and usually guidelines within which students must respond to the tasks. There is usually no simple correct answer expected on a constructed-response item, and so responses cannot be scored dichotomously as incorrect (0) or correct (1). Answers to constructed-response assessments are scored using a rating scale or partial-credit scale. These scales typically cover anywhere from 3 to 6 points, with each score point defining a different qualitatively described level of performance. The rating scales may begin at 0 or 1. Often, special codes outside the range of the rating scale are used to indicate responses that are blank, illegible, not responsive, or unrelated to the question. Students' constructed responses are scored by using a scoring rule or model called a scoring rubric. There are four major types of scoring rubrics: (1) holistic; (2) modified holistic; (3) analytic; and (4) modified analytic.

Holistic rubrics employ a set of model answers or responses ordered from the lowest-quality work or response that defines the bottom of the scale (e.g., a 0 or 1) to the highest-quality work or response that defines the top of the scale (e.g., a 4). These models are called benchmarks or exemplars. Judges rate students' work by identifying the benchmark that the work most closely matches and assigns the score point of that benchmark to the work. Holistic scoring provides only general information about students with limited information about specific strengths and weaknesses.

Modified or focused holistic rubrics are derived from benchmarks or exemplars and involve the explication of the relevant critical features that differentiate the quality of the work at each of the ordered score points. Students receive a single score, which reflects the nature of the composition, word usage, and grammar characteristic of papers at the 1, 2, 3, and 4 score point levels. These are explicitly described in a modified holistic rubric. Students' papers are evaluated against these substantively defined score points and are assigned the score at which their work best matches the score point definition. Modified holistic scoring provides instructional relevant information about students' strengths and weaknesses.

Analytic rubrics involve defining several specific dimensions of the work to be scored, such as composition, word usage, and grammar, and then defining a rating scale for each dimension. Students receive a set of scores, with one score for each dimension. Analytic rubrics are especially useful in identifying students' strengths and weaknesses.

Modified analytic rubrics are derived from analytic rubrics and involve adding together the scores or ratings assigned to each dimension. This provides a single overall score. The total score provided from a modified analytic rubric is useful in providing a general, overall idea of students' achievement or ability but does not provide useful information about students' strengths and weaknesses.

Assessment Development Tools

(E6–12) Item Specifications
(E6–13) Test Specifications

E6–12

Measurement Category: Assessment Development Tools
Concept/Procedure: Item Specifications
Description: Item specifications define the critical characteristics of the items that can be used on an assessment. Item specifications prescribe what is allowed and what is not allowed in the stimulus materials, tasks, questions, and incorrect and correct answers when selected response formats are used. Item specifications often include details describing the length, complexity, grade level, and other features of the words, sentences, and passages used in the assessment. Specifications are often provided for the context used in reading, writing and other subject areas when constructed-response formats are used. In mathematics, item specifications often define how many steps a problem can require, the algorithms that may be needed, the nature and size of the numbers (e.g., integers, fractions, mixed numbers, 1–, 2–, and 3–digits). The nature and characteristics of incorrect answer are often specified. This might include incorrect answers obtained by using an incorrect arithmetic operation, wrong algorithm, or the solution at a preliminary step in a multiple-step problem.

Item specifications are a critical part of the assessment development process and are very important in building assessment validity.

E6–13

Measurement Category: Assessment Development Tools
Concept/Procedure: Table of Specifications
Description: The table of specifications, sometimes called the test blueprint, defines what is to be included on an assessment and is vital for developing and demonstrating assessment validity (**E6–43** to **E6–46**). The table of specifications defines what is assessed along two dimensions. One is the substantive aspect of the assessment, that is, the facts, terms, principles, and procedures that are to be assessed. The other dimension is the cognitive or intellectual processes that students will be required to use in responding to the assessment questions and tasks. Cognitive level might be defined, for example, in terms of knowledge, comprehension, application, and analysis. These terms would need more detailed explanation and examples to be useful in a table of specifications. Tables of specifications are often presented in a two-way table (see table) with rows listing elements of content and columns defining cognitive levels. Each cell in such a table identifies a content-process element that is eligible for assessment.

The number of items used to assess each content-process element is written in the corresponding cell. The totals in the last column show how many items are used to assess each content element, and the totals in the last row show how many items are used to assess each cognitive level. The number in the bottommost right cell shows the total number of items on the assessment. All of the numbers in the table of specifications can be converted to proportions or percentages to show the relative emphasis given to various parts of the content at different cognitive levels. The table of specifications is often a very good answer to the question, What does the test measure?

Content	Cognitive Level				Number of Items by Content
	Knows	Understands	Applies	Analyzes	
1					
2					
3					
Number of Items, Cognitive Level					

A very valuable application of the table of specifications involves developing such a table for an existing test to define exactly what the test is assessing. Educators are often surprised to see exactly what an assessment they have been using actually measures.

Approaches to Measurement

(**E6–14**) Classical Test Theory (CTT)
(**E6–15**) Item Response Theory (IRT)

E6–14
Measurement Category: Approaches to Measurement
Concept/Procedure: Classical Test Theory (CTT)
Description: Classical test theory (CTT) is the basic approach used traditionally in all educational and psychological measurement. CTT was the only approach to measurement until the development of modern test theory or item response theory (IRT) (**E6–15**). CTT is concerned with the scores that people make on various tests and is based on the following fundamental model:

$$O = T + e$$

where

O = a person's observed score

T = a person's true score

e = the error made in measuring the person

A person's "true score" is a theoretical ideal representing the score that a person would be expected to make if there were no errors in measurement. CTT assumes that the mean of the errors is zero, that the errors are not correlated with the true score, and that the errors of measurement are not correlated with each other.

Application: Classical test theory is ubiquitously used, and its basic procedures are employed in virtually all test settings. Fundamental concepts such as item difficulty and test reliability and validity are integral parts of CTT. Most classroom teachers, knowingly or not, employ CTT principles and procedures when they score students' tests.

Data: CTT procedures apply to virtually all types of item data and test scores.

Limitations: CTT has several major limitations related to the fact that the characteristics of the people taking the tests and the characteristics of the items and the test itself are confounded. For example, if students answer an average of 95% of the items on a test correctly, there are no data that allow one validly to conclude that the test was easy or that the students were smart and well prepared or both. This problem plays out in two ways. First, all information about test items and tests is dependent on the sample of students who take the tests. For example, a test item answered correctly by 90% of the students might seem to be easier than an item on a different test answered correctly by only 60% of the students. The percentage of students answering an item correctly, however, might reflect the characteristics of the sample, not the inherent difficulty of the item. Second, all scores and score interpretations are test form specific, and, therefore, scores are not directly comparable across forms. For example, two students with scores of 40 on two different 50-item mathematics tests given at the same grade levels may have the same raw score. The identical scores of 40 on the two tests, however, are not sufficient evidence for saying that the students have the same mathematical abilities. The two tests may not measure the same mathematics content, and, even if they did, one test might be measuring the mathematical ability at a more demanding and higher cognitive level.

Comments: CTT has been very useful for decades and will continue to be a mainstay for most educational measurement applications. Many policy leaders and decision makers misuse the results of CTT analyses by jumping to erroneous conclusions about the causes that explain the results of a CTT analysis. For example, when students score very well on a test, some leaders might conclude that the test was too easy, ignoring the alternative explanation that students received well-targeted effective instruction and studied hard. Conversely, when students score poorly on a test, some leaders might conclude that instruction was ineffective and students did not study, ignoring the alternative explanation that the content of the test was very demanding and difficult.

Formula: See the formula in *Description.*

E6–15

Measurement Category: Approaches to Measurement

Concept/Procedure: Item Response Theory (IRT)

Description: Item response theory refers to a broad array of psychometric models and procedures used to support large-scale assessment programs. All IRT models are designed to estimate the probability that a given student will correctly answer a particular test item. The ability of the students is a part of all IRT models. IRT models differ in the characteristics of the items that they employ. The three common IRT models and the item characteristic(s) that each model employs are as follows:

IRT Model	Item Characteristic(s) Modeled
One-parameter	Item Difficulty
Two-parameter	Item Difficulty, Item Discrimination
Three-parameter	Item Difficulty, Item Discrimination, Guessing

IRT involves the estimation of model parameters, which yields numeric values for students' abilities, item difficulties, discriminations, and the guessing parameters. These values are used in the model to estimate expected values for student ability and item characteristics. These are used, in turn, in various ways to assess the fit of the data to the model.

Application: IRT is the basis for virtually all commercial tests, statewide testing programs, and many district assessment programs.

Data: IRT models were initially developed for dichotomously scored items, but IRT models were quickly developed for partial credit and rating scale data.

Limitations: IRT procedures are based on two major assumptions that make their applicability more or less appropriate depending on the extent to which the assumptions are met. The assumption of unidimensionality suggests that all items measure the same underlying trait. The assumption of item independence suggests that the probability that students will correctly answer a given item is not influenced by their performance on any other items.

All IRT analyses require specialized computer software, and most software for the two- and three-parameter models requires samples approaching 1,000 students to work effectively.

Comments: There is some division among measurement experts about the use of the one-parameter model compared to the use of the two- or three-parameter model. Proponents of the one-parameter model assert that they are modeling underlying or latent traits (person ability and item difficulty) and are concerned with whether the data fit the model. They would contend that the two- and three-parameter models are modeling observed characteristics of the data and are concerned with whether the model fits the data. Proponents of the two- and three-parameter models would point out that data from test items show variation in item discrimination and that guessing can certainly occur on selected-response items. It follows that having discrimination and guessing as part of the IRT model would more accurately reflect real data and improve model-data fit. The various IRT models give very similar results in many applications. Which IRT model is used depends on a wide range of factors, including the purpose of the test, the need to produce equivalent measures of students' ability using different forms of the test, and the availability of technical expertise and software.

Formula: The mathematics of IRT models are beyond the scope of this chapter and book. Listed here are some helpful and important references: Crocker and Algina (1985), Lord and Novick (1968), Rasch (1980), Wright and Stone (1980).

E6–16 SCORE INTERPRETATION AND SCALES

Students' performance on a test or any other type of assessment can be interpreted and reported in a variety of forms using a number of different scaling techniques. There are two major frameworks used to interpret students' test scores: norm-referenced and criterion-referenced. Within these frameworks, many scales can be used to report student scores. The most common scale is the simple raw score, the number of items answered correctly or points earned. From the raw score, a number of derived scores are commonly used in assessment activities. This section offers a description of the scales most commonly used to report students' achievement.

Frames of References for Interpretation

> **(E6–17)** Norm-referenced
> **(E6–18)** Criterion-referenced

E6–17
Measurement Category: Frames of Reference for Interpretation
Concept/Procedure: Norm-referenced
Description: Norm-referenced test (NRT) interpretations of students' scores describe students' performance relative to the performance of other students. A normative interpretation does not describe what students know and are able to do but how students' scores compare to the scores of students in the norm sample. The most common NRT interpretation is the percentile or percentile rank (**E4–11**). A student with a test score in the 80th percentile, for example, has scored as well or better than 80% of the students in the norm sample. Grade equivalents, stanines, normalized T-scores, and normal curve equivalents are other examples of norm-referenced score interpretations.

E6–18
Measurement Category: Frames of Reference for Interpretation
Concept/Procedure: Criterion-Referenced
Description: Criterion-referenced test (CRT) interpretations of students' test scores describe students' performance in terms of specific and well-defined elements or domains of knowledge and skills. The knowledge and skills used to describe students' achievement may include educational objectives and goals, curriculum domains, or content standards. Criterion-referenced test interpretations are sometimes called objective-referenced, curriculum-referenced, standard-referenced, or standards-based. Criterion-referenced interpretations attempt to provide information about what students actually know and are able to do, not how well they are doing relative to other students.

Types of Scores and Scales

> **(E6–19)** Raw Score
> **(E6–20)** Standardized Score, Z-score
> **(E6–21)** Standardized Score, T-score
> **(E6–22)** Standardized Score, General Form
> **(E6–23)** Grade Equivalent
> **(E6–24)** Percentile
> **(E6–25)** Normalized T-score
> **(E6–26)** Normal Curve Equivalent (NCE)
> **(E6–27)** Stanine

E6–19

Measurement Category: Types of Scores and Scales

Concept/Procedure: Raw Score

Description: The raw score is the total number of points earned on an assessment. This might be the test items answered correctly on a multiple-choice test, the number of points awarded on a short-answer or essay question, or a combination of both.

Application: The raw score is the fundamental unit for interpreting achievement on an assessment and the basis for all derived scale scores.

Data: The raw score is the number of points or marks earned on an assessment.

Limitations: Raw scores cannot be compared across tests since they vary in the number of items and relative difficulty. Raw scores provide limited basis for interpretation without additional information. The additional information might be the scores of other students, which would facilitate a norm-referenced interpretation. Information about the content measured by the assessment and the relative difficulty of the items could facilitate a criterion-referenced or standards-based interpretation.

Comments: The raw score is the basic unit for test interpretation and reporting.

Formula: The raw score is the sum of the number of items answered correctly or points earned.

E6–20

Measurement Category: Types of Scores and Scales

Concept/Procedure: Standardized Scores, Z-Score

Description: Standardized scores are transformations of raw scores so that the standardized scores have a predetermined mean (**E4–2**), variance (**E4–7**), and standard deviation (**E4–8**). Z-scores are standardized to have a mean of 0 and a standard deviation of 1.

Application: Standardizing test scores facilitates interpretation since the standardized scores are referenced to a known mean and standard deviation.

Data: Test scores that are interval or ratio level can be standardized.

Limitations: Standardizing a set of test scores does not change the skew (**E4–12**) or kurtosis (**E4–13**). Standardizing the mean and standard deviation does not normalize data that are not normally distributed.

Comments: The z-score transformation allows for a norm-referenced interpretation if the original test scores follow or approximate the normal distribution. The z-score transformation is used as the basis for other standardization with other means and standard deviations.

Formula:

$$Z = \frac{(X - \overline{X})}{SD}$$

where
X = students' scores,
$\overline{X}$ = the mean of the scores
SD = the standard deviation of the scores

E6–21

Measurement Category: Types of Scores and Scales

Concept/Procedure: Standardized Scores, T-Score, Linear or Non-Normalizing Standardization

Description: Standardized scores are transformations of raw scores so that the standardized scores have a predetermined mean (**E4–2**), variance (**E4–7**), and standard deviation (**E4–8**). T-scores are standardized to have a mean of 50 and standard deviation of 10. The resulting T-score distribution has a new mean and standard deviation, but the overall shape of the score distribution is not changed. If the original scores were not normally distributed, the new T-scores will not be normally distributed.

Application: Standardizing test scores facilitates interpretation since the standardized scores are referenced to a known mean and standard deviation.

Data: Test scores that are interval- or ratio-level can be standardized.

Limitations: Standardizing a set of test scores does not change the skew (**E4–12**) or kurtosis (**E4–13**). Standardizing the mean and standard deviation does not normalize data that are not normally distributed.

Comments: The T-score transformation allows for a norm-referenced interpretation if the original test scores follow or approximate the normal distribution. The T-score transformation is often used to eliminate the negative values ($Z < 0$) that occur with Z-scores.

Formula:

$$T = 10 \cdot Z + 50$$

where
Z = students' scores in Z-score form (**E6–20**)

E6–22

Measurement Category: Types of Scores and Scales

Concept/Procedure: Standardized Scores, General Expression

Description: Standardized scores are transformations of raw scores so that the standardized scores have a predetermined mean (**E4–2**), variance (**E4–7**), and standard deviation (**E4–8**). Raw scores can be standardized to have any mean and standard deviation desired. Raw scores must first be turned into Z-scores (**E4–20**) to standardize them further.

Application: Standardizing test scores facilitates interpretation since the standardized scores are referenced to a known mean and standard deviation.

Data: Test scores that are interval- or ratio-level can be standardized.

Limitations: Standardizing a set of test scores does not change the skew (**E4–12**) and kurtosis (**E4–13**). Standardizing the mean and standard deviation does not normalize data that are not normally distributed.

Comments: Standardizing test scores allows for a norm-referenced interpretation if the original test scores follow or approximate the normal distribution. The Z-score transformation is used as the basis for other standardization with other means and standard deviations.

Formula:

Standard Score = (SD) Z + M
where
SD = the desired standard deviation
Z = a student's score expressed as a Z-score (**E6–20**)
M = the desired mean

E6–23

Measurement Category: Types of Scores and Scales

Concept/Procedure: Grade Equivalent (GE)

Description: Grade equivalent scores or GE scores are standardized normative scores expressed with an integer for the grade level and a decimal value representing a month within the school year. The months are numbered with October counting as the first month. A GE of 6.6, for example, indicates performance typical of sixth grade students in March.

Application: Many tests are given within specific grades during narrowly defined test administration periods of two to three weeks. This test administration arrangement invites and facilitates the development and use of grade equivalents.

Data: Grade equivalent scores can be derived for any set of tests that span multiple years.

Limitations: There are a number of very serious limitations to the use of grade equivalent scores, and such scores are often misunderstood and misinterpreted. Like all norm-referenced scores, they do not indicate what students actually know and are able to do. GEs are not prescriptive; that is, they do not define what students ought to know at a particular point in a given grade, nor do they define where students ought to be placed in an instructional sequence. GE scores are not equal interval scores, nor are they comparable across tests.

Comments: Grade equivalents are so prone to misinterpretation that many assessment specialists recommend against their use. One common and egregious misinterpretation can be illustrated by considering a sixth grade student with a GE of 7.4. This score does not mean that the child is achieving at the seventh grade, fourth month level and, therefore, should be advanced. Rather, it means that the score obtained on the sixth grade test is the score that one would expect if a child in the seventh grade, fourth month had taken the sixth grade test.

Formula: GE scores are derived by standardizing scores as described in (**E6–22**) and using the mean for a given grade and month of test administration. Values for the month within and across years are obtained by using interpolation and extrapolation.

E6–24

Measurement Category: Types of Scores and Scales

Concept/Procedure: Percentile, Percentile Rank, or Percentile Score

Description: A percentile reports a students' score in terms of the percentage of students who made that same score or a lower score. Scoring in the 80th percentile means that the score obtained was as high or higher than the score made by 80% of the students in the norming sample. Percentiles are usually based on a national norm sample, but state, local, and other specialized norms are sometimes available.

Application: Percentiles provide a relative standard for comparing students' performance. For example, a student who scored in the 80th percentile in reading and the 70th percentile in mathematics did relatively better in reading than in mathematics.

Data: Norms can be developed for all test data that are ordinal-, interval-, or ratio-level.

Limitations: Percentile scores provide information about students' achievement relative to that of other students in the norm sample. Percentiles do not indicate the content and skills that students actually know and are able to do. In addition, the norms may be based on a sample representative of some population (**E5–1** to **E5–3**), but a particular student or group of students may not be well represented by that population. Finally, percentiles do not provide equal-interval data. Hence, arithmetic and statistical operations, such as calculating the mean, standard deviation, or gains, should not be performed on percentile scores.

Comments: Percentiles are popular, widely used, and often misunderstood and misused. Percentiles based on national norms do not necessarily reflect relative achievement on local or state content standards or curriculum.

Formula: A percentile is a position on the cumulative proportion frequency distribution (**E4–11**) expressed as a percentage by multiplying the proportion by 100.

E6–25

Measurement Category: Types of Scores and Scales

Concept/Procedure: Normalized T-Scores

Description: As mentioned in **E6–20** to **E6–22**, standardizing test scores by changing the mean and standard deviation does not produce a normal distribution of scores unless the original score distribution was itself normally distributed. A normalizing standardization can be used to transform the original scores into a new scale that is normally distributed and has any desired mean and standard deviation. Normalizing standardizations are called area conversion.

Application: Normalizing transformations can be applied to all test score distributions, although care should be taken in attempting to normalize data that are severely nonnormal. Normalizing standardizations are especially appropriate when there is good reason to believe that the distribution in the population is normal but the distribution in the norm sample departs modestly from normality.

Data: Most forms of test score data can be normalized.

Limitations: Normalized T-scores should not be confused with linear T-scores (**E4–21**). Normalized scores are sometimes difficult to explain.

Comments: Normalized standard scores facilitate score interpretation.

Formula: Normalizing standard scores are produced by first expressing the original scores in terms of percentiles (**E6–24**). The Z-score that each percentile represents in the normal distribution is then matched and used in place of the corresponding original raw score for each student. A student's Z-score derived in this fashion is then standardized as in (**E6–21**) by the formula,

$$T = 10z + 50$$

where

z = the normal distribution z corresponding to the percentile rank position of the original raw score. This is not the Z as defined in **E6–20**.

E6–26

Measurement Category: Types of Scores and Scales

Concept/Procedure: Normal Curve Equivalent (NCE)

Description: The normal curve equivalent (NCE) score is a normalizing standardization of the test scores. A normalizing standardization can be used to transform the original scores into a new scale that is normally distributed and has any desired mean and standard deviation. Normalizing standardizations are called area conversion. The NCE scale is equal-interval and thus an appropriate scale for arithmetic and statistical calculations. The NCE scale is standardized so that NCE scores of 1 and 99 correspond to the 1st and 99th percentiles, respectively.

Application: Normalizing transformations can be applied to all test score distributions, although care should be taken in attempting to normalize data that are severely nonnormal. Normalizing standardizations are especially appropriate when there is good reason to believe that the distribution in the population is normal but the distribution in the norm sample departs modestly from normality. NCE scores should be used in any applications in which data will be subject to statistical analysis. Percentiles can be transformed into NCE scores, the analyses can be performed on the NCE scores, and then the results can be retransformed back into percentile scores.

Data: NCE scores can be calculated from any set of test scores. Commercial standardized test results routinely report NCE scores.

Limitations: NCE scores can be difficult to explain and can be computationally cumbersome if they have to be calculated locally.

Comments: NCE scores should be used in any applications in which data will be subject to statistical analysis. NCE scores, not percentiles, must be used when measuring the effects of instruction or growth over time or comparing groups.

Formula: NCEs are a normalized standard score. Normalizing standard scores are produced by expressing the original scores in terms of percentiles (**E6–21**). The z-score that each percentile represents in the normal distribution is then matched and used in place of the corresponding original raw score for each student. Students' z-transformed scores derived in this fashion are then standardized into NCE form by:

NCE= 21.06z + 50

where

z = the normal distribution z corresponding to the percentile rank position of the original raw score. This is not the Z as defined in (**E6–20**).

E6–27

Measurement Category: Types of Scores and Scales

Concept/Procedure: Stanine, Standardized Nine-Point Scale, Normalized

Description: Stanine scores are nine-category, normalized standard scores with a mean of 5 and standard deviation of 2. Each stanine represents one-half of a standard deviation of the original scale except for stanines 1 and 9. Stanines 2 through 8, therefore, form an equal-interval scale. Stanine 5 is the center of the distribution and includes scores that fall between the 40th and 59th percentile. The relationship between stanine scores and the normal distribution is shown:

Stanine	Percentiles Included
9	98–99
8	89–95
7	77–88
6	60–76
5	40–59
4	23–39
3	11–22
2	4–10
1	1–3

Application: Stanines are popular among educators and provide a simple way to describe students' achievement.

Data: Normalizing scores like stanines can be calculated for all test score distributions, although care should be taken in attempting to normalize data that are severely nonnormal.

Limitations: Stanines provide very broad categories of student achievement and thus make it difficult to make fine distinctions among students. Stanines provide limited precision for measuring the effects of instruction or students' growth in general.

Comments: Stanine scores are sometimes simplified further by grouping and characterizing stanines 1, 2, and 3 as "low" performance; stanines 4, 5, and 6 as "medium" performance; and stanines 7, 8, and 9 as "high" performance.

Formula: Normalizing standard scores are produced by expressing the original scores in terms of percentiles (**E6–24**). The z-score that each percentile represents in the normal distribution is then matched and used in place of the corresponding original raw score for each student. Students' z-scores derived in this fashion are then standardized as in (**E6–22**) by the formula,

Stanine = 2z + 5
where
z = the normal distribution z corresponding to the percentile rank position of the original raw score. This is not the Z as defined in (**E6–20**).

E6–28 ITEM ANALYSIS AND REVIEW

Item analysis refers to a set of procedures used to review the quality of the items on a test. Item analysis can be applied to small samples, but the results must be interpreted with care. Results based on small samples may not provide accurate information about how the items will function on tests taken by the larger population of students for whom the test is intended. Considerable care should be taken in interpreting the results of an item analysis. All interpretations of item analysis information should take into consideration the broader context, including the content and curriculum standards being assessed, the instructional emphases given by teachers, and students' opportunities to learn. Any special characteristics of the students that might influence the results of the item analysis should be examined.

Item Analysis

> (**E6–29**) Item Difficulty
> (**E6–30**) Item Discrimination
> (**E6–31**) Distractor Analysis

E6–29

Measurement Category: Item Analysis
Concept/Procedure: Item Difficulty or p-Value
Description: The classical item difficulty is simply the proportion of people who answer an item correctly after the item is scored 0 or 1 (incorrect or correct). A relatively low number, such as .30, indicates a difficult item with only 30% of the respondents answering correctly. An item difficulty of .90 indicates an easy item with 90% of the respondents answering correctly. The item difficulty is frequently referred to as the item "p-value," indicating the proportion of students answering the item correctly. The item difficulty is the mean response that people make if the item is a rating scale question with ordered responses such as "Strongly Disagree," "Disagree," "Agree," and "Strongly Agree," scored 1, 2, 3, and 4, respectively.
Application: The item difficulty is an essential feature of any evaluation of item and test quality. The item difficulty is used to identify relatively easy and difficult test questions or survey questions that are difficult or easy for respondents to endorse. In traditional norm-referenced testing, most items are selected to have difficulties roughly in the .40 to .60 range. In criterion-referenced or standards-referenced assessment, one would expect item difficulties to be generally above .60 or .70, assuming that the content standards are reasonable and appropriate and that effective instruction has taken place.
Data: Item difficulty for test questions is calculated after the data have been scored with 0 for an incorrect answer and 1 for a correct answer. In surveys and questionnaires, the

data are ordered categories such as "Strongly Disagree," "Disagree," "Agree," and "Strongly Agree," or "Never," "Rarely," "Sometimes," and "Always." These categories are represented by ordered integers 1, 2, 3, and 4. Any number of ordered categories may be used. Low to high is preferred so that low attitudes (negative) and high attitudes (positive) correspond to low and high numbers, respectively.

Limitations: Item difficulty is easily and often misinterpreted. An item difficulty of .90, for example, is often described simply as reflecting an "easy item." This simple interpretation may be misleading and even incorrect. (See the *Comments* section.) The proper interpretation of item difficulty for survey and questionnaire items is dependent on the nature of the question (positive or negative) and the direction used to order the choices.

Comments: Inferences about why an item has a particular difficulty value must be made carefully and must consider many factors. For example, a relatively high difficulty value like .90 may represent the impact of excellent instruction and hard work and focused study by students, an item measuring relatively simple content or content from an earlier point in the instructional sequence, or an item that is a simple representation of the content. The conclusion that an item with a difficulty of .90 is an easy item may be very misleading because the explanation for the large proportion of correct answers may be related to curriculum, instruction, or the work of the students.

Formula: The item difficulty is simply the mean response to an item and is calculated as defined in **(E4–2)**.

E6–30

Measurement Category: Item Analysis
Concept/Procedure: Item Discrimination
Description: The item discrimination refers to the extent to which an item differentiates between the relatively high-scoring students and relatively low-scoring students. The item discrimination is the difference between the item difficulty **(E6–29)** for a relatively high-scoring group and the item difficulty for a relatively low-scoring group. The relatively high- and low-scoring groups can be defined in a variety of ways, including simply the students above and below the mean score **(E4–2)**. Traditionally, the high- and low-scoring groups are defined as the upper and lower 27% of the cumulative score distribution **(E4–11)**.

Item discrimination can be negative or positive. Negative discriminations indicate that a larger proportion of students in the relatively low-scoring group is answering the item correctly in contrast to the students in the relatively high-scoring group. Negative discriminations indicate serious flaws in an item or that the item may be incorrectly keyed. Discrimination values below .20 are considered low, between .21 and .50 moderate, and above .50 high.

A very common statistic used as an estimate of item discrimination is the correlation coefficient between the item and the total test score **(E4–19)**. The item-total correlation does not yield a numeric value identical to the difference between the proportion of students in the upper and lower groups answering an item correctly. The item-total correlation does identify the same items as having negative, relatively low, moderate, or high discriminations.

Application: The item discrimination is a valuable index used to assess item quality. The item discrimination essentially provides an indication of whether people's responses to an item are consistent with their responses to the rest of the items on a test. In this way, item discrimination indicates how well an item fits in with the other items on a test or survey.

Data: The item discrimination can be calculated on items that are scored dichotomously (0,1) and also for survey and questionnaire items that have ordered category responses such as "Strongly Disagree," "Disagree," "Agree," and "Strongly Agree," or "Never," "Rarely," "Sometimes," and "Always." These categories are represented by ordered integers 1, 2, 3, and 4.

Limitations: Item discrimination cannot be interpreted by itself but must be examined along with other item and test analysis information. An item discrimination is highly related to, and limited by, the item difficulty **(E6–29)**. Items with very low or very high difficulty values may not have moderate discrimination values and cannot have high discrimination values. Like all item and test statistics, item discrimination based on small samples should be interpreted with great care.

Comments: As mentioned under *Limitations*, item discrimination is related to, and limited by, the item difficulty. An item with a difficulty above .90 and close to 1.00, for example, will have a discrimination value close to 0.00. There must be a nearly equal proportion of students in the upper- and lower-scoring groups answering an item correctly as the total proportion of all students answering the item correctly approaches 1.00. A very common statistic used as an estimate of item discrimination is the correlation coefficient between the item and the total test score.

Formula: Item analysis software such as ITEMAN (see Section D, Part 3) routinely calculates item discrimination. The item-total correlation method for estimating item discrimination uses the point-biserial **(E4–19)** and biserial **(E4–20)** correlation coefficients.

E6–31

Measurement Category: Item Analysis

Concept/Procedure: Distractor Analysis

Description: Distractor analysis examines the characteristics of the incorrect answer choices for a test item. The distractor analysis includes the proportion of students selecting each incorrect answer, that is, each distractor's difficulty or p-value **(E6–29)** and the discrimination value **(E6–30)** of each distractor.

Application: The distractor analysis is a valuable tool for detecting flawed or weak test items and items that are not aligned with curriculum standards and instructional emphasis. Careful attention must be paid to understanding any distractor chosen by no students or few students; distractors chosen more often than the correct answer; and distractors with negative discrimination values.

Data: Distractor analysis is applied to students' responses to each question before the data are scored into 0s (incorrect) and 1s (correct).

Limitations: Distractor analysis information cannot be interpreted by itself but must be examined along with other item and test analysis information. Distractor analysis data are highly related to, and limited by, the item difficulty **(E6–29)**. The proportion of students who can select any incorrect answer is equal to one minus the proportion of students selecting the correct answer. Thus, an item with a p-value of .90 has only 10% of the students who can select any and all of the incorrect answers.

Comments: Care must be taken in making inferences about why students might choose a particular distractor or why some distractors might be chosen rarely, if at all. There is nothing intrinsically wrong with a distractor simply because few students select it. Items on criterion-referenced tests, covering material that is well taught and carefully studied, may have high p-values and therefore no students, or a small proportion of students, selecting each distractor.

Formula: Distractor analysis includes the proportion (or percentage) of students and the discrimination value (**E6–30**) for each distractor.

DIFFERENTIAL ITEM FUNCTIONING (DIF)/ ITEM BIAS

Differential item functioning (DIF) is the more technical expression for what is commonly called item bias analysis. Care must be taken in interpreting DIF and DIF analyses. DIF and all DIF procedures can detect only that two identifiable groups, for example, girls and boys, have different levels of achievement on a test question even when overall differences between the groups have been controlled statistically. The cause or causes for the difference cannot be identified through any item or test analysis procedure. There are a number of ways in which an item may function differently or be biased for a particular group. One possibility is that the items have substantially different meanings for the two groups or that one group might have the advantage of special familiarity with the content. For example, boys might be favored on a reading comprehension test by the use of sports-related passages and questions that are easier if one is familiar with the particulars of the sport. Most test developers avoid such obvious problems. Differential group performance can also reflect differences in instructional time, instructional effectiveness, opportunity to learn, different emphasis on some course material compared to other material, and variation in students' study habits. Such factors as these may lead to item DIF statistics of concern, but, in such circumstances, the items are reflecting group differences, not causing them.

Differential Item Functioning (DIF)

(**E6–32**) Item Sensitivity Review Panels
(**E6–33**) Delta Measures of Item Difficulty
(**E6–34**) Chi-Squared Based Approaches
(**E6–35**) Item Response Theory (IRT) Approaches

E6–32
Measurement Category: Differential Item Functioning
Concept/Procedure: Item Sensitivity Review Panels
Description: The use of an item sensitivity review panel is a standard feature in carefully developed assessment programs. Panels of qualified experts review all aspects of the test items, including stimulus materials, questions, and options. The panel members are asked to identify and describe any item or item features that might be offensive to

some group of students. Panelists are asked to identify any item or item feature, unrelated to what the item is designed to measure, that might make the item relatively easier or relatively more difficult for groups of students. Panel members are often asked to provide a written explanation or rationale for their judgments.

Application: The use of a sensitivity review panel is essential for any assessment for which high stakes are attached and is recommended in most assessment settings.

Data: Sensitivity review panels review item **(E6–12)** and test specifications **(E6–13)**, results from empirical DIF analyses, and item analysis information **(E6–29** to **E6–31)**. The results of a sensitivity review are often presented in tabular form by showing the number or percentage of judges who note a problem with each item. A narrative is generally produced describing each judge's rationale for noting a concern with an item.

Limitations: The qualifications of the panel members and the directions and criteria that they are directed to use strongly influence the value of a sensitivity review. Judges should be familiar with the developmental capacity of the students, the curriculum expectations, all aspects of the content being assessed, and the instruction that students receive. Sensitivity review panels should include members from identifiable ethnic, racial, religious, social, and perhaps regional groups. Membership in such groups, however, does not necessarily mean that a person understands and reflects the views of that group or meets the other important qualifications. Members of sensitivity review panels should be given clear guidelines or criteria for evaluating the quality of the test items. For example, the nature and level of language that a test is designed to measure and use should be stated in guidelines for the panelists. Technical language is appropriate on a test designed to measure technical materials, even though many students may not encounter such language in their everyday lives.

Comments: The work of a sensitivity review panel is greatly enhanced by the careful selection of qualified panelists and the use of clear and explicit guidelines and criteria.

Formula: Not applicable.

E6–33

Measurement Category: Differential Item Functioning

Concept/Procedure: Delta Measures of Item Difficulty

Description: Item difficulties are the basis for an approach to detecting differential item functioning (DIF) involving the calculation of item deltas. The item difficulty is treated as a proportion under the normal distribution, and the normal deviate z-statistic that corresponds to that proportion is used for the item. The item delta for a group is derived by multiplying the z-statistic by 4 and adding 13. The item delta is calculated for the comparison groups of interest and compared graphically and by regression analysis to identifying regression outliers.

Application: The delta method has been used for some time to detect items on which groups might perform quite differently.

Data: This method applies best to dichotomously scored items.

Limitations: There is no exact test for the statistical significance of deltas, and the results of a delta analysis may be difficult to interpret. As with all statistical tests of DIF, the statistical tests do not necessarily demonstrate item bias.

Comments: The delta method can be useful and informative, but other methods are used more often.

Formula: A z-statistic is derived as described earlier and then is transformed by:

$$Delta = 4z + 13$$

E6–34

Measurement Category: Differential Item Functioning

Concept/Procedure: Chi-Square-Based Approaches

Description: A set of DIF procedures has been developed that are based on the chi-square statistic. The basic strategy involves forming three-way contingency tables. The three factors are group membership (e.g., females, males), scored item response (0, 1), and score group membership. Score groups are formed by defining ranges of raw scores that set the group boundaries. For example, three groups could be formed based on total test scores on a 60 item test and defined as low (scores of 0 to 20), medium (scores of 21 to 40), and high (scores above 40) groups. The chi-squared statistic is used to test for any significant group differences. Forming groups with homogeneous test scores is designed to control for differences in basic group performance.

Application: The chi-square DIF approach is well established and very commonly used. The chi-square approach is used as a regular part of item development and analysis.

Data: The chi-square approaches can be applied to dichotomous data as well as rating scale and partial-credit items.

Limitations: The number of score groups and the manner in which the score groups are formed can strongly influence the results. As with all statistical tests of DIF, the statistical tests do not necessarily demonstrate item bias.

Comments: The Mantel-Haenszel is the most commonly used chi-square approach.

Formulá: See (**E4–61**).

E6–35

Measurement Category: Differential Item Functioning

Concept/Procedure: Item Response Theory (IRT) Approaches

Description: Item response theory (**E6–15**) is used in a number of ways to detect item DIF, but two basic approaches are most common. The first approach involves comparing item parameter estimates derived from the two groups of interest. For example, the IRT estimates of item difficulties based on a sample of boys can be compared to the IRT estimates of item difficulties for the same items based on a sample of girls. The comparison of the item difficulty estimates is the most commonly examined difference. The second approach involves comparing the area under the item characteristic curves for the two groups of interest.

Application: The IRT approaches are used frequently and can be applied to a wide range of data.

Data: IRT-based DIF analyses can be used in any setting in which IRT models are applied.

Limitations: The IRT approaches are somewhat complicated and require reasonably large sample sizes. As with all statistical tests of DIF, the statistical tests do not necessarily demonstrate item bias.

Comments: IRT models are the basis for most large-scale testing programs.
Formula: See **(E6–15)**.

E6–36 CRITERIA FOR EVALUATING TEST QUALITY: RELIABILITY AND VALIDITY

Reliability and Related Concepts and Procedures

Reliability refers to the consistency or stability of scores obtained from a test. A test must be reliable if the test results are to be credible and useful. For example, we need to know that a test proposed as a high school graduation requirement is reliable before its use could be recommended for such an important decision. Different types of reliability are designed to answer different questions. Test-retest reliability answers the question: Will we obtain the same test results if students take the test again? Alternate form reliability answers the question: Will we obtain the same test results if students take different forms of a test that are supposed to measure the same knowledge and skills? Internal consistency reliability answers the question: Are the scores we obtain from a test providing similar scores for students using various subsets of items on the test?

Reliability is influenced by a number of factors. Longer tests with many items are more reliable than shorter tests with few items. All tests are more reliable when taken by students with heterogeneous test scores showing a wide range of scores than when taken by students whose tests scores are homogeneous showing a narrow range of scores. Tests that are moderately difficult for the students taking them are more reliable than tests that students find very easy or very hard.

Several reliability coefficients are correlation coefficients, and all reliability coefficients range, in theory, from 0.00 to 1.00. The reliability required of a test depends on the importance of the decision that will be made based on the test results and whether the decision is final. In general, tests used to make important and definitive decisions about students should have reliabilities of at least .85 or greater and more often greater than .90 depending on the consequences of the test results.

The major aspects of reliability include:

    (E6–37) Test-Retest Reliability
    (E6–38) Alternate Form Reliability, Parallel Form Reliability
    (E6–39) Internal Consistency, Split-Half Reliability
    (E6–40) Spearman-Brown Prophecy Formula
    (E6–41) Internal Consistency, Kuder-Richardson 20 (KR-20)
    (E6–42) Internal Consistency, Coefficient Alpha
    (E6–43) Inter-rater Agreement or Consistency
    (E6–44) Standard Error of Measurement
    (E6–45) Classification Reliability
    (E6–46) Generalizability

E6–37

Measurement Category: Reliability
Concept/Procedure: Test-Retest Reliability

Description: Test-retest reliability is an index of the stability or consistency of test scores over some period of time when the same group of students takes the same test twice. The test-retest reliability coefficient is the correlation (**E4–16**) between students' scores when taking the test a first time and their scores when taking the same test a second time.

Application: Test-retest reliability is extremely valuable in deciding if a test can be used to measure change over time. Tests that do not have a high level of test-retest reliability should not be used to measure progress, growth, the impact of an intervention, or any type of change over time. Tests with low test-retest reliability may show differences between time 1 (a pretest) and time 2 (a posttest) that are due to instability or lack of reliability of the test, instead of actual growth or progress.

Data: Test-retest reliability is calculated on two sets of test data obtained from students taking the same test twice.

Limitations: The calculation of test-retest reliability involves students' taking the same test twice. The intervening length of time and some events that might occur between the two test administrations influence test-retest reliability. It is important to know that all students took the tests on both occasions and that no subgroups of students had exposure to the test content between the two test administrations.

Comments: The test-retest reliability should be obtained for any test that students are likely to take two or more times. It is especially important to know the test-retest reliability of any test that will be used to measure growth, progress, or the impact of an intervention.

Formula: The test-retest reliability coefficient is the correlation coefficient between the two sets of scores obtained when students take the same test twice (**E4–16**).

E6–38

Measurement Category: Reliability

Concept/Procedure: Alternate Form Reliability, also called Parallel Form Reliability

Description: Alternate form reliability is an index of consistency of test scores when the same group of students takes two forms of the same test. Alternate or parallel test forms are designed to measure the same content, at the same skill levels, in the same context, using the same assessment format. The alternate form reliability coefficient is the correlation (**E4–16**) between students' scores on each of the two forms.

Application: Alternate form reliability is an important characteristic of tests that are used to measure change. Tests with high alternate form reliability are especially useful for measuring progress, growth, the impact of an intervention, or any type of change over time.

Data: Alternate form reliability is calculated on two sets of test scores obtained from students taking two parallel forms of a test.

Limitations: The calculation of alternate form reliability involves students' taking two forms of the same test. It is influenced by the length of time between the two test administrations, events that might occur between the two testing times, and the order in which students take the two forms. Ideally, the time between test administrations should be a matter of days and no more than a few weeks. Students should be randomly assigned (**E5–15**) into two groups, each of which takes the two forms in a different order.

Comments: The alternate form reliability is an important characteristic of any test used to measure students' progress or the impact of an instructional program. Alternate forms of tests have an advantage over using the same test twice (test-retest) because students do not see exactly the same test questions when they take the second test.

Formula: The alternate form reliability coefficient is the correlation coefficient (**E4–16**) between the two sets of scores obtained when students take each of the two test forms.

E6–39

Measurement Category: Reliability

Concept/Procedure: Internal Consistency, Split-Half Reliability

Description: Split-half reliability is the consistency between students' performance on two halves of a test. The two half-tests are often composed of the odd items and the even items, yielding the odd-even split-half reliability. The split-half reliability coefficient is the correlation (**E4–16**) between students' scores on the two halves of the test.

Application: Split-half reliability is an important indicator of reliability when students' performance on a test is represented by a single total score. The use of a single total score assumes that one unitary or unidimensional ability, skill, or body of knowledge is being tested. If this assumption is true, all of the items on a test should be measuring the same trait, and hence there should be a high degree of consistency between students' performance when measured on subsets of the test items.

Data: The split-half reliability is calculated on students' test scores from two halves of a test. The two halves are often composed of the odd and the even items, but other ways of dividing the items may be used.

Limitations: The split-half reliability for a total test, like all measures of internal consistency, is not completely appropriate if the test is composed of subscales and if test results will be reported at the subscale level. In such cases, the reliability of the subscales should be determined and reported. The reliability of any test is directly related to test length: longer tests are more reliable than shorter tests. It is important to note that split-half reliability is based on artificially constructed tests that are half the length of the original test, the reliability of which needs to be determined. The correlation between these two half-length tests is an underestimate of the reliability of the original full-length test. This underestimation of the test reliability can be adjusted using the Spearman-Brown prophecy formula (**E6–40**) to yield the reliability of the original test at its full length. Finally, internal consistency reliability is not appropriate if the test has a specific time limit (e.g., is speeded) and will not be completed by some students.

Comments: Split-half reliability and adjusted split-half reliability are standard indices of test quality that should be reported for any test or test subscales on which students' performance is reported. It is important to consider the structure and organization of a test in deciding how to divide it into two halves. For example, if a test is designed to measure three content areas, then items within the content areas should be randomly assigned to each of the two half-tests used to calculate the split-half reliability.

Formula: The split-half reliability coefficient is the correlation (**E4–16**) between students' scores on the two halves of the test. The adjusted split-half reliability is the split-half reliability coefficient adjusted for test length using the Spearman-Brown prophecy formula (**E6–40**).

E6–40

Measurement Category: Reliability

Concept/Procedure: Spearman-Brown Prophecy Formula

Description: The Spearman-Brown prophecy formula is used to adjust the correlation co-efficient used to estimate the split-half reliability **(E6–39)**. The adjustment increases the size of the reliability coefficient to the value that it would be for a test that has the actual number of items as the original test.

Application: It is important to use the Spearman-Brown formula to adjust for test length because otherwise the estimate of split-half reliability will be systematically too low.

Data: The Spearman-Brown formula is applied to the correlation coefficient obtained when students' scores on two halves of a test are correlated.

Limitations: How the two halves of a test are constructed can influence the Spearman-Brown adjustment.

Comments: It is important to note when reading a technical manual or reporting split-half reliability whether the Spearman-Brown formula has been applied.

Formula:

$$\text{Adjusted Reliability} = \frac{2r}{1+r}$$

where
r = the split-half reliability

E6–41

Measurement Category: Reliability

Concept/Procedure: Internal Consistency, Kuder-Richardson Formula 20

Description: The Kuder-Richardson formula 20, commonly called the KR-20, is an index of internal consistency like split-half reliability but does not require splitting the test into halves. The KR-20 is an estimate of the average of all the split-half reliabilities that one could generate dividing a test into two halves using every possible combination.

Application: The KR-20 applies only to tests composed of items that are scored dichoto-mously with 0 indicating an incorrect answer and 1 a correct answer. Nevertheless, the KR-20 is very useful since it is based on a single test administration and does not re-quire dividing a test into two halves.

Data: The KR-20 is applied to tests with dichotomously scored items. The variance **(E4–7)** or standard deviation **(E4–8)** of the test must be known as well as the difficulty of each item **(E4–29).**

Limitations: The KR-20 applies only to tests composed of items scored dichotomously as 0 and 1 and, as such, is a special case of coefficient alpha **(E6–42)**. Like all internal consistency reliabilities, the KR-20 is not appropriate if the test is time-limited (speeded) and will not be completed by some students.

Comments: The KR-20 is a commonly reported and used index of internal consistency re-liability.

Formula:

$$KR\text{-}20 = \frac{n}{n-1}\left(1 - \frac{\sum p_i q_i}{S_t^2}\right)$$

where

n $\quad$ = the number of items

$\sum p_i q_i$ = the sum of the item variances

S_t^2 $\quad$ = the variance of the test scores

E6–42

Measurement Category: Reliability

Concept/Procedure: Internal Consistency, Coefficient Alpha

Description: Coefficient alpha is the most general version of internal consistency reliability. It does not require dividing a test into two halves and that test items be scored dichotomously.

Application: Coefficient alpha can be calculated on test data scored dichotomously (0,1) and on test data scored on a rating scale such as 1, 2, 3, 4, etc. Coefficient alpha is applicable to tests that use items scored dichotomously and items scored on a rating scale.

Data: Coefficient alpha is appropriate for data scored dichotomously or data from an ordinal rating scale. The variance (**E4–7**) or standard deviation (**E4–8**) of the test must be known, as well as the difficulty of each item (**E6–29**).

Limitations: Like all internal consistency reliabilities, alpha is not appropriate if the test must be completed in a fixed period of time and will not be completed by some students.

Comments: Coefficient alpha is a commonly reported and frequently used index of internal consistency reliability.

Formula:

$$\alpha = \frac{n}{n-1}\left(1 - \frac{\sum \sigma_i^2}{S_t^2}\right)$$

where

n $\quad$ = the number of items

$\sum \sigma_i^2$ = the sum of the item variances

S_t^2 $\quad$ = the variance of the test scores

E6–43

Measurement Category: Reliability

Concept/Procedure: Inter-rater Agreement or Consistency

Description: Inter-rater agreement is often referred to as inter-rater reliability and describes the extent to which two (or more) judges assigned the same values when rating students' work. Inter-rater consistency can be calculated and reported in terms of a correlation coefficient or the percentage of times two judges assign the same ratings to the same students' work.

Application: Interrater consistency is an important characteristic of an assessment system in which students' performance or the products that they create are evaluated. Indices of interrater agreement provide a basis for knowing the extent to which students' ratings are fair and reflect the quality of their work and not the bias of the judges rating that work.

Data: Inter-rater consistency is calculated on ordinal ratings (e.g., 1, 2, 3, 4, etc.) made by two or more judges evaluating the same students' work.

Limitations: The narrow range of many rating scales, usually 4 to 7 score points, makes the appropriateness of using the correlation coefficient questionable. In addition, indices of inter-rater agreement can be misleading in two ways. First, two raters may have very highly correlated ratings, even though one rater is consistently rating higher or lower than the other. Second, two raters may have a high percentage of agreements in their ratings, but the disagreements may be systematic such that one rater is consistently higher or lower when there is a difference in the two ratings.

Comments: Inter-rater consistency is an essential characteristic of assessment programs that evaluate performance assessments such as students' writing. In addition to reporting the percentage of exact agreements between two or more judges, it is useful and informative to report the percentage of ratings in which judges differ by 1 point, 2 points, etc.

Formula: Inter-rater agreement based on the correlation approach uses the correlation coefficient (**E4–16** or **E4–17**). The percentage of inter-rater agreement is

$$\text{Percent Agreement} = 100 \times \frac{\text{Number of agreements}}{\text{Total number of paired ratings}}$$

E6–44

Measurement Category: Reliability—Related Concept and Procedure

Concept/Procedure: Standard Error of Measurement

Description: All tests have a margin of error, and the standard error of measurement (SEM) shows how precisely or accurately a test measures a student's score. Conceptually, the SEM is the standard deviation (**E4–8**) of the scores that one would expect to see if a student could be measured over and over on the same test. Tests that are more reliable have smaller SEMs than less reliable tests. If a test were perfectly reliable, there would be no error, and the SEM would be zero.

Application: The SEM is important for interpreting students' test scores and should be taken into account when any important and definitive decisions are made about students based on test scores.

Data: The SEM is calculated using the standard deviation of the test (**E4–8**) and the reliability of the test.

Limitations: The SEM is not exactly the same at all points in the test score range. In general, the SEM is smaller toward the center of the score range and larger at the bottom and top of the score range. Also, it is important to note that SEMs reported by test publishers are based on national norm samples and may not be applicable to particular groups of students who differ from the norm group on some important characteristics.

Comments: The SEM is used to construct a confidence interval around students' test scores. The confidence interval is a score range within which students' true scores are most likely located. A specific level of probability can be used to define "most likely." For example, a score range of ± 1 SEM defines a score range with a 68% probability of including students' true scores; a score range of ± 2 SEMs defines a score range with a 95% probability of including students' true scores; and a score range of ± 3 SEMs defines a score range with a 99% probability of including students' true scores. SEMs can be calculated and expressed in terms of raw scores or scale scores and should be reported in the scale that is used to report students' scores.

Formula:

$$\text{SEM} = S_y \sqrt{1 - \text{reliability}}$$

where S_y = standard deviation of the test scores

E6–45

Measurement Category: Reliability—Related Concept or Procedure
Concept/Procedure: Classification Reliability
Description: The classification of students into specific categories, such as proficient or nonproficient, employs the concept of reliability in a special way. If two tests are supposed to be equivalent, then a certain consistency (reliability) should be observed in the classification of students who take both test forms. The possible classification outcomes for two test forms are shown:

Test Form B

Test Form A		Proficient	Nonproficient
	Proficient	11	10
	Nonproficient	01	00

The sum of the proportion of students in the 11 and 00 categories is an estimate of the classification consistency.

The classification consistency is inflated by the fact that a certain proportion of students would receive a consistent classification just by chance. Thus, the kappa index is used. Kappa controls for the chance probability that students receive the same classification.

Application: Some indication of classification or decision consistency is important in any testing situation that can lead to important decisions about students, teachers, or school programs. All high-stakes tests, such as graduation tests, should report kappa or some other index of decision reliability.

Data: Classification reliability can be calculated around any decision point or cut score.

Limitations: Classification reliability is influenced by the location of the cut score on the scale, the length of the tests, and the shape of the score distributions on the two tests. There are no exact significance levels for kappa.

Comments: Classification reliability is an essential statistic in any technical report for high-stakes tests.

Formula:

$$\text{kappa} = \frac{P - P_c}{1 - P_c}$$

where
P = proportion of agreements
P_c = chance probability of agreements

E6–46

Measurement Category: Reliability—Related Concept or Procedure

Concept/Procedure: Generalizability

Description: Generalizability is actually a comprehensive theory and set of procedures, not a single, specific procedure. Generalizability is concerned with determining what proportion of the variation in students' scores can be attributed to various factors or facets. For example, consider a situation in which students responded to three open-ended science tasks or questions and two different raters scored their responses. Variation in students' scores can be accounted for by differences among students, tasks, and raters. There would be serious concerns about the assessment if most of the variation were attributable to tasks or raters. Such situations would indicate that variation in students' scores was mostly influenced by which tasks students took and who rated their work. In many respects, generalizability uses many of the same concepts and procedures as analysis of variance (**E4–70**) and focuses on the proportion of variance accounted for by various factors.

Application: Generalizability is very important in evaluating complex assessment situations involving different assessment formats, variation in questions or tasks, and different raters.

Data: Generalizability theory can be applied to virtually any type of assessment data.

Limitations: Many practitioners are not familiar with generalizability analyses, the results of which can be complex and sometimes difficult to explain.

Comment: Generalizability analyses are especially helpful in exploring questions about the number of assessment tasks or raters that are needed to obtain stable scoring. Most measurement situations would involve what are known as G studies.

Formula:

Validity

Validity is the most critical feature of any assessment or assessment program. Tests and other forms of assessment that are used to make important decisions about students should be held to a very high standard of validity. Validity is used today to refer to the extent to which evidence has been collected and supports the inferences that the assessments are used to make. Evidence from a wide variety of sources can be used to document the validity of an assessment. Traditional measurement describes three types of validity (**E6–47** to **E6–50**). More recently, validity is viewed as an integrated and unified characteristic of an assessment. Readers interested in more information about validity and all other aspects of measurement are urged to examine *The Standards for Educational and Psychological Testing* by the American Educational Research Association, American Psychological Association, and the National Council on Measurement in Education (1999).

(**E6–47**) Content Validity
(**E6–48**) Criterion-Related Validity, Concurrent
(**E6–49**) Criterion-Related Validity, Predictive
(**E6–50**) Construct Validity
(**E6–51**) Validity Related to Consequences

E6–47

Measurement Category: Validity
Concept/Procedure: Content
Description: Content validity is the extent to which an assessment includes the content that it should cover and does not include other material. The term "content" is used broadly to include three features of the material: first, content in the usual sense of the facts, terms, principles, and procedures; second, content as related to the appropriate cognitive or intellectual level of activity, for example, knowledge level compared to analysis level; and third, content as regarding the context within which the assessment material and questions are presented, for example, real-life contexts for problem solving. The content of an assessment should be representative of the content that has been specified for learning and teaching and be relevant to the specified content domain.

Content validity is established substantially through judgmental processes involving educational experts knowledgeable with the content standards, the curriculum employed, the instruction provided, and the characteristics of the students to be assessed. These experts review all aspects of the assessments, stimulus materials, questions, possible answers, and scoring rubrics. These experts then evaluate the items using a rating form indicating the extent to which the assessments are representative of the specified content domain.

Application: Content validity is an essential part of any assessment or assessment program. It is the cornerstone of any standards-based assessment program and an absolute requirement for any high-stakes assessment. Attempts to bring about curriculum reform through assessment require a high degree of content validation.

Data: Content validity is a judgmental process in which the data examined include a comprehensive and explicit statement of the content domain or curriculum standards and all the materials used for the assessment of the content domain or curriculum standards.

Limitations: Content validity is limited by the degree to which the content domain and content standards are explicit and comprehensive and also by the qualifications and expertise of the judges evaluating the assessment materials.

Comments: The content validity process is used to evaluate the extent to which the assessment is aligned with the curriculum. Content reviews typically utilize a carefully selected and qualified content review committee. The evaluation of the appropriateness of the cognitive task demands and the contexts used in the assessments (e.g., names, places, activities, situations) are critical aspects of the content validation process.

Formula: The results of a content validation review are often presented in a narrative form that includes the percentage of items or assessments that match the content specifications. The content validation should provide an overall description of how well the assessment represents the intended content. The content validation must also be explicit and detailed in describing specific content elements that are underrepresented or overrepresented in terms of the material covered, the cognitive levels assessed, and the context employed.

E6–48

Measurement Category: Validity

Concept/Procedure: Criterion-Related Validity, Concurrent Validity

Description: A new assessment designed to measure certain domains of knowledge or particular abilities or skills should be systematically related to other indicators of that knowledge or those abilities or skills. For example, a new assessment designed to measure students' mathematics problem-solving ability should be related to other indicators of mathematics problem-solving ability. The "other indicators" are called criterion variables or criterion measures. Assuming that the criterion measures are themselves valid (see *Limitations* below), a strong relationship between the new assessment and the criterion is evidence supporting the validity of the new assessment. Useful criterion indicators can be scores from other tests, teacher ratings, and observations of students' work. Concurrent validity evidence also includes consideration of criterion measures to which the new assessment should be uncorrelated, have a low correlation, or even be negatively correlated. If a consideration of the construct being measured by a new assessment suggests that it should be uncorrelated or have a negative correlation with some criterion variable, then a low or negative correlation coefficient between the new assessment and the criterion variable is evidence of concurrent validity.

Application: Concurrent validity is an important aspect of any validity investigation and should be routinely reported in technical manuals for commercial assessment and any assessment used for high-stakes purposes.

Data: Concurrent validity data include scores or ratings on the assessment being investigated and the criterion variable or variables.

Limitations: There are two serious limitations to concurrent validity. First, there must be strong reason to believe that criterion variables themselves are valid. Concurrent validity evidence is of little value if the validity of the criterion variable is questionable. Standardized, norm-referenced test scores, for example, are not necessarily useful criterion variables for curriculum-referenced or standards-based assessments. Second, the value of a new assessment should be reviewed if its correlation with an available criterion is very high. Educators must be certain that a new assessment is worth the effort and expense if it correlates at .8 (see **E4–16**) or higher with an existing measure.

Comments: Concurrent validity is an important feature of any assessment program that employs multiple measures. The intercorrelations among a set of measures used to describe the achievement or ability of a student or group of students should be determined and reported. Highly correlated measures may be redundant, while measures with low correlations may provide information about unique components of the characteristic being measured.

Formula: Current validity is generally reported in terms of the correlation between the new assessment and the criterion measure (**E4–16, E4–17**).

E6–49

Measurement Category: Validity

Concept/Procedure: Criterion-Related Validity, Predictive Validity

Description: Predictive validity is information about the accuracy with which an assessment predicts subsequent achievement or behavior. The future achievement or behavior serves as the criterion measure or variable. Predictive validity is an essential requirement for assessments used to make selection decisions (**E6–2**) when the decision uses current assessment data as a basis for deciding who will achieve or benefit most from future instruction or other future activity.

Application: A very common educational application is the use of the Scholastic Assessment Test (SAT I and II) employed to predict which students will most likely have high levels of achievement in postsecondary educational institutions. Assessments used for placement purposes would generally require the demonstration of predictive validity.

Data: Predictive validity analysis uses assessment data from two points in time. These are data from the assessment being studied and data from the criterion measure. The data are generally test scores, but the basic approach could be applied to a variety of assessment procedures, including teachers' ratings of students, evaluations of students' work, or systematic observations of behavior.

Limitations: The validity and importance of the criterion variable must be established, and often this is a matter of professional judgment. Also, it is essential to show that the predictive validity evidence is obtained from, or at least applicable to, the students who will be taking the assessment. In general, predictive validity evidence is based on group-based correlational evidence. The prediction does not apply with equal accuracy to all students. Furthermore, the correlational evidence does not support a causal interpretation.

Comments: Great care should be taken in using predictive validity evidence to exclude students from programs or activities. Important decisions about students should be based on multiple sources of information. In addition, the students who might need a program the most could be the very students predicted to do poorly in the program.

Formula: Predictive validity studies are generally based on the use of regression analysis (**E4–32 to E4–39**).

E6–50

Measurement Category: Validity

Concept/Procedure: Construct Validity

Description: A construct is a general multicomponent ability, aptitude, or personality characteristic. Constructs are not directly observed but are inferred (or constructed) from test scores and other observed behaviors. Constructs are used to explain complex sets of observed behaviors. Such abilities as mathematics problem solving, reading readiness, reading comprehension, and academic self-concept are examples of constructs. A detailed and comprehensive description of a construct is required before any attempt to assess it is possible. The description must include an explication of all the construct's components and the interrelationships among the components. Construct validity requires demonstrating that the assessment reflects all the components of the construct and does not reflect variables that are not part of the construct. The inclusion of all construct components in an assessment is referred to as construct representation. If a critical component is not reflected in the assessment, the assessment suffers from construct underrepresentation. If an assessment reflects the influence of student characteristics not relevant to the construct, it is said to suffer from construct-irrelevant variation.

Application: Many important educational variables are constructs, like those previously mentioned as well as most abilities characterized as higher-order thinking skills. Construct validity is essential for assessments that purport to measure these important constructs since they are often used to make important decisions about students and the efficacy of educational programs.

Data: Multiple sources of evidence are generally required to substantiate construct validity. These data sources might include a variety of test scores, teacher ratings, and samples of students' work.

Limitations: Many important educational constructs are ill defined or undefined, despite the fact that educators use them quite frequently (e.g., problem solving, higher-order thinking, etc). The lack of a clear construct definition limits the extent to which construct validity can be demonstrated. Developing substantial evidence for construct validity requires planning, effort, resources, time, and care. In many educational settings, assessment development is on an accelerated schedule, and these requirements are not available and/or not brought to bear on the assessment validation process.

Comments: Construct validity often involves combining the results from a number of validity studies. A detailed content validity (**E6–47**) investigation would always be included, and multiple demonstrations of criterion-related validity would typically be involved (**E6–48, E6–49**).

Formula: See **E6–47**, **E6–48**, and **E6–49**.

E6–51

Measurement Category: Validity

Concept/Procedure: Validity Related to Consequences

Description: Many measurement experts have discussed and applied the concept of consequential validity. The basic idea is that the validity of an assessment should consider and take into account consequences that accrue to the use of the assessment. This point of view suggests that a validity analysis of an assessment should collect and include information about any serious negative impact that the use of the assessment may have on students. It is especially important to document whether certain aspects of an assessment not related to its primary purpose have a negative impact on students. For example, it would be especially problematic if the results of a mathematics test had negative consequences for students and the test used an unnecessarily high language level in presenting the questions.

Application: Evidence related to the consequences of assessment can be collected in a wide range of assessment situations.

Data: A variety of qualitative and quantitative data can be used to describe the consequences of an assessment.

Limitations: It is difficult to separate consequences related to an assessment instrument from consequences related to the misuse of valid assessment information.

Comments: Not all measurement experts agree that consequences should be included as an aspect of assessment validity. The misuse of test results by educators and elected officials, for example, may have negative consequences for students. Some measurement experts contend that such people, not the test, should be held accountable for actions that have negative consequences.

Formula: Consequential validity does not refer to a specific statistic or procedure. Documenting the consequences of an assessment may include information from a variety of qualitative and quantitative sources.

E6–52 TEST EQUATING AND STANDARD SETTING

Test equating and standard setting are two important aspects of a comprehensive assessment program. Test equating and standard setting are not directly related procedures. They are covered together here in this final section so that the chapter provides readers with a comprehensive reference source of important measurement concepts, principles, and procedures.

Test equating refers to the process of determining whether or to what extent scores on different tests or different forms of the same test have the same meaning. Test equating allows educators to determine what scores on one test are equivalent to scores on a different test. Standard-setting procedures are employed to set cut scores or performance levels on various tests. Some tests employ a single cut score resulting in two classifications of students (e.g., pass or fail), while other tests have multiple cut scores with multiple classifications (e.g., novice, proficient, or advanced).

> (**E6–53**) Equating
>> Linear
>> Equipercentile
>> Item Response Theory (IRT) Approaches
>
> (**E6–54**) Standard Setting
>> Test- and Item-Focused Approaches
>> Student-Focused Approaches

E6–53

Measurement Category: Test Equating

Concept/Procedure: Equating: Linear, Equipercentile, and Item Response Theory (IRT) Approaches

Description: Equating refers to the process of establishing the correspondence between the scores on one test and the scores on a second test. The nature of the correspondence can range from simply linking or matching up the scores, to the claim that the equated scores have the same meaning in terms of what students know and are able to do. Two tests are generally considered equated if they measure the same construct and have the same reliability and if students' percentile ranks on the two tests are the same. There are many different procedures for equating and many variations on the different procedures.

Linear equating refers to procedures in which a linear transformation of the form $Y = a(X - c) + d$ is used. Y and X are the two tests to be equated. The values for a, c, and d reflect the data collection design and characteristics of the data for Y and X.

Equipercentile equating matches scores on Y and X that correspond to the same percentile rank. Finally, IRT methods can be employed to equate tests or to develop a bank of test items equated to a common scale from which equated test forms can be constructed. There are many equating strategies and procedures within the IRT approach.

Application: Equating is an essential component of all large-scale assessment programs. Equated forms are needed to ensure that students taking different test forms are being measured on the same scale. Equated test forms are also an important aspect of test security.

Data: Data from many different types of assessments can be equated or at least linked.

Limitations: All equating procedures are based on a number of assumptions, and the validity of the assumptions should be examined carefully. In addition, most equating is fairly complex and requires technical expertise and experience.

Comments: Equating is essential for all large-scale testing programs. Computer software needed to perform equating is becoming more readily available (see Section D, Chapter 3).

Formula: The technical details of equating are beyond the scope of this work but are well described in Kolen and Brennan (1995), *Test Equating: Methods and Practices.*

E6–54

Measurement Category: Standard Setting

Concept/Procedure: Standard Setting: Test- and Item-Focused Approaches, Student-Focused Approaches

Description: Standard setting refers to a wide array of procedures for setting a standard or cut score on a test. The cut score might separate pass/fail or master/nonmaster. Multiple cut scores can be used to define several categories such as novice, proficient, and advanced. It is important to recognize that all standards or cut scores are the products of human judgment and represent not truth but rather consensus. Standard-setting activities involve, or should involve, a qualified group of standard-setting judges. The judges must be familiar with the test content, the developmental level of the students, and the instruction that the students have been receiving.

Standard-setting procedures are divided into test- or item-focused procedures and student-focused procedures. The most widely used item-focused approach is called the Angoff procedure. In this procedure, judges review each item carefully and are asked to estimate the proportion of the students who score right at the cut score that would correctly answer the item. The sum of these estimated proportions for all the items yields each judge's preliminary cut score. The judges generally see the distributions of the cut scores set by all the judges and the impact that the tentative cut scores would have on student passing rates. Judges can revise their cut scores based on this information.

The bookmark approach has judges examine the items in a different way. The test items are ordered from easy to hard in a booklet. Judges are asked to read each item and decide if a person at the cut score would correctly answer the item at some level of probability. If so, the judge goes to the next item and continues until finding the item that the student at the cut score will probably not answer correctly. This point is then used to identify the judge's tentative cut score.

The most commonly used student-focused approach is called the contrasting group design. This approach uses classroom teachers as judges. The teachers are given definitions of what students in the various categories (e.g., novice, proficient, advanced) know and are able to do. Next, teachers are asked to examine their class rosters and to identify which category each student best matches. The actual scores that students make on the test are then used to find the score points that maximize the separation between the groups. Obviously, the teachers must not know students' scores before they do their ratings. A variation on this approach involves the use of "undecided" categories between the novice and proficient categories and between the proficient and advanced categories. The median scores of students in these undecided categories define the cut scores.

Application: A systematic standard-setting procedure should be used whenever a cut score is to be set. There are no "true" or "correct" cut scores, but these procedures help ensure fairness and due diligence.

Data: Standards can be set on a wide range of assessments.

Limitations: The logistics of some of the standard-setting procedures can be quite cumbersome.

Comments: The capricious selection of a cut score by groups unfamiliar with the students, the test content, and the instruction that students receive is unfair and unwise and may be illegal in high-stakes situations. Folk wisdom concern with such "magic" numbers as 80% of the items correct as the definition of mastery has no basis in reason or fact. The actual content of the specific items on a test can drastically change the meaning of 80% correct.

Formula: The technical details of various standard-setting procedures are beyond the scope of this work but are well described in Cizek (2001).

RESOURCES FOR REVIEWING AND EVALUATING TESTS

Buros

The most valuable, all-purpose resource for evaluating tests is the most current edition of the *Mental Measurement Yearbook,* published by the Buros Institute of Mental Measurement: Plake, B. S., and Impara, J. C. (Eds.). (2001). *The Fourteenth Mental Measurement Yearbook.* Lincoln, NE: The Buros Institute.

The Buros Institute web site is also very useful: www.unl.edu/buros.

ERIC/AE Test Locator

The ERIC/AE Test Locator is a joint project of the ERIC Clearinghouse on Assessment and Evaluation, the Library and Reference Services Division of ETS, the Buros Institute of Mental Measurement at the University of Nebraska in Lincoln, the Region III Comprehensive Center at GW University, and Pro-Ed test publishers.

The ERIC/AE Test Locator is located at: http://ericae.net/testcol.htm. This valuable Web page includes:

> ETS/ERIC Test File
> Test Review Locator
> Buros/ERIC Test Publisher Locator
> Buros Classified Subject Index
> CEEE/ERIC Test Database (tests commonly used with LEP students)
> Code of Fair Testing Practices
> Test Selection Tips

REFERENCES AND RESOURCES

American Educational Research Association, American Psychological Association, and National Council on Measurement in Education. (1999). *Standards for Educational and Psychological Testing*. Washington, DC: American Psychological Association.

Brennan, R. L. (1983). *Elements of Generalizability Theory*. Iowa City: American College Testing Programs.

Cizek, G. J. (Ed.). (2001). *Setting Performance Standards: Concepts, Methods, and Perspectives*. Mahwah, NJ: Lawrence Erlbaum Associates.

Crocker, L., and Algina, J. (1985). *Introduction to Classical and Modern Test Theory*. New York: CBS.

Haladyna, T. M. (1994). *Developing and Validating Multiple Choice Test Items*. Hillsdale, NJ: Lawrence Erlbaum Associates.

Kolen, M. J., and Brennan, R. L. (1995). *Test Equating: Methods and Practices*. New York: Springer-Verlag.

Lord, F. M., and Novick, M. R. (1968). *Statistical Theories of Mental Test Scores*. Reading, MA: Addison-Wesley.

Rasch, G. (1980). *Probabilistic Models for Some Intelligence and Attainment Tests/ George Rasch; with a Foreword and Afterword by Benjamin D. Wright*. Chicago: University of Chicago Press.

Wright, B. D., and Stone, M. H. (1980). *Best Test Design*. Chicago: Mesa Press.

CHAPTER 7

A Summary of Graphical Procedures for Examining, Summarizing, and Reporting Data[*]

INTRODUCTION

A wide variety of graphical procedures has been developed for exploring data, summarizing the results of various data analyses, and reporting research results to different audiences. Many educators find these graphical techniques extremely useful for several reasons. First, they are not dependent on knowledge of formal statistical procedures. Second, they can often capture and show clearly in simple, easy-to-understand figures, charts, or graphs the most important information contained in a large amount of data. Finally, carefully developed visual displays of data can communicate very effectively to a variety of audiences. In contrast, many such audiences might find statistical tables and numeric displays uninformative and perhaps even intimidating.

It is important to note that visual displays should not be used as substitutes for appropriate statistical analyses. Rather, visual displays and statistical analyses should be used in a complementary fashion. Visual displays can be used to explore data as a guide to statistical analyses, as a way to summarize key statistical results, and as a dissemination tool.

This chapter contains 13 of the most commonly used visual displays. There are many variations of these graphs and charts, and many other types of visual displays could be included. The graphs and charts included in this chapter constitute the visual displays that educators are most likely to encounter and employ. SPSS 10 (Norusis, 2000) was used to prepare most of the visual displays in this chapter. Many other programs can be used to develop these displays, including spreadsheet, database, and word-processing programs found in many typical office applications.

Graphical Procedures and Visual Displays

> (**E7–1**) Histogram
> (**E7–2**) Bar Chart, Simple
> (**E7–3**) Bar Chart, Clustered
> (**E7–4**) Bar Chart, Stacked
> (**E7–5**) Pie Chart
> (**E7–6**) Line Chart, Simple
> (**E7–7**) Line Chart, Multiple
> (**E7–8**) Drop-line Chart

*This chapter was prepared by Joseph M. Ryan and Sharon Osborn Popp.

(**E7–9**) Stem-and-Leaf Plot
(**E7–10**) Box Plot, Simple
(**E7–11**) Box Plot, Clustered
(**E7–12**) Scatterplot
(**E7–13**) Scatterplot Matrix

PROFILES OF GRAPHICAL PROCEDURES AND VISUAL DISPLAYS

E7–1

Visual Display: Histogram

Description: The histogram is used to display the frequency distribution of a continuous variable. Contiguous vertical bars represent equal subsets of score values and are displayed on the x-axis. Subsets of scores in each bar are called class intervals or bins. The height of each bar represents the frequency of data values within a class interval and is labeled along the y-axis. The y-axis should be drawn about two-thirds as long as the x-axis. Class-interval midpoints are used to label each bar.

Application: Shows the shape of a variable's distribution. Often used to show the dispersion of student test scores.

Data: Any continuous variable may be represented with a histogram.

Limitations: The size of class intervals represented by each bar may affect the appearance of the histogram, particularly with small samples. Reconfiguring the histogram with different class-interval sizes may prevent a misleading display. A small sample may be better viewed with one class interval for each possible score value.

General Comments: Histograms offer quick insight into the spread of a variable.

Example:

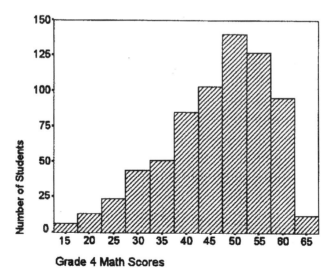

E7–2

Visual Display: Bar Chart, Simple

Description: Shows frequency or percentages of nominal or ordinal categories. Summary statistics of continuous variables may also be displayed in bars. Noncontiguous vertical bars represent each category or variable and are displayed on the x-axis. The y-axis represents the frequency, percentage, or level of summary value.

Application: Often used to show frequencies or percentages of demographic variables (e.g., gender, geographic region, ethnicity) or response categories (e.g., survey data). Can be used to compare summarized values of different variables (e.g., average absentee rates at different schools).

Data: Categorical or continuous variables can be represented in bar charts, depending on the purpose of the display. Data with negative values can also be displayed, using bars that extend downward from the x-axis.

Limitations: The scale on the y-axis must be carefully chosen to provide the most informative range of values. A zero should be used as the scale minimum, where appropriate, to prevent exaggeration of small differences among bars.

General Comments: Bar charts are widely used and easily understood.

Example:

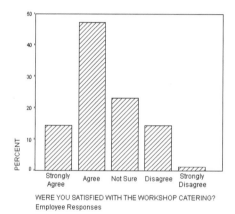

WERE YOU SATISFIED WITH THE WORKSHOP CATERING?
Employee Responses

E7–3

Visual Display: Bar Chart, Clustered

Description: A clustered bar chart is a bar chart that splits the frequencies, percentages, or summary values for display into separate categories of another variable. Each category comprises contiguous bars that represent the categories in the other variable. A legend defines the cluster variable.

Application: May be used to break down values displayed in a simple bar chart by any other categorical variable of interest to observe possible differences among groups, treatments, or demographic variables. Also, summaries on a continuous variable can be compared against two categorical variables.

Data: Clusters are categorical, usually nominal variables.

Limitations: Too many cluster categories can make comparisons more difficult.

General Comments: Clustered bar charts are extremely versatile. Switching the main variable with the clustered variable can provide a different perspective.

Example:

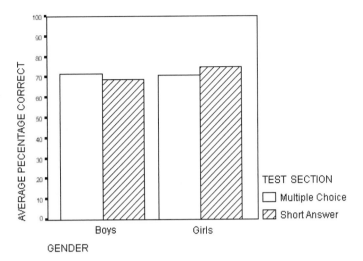

E7–4

Visual Display: Bar Chart, Stacked

Description: A stacked bar chart is a bar chart that splits the frequencies, percentages, or summary values for display into separate categories of another variable or separate, related variables. The bar that represents each category along the x-axis is divided into segments that are defined by another categorical variable. The bar segments are identified in a legend.

Application: The stacked bar chart is useful for presenting total values of categories or variables along with a breakdown by another variable of interest within the total.

Data: Bar segmenting variables are categorical, usually nominal variables, or related sets of variables.

Limitations: The size of bottom segments in a stacked bar chart can be judged precisely, but the size of upper segments may be difficult to estimate. A stacked bar should not be used unless it is meaningful to combine the categories or set of variables into totals for each x-axis value.

General Comments: A stacked bar is an efficient way to display the relationship between individual segments and whole values.

Example:

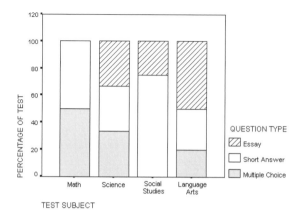

E7–5

Visual Display: Pie Chart

Description: A pie chart is used to display the division of a whole into several subgroups. A circle, or "pie," represents all values in a variable, and the area of each slice is proportional to the number of values in a category. Each slice is labeled and depicted by a different color or texture.

Application: Often used as a presentation display to show and compare relative size of categories that constitute a whole. Demographic and descriptive variables are commonly presented in pie charts.

Data: Any categorical variable can be used in a pie chart. Nominal variables are preferable over ordinal, which may confuse interpretation if the order is not related to size.

Limitations: Small differences in slice angles may be difficult to discern. A large number of categories reduces the effectiveness of the display.

General Comments: Very commonly used and intuitively easy to interpret.

Example:

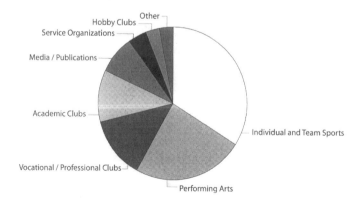

EXTRACURRICULAR ACTIVITIES:
STUDENT PARTICIPATION

E7–6

Visual Display: Line Chart, Simple

Description: A line chart displays the values of a variable in order and connects successive values with lines. Variable values of a categorical variable are labeled at equal intervals along the x-axis, and summary values of a continuous variable are displayed on the y-axis. Also, a categorical variable may be plotted against its frequency or percentage at each value.

Application: The line that connects successive points makes line charts ideal for observing data recorded over time.

Data: Any continuous variable (test scores, earnings, etc.) combined with a categorical series variable may be used when examining trends or differences over time.

Limitations: The series variable in a line chart is spaced at equal intervals. Data collected over unequal intervals may not be appropriate for a line chart.

General Comments: Line charts are easy to create and understand.

Example:

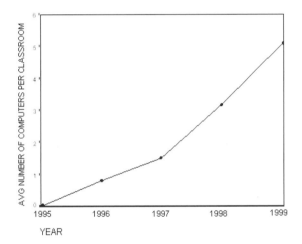

E7–7

Visual Display: Line Chart, Multiple

Description: The multiple-line chart displays several variables (or groups within a variable) in lines against a common sequence. All variables are measured on the same y-axis variable and in the same units. Different lines are distinguished by color, texture, or point symbol. A legend identifies the variables.

Application: Multiple-line charts show how several sequences move together. They are most useful when the sequences plotted are directly comparable (e.g., costs of similar services or achievement of students in similar schools over time).

Data: A combination of one categorical series variable and several comparable continuous variables may be used, or a series variable with a single continuous variable broken down by groups can be used.

Limitations: Limit the number of variables or groups to facilitate interpretation. Also, variables for comparison in a multiple line chart need to be selected with great care. The variables should be measured in the same units and cover approximately the same range of units to avoid a misleading display. Standardizing variables may allow for comparison when units differ.

General Comments: Multiple-line charts provide insight into differences in trends across groups.

Example:

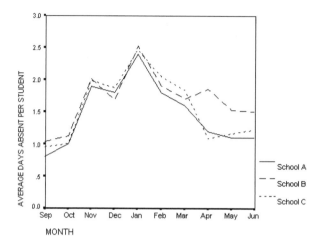

E7–8

Visual Display: Drop-Line Chart

Description: The drop-line chart is similar to a multiple-line chart but emphasizes the relationship among the data values that correspond to each x-axis variable or category. The categories being compared are represented by different symbols, identified in a legend. The symbols at each x-axis value are connected by vertical lines. The y-axis represents the continuous variable on which the categories or variables are being compared.

Application: A drop-line can be used to show differences over time for separate, but comparable, groups (e.g., average teacher salary for two districts over different years) or can show different individual or summary values of the same measure for different variables or categories (e.g., pretest and posttest performance for a set of students).

Data: Drop-lines require one continuous variable and two categorical variables (one to distinguish the drop-line points and one to define the values along the x-axis).

Limitations: Too many categories defining the drop-line points (i.e., more than two or three) can create a confusing display, particularly if the categories do not show a clear pattern across the x-axis values. Breaking down the x-axis variable or limiting the categories for display can help.

General Comments: Well-constructed drop-line charts provide information about several variables at once and are easy to interpret.

Example:

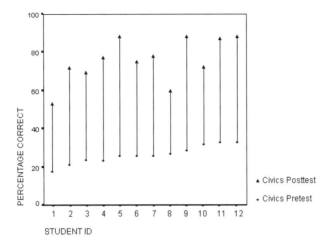

E7–9

Visual Display: Stem-and-Leaf Plot

Description: A stem-and-leaf plot is used to show the frequency distribution (**E4-11**) of a set of numbers. With two-digit numbers, the "stem" is the first digit, and the "leaf" is the second digit. Generally, each stem appears once, with each leaf listed as many times as it occurs, set apart from the stem. The number of leaves is the frequency for each stem.

Application: Displays the distribution of a set of numbers while showing each value that occurs. Useful for relatively small data sets, such as showing classroom test scores.

Data: Almost any continuous variable may be represented, but two-digit numbers, such as test scores or percentage of correct scores, work best in this format.

Limitations: The stem-and-leaf plot may not be the best format to examine large data sets, since stems will become fractions of the usual 10-point intervals and may be less easy to interpret. Data sets with values over two digits can also be shown in a stem-and-leaf plot but may also be less easily interpreted.

General Comments: Stem-and-leaf plots can be easily produced by hand to visually organize a set of numbers.

Example:

Percentages correct for 26 students
on a classroom test

Frequency	Stem & Leaf
1	4 . 8
2	5 . 45
4	6 . 6789
8	7 . 01457799
7	8 . 3335788
4	9 . 2336

Stem width: 10
Each leaf: 1 case(s)

E7–10

Visual Display: Box Plot, Simple

Description: A box plot, also called box-and-whiskers plot, summarizes the distribution of a variable. Box plots are used to simultaneously observe the distributions of comparable variables or subgroups of a variable. The "box" represents the middle half of the data values and extends from the 25th percentile to the 75th percentile. The median is represented by the horizontal line in the box. The "whiskers" extend to the data values up to 1.5 times the length of the box. "Outliers" fall between 1.5 and 3 times the box length and are designated by circles; "extremes" fall beyond 3 times the box length and are designated by asterisks.

Application: Box plots facilitate visual comparisons among variables or groups, such as score distributions among groups of students. Survey responses may also be viewed for a quick comparison of response distributions.

Data: Any continuous or ordinal variable combined with a categorical variable or several comparable continuous variables may be used.

Limitations: Box plots that compare ordinal variables may provide a quick overview of response pattern differences among many variables but should not be substituted for the specific detail displayed in individual histograms or bar charts.

General Comments: Box plots are somewhat unfamiliar, but with a little practice, they can be very useful for identifying patterns among groups or sets of variables.

Example:

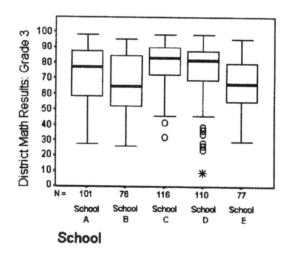

E7–11

Visual Display: Box Plot, Clustered

Description: A clustered box plot summarizes and allows comparison among the distributions of comparable variables or subgroups of a variable, broken down by an additional, discrete variable of interest. The clustered box plot shows pairs, or clusters, of boxes along the x-axis categories or separate variables. A legend identifies the cluster variable categories.

Application: Used to facilitate visual comparisons among categories, such as gender, within groups or sets of variables.

Data: A categorical variable, usually nominal, can be a cluster variable, added to the combination of continuous and categorical variables or set of comparable continuous variables.

Limitations: Two or three categories of the cluster variable may be all that can be displayed without cluttering the visual presentation.

General Comments: Once familiar, the clustered box plot can be an easy way to gain insight into large amounts of data.

Example:

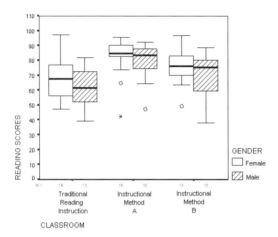

E7–12

Visual Display: Scatterplot

Description: Scatterplots display the relationship between two variables. Each point in the scatterplot represents the values on each variable for a particular case. Where the distinction is appropriate, it is conventional to plot a dependent variable on the y-axis and an independent variable on the x-axis.

Application: Scatterplots may be used to show how more or less of something (e.g., years employed, calories consumed, or hours spent playing video games) may be related to something else (e.g., salary, weight, or grades). Scatterplots are also used to examine how closely related two things may be (e.g., achievement on state- and district-level tests).

Data: Continuous variables are generally used in scatterplots. Methods exist, however, to display categorical variables in scatterplot format, such as sunflower plots.

Limitations: Relationships between variables in a scatterplot may not be easily seen if one or both variables have skewed or irregular distributions. Power transformations may be helpful in these cases, but interpretation may be more complicated.

General Comments: Scatterplots are very versatile. Groups of cases that depart from the displayed relationship can be easily identified and explored. Regression lines may be placed through the plot and subgroups may be color- or symbol-coded.

Example:

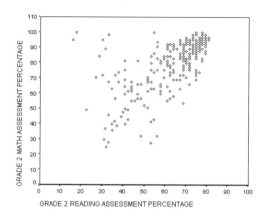

E7–13

Visual Display: Scatterplot Matrix

Description: A scatterplot matrix displays scatterplots for all possible pairs of several variables simultaneously. The scatterplot matrix contains the same number of rows and columns as there are chosen variables. The first variable is plotted along the y-axis for all plots in the first row and plotted along the x-axis for all plots in the first column. The second variable is on the y-axis for the second row and the x-axis for the second column, and so on.

Application: Scatterplots are especially good for visually inspecting the relationship among several different independent variables to identify multicollinearity.

Data: As with standard scatterplots, continuous variables are used in scatterplot matrices.

Limitations: Scatterplot matrices generally do not contain axis labels or units, so the user needs to be familiar with the format.

General Comments: Scatterplot matrices allow for a quick review of multiple bivariate relationships. Each plot is presented twice, once with the x and y axes reversed, providing a new perspective.

Example:

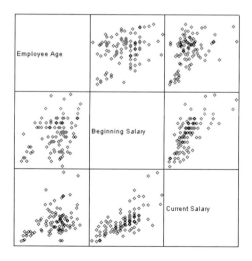

REFERENCES AND RESOURCES

Behrens, J. T., and Smith, M. L. (1996). Data and Data Analysis. In D. C. Berliner, and R. C. Calfee, (Eds.), *Handbook of Educational Psychology* (pp. 945–989). New York: Simon and Schuster Macmillan.

Cleveland, W. S. (1993). *Visualizing Data*. Summit, NJ: Hobart Press.

Norusis, M. J. (2000). *SPSS 10.0 Guide to Data Analysis*. Upper Saddle River, NJ: Prentice-Hall.

Tukey, J. W. (1977). *Exploratory Data Analysis*. Reading, MA: Addison-Wesley.

Velleman, P. F. (1997). *Data Desk Handbook*. Ithaca, NY: Data Description.

Wainer, H. (1992). Understanding Graphs and Tables. *Educational Researcher* 21 (1), 14–23.

Wainer, H., and Thissen, D. (1981). Graphical Data Analysis. In M. R. Rosenzweig and L. W. Porter (Eds.), *Annual Review of Psychology* (pp. 191–241). Palo Alto, CA: Annual Reviews.

CHAPTER 8

A Research Process Checklist

INTRODUCTION

This Research Process Checklist is designed to provide general guidelines for conducting educational research. This checklist can be used as a planning guide before a research study begins, as a review procedure for a research study in progress, or as a standard for evaluating completed research.

The checklist is organized around five major steps in the research process. These steps are:

1. **Defining the Research Question and the Nature of the Research**

   Information related to this step is contained in Section E, Chapter 2, *Linking Research Questions to Research Designs and Statistical Procedures.*

2. **Defining Variables, Subjects, and the Research Design**

   Information related to this step is contained in Section E, Chapters 3, *A Summary of Research Designs* and Chapter 5, *A Summary of Sampling Techniques.*

3. **Verifying the Objectivity, Reliability, and Validity of Observation Instruments and Procedures**

   Information related to this step is contained in Section E, Chapter 6, *A Summary of Measurement Concepts, Approaches, and Procedures.*

4. **Analyzing Data**

   Information related to this step is contained in Section E, Chapter 4, *A Summary of Statistical Procedures.*

5. **Interpreting Research Results**

   Information related to this step is contained throughout this section of the book.

The major issues that must be addressed in each step of the research process are enumerated in the checklist. The listing of issues is appropriate for a large variety of research studies but may not be appropriate in all cases. Depending on the nature of a particular study, certain of these issues might be ignored, while other issues, not listed in this general checklist, might be addressed.

THE CHECKLIST

Defining the Research Question and the Nature of the Research

1. _____Specify the research problem in clear and explicit terms.
2. _____Review the literature related to the research problem.
   _____A. Review substantive/conceptual issues.

_____B. Review technical/methodological issues.

_____C. Enumerate recommendations for improving research offered by those conducting previous research.

3. Determine whether the research question deals with:

    _____A. Description (See **E2**, Part 1)

    _____B. Relationships or Correlation (See **E2**, Part 2)

    _____C. Differences (See **E2**, Part 3)

4. _____Specify each research hypothesis to be explored in the study.

5. Classify the research approach as:

    _____A. Descriptive.

    _____B. Correlational.

    _____C. Quasi-experimental.

    _____D. Experimental.

6. _____Specify delimitations of the study.

7. _____Specify operating assumptions.

Defining Variables, Subjects, and the Research Design

Variables

8. Specify a constitutive or conceptual definition of each of the following:

    _____A. All independent variables.

    _____B. All dependent variables.

    _____C. All controlled extraneous variables.

    _____D. All other extraneous variables.

9. Specify an operational definition of each of the following:

    _____A. All independent variables.

    _____B. All dependent variables.

    _____C. All controlled extraneous variables.

    _____D. All other extraneous variables.

Subjects

10. _____Specify the target population.

11. _____Specify the accessible population.

12. _____Specify the procedures that will be used for sample selection.

13. _____Identify any limitations to generalizability due to the sample selection procedure.

14. _____When appropriate, specify procedures for assigning subjects to treatment groups.

15. _____Specify review procedures for assuring compliance with guidelines for ethical use of human subjects.

16. _____Specify procedures for obtaining subjects' informed consent to participate in the study.

Research Design

17. Specify procedures for controlling extraneous variables:
    _____A. Design Procedures.
    _____B. Statistical Procedures.
18. Summarize the overall research design, specifying:
    _____A. The nature of the research. (See #3 and #5).
    _____B. The number and nature of any groups (i.e., experimental, control).
    _____C. The number and sequence of observations made on the groups (e.g., pretests, posttests).

Verifying the Objectivity, Reliability, and Validity of Observation Instruments and Procedures

19. Will the independent, dependent, control, and extraneous variables be observed using:
    _____A. Currently available instruments/procedures.
    _____B. Instruments/procedures developed for this research.
20. If instruments/procedures for observing variables will be developed (19, B), specify:
    _____A. Procedures for developing the instrument(s).
    _____B. Procedures for pilot-testing the instrument(s).
21. _____Specify evidence that the instruments and procedures used to observe the independent, dependent, control, and extraneous variables (Steps 9, 19, 20) are objective.
22. _____Specify evidence that the instruments and procedures used to observe the independent, dependent, control, and extraneous variables (Steps 9, 19, 20) are reliable.
    _____A. For each variable, specify the index of reliability used.
23. _____Specify evidence that the instruments and procedures used to observe the independent, dependent, control, and extraneous variables (Steps 9, 19, 20) are valid.
    _____A. For each variable, specify how of validity is established.

Analyzing Data

24. Specify the procedures that will be used to provide basic descriptive information:
    _____A. Visual displays of data (e.g., graphs, charts, etc.).
    _____B. Descriptive statistics.
    _____C. Indices of relationships.
25. _____Specify the statistical hypothesis that corresponds to each research hypothesis described in Step 4.
26. _____Specify the appropriate statistical procedure for testing each hypothesis stated in Step 25.
    _____A. Indicate the significance level for inferential tests.

_____B. Indicate possible violations of assumptions or other limitations of the procedures.

Interpreting Research Results

Internal Validity

27. Determine the internal validity of the study:
_____A. Enumerate threats to internal validity that must be assessed in interpreting the results of the study.
_____B. Evaluate the internal validity of the study.

External Validity

28. Determine the external validity of the study:
_____A. Enumerate threats to external validity that must be assessed in interpreting the results of the study.
_____B. Evaluate the external validity of the study.

Findings, Conclusions, and Recommendations

29. _____Summarize the study's findings.
30. _____Provide conclusions based on the study.
31. _____Describe how the results of the study related to the findings from previous research on the problem.
32. Provide recommendations based on the study.
_____A. Substantial recommendations.
_____B. Methodological recommendations.

SECTION F

ORGANIZATIONS IN EDUCATION

Melvyn N. Freed

CHAPTER 1

Directory of National and Regional Organizations in Education

INTRODUCTION

The fabric of education in America comprises a diverse array of national and regional organizations that support the educational system. These bodies are dedicated to promotion of specific academic disciplines, governance, dissemination of information, accreditation, student affairs, faculty welfare, professional development, lobbying for education, and myriad other purposes. They, in cooperation with local school districts and college campuses, are the voice of American education along with the American public. They marshal the different sectors in education and provide a collaborative presence on regional and national levels.

A rich source of information in their particular areas of interest, these organizations often sponsor Web sites on the Internet and publish documents—periodicals, books, special reports—that describe the conditions and status of their sector of American education. The researcher should not overlook these important resources.

To help the researcher, these organizations have been classified according to their type and by the subject areas of the data they collect. In Chapter 2 of this section, there are detailed profiles of these education organizations, which are listed alphabetically. The organizations presented herein represent a select list due to space limitations. For an even more comprehensive list, see the *Encyclopedia of Associations*.

Chapter 1 of this section lists education organizations by type. Readers who require assistance with identifying organizations in an area of professional activity (e.g., accreditation) should first consult "Education Organizations by Type." Next, readers should turn to Chapter 2 and read the profile of that organization. This profile contains the organization's contact information, its primary purpose, programs of service, major publications, membership information, kinds of data collected, and, when applicable, a statement on research grant programs that it sponsors.

Organizations are also categorized according to the kinds of data that they collect. The profile section titled "Data Collected" refers to either raw data or the maintenance of a library of data sources. An organization may be a primary or secondary source. Sometimes the data are unpublished and are for in-house use. Check the list of organizations under the subject classification and then refer to Chapter 2 for the selected organization's profile.

EDUCATION ORGANIZATIONS BY TYPE

Accreditation

AACSB International
Council for Higher Education Accreditation

Middle States Commission for Elementary Schools
Middle States Commission on Higher Education
Middle States Commission on Secondary Schools
National Council for Accreditation of Teacher Education
New England Association of Schools and Colleges
North Central Association of Colleges and Schools, Commission on
    Accreditation and School Improvement
North Central Association of Colleges and Schools, the Higher Learning
    Commission
Northwest Association of Schools and Colleges, Commission on Colleges
Northwest Association of Schools and Colleges, Commission on Schools
Southern Association of Colleges and Schools
Western Association of Schools and Colleges, Accrediting Commission for
    Community and Junior Colleges
Western Association of Schools and Colleges, Accrediting Commission for
    Schools
Western Association of Schools and Colleges, Accrediting Commission for
    Senior Colleges and Universities

Associations of Professionals

American Association of Collegiate Registrars and Admissions Officers
American Association of School Administrators
American Association of University Professors
American College Personnel Association
American Conference of Academic Deans
American Counseling Association
American Educational Research Association
Association for Continuing Higher Education
Association for Institutional Research
Association for Supervision and Curriculum Development
Association of Higher Education Facilities Officers
Association of Schools of Allied Health Professions
College and University Professional Association for Human Resources
Council for Exceptional Children
Council of Chief State School Officers
International Reading Association
Music Teachers National Association
National Association for Gifted Children
National Association of Elementary School Principals
National Association of Pupil Services Administrators
National Association of State Directors of Teacher Education and Certification
National Association of Student Financial Aid Administrators
National Association of Student Personnel Administrators
National Council of Teachers of English
National Council of University Research Administrators

National Council on Measurement in Education
North American Association of Educational Negotiators
Society for College and University Planning
State Higher Education Executive Officers
University Continuing Education Association

Associations of Institutions

AACSB International
American Association of Colleges for Teacher Education
American Association of Community Colleges
American Association of State Colleges and Universities
American Conference of Academic Deans
Association of American Colleges and Universities
Association of American Universities
Council of Graduate Schools in the United States
National Association of Independent Colleges and Universities
National Association of Independent Schools
National Association of State Universities and Land-Grant Colleges

Broad-Scope National Organizations

American Association for Higher Education
American Council on Education
National PTA (National Parent-Teacher Association)

Educational Resources Information Center (ERIC)

ERIC Clearinghouses

Adult, Career, and Vocational Education
Assessment and Evaluation
Community Colleges
Counseling and Student Services
Disabilities and Gifted Education
Educational Management
Elementary and Early Childhood Education
Higher Education
Information and Technology
Languages and Linguistics
Reading, English, and Communication
Rural Education and Small Schools
Science, Mathematics, and Environmental Education
Social Studies/Social Science Education
Teaching and Teacher Education
Urban Education

ERIC Adjunct Clearinghouses

    Child Care
    Clinical Schools
    Educational Opportunity
    Entrepreneurship Education
    ESL Literacy Education
    International Civic Education
    Service Learning
    Test Collection
    U.S.-Japan Studies

ERIC Affiliate Clearinghouse

    National Clearinghouse for Educational Facilities

Governance Associations

    Association of Governing Boards of Universities and Colleges
    National Association of State Boards of Education
    National S+chool Boards Association
    State Higher Education Executive Officers

Regional Educational Laboratories

    AEL, Inc.
    Laboratory for Student Success
    Mid-Continent Research for Education and Learning
    North Central Regional Educational Laboratory
    Northeast and Islands Regional Educational Laboratory at Brown University
    Northwest Regional Educational Laboratory
    Pacific Resources for Education and Learning
    SERVE
    Southwest Educational Development Laboratory
    WestEd

Other Education Organizations

    Academy for Educational Development
    ACT, Inc.
    Association for Direct Instruction
    Association for the Study of Higher Education
    The College Board
    Educational Research Service
    Educational Testing Service
    High/Scope Educational Research Foundation

National Council on Economic Education
National Board for Professional Teaching Standards
National Center for Higher Education Management Systems
National Center for Education Statistics
National Society for the Study of Education
Western Interstate Commission for Higher Education

EDUCATION ORGANIZATIONS BY FIELD OF DATA COLLECTED

Academic Fields (Characteristics and Status)

AACSB International
American Association of Colleges for Teacher Education
American Counseling Association
Association of Schools of Allied Health Professions

Academic Programs

American Association of Colleges for Teacher Education
Association for Supervision and Curriculum Development
Association of American Colleges and Universities
Council of Graduate Schools in the United States
Educational Research Service
High/Scope Educational Research Foundation
National Association of State Directors of Teacher Education and Certification
National Council on Economic Education
State Higher Education Executive Officers
University Continuing Education Association

Accreditation Information

AACSB International
American Council on Education
American Counseling Association
Council for Higher Education Accreditation
Middle States Commission on Elementary Schools
Middle States Commission on Higher Education
Middle States Commission on Secondary Schools
National Council for Accreditation of Teacher Education
New England Association of Schools and Colleges
North Central Association of Colleges and Schools, Commission on
        Accreditation and School Improvement
North Central Association of Colleges and Schools, The Higher Learning
        Commission
Northwest Association of Schools and Colleges, Commission on Colleges
Northwest Association of Schools and Colleges, Commission on Schools

Southern Association of Colleges and Schools
Western Association of Schools and Colleges, Accrediting Commission for Community and Junior Colleges
Western Association of Schools and Colleges, Accrediting Commission for Schools
Western Association of Schools and Colleges, Accrediting Commission for Senior Colleges and Universities

Business-Higher Education Linkages

AACSB International
American Council on Education
Western Interstate Commission for Higher Education

Certifications, Licenses, and Permits

National Association of State Directors of Teacher Education and Certification
National Board for Professional Teaching Standards

Educational Finance

American Association of State Colleges and Universities
American Council on Education
Laboratory for Student Success
National Association of Independent Colleges and Universities
National Association of Independent Schools
National Association of State Boards of Education
National Association of State Universities and Land-Grant Colleges
National Center for Education Statistics
National Center for Higher Education Management Systems
National School Boards Association
State Higher Education Executive Officers
Western Interstate Commission for Higher Education

Leaders in Education (Characteristics)

American Association of School Administrators
American Council on Education
College and University Professional Association for Human Resources
Laboratory for Student Success
National Association of Elementary School Principals
National Association of Pupil Services Administrators

Educational Research and Information

AEL, Inc.

Educational Research Service
Educational Resources Information Center (ERIC)
Laboratory for Student Success
Mid-Continent Research for Education and Learning
National Center for Education Statistics
North Central Regional Educational Laboratory
Northeast and Islands Regional Educational Laboratory at Brown University
Northwest Regional Educational Laboratory
Pacific Resources for Education and Learning
SERVE
Southwest Educational Development Laboratory
WestED

Faculty Characteristics

AACSB International
American Association of Community Colleges
American Association of State Colleges and Universities
American Association of University Professors
American Council on Education
College and University Professional Association for Human Resources
Laboratory for Student Success
National Association of Independent Colleges and Universities
National Association of Independent Schools
National Association of State Universities and Land-Grant Colleges
National Center for Education Statistics
National Center for Higher Education Management Systems

Gifted Students and Students with Disabilities

Council for Exceptional Children
ERIC Clearinghouse on Disabilities and Gifted Education
National Association for Gifted Children

Governance

Association of Governing Boards of Universities and Colleges
National Association of State Boards of Education
National School Boards Association
North American Association of Educational Negotiators
State Higher Education Executive Officers

Miscellaneous National-Regional Descriptive Data

American Association of State Colleges and Universities
American Council on Education

Council of Chief State School Officers
Educational Testing Service
National Association of Independent Schools
National Association of State Boards of Education
National Association of State Universities and Land-Grant Colleges
National Center for Education Statistics
National Center for Higher Education Management Systems
National School Boards Association
State Higher Education Executive Officers
Western Interstate Commission for Higher Education

Physical Facilities

Association of Higher Education Facilities Officers
National Clearinghouse for Educational Facilities [See Educational Resources
    Information Center (ERIC)]

Reading

ERIC Clearinghouse on Reading, English, and Communication
International Reading Association

Student Characteristics and Performance

AACSB International
ACT, Inc.
AEL, Inc.
American Association of Community Colleges
American Association of State Colleges and Universities
American College Personnel Association
American Council on Education
The College Board
Educational Research Service
Educational Testing Service
High/Scope Educational Research Foundation
Laboratory for Student Success
Mid-continent Research for Education and Learning
National Center for Education Statistics
National Center for Higher Education Management Systems
North Central Regional Educational Laboratory
Northeast and Islands Regional Educational Laboratory at Brown University
Northwest Regional Educational Laboratory
Pacific Resources for Education and Learning
SERVE
Southwest Educational Development Laboratory
WestEd
Western Interstate Commission for Higher Education

Student Financial Aid

American Council on Education
The College Board
National Association of Independent Colleges and Universities
National Association of Student Financial Aid Administrators
National Center for Education Statistics
National Center for Higher Education Management Systems
State Higher Education Executive Officers
Western Interstate Commission for Higher Education

CHAPTER 2

Profiles of National and Regional Organizations in Education

AACSB International
(Association to Advance Collegiate Schools of Business)
Suite 300
600 Emerson Road
St. Louis, MO 63141
(314) 872-8481
Fax: (314) 872-8495
E-mail: info@aacsb.edu
http://www.aacsb.edu

Purpose: AACSB International is an association of educational institutions, corporations, and other organizations that are devoted to the promotion and improvement of higher education in business administration and management. It provides global leadership in advancing management education through accreditation and the fostering of international interchanges, key business linkages, and the sharing of best practices.

Services: As the worldwide professional organization for collegiate management education, AACSB International provides accreditation services for quality assurance and continuous improvement; professional development through conferences and seminars; knowledge services, including trends and effective practices; and professional publications, including trend reports and research and news services on current and emerging management education issues.

Major Publications: Newsline, Accreditation Standards Manual, Accreditation Handbook, Guide to Undergraduate Business Programs in the USA, Guide to Graduate Business Programs in the USA, Guide to Doctoral Programs in Business and Management in the USA (The latter is in collaboration with Education International.)

Type of Membership: Institutional

Membership Requirements: Educational members must be collegiate institutions that offer degree programs in business and management at the undergraduate and/or graduate levels. In the United States, the parent institution must be regionally accredited. Outside the United States, educational members must be recognized and/or accredited by a government decree, as in the award of "university status," or demonstrate approval of its academic programs through membership in, or recognition by, one or more appropriate professional or government organizations within the applicable region or country. Programs must have been in existence for a minimum of five years with program completion and graduation by students who were admitted in two different enrollment cycles.

Corporate and business sector members include organizations that demonstrate a direct and strategic interest or relationship to supporting quality and continuous improvement in collegiate management education. To be eligible for nonprofit organizational membership, an organization must be a nonprofit academic or professional association having individual members.

Data Collected: AACSB International collects a wide array of data on the academic programs, faculty, staff, students, and operations of collegiate schools of business.

Academy for Educational Development (AED)

1825 Connecticut Avenue, NW
Washington, DC 20009
(202) 884-8000
Fax: (202) 884-8400
E-mail: admindc@aed.org
http://www.aed.org

Regional Office: 100 Fifth Avenue
New York, NY 10011
(202) 243-1110
Fax: (202) 627-0407

Purpose: Dedicated to solving social problems in the United States and abroad via education, training, research, innovative program design, policy analysis, and social marketing.

Services: Has more than 225 programs and projects in the United States and foreign countries. Program areas encompass health, training, democracy, environment and energy, education, and youth. Offers consulting and strategic planning, information exchange and technical assistance, qualitative and quantitative research, training and capacity building, technology assessment and design, and social marketing and communication for behavior change.

Major Publications: Annual report. Additionally, prepares special project and program reports.

Type of Membership: NA
Data Collected: NA

ACT, Inc.

2201 North Dodge Street
P.O. Box 168
Iowa City, IA 52243
(319) 337-1000
Fax: (319) 337-3020
http://www.act.org

Regional Offices: Washington, DC Office
Suite 340
One Dupont Circle, NW

Washington, DC 20036
(202) 223-2318

Western Region
Sacramento Office
Suite 262
10419 Old Placerville Road
Sacramento, CA 95827
(916) 361-0656

Denver Office
Cherry Creek Place I, Suite 218
3131 South Vaughn Way
Aurora, CO 80014
(303) 337-3273

Midwestern Region
Chicago Office
Suite 300
300 Knightsbridge Parkway
Lincolnshire, IL 60069
(847) 634-2560

Ohio Office
Suite A
412 East Wooster Street
Bowling Green, OH 43402
(419) 352-5317

Southwestern Region
Suite B-228
8303 MoPac Expressway, North
Austin, TX 78759
(512) 345-1949

Eastern Region
Pine West Plaza IV
Washington Avenue Extension
Albany, NY 12205-5510
(518) 869-7378

Southeastern Region
Atlanta Office
Suite 320
3355 Lenox Road, NE

Atlanta, GA 30326
(404) 231-1952

Florida Office
Suite A
1315 East Lafayette Street
Tallahassee, FL 32301
(850) 878-2729

Educational Technology Center
Executive Plaza I, Suite 200
11350 McCormick Road
Hunt Valley, MD 21031
(410) 584-8000

Purpose: Provides assessment, research, information, and program management services for educational planning, career planning, and workforce development. Develops instruments, techniques, and methods necessary to fulfill its mission.

Services: The Educational Planning and Assessment System (EPAS) consists of a series of integrated programs that serve students in grades eight through high school graduation by providing information on academic strengths and weaknesses in English, math, reading, and science reasoning. EPAS also identifies interests and assesses work-related abilities. It provides data and guidance for instructional support and curriculum evaluation.

Career planning is another service area and is implemented with UNIACT and the World-of-Work Map. Interest assessments are administered, and students are assisted with identifying career fields that are compatible with their abilities and interests.

Workforce development is another service area that is provided via the Work Keys Program. This program helps students and workers acquire work-related skills and prepare for success in the modern workplace. It measures a range of job-related skills.

Finally, ACT provides customized measurement and research services for client organizations, such as the Medical College Admission Test (MCAT), the Law School Admission Test (LSAT), the Multistate Bar Examination (MBE), and the Fundamentals of Engineering Examination. ACT is the processor of Federal Applications for Student Aid (FAFSA). These and other services constitute the service program of ACT, which helps students to learn about themselves, identify realistic career goals, and establish a reasonable match between themselves and a postsecondary education institution.

Major Publications: ACT issues many publications related to its areas of service.

Type of Membership: NA

Data Collected: ACT is continuously collecting data in its sundry areas of service. These include state and national performance on the ACT Assessment, information about academic skills, course grades, career interests, workplace skills, and information for recruitment and enrollment management.

AEL, Inc.
(Appalachia Educational Laboratory)
1031 Quarrier Street (Zip code 25301)
P.O. Box 1348
Charleston, WV 25325-1348
(800) 624-9120
(304) 347-0400
Fax: (304) 347-0487
E-mail: aelinfo@ael.org
http://www.ael.org/rel/

Purpose: As a component of the U.S. Regional Educational Laboratory Network, AEL's mission is to link knowledge gained from educational research to the teaching and learning processes. This regional laboratory's primary service region is Kentucky, Tennessee, Virginia, and West Virginia. The laboratory seeks to transform low-performing schools into high-performing learning communities. Concomitant with the foregoing, it also serves as a National Leadership Area in identifying emerging technologies and determining their application to education.

Services: This regional laboratory works with schools, school districts, and states in rural areas to develop, test, and refine educational products and processes that address needs identified by local educators. It provides R&D, technical assistance, the exchange of information, professional development, planning, and evaluation of the educational process. Furthermore, it seeks ways to enhance the educational process with the infusion of high tech into the classroom. This lab collects the most relevant research on educational technology and disseminates promising practices and exemplary strategies to the education community.

AEL also operates the Eisenhower Regional Consortium for Mathematics and Science Education, the Region IV Technical Assistance Comprehensive Center, and the ERIC Clearinghouse on Rural Education and Small Schools.

Major Publication: The Link, The Rural Educator, and sundry other publications that are related to special programs and projects.

Type of Membership: NA

Data Collected: Student achievement (K–12) and other miscellaneous data related to the lab's mission.

American Association for Higher Education (AAHE)
Suite 360
One Dupont Circle, NW
Washington, DC 20036
(202) 293-6440
Fax: (202) 293-0073
http://www.aahe.org

Purpose: By bringing individuals together who are involved in the higher education process, AAHE provides a forum for the discussion of critical issues in American higher education. It seeks constructive change that results in the development of institutions and individuals engaged in higher education. Through the exchange of ideas, AAHE's programs foster improvement in teachers, learners, administrators, and policymakers.

Services: The mission of this organization is pursued through its conferences and projects. It sponsors the annual AAHE National Conference on Higher Education, the AAHE Conference on Faculty Roles and Rewards, the AAHE (Student) Assessment Forum, the AAHE Teaching Initiatives project, and other programs that advance its purpose.

Major Publications: AAHE Bulletin and *Change Magazine* (in cooperation with Heldref Publications)

Type of Membership: Individual

Membership Requirements: Interest in higher education

American Association of Colleges for Teacher Education (AACTE)

Suite 300
1307 New York Avenue, NW
Washington, DC 20005
(202) 293-2450
Fax: (202) 457-8095
E-mail: aacte@aacte.org
http://www.aacte.org

Purpose: An association of colleges and universities that prepare teachers and principals for K–12 schools. Provides leadership for enhancing the quality of teacher-education programs.

Services: Sponsors conferences on the preparation of professional educators, organizes task forces that work on issues related to teacher education, offers technical assistance to colleges and universities that prepare teachers for K–12, provides professional development for college faculty and deans involved in teacher education, and offers services on governmental relations.

Major Publication: The Journal of Teacher Education

Type of Membership: Institutional and organizational

Membership Requirements: The college must be accredited by its regional accrediting agency and offer programs that ultimately lead to a teacher-education degree.

Data Collected: A variety of data on programs in teacher education. These data include enrollment statistics, faculty, program information, and other relevant data on the field.

American Association of Collegiate Registrars and Admissions Officers (AACRAO)

Suite 520
One Dupont Circle, NW
Washington, DC 20036
(202) 293-9161
Fax: (202) 872-8857

E-mail: info@aacrao.org

http://www.aacrao.com

Purpose: This is the professional association for collegiate registrars and admissions officers. As such, it advances the policies and practices of records management and admissions for institutions of higher education.

Services: Identifies and promotes standards and best practices in enrollment management, academic records management, information technology, and student services. Sponsors conferences and workshops that implement its purposes.

Major Publication: College and University

Type of Membership: Individual and institutional

Membership Requirements: Institutional membership is open to postsecondary degree-granting institutions that are accredited by an accrediting agency that has been approved by the Council for Higher Education Accreditation (CHEA). Individual membership is extended to those persons in higher education whose professional responsibilities, activities, or interests are consistent with those of AACRAO members. Membership is also available to those persons who represent an organization that, while noncollegiate, is determined to have purposes that are parallel with those of AACRAO.

Secondary school membership is extended to registrars, counselors, or other persons at a high school who would benefit from membership in AACRAO. Student membership is available to graduate students who are interested in joining this organization and whose application is recommended by an active AACRAO voting member. Retired membership is available to former members who are retired.

American Association of Community Colleges (AACC)

Suite 410

One Dupont Circle, NW

Washington, DC 20036

(202) 728-0200

Fax: (202) 833-2467

E-mail: employee's first initial, last name@aacc.nche.edu

http://www.aacc.nche.edu

Purpose: The national advocate for two-year degree-granting institutions of higher education. Promotes their welfare and functions as their voice before different forums. Serves as a resource for its members.

Services: Provides services to member two-year community colleges in the areas of policy initiatives, research and information, professional development, advocacy, and coordination. Lobbies the federal government on behalf of its member colleges and sponsors conferences.

Major Publications: Community College Journal and *Community College Times*

Type of Membership: Institutional and individual

Membership Requirements: Institutional memberships are open to two-year, associate degree-granting colleges that are accredited or that are in the process of becoming accredited by one of the six regional accrediting agencies. Institutional membership is also available to state agencies of higher education and to district offices of multicommunity college systems.

Any nonprofit organization that is interested in education issues or any educational institution that is not eligible for institutional membership may affiliate as an educational associate member. Administrators, faculty, students and other individuals who are interested in higher education issues may join as individual associate members. Other membership categories include lifetime individual members, international associate members, and corporate members.

Data Collected: Collects, analyzes, and disseminates information on state, national, and international trends of interest to community colleges. Data sets include enrollment statistics, degrees awarded, number of institutions, student employment success, and more. A major source of information on community colleges.

American Association of School Administrators (AASA)
1801 N. Moore Street
Arlington, VA 22209
(703) 528-0700
Fax: (703) 528-2146
E-mail: info@aasa.org
http://www.aasa.org

Purpose: A professional association for school administrators and professors of educational administration. Offers programs and services that address the needs and interests of those in educational administration as they strive to build and maintain high-quality public education.
Services: Sponsors the National Conference on Education. Offers specialized conferences on specific topics and serves as an advocate for public education.
Major Publication: The School Administrator
Type of Membership: Individual
Membership Requirements: Must either be employed or actively interested in educational administration.
Data Collected: Demographic information on superintendents of education.

American Association of State Colleges and Universities (AASCU)
5th Floor
1307 New York Avenue
Washington, DC 20005
(800) 542-2062
(202) 293-7070
Fax: (202) 296-5819
E-mail: employee's last name, first initial@aascu.org
http://www.aascu.org

Purpose: An association of state-supported colleges and universities that offer the baccalaureate and higher degrees. Represents the interests of these institutions of higher education to the public and before legislative bodies. Promotes the welfare of public colleges and universities.

Services: Assists with governmental relations germane to public policy issues. Provides programs for academic leadership development, public policy analysis, and advocacy.

Major Publications: State Issues Digest, Public Policy Agenda, Perspectives, Annual Report, EdLines, and *Memo: To the President*

Type of Membership: Institutional

Membership Requirements: Regionally accredited, state-supported, and state-controlled institutions of higher education with programs that confer the baccalaureate or higher degree.

Data Collected: Information on state funding of higher education, accountability measures, tuition and fees, and other institutional characteristics. Also assembles data on sundry state policy topics.

American Association of University Professors (AAUP)
Suite 500
1012 14th Street, NW
Washington, DC 20005
(800) 424-2973
(202) 737-5900
Fax: (202) 737-5526
E-mail: aaup@aaup.org
http://www.aaup.org

Purpose: The professional association for faculty in American colleges and universities. Establishes and advances standards for academic due process and faculty participation in academic decision making. Protects academic freedom and tenure. Furthers the standards and ideals of the profession.

Services: Processes inquiries on issues of academic freedom and tenure. Endeavors to ensure that standards governing professional relationships are not violated. Becomes involved in legislative affairs at the state and federal levels as an advocate for higher education. Publishes an annual report on faculty salaries in higher education. When requested by an AAUP chapter, provides advice on collective bargaining.

Major Publications: Academe, Annual Report on the Economic Status of the Profession (Faculty Salary Report), and periodic policy documents and reports.

Type of Membership: Individual

Membership Requirements: Full-time membership requires a faculty appointment at an accredited college or university. Sustaining membership categories are available for administrators, graduate students, and others.

Data Collected: Faculty salary and benefits. Also, faculty demographics.

American College Personnel Association (ACPA)
Suite 300
One Dupont Circle, NW
Washington, DC 20036

(202) 835-2272
Fax: (202) 296-3286
E-mail: info@acpa.nche.edu
http://www.acpa.nche.edu

Purpose: A professional association for persons who are either employed, interested in, or preparing to be employed in college student personnel services. Fosters the full development of students in higher education.

Services: Provides services to its members through the 32 state and international divisions and the 16 functional area commissions. Sponsors an annual convention and offers placement services. Conducts a midlevel management institute and regional workshops on current issues in the field.

Major Publications: Journal of College Student Development, About Campus: Enriching the Student Learning Experience

Type of Membership: Individual and institutional

Membership Requirements: Be employed in a faculty or professional student affairs position on a college campus or in a nonprofit systemwide or governmental agency. Membership is also available to full-time graduate students and to persons retired from the field. Institutions of higher education may have an institutional membership.

Data Collected: Demographics of the ACPA membership

American Conference of Academic Deans (ACAD)

1818 R Street, NW
Washington, DC 20009
(202) 387-3760
Fax: (202) 265-9532
E-mail: ereilly@acad-edu.org
http://www.acad-edu.org

Purpose: A national organization of chief academic officers and deans in two-year and four-year colleges. Provides opportunities for members to meet and discuss matters of common interest related to administering programs of liberal education. Fosters the development of academic leadership.

Services: The primary service is to provide annual and regional meetings for the presentation and discussion of major topics and problem areas that are important to academic administrators and liberal education.

Major Publication: Resource Handbook for Academic Deans

Type of Membership: Individual

Membership Requirements: Must be an academic administrator responsible for the instructional program in a two- or four-year college. Titles may include provost, vice president for academic affairs, dean, assistant or associate dean.

American Council on Education (ACE)

One Dupont Circle, NW
Washington, DC 20036

(202) 939-9300

E-mail: pubs@ace.nche.edu

http://www.acenet.edu

Purpose: ACE represents all accredited postsecondary education institutions as well as national and regional higher education associations. A major function of this organization is to coordinate the interests of all segments of higher education into a single voice.

Services: As the principal umbrella organization representing higher education in America, ACE provides many services that include representing higher education before the U.S. Congress, the Supreme Court, and the federal courts; conducting research and analyzing data on American higher education; working with colleges and universities to assist them in such areas as management and leadership, accreditation, and self-regulation; helping shape international education policy at the federal level and working with the nation's campuses and higher education groups in international matters; assisting the off-campus student by reviewing and assigning credit equivalencies for those attending business-sponsored and other courses and military training; sponsoring an annual conference on American higher education; issuing different professional publications; and offering other services to the higher education community.

Major Publications: The Presidency, Higher Education and National Affairs, Fact Book on Higher Education, the ACE/Praeger Series on Higher Education, and sundry monographs on special topics and research in higher education.

Type of Membership: Institutional

Membership Requirements: Must be either an accredited, degree-granting, postsecondary education institution, higher education association, or a nonprofit organization that is concerned with higher education.

Data Collected: Freshman norms, list of accredited postsecondary education institutions, list of accredited institutions offering external degrees, student aid, demographics on minorities in postsecondary education, presidential database, women in higher education, international programs, business/higher education linkages, and other data on higher education. The *Fact Book on Higher Education* is a digest of data and is published annually.

American Educational Research Association (AERA)

1230 17th Street, NW

Washington, DC 20036

(202) 223-9485

Fax: (202) 775-1824

E-mail: outreach@aera.net

http://www.aera.net

Purpose: Concerned with the improvement of the educational process through the encouragement of scholarly inquiry related to education, the dissemination of research results, and their practical application. This is the most prominent international organization dedicated to advancing educational research and its application to the advancement of learning.

Services: Publishes scholarly research journals, conducts a program of professional development in educational research, monitors legislative activities and public policy at the federal level, disseminates current research findings, and convenes an annual meeting on educational research for its members.

Major Publications: Educational Researcher, Educational Evaluation and Policy Analysis, American Educational Research Journal, Journal of Educational and Behavioral Statistics, Review of Educational Research, and *Review of Research in Education.* In addition to the foregoing periodicals, AERA publications include the *Encyclopedia of Educational Research, Handbook of Research on Curriculum, Experimental and Quasi-Experimental Designs for Research on Teaching, Handbook of Research on Educational Administration, Handbook of Research on Teaching, Complementary Methods for Research in Education,* and others.

Type of Membership: Individual

Membership Requirements: Active memberships are available to those who present satisfactory evidence of active interest in educational research and who have professional training at least at the master's degree level or the equivalent. Associate membership is for those persons who have an interest in educational research and who subscribe to the purposes of AERA but do not qualify for active membership.

Data Collected: Through the Professional Outreach Program, AERA disseminates current research findings.

American Counseling Association (ACA)

5999 Stevenson Avenue
Alexandria, VA 22304
(800) 347-6647
(703) 823-9800
Fax: (703) 823-0252
E-mail: aca@counseling.org
http://www.counseling.org

Purpose: Dedicated to the growth and enhancement of the counseling profession. Assists counseling professionals develop their skills by providing continuing education credits and opportunities, leadership training, and advocacy services. Serves as an association of associations in the counseling field with 18 divisions that are themselves associations of professionals. ACA is the largest counseling organization in the world.

Services: Among ACA's services are accreditation of counselor education programs, sponsorship of an annual convention for the counseling profession, and a variety of professional publications.

Major Publications: Among the professional journals of the ACA are *Counselor Education and Supervision, Journal of College Counseling, Journal of Counseling and Development, Journal of Multicultural Counseling and Development,* and *Measurement and Evaluation in Counseling and Development.*

Type of Membership: Individual

Membership Requirements: Professional membership is for persons who have a master's degree or higher in counseling or a closely related field from an accredited college or university. Regular membership is extended to those individuals whose interests and activities are compatible with those of ACA but who do not qualify for professional membership. Student membership is for those persons who are enrolled at least half-time in a college or university program.

Data Collected: An array of data and information pertaining to professional counseling.

Association for Continuing Higher Education (ACHE)

Trident Technical College
P.O. Box 118067, CE-M
Charleston, SC 29423-8067
(800) 807-2243
(843) 574-6658
Fax: (843) 574-6470
E-mail: zpwhelanw@trident.tec.sc.us
http://charleston.net/org/ache/

Purpose: Dedicated to the promotion of lifelong learning and excellence in continuing higher education. Encourages professional networks, research, and the exchange of information on continuing higher education.

Services: Sponsors regional and national meetings that provide forums for the discussion of theoretical and practical aspects of continuing higher education. Provides services to strengthen continuing education programs.

Major Publications: Journal of Continuing Higher Education and *Proceedings* (report of the association's annual meeting).

Type of Membership: Individual and institutional

Membership Requirements: Institutions must have a continuing education program and be regionally accredited. Individuals must be engaged in the delivery of continuing education at the college or university level.

Research Grants: ACHE sponsors grants for individuals who are conducting research on continuing higher education.

Association for Direct Instruction (ADI)

P.O. Box 10252
Eugene, OR 97440
(800) 995-2464
(541) 485-1293
Fax: (541) 683-7543
E-mail: brywick@adihome.org
http://www.adihome.org

Purpose: Promotes and disseminates information on effective research-based educational methods and materials with emphasis on Direct Instruction programs (DI). Provides support for teachers and other educators who use the direct instruction method. DI is a method of instruction that focuses on reading, language, spelling, writing, and math.

Services: Conducts workshops and training conferences that teach educators how to implement the direct instruction method. Instructs on the methodology and special materials used in the DI process.

Major Publication: Effective School Practices

Type of Membership: Individual and institutional

Membership Requirements: Interest in the purpose of ADI and payment of dues.

Association for Institutional Research (AIR)

114 Stone Building
Florida State University
Tallahassee, FL 32306-4462
(850) 644-4470
Fax: (850) 644-8824
E-mail: air@mailer.fsu.edu
http://www.airweb.org

Purpose: Dedicated to facilitating the decision-making process in higher education. An association of professionals who are engaged in institutional research via management research, policy analysis, and planning. Promotes a code of professional ethics germane to the collection, management, and dissemination of institutional data within institutions of higher education.

Services: Conducts professional development programs for practitioners in institutional research by sponsoring national conferences (forums) and institutes and through publications. Provides leadership in advancing the field of institutional research.

Major Publications: Research in Higher Education, New Directions for Institutional Research, AIR Currents, Strategies for the Practice of Institutional Research, and *Handbook of Higher Education*

Type of Membership: Individual and institutional

Membership Requirements: Individual membership is for those persons who have an interest in institutional research and those engaged in its practice. Institutional membership is for a specific campus, system office, agency, or other organization in higher education.

Research Grants: Supported by the National Center for Education Statistics and the National Science Foundation, funding is available for research grants to doctoral students, staff and faculty of postsecondary educational institutions, and practitioners in the field of education. For more information, visit the AIR Web site listed earlier or telephone.

Association for the Study of Higher Education (ASHE)

202 Hill Hall
University of Missouri at Columbia
Columbia, MO 65211-2190
(573) 882-9645
Fax: (573) 884-2197

E-mail: ashe@coe.missouri.edu

http://www.ashe.missouri.edu

Purpose: An organization of scholars and higher education faculty, administrators, and graduate students who are interested in the research, study, and practice of higher education.

Services: Promotes collaboration among ASHE's members and others who approach higher education as a field of study. Sponsors conferences and scholarly publications.

Major Publications: The Review of Higher Education, ASHE Reader Series on Higher Education, and the *ASHE-ERIC Report Series*

Type of Membership: Individual

Membership Requirements: Interest in the study of higher education and the scholarly research associated with it.

Association for Supervision and Curriculum Development (ASCD)

1703 N. Beauregard Street

Alexandria, VA 22311

(800) 933-2723

(703) 578-9600

Fax: (703) 575-5400

http://www.ascd.org

Purpose: A professional association for curriculum supervisors and others who are interested in the development, improvement, and evaluation of curricula.

Services: To promote curriculum and professional development, ASCD provides information and consulting services, curriculum institutes, print and electronic publishing, video- and CD-ROM-based programs, and an annual conference.

Major Publication: Educational Leadership

Type of Membership: Individual

Membership Requirements: Commitment to ASCD's mission and beliefs

Data Collected: Curriculum trends, demographic data on the membership, and annual status reports from affiliates.

Association of American Colleges and Universities (AAC&U)

1818 R Street, NW

Washington, DC 20009

(202) 387-3760

Fax: (202) 265-9532

http://www.aacu-edu.org

Purpose: Advance and strengthen undergraduate liberal education.

Services: Provides consultative services for the improvement of undergraduate liberal education and offers professional development institutes and workshops and professional publications.

Major Publications: Liberal Education, On Campus with Women, Peer Review

Type of Membership: Individual and institutional

Membership Requirements: Institutional membership is limited to accredited colleges and universities. Individual memberships are restricted to faculty and administrators on campuses that are institutional members.

Data Collected: Trends in general education, diversity and learning, and educational reform in higher education.

Association of American Universities (AAU)

Suite 550
1200 New York Avenue, NW
Washington, DC 20005
(202) 408-7500
Fax: (202) 408-8184

Purpose: An association of public and private research and doctoral degree-granting universities. Emphasizes the pursuit of excellence in undergraduate, graduate, and professional programs with much consideration given to academic research. Provides a forum for the presidents and chancellors of these institutions to exchange information of common interest and to develop policies that promote strong programs of research and scholarship.

Services: Coordinates federal relations activities for member institutions, conducts policy studies, and sponsors meetings and conferences for its membership.

Type of Membership: Institutional

Membership Requirements: Membership is by invitation, and new members must be approved by three-fourths of the member institutions. The criteria include, but are not limited to, high-quality degree and research programs.

Association of Governing Boards of Universities and Colleges (AGB)

Suite 400
One Dupont Circle, NW
Washington, DC 20036
(800) 356-6317
(202) 296-8400
Fax: (202) 223-7053
E-mail: tomi@agb.org
http://www.agb.org

Purpose: To strengthen the governing boards of public and private colleges and universities and their affiliated foundation boards by serving as a resource to trustees and chief executives.

Services: Conducts a national conference on trusteeship, operates leadership forums for foundation boards, and provides information services for boards of trustees and foundation boards.

Major Publications: Trusteeship, Priorities, and special reports

Type of Membership: Institutional

Membership Requirements: The college or university must either be accredited or be a candidate for accreditation by a regional or specialized accrediting agency that is recognized by the Council for Higher Education Accreditation.

Data Collected: Information relating to governance of institutions of higher education, trusteeship, and the academic presidency. Examples include institutional and board policies, model documents, bylaws, and presidential assessment.

Association of Higher Education Facilities Officers (APPA)

1643 Prince Street
Alexandria, VA 22314
(703) 684-1446
Fax: (703) 549-2772
E-mail: info@appa.org
http://www.appa.org

Purpose: The professional association for administrators of the physical plants of colleges and universities. Provides leadership for the management of higher education facilities. Promotes excellence in the administration, operation, care, planning, and development of such facilities.

Services: Sponsors an annual national meeting, seminars, workshops, and institutes on the management of higher education facilities. Publishes professional literature for the field.

Major Publication: Facilities Manager

Type of Membership: Institutional

Membership Requirements: Institutional membership is for accredited, degree-granting institutions of higher education. Affiliate membership is available to school districts, hospitals, museums, municipalities, and other nonprofit organizations.

Data Collected: Annually, collects data on the construction and operating costs of physical plants of colleges and universities. These include utilities, salaries, fringe benefits, and other associated costs.

Association of Schools of Allied Health Professions (ASAHP)

Suite 500
1730 M Street, NW
Washington, DC 20036
(800) 497-8080
(202) 293-4848
Fax: (202) 293-4852
E-mail: asahp1@asahp.org
http://www.asahp.org

Purpose: ASAHP is the professional umbrella organization for allied health education. It strives to advance education, research, and service in the field of allied health professions. This association addresses critical issues such as health care legislation, personnel preparation, professional standards, and technological advances in the health care field.

Services: Government relations, leadership development, public policy analysis and development regarding allied health, data collection, dissemination of information, sponsorship of a national conference and other meetings for the profession, and professional publications.

Major Publication: Journal of Allied Health, Trends

Type of Membership: Individual and institutional

Membership Requirements: Institutional members must have an allied health program that awards a degree or certificate in one or more of the allied health professions. Individual membership is for persons who are employed in an allied health education program or who are career professionals in the field. In either situation, the individual must be employed by an institutional member. Agency and individual member affiliation is available for organizations and persons who are interested in the mission and purpose of ASAHP but do not meet the criteria of institutional membership.

Data Collected: Annually assembles descriptive data on allied health education programs, including characteristics of the faculty, student enrollment, operating budgets, clinical income, and more. Also, collecting national workforce data on the allied health professions.

College and University Professional Association for Human Resources (CUPA-HR)
Suite 301
1233 20th Street, NW
Washington, DC 20036
(202) 429-0311
Fax: (202) 429-0149
http://www.cupahr.org

Purpose: Promotes the effective management and development of human resources in higher education. A professional association for human resource personnel in institutions of higher education.

Services: Provides conventions, seminars, and workshops related to human resource management in higher education. Conducts a public policy program to educate and represent members concerning judicial, regulatory, and legislative affairs in this field. Also conducts annual salary surveys of administration and faculty in higher education and special studies germane to human resource management.

Major Publications: CUPA-HR Journal, Administrative Compensation Survey, Mid-Level Administrative/Professional Salary Survey, National Faculty Salary Survey (public and private institution versions)

Type of Membership: Mostly institutional; however, associate, corporate, individual, international, retiree, and student memberships are also available.

Membership Requirements: See CUPA-HR Web site cited.

Data Collected: Median salary data on administrative and midlevel administrative/professional positions in higher education. Organized by enrollment size of campus, operating budget, institutional classification, and other criteria. Also conducts separate annual faculty salary surveys of public and private colleges and universities. These reports include average, high, and low salary data based on the 9- or 10-month academic year for faculty ranks, researcher levels, and discipline/major fields.

The College Board (College Entrance Examination Board [CEEB])
45 Columbus Avenue
New York, NY 10023
(212) 713-8000
Fax: (212) 713-8282
http://www.collegeboard.com

Regional Offices:

    Middle States Regional Office
        Suite 410
        3440 Market Street
        Philadelphia, PA 19104
        (215) 387-7600

    Midwestern Regional Office
        Suite 1001
        One Rotary Center
        1560 Sherman Avenue
        Evanston, IL 60201
        (847) 866-1700

    New England Regional Office
        470 Totten Pond Road
        Waltham, MA 02451
        (781) 890-9150

    Southern Regional Office
        Suite 340
        100 Crescent Centre Parkway
        Tucker, GA 30084
        (770) 908-9737

    Southwestern Regional Office
        Suite 2000
        4330 South MoPac Expressway
        Austin, TX 78735
        (512) 891-8400

Western Regional Office
Suite 480
2099 Gateway Place
San Jose, CA 95110
(408) 452-1400

Purpose: An association of schools, colleges, universities, and other educational organizations dedicated to serving college-bound students with programs and services in college admissions, guidance, assessment, financial aid, and enrollment.

Services: Among the services provided are the National Forum for the discussion of national issues and trends; special conferences concerned with connecting students to college; College Access Services, which include standardized tests such as the SAT, PSAT/NMSQT, the Advanced Placement Program, and Pacesetter; adult learning services; college scholarship service; data and special services; minority activities; research and development; and publications.

Major Publications: The College Board offers a wide assortment of publications related to its mission and services. Those interested should write for a copy of *College Board Publications*. Also, the College Board publishes *College Board News* and *College Board Review*. See the College Board's Web site cited.

Type of Membership: Institutional

Membership Requirements: Be accredited by a regional accrediting association and make use of the College Board's services.

Data Collected: College admissions, student characteristics, student finances, placement, and other data related to the College Board's programs.

Council for Exceptional Children (CEC)

1110 N. Glebe Road
Arlington, VA 22201
(800) 224-6830
(703) 620-3660
Fax: (703) 264-1637
E-mail: service@cec.sped.org
http://www.cec.sped.org

Purpose: A professional organization dedicated to improving educational opportunities for individuals with exceptional traits (i.e., gifted students and those with disabilities). CEC advocates for appropriate governmental policies, sets professional standards, advocates for underserved individuals with exceptional traits, and assists professionals in gaining resources necessary for maximizing educational success.

Services: Sponsors conferences, institutes, and workshops on topics and issues in special education. In cooperation with NCATE, conducts accreditation of special education programs in colleges and universities. Sets standards for the preparation and certification of special educators and professional practice. Provides professional development programs and serves as a public policy advocate on special education.

Major Publications: Exceptional Children, Teaching Exceptional Children, and *CEC Today*

511

Type of Membership: Individual

Membership Requirements: Professional membership is for individuals who are professionally employed in education. Associate membership is for parents or paraprofessionals interested in the education of students with exceptional traits. Student membership is for undergraduate and graduate students who are so certified by a faculty adviser.

Data Collected: Abstracts and disseminates professional literature on resources and successful strategies used in the education of individuals with disabilities and/or gifts and talents.

Council for Higher Education Accreditation (CHEA)

Suite 510
One Dupont Circle, NW
Washington, DC 20036
(202) 955-6126
Fax: (202) 955-6129
E-mail: chea@chea.org
http://www.chea.org

Purpose: Recognizes organizations that accredit institutions of higher education, provides national leadership to advance self-regulation of postsecondary education institutions through accreditation, and serves as the primary national voice for voluntary accreditation to the federal government, general public, and the international community. Works to achieve quality assurance through voluntary accreditation.

Services: Facilitates coordination among accrediting bodies; assists with the improvement of the accrediting process by fostering high standards and practices by accrediting agencies; conducts research and disseminates information about regional, national, and specialized accreditors; sponsors meetings and conferences on issues related to higher education accreditation; provides mediation and dispute-resolution services; serves as a national leader in identifying and articulating emerging issues in quality assurance; and supports a good-practices database.

Major Publication: CHEA Almanac of External Quality Review

Type of Membership: Institutional

Membership Requirements: Membership is extended to national, regional, and specialized higher education accrediting organizations that have been recognized by CHEA. Membership is also granted to colleges and universities that are accredited by an organization recognized by CHEA and who pay the required dues. Finally, membership is granted to organizations related to higher education that do not accredit but whose activities are consistent with the purposes of CHEA and who pay the requisite dues.

Data Collected: Descriptive data on member accrediting bodies, including scope of operations, profiles of institutions and programs accredited, accrediting procedures, requirements for accreditation, contact information, and other related data.

Council of Chief State School Officers (CCSSO)

Suite 700

One Massachusetts Avenue, NW
Washington, DC 20001
(202) 408-5505
Fax: (202) 408-8072
http://www.ccsso.org

Purpose: The professional organization for the state superintendents and commissioners of education. Assists these chief state school officers and their agencies with the fulfillment of their responsibilities.

Services: Conducts special projects that address educational concerns at the state level. Offers professional development programs for chief state school officers. Operates three major programs: the State Education Assessment Center, the State Leadership Center, and the Resource Center on Educational Equity.

Major Publications: Directory of State Education Agencies, State Education Indicators with a Focus on Title 1, State Indicators of Science and Mathematics, Status Report: State Systemic Education Improvements

Type of Membership: Individual

Membership Requirements: Must be the chief school officer in the state, District of Columbia, or U.S. territory.

Data Collected: Maintains information about effective state education programs, student learning standards and assessments, programs that serve the needs of at-risk children, middle-school programs, mathematics and science program content and participation, evaluation and assessment information on teachers and educational leaders, early childhood programs, school-to-career transition, and other topics and programs. Does not collect data on individual school districts.

Council of Graduate Schools in the United States (CGS)
Suite 430
One Dupont Circle, NW
Washington, DC 20036
(202) 223-3791
Fax: (202) 331-7157
http://www.cgsnet.org

Purpose: Works for the improvement and advancement of graduate education. Serves as a medium of communication among graduate schools and between them and governmental agencies.

Services: Offers consultation, association, and governmental relations services, sponsors an annual conference on graduate education, and conducts summer workshops for new graduate deans. Also issues policy statements and position papers on graduate education.

Major Publication: Communicator

Type of Membership: Institutional

Membership Requirements: Accredited colleges and universities in the United States that offer graduate degrees in at least three distinct fields.

Data Collected: Descriptive information about graduate enrollments and graduate degrees awarded in the U.S.

Educational Research Service (ERS)

2000 Clarendon Boulevard
Arlington, VA 22201
(800) 791-9308
(703) 243-2100
Fax: (703) 243-5971
E-mail: ers@ers.org
http://www.ers.org

Purpose: Provides educational research and information for public school districts K–12.

Services: Searches the literature for information that has been requested. Under contract, performs customized research for school districts. Publishes reports and periodical literature.

Major Publications: ERS Spectrum, ERS Bulletin, ERS Informed Educator Series, Successful School Practices

Type of Membership: Individual and institutional

Membership Requirements: Individual membership is open to everyone. Institutional membership is limited to school districts K–12 and educational agencies.

Data Collected: An array of data on K–12, including national statistics on salaries and wages for public school employees. Also has data on budgeting and staffing of school districts. Serves as a secondary source of information on academic performance, program success, and other topics in education.

Educational Resources Information Center (ERIC)

National Library of Education
Office of Educational Research and Improvement (OERI)
U.S. Department of Education
400 Maryland Avenue, SW
Washington, DC 20202-5721
(800) 424-1616
Fax: (202) 205-7759
E-mail: eric@inet.ed.gov
http://www.ed.gov
http://www.accesseric.org (reference and referral component of ERIC)

Purpose: This is the federally funded national information network for education and related disciplines. Its purpose is to assemble and disseminate information from research and other sources. Central to ERIC is its database containing approximately 1 million abstracts of documents and journal articles on educational research and practice.

Services: To implement the mission of ERIC, subject-oriented centers known as clearinghouses have been established where educational literature is received, abstracted, indexed, stored, and disseminated. Adjunct clearinghouses, funded by other sources, function within the broader scope of their associated clearinghouses and, for the most part, duplicate the services of the clearinghouses as the adjunct specializes in a more narrow field.

ERIC document résumés (research and technical reports, conference papers, teaching guides, program descriptions, etc.) that have been collected are cataloged and indexed in *Resources in Education* (RIE). Also the clearinghouses catalog and index articles that appear in professional education journals and the résumés of these articles are reported in *Current Index to Journals in Education* (CIJE). The master list of headings used to index and search the ERIC system is to be found in the *Thesaurus of ERIC Descriptors*.

To access the ERIC database, there are multiple points of entry. The researcher may use the Internet Web site of a particular clearinghouse or adjunct clearinghouse or use a CD-ROM at a participating library. The http://www.accesseric.org Web site is a place to start, as is http://www.askeric.org. The latter is a personalized entry to ERIC that allows for customized educational questions to be asked, and an e-mail response is subsequently generated.

ERIC Clearinghouses

ADULT, CAREER, AND VOCATIONAL EDUCATION
Center on Education and Training for Employment
Ohio State University
1900 Kenny Road
Columbus, OH 43210
(800) 848-4815, Extension 2-7069
(614) 292-7069
Fax: (614) 292-1260
E-mail: ericacve@postbox.acs.ohio-state.edu
http://ericacve.org

ASSESSMENT AND EVALUATION
1129 Schriver Laboratory
Department of Measurement, Statistics, and Evaluation
University of Maryland, College Park
College Park, MD 20742
(800) 464-3742
(301) 405-7449
Fax: (301) 405-8134
E-mail: ericae@ericae.net
http://ericae.net

COMMUNITY COLLEGES
University of California at Los Angeles
3051 Moore Hall

405 Hilgard Avenue
P.O. Box 951521
Los Angeles, CA 90095-1521
(800) 832-8256
(310) 825-3931
Fax: (310) 206-8095
E-mail: ericcc@ucla.edu
http://www.gseis.ucla.edu/ERIC/eric.html

COUNSELING AND STUDENT SERVICES
School of Education
201 Ferguson Building
University of North Carolina at Greensboro
P.O. Box 26171
Greensboro, NC 27402-6171
(800) 414-9769
(336) 334-4114
Fax: (336) 334-4116
E-mail: ericcass@uncg.edu
http://ericcass.uncg.edu

DISABILITIES AND GIFTED EDUCATION
Council for Exceptional Children
1110 N. Glebe Road
Arlington, VA 22201
(800) 328-0272
Fax: (703) 620-2521
E-mail: ericec@cec.sped.org
http://ericec.org

EDUCATIONAL MANAGEMENT
University of Oregon
Dept. 5207
1787 Agate Street
Eugene, OR 97403-5207
(800) 438-8841
(541) 346-5043
Fax: (541) 346-2334
E-mail: ppiele@oregon.uoregon.edu
http://eric.uoregon.edu

ELEMENTARY AND EARLY CHILDHOOD EDUCATION
Children's Research Center

University of Illinois at Urbana-Champaign
51 Gerty Drive
Champaign, IL 61820
(800) 583-4135
(217) 333-1386
Fax: (217) 333-3767
E-mail: ericeece@uiuc.edu
http://ericeece.org

HIGHER EDUCATION
George Washington University
Suite 630
One Dupont Circle, NW
Washington, DC 20036
(800) 773-3742
(202) 296-2597
Fax: (202) 452-1844
E-mail: eric-he@eric-he.edu
http://www.eriche.org

INFORMATION AND TECHNOLOGY
Syracuse University
Suite 160
621 Skytop Road
Syracuse, NY 13244
(800) 464-9107
(315) 443-3640
Fax: (315) 443-5448
E-mail: eric@ericir.syr.edu
         askeric@askeric.org
http://ericir.syr.edu/ithome
AskERIC Web site: http://www.askeric.org

LANGUAGES AND LINGUISTICS
Center for Applied Linguistics
4646 40th Street, NW
Washington, DC 20016
(800) 276-9834
(202) 362-0700
Fax: (202) 363-7204
E-mail: eric@cal.org
http://www.cal.org/ericcll

READING, ENGLISH, AND COMMUNICATION
Indiana University
Suite 140
Smith Research Center
2805 East 10th Street
Bloomington, IN 47408
(800) 759-4723
(812) 855-5847
Fax: (812) 856-5512
E-mail: ericcs@indiana.edu
http://www.indiana.edu/~eric_rec

RURAL EDUCATION AND SMALL SCHOOLS
AEL, Inc.
1031 Quarrier Street
P.O. Box 1348
Charleston, WV 25325-1348
(800) 624-9120
(304) 347-0400
Fax: (304) 347-0467
E-mail: ericrc@ael.org
http://www.ael.org/eric

SCIENCE, MATHEMATICS, AND ENVIRONMENTAL EDUCATION
Ohio State University
1929 Kenny Road
Columbus, OH 43210
(800) 276-0462
(614) 292-6717
Fax: (614) 292-0263
E-mail: ericse@osu.edu
http://www.ericse.org

SOCIAL STUDIES/SOCIAL SCIENCE EDUCATION
Indiana University
Social Studies Development Center
2805 East 10th Street, Suite 120
Bloomington, IN 47408
(800) 266-3815
(812) 855-3838
Fax: (812) 855-0455
E-mail: ericso@indiana.edu
http://www.indiana.edu/~ssdc/eric_chess.htm

TEACHING AND TEACHER EDUCATION
American Association of Colleges for Teacher Education
Suite 300
1307 New York Avenue, NW
Washington, DC 20005
(800) 822-9229
(202) 293-2450
Fax: (202) 457-8095
E-mail: query@aacte.org
http://www.ericsp.org

URBAN EDUCATION
Institute for Urban and Minority Education
Main Hall, Room 303, Box 40
Teachers College
Columbia University
New York, NY 10027-6696
(800) 601-4868
(212) 678-3433
Fax: (212) 678-4012
E-mail: eric-cue@columbia.edu
http://eric-web.tc.columbia.edu

ERIC Adjunct Clearinghouses

CHILD CARE
National Child Care Information Center
2nd Floor
243 Church Street, NW
Vienna, VA 22180
(800) 616-2242
Fax: (800) 716-2242
E-mail: info@nccic.org
http://nccic.org

CLINICAL SCHOOLS
American Association of Colleges for Teacher Education
Suite 300
1307 New York Avenue, NW
Washington, DC 20005
(800) 822-9229
(202) 293-2450
Fax: (202) 457-8095

E-mail: query@aacte.org
http://www.ericsp.org

EDUCATIONAL OPPORTUNITY
National TRIO Clearinghouse
Council for Opportunity in Education
Suite 900
1025 Vermont Avenue, NW
Washington, DC 20005
(202) 347-2218
Fax: (202) 347-0786
E-mail: clearinghouse@hqcoe.org
http://www.trioprograms.org/clearinghouse

ENTREPRENEURSHIP EDUCATION
A325G Moore Hall
University of California at Los Angeles (UCLA)
405 Hilgard Avenue
Los Angeles, CA 90095-1521
(888) 423-5233
(310) 206-9549
Fax: (310) 206-8095
E-mail: celcee@ucla.edu
http://www.celcee.edu

ESL LITERACY EDUCATION
National Clearinghouse for ESL Literacy Education
Center for Applied Linguistics
4646 40th Street, NW
Washington, DC 20016
(202) 362-0700, Extension 200
Fax: (202) 363-7204
E-mail: ncle@cal.org
http://www.cal.org/ncle

INTERNATIONAL CIVIC EDUCATION
Social Studies Development Center
Indiana University
Suite 120
2805 East 10th Street
Bloomington, IN 47408
(800) 266-3815
(812) 855-3838

Fax: (812) 855-0455
E-mail: patrick@indiana.edu

SERVICE LEARNING
University of Minnesota
R-460 VoTech Building
1954 Bufford Avenue
St. Paul, MN 55108
(800) 808-7378
(612) 625-6276
Fax: (612) 625-6277
E-mail: serve@tc.umn.edu
http://umn.edu/~serve

TEST COLLECTION
Educational Testing Service
Princeton, NJ 08541
(609) 734-5689
Fax: (609) 683-7186
E-mail: library@ets.org
http://ericae.net/testcol.htm

UNITED STATES-JAPAN STUDIES
Social Studies Development Center
Indiana University
Suite 120
2805 East 10th Street
Bloomington, IN 47408
(800) 266-3815
(812) 855-3838
Fax: (812) 855-0455
http://www.indiana.edu/~japan

ERIC Affiliate Clearinghouse

NATIONAL CLEARINGHOUSE FOR EDUCATIONAL FACILITIES
National Institute of Building Sciences
Suite 700
1090 Vermont Avenue, NW
Washington, DC 20005
(888) 552-0624
(202) 289-7800
Fax: (202) 289-1092

E-mail: ncef@nibs.org
http://www.edfacilities.org

Educational Testing Service (ETS)
Rosedale Road
Princeton, NJ 08541
(609) 921-9000
Fax: (609) 734-5410
E-mail: etsinfo@ets.org
http://www.ets.org

Regional Offices:

Washington, DC, Office
Suite 900
1800 K Street, NW
Washington, DC 20006
(202) 659-0616
Fax: (202) 659-8075
E-mail: DCO@ets.org

California Field Office
Trans Pacific Centre
Suite 310
1000 Broadway
Oakland, CA 94607
(510) 873-8000
Fax: (510) 873-8118
E-mail: OAK@ets.org
http://www.ets.org/regions/oak.html

Florida Field Office
Region XIV Comprehensive Center
Suite 312
1000 N. Ashley Drive
Tampa, FL 33602
(800) 756-9003
(813) 307-6100
Fax: (813) 228-0632
E-mail: thensley@ets.org
http://www.ets.org/ccxiv

Puerto Rico Field Office
Suite 315
American International Plaza
250 Munoz Rivera Avenue
Hato Rey, PR 00918
(787) 753-6363
Fax: (787) 250-7426
E-mail: PRO@ets.org

Purpose: ETS is chartered to "engage in, undertake, and carry on services, research, and other activities in the field of educational testing and such other activities as may be appropriate to such purpose."

Services: Provides a number of testing programs (e.g., SAT, GRE, GMAT) and services for admissions, selection, placement, and guidance for educational objectives as well as occupational licensing and certification through its subsidiary, the Chauncey Group International. Advisory services and a research program complement the testing programs.

Major Publications: Access. Also publishes occasional papers from the ETS Policy Information Center and the Office of Public Leadership.

Data Collected: A continuing survey (National Assessment of Educational Progress) of the knowledge, skills, understanding, and activities of young Americans. Sundry data gathered from the College Board Admissions Testing Program, Graduate Record Examination, and Test of English as a Foreign Language.

Research Grants Program: ETS Predoctoral Fellowship Program (summer), ETS Postdoctoral Fellowship Program, and the NAEP Visiting Scholar Program. For more information, contact ETS.

High/Scope Educational Research Foundation

600 North River Street
Ypsilanti, MI 48198
(734) 485-2000
Fax: (734) 485-0704
E-mail: info@highscope.org
http://www.highscope.org

Purpose: This internationally renowned educational research foundation has established educational programs in preschool through high school that are based on interactive learning and founded on the outcomes of research. Its approach to learning has been heralded in countries worldwide as it is called upon to implement its approach to early childhood education, elementary education, and secondary education. The foundation states that its goal is to "promote the learning and development of children worldwide from infancy through adolescence and to support and train educators and parents as they help children learn."

Services: Provides educational programs preK–12 and training for educators and parents and offers an extensive array of publications. Engages extensively in research and evaluation and curriculum development. Serves as a consultant to schools worldwide as it implements the High/Scope approach to teaching and learning. Its programs have caused High/Scope to be recognized worldwide for its work in early childhood care.

Major Publication: High/Scope Resource

Type of Membership: Individual and institutional

Membership Requirements: High/Scope certification through successful completion of the High/Scope training programs and demonstrated competence.

Data Collected: Data on the effectiveness of the High/Scope programs preK–12. Also has been conducting a longitudinal study for 34+ years on the effectiveness of three pre-school curriculum models. Individuals who were selected in 1967 at ages three and four have been followed into adulthood. Has also assembled profiles on the condition and characteristics of the care and education of preschool-age children in 15 countries.

International Reading Association (IRA)

800 Barksdale Road
P.O. Box 8139
Newark, DE 19714-8139
(302) 731-1600
Fax: (302) 731-1057
http://www.reading.org

Purpose: An association of reading specialists, classroom teachers, supervisors, college teachers, researchers, administrators, librarians, parents, and others who are interested in improving the quality of reading instruction at all levels and who seek to promote the lifetime reading habit among all people. The IRA promotes high levels of literacy and pursues equitable access to quality reading instruction.

Services: Sponsors regional and national conferences and the World Congress on Reading. Provides leadership and support for literacy activities throughout the world. Offers a volunteer consultancy on literacy to developing countries. Supports teacher education, curriculum reform, and classroom innovation. Serves as a clearinghouse on reading research. Publishes numerous journals and special reports. Conducts a placement service for its members.

Major Publications: The Reading Teacher, Journal of Adolescent & Adult Literacy, Reading Research Quarterly, Lectura y vida, Reading Online, Reading Today. Also publishes books, videotapes, and electronic products on reading and related topics.

Type of Membership: Institutional and individual memberships from 99 countries.

Membership Requirements: Open to all persons who are interested in the goals of the association and who pay the required membership fee.

Data Collected: Maintains an information clearinghouse on a variety of research data related to reading and the teaching of reading.

Research Grants Programs: Offers numerous monetary awards for outstanding contributions to the field of literacy.

Laboratory for Student Success (LSS)

Temple University Center for Research in Human Development and Education

9th Floor, Ritter Annex
1301 Cecil B. Moore Avenue
Philadelphia, PA 19122-6091
(800) 892-5550
(215) 204-3000
Fax: (215) 204-5130
E-mail: lss@vm.temple.edu
http://www.temple.edu/lss/

Purpose: This laboratory is a component of the U.S. Regional Educational Laboratory Network. As such, it serves the region of Delaware, Maryland, New Jersey, Pennsylvania, and the District of Columbia. Working with schools, school districts, state departments of education, service providers, institutions of higher education, and professional associations, LSS searches for successful strategies and programs for student achievement in pre-kindergarten to postsecondary education. It then engages in activities that disseminate this information for the purpose of raising the achievement level of the neediest students in rural and urban communities. LSS National Leadership Area is educational leadership.

Services: LSS services facilitate the transformation of research-based knowledge into useful tools that can be integrated into the classroom. This lab sponsors professional development seminars and workshops, advanced study programs, and technical assistance. The educational community in the mid-Atlantic region is provided technical and instructional leadership to enable it to benefit from emergent technologies for learning. Assistance is given to promote school reform by bringing an awareness to what makes schools work in their mission to facilitate student learning.

In the implementation of its educational leadership mission, LSS has developed the Mid-Atlantic Educational Leadership Think Tank, which has a Web-based leadership development information resource called the E-Lead Directory. It facilitates the sharing of information about specific leadership development models that offer the greatest likelihood of success in specific environments and contexts.

Major Publications: Spotlight on Student Success, The CEIC Review (Center on Education in the Inner Cities), *Partnerships.* In addition, the laboratory publishes a series of reports and monographs that disclose the findings of research in which they have been involved. Furthermore, special reports are published throughout the year on sundry topics related to the activities of LSS.

Type of Membership: NA

Data Collected: Student achievement, faculty development, comprehensive school reform, educational finance.

Mid-Continent Research for Education and Learning (McREL)

Suite 500
2550 S. Parker Road
Aurora, CO 80014
(303) 337-0990
Fax: (303) 337-3005

E-mail: info@mcrel.org
http://www.mcrel.org

Purpose: McREL is a member of the U.S. Regional Educational Laboratory Network with its service region consisting of the states of Colorado, Kansas, Missouri, Nebraska, North Dakota, South Dakota, and Wyoming. As a component of the educational laboratory system, its purpose is to collect, organize, and disseminate to the educational community information derived from research for the purpose of enhancing the effectiveness of schools. Its National Leadership Area is standards-based instructional practice, the implementation of which engages the lab in identifying the best instructional practices and publishing these for others to use as a guide. Furthermore, McREL endeavors to help school districts adopt these standards and align instructional practices with them.

Services: In furtherance of its mission, McREL provides research and development (R& D), technical assistance to schools, and assessment services. It conducts various programs for disseminating information that will reform classroom practices, where needed, and stimulate educational leadership in the pursuit of transforming low-achieving schools into high performing centers.

Major Publications: Noteworthy and *Changing Schools*

Type of Membership: NA

Data Collected: Information on effective standards-based instructional practices, successful curricula, and student achievement.

Middle States Commission on Elementary Schools (MSCES)

Middle States Association of Colleges and Schools
GSB Building
Suite 618
One Belmont Avenue
Bala Cynwyd, PA 19004
(610) 617-1100
Fax: (610) 617-1106
E-mail: info@ces-msa.org
http://www.ces-msa.org

Purpose: Accredits public, independent, and religious schools serving students in grades preK–8; however, accreditation can be extended through grade 12 depending on the organizational structure of the school or school district. The service region encompasses New York, New Jersey, Pennsylvania, Delaware, Maryland, the District of Columbia, Puerto Rico, and the U.S. Virgin Islands. Also accredits international schools in Africa, Europe, and in the Mid- and Near-East.

Services: Guides schools through the self-study and evaluation process. Provides exchanges among accredited schools through its electronic directory and Web site.

Major Publications: Publishes a variety of self-study protocol documents for schools engaged in the accreditation process.

Type of Membership: Institutional

Membership Requirements: Meet the standards for accreditation.

Data Collected: Institutional characteristics of accredited schools and performance of students in those schools.

Middle States Commission on Secondary Schools (MSCSS)

Middle States Association of Colleges and Schools
3624 Market Street
Philadelphia, PA 19104
(215) 662-5603
Fax: (215) 662-0957
E-mail: info@css-msa.org
http://www.css-msa.org

Purpose: Accredits public, independent, and religious schools serving students in grades 6–12. (*Note:* For grades 6–8, there is an overlap between the Middle States Commission on Elementary Schools and the Commission on Secondary Schools.) The service region encompasses New York, New Jersey, Pennsylvania, Delaware, Maryland, the District of Columbia, Puerto Rico, and the U.S. Virgin Islands. Also accredits international schools in Africa, Europe, and in the Mid- and Near-East.
Services: Assists schools through the self-study and evaluation process.
Major Publications: Publishes a variety of self-study protocol documents for schools engaged in the accreditation process.
Type of Membership: Institutional
Membership Requirements: Meet the standards for accreditation.
Data Collected: Student performance and characteristics of accredited schools.

Middle States Commission on Higher Education (MSCHE)

Middle States Association of Colleges and Schools
3624 Market Street
Philadelphia, PA 19104
(215) 662-5606
Fax: (215) 662-5501
E-mail: info@msache.org
http://www.msache.org

Purpose: Accredits public and private institutions of higher education in the District of Columbia and in the states of Delaware, Maryland, New Jersey, New York, and Pennsylvania. Also accredits in Puerto Rico, the U.S. Virgin Islands, and locations overseas.
Services: Provides guidance in the self-study and evaluation process for colleges and universities preparing for accreditation or reaccreditation. Conducts training workshops for evaluators and institutions of higher education. Sponsors conferences on issues in higher education that affect quality.
Major Publications: Directory: Accredited Membership and Candidates for Accreditation and *Proceedings of the Annual Conference*
Type of Membership: Institutional

Membership Requirements: Meet the standards for accreditation.

Data Collected: Annual profiles of member colleges and universities that include institutional type, graduation data, enrollment, instructional personnel, distance learning, study abroad, financial data, and more.

Music Teachers National Association (MTNA)

Suite 505
441 Vine Street
Cincinnati, OH 45202
(513) 421-1420
Fax: (513) 421-2503
E-mail: mtnanet@mtna.org
http://www.mtna.org

Purpose: Professional organization of music teachers at all levels and in all sectors of education. Endeavors to raise the level of music performance, understanding, and teaching.

Services: Offers national professional certification of music teachers; sponsors music performance competition at the local, state, and national levels; and convenes a national convention.

Major Publication: American Music Teacher

Type of Membership: Individual, institutional, corporate

Membership Requirements: Membership in MTNA is automatic after having become a member of an affiliated state association.

National Association for Gifted Children (NAGC)

Suite 550
1707 L Street, NW
Washington, DC 20036
(202) 785-4268
Fax: (202) 785-4248
http://www.nagc.org

Purpose: To serve as a public advocate for the educational needs of gifted students. Educate parents, teachers, and other professionals about these needs.

Services: To promote the education of the gifted, conducts training institutes and an annual conference for parents and educators, disseminates research-based information, and serves as a liaison for national legislation on the gifted.

Major Publications: Gifted Child Quarterly, Parenting for High Potential

Type of Membership: Individual and institutional

Membership Requirements: Anyone who supports the purpose of NAGC and who pays the annual dues.

Data Collected: Maintains information on gifted education that includes lists of private schools for the gifted, outstanding programs for gifted students, summer opportunities for the gifted, graduate programs in gifted education, contact persons for each state, and contacts within special areas of gifted education.

National Association of Elementary School Principals (NAESP)

1615 Duke Street
Alexandria, VA 22314
(800) 386-2377
(703) 684-3345
Fax: (800) 396-2377 or (703) 548-6021
E-mail: naesp@naesp.org
http://www.naesp.org

Purpose: A professional organization that serves elementary and middle school principals, assistant principals, and related professional educators in the United States, Canada, and overseas. NAESP's goals are to sustain and promote the professional qualifications and leadership effectiveness of its members. This organization represents the elementary and middle school sector of education to the state and federal governments, the news media, and other arenas of interest.

Services: Sponsors the National Principal's Resource Center, which provides publications, compact discs (CDs), videos, and other resources to facilitate the work of principals in elementary and middle schools. Within NAESP's Web site is the "Principal's Electronic Desk," which offers a variety of services to principals. Conducts the National Fellows Program, which offers weeklong professional development. The Leadership Academy is designed to keep principals abreast of developments in educational leadership, curriculum, and critical issues in education. The Summer Leadership Institute explores current educational trends and issues.

Major Publications: Principal (magazine), *Research Roundup, Communicator, Streamlined Seminar, Here's How, Report to Parents,* the *Standards Series,* and the *Essentials Series*

Type of Membership: Individual and institutional

Membership Requirements: Active membership is for persons employed as a principal or assistant principal in an elementary or middle school. Associate members are college and university faculty and other interested nonprincipals. Institutional membership is for educational institutions and libraries.

Data Collected: Conducts decennial studies of the principalship. Annually surveys salaries and benefits of principals. Publishes the *Standards Series,* which focuses on the principles and practices of elementary and middle school education. NAESP is a cosponsor of the Educational Research Service, which conducts sundry studies in education. (*Note:* See profile of ERS [p. 514]).

National Association of Independent Colleges and Universities (NAICU)

Suite 700
1025 Connecticut Avenue, NW
Washington, DC 20036
(202) 785-8866

Fax: (202) 835-0003
http://www.naicu.edu

Purpose: Serves as the voice for the independent colleges and universities in America. Represents these institutions in legislative matters to the federal government. Functions as a voluntary consortium of the independent sector of U.S. higher education. Provides a forum for its member institutions to exchange ideas among themselves and, through unity, promote their common interests. Supports fiscal and tax policies that provide maximum encouragement for charitable giving to independent institutions of higher education.

Services: Lobbies the federal government on behalf of the independent colleges and universities, informs its members of key federal decisions that affect their institutions, provides access to congressional and administration leaders, assists with media relations, conducts research, and disseminates data on policies and issues that affect the independent sector of higher education. Provides technical services to state associations of independent colleges and universities that assist them in developing public policies that sustain independent higher education at the state level. Convenes an annual meeting of the membership.

Major Publication: Independent Colleges and Universities: A National Profile

Type of Membership: Institutional

Membership Requirements: Must be an accredited, not-for-profit, independent college or university. Membership is also extended to state associations of independent colleges and universities and to national and regional organizations that represent this type of institution of higher education.

Data Collected: Directly or indirectly, gathers institutional descriptive data on independent colleges and universities. These data include enrollment, student financial aid, degrees granted, institutional finances, and other data that help to better understand the independent sector of higher education.

National Association of Independent Schools (NAIS)

1620 L Street, NW
Washington, DC 20036
(202) 973-9700
Fax: (202) 973-9790
http://www.nais.org

Purpose: The national voice for independent elementary and secondary education. Assists and strengthens independent, precollegiate schools by providing professional development and support services so they may better serve their students.

Services: Provides services to schools in the United States and abroad in addition to local, state, regional, and special-purpose associations of independent schools. These services include assistance with business management, fund-raising, admissions, financial aid, and public relations. Also provides academic services, workshops, and professional publications. Convenes an annual conference, offers school leadership workshops, and prepares statistical reports for member schools.

Major Publication: Independent School Magazine

Type of Membership: Institutional

Membership Requirements: Schools must be governed by independent boards of trustees, be nonprofit, and be fully accredited by an accepted accrediting association. Furthermore, schools must belong to a state or regional association of independent schools that has been approved by NAIS. Finally, to be accepted, a school must operate under a policy of nondiscrimination.

Data Collected: Statistics that are collected on independent elementary and secondary schools include enrollment trends, tuition, financial operations, teacher and administrative salaries, and more.

National Association of Pupil Services Administrators (NAPSA)

P.O. Box 783
Pittsford, NY 14534-0783
(716) 223-2018
Fax: (716) 223-1497
E-mail: napsa@rochester.rr.com
http://napsa.com

Purpose: NAPSA is a national organization of school administrators who are charged with districtwide administration of pupil services. Its goals are to promote pupil services in school systems, to provide a means of professional growth and communication among pupil services administrators, and to create an awareness of the role and function of pupil services and the administrators of these services.

Services: Among the services offered are training programs for new pupil service administrators, an annual conference, professional publications, and other services for the implementation of the organization's goals.

Major Publications: NAPSA News, NAPSA Notes

Type of Membership: Individual

Membership Requirements: Membership is extended to school district administrative personnel who are officially designated as having districtwide (or, in large school systems, subdistrict-wide or levelwide) administrative responsibility and who provide professional leadership for staff in two or more areas of pupil services. Also eligible for membership are professional personnel of universities or of county, state, regional, or federal departments of education who are officially designated as having administrative responsibility and/or provide professional leadership in the development of programs of pupil services or who are engaged in the professional preparation of pupil services staff and administrators.

Data Collected: Descriptive statistics of the members.

National Association of State Boards of Education (NASBE)

Suite 100
277 S. Washington Street
Alexandria, VA 22314
(703) 684-4000
Fax: (703) 836-2313

E-mail: boards@nasbe.org

http://www.nasbe.org

Purpose: A private, nonprofit association that represents state and territorial boards of education. The principal objectives are to strengthen state leadership in education policy-making, promote excellence in the education of all students, advocate equality of access to educational opportunity, encourage cooperation among state boards of education, and promote responsible lay governance of public education.

Services: Provides technical assistance to state boards of education, operates a clearinghouse on state education policies, convenes conferences, and offers training for new state board members. Upon request, assists with the selection of chief state school officers.

Major Publication: The State Education Standard

Type of Membership: State boards of education

Data Collected: Collects information on state boards of education.

National Association of State Directors of Teacher Education and Certification (NASDTEC)

39 Nathan Ellis Highway

PMB #134

Mashpee, MA 02649-3267

(508) 539-8844

Fax: (508) 539-8868

E-mail: nasdtec@mediaone.net

http://www.nasdtec.org

Purpose: Dedicated to providing leadership and support to those professionals who are responsible for the preparation, certification or licensure, ethical and professional practice, and continuing professional development of educators. Facilitates the adoption and implementation of high standards for the preparation of candidates who seek certification or licensure as educators.

Services: Provides services that fulfill the mission of the organization. Disseminates information on the use of technology and other methodologies that enhance the management of certification and licensure systems. Makes available current information on requirements and procedures about the preparation and certification of educators. Facilitates the mobility of certified educators. Promotes communication among entities that are responsible for the preparation, certification, and professional development of educators. The foregoing are accomplished with conferences, a clearinghouse of information, and publications.

Major Publications: NASDTEC Manual, NASDTEC Communicator, and occasional issue papers

Type of Membership: Institutional

Membership Requirements: Members are state or jurisdictional agencies that have major administrative responsibility for the preparation, certification, or licensure of professional personnel for schools or for the related professional standards and practices governing such procedures.

Data Collected: Maintains data on teacher education programs and the certification or licensure requirements that are being implemented in each state.

National Association of State Universities and Land-Grant Colleges (NASULGC)
Suite 400
1307 New York Avenue, NW
Washington, DC 20005
(202) 478-6040
Fax: (202) 478-6046
http://www.nasulgc.org

Purpose: NASULGC serves as the voice of public higher education and its land-grant universities as it expresses their priorities and positions to the federal and state legislative and administrative branches of government. This organization also promotes support of its members in the private sector. In addition to focusing on legislative matters, emphasis is on academic structure and curricula, research, urban affairs, educating the disadvantaged, enhancing student access and opportunities, fostering changes in higher education that ensure the societal relevance of colleges and universities, and promoting a global perspective among its members.

Services: The principal service is to represent the state and land-grant universities to the Congress, the executive branch, and various federal agencies on policy and program issues. The different offices within NASULGC work to implement the priorities of the association. Convenes an annual conference of its members.

Major Publications: NASULGC People and Programs, Newsline

Type of Membership: Institutional

Membership Requirements: Must be a publicly supported institution of higher education with substantial research programs. Member institutions offer the doctoral degree.

Data Collected: Descriptive data on member universities.

National Association of Student Financial Aid Administrators (NASFAA)
Suite 400
1129 20th Street, NW
Washington, DC 20036
(202) 785-0453
Fax: (202) 785-1487
E-mail: ask@nasfaa.org
http://www.nasfaa.org

Purpose: A professional association of student financial aid administrators in institutions of higher education. Promotes the effectiveness of these administrators and encourages programs that remove financial barriers to student enrollment and retention in postsecondary education.

Services: Provides training and technical assistance in student financial aid for staff in colleges and universities who administer financial aid programs. Serves as a voice in matters of student financial aid that are before Congress.

Major Publications: Journal of Student Financial Aid, Student Aid Transcript, The Advisor, Encyclopedia of Student Financial Aid

Type of Membership: Individual and institutional

Membership Requirements: Institutional membership is open to institutions of higher education. Affiliate membership is for individuals who are employed full-time by a postsecondary education institution, and constituent membership is for educational associations, governing agencies, and other educational organizations, and for individuals interested in the effective administration of student financial aid but who are not employed full-time by a college or university. Student membership is open to persons who are enrolled full-time in an institution of postsecondary education and who are interested in the aims of NASFAA.

Data Collected: Assembles information on the availability of student financial aid and legislative matters pertaining thereto.

National Association of Student Personnel Administrators (NASPA)

Suite 418
1875 Connecticut Avenue, NW
Washington, DC 20009
(202) 265-7500
Fax: (202) 797-1157
E-mail: office@naspa.org
http://www.naspa.org

Purpose: The professional association of college student personnel administrators. Provides professional development for its members and is a leader in policy development for the enhancement of student learning on college campuses.

Services: Organizes national and regional workshops, institutes, and symposia on issues and topics on college student affairs. Convenes an annual conference and represents its members on issues central to the responsibilities of student personnel officials. Publishes books, papers, and references.

Major Publications: NASPA Journal, Net Results

Type of Membership: Individual and institutional

Membership Requirements: Institutional membership is for accredited postsecondary education institutions; professional affiliate membership is for student affairs administrators or staff at member institutions; associate affiliate membership is for student affairs administrators at nonmember colleges or universities or those employed in postsecondary institutions not eligible for membership. There are also membership categories for former members who are now retired and for graduate students enrolled in student affairs programs.

Data Collected: Collects data on membership that are reported in aggregate.

National Board for Professional Teaching Standards (NBPTS)
Suite 400
26555 Evergreen Road
Southfield, MI 48076
(800) 228-3224
(248) 351-4444
Fax: (248) 351-4170
E-mail: info@nbpts.org
http://www.nbpts.org/nbpts/

Regional Office:
Suite 1401
2200 Clarendon Boulevard
Arlington, VA 22201
(703) 465-2700
Fax: (703) 465-2715

Purpose: The mission of NBPTS is to establish high standards for what accomplished teachers should know and be able to do, to develop and operate a national voluntary system that assesses and certifies teachers who meet these standards, and to advance related education reform for the purpose of improving student learning.

Services: The following programs have been established:

1. Standards have been created for K–12 teachers in nearly 30 fields. These national standards describe the critical aspects of teaching that distinguish accomplished practice.
2. National Board Certification, which is a performance-based assessment process that measures teachers against the National Board's standards.
3. National Board Certified Teacher Program, which fosters the movement of teachers who have been certified by the National Board into roles as professional experts, education leaders, education policymakers, and public opinion leaders in the education system.
4. Information and support services for candidates who are going through the National Board certification process.
5. Providing technical assistance to state and local policymakers, teachers' unions, and academic associations interested in supporting National Board Certification.

Major Publications: Accomplished Teacher, What Teachers Should Know and Be Able to Do, Q&A: What Every Teacher Should Know, Assessment and Scoring Kits, Portfolio Samplers

Type of Membership: NA

Data Collected: The National Board collects and maintains data on candidates who are seeking National Board certification and on National Board certified teachers. The data include teaching experience and other descriptive statistics.

National Center for Education Statistics (NCES)

U.S. Department of Education
1990 K Street, NW
Washington, DC 20006
(202) 502-7300
Fax: (202) 502-7466
E-mail: nceswebmaster@ed.gov
http://www.nces.ed.gov

Purpose: The principal federal government agency that is responsible for collecting and reporting data on the condition of education in the United States.

Services: Primarily via the Internet and printed publications, organizes and disseminates statistical data on education at all levels in the United States. Encompasses the full spectrum of education. (*Note:* See Section B, Chapters 1 and 2 of this book for further information on NCES and its services on the Internet.)

Major Publications: Condition of Education, Digest of Education Statistics, and numerous other publications.

Data Collected: Among the surveys conducted by NCES are the following:

1. Common Core of Data
2. Integrated Postsecondary Education Data System
3. Numerous longitudinal studies
4. National Assessment of Educational Progress
5. Survey of Recent College Graduates
6. Public/private school surveys

Visit the NCES Web site for more information.

National Center for Higher Education Management Systems (NCHEMS)

P.O. Box 9752
Boulder, CO 80302-9752
(303) 497-0301
Fax: (303) 497-0338
E-mail: nchems@nchems.org
http://www.nchems.org

Purpose: A nonprofit corporation that helps colleges and universities improve their management capabilities. NCHEMS bridges the gap between research and practice by placing the latest management strategies and tools in the hands of working collegiate administrators.

Services: Conducts specific research, consulting, or development projects contracted by institutions of higher education, consortia, state agencies, or others related to higher education. Maintains a higher education management system database and operates an information service, operates management training seminars, and issues numerous publications that disseminate concepts, principles, and strategies germane to collegiate management practices.

Type of Membership: Institutional

Membership Requirements: Be supportive of the mission of NCHEMS and pay the annual fee.

Data Collected: Uses the data collected by the Integrated Postsecondary Education Data System, operated by the National Center for Education Statistics and other external databases.

National Council for Accreditation of Teacher Education (NCATE)
Suite 500
2010 Massachusetts Avenue, NW
Washington, DC 20036
(202) 466-7496
Fax: (202) 296-6620
E-mail: ncate@ncate.org
http://www.ncate.org

Purpose: The national professional accrediting body for elementary and secondary teacher education.

Services: Pursues activities in the fulfillment of its mission of accrediting teacher education programs throughout the nation.

Major Publications: Guide to College Programs in Teacher Preparation; Professional Standards for Accreditation for Schools, Colleges, and Departments of Education; Annual List of Accredited Programs

Type of Membership: Institutional and organizational

Membership Requirements: In addition to professional organizations and associations, members are those institutions of higher education whose teacher education programs have been accredited by NCATE. Criteria for accreditation membership are specified in *Professional Standards for Accreditation for Schools, Colleges, and Departments of Education.*

Data Collected: Publishes a list of NCATE-accredited programs in professional elementary and secondary education organized by field within professional education and degree level at each collegiate institution.

National Council of Teachers of English (NCTE)
1111 W. Kenyon Road
Urbana, IL 61801
(800) 369-6283
(217) 328-3870
Fax: (217) 328-0977
E-mail: public_info@ncte.org
http://www.ncte.org

Purpose: A professional association dedicated to improving the teaching and learning of English and the language arts at all levels of education.

Services: Publishes professional journals and books, holds conventions and conferences, and offers members opportunities for networking with other teachers with similar interests.

Major Publications: Language Arts (elementary education); *English Journal* (secondary education); *College English; Talking Points; Voices from the Middle; Primary Voices, K–6; School Talk; Classroom Notes Plus; English Education; The Council Chronicle; English Leadership Quarterly; College Composition and Communication; Teaching English in the Two-Year College; Research in the Teaching of English; Quarterly Review of Doublespeak*

Type of Membership: Individual and institutional

Membership Requirements: Be involved in the teaching and/or research of English and/or the language arts or be a nonpractitioner with an interest in these fields.

Research Grant Programs: The NCTE Research Foundation sponsors grants-in-aid and teacher-research programs for members who are conducting research in the field of English and/or the language arts. For further information, contact the NCTE Research Foundation at the address, toll-free telephone number, or fax number cited.

National Council of University Research Administrators (NCURA)
Suite 220
One Dupont Circle, NW
Washington, DC 20036
(202) 466-3894
Fax: (202) 223-5573
E-mail: info@ncura.edu
http://www.ncura.edu

Purpose: Professional organization of persons involved in the administration of sponsored research programs in colleges and universities. Promotes the development of effective policies and practices related to the administration of sponsored research programs. Provides a forum through national and regional meetings for the exchange of information pertaining to sponsored programs. Facilitates the professional development of its members.

Services: Offers in-service training for sponsored research administrators in grant and contract administration. Convenes workshops and a national conference and publishes professional literature of interest to its members.

Major Publications: NCURA Journal, NCURA Newsletter

Type of Membership: Individual

Membership Requirements: Regular membership is for those persons who are engaged in the administration of sponsored research programs in an institution of higher education. Associate membership is for individuals who are not qualified for regular membership but whose responsibilities are related to the administration of such programs.

National Council on Economic Education (NCEE)
2nd Floor
1140 Avenue of the Americas

New York, NY 10036
(800) 338-1192
(212) 730-7007
Fax: (212) 730-1793
E-mail: ncee@eaglobal.org
http://www.nationalcouncil.org

Purpose: To promote and improve the study of economics, K–12. NCEE has a network of 46 state Councils on Economic Education and 275 university-based centers for economic education in the United States.

Services: Develops teaching materials and trains teachers for economic education. These materials and services form a comprehensive program in economic education for K–12. Works to develop state and national content standards in economics. Conducts research and evaluation on materials and strategies for teaching economics.

Major Publication: Request the NCEE catalog of textbooks for economics.

Type of Membership: Institutional

Membership Requirements: Institutions must make a commitment to offer and support economic education.

Data Collected: Among the data that are collected on a regular basis are (1) school district participation in economic education; (2) number of teachers trained in economic education; (3) national, regional, and local test data on economics; and (4) other related information.

National Council on Measurement in Education (NCME)

1230 17th Street, NW
Washington, DC 20036
(202) 223-9318
Fax: (202) 775-1824
http://www.ncme.org

Purpose: An organization for professionals who are involved in assessment, evaluation, testing, and other areas of educational measurement.

Services: Provides opportunities for persons engaged in the construction and use of standardized tests, new forms of assessment, and program evaluation to come together and discuss matters of mutual professional interest. Offers professional development seminars at its annual meeting. Publishes professional journals for its members and instructional materials in educational measurement for teachers and others.

Major Publications: The Journal of Educational Measurement, Educational Measurement: Issues and Practice, The NCME Quarterly Newsletter

Type of Membership: Individual

Membership Requirements: Interest in the professional mission of NCME and payment of the annual dues.

National PTA (National Parent-Teacher Association)

Suite 2100

330 N. Wabash
Chicago, IL 60611
(800) 307-4782
(312) 670-6782
Fax: (312) 670-6783
E-mail: info@pta.org
http://www.pta.org

Regional Offices: There are 54 regional offices whose addresses and telephone numbers are to be found on the Web site cited.

Purpose: To promote the welfare of children and youth in home, school, and community. An association of parents and educators. Fosters legislation that benefits the children of America.

Services: Provides advocacy and leadership in fostering the welfare of children. Also provides parent training and an array of resources on the organization's Web site for parents and teachers.

Major Publication: Our Children (magazine)

Type of Membership: Individual

Membership Requirements: A commitment to the welfare of children

Information Collected: Information on preK–12 educational issues, child welfare, and health and safety issues that are germane to children.

National School Boards Association (NSBA)

1680 Duke Street
Alexandria, VA 22314
(703) 838-6722
Fax: (703) 683-7590
E-mail: info@nsba.org
http://www.nsba.org

Purpose: The national association for local school boards and their state associations. Represents public elementary and secondary education governance before federal agencies and national organizations that affect education. Fosters the public's understanding of the role of local school boards in the governance of public schools.

Services: In addition to representing the interests of the nation's school boards before Congress and federal agencies, NSBA provides education and training for school board members, offers technical assistance to school boards, operates a program that advances public education through the best use of technology in the classroom, and has a service for school board attorneys that focuses on issues of school law. Convenes an annual convention that fosters leadership development for the nation's local school board members.

Major Publications: American School Board Journal, School Board News

Type of Membership: Institutional

Membership Requirements: NSBA is a federation of state school board associations.

Data Collected: (1) Annual review of state support for public education, (2) demographic data on state school board associations, (3) descriptive data on public education in urban and nonurban school districts, and (4) other information related to its mission.

National Society for the Study of Education (NSSE)
College of Education, Mail Code 147
University of Illinois at Chicago
1040 W. Harrison Street
Chicago, IL 60607
(312) 996-4529
Fax: (312) 996-6400
E-mail: nsse@uic.edu

Purpose: To focus attention on enduring issues of policy and practice in education and to assemble the best theoretical and practical knowledge on a topic. Also, to explore the implication of that knowledge for practice, research, and policy in education.

Services: Publishes two yearbooks each April. These yearbooks are organized around a theme. Previous topics have included technology in education, professional development of teachers, bilingual education, and adolescence. Scholars who are recognized experts in a relevant field are invited to contribute chapters.

Major Publications: The thematic yearbooks mentioned above.

Type of Membership: Individual

Membership Requirements: Interest in the purpose of NSSE and payment of dues.

New England Association of Schools and Colleges (NEASC)
209 Burlington Road
Bedford, MA 01730
(781) 271-0022
Fax: (781) 271-0950
E-mail: cihe@neasc.org
http://www.neasc.org

Purpose: A regional accrediting organization for public and private colleges and universities, vocational-technical schools, and elementary and secondary schools in Connecticut, Maine, Massachusetts, New Hampshire, Rhode Island, and Vermont.

Services: Evaluates and accredits the aforementioned schools and colleges; conducts workshops on evaluation and accreditation; and holds an annual convention.

Major Publications: Roster of Membership, NEASC Notes

Type of Membership: Institutional

Membership Requirements: Fulfill the criteria for accreditation.

Data Collected: Regarding the schools accredited in the association's region, enrollment, educational programs being offered, and other information assembled related to accreditation.

North American Association of Educational Negotiators (NAEN)

122 White Pine Drive
Springfield, IL 62707
(217) 529-7902
Fax: (217) 529-7904
E-mail: naen@aol.com
http://www.naen.org

Purpose: An association for school labor relations professionals. Serves as a network for educational negotiators, enhancing their communications and acting as source of information as they engage in labor negotiations for their school districts.

Services: Keeps members current on trends in collective bargaining among school districts, effective negotiating strategies, key court decisions, emerging legislation, and other related developments. Sponsors an annual conference for its members. Also convenes regional seminars designed to facilitate labor relations practices.

Major Publication: The Bulletin

Type of Membership: Individual and institutional

Membership Requirements: Must be an active educational negotiator for management in a school district.

Information Collected: Trends in collecting bargaining, court decisions, new legislation on employee relations, and other related information.

North Central Association of Colleges and Schools (NCA)

The Higher Learning Commission
Suite 2400
30 North LaSalle Street
Chicago, IL 60602
(800) 621-7440
(312) 263-0456
Fax: (312) 263-7462
E-mail: info@ncacihe.org
http://www.ncahigherlearningcommission.org

Purpose: The Higher Learning Commission of the NCA accredits degree-granting institutions of higher education in the states of Arizona, Arkansas, Colorado, Illinois, Indiana, Iowa, Kansas, Michigan, Minnesota, Missouri, Nebraska, New Mexico, North Dakota, Ohio, Oklahoma, South Dakota, West Virginia, Wisconsin, and Wyoming.

Services: Evaluates and accredits postsecondary education institutions. Conducts a candidacy program for applying institutions. Administers the Academic Quality Improvement Project, an alternative model for accreditation that leads participant institutions through continuous self-examination of systemic processes.

Major Publications: Handbook of Accreditation, A Collection of Papers on Self-Study and Institutional Improvement

Type of Membership: Institutional

Membership Requirements: Satisfy the requirements for accreditation.

Data Collected: Maintains descriptive institutional data on affiliated postsecondary education institutions. Included in these are contact information, academic calendar, enrollments, number of majors at each degree level, and a myriad of other data and information gleaned from self-study reports of individual institutions.

Research Grant Programs: Small research grants are occasionally available for scholarly studies related to accreditation. For further information, contact the executive director of the commission.

North Central Association of Colleges and Schools (NCA)

Commission on Accreditation and School Improvement
Arizona State University
P.O. Box 873011
Tempe, AZ 85287-3011
(800) 525-9517
(480) 965-8700
Fax: (480) 965-9423
E-mail: nca@ncacasi.org
http://www.ncacasi.org

Purpose: The Commission on Accreditation and School Improvement of the NCA accredits elementary schools, middle schools, high schools, and nondegree-granting postsecondary schools in the states of Arizona, Arkansas, Colorado, Illinois, Indiana, Iowa, Kansas, Michigan, Minnesota, Missouri, Nebraska, New Mexico, North Dakota, Ohio, Oklahoma, South Dakota, West Virginia, Wisconsin, and Wyoming. It ensures that its members engage in the continuous process of school improvement.

Services: Evaluates and accredits K–12 schools and nondegree postsecondary schools in the states cited earlier. Facilitates efforts for school improvement.

Major Publication: Journal of School Improvement

Type of Membership: Institutional

Membership Requirements: Satisfy the requirements for accreditation.

Data Collected: Maintains data on its member schools. Includes demographic information on the schools, student performance data, and information on school improvement goals.

North Central Regional Educational Laboratory (NCREL)

Suite 200
1120 East Diehl Road
Naperville, IL 60563
(800) 356-2735
(630) 649-6500
Fax: (630) 649-6700
E-mail: info@ncrel.org
http://www.ncrel.org

Purpose: NCREL is one of the 10 regional educational laboratories and serves the states of Illinois, Indiana, Iowa, Michigan, Minnesota, Ohio, and Wisconsin. As with the other regional laboratories, a portion of its mission is to promote educational research and development and to assemble information gathered therefrom and disseminate it to the educational community. The lab seeks to assist schools and school districts become centers of excellence.

This lab's National Leadership Area is educational technology. The purpose of this specialty is to engage in activities and programs that find ways to assist schools integrate technology into the classroom.

Services: This regional educational laboratory provides research-based resources and assistance to educators and policymakers in its region. Areas of emphasis include educational applications of technology, improving literacy, professional development, math and science, and evaluation. As a national leader in educational technology, NCREL synthesizes research and evaluation studies on educational technology, maintains a Web-based library on the development and performance of high-tech schools, and makes available strategies that schools in poverty areas should undertake to become effective high-technology educational institutions. Technical assistance is provided to these schools.

Major Publications: Learning Point Magazine and a variety of specialty publications consistent with the lab's mission.

Type of Membership: NA

Data Collected: Collects data on key educational issues derived from national, regional, and state sources. These include information on educational technology, student performance, and a diversity of other data pertaining to the lab's purpose of collecting, synthesizing, and disseminating research-based information in education.

Northeast and Islands Regional Educational Laboratory at Brown University (LAB at Brown)

Suite 300
222 Richmond Street
Providence, RI 02903
(800) 521-9550
(401) 274-9548
Fax: (401) 421-7650
E-mail: info@lab.brown.edu
http://www.lab.brown.edu

Purpose: A regional educational laboratory sponsored by the U.S. Department of Education that serves primarily Connecticut, Maine, Massachusetts, New Hampshire, New York, Rhode Island, Vermont, Puerto Rico, and the Virgin Islands. It identifies, synthesizes, and disseminates information derived from educational research with a primary focus on culturally diverse students as its National Leadership Area.

The lab seeks to identify strategies for the effective implementation of programs and practices that address the needs of diverse students. Its mission is to be a national repository of information on this segment of the student population and to facilitate transforming low-performing schools into high-achieving schools.

Services: The mission of this laboratory is pursued through its programs of technical assistance, applied research, information dissemination, teacher development, and collaborative leadership. It works with the leaders of school districts to enhance academic programs and reform schools, especially those schools with culturally diverse students.

Major Publications: Two regular publications are *Perspectives on Policy and Practice* and *Ed Notes.* Also published are books, pamphlets, and other types of materials that emerge from the numerous programs sponsored by this laboratory.

Type of Membership: NA

Data Collected: As a regional educational laboratory, this lab is constantly collecting a variety of data germane to its mission. These data include student achievement and comprehensive school reform, strategies for teaching diverse students, and model curricula.

Northwest Association of Schools and Colleges (NASC)

Commission on Colleges
Suite 120
11130 N.E. 33rd Place
Bellevue, WA 98004
(425) 827-2005
Fax: (425) 827-3395
E-mail: employee's last name@cocnasc.org
http://www.cocnasc.org

Purpose: Accredits colleges and universities in the states of Alaska, Idaho, Montana, Nevada, Oregon, Utah, and Washington.

Services: Evaluates and accredits institutions of higher education in the states previously named. Publishes materials pertaining to accreditation and convenes an annual conference.

Major Publication: Accreditation Handbook

Type of Membership: Institutional

Membership Requirements: Meet the standards for accreditation.

Data Collected: Assembles descriptive statistics on member institutions of higher education, including enrollment, degrees granted, research productivity, academic programs, financial data, and more.

Northwest Association of Schools and Colleges (NASC)

Commission on Schools
1910 University Drive
Boise, ID 83725
(208) 426-5725
Fax: (208) 426-5729

E-mail: employee's last name@boisestate.edu
http://www2.idbsu.edu/nasc

Purpose: Accredits elementary schools, middle schools, and high schools in the states of Alaska, Idaho, Montana, Nevada, Oregon, Utah, and Washington. Also conducts accreditation activities overseas.
Services: Evaluation and accreditation of K–12 schools in the areas previously cited.
Major Publications: Proceedings and Directory, Report
Type of Membership: Institutional
Membership Requirements: Satisfy the standards for accreditation.
Data Collected: Descriptive information on each school, such as type of program, enrollment, size of staff, and more.

Northwest Regional Educational Laboratory (NWREL)
Suite 500
101 SW Main Street
Portland, OR 97204
(800) 547-6339
(503) 275-9500
Fax: (503) 275-9489
E-mail: info@nwrel.org
http://www.nwrel.org

Purpose: As 1 of the 10 U.S. regional educational laboratories, NWREL serves the region of Alaska, Idaho, Montana, Oregon, and Washington. Its mission is to conduct applied research and development in the region's schools and to place the results of the research into practice for the purpose of improving education. Its National Leadership Area is Re-Engineering Schools for Improvement.

The lab seeks to apply what is known about educational standards, school organization, and comprehensive reform to transforming low-performing schools into high-performing learning centers. Its services are for all schools, particularly those with high concentrations of diversity and poverty.
Services: NWREL's services include applied research, development, dissemination of research-based information, school improvement, technical assistance to schools, teacher development, and assistance with assessment and evaluation in the schools.
Major Publication: Northwest Education
Type of Membership: NA
Data Collected: As a regional educational laboratory, it collects sundry data in the implementation of its mission and National Leadership Area. This includes data on effective programs and strategies for teaching and learning. Serves as a repository of educational information in its service region.

Pacific Resources for Education and Learning (PREL)
25th Floor
1099 Alakea Street

Honolulu, HI 96813-4321
(808) 441-1300
Fax: (808) 441-1385
E-mail: askprel@prel.org
http://www.prel.org

Regional Offices:

American Samoa Service Center
P.O. Box 1995
Pago Pago, AS 96799
(684) 699-7936
Fax: (684) 699-7936
E-mail: amssc@prel.org

Chuuk Service Center
P.O. Box 697
Weno, Chuuk FM 96942
(691) 330-5449
Fax: (691) 330-5450
E-mail: chuuksc@prel.org

CNMI Service Center
(Commonwealth of the Northern Mariana Islands)
P.O. Box 504449
Saipan, MP 96950
(670) 323-6000
Fax: (670) 323-7735
E-mail: cnmisc@prel.org

Guam Service Center
P.O. Box 326359
Hagatna, GU 96932
(671) 475-0215
Fax: (671) 478-0215
E-mail: guamsc@prel.org

Pohnpei Service Center
P.O. Box 1919
Kolonia, Pohnpei FM 96941
(691) 320-2112
Fax: (691) 320-4989
E-mail: pohnpesc@prel.org

Palau Service Center
Palau Community College
P.O. Box 9
Koror, PW 96940
(680) 488-8130
Fax: (680) 488-8131

RMI Service Center
(Republic of the Marshall Islands)
P.O. Box 1186
Majuro, MH 96960
(692) 625-2343
Fax: (692) 625-2345
E-mail: rmisc@prel.org

Yap Service Center
P.O. Box 985
Colonia, Yap FM 96943
(691) 350-4382
Fax: (691) 350-4380
E-mail: yapsc@prel.org

Purpose: PREL is a component of the Regional Educational Laboratory Network of the U.S. Department of Education. Its primary service region is in the Pacific and encompasses American Samoa, Commonwealth of the Northern Mariana Islands, Federated States of Micronesia (Chuuk, Kosrae, Pohnpei, and Yap), Guam, Hawaii, Republic of the Marshall Islands, and the Republic of Palau. The lab's National Leadership Area is Curriculum and Instruction Related to Reading and Language Mastery. As with the other regional laboratories, PREL collects educational information, synthesizes it, and disseminates it to the educational community. It specializes in gathering information on reading and language mastery for use in the schools.

Services: PREL helps schools in the Pacific Region by providing research, collection, and dissemination of research-based information, providing professional development of teachers, technical assistance, development opportunities, distance education, and evaluation services. Its services emphasize reading and language mastery; however, its scope reaches beyond this specialization.

Major Publications: This regional laboratory publishes briefing papers on a variety of timely educational topics.

Type of Membership: NA

Data Collected: Descriptive statistics on the schools and students in the Pacific Region.

Regional Educational Laboratories (REL)
Office of Educational Research and Improvement
U.S. Department of Education

Room 504B
555 New Jersey Avenue, NW
Washington, DC 20208
(202) 219-2235
http://www.relnetwork.org

Purpose: Supported by the U.S. Department of Education, Office of Educational Research and Improvement, the Regional Educational Laboratory network consists of 10 regional laboratories that provide educational information based on research and best practices. Each collects, synthesizes, and disseminates information that facilitates school improvement in its primary service region. In addition, each laboratory has a national specialty area for which it serves as a resource. The labs work with community members, policymakers, local and state educators, and others in the pursuit of upgrading the schools in their respective regions.

Services: The labs provide consultation, publish documents that disclose useful strategies and practices for classroom instruction and management, create instructional materials for use by teachers and students, offer professional development for teachers and administrators, and disseminate a potpourri of research findings and best practices for use in schools.

The Regional Educational Laboratories: For a profile of each of the following regional laboratories, see its individual alphabetical listing in this chapter.

SERVE

2nd Floor
915 North Ridge Street
Greensboro, NC 27403
(800) 755-3277
(336) 315-7400
Fax: (336) 315-7457
E-mail: info@serve.org
http://www.serve.org

Regional Offices:

> Florida Office
> Suite 400
> 1203 Governor's Square Boulevard
> Tallahassee, FL 32301
> (800) 352-6001
> (850) 671-6000
> Fax: (850) 671-6020
>
> Georgia Office
> Suite 1110
> 41 Marietta Street, NW
> Atlanta, GA 30303
> (800) 659-3204
> (404) 893-0100
> Fax: (404) 577-7812

Purpose: SERVE is 1 of the 10 regional educational laboratories sponsored by the U.S. Department of Education. Its primary service region is the states of Alabama, Florida, Georgia, Mississippi, North Carolina, and South Carolina. This lab focuses on transforming low-performing schools into high-performing educational learning centers. To achieve this objective, SERVE engages in research and development activities with schools and other agencies in its region. It collects data based on educational research and searches for successful methods and strategies that have improved the learning process. The lab disseminates information, provides technical assistance, and assists with teacher development.

    The National Leadership Area for SERVE is Expanded Learning Opportunities. This involves working with preschool, after-school, latchkey, and summer programs and, through research, identifying the most effective practices among these programs and then disseminating this information.

Services: Research and development, educational product development, technology support, assessment and evaluation, and publications are among the primary services of this lab. It endeavors to work with school districts regarding comprehensive school reform, offer new and effective products and strategies for change, and serve as a catalyst in working with school and community leaders in upgrading schools, especially among low-income and culturally diverse communities.

Major Publications: SERVE publishes a large variety of titles in the fulfillment of its mission. Some of these titles are *Reducing School Violence: A Framework for School Safety; Designing Teacher Evaluation Systems That Support Professional Growth; Ramping Up Reform: Aligning Education Rhetoric, Resolve, and Results; Improving Basic Education for All Learners: The Role of Arts Education;* and *Improving Reading: Southeastern School Strategies.*

Type of Membership: NA

Data Collected: Information on school reform, assessment of student achievement, and data on the effectiveness of research-based educational products that have been developed.

Society for College and University Planning (SCUP)

311 Maynard Street
Ann Arbor, MI 48104
(734) 998-7832
Fax: (734) 998-6532
E-mail: scup@scup.org
http://www.scup.org

Purpose: Focuses on the promotion, advancement, and application of effective planning in higher education. Addresses the full scope of higher education planning. Geographically, the membership comes from 30 countries, and their roles in higher education encompass college and university presidents, provosts, vice presidents, deans, financial officers, facilities personnel, information technology directors, and others.

Services: Sponsors workshops, forums, conferences, and other services that bring professionals together who are engaged in the planning process in higher education.

Major Publications: Planning for Higher Education, SCUP Membership Directory, Transforming Higher Education: A Vision for Learning in the 21st Century

Type of Membership: Individual, institutional, and nonuniversity organizations (including corporations)

Membership Requirements: Have an interest in higher education planning and pay the required membership dues.

Southern Association of Colleges and Schools (SACS)

1866 Southern Lane
Decatur, GA 30033
(800) 248-7701
(404) 679-4500
Fax: (404) 679-4556
http://www.sacs.org

Purpose: Accredits elementary schools, middle schools, secondary schools, and institutions of higher education in the states of Alabama, Florida, Georgia, Kentucky, Louisiana, Mississippi, North Carolina, South Carolina, Tennessee, Texas, and Virginia.

Services: Evaluates and accredits schools and colleges in the states previously listed. Conducts workshops and seminars provides and consulting assistance related to accreditation.

Major Publication: Proceedings (of the annual meeting)

Type of Membership: Institutional

Membership Requirements: Meet the standards for accreditation.

Data Collected: Descriptive statistics of each school and college that has been accredited by SACS.

Southwest Educational Development Laboratory (SEDL)

211 East Seventh Street
Austin, TX 78701

(800) 476-6861
(512) 476-6861
Fax: (512) 476-2286
E-mail: info@sedl.org
http://www.sedl.org

Purpose: SEDL is a member of the Regional Educational Laboratory Network under the sponsorship of the U.S. Department of Education. Its primary service region consists of the states of Arkansas, Louisiana, New Mexico, Oklahoma, and Texas. The mission of this laboratory is to improve the effectiveness of school systems in its region by linking the findings of research with educational practice. This lab works with educators, decision makers in education, and parents in this process. As with the other regional laboratories, SEDL seeks to identify, synthesize, and disseminate information that will enhances learning. Special regional focus is given to improving student performance in reading and mathematics.

The National Leadership Area of SEDL is Family and Community Involvement with Schools. Utilizing SEDL's partnership with the Charles A. Dana Center at the University of Texas, national leadership is being given to ascertaining ways that families and communities can become effective agents in creating high-performing schools. SEDL's research and development activities identify the best practices and then produce products that enhance parental and community involvement in the improvement of low-performing schools, especially those whose students have high concentrations of poverty and diverse languages and cultural backgrounds.

Services: SEDL develops research-based resources in the implementation of its mission. These include interactive Web tools, instruments, multimedia training modules, audio- and videotapes, briefing papers, and reports. These resources, which are for sale and available on-line at http://www.sedl.org/pubs/, cover the topics of improving student learning, increasing student literacy through improved teaching of reading, teaching mathematics and science, integrating educational technology into teaching, improving teacher and administrator quality, and engaging family and community in student learning.

Major Publication: SEDLetter

Type of Membership: NA

Data Collected: The kinds of data collected are consistent with the programmatic mission of this laboratory and vary as different contracts with school districts are created. Among the data sets collected are performance data on student achievement. As a component of the Regional Educational Laboratory program, it assembles information on the best educational practices as revealed by research.

State Higher Education Executive Officers (SHEEO)
Suite 2700
707 Seventeenth Street
Denver, CO 80202
(303) 299-3686
Fax: (303) 296-8332

E-mail: sheeo@sheeo.org
http://www.sheeo.org

Purpose: The national professional organization for chief executive officers who serve statewide coordinating boards and governing boards of postsecondary education. The primary objectives include developing the interest of the states in supporting quality higher education, promoting the importance of state planning and coordination of higher education, improving the competence of the staffs of statewide coordinating and governing boards, and serving as the collective voice of higher education executive officers at the state and federal levels.

Services: Serves as a clearinghouse for information on higher education. Administers the SHEEO/NCES Communication Network and participates in an electronic mail system on the Internet that facilitates the fast exchange of information among SHEEO's members. Conducts policy studies on state planning, school and college articulation, tuition policy, financing, student achievement, technology, and other topics of interest to its members. Convenes professional development seminars for staff members of state higher education agencies and sponsors governmental relations activities. Provides forums that involve state higher education executive officers, legislators, governors, institutional representatives, and other leaders in higher education.

Major Publications: Directory of Professional Personnel and other annual publications that include a survey of staffing and salary information in higher education.

Type of Membership: The regular members are the full-time chief executive officers of statewide governing and coordinating boards of higher education.

Membership Requirements: The aforementioned boards must have statutory responsibility for public higher education.

Data Collected: Policy studies of state coordinating and governing boards of higher education. Diverse descriptive data are collected, including higher education finances, academic programs, admissions standards, enrollment, student aid, and other descriptive statistical data.

University Continuing Education Association (UCEA)
Suite 615
One Dupont Circle, NW
Washington, DC 20036
(202) 659-3130
Fax: (202) 785-0374
E-mail: postmaster@nucea.edu
http://www.nucea.edu

Purpose: To promote high-quality continuing higher education, represent the broad interests of continuing higher education before governmental bodies and other forums, develop and disseminate timely information and research about continuing higher education, and provide professional development services for leaders in this field.

Services: Conducts professional development programs that include regional and national conferences and different special interest meetings; operates an extensive and diverse publications program; maintains an office of governmental relations germane to continuing higher education issues; and serves as an information resource for its members.

Major Publications: Continuing Higher Education Review, Lifelong Learning Trends

Type of Membership: Individual and institutional

Membership Requirements: Institutions must be accredited, degree-granting colleges or universities and be involved in continuing higher education. Individuals must be professionals in continuing education at member institutions.

Data Collected: Maintains national data on continuing higher education programs that are being offered by its members. Data include the type of programs, size, budgets, enrollment, funding sources, and other data.

WestEd

730 Harrison Street
San Francisco, CA 94107
(415) 565-3000
Fax: (415) 565-3012
E-mail: tross@wested.org
http://www.wested.org

Purpose: WestEd is one of the regional educational laboratories that are sponsored by the U.S. Department of Education. Its primary service region consists of the states of Arizona, California, Nevada, and Utah. As with the other labs, its mission is the improvement of education, especially in low-performing schools within a culturally deprived and mobile community. It searches for the best educational practices that have been identified through research and disseminates this information. The lab provides technical assistance and fosters programs for the professional development of teachers.

WestEd's National Leadership Area is Assessment of Educational Achievement. In fulfillment of this specialty area, the lab focuses, in depth, on the area of educational assessment, ascertaining procedures and processes for developing and conducting valid educational assessment, exploring issues and policies of assessment, working with states in the development of assessment programs, and studying the area of accountability for student achievement. The outcomes of this program are disseminated to the community.

Services: The services of WestEd are provided in the categories of standards and accountability, teacher quality, leadership, and linkages between schools and communities. These services consist of research and development, evaluation, technical assistance, and policy analysis.

Major Publications: The principal publication of WestEd is titled *R and D Alert*; however, this lab also publishes sundry other documents that include knowledge and policy briefs, guidebooks, research reports, surveys, case studies, and directories.

Type of Membership: NA

Data Collected: Albeit WestEd does not collect raw data, it is a resource for acquiring research-based information on its region because it is a repository for published research reports that have been issued by various schools and educational organizations in the states that it serves.

Western Association of Schools and Colleges (WASC)

Accrediting Commission for Community and Junior Colleges
3402 Mendocino Avenue
Santa Rosa, CA 95403
(707) 569-9177
Fax: (707) 569-9179
E-mail: accjc@aol.com
http://www.wascweb.org

Purpose: Accredits public and private postsecondary education institutions that offer one or more educational programs of two academic years in length and that grant the associate degree. The commission's service region encompasses California, Hawaii, and Guam.

Services: Evaluates and accredits two-year degree programs in the areas previously cited. Provides counsel and assistance to developing and established institutions, offers guidance to institutions that are in the self-study process, and sets standards for accreditation.

Major Publications: Handbook of Accreditation, Guide to Self-Study and Reports, Evaluator Handbook, Team Chair Handbook

Type of Membership: Institutional

Membership Requirements: Satisfy the criteria for accreditation.

Data Collected: Descriptive statistics of member institutions, including programs, enrollment, finances, and more.

Western Association of Schools and Colleges (WASC)

Accrediting Commission for Schools
Suite 200
533 Airport Boulevard
Burlingame, CA 94010
(650) 696-1060
Fax: (650) 696-1867
E-mail: mail@acswasc.org
http://www.wascweb.org

Purpose: Accredits public and private schools, preK–12, in California, Hawaii, and Guam.

Services: Provides guidance in the accreditation process and implements standards of accreditation.

Major Publication: WASC Directory (of accredited schools)

Type of Membership: Institutional

Membership Requirements: Satisfy the requirements for accreditation.

Data Collected: Descriptive statistics on member schools, including programs, faculty, enrollment, and more.

Western Association of Schools and Colleges (WASC)

Accrediting Commission for Senior Colleges and Universities

Suite 100
985 Atlantic Avenue
Alameda, CA 94501
(510) 748-9001
Fax: (510) 748-9797
E-mail: wascsr@wascsenior.org
http://www.wascweb.org

Purpose: Accredits colleges and universities in California, Hawaii, and Guam.
Services: Provides guidance in the self-study process and implements the standards for accreditation.
Major Publication: Handbook of Accreditation
Type of Membership: Institutional
Membership Requirements: Meet the standards for accreditation.
Data Collected: Descriptive statistics on member institutions, including enrollment, tuition, fees, institutional finances, and degree programs.

Western Interstate Commission for Higher Education (WICHE)
1540 30th Street
P.O. Box 9752
Boulder, CO 80301-9752
(303) 541-0200
Fax: (303) 541-0291
E-mail: execdir@wiche.edu
http://www.wiche.edu

Purpose: An interstate compact of 15 western states dedicated to maximizing excellence in higher education. A collaborative effort to meet the needs of higher education and personnel resources in the western region of the United States.
Services: Among the services offered by WICHE is the Student Exchange Program, which promotes the sharing of educational resources, thus reducing the need for costly and duplicative programs. The Policy Analysis and Research Program provides data to higher education and government officials that assist them in formulating policy decisions and in addressing higher education issues. The Mental Health Program coordinates regional efforts to share information and resources to meet changing mental health needs. To help states and institutions adopt new technologies for the improvement of education, WICHE supports the Western Cooperative for Educational Telecommunication. Workshops, forums, and seminars are conducted in the pursuit of WICHE's mission.
Major Publications: Publishes an extensive variety of special reports and monographs. For a bibliography of current publications, see http://www.wiche.edu/Pubs/currentpubs.htm on the WICHE Web site.
Type of Membership: State memberships
Membership Requirements: Full state membership is restricted to the interstate compact members, namely, the states of Alaska, Arizona, California, Colorado, Hawaii, Idaho,

Montana, Nevada, New Mexico, North Dakota, Oregon, South Dakota, Utah, Washington, and Wyoming. Affiliated state memberships are available to those states that are geographically contiguous to the western region.

Data Collected: WICHE collects a wide array of data. Included are elementary and secondary grade progression rates for the 50 states; higher education tuition, fees, and enrollment trends; personnel and state financial resources; demographic changes and student migration; financial aid resources; and other data related to higher education.

Index

About the Authors

MELVYN N. FREED, Ph.D., has served extensively in higher education as a faculty member and administrator. He is former vice president for administration at Arkansas State University and Governors State University (Illinois).

ROBERT K. HESS, Ph.D., is Associate Professor of Educational Research and Measurement at Arizona State University, West.

JOSEPH M. RYAN, Ph.D., is director of the Research Consulting Center and Professor of Education at Arizona State University, West.